I0888453

Competition Law in India

Competition Law in India

A Practical Guide

Second Edition

Abir Roy

Wolters Kluwer

Published by:
Kluwer Law International B.V.
PO Box 316
2400 AH Alphen aan den Rijn
The Netherlands
E-mail: lrs-sales@wolterskluwer.com
Website: www.wolterskluwer.com/en/solutions/kluwerlawinternational

Sold and distributed by:
Wolters Kluwer Legal & Regulatory U.S.
920 Links Avenue
Landisville, PA 17538
United States of America
E-mail: customer.service@wolterskluwer.com

ISBN 978-94-035-3137-3

e-Book: ISBN 978-94-035-3147-2
web-PDF: ISBN 978-94-035-3157-1

© 2024 Kluwer Law International BV, The Netherlands

All rights reserved. No part of this publication may be reproduced, stored in a retrieval system, or transmitted in any form or by any means, electronic, mechanical, photocopying, recording, or otherwise, without written permission from the publisher.

Permission to use this content must be obtained from the copyright owner. More information can be found at: www.wolterskluwer.com/en/solutions/legal-regulatory/permissions-reprints-and-licensing

About the Author

Abir Roy is the Co-Founder of Sarvada Legal, a law firm based in New Delhi, India. He heads the antitrust practice at Sarvada Legal. He is a counsel specializing in competition law and he regularly represents clients across judicial and quasi-judicial forums in India. Abir has represented clients on competition law issues across all industry segments, including technology, e-commerce, digital markets.

Abir has also been recognized as a leading practitioner in competition law by Whos Who Legal, Chambers & Partners, Legal 500 and Asia Law.

Abir is also a visiting lecturer on Competition Law at Symbiosis Law University, Noida & LawSikho, a leading online legal education portal.

Table of Contents

About the Author v

List of Abbreviations xvii

Foreword xxiii

Acknowledgements xxvii

CHAPTER 1
Introduction to Competition Law 1
§1.01 March Towards Competition Law 1
[A] The Aim and Objective of the Competition Act 2
[B] The Purpose Behind Enforcing the Competition Act 4
§1.02 Procedure for Inquiry 7
[A] Initiation of the Case 9
[B] Prima Facie Case 11
[C] Investigation and Inquiry Process 12
[D] The Scope of DG's Investigation 15
[E] Standard of Proof 17
[F] Further Investigation/Enquiry 17
§1.03 Enforcement Powers of the CCI 19
[A] Penalties and Directions on Companies/Group 19
[B] Penalties on Directors/Officers-in-Charge 24
[C] Advocacy Remedy 27
[D] Fines for Non-cooperation/Furnishing False Information 27
[E] Interim Relief 28
[1] Stage of Granting Interim Relief 29
[2] Conditions to Grant Interim Relief 29
[a] Stronger Prima Facie Case 30

[b] Necessary to Issue Interim Order or Balance of Convenience 30
[c] Irreparable Harm 31
§1.04 Competition Law Compliance 32
§1.05 Appeal Provisions 33
[A] Appealable Orders 34
[1] Section 26(2) of the Competition Act 34
[2] Section 26(2A) of the Competition Act 34
[3] Section 26(6) of the Competition Act 34
[4] Section 26(9) of the Competition Act 35
[5] Sections 27, 28 and 31 of the Competition Act 35
[6] Section 32 of the Competition Act 35
[7] Section 33 of the Competition Act 35
[8] Section 38 of the Competition Act 35
[9] Section 39 of the Competition Act 35
[10] Sections 43, 43A, 44 and 45 of the Competition Act 36
[11] Section 46 of the Competition Act 36
[B] Pre-deposit of Penalty Amount for Appeal 36
§1.06 Private Action 37
§1.07 Due Process 37
[A] Quorum of CCI 39
[B] Principles of Natural Justice and Due Process of Law 41
[1] Parties Must Be Heard Before the Final Order 41
[2] CCI Must Record Reasons in Its Administrative Order as Well as Adjudicatory Order 42
[3] CCI Must Display Application of Its Mind and Follow Due Process of Law 43
[C] Problem of 'Revolving Door' Practice in CCI 44
§1.08 Jurisdictional Boundary of CCI 44
[A] CCI's Conflict and Co-existence with Other Regulatory Authorities 44
[B] Jurisdiction of CCI in Data Privacy and Data Management 48
[C] Contractual Remedies Can Simultaneously Co-exist with the Competition Act 49
§1.09 Scope of Judicial Review under Article 226 of the Constitution of India, 1950 51
§1.10 Power of Recall 52
§1.11 Settlement or Commitment under the Competition Act 53
[A] Legal Framework for Settlement and Commitment 53
[B] Procedure of Settlement and Commitment 55
[C] The Challenges Ahead 56
§1.12 Sector Inquiry 57
[A] E-Commerce Market 58
[B] Telecom Sector 58

[C] Pharmaceutical Sector 58
[D] Cab Aggregators 59
[E] Film Distribution Chain 59
§1.13 Consumer 60
§1.14 Enterprise 62
§1.15 Relevant Market 65
[A] Relevant Product Market 67
[B] Relevant Geographic Market 68
[C] Trends of the CCI 68
[1] Starting Point of Analysis 69
[2] Analysis in Multi-sided Markets Is from the Perspective of Affected Parties 69
[3] Relevant Geographic Market Can Only Be India 70
[4] Online Versus Offline Distribution Model 71
[5] Aftermarket Versus Unified Systems Market 73
[6] Lack of Scientific Sampling 75
[7] Relevant Markets for Section 3(4) of the Competition Act Need Not Be Precisely Delineated 75
[8] No Static Approach to Relevant Market Analysis 76
§1.16 Conclusion 77

CHAPTER 2
Anti-competitive Agreements and Competition Law 79
§2.01 Legal Framework 79
§2.02 Legal Framework of Cartels in India 80
§2.03 Existence of an Agreement 81
§2.04 Standard of Proof 86
§2.05 Direct Evidence 91
§2.06 Indirect Evidence: Role of Circumstantial Evidence 100
[A] Communication Evidence 102
[1] Frequent Meetings among Competitors 102
[2] Publication of Price Bulletin 104
[3] Commonality of Key Business Personnel 105
[4] Other Evidence 106
[B] Economic Evidence 108
[1] Analysis of Final Price in Comparison to the Input Price 109
[2] Price Correlation Exercise for All Market Participants 110
[3] Production Capacity and Capacity Utilization 111
[4] Profit Margin of the Market Participants 113
[5] Economic Evidence to Establish Bid Rigging 113
[a] Bid Price Versus Input Price 113
[b] Cover Bids 114
[c] Sub-contracting 114

[d] Other Economic Evidence for Establishing Bid Rigging Cartel 114
§2.07 Single Economic Entity 122
§2.08 Determination of Relevant Market 124
§2.09 Types of Cartel 124
[A] Price Fixing 125
[B] Output Controls/Limiting Production 126
[C] Market Sharing 127
[D] Bid Rigging 128
[1] Role of the Procurement Authority in Bid Rigging Inquiries 131
[E] Hub-and-Spoke Cartel 134
§2.10 Structural Factors Aiding Cartelization 135
[A] Highly Concentrated/Oligopolistic Market 135
[B] Demand and Supply Conditions 136
[C] Homogeneous Product 137
[D] Active Trade Association 137
§2.11 AAEC in India 139
[A] Creation of Barriers to Dissuade New Entrants/Existing Player to Expand in the Market 141
[B] Foreclosure of Competition by Hindering Entry into the Market 141
[C] Accrual of Benefits to Consumers 141
[D] Improvements in Production or Distribution or Promotion of Technical, Scientific and Economic Development 142
§2.12 Trade Association 143
[A] Boycott 145
[B] No Objection Certificate 146
[C] PIS Approval 147
[D] Fixing of Trade Margins 147
§2.13 Joint Venture Defence 148
§2.14 Leniency Regime 149
[A] Legal Framework for Leniency Application 150
[B] Process of Filing Lesser Penalty/Lesser Penalty Plus Application 150
[C] Priority Status of the Lesser Penalty Applicant and Lesser Penalty Plus Applicant 151
[D] Evaluation of Lesser Penalty/Lesser Penalty Plus Application 153
[1] Vital Disclosure to Establish the Cartel 153
[2] Other Conditions to Evaluate a Lesser Penalty/Lesser Penalty Plus Application 154
[E] Trend of CCI in Adjudicating Lesser Penalty Applications 154
§2.15 Legal Framework for Vertical Agreement 162
§2.16 Types of Vertical Agreements 163
[A] Tie-In Arrangement 164
[B] Exclusive Dealing Agreement 166

[C] Exclusive Distribution Agreement 167
[D] Refusal to Deal 168
[E] Resale Price Maintenance 172
§2.17 Essential Conditions Necessary to Establish Vertical Anti-competitive Agreement 175
[A] Delineation of Relevant Markets of the Parties 175
[B] Significant Market Power in the Relevant Market 177
§2.18 Factors to Determine AAEC in India 180
[A] Negative Factors 180
[B] Positive Factors 182
[1] Business Justifications or Rationales 183
§2.19 Exemption under Section 3 of the Competition Act 184
§2.20 Conclusion 185

CHAPTER 3
Abuse of Dominance and Competition Law 187
§3.01 Legislative Framework 187
[A] Textual Interpretation of Section 4 of the Competition Act 187
[B] Dominance Per Se Is Not Illegal 188
[C] Procedure Adopted in an Abuse of Dominance Investigation 189
§3.02 Position of Strength 190
[A] Parameters of Dominance under the Competition Act 192
[1] Operate Independently of Competitive Forces Prevailing in the Relevant Market 192
[2] Affect Its Competitors or Consumers or the Relevant Market in Its Favour 193
[B] Special Responsibility of a Dominant Player 196
[C] Collective Dominance 197
§3.03 Examining Position of Strength by Conduct of the Enterprise 199
[A] *NSE* Case 200
[1] Can NSE Sustain Zero Pricing Policy in the Relevant Market Long Enough to Outlive Effective Competition? 201
[2] Does the Policy of NSE to Provide Complete Transaction Waivers Make Any Commercial Sense? 201
[3] Would the NSE Be in a Position to Provide Complete Transaction Waivers Endlessly Had It Not Have Such Financial Muscle? 201
§3.04 Indices of Dominance: 'All or Any Factor' 202
[A] Market Share 203
[1] Market Share Is Not the Sole Criterion for Determining Dominance 204
[B] Strength of the Enterprise Vis-à-Vis the Competitors 206
[C] Economic Power of the Enterprise Including Commercial Advantages over Competitors 208

[1] Network Effects 209
[D] Consumer Dependence 211
[E] Entry Barriers 213
[1] Legal Barriers to Entry 214
[2] Strategic Barriers to Entry 214
[F] Countervailing Buyer Power 216
[G] Statutory Monopoly 219
[H] Using the Regulatory Power to Enter Commercial Activities 222
[I] Other Factors 223
§3.05 Abuse of Dominance 225
[A] Statutory Scheme 225
§3.06 Types of Abuse 226
[A] Unfair Terms and Conditions 226
[1] Discriminatory Conditions 231
[2] Analysis of Specific Unfair Terms and Conditions 234
[B] Unfair and Discriminatory Pricing 245
[1] Excessive Pricing 246
[a] The CCI Is Not a Price Regulator 251
[2] Predatory Pricing 252
[3] Determination of Cost 252
[4] Differential Pricing 259
[a] Meeting Competition Defence 260
[C] Limiting or Restricting Production and Technical Development 261
[D] Denial of Market Access 262
[1] Freedom to Choose Trading Partners 263
[2] Essential Facilities Doctrine 265
[3] 'In Any Manner': Expression of Wide Import 266
[a] Denial of Market Access Includes Non-price Parameters Also 271
[E] Imposing Supplementary Obligations 273
[F] Leveraging of Dominant Position 275
§3.07 Objective Justification 278
[A] Effects Doctrine 280
[B] IPR as a Defence 283
§3.08 Conclusion 284

CHAPTER 4
Mergers and Competition Law 285
§4.01 Introduction 285
§4.02 Threshold Limits 285
[A] Parties to the Combination 286
[B] Group Thresholds 286
[C] Deal Value Thresholds 287
§4.03 Target Level/*De Minimis* Exemption 288

[A] Asset and Turnover Details 289
[1] Scope of *De Minimis* Exemption 289
[2] Proof of AAEC Is Necessary to Investigate a Combination Which Has Availed the Target Exemption 291
[B] Calculation on a Consolidated Basis 293
[C] Regulation 5(9) 294
§4.04 Shares 295
§4.05 Group 296
§4.06 Control 298
[A] Meaning of Control 299
[1] Control Includes the Ability to Exercise Material Influence 301
[2] Beneficial Ownership Is not Necessary to Establish Control 304
[B] Indices of Control 304
[C] Joint Versus Sole Control 306
§4.07 Calculation of Asset Value 308
§4.08 Calculation of Turnover 310
§4.09 Key Issues in Accounting 310
§4.10 Obligation to Notify a Combination 311
[A] Pre-filing Consultation 312
[B] Responsibility to File the Merger Notification 312
[1] Triggering Events 314
[C] Single Notice in Case of an Interconnected Transaction 319
[D] Substance over Form 324
[E] Form of Filing 325
[F] Green Channel 325
§4.11 Penalty for Non-filing 326
[A] Gun Jumping 327
[1] Part/pre-payment of Consideration 331
[2] Escrow Arrangements 333
[3] Interim Conditions 335
[B] Importance of Mitigating Factors 335
§4.12 Exclusions and Exemption 336
[A] Acquisition by Public Financial Institution, Foreign Portfolio Investor, Bank or Category I Alternative Investment Fund 336
[B] Exempt Transactions 336
[1] Schedule I Item 1 337
[a] 'Solely as an Investment' 339
[b] 'In the Ordinary Course of Business' 342
[2] Schedule I Item 1A 344
[3] Schedule I Item 2 345
[4] Schedule I Item 3 346
[5] Schedule I Item 4 348
[6] Schedule I Item 5 348

[7] Schedule I Item 6 349
[8] Schedule I Item 7 349
[9] Schedule I Item 8 349
[10] Schedule I Item 9 351
[11] Schedule I, Item 10 352
[12] Sector-Specific Exemptions: Government Notifications 352
[C] Open Market Purchases 353
§4.13 Treatment of Offshore Combinations 354
§4.14 Procedure for Investigation of a Combination 356
[A] Phase I 356
[B] Phase 2 358
[1] Role of Third Parties 359
[C] Voluntary Modifications 362
§4.15 Types of Mergers 364
[A] Horizontal Mergers 364
[1] Issues with Horizontal Mergers 365
[B] Vertical Mergers 366
[1] Fear of Foreclosure 366
[2] Entry Blocking 367
[3] Price Squeezes 367
[C] Conglomerate Mergers 367
[1] The Theory of Deep Pockets 367
[2] Raising Barriers to Entry 368
[3] Loss of Potential Competition 368
§4.16 Substantive Analysis of Combinations 368
[A] Combined Market Share 369
[B] Presence of Overlaps 370
[C] Barriers to Entry 372
[D] Buyer Power 373
[E] Presence of a Sectoral Regulator 374
[F] Role of Efficiencies as a Defence 375
§4.17 Commitments 376
[A] Behavioural Commitments 377
[B] Structural Commitments 381
§4.18 Penalty for Making False Statement or Omission to Furnish Material Information 385
§4.19 Mismatch of Timeline and Remedies: The Clash Between Twin Regulators 387
§4.20 Conclusion 388

CHAPTER 5
Intellectual Property and Competition Law 389
§5.01 Friends in Disagreement 389
§5.02 Jurisdiction of the CCI over IPR Issues 390

	[A]	MRTP Commission	390
	[B]	Challenges to CCI's Jurisdiction	391
		[1] Competition Act Versus Copyright Act	391
		[2] Competition Act Versus Patents Act	394
§5.03	Scope of the IPR Exemption		404
	[A]	Reasonable Restrictions	405
	[B]	Coverage of IPR Exemption	406
		[1] Reasonability Depends on Facts and Circumstances	410
	[C]	Applicability of Section 3(5) to Trade Secrets	413
	[D]	Applicability of IPR Defence to Section 4	413
§5.04	Anti-competitive Practices Emanating out of IPRs		415
	[A]	Standard Essential Patents	415
	[B]	Pricing Abuse	417
		[1] Excessive Pricing	418
		[2] Differential Pricing	420
		[3] Minimum Commitment Charge	422
		[4] The Advocacy Initiatives of the CCI	423
	[C]	Non-pricing Abuse	423
		[1] Onerous Terms in the Licence Agreement	423
		[2] Denial of Market Access by Fraudulent Litigation	425
		[3] Advocacy Initiatives of CCI	428
§5.05	Refusal to Deal and Compulsory Licensing		429
	[A]	Decisional Practice of CCI	430
		[1] Refusal to Deal	430
		[2] Compulsory Licensing	432
	[B]	Practical Guidance	433
§5.06	IP Remedies in Mergers		434
	[A]	Remedies Issued by CCI	435
§5.07	Conclusion		436

CHAPTER 6
Digital Markets and Competition Law 437

§6.01	Introduction		437
§6.02	Market Definition		438
	[A]	Substitutability of Online and Offline Markets	438
	[B]	Platform Markets	440
	[C]	Wider Scope of Relevant Geographic Market	442
§6.03	Characteristic Features of Digital Markets		442
	[A]	Multi-sided Markets	442
		[1] Network Effects	443
		[2] Tipping Effect	447
		[3] Creation of an Ecosystem	448
	[B]	Economies of Scale	449
	[C]	Switching Costs	450

[D] Multi-homing 452
[E] Prevalence of Zero-Price Strategy 453
[F] Access to Data 454
[1] Using Data as a Competitive Advantage 455
[2] Data as a Tool to Create Revenue and New Business Verticals 456
[G] Across Platform Parity Agreements 457
[1] Free Riding 460
§6.04 Emerging Digital Markets 462
[A] Technology 462
[1] Concept of Gatekeepers 462
[B] Social Media and Communication 464
[C] Online Search 466
[D] Digital Advertising 467
[E] E-Commerce 468
[F] Aggregation 471
[1] Online Cab Aggregation 471
[2] Online Food Services Aggregation 472
[3] Online Travel Services Aggregation 473
§6.05 Trends from Decisional Practice 474
[A] Exploitative and Exclusionary Abuse 474
[B] Special Responsibility 477
[C] Efficiency Gains and Competition Harms in Mergers 477
[D] Protection of Incentives to Innovate 479
§6.06 Regulatory Intervention 480
[A] Competition Law (Amendment) Act, 2022 481
[1] Deal Value Threshold 481
§6.07 Digital Competition Act 482
[A] Digital Markets Act: The European Approach 482
[B] Does India Need a Digital Competition Act? 483
§6.08 Conclusion 485

Index 487

List of Abbreviations

APPAs	Across Platform Parity Agreements
ARM	Active Risk Management
ASG	Additional Solicitor General
ABNL	Aditya Birla Nuvo Limited
AIOCD	All India Organization of Chemists and Druggists
APT	Aluminium Phosphide Tablets
ACC	Android Compatibility Commitment Agreement
Anr.	Another
AFA	Anti-fragmentation Agreement
app	Application
APIC	Application Programme Interface Code
APIs	Application Programming Interface
AAEC	Appreciable Adverse Effect on Competition
Apr.	April
AV	Audio-Visual
Aug.	August
ATF	Aviation Rurbine Fuel
Baxalta	Baxalta Incorporated
Bayer	Bayer Aktiengesellschaft
BCDA	Bengal Chemists and Druggists Association
BPCL	Bharat Petroleum Corporation Limited
Bharti/Airtel	Bharti Airtel Limited
BTL	Bharti Telemedia Limited
BCCI	Board of Cricket Control in India

B2B	Business-to-Business
CPPIB	Canada Pension Plan Investment Board
Combination Regulations	CCI (Procedure in regard to the transaction of business relating to Combinations) Regulations, 2011
CMA	Cement Manufacturers Association
CCA	Commercial Cooperation Agreement
Competition Act	Competition Act, 2002
COMPAT	Competition Appellate Tribunal
CCI	Competition Commission of India
Draft Regulations	Competition Commission of India (Combinations) Regulations, 2023
CAGR	Compound Annual Growth Rate
CSC	CSC e-Governance Services India Limited
CD	Currency Derivates
Dec.	December
DIPP	Department of Industrial Policy and Promotion
DMA	Digital Markets Act
DG	Director General
DCP	Discount Control Mechanism
DGCI	Drug Controller General of India
EIPL	East India Petroleum Pvt. Ltd
etc.	Et cetera
EUR	Euro
EC	European Commission
ECJ	European Court of Justice
EU	European Union
FRAND	Fair, Reasonable, and Non-Discriminatory
Feb.	February
FIH	Federation of Indian Hockey
FPBAI	Federation of Publishers' and Booksellers' Associations in India
F&B	Food and Beverage
FCI	Food Corporation of India
FIPB	Foreign Investment and Promotion Board, Ministry of Finance
FAQs	Frequently Asked Questions
FSA	Fuel Supply Agreements

FSC	Fuel Surcharge
FCPL	Future Coupons Private Limited
FRL	Future Retail Limited
GSDA	Global Separation and Distribution Agreement
GMR	GMR Hyderabad International Airport Limited
GMS	Google Mobile Services
GPBS	Google Play Billing System
High Level Committee	High Level Committee on Competition Policy and Law Report, 2000
HPCL	Hindustan Petroleum Corporation Ltd.
HUL	Hindustan Unilever Limited
HI	Hockey India
Ibid.	Ibidem
i.e.	Id est
IDOs	Incumbent Dominant Operators
IDMA	Indian Drugs Manufacturers' Association
IMFL	Indian Made Foreign Liquor
IOCL	Indian Oil Corporation Limited
INR	Indian Rupee
ICAI	Institute of Chartered Accounts of India
IPR	Intellectual Property Rights
iOS	iPhone Operating System
Jan.	January
Jio	Jio Platforms Limited
Jul.	July
Jun.	June
KAFF	KAFF Appliances (India) Pvt. Ltd.
KFCC	Karnataka Film Chamber of Commerce
KCCL	Kerala Communicators Cable Limited
KFEF	Kerala Film Exhibitors Federation
KFinvest	Kingfisher Finvest India Limited
Lakshdeep	Lakshdeep Investments & Finance Private Limited
LOC	Letter of Consent/Cooperation
LMIL	Lion Meadow Investment Limited
iBall	M/s Best IT World (India) Private Limited
Life Cell	M/s Life Cell India Pvt. Ltd.
MAHAGENCO	Maharashtra State Power Generation Co. Ltd.

MMBL	Mahyco Monsanto Biotech India Pvt. Ltd.
MMT	MakeMyTrip
MMT-Go	MakeMyTrip-Go Ibibo
MTO	mandatory tender offer
MCFL	Mangalore Chemicals and Fertilizers Limited
Mar.	March
MRP	Maximum Retail Price
MCX-SX	MCX Stock Exchange
MOU	Memorandum of Understanding
MOP	Minimum Operating Price
MCA	Ministry of Corporate Affairs
MoR	Ministry of Railway
MADA	Mobile Application Distribution Agreement
MRTP	Monopolies and Restrictive Trade Practice
Monsanto	Monsanto Company
MFN	Most Favoured Nation
MSOs	Multi-system Operators
MAFFFL	Mumbai Aviation Fuel Farm Facility Limited
NCLAT	National Company Law Appellate Tribunal
NECC	National Egg Co-ordination Committee
NSE	National Stock Exchange
NDA	Non-Disclosure Agreement
NOC	Non-objection Certificate/No-Objection Certificate
Nov.	November
Oct.	October
OTAs	Online Travel Aggregators
OS	Operating System
OYO	Oravel Stays Private Limited
OECD	Organisation for Economic Co-operation and Development
OPPI	Organization of Pharmaceutical Producers of India
OEMs	Original Equipment Manufacturers
OESs	Original Equipment Suppliers
Ors.	Others
OTT	Over the Top
p.	Page
para.	Paragraph

PAs	Payment Aggregators
POIs	Point of Interconnection
POS	Point of Sale
PPA	Power Purchase Agreement
PAA	Preferential Allotment Agreement
PFC	Pre-filing Consultation
PIS	Product Information Service
RGIA	Rajiv Gandhi International Airport Hyderabad
RSBY	Rashtriya Swasthya Bima Yojna
ReNew	ReNew Energy Global plc
Big Tech Report	Report of the Parliamentary Standing Committee on Finance on Anti-Competitive Practices by Big Tech Companies, 2022
R&D	Research and Development
RBI	Reserve Bank of India
RSA	Revenue Sharing Agreement
ROFO	Right of First Offer
Schott Kaisha	Schott Kaisha Private Ltd
Takeover Code	SEBI (Substantial Acquisition of Shares and Takeovers) Regulations, 2011
SEBI	Securities and Exchange Board of India
Sep.	September
SPA	Share Purchase Agreement
SSHA	Share Subscription and Shareholders' Agreement
SHA	Shareholders Agreement
SSNIP	Small but Significant and Non-Transitory Increase in Price
SDK	Software Development Kits
FCM	Soluble Ferric Carboxymaltose
SALPG	South Asia LPG Company Pvt. Ltd.
SJM	St. Jude Medical, Inc.
SEPS	Standard Essential Patents
SIPL	Star India Private Limited
SHRIL	Sterling Holiday Resort India Limited
SAI	Stock Availability Information
SFL	Sundaram Finance Limited
SC	Supreme Court
SIDIs	Systematically Important Digital Intermediaries

TRAI	Telecom Regulatory Authority of India
TSPs	Telecom Service Providers
Telenor South Asia	Telenor South Asia Investment Pte Limited
Telenor India	Telewings Communications Services Private Limited
TOIL	Tesco Overseas Investments Limited
TRIPS Agreement	The Agreement on Trade-Related Aspects of Intellectual Property Rights
TPAP	Third-Party Apps
TCIL	Thomas Cook India Ltd.
TMM Act	Trade and Merchandise Marks Act, 1958
TFEU	Treaty on the Functioning of the European Union
THL	Trent Hypermarket Limited
Twin Star	Twin Star Technologies Limited
UAE	United Arab Emirates
UBHL	United Breweries (Holdings) Limited
UK	United Kingdom
UPI	United Payment Interface
USL	United Spirits Limited
USD	United States Dollar
US	United States of America
UPGMS	Uttar Pradesh Glass Manufacturers Syndicate
UAPMB	Uttarakhand Agricultural Produce Marketing Board
VAS	Value-Added Services
ZACL	Zuari Agro Chemicals Limited
ZFCL	Zuari Fertilisers and Chemicals Limited

Foreword

Law, they say, is jargonized common sense. The difficulty only is in overcoming the jargon associated with the law before embracing the underlying common sense. In the case of a highly complex and technical area such as competition law, the use of jargon is inevitable due to the nature of the subject. Given the fact that competition law is essential and integral to the economy, the Need of the Hour is a book that can deftly address the issues and present them in simple and easily readable prose. This is where the author - Shri Abir Roy - has done yeoman service to the citizenry by releasing the second edition of his book - *Competition Law in India: A Practical Guide*.

The first edition of this book was published in 2016. Thereafter, the author has taken pains to incorporate subsequent developments in the law and the statutory regime. The clarity with which the concepts have been handled in this book bears testimony to the surefootedness that the author brings to bear while navigating the thickets of competition law. His passion for the subject and the corresponding mastery is evident from the in-depth analysis that this intricate subject has received at his hands. The author has not hesitated to take on abstract concepts and explain them to the reader by breaking them down into easily comprehensible points. The book maintains a seamless flow from one chapter to another, employing a smooth narrative style without compromising on the quality of the content.

This book stands out for its ability to succinctly explore the fundamental concepts integral to the Competition Act. It provides meticulous references and analyses of the decisional patterns of both the Competition Commission of India and the adjudicatory bodies including the Apex Court. In the chapter dedicated to Anti-Competitive Agreements, the book illustrates how the regulator utilizes both direct and circumstantial evidence to uncover arrangements between parties that have potential anti-competitive effects. The author astutely highlights the regulator's predominant reliance on circumstantial evidence to infer the existence of an *agreement* where the market participants are 'instructed based on *nods and winks*'. Given the nature of such circumstantial evidence, one should however expect the regulators and adjudicatory bodies to bear in mind the caution administered in words memorable by Baron Alderson J. in *R. v. Hodge* [(1838) 2 Lew 227]:

> The mind was apt to take a pleasure in adapting circumstances to one another, and even in straining them a little, if need be, to force them to form parts of one connected whole; and the more ingenious the mind of the individual, the more likely was it, considering such matters, to overreach and mislead itself, to supply some little link that is wanting, to take for granted some fact consistent with its previous theories and necessary to render them complete.

Furthermore, in the same chapter, the book extensively references various forms of cartels, encompassing vertical and horizontal agreements, that are covered by the Act. It elaborates on the key identifiers of each agreement and elucidates the regulator's perspective on such agreements. As the author rightly observes, cartelization, like conspiracies, is shrouded in secrecy. Akin to criminal law, uncovering such conspiracies is a challenge for the regulator. Given the similarities between conspiracies in criminal law, and cartels governed by competition law, this would be a great opportunity for creative lawyers to cross-pollinate from the former to the latter, to devise yardsticks that the regulator can utilize to govern cartels. As the author predicts, one would expect that there would be stronger enforcement and stricter stance taken by the regulator towards cartels.

A noteworthy aspect of this book is the author's meticulous consideration of the Amendments introduced to the Competition Act in 2023. Each chapter of the book examines how these amendments address key concerns and delves into the conscious decisions made by legislators while introducing these amendments. For instance, in the chapter on Anti-Competitive Agreements, there is a reference to how the Act has been amended to regulate all parties which could be part of a *hub-and-spoke cartel*. The chapter on 'Mergers' discusses how the Amendments made to the CCI Regulations in 2023 have resulted in the inclusion of every valuable consideration in determining the *deal value threshold* for the purpose of notification to the Regulator. Further, the chapter on Abuse of Dominant Position also explores the absence of statutory recognition for *collective dominance* by multiple enterprises, which is different from the Treaty on the Functioning of the European Union – an aspect which is sub-judice in India. This meticulous effort renders the book a valuable resource for readers who are keen on tracking the evolution of competition law in India.

The enormous hard work of the author in simplifying complex jargon becomes evident through the tremendous effort undertaken in punctuating each chapter with tools such as graphs, charts, diagrams, and comparative tables to enhance the reader-friendly nature of the text. In the chapter on 'Mergers', for instance, the author adeptly traverses through challenging topics such as the calculation of *asset value* and *turnover* using illustrative tables. The discussion on how the regulator perceives the transfer of control of an entity is also duly supported by diagrammatic representations, elucidating intricate company structures and control dynamics. Further, in the same chapter, the author pithily discusses the concept of *Gun Jumping* – another jargon associated with the Act which refers to parties consummating a transaction even before notifying the Competition Commission of India. The author takes care to carve out and emphasize that only *Substantive Gun Jumping* would fall foul of the law. To substantiate, the author, as he has done with other chapters, populates the text with multiple circumstances which would be considered *Substantive Gun Jumping*. These are, as the author points out, cases where there is sharing of commercially sensitive information, allocation of customers, or undertaking joint marketing efforts while waiting for approval from the Regulator. Each such instance is dealt with in substantial detail, making the concepts accessible to any reader.

The chapter on intellectual property and competition law offers a virtual treat to the discerning reader. It delves into protection entitled to intellectual property rights, offering a nuanced discussion on the delicate balance between safeguarding these rights and ensuring fair access in the realm of competition. The author captures how the intellectual property regime and competition law function like two *friends in disagreement*, since both of them continue to work in tandem, one complementing the other, while their objectives may appear diametrically opposed and daggers drawn. The analysis distinguishes between the safeguarding of intellectual property rights and the abuse of the same. Further, the chapter discusses the expanded protection of Intellectual Property Rights introduced under the 2023 amendment. It engages in discussion on the legislative choices regarding the extension (or lack thereof) of intellectual property rights protection in cases involving a dominant player in the market. This recognizes the blurring lines between the impact of protecting such rights in anti-competitive agreements and situations involving a dominant player in the market. The analysis by the author arrests the attention of the reader and makes for compelling reading.

A whole chapter has been devoted to digital markets and competition law, offering an in-depth perspective for the readers. The author grapples with the subtle issue of how online and offline channels of distribution are interdependent, and sometimes substitutable, which impacts the meaning of *relevant market* under the Competition Act. The author rightly concludes that in defining a market in the digital space, the definition cannot be fossilized and must keep pace with the times. The chapter delves into pricing strategies adopted in multisided platforms and addresses the rapid accumulation of market power in such platforms. The approach of the Competition Commission of India emphasizing the assessment of the interdependence of different sides to a transaction and determining whether appreciable adverse effects of competition are felt by both sides have been highlighted. In an interesting passage, the author sows the seed for a future Digital Competition Act, to identify and regulate the small number of digital players, termed as *Systematically Important Digital Intermediaries* (SIDI) in order to ensure free and fair markets.

This is a book that must adorn the library of anyone and everyone who is concerned with competition law. I am sure the legal community, especially, young legal professionals will make the best use of the book to acquire mastery over this technical and complex but nevertheless fascinating subject.

I wish the book all success and Abir many more books to his pen.

Justice K.V. Viswanathan

Judge, Supreme Court of India

Acknowledgements

While working on the second edition of the book, I realized that with so much which has happened in the Indian competition law circles in the last eight years, it would be a mammoth task to revise this book, and may I add, it was essentially and for all practical purposes, writing a new book.

With the existing work pressures and jostling between work deliverables and other personal commitments, writing the second edition of my book seemed a herculean task. This book would not have been possible without the support of my family (my parents; my wife, Neha; my five-year-old lifeline, Aryana; and my pet, Biscuit). Their support and encouragement have been invaluable throughout since I had to keep on working at odd hours and miss much of our family time.

Having said that, I would be remiss in my duty if I did not acknowledge the contribution of two people, without whom this book would not have been possible.

The first person I would like to thank is Shreya Kapoor. Shreya is a final-year law student at National Law University Odisha. My association with Shreya started when she interned with Sarvada in her third year, and since then, it has been a matter of great fortune for Sarvada and me personally that she has been working with me and her analysis is exceptional. She has a keen interest in competition law and has actively contributed to legal scholarship on the subject through several publications. Beyond academic excellence, Shreya has actively engaged in internships at prestigious law firms, leveraging practical experience to complement theoretical knowledge. She has also excelled in moot court competitions and debates focusing on the domain of competition law.

The second person I would like to thank is Sasthibrata Panda. My association with Sasthi also dates back more than eighteen months, when I first saw him assisting a lawyer on an antitrust matter while he was still a law student. Thereafter, Sasthi interned in my office last year when he was in his final year, and since then, he has been a part of Sarvada Legal. He completed his BA LLB degree from DSNLU, Vishakhapatnam. Sasthi has assisted in matters before the Hon'ble Supreme Court of India, High Courts, Tribunals & quasi-judicial bodies such as the National Company Law Appellate Tribunal (NCLAT), Competition Commission of India, etc.

I am extremely proud of the fact that both Shreya and Sasthi are part of the competition law practice at Sarvada Legal, and their assistance has been invaluable. Like I said, this book would not have been possible without them.

CHAPTER 1

Introduction to Competition Law

§1.01 MARCH TOWARDS COMPETITION LAW

Competition law is intended to protect competition in the market in order to maximize consumer welfare. A robust competition law and policy is quintessential for enhancing efficiency and consumer welfare. The Competition Act, 2002 ('Competition Act') was enacted with the intention of preventing anti-competitive practices which would have an adverse effect on the market and its market participants. It seeks to protect the market participants and promote competition since effective competition helps the consumer to get the best quality product at the most competitive price. An effective competition law regime helps to attain efficiencies which ensure the application of laws, rules and regulations to ensure businesses and companies compete fairly with each other. This encourages enterprises to attain efficiency, creates a wider choice for consumers and helps reduce prices and improve quality of products/services. While the idea of perfect competition may be a farfetched concept in most industries, effective competition is the goal of any competition law dispensation. Effective competition is to be assessed in terms of rivalry among firms, low barriers and where no single firm can influence the market conduct. The aim and objective of the Competition Act were explained by the Supreme Court in *Competition Commission of India v. Steel Authority of India Limited* ('*SAIL* case'),[1] where it was said that the purpose of the Competition Act is to control the concentration of an industry from the hold of a particular market participant and prevent monopolies or similar kinds of concentration in an industry. Competition law is not against attaining monopolistic power, but it abhors the misuse of the monopolistic power to harm the market system and stakeholders. The primary purpose of the competition law is to increase competition in the market, protect the cost of the product, prevent losses to society and product quality, and safeguard other

1. *Competition Commission of India v. Steel Authority of India Limited* [2010], (SC) (2010) 10 SCC 744, para. 5.

competitors. The Supreme Court held that the perfect competition is the economic model where the market is competitive. Similarly, in *Competition Commission of India v. Bharti Airtel Ltd.* ('*Bharti Airtel* case'),[2] the Supreme Court observed that the Competition Act was enacted to bring out the paradigm shift in terms of globalization and economic development in India. This Competition Act would be anathema to unfair trade practices which cause an adverse effect on the market and ensure fair competition.

[A] The Aim and Objective of the Competition Act

The aim and objective of the Competition Act have been discussed in *Excel Crop Care Ltd. v. Competition Commission of India* ('*Excel Crop* case'),[3] and it was said that the purpose behind enacting the Competition Act was to prohibit anti-competitive practices and promote market's competition, consumer welfare and fair trade. The Competition Act sets the 'rules of the game' to ensure effective competition in order to bring economic efficiency, economic growth and development and consumer welfare in the market. The benefits of the Competition Act have been elaborated below:

(i) Economic Efficiency: In a competitive market, market participants must make effective use and allocation of the resources by forcing market participants to produce at the lowest cost and sell the product at a competitive price. The main advantage of a competitive market is the continuous pressure on the market participants to use resources in a manner that keeps costs down without compromising the quality of products. This always favors the consumer as the market participants must constantly strive to invest in research and development to provide a better deal to the consumer.

(ii) Economic Growth and Development: The competitive force in the market brings economic growth to the country by rapidly reallocating resources and increasing the value of the products and services in the market. The growth of the economy is one of the major indicators of economic development. Economic development shows the improvement in literacy rates, reduction in mortality rates, easy market entry and exit, development in innovation, improvement in physical infrastructure and overall economic welfare of the country. Thus, with economic growth and development, the economic efficiency of the country will improve, and there will be optimal usage of products and services.

(iii) Consumer Welfare: The ultimate beneficiary of competition is the consumer. Consumers will get better choices, better quality at a cheaper rate, improve their bargaining position in the market, etc. Along with the

2. *Competition Commission of India v. Bharti Airtel Ltd.* [2019], (SC) (2019) 2 SCC 521, para. 81.
3. *Excel Crop Care Ltd. v. Competition Commission of India* [2017], (SC) (2017) 8 SCC 47, para. 29; *Competition Commission of India v. State of Mizoram* [2022], (SC) (2022) 7 SCC 73, paras 7, 21-25.

remedies provided in the consumer laws, the end-consumers can use the tenets of the Competition Act to resolve the issue of market failures.

The Supreme Court in *Excel Crop* case also noted a few more benefits of the Competition Act, such as an improvement in employment rate, better industrial and trade policies, an improvement in the workplace environment, an increase in foreign investment, benchmarking by exposing inferior performance, etc.

Again, the ratio on the purpose of the Competition Act in *Excel Crop* case was re-emphasized by the Supreme Court in *Rajasthan Cylinders & Containers Ltd. v. Union of India* ('*LPG-I* case').[4] In *LPG-I* case, it was held that the Competition Act not only intends to eliminate anti-competitive practices but also to promote and sustain competition in the market. The CCI should enforce the Competition Act to curb the practices which will harm the competition. Hence, effective enforcement is important to prohibit practices having adverse effects on the competition as well as to deter future anti-competitive practices.

As discussed above, the primary objective of the Competition Act is to promote economic efficiency through effective enforcement of competition to create a market responsive to consumer preferences. Competition law is to promote economic efficiency by using competition as one of the means of assisting in the creation of a market responsive to consumer preferences.[5] The advantages of having an effective competition regime are threefold:

(i) Allocative efficiency, which ensures the effective allocation of resources. Allocative efficiency can be achieved only if all firms are of sufficient size to realize significant economies of scale, and markets are either competitively structured (i.e., they comprise a significant number of producers) or entry barriers are low. In such cases, all companies are price takers, and the demand and supply forces in the market determine the price. Allocative efficiency is attained when prices are equated to marginal costs, which is a condition for perfect competition.
(ii) Productive efficiency, which ensures that costs of production are kept at a minimum.
(iii) Dynamic efficiency, which promotes innovative practices. Dynamic efficiency refers to the development of new products. This can be done by ensuring proper reward to the inventor in lieu of developing and disclosing the invention to the public.

A high level committee on Competition Policy and Law ('High Level Committee') was formed to examine the various aspects and accordingly suggest keeping in view the competition policy of India. On 22 May 2022, the High Level Committee submitted its report, and thereafter, the Competition Act, 2002 came into operation on 12

4. *Rajasthan Cylinders & Containers Ltd. v. Union of India* [2020], (SC) (2020) 16 SCC 615, para. 80.
5. *SAIL* case, paras 6, 7, 125; in *Competition Commission of India v. Fast Way Transmission (P) Ltd.* [2018], (SC) (2018) 4 SCC 316, para. 12.

December 2003. The Competition Act was enacted as a response to market liberalization, ease of doing business by opening up India's economy and removing the strict government restrictions.

In India, a High Level Committee was constituted to examine its various aspects and make suggestions keeping in view the competition policy of India. This Committee made recommendations and submitted its report on 22 May 2002. After the completion of the consultation process, the Competition Act was enacted. As per the statement of objects and reasons of the Competition Act, this enactment is India's response to the opening up of its economy, removing controls, and resorting to liberalization. The natural corollary of this is that the Indian market should be geared to face competition from within the country and outside.

[B] The Purpose Behind Enforcing the Competition Act

The natural corollary of the Competition Act is to bring evolution to the Indian market by creating a competitive force within the country and outside.[6] So, with the avowed objective of a free-market economy, it was felt essential to have a quasi-judicial body to ensure that the practices which have an adverse effect on competition in India are prevented. And thereby, to ensure effective enforcement and fulfil the purpose of the Competition Act, a quasi-judicial body, namely the CCI, was established under section 7 of the Competition Act. Apart from the CCI, the Competition Act provides for the appointment of the Director General (DG) under section 16(1) of the Competition Act. The DG is a specialized investigating wing or the investigatory arm of the CCI. The various provisions of the Competition Act deal with the establishment, powers and functions as well as the discharge of adjudicatory functions by the CCI. Under the scheme of the Competition Act, the CCI is vested with inquisitorial, investigative, regulatory, adjudicatory and advocacy functions.

Further, the proviso of section 18 of the Competition Act states that for better enforcement, the CCI can have tie-ups with other Indian government agencies and foreign competition agencies. For international cooperation and promotion of competition law, CCI has signed a memorandum of understanding with the DG for Competition of the European Commission, the Australian Competition and Consumer Commission, the Japan Fair Trade Commission, etc. Such cooperation will help the competition agencies exchange information, share best practices and conduct various capacity-building programmes. Also, on 22 November 2022,[7] the Union Finance Ministry through a notification mandated the CCI to share information with the Enforcement Director, directly or indirectly. So, keeping in view the economic development of the country as a whole, a positive role has been given to the CCI to enforce the competition law in India.

---

6. *Coal India Limited and Another v. CCI and Another* [2023], (SC) 2023 SCC OnLine SC 740, para. 67.
7. Notification No. G.S.R. 832(E), dated 22 Nov. 2022.

Chapter II of the Competition Act can be referred to as the heart and soul of the competition law. Chapter II spells out three substantial provisions of the Competition Act because it prohibits the practices which are anathema to the concept of fair and competitive market. The substantive provisions of the Competition Act were notified in a phased manner, provisions relating to anti-competitive agreements (section 3) and abuse of dominance (section 4) were notified in May 2009, and provisions with respect to merger control (sections 5 and 6) were notified in June 2011.

To fulfil the purpose of the Competition Act, the CCI must prohibit such practices to create a healthy competition in the market. Because the aim and objective of the Competition Act clearly show that the enterprises that independently determine their commercial policies are prohibited from indulging in agreements which affect the competition adversely or concerted practices by taking advantage of their dominant position in their markets.[8] As the aim and objective also prohibit future anti-competitive effects, the parties before entering into a combination must notify the CCI by showing that the combination will not adversely affect the competition.[9]

The Competition Act in totality has a significant departure from the letter and spirit of the erstwhile Monopolies and Restrictive Trade Practices Act, 1969. The Competition Act is premised on the effect theory, which means the primary purpose of the Competition Act is to prevent practices which cause or are likely to cause an anti-competitive effect on the market. It does not condemn monopoly per se but rather focuses on the enterprise's use of the monopoly status. Further, the earlier Monopolies and Restrictive Trade Practices Commission had very limited enforcement powers since they could not penalize any enterprise. Their power was limited to passing cease and desist orders. Conversely, the Competition Act has empowered the CCI to penalize a delinquent enterprise, apart from passing ceasing-and-desist orders and also ordering for modification of the business practices. The penalties which are imposed by the CCI are one of the highest economic penalties in India. Also, the CCI can pass directions to modify the business practices by imposing behavioural remedies[10] under section 27 of the Competition Act and modify the structure of the enterprises by passing structural remedies[11] under section 28 of the Competition Act. In the context of anti-competitive agreements and abuse of dominance, CCI generally passes behavioural changes in terms of the enterprise's conduct with other market participants and end customers. In relation to merger control, under section 31 of the Act, structural and/or behavioural remedies are imposed through commitments on the parties to the combination. Further, the CCI, unlike its predecessor regime, has extraterritorial jurisdiction; i.e., the

8. *CCI v. Coordination Committee*, (2017) 5 SCC 17, para. 45. Also see, *Excel Crop* case, (2017) 8 SCC 47, paras 21, 26.
9. *SCM Solifert Ltd. v. CCI*, (2018) 6 SCC 631, para. 18.
10. *See*, OECD, Remedies and Commitments in Abuse Cases, p. 5. Behavioural Remedies are the remedies which mandates an enterprise to conduct in a particular manner, for example, with regard to pricing clauses, contractual obligations, etc.
11. *See*, OECD, Remedies and Commitments in Abuse Cases, p. 5. Structural Remedies are the remedies which involve changes to the structure of an enterprise, thereby effectively changing the structure of the market.

CCI can investigate the practices of companies based outside India if their conduct causes any anti-competitive effects in India.

Further, the Competition Act seeks to maintain a level playing field between the private and the public sector and seek competitive neutrality; i.e., government or state-owned enterprises should not use their legislative or fiscal powers to advantage their own businesses over the private sector. The provisions of the Competition Act are applicable to any enterprise which carries on economic activity, irrespective of whether it is publicly or privately owned. We will see from the definition of enterprise, discussed in detail below, that all the commercial activities of the government, excluding the sovereign functions (energy, currency, defence and space), come under the provisions of the Competition Act and that no antitrust exemptions are applicable to such state-owned enterprise. In fact, the CCI has penalized state-owned enterprises, like Coal India, since they have indulged in activities which constitute abuse of dominance. The erstwhile Competition Appellate Tribunal (COMPAT) also upheld the order passed by the CCI against Coal India. Thereafter, in *Coal India Ltd. v. CCI and Another* ('*Coal India* case'),[12] Coal India appealed before the Supreme Court by arguing that Coal India is a monopoly created by the Coal Mines (Nationalization) Act, 1973 with an objective of protecting it from challenges, and is guarded under Article 31B of the Constitution of India, 1950.[13] Article 31B validates certain enactments (such as, the Coal Mines (Nationalization) Act, 1973) which have been inserted under the Ninth Schedule of the Constitution of India, 1950. Coal India also relied upon section 19(4)(g) of the Competition Act to say that Coal India is not a dominant player under the Competition Act because Coal India is dominant due to a statute; hence, it should be treated differently that an ordinary dominant player. It was argued that Coal India was created under the said statute for the equitable distribution of coal in order to secure the 'common good' under Article 39(b) of the Constitution of India, 1950.[14] Accordingly, Coal India took support of Article 39(b) of the Constitution of India, 1950, to say that it has not violated the Competition Act because it is following the principle of 'common good' while distributing minerals and resources of the highest importance for India's economy. Hence, the provisions of the Competition Act will not be applicable to the conduct of Coal India because Coal India is an instrument of the state, and its conduct is in accordance with the directive principles under Article 39(b). Furthermore, it was also argued that there is no abuse of dominance under section 4(2)(a) and (b) of the Competition Act because the conduct of Coal India relating to the pricing and production of coals is based on the constitutional mandate under Article 39(b) and the objective of Coal Mines (Nationalization) Act, 1973. Additionally, it was also argued

12. *Coal India Limited and Another v. CCI and Another* [2023], (SC) 2023 SCC OnLine SC 740, paras 7-13, 88, 98, 99, 100, 101, 105, 119, 122.
13. Article 31B of the Constitution of India, 1950, says that the enactments placed in the ninth schedule of the Constitution of India shall not become void on the ground that they violate fundamental rights and no judicial review is possible against such enactments.
14. Article 39(b) of the Constitution of India, 1950, states that the state can enact laws to secure control of the resources of the community, and the distribution of the resources must subserve the common good.

that section 28 of the Coal Mines (Nationalization) Act, 1973 is a non-obstante clause; hence, it prevails over the Competition Act.

However, the Supreme Court, after taking consideration of all the arguments, dismissed the appeal. The Supreme Court held that the purpose of the Competition Act is to attain faster economic growth in India and foster competitive economy. To achieve the purpose, public sector companies or bodies created under statutes cannot abuse their dominance. The parliament was aware of the Coal Mines (Nationalization) Act, 1973, while including bodies created under statute within the purview of the term 'enterprise' under section 2(h) of the Competition Act. This shows that Coal India is an enterprise, and it can't evade its obligation under the Competition Act. Only those enterprises which are engaged in sovereign activities are exempt, but Coal India was not involved in any such sovereign activities. The Supreme Court then noted that the expression in section 19(4)(g) of the Competition Act regarding creating monopolies under statutes for determining the existence of dominant player shows the intention of the legislature to bring Coal India within the ambit of the Competition Act. Regarding the application of Article 31B of the Constitution of India, 1950, the Supreme Court held that the said article provides constitutional immunity from being challenged for violating fundamental rights and being invalidated by the courts. The said article protects the entities which are created under statutes, but these entities are not immunized from their anti-competitive conduct by acting with caprice, unfairly or discriminating against similarly situated persons or things with different conditions. The term 'common good' in Article 39(b) means achieving the highest good of the maximum number of people. But to serve the purpose of 'common good' and attain the goals in the directive principles, the principles of competition law must also be harmoniously construed along with the goals of directive principles. Finally, on the point of non-obstante provision under the Coal Mines (Nationalization) Act, 1973, the Supreme Court looked at the purpose of the Competition Act and held that the Competition Act will prevail over the Coal Mines (Nationalization) Act, 1973.

§1.02 PROCEDURE FOR INQUIRY

A detailed procedure has been established under the Competition Act and the regulations of the CCI with respect to the investigation process for a violation under sections 3 and 4 of the Competition Act. Merger filings and procedures have been dealt with in Chapter 4.

A diagrammatic illustration of key stages of inquiry under the Competition Act is as follows:

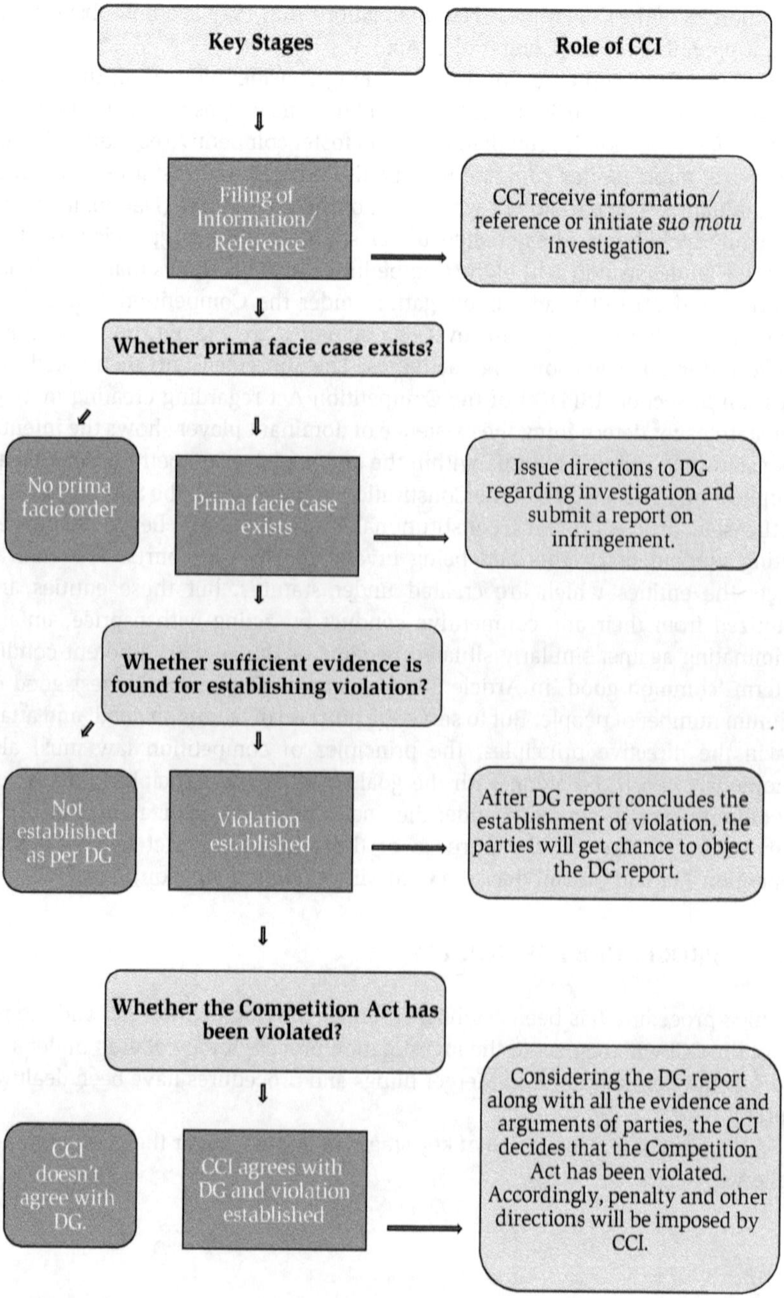
Key Stages
Role of CCI
Filing of Information/ Reference
CCI receive information/ reference or initiate suo motu investigation.
Whether prima facie case exists?
No prima facie order
Prima facie case exists
Issue directions to DG regarding investigation and submit a report on infringement.
Whether sufficient evidence is found for establishing violation?
Not established as per DG
Violation established
After DG report concludes the establishment of violation, the parties will get chance to object the DG report.
Whether the Competition Act has been violated?
CCI doesn't agree with DG.
CCI agrees with DG and violation established
Considering the DG report along with all the evidence and arguments of parties, the CCI decides that the Competition Act has been violated. Accordingly, penalty and other directions will be imposed by CCI.

[A] Initiation of the Case

The informant, i.e., the person who wishes to complain about a conduct to the CCI, would make such information available in writing to the CCI by paying the requisite filing fee outlining in detail the facts, evidence in support and the alleged contravention of the provisions of the Competition Act. The information could also be made by way of reference by the Central Government, State Government, statutory authority or on its own knowledge as provided under section 19(1)(a) of the Competition Act. Hence, the CCI can initiate an inquiry under section 26 of the Competition Act under the following three conditions:[15]

(i) information given under section 19;
(ii) reference made by the Government or a statutory authority; or
(iii) on its own motion ('*suo motu*').

It must be noted that under the Competition Act, there is no *locus standi* requirement; i.e., it is not necessary that the affected party only can file information. As a part of the information, it is not required for the informant to show how it has been harmed by the conduct of the alleged infringer. This is a precise reason why the term 'information' is used in the Competition Act and not 'complaint'. Before the Competition Act was notified in 2009, the term used in the Competition Act was filing of a 'complaint' which was changed to filing of 'information' in 2007. One of the major reasons for this change was that the legislature did not want to have a *locus standi* requirement. Further, the use of the word 'complaint' would mean an adversarial proceeding which is not the case with 'information' being used. There have been instances where the informant has filed the information, and the CCI has proceeded with the investigation and final orders, even when the informant is not present during the course of proceedings.

On the issue of *locus standi* under the Competition Act, the NCLAT in *Samir Agrawal v. Competition Commission of India and Others*[16] erred in holding that the informant had no right to file an information because he was neither aggrieved nor prejudiced by the conduct of the cab aggregators. The substantial question of law was whether a 'person' would mean any natural person irrespective of whether he was a consumer who suffered harm or a person whose legal rights have been harmed by the anti-competitive activity. The NCLAT held that CCI cannot take cognizance against the allegation of violation under sections 3 and/or 4 because the informant never suffered harm at the hands of the cab aggregators while using the apps as a consumer, so he has no locus to file an information. On an appeal against the judgment of the NCLAT, the Supreme Court in *Samir Agrawal v. CCI and Others* ('*Cab aggregator* case')[17] set aside

15. *Coal India* case, para. 90.
16. *Samir Agrawal v. Competition Commission of India and Others* [2020], (NCLAT) Competition Appeal (At) No. 11 of 2019, paras 10, 15, 16, 17.
17. *Samir Agrawal v. CCI and Others* [2021], (SC) (2021) 3 SCC 136, paras 14-17, 21; *Flipkart Interned Pvt. Ltd. and Others v. CCI and Others*, Writ Appeal No. 562 of 2021, paras 29, 35, 36, the Karnataka High Court rejected the argument that the person who filed the information was

the reasoning of the NCLAT on the issue of the *locus standi*. The Supreme Court said that the term 'any person' as defined in section 2(l) of the Competition Act is a wide and inclusive definition. Further, by looking at section 19(1)(a) of the Competition Act, it was held that an information can be filed by any person irrespective of the person being affected or not. As the proceeding under the Competition Act is a proceeding in rem which affects the public interest at large, anyone can file an information under section 19(1)(a) of the Competition Act. Thus, the informant need not be personally aggrieved by the anti-competitive agreement and/or the abuse of dominance.

Information is essentially made by a person or by way of reference from another authority. The purpose of information is to inform the CCI of an anti-competitive practice, and it is up to the CCI to determine whether the information has any merit and whether the factual situation mentioned in the information warrants any further investigation by the DG. The CCI is not bound by the issues and pleadings taken in the information and can go beyond the scope of the information and ask the DG to investigate additional grounds.

Further, unlike in a complaint scenario, there is no mechanism under the Competition Act to withdraw an information. Once information is made, it is up to the CCI to decide whether a fit case exists for further investigation or to close the matter.[18] The informant need not be present throughout the proceedings, and the CCI can pass appropriate orders based on the facts and circumstances of the case. Furthermore, it must be noted that the Competition (Amendment) Act, 2023 incorporated a statutory limitation of three years, which means CCI shall not initiate an inquiry against a matter unless the information or reference under section 19(1) of the Act is filed within three years. Also, the said amendment introduced the principle of res judicata in the Competition Act. Now, the CCI may refuse inquiry if a similar matter has already been decided under section 26(2A) of the Competition Act. However, it is important to note that section 26(2A) uses the term 'Commission may not inquire'. Therefore, it gives discretion to the CCI to interfere and there is no strict prohibition. There may be a situation where conduct which was not considered to be anti-competitive earlier by the CCI becomes anti-competitive with a change in market dynamics over a period of time, development in competition law jurisprudence or for any other reason. Considering the fact that the market is very dynamic and is constantly changing, the Karnataka High Court in *Flipkart Interned Pvt. Ltd. and Others v. Competition Commission India and Others*[19] held that just because CCI had looked into some matter previously, it does not

---

not an aggrieved person but was sponsored by someone else. The High Court reiterated the ratio of Supreme Court in *Samir Agrawal v. CCI and Others* and held that the Competition Act allows any person and not just an aggrieved person to file an information under section 19 of the Competition Act.

18. *Bharti Airtel* case, para. 1.
19. *Flipkart Interned Pvt. Ltd. and Others v. Competition Commission India and Others* [2021], (Karnataka High Court) Writ Appeal No. 562 of 2021, para. 42; *WhatsApp LLC and Another v. Competition Commission of India and Another* [2022], (Delhi High Court) 2022 SCC OnLine Del 2582, para. 36.

stop the CCI under the principle of res judicata from looking into any information subsequent to the development of new practices.

[B] Prima Facie Case

When such information mentioned above is received, the CCI is expected to satisfy itself and express its opinion on whether a prima facie case exists from the record produced before it and then to pass a direction to the DG to cause an investigation to be made into the matter under section 26(1) of the Competition Act. However, if the CCI is of the opinion that there exists no prima facie case based on the information placed before it, it may close the matter under section 26(2) of the Competition Act.

The Supreme Court of India has succinctly described the ambit of the direction passed under section 26(1) of the Competition Act in the case of *SAIL*.[20] The Supreme Court noted that the direction of the CCI under section 26(1) of the Competition Act, for the formation of a prima facie opinion requesting the offices of the DG to investigate the matter, is a direction *simpliciter* to cause an investigation into the matter. The Supreme Court noted that issuance of such a direction is an administrative direction to one of its own wings departmentally and is made without entering upon any adjudicatory process. It does not effectively determine any right or obligation of the parties to the *lis*. The Supreme Court further noted that a direction under section 26(1) of the Competition Act does not entail civil consequences for any person. In fact, in all the prima facie orders made by the CCI, it is clearly stated that the CCI makes clear that nothing stated in the prima facie order shall be tantamount to a final expression of opinion on the merit of the case, and the DG shall conduct the investigation without being swayed in any manner whatsoever by the observations made herein.

It must be noted herein that although the prima facie order is a direction *simpliciter* akin to an administrative function, the Gujarat High Court in *Vardayani Offset v. Competition Commission of India and Other*[21] quashed a prima facie order against the allegation of bid rigging because the CCI failed the test of legality by not recording reasons while passing the prima facie order. Also, it was impossible to read the prima facie order because it was heavily redacted. So, based on the reasoning of the *SAIL* case, the Gujarat High Court reiterated that the CCI may not record detailed reasons, but it must record some or minimum reasons to show that a prima facie case exists. Hence, the CCI failed to satisfy the basic requirement of a prima facie order, which expresses the mind of the CCI.

Another issue that was deliberated in detail by the Supreme Court in the *SAIL* case[22] was whether a notice of hearing had to be given to the informant or the alleged infringer prior to passing an order under section 26(1) of the Competition Act. It was noted by the Supreme Court, based on the statutory scheme of the Competition Act that the direction under section 26(1) of the Competition Act could be issued by the CCI

20. *SAIL* case, para. 38.
21. *Vardayani Offset v. Competition Commission of India and Other* [2020], (Gujarat High Court) MANU/GJ/1046/2020, paras 7, 10, 12, 17.
22. *SAIL* case, paras 21, 31, 91, 71.

with or without hearing the party against whom the information has been filed. Section 19(1) of the Competition Act does not mandate a requirement of notice to be given to the informant, affected party or any other person at the stage of deciding whether a prima facie case exists or not. Such parties cannot claim the right to notice or hearing as a matter of right, but it is always open to the CCI to call any 'such person' to render assistance or produce such records as the CCI may consider appropriate.

The relevant observations made by the Supreme Court in the *SAIL* case, in this regard, are that the proceeding under section 26(1) is the very beginning of the procedure against the matter raised under section 19(1) of the Competition Act. Unlike an adjudicatory proceeding which requires the CCI to hear the parties before passing a prima facie order, proceeding under section 26(1) is merely an administrative function and the power of CCI under section 26(1) is characteristic of an inquisitorial and regulatory power. The statutory language of section 26(1) of the Competition Act does not mandate the CCI to issue notice or allow the parties to claim *audi alteram partem* as a matter of right. CCI at this stage does not deal with the rights of the parties and only forms a prima facie opinion directing the DG to submit an investigation report or close the inquiry under section 26(2) of the Competition Act. However, this exclusion of *audi alteram partem* at the initial stage does not vitiate the due process of law because an opportunity for a full hearing will be given before final disposal of the matter. After the CCI forms prima facie opinion and subsequently receives the DG investigation report, thereafter, the CCI has to invite written submissions and oral hearings from the parties concerned. This means that before reaching the final decision, the concerned parties will get an opportunity to raise objection to or support the DG report and argue before CCI.

[C] Investigation and Inquiry Process

Once the CCI has found that there exists a prima facie case for violation of the provisions of section 3 and/or section 4 of the Competition Act, it will direct the offices of the DG to conduct a detailed investigation under section 26(1) of the Competition Act.

The inquiry process of the CCI and the investigation process of the DG have been distinctly separated in the Competition Act. The CCI acts as the watchdog on anti-competitive practice, whereas the DG is the investigative wing which assists the inquiry process by finding the facts and evidence. In the *SAIL* case,[23] the Supreme Court dealt with an important distinction between the terms 'inquiry' and 'investigation' in the context of section 26 of the Competition Act. An 'inquiry', as defined under Regulation 18(2) of the Competition Commission of India (General) Regulations, 2009 ('General Regulations'), is deemed to have commenced once the CCI provides the DG with a direction to investigate under section 26(1) of the Competition Act. The terms 'inquiry' and 'investigation' are often treated as synonyms; however, the Supreme Court clarified that both are different under the Competition Act. The inquiry continues

23. *SAIL* case, paras 115, 116.

until the final order is passed by the CCI, whereas an investigation is merely a part of the process of inquiry. Thus, inquiry also includes the phase after the investigation, where the CCI considers the DG's investigation report and hears the objections of the parties.

In terms of Regulation 18(2) of the General Regulations, once the CCI has directed the DG to investigate the matter, it is deemed that an inquiry has commenced. Then, the CCI considers the DG's investigation report and the objections and submissions made by the concerned parties. This inquiry will continue till the time a final order gets passed under section 27 or 26(6) of the Competition Act[24] or when the CCI, by not agreeing to the DG investigation report's finding on contravention, passes a final order holding the parties not liable. Further, under Regulation 20(4) of the General Regulations, the DG report should contain his findings of each of the allegations made in the information or reference, together with all evidence collected during the investigation.

On a concomitant reading of section 36(2) with section 41(2) of the Competition Act, both the CCI and DG have been vested with the wide and sweeping power of a civil court while discharging their functions. Sections 36(2) and 41(2) empower them to summon and examine any person, issue commissions for the examination of witnesses and documents, and render assistance or production of evidence.[25] Further, evidence is collected in the context of section 36(4) of the Competition Act, read with Regulation 41 of the General Regulations. While the DG investigates, subject to confidentiality, the concerned parties can apply inspection and certified copies of documents as per Regulation 37 of the General Regulations.[26] The DG is further empowered for the search and seizure of documents by section 41(3) of the Competition Act. The detailed procedure for conducting an investigation is contained in section 41, read with section 36 and Regulations 20, 21, 35, 41, 42 and 45 of the General Regulations.

Also, even in the absence of any particular provision, the CCI has some inherent power, such as to review or recall an illegal order. In *Google Inc. and Others v. CCI and Another*,[27] Google filed a writ petition before the Delhi High Court, praying to direct CCI for the recall of its prima facie order which has been passed without following the principles of natural justice. It was further noted that the omission of section 37 of the Competition Act, which empowered the CCI to review its order prior to the omission, cannot be a conclusive indication of the legislature's intention to take away the CCI's power to review. The High Court concluded that the prima facie order directing the DG to investigate can be reviewed or recalled by the CCI. To avoid any delay in the investigation process, the High Court directed the CCI to dispose of the application for review or recall on the very first date without entertaining any lengthy arguments or going into the merits of the case.

24. *SAIL* case, para. 116.
25. *Google Inc. and Others v. CCI and Another*, [2015], (Delhi High Court) 2015 SCC OnLine Del 8992, para. 18(c).
26. *Vardayani Offset v. Competition Commission of India and Other* [2020], (Gujarat High Court) MANU/GJ/1046/2020, para. 15.2.
27. *Google Inc. and Others v. CCI and Another*, [2015], (Delhi High Court) 2015 SCC OnLine Del 8992, paras 8, 18, 18(ZA), 18(ZQ), 18(ZT), 20-24.

Chapter 2 shows the various techniques used by the DG to investigate a case of cartels. As a matter of practice, the DG has been collecting evidence in the form of personal/official e-mails, e-mail dumps, telephonic records, minutes of the meeting, travel details, physical meetings and conferences, etc. Further, the DG has not only relied on the traditional modes of collecting evidence, i.e., issuance of information requests and depositions followed by written submissions but also conducted raids on the premises of the companies. Section 41(3) of the Competition Act empowers the DG with investigative tools, and one of the effective investigative tools is to conduct raids. Such raids are known as 'dawn raid' which means an unannounced inspection by the DG on the parties that have violated or are likely to violate the Competition Act. The DG has broad power while conducting a dawn raid and may search and seize documents (including electronic data residing on electronic devices), office premises and other properties of the parties. A dawn raid is also known as an on-site inspection or surprise inspection. In September 2014, the DG conducted the first dawn raid by its unannounced search and seizure operation on JCB Limited, a leading player in the earth-moving and construction equipment industry. The legality of the dawn raid was thereafter challenged by the JCB Limited before the Delhi High Court, and the said High Court passed an ad interim order restraining the DG and the CCI from utilizing the seized material to pass a final report and final order, respectively. Then CCI filed a special leave petition before the Supreme Court challenging the Delhi High Court's interim order. The Supreme Court in *CCI v. JCB (India) Ltd.*[28] vacated the interim order and held that the High Court erred in restraining the statutory authority of DG to conduct a fair investigation. Reading section 41(3) of the Competition Act with section 240-A of the Companies Act, 1956, the DG has been expressly conferred with the power to investigate anti-competitive behaviours via search and seizure. The Supreme Court was of the view that the High Court's blanket restrains on analysing the seized material for the purpose of investigation. Hence, vacating the interim order of the Single Bench of the High Court, the Supreme Court remitted back to the Division Bench of the High Court. After the Supreme Court passed this judgment in 2019, many dawn raids were carried out by the DG. For instance, only in the year 2022 the DG conducted dawn raids on e-commerce platforms like Flipkart and Amazon,[29] mining services companies,[30] tyre companies,[31] and cement companies.[32]

If the DG recommends that there is contravention of the provisions of the Competition Act, the said recommendation also is not binding on the CCI, and it may

---

28. *CCI v. JCB (India) Ltd.* [2020], (SC) (2020) 17 SCC 446, paras 13-18.
29. Business Standard, Top traders body CAIT lauds CCI raids on Amazon sellers Cloudtail, Appario, 28 Apr. 2022, available at: https://www.business-standard.com/article/companies/top-traders-body-cait-lauds-cci-raids-on-amazon-sellers-cloudtail-appario-122042800642_1.html.
30. Deccan Herald, CCI raids engineering firms after Coal India antitrust complaint, 6 May 2022, available at: https://www.deccanherald.com/national/east-and-northeast/cci-raids-engineering-firms-after-coal-india-antitrust-complaint-1106982.html.
31. Business Today, CCI conducts raids on tyre companies CEAT, Apollo, Continental: Report, 30 Mar. 2022, available at: https://www.businesstoday.in/latest/corporate/story/cci-conducts-raids-on-tyre-companies-ceat-apollo-continental-report-327911-2022-03-30.

enquire into the matter if in its opinion a further inquiry is called for or it may if it does not agree with the DG, close the matter forthwith. If the CCI agrees with the DG, it can proceed to pass appropriate orders in terms of sections 27, 28 and 31 of the Competition Act.

Based on the above, it can be seen from the scheme of the Competition Act that the recommendations of the DG are not binding on the CCI. Also, NCLAT in *Hyundai Motor India Ltd. v. Competition Commission of India and Others*[33] noted that the DG's report is merely an opinion primarily to assist the CCI in appreciation of evidence in arriving at the final conclusion; hence, it is not binding at all. Further, the scheme of the Competition Act does not restrict the scope of DG's investigation into any matter which was not considered by the CCI, while forming a prima facie opinion under section 26(1) of the Competition Act.

[D] The Scope of DG's Investigation

It must be noted herein that a plain reading of the Competition Act would show that under the provisions of the Competition Act, the DG has no *suo moto* powers of investigation, and they can act and investigate a matter only if it is directed by the CCI. This is a marked difference from the earlier Monopolies and Restrictive Trade Practices regime where the DG had *suo moto* powers of investigation under the Monopolies and Restrictive Trade Practices Act, 1969.

However, the scope of the DG's investigation should not be limited to the direction of the CCI's prima facie order, and it must involve analysis of the facts from all angles and finding out every possible violation of the Competition Act. The DG's scope of the investigation was sufficiently discussed in the *Excel Corp* case.[34] In this case, the inquiry was initiated by the CCI based on information from the Chairman and Managing Director of Food Corporation of India (FCI). It was alleged that four manufacturers of Aluminium Phosphide Tablets (APT) have formed a bid rigging cartel by quoting identical rates in the tenders floated by FCI. Accordingly, a prima facie order was passed to initiate investigation, and ultimately, the APT manufacturers were held liable for rigging several tenders. One of the contentions of the APT manufacturers was that there was no specific prima facie direction by the CCI directing the DG to investigate the 2011 tender, so the DG couldn't investigate the tender. The Supreme Court held that the DG should not be restricted from investigating outside the scope of the prima facie order. The purpose of the investigation by the DG is to cover all the necessary facts to see whether there is any contravention of the Competition Act by the enterprise(s) whose conduct needs to be investigated. Though the information is the

32. Business Standard, Competition Commission conducts searches at India Cements' Chennai office, 23 Dec. 2022, available at: https://www.business-standard.com/article/companies/competition-commission-conducts-searches-at-india-cements-chennai-office-122122201123_1.html.
33. *Hyundai Motor India Ltd. v. Competition Commission of India and Others* [2018], (NCLAT) Competition Appeal No. 06 of 2017, para. 37.
34. *Excel Corp* case, paras 44, 45.

starting point of the investigation, the DG can carry out a further investigation if another enterprise is also involved in the violation of the Competition Act or if other facts reveal another violation of the Competition Act. Since the prima facie order gets passed in an initial stage, it is not possible to foresee and predict all the violations of the Competition Act. Hence, the DG would be well within its power to include the violation and the enterprise(s) revealed during the investigation. Further, the Delhi High Court in *Cadila Healthcare Ltd. and Others v. Competition Commission of India*[35] noted that the CCI investigated Cadila Healthcare Ltd. which is not impleaded as the Opposite Party in the prima facie order. Cadila Healthcare Ltd. objected to the investigation being conducted by the DG, but the High Court held that the DG's scope of investigation shall not be restricted only to the enterprises named in the prima facie order.

Similarly, in *Competition Commission of India v. Grasim Industries Ltd.*,[36] the Delhi High Court held that the DG could *suo motu* expand its scope of the investigation beyond the prima facie order to investigate Grasim Industries for the violation of section 3 of the Competition Act, and allowed the DG to investigate Grasim Industries for abusing its dominant position under section 4 of the Competition Act. The Delhi High Court relied upon the observation made by the same court in *Cadila Healthcare Limited v. CCI*, where it was held that DG can travel outside the prima facie opinion to investigate an anti-competitive behaviour which was not even mentioned in the order under section 26(1) of the Competition Act. Further, the Delhi High Court relied on the *SAIL case* and *Excel Crop case* to reiterate that the prima facie opinion at the stage of issuing directions to the DG does not restrict the scope of the investigation. The stage when the directions are issued under section 26(1) of the Competition Act is a very early stage of inquiry; hence, CCI could not foresee or predict all the anti-competitive behaviour and the parties who are engaged in it. Similarly, the High Court also noted that the CCI directed the DG to investigate 'the matter', and this was broad enough to enable the DG to investigate all the anti-competitive behaviour that will come to the notice of the DG while undertaking the investigation. As the language of prima facie opinion also plays an important role for DG while conducting the investigation, using broad language helps the DG to investigate in an unrestricted manner.

To protect the purpose of the Competition Act, ensure fair competition and prohibit anti-competitive trade practices in the market, the DG can expand its scope of investigation in order to include facts, additional enterprise and additional information that were not present in the prima facie order.

35. *Cadila Healthcare Ltd. & Ors. v. Competition Commission of India* [2018], (Delhi High Court) 2018 SCC OnLine Del 11229, para. 43. An appeal is pending before the Supreme Court. *See*, *Cadila Healthcare Ltd. v. Competition Commission of India*, (SC) SLP(C) No. 030641/2018.
36. *Competition Commission of India v. Grasim Industries Ltd.* [2019], (Delhi High Court) 2019 SCC OnLine Del 10017, paras 35, 40, 41, 42, 44, 45, 48, 49-52. An appeal is pending before the Supreme Court. *See*, *M/s Grasim Industries Ltd. v. CCI*, SLP(C) No. SLP(C) No. 008546/2020.

[E] Standard of Proof

The standard of proof required for proving a case of contravention under the Competition Act is that of 'preponderance of probability' akin to civil law; the DG brings forth evidence which includes a mix of direct and circumstantial evidence. The reason behind applying 'preponderance of probability' instead of 'beyond reasonable doubt' as standard of proof is because of the difficulty in finding direct evidence to prove the allegations against the contravention under the Competition Act. Generally, in cartel cases,[37] there is rarely any direct evidence to establish the anti-competitive agreement as the concerted practice takes place in a clandestine manner. So, in most cartel cases, the cartelization was inferred from a number of co-incidences and indicia which were taken together to constitute evidence of the contravention of section 3(3) of the Competition Act.[38] Hence, for efficient enforcement and to fulfil the purpose of the competition law, CCI has set the standard of proof on the basis of the benchmark of preponderance of probability.

[F] Further Investigation/Enquiry

Once the DG submits his report to the CCI, a copy of the said report is required to be forwarded to the parties concerned, including the Central Government, State Government, or Statutory Authority in case the investigation was directed on a reference received from such Government/Authority. This exercise is required to be undertaken irrespective of whether the DG reports a contravention of the provisions of the Competition Act or otherwise. In case the DG recommends that no contravention of the provisions of the Competition Act is made, the CCI is required to invite objections or suggestions on the said report from the Central Government, or the State Government, or the Statutory Authority of the parties concerned, as the case may be. Such a report is then required to be considered by the CCI in light of the objections or suggestions received by it. If the CCI, on consideration of the matter in light of the objections or suggestions, if any, received by it, agrees with the DG, the matter is closed forthwith.

However, the recommendation made by the DG in this regard is not binding on the CCI,[39] and after considering the said report in light of the objections or suggestions received by it, if the CCI is of the opinion that further investigation is required, it may direct such further investigation into the matter by the DG. The CCI, instead of directing further investigation by the DG, may also cause a further inquiry to be made into the matter, or it may itself hold a further inquiry into the matter. There is a detailed

37. *GAIL (India) Limited v. PMP Infratech Private Ltd. and Another*, Case No. 41 of 2019, para. 35; *In Re: Anti-competitive conduct in the paper manufacturing industry*, *Suo Motu* case No. 05 of 2016, para. 153; *Mr. Rizwanul Haq Khan v. Mersen (India) Pvt. Ltd. and Another*, Reference Case No. 02 of 2016, para. 44, *in re, alleged cartelization by steel producers*, RTPE 09 of 2008, para. 111.
38. *Builders Association of India v. Cement Manufacturers' Association & Ors.*, Case No. 29 of 2010, para. 183.
39. *Google Inc. and Others v. CCI and Another*, 2015 SCC OnLine Del 8992, para. 18(ZJ).

procedure for further investigation and inquiry under the Competition Act when the DG report records that there is no violation under sections 3 and 4 of the Competition Act.

A diagrammatic illustration of the key stages of proceeding for further investigation/inquiry under the Competition Act is as follows:

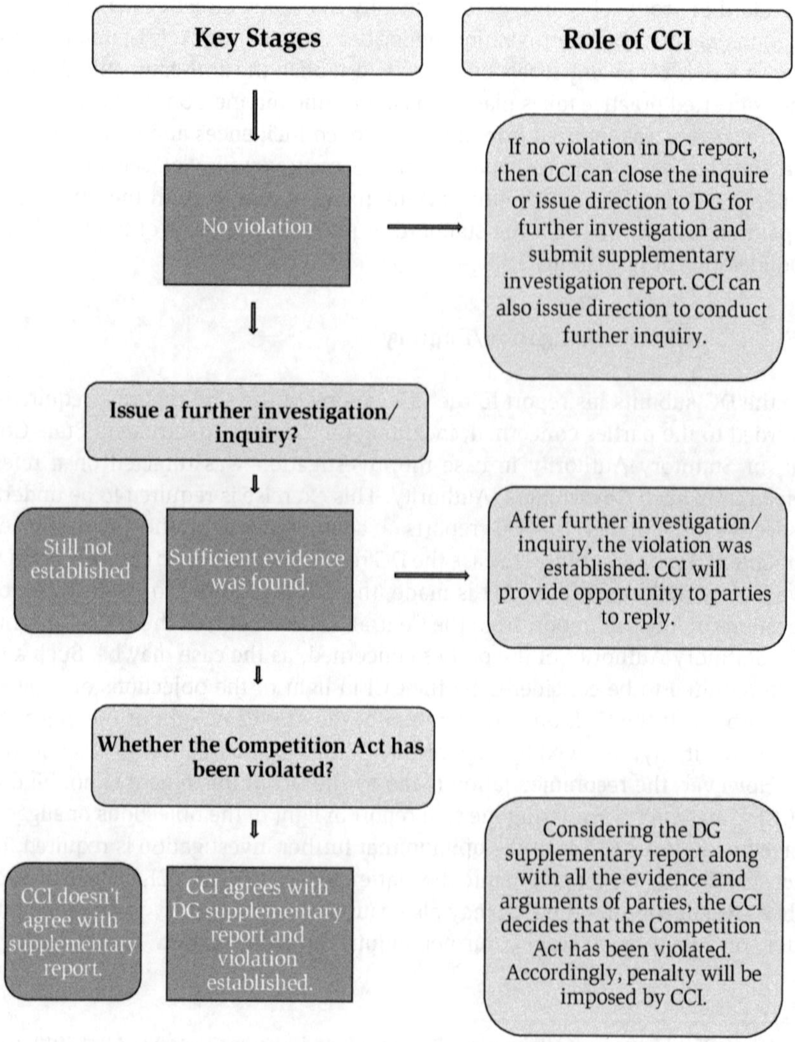

On the CCI's power to direct DG for further investigation, the NCLAT in *Amit Mittal v. DLF and Others*[40] made some important observations. In this case, an appeal

40. *Amit Mittal v. DLF and Others* [2022], (NCLAT) Competition Appeal (AT) No. 82 of 2018, paras 18-23.

was filed against the CCI's order passed under section 26(6) of the Competition Act. In the CCI's order, the DG's main investigation report disclosed that DLF is abusing its dominant position under section 4(2)(a)(ii) of the Competition Act, but the CCI directed the DG to further investigate and submit a supplementary investigation report under section 26(7) of the Competition Act read with Regulation 20(6) of the General Regulations. In the supplementary investigation report, the DG found that DLF is not a dominant player in the relevant market; therefore, the question of abuse of dominance will not arise. Accordingly, the CCI passed an order to close the proceeding against DLF for the violation of section 4(2)(a)(ii) of the Competition Act. At the appellate stage, the NCLAT held that the CCI can direct the DG for further investigation only if the DG finds there is no contravention of the Competition Act in its main investigation report as per section 26(5) of the Competition Act. Hence, section 26(5) is a prerequisite to pass an order for further investigation under section 26(7) of the Competition Act. Thereby, NCLAT remitted the matter back to CCI and directed the CCI to pass an order based on the main investigation report of the DG. The NCLAT's order was subsequently stayed by the Supreme Court, and the fate of the CCI's order is still undecided.[41] There is enough indication in the Competition Act to suggest that the restrictive interpretation adopted by NCLAT may not stand judicial scrutiny from the Supreme Court.

After conducting further inquiry, if the DG's supplement investigation report recommends that there is a contravention of the provisions of the Competition Act, the said recommendation also is not binding on the CCI, and it may enquire into the matter if in its opinion a further inquiry is called for or it may if it does not agree with the DG, close the matter forthwith. If the CCI agrees with the DG, it can proceed to pass appropriate orders in terms of sections 27, 28 and 31 of the Competition Act.

§1.03 ENFORCEMENT POWERS OF THE CCI

[A] Penalties and Directions on Companies/Group

The Competition Act regulates the manner in which businesses should operate in the market. It has emerged as the most important piece of economic legislation governing both behavioural and structural aspects of a business. Every company should take into consideration the legal issues of competition relating to both inorganic growth and behavioural models adopted by companies. The CCI is emerging as a market regulator in India which is as assertive as the market regulators in developed jurisdictions. Unlike the predecessor regime which lacked teeth, the Competition Act provides for extensive enforcement powers. The CCI can impose a monetary penalty of up to 10% of the average turnover of the last three preceding financial years on every enterprise for abuse of dominance or for entering into anti-competitive agreements. A still higher penalty is reserved for cartel activities where the penalty can extend up to three times the amount of profits or 10% of the turnover during the period of the existence of the

41. Stay order dated 17 Mar. 2023, *Competition Commission of India v. Amit Mittal and Others*, (SC) Civil Appeal 1486 of 2023.

cartel, whichever is higher. Further, the CCI has the powers to modify terms of agreements, modify business practices, declare agreements to be void, direct division of an enterprise, etc. In essence, apart from monetary penalties, the CCI can also direct enterprises to change the manner of conducting their business operations. Therefore, we see that the law enables the CCI to have vast powers to prevent practices which have an anti-competitive effect. The CCI has also used its powers under the Competition Act to penalize a large number of companies.

The CCI is using the vast powers provided to it under the Competition Act to levy penalties. However, the manner in which the penalties are being imposed is not very structured and clear. It is apposite to note that India has moved from a regime of no penalties for anti-competitive activities (under the Monopolies and Restrictive Trade Practices Act, 1969) to a regime of heavy penalties and liabilities. As mentioned above, the CCI can penalize up to 10% of the average turnover of the parties, and further, a higher penalty is reserved for cartel activities. In 2023, the Competition Act was amended to clarify that turnover means the global turnover derived from all the products and services of the parties. While a headroom of penalties has been provided under the Competition Act (from 0.1% to 10%), the CCI, in their orders, do not spell out any reason for granting, say, penalties of 5% of average turnover or 9% of the average turnover. It is a well-established principle laid down by the Supreme Court that the CCI and NCLAT are quasi-judicial authorities, and hence, their orders must be speaking orders; i.e., the orders must clearly spell out reasons which show application of mind. Having said that, the orders of the CCI do not spell out the reason for quantum of the penalty. This is the same reason why when the matter goes up in appeal before the NCLAT, one of the hotly contested topics in the appellate forum is the quantum of penalty. Since the CCI effectively determines the rights and liabilities of the parties, and the penalties that are imposed by them are the highest economic penalties in India, it is essential that due reasons are provided in the order of the quantum of penalty. Such reasons for penalties are required to determine proportionality by a higher forum, and indeed, it is a part of due process.

In this regard, it is apposite to note the observations in the case of *Excel Crop* case,[42] where the Supreme Court relied on the decision of the Competition Appeal Court of South Africa in *Southern Pipeline Contractors v. Competition Commission* to hold that imposition of the penalty on the total turnover would be inequitable for a multi-product company. The Supreme Court looked beyond the literal interpretation and applied rule of purposive interpretation while interpreting section 27(b) of the Competition Act and held that there is no justification for including other products of such companies if the contravention of the Competition Act involves one specific unit or business. So, any penalty imposed under the Competition Act should be imposed only on the 'relevant turnover', i.e., the turnover of the specific unit or business of a multi-product company, with respect to which the violation has taken place. The Supreme Court applied the principle of proportionality to arrive at this conclusion and believed that imposing a penalty on the total turnover of multi-product companies

42. *Excel Crop* case, paras 80, 84, 91, 94, 95, 96, 106-108, 111-114.

would be grossly disproportionate to the degree of contravention. Hence, by looking at the principle of proportionality, the CCI can't impose more than a 10% penalty on the company's relevant turnover. Having said that, the Supreme Court discussed a two-step calculation approach to calculate the penalty. The first step would be determination of the relevant turnover based on audited financial statements or any other reliable records. In the second step, the aggravating and mitigating circumstances while imposing an appropriate percentage of penalty.

Furthermore, the Supreme Court also looked at the guidelines of foreign competition agencies, such as the European Commission and the United Kingdom's Office of Fair Trade, to suggest that guidelines for the calculation of penalty need to be framed to ensure proportionality while imposing penalty. It was further noted that imposing penalty on the relevant turnover aligns with the purpose of the Competition Act because if penalty is calculated based on total turnover, then it will result in over-deterrence and stifle the economy of the country.

So, the penalties under section 27(b) of the Competition Act must be calculated as per the relevant turnover, or else an excessively high penalty may be imposed which will ultimately harm the economic growth, investment, entrepreneurship, employment and the interest of national economy, which is not the intention of the Competition Act. However, in 2023, the Competition Act was amended to impose penalties on the global turnover of the companies, which need not be limited specifically to the infringing products. This might result in discouraging investors and has the potential to have far-reaching implications on multinational companies to do business in India. This amendment may, thus, be the subject matter of judicial scrutiny in future appropriate cases for including all the units and businesses (all over the world) of the company while calculating the penalty under section 27(b) of the Competition Act since it may be argued that it is against the principle of proportionality as was laid down by the Supreme Court in the *Excel Crop* case (discussed *supra*).

Apart from the monetary penalties, the decisional practice of the CCI would show that under section 27 of the Competition Act, it has also directed the enterprise to change its business practice, for example, by directing cease-and-desist order and behavioural remedies. In the case of *Shri Shamsher Kataria v. Honda Siel Cars India Ltd. and Others* ('*Automobile spare parts* case'),[43] the CCI imposed the following behavioural remedies on the automobile manufacturers:

(i) allow suppliers to sell spare parts in the open market without any restriction on independent repairers;
(ii) the automobile manufacturers must develop an effective system regarding the availability of spare parts and diagnostic tools in the market, sell spare parts under fair and reasonable terms, and train independent and provide technical support to repairers;
(iii) to decrease the prices and provide more choices to the consumers;
(iv) automobile manufacturers should standardize the increasing number of different spare parts;

43. *Shri Shamsher Kataria v. Honda Siel Cars India Ltd. and Others*, Case No. 03 of 2011, para. 22.3.

(v) the automobile manufacturers shall not impose any restrictive condition that warranties would be cancelled if the consumer avails of services of any independent repairer;
(vi) the automobile manufacturers have to be transparent regarding the information of the spare parts, their maximum retail prices (MRPs), and any such information by publishing such information on their websites.

Similarly, the CCI in *Federation of Hotel & Restaurant Associations of India and Others v. MakeMyTrip and Others* ('*MMT-Go* case')[44] passed a set of directions to MakeMyTrip for abuse of dominance and vertical anti-competitive agreement with OYO to delist the inventories of competitors of OYO. The CCI imposed the following direction on the MakeMyTrip:

(i) remove the price and room availability parity obligation and remove the exclusive conditions from the agreement with hotels;
(ii) MakeMyTrip must impose fair conditions on the hotels; there must be transparent disclosures regarding the non-availability of inventories on MakeMyTrip's platform, etc.;
(iii) listing of hotels on fair, reasonable and non-discriminatory terms.

In *Umar Javeed and Others v. Google LLC*,[45] the CCI found Google to be abusing its dominant position in the Android ecosystem. The CCI ordered the following behavioural remedies on Google:

(i) Google shall prohibit mandating the smartphone manufacturers to pre-install Google's app and allow the smartphone manufacturers to decide on the pre-installation of apps.
(ii) Google shall not bundle Play Store services with its other services.
(iii) Google shall not offer any incentives for ensuring exclusivity for its search services and for not selling Android fork devices.
(iv) Google shall not impose any anti-fragment obligations on smartphone manufacturers by restricting them from manufacturing Android fork devices.
(v) Google shall allow the end-users to set the default search engine for all search entry points in the minimum steps possible.

In the app store market, CCI passed some behavioural remedies on Google for violating section 4 of the Competition Act in *XYZ and Others v. Alphabet Inc. and Others*.[46] CCI passed the following remedies:

(i) Google shall allow app developers to use any third-party billing system without imposing any adverse measurers.

44. *Federation of Hotel & Restaurant Associations of India and Others v. MakeMyTrip and Others*, Case No. 14 of 2019 and 01 of 2020, para. 312.
45. *Umar Javeed and Others v. Google LLC*, Case No. 39 of 2018, para. 617.
46. *XYZ and Others v. Alphabet Inc and Others*, Case No. 07 of 2020, 14 and 35 of 2021. para. 395.

(ii) Google shall not restrict any app developers from communicating with end-users about their apps and offers.
(iii) Google shall not restrict end-users from accessing all the features of the app developers and shall not impose any unfair pricing conditions on app developers.
(iv) the criteria for the application of fees and payment policy of Google shall be transparent, and Google shall not impose any discriminatory conditions for using third-party billing systems.
(v) the policy relating to the collection and processing of data from the app developers must be transparent, and Google shall allow the app developers to access the data collected through the concerned app.

Further, as per the Competition (Amendment) Act, 2023, the CCI can accept the commitment of the enterprise in terms of change in their anti-competitive agreements and abusive practices.

In case of combinations, the CCI has the power to give behavioural and/or structural remedies under section 31 of the Competition Act by issuing or accepting commitments of the parties. For instance, in relation to the merger agreement between Zee Entertainment and Sony,[47] a structural remedy was proposed by Zee, to divest its three channels. The proposal to divestiture of channels was accepted by CCI to avoid potential harm to Zee's business users as well as its end-users.

Behavioural remedies were undertaken by Google for acquiring a non-controlling minority stake of 1.28% in Airtel.[48] It was noted that Google already had a stake in Jio and through this proposed combination, it was also acquiring a stake in Airtel (which is a competitor of Jio). Therefore, the CCI pointed out the possibility of the flow of competitively sensitive information between Airtel and its competing firm, i.e., Jio. Accordingly, Google proposed a modification in their Co-Marketing Agreement by saying that it will maintain an appropriate firewall to prevent the flow of competitively sensitive information between Airtel and Jio. The parties further undertook, that they will comply with all applicable privacy and data protection laws governing customer and/or consumer data and will not share customer data with each other. These cases and concepts have been discussed in the appropriate portions of the book.

Thus, the Competition Act provides for vast sweeping powers provided to the CCI. Further, the CCI may pass behavioural remedies to modify the anti-competitive agreements which have been found to be in contravention of section 3 of the Competition Act. However, as per the strict interpretation of the statute, the power to modify the agreement is limited to the agreements which are in contravention of section 3 can only be modified. In *DLF Ltd. and Others v. Competition Commission of*

47. Culver Max Entertainment Private Limited, Zee Entertainment Enterprises Limited, Bangla Entertainment Private Limited, and Essel Group Participants, Combination Registration No. C-2022/04/923, 4 Oct. 2022.
48. Google International LLC and Bharti Airtel Limited, Combination Registration No. C-2022/03/913, para. 24.

India and Others,[49] the erstwhile COMPAT said that under section 27 of the Competition Act, the CCI is empowered to modify the agreements for violating section 3. However, the same is not possible for the violation of section 4. The erstwhile COMPAT interpreted section 27 to say that the wording of the said provision clearly states that the CCI can order to modify the which are in contravention of section 3 of the Competition Act, and the said provision is silent about the CCI's power to modify agreement for the contravention of section 4 of the Competition Act.

Nevertheless, as noted above, the decisional practice of CCI shows that it may completely or partially modify the agreements which are in contravention of section 4 of the Competition Act.

Furthermore, for conducts that amount to anti-competitive agreement or abuse of dominance, CCI has the power to pass orders against the entire group that holds control over the entity and not limit the penalty only on the concerned entity, which committed the contravention. The group may be penalized if it holds responsibility (direct attribution) or even contributes (acts in common) towards such anti-competitive/abusive conduct. The penalty clause (proviso of section 27(g) of the Competition Act) which is rather loosely worded may be interpreted to impose liability on the group companies akin to the concept of joint and several liability, often found in tortious claims. Similarly, the penalty may be imposed on the global turnover of the group. Further, in case of abuse of dominance, the CCI has been given the power to order the division of the enterprise.

Considering the vast enforcement powers under the Competition Act, every enterprise must ensure that their practices are in compliance with the provisions of the Competition Act, as non-compliance will result in huge penalties, apart from consequential cascading effects such as reputational loss and change in business practices. Further, the Competition Act is applicable to all companies, irrespective of the size of the company and the sector. Even a loss-making company has no safety net prescribed under the Competition Act, and penalties can be imposed on such loss-making companies as a percentage of their turnover. In this climate of inflow of investments into India, it is critical that the enterprises undertake a thorough due diligence of the target enterprise for competition law violations prior to acquisition since the liabilities of the target enterprise may flow to the acquirer.

[B] Penalties on Directors/Officers-in-Charge

Companies are a juristic person as they have no mind of their own; thus, CCI can penalize the officer-in-charge who is responsible for the conduct of the company during the time when the contravention took place. Unless the officer-in-charge shows that he diligently tried to prevent the contravention of the Competition Act or the contravention was committed without his knowledge, he will be deemed to be responsible for the

49. *DLF Ltd. and Others v. Competition Commission of India and Others* [2014], (COMPAT) MANU/TA/0012/2014, para. 74. An appeal is pending before the Supreme Court against this erstwhile COMPAT's order. *See*, *DLF Home Developers Ltd v. CCI and Another*, Civil Appeal No. 019945 of 2017.

anti-competitive conduct of the company.[50] Hence, apart from fining the companies or trade associations, as the case may be, the CCI can also penalize directors, managers, secretaries and any other officers-in-charge of companies under section 48 of the Competition Act.

Directors owe a fiduciary duty towards the stakeholders of the company and further in a general manner to the government and the public at large. The directors must, therefore, have to identify the risks of competition law violations since failure to take note of competition law provisions can result in heavy penalties, which affect the bottom line of the company. The directors face a real risk of non-compliance, considering the rigorous regulatory regime brought in by the CCI. Under section 48 of the Competition Act, the CCI can proceed against directors and officers-in-charge of the company (e.g., Managing Director, Director, Chief Executive Officer, Chief Operating Officer, etc.) for conducting the business of a company at that relevant point of time when the violation of the Competition Act was committed by the concerned company. The threshold is quite high for a managing director to avail the due diligence exemption. A chain of evidence must be clearly shown and demonstrated by the director to show that he undertook all actions to prevent the commission of the contravention. Such evidence may be in terms of proper training being imparted to employees or business partners of the company, undertaking periodic competition compliance training and manual, etc. The CCI generally do not accept the defence raised by such officer of a company, in terms of section 48(2) of the Competition Act, that the contravention committed by the company was committed without his knowledge.[51]

The erstwhile COMPAT, too, has stressed that the directors and the officers-in-charge responsible to the company be aware of the provisions of the Competition Act and ensure that their activities (like pricing policy, etc.) are in compliance with the provisions of the Competition Act. In fact, the erstwhile COMPAT in the *National Stock Exchange (NSE)* case (discussed in Chapter 3) has referred to the fiduciary duty of the director to undertake the activities of the company in compliance with the provisions of the Competition Act. The erstwhile COMPAT opined that directors must be aware of the provisions of the Competition Act, as the duty of the director is very onerous in ensuring that the business of the company is run in a competition law-compliant manner.

If one sees the pattern of the CCI, the CCI directs the offices of the DG in their prima facie order under section 26(1) of the Competition Act to investigate the role of persons who were in charge of the company when the violation of the Competition Act was committed. The reason behind such a pattern is that while conducting an inquiry against the company, the CCI should simultaneously proceed against the officer-in-charge as well. Further, the officer-in-charge must get an opportunity to be heard and raise objection against the proceeding against it. If the CCI holds a person liable without

50. *A.N. Mohana Kurup v. Competition Commission of India* [2016], (COMPAT) 2016 SCC OnLine Comp AT 423, para. 29.
51. *In Re: Cartelisation by broadcasting service providers by rigging the bids submitted in response to the tenders floated by Sports Broadcasters*, *Suo Motu* Case No. 02 of 2013, para. 112.

providing an opportunity or does not hear the person, then the order will be vitiated due to violation of the principles of natural justice.[52] Also, the insights provided by the officer-in-charge would help the CCI analyse the matter holistically and pass a well-reasoned order. Most importantly, this would protect the principles of natural justice of the officer-in-charge by allowing them to raise objections during the inquiry process.[53]

Nevertheless, even if the prima facie order has not explicitly directed DG to investigate the officer-in-charge, the DG is still duty-bound to investigate all the officer-in-charge.[54] This is done to ensure that directors and officers-in-charge are made vicariously liable for the violations of the company, lift the corporate veil and penalize the persons who were responsible for the conduct of the company.

It is important to note that a finding against the company is a pre-requisite to impose penalty on the officer-in-charge. As per the erstwhile COMPAT in *A.N. Mohan Kurup v. Competition Commission of India*,[55] proceeding under section 48 of the Competition Act can't be invoked against the officer-in-charge of the company unless there is an affirmative finding against the company. It is important to note that if the CCI could not find any contravention of the Competition Act by the company, then the CCI could not penalize the officer-in-charge of the company under section 48 of the Competition Act. Nevertheless, the CCI can simultaneously conduct an inquiry under section 26 of the Competition Act against the company and its officer-in-charge. The Delhi High Court, in *Pran Mehra v. Competition Commission of India*,[56] said that for efficacious and expeditious inquiry, there can't be two separate proceedings, one in respect of the company and another proceeding for the officer-in-charge. Thus, while the officer in charge will be held liable only if the company is found to be in violation of the Competition Act, the proceedings against the company and the directors can carry on simultaneously. This Delhi High Court judgement was re-emphasized by CCI in *Ministry of Agriculture and Farmers Welfare v. M/s Mahyco Monsanto Biotech (India) Limited*,[57] to hold that when an inquiry under section 26 of the Competition Act is carried out, the finding of contravention has to be first recorded against the company. Pursuant to a finding of an anti-competitive conduct against the company, the question of the personal liability of officers arise. However, the findings against both the company and its officer-in-charge would be in the same order.

52. *A.N. Mohana Kurup v. CCI*, Appeal No. 05 of 2016, para. 34.
53. *Ministry of Agriculture and Farmers Welfare v. M/s Mahyco Monsanto Biotech (India) Limited*, Ref. 02/2015, 107/2015, 03/2016, Ref. 01/2016 and 10/2016, paras 32, 33. The Delhi High Court in *Cadila Healthcare Ltd. and Others v. Competition Commission of India and Others* [2018], (Delhi High Court) 252 (2018) DLT 647, paras 68, 69, validated the reasoning of *Ministry of Agriculture and Farmers Welfare v. M/s Mahyco Monsanto Biotech (India) Limited* and held that power to investigate can be *suo motu* expanded to proceed against the officer in charge.
54. *Ministry of Agriculture and Farmers Welfare v. M/s Mahyco Monsanto Biotech (India) Limited*, Ref. 02/2015, 107/2015, 03/2016, Ref. 01/2016 and 10/2016, para. 35.
55. *A.N. Mohana Kurup v. Competition Commission of India* [2016], (COMPAT) 2016 SCC OnLine Comp AT 423, paras 29, 30.
56. *Pran Mehra v. Competition Commission of India* [2015], (Delhi High Court) 2015 SCC OnLine Del 7929, paras 1, 5, 6.
57. *Ministry of Agriculture and Farmers Welfare v. M/s Mahyco Monsanto Biotech (India) Limited*, Ref. 02/2015, 107/2015, 03/2016, Ref. 01/2016 and 10/2016, paras 30, 32, 33, 35.

As a practical step, once the CCI has identified that the company is in contravention of the provisions of the Competition Act, it asks for the last three years' income tax statements of the directors so that they can levy a penalty as a percentage of the income of the directors, as shown in the income tax statement. Further, the CCI has not only levied penalties on officers-in-charge but also barred the President and General Secretary of Kerala Film Exhibitors Federation (KFEF), an association representing 315 film theatres in Kerala, from participating in the association's affairs, including its administration, management and governance, for a period of two years.[58] Therefore, apart from penalties, they can ask a person to leave the management of the company.

[C] Advocacy Remedy

Apart from penalties and directions to companies and directors, CCI also awarded an advocacy-based remedy. Under the power under section 27(g) of the Competition Act, the CCI in *Madhya Pradesh Chemists and Distributors Federation (MPCDF) v. Madhya Pradesh Chemists and Druggist Association (MPCDA) and Others*[59] had awarded advocacy based remedy to a trade association by mandating the trade associations to organize competition awareness and compliance programmes for all its members. Similarly, in *Re, M/s. Crown Theatre v. Kerala Film Exhibitors Federation (KFEF)*,[60] it mandated the trade association to organize, in letter and in spirit, at least five competition awareness and compliance programmes over the next six months in the State of Kerala for its members and the same was directed to get commenced before the expiry of sixty days from the receipt of the order by trade association. This is path-breaking, considering that the CCI has now mandated a trade association to follow competition compliance sessions, which earlier was generally recommended.

Thus, the other trade associations and companies must take note of the latest order and amendments to put in place an efficient competition compliance programme to educate their members about competition law. Having in place an effective competition compliance programme may act as a mitigating factor in competition law proceedings.

[D] Fines for Non-cooperation/Furnishing False Information

The Competition Act also provides the power to the CCI to levy fines on any person or company who fails to comply with the direction of the CCI or the DG in furnishing information or deposing on oath or other directions issued by the CCI or DG to collect information. Failure to comply with such directions is punishable with a fine which may extend up to INR 1 lakh for each day during which such failure continues subject to a maximum of INR 1 crore, as may be determined by the CCI.

58. In *Re: M/s. Crown Theatre v. Kerala Film Exhibitors Federation (KFEF)*, Case No. 16 of 2014, para. 9(d), (e).
59. Case No. 64 of 2014, para. 161.
60. Case No. 16 of 2014, para. 9(f). Also *see*, *XYZ v. Tamil Film Producers Council and Others*, Case No. 07 of 2018, para. 58.

Further, in the event that any person makes a false statement, omits to state any material facts, or wilfully alters/hides any document knowing it to be material before the CCI or the DG, such person shall be liable to a penalty which shall not be less than INR 50 lakhs, but which may extend to INR 1 crore, as may be determined by the CCI. Similarly, for non-furnishing information on combinations, the CCI can impose a penalty which may extend to 1% of the total turnover, assets, or the value of the transaction. In *Amazon.com NV Investment Holdings LLC. v. CCI and Others*,[61] wherein the NCLAT upheld the order of the CCI which revoked the approval granted to Amazon's acquisition of Future Coupon Private Ltd.[2] It was held that Amazon was misleading and inadequately disclosures its strategic intent of the transaction. It was found that the said transaction was not a mere investment in Future Coupon Private Limited but a strategy of Amazon to become the single largest shareholder of Future Retail Limited (FRL). Thereby, the acquisition process was suspended, and sections 43A, 44 & 45 of the Competition Act were applied to impose a monetary penalty on Amazon because it failed to disclose certain material facts as per section 6(2) of the Competition Act. Under section 45(2) of the Competition Act, Amazon was directed to file a notice in Form II, which will disclose the material facts of the Amazon and Future deal in a detailed manner. Furthermore, the NCLAT upheld the CCI's direction to revoke the approval by pointing out that section 45 (2) of the Competition Act clearly points out that the CCI may also pass such other order as it deems fit. In terms of monetary penalties, the NCLAT also upheld the penalty of INR 200 crores under section 43A but reduced the penalty under sections 44 and 45 from INR 2 crores to INR 1 crores. Thus, the total penalty imposed under sections 43A, 44 and 45 of the Competition Act is INR 201 crores. Soon after the NCLAT passed its order, Amazon filed an appeal against the order of NCLAT before the Supreme Court, and the recovery proceeding against the penalty was stopped by the Supreme Court.[62]

Moreover, making false statements or omissions to provide any material information for the combination shall not be less than INR 50 lakhs but may extend to INR 5 crores, as may be determined by the CCI.

[E] Interim Relief

The Competition Act also provides the power to the CCI to provide interim relief under section 33. A plain reading of section 33 of the Competition Act says that the CCI has the discretionary power to issue an interim relief to temporarily restrict contravention of section 3(1), or 4(1) or 6(1) of the Competition Act. The procedure for the interim order has to be mandated according to Regulation 31 of the General Regulation, 2009. Interim relief is a competition enforcement tool that can be used to prohibit anti-competitive activities till the completion of the inquiry. Further, the CCI is empowered to reverse or modify its interim order, and the CCI also has the power to pass an

61. Competition Appeal (at) No. 1 of 2022, paras 263. 284, 314, 316, 318, 326, 330-333, 339, 340, 345, 346, 375, 376.
62. *Amazon.com NV Investment Holdings LLC. v. CCI and Others*, Civil Appeal No. 004974 of 2022.

ex-parte interim order. However, after passing an ex parte interim order, the CCI shall give a short notice to hear the parties.[63] Regulation 31(2) of the General Regulations mandates that the CCI shall hear the parties against whom such an order has been passed as soon as possible.

[1] Stage of Granting Interim Relief

Once the inquiry has begun, the CCI can exercise the powers vested under section 33 of the Competition Act. The Supreme Court, in the *SAIL* case,[64] has observed that at the stage of section 33 proceedings, the CCI is required to record a satisfaction that there has been contravention of the provisions of sections 3, 4 or 5 of the Competition Act and such contravention has been committed, continues to be committed or is about to be committed. This satisfaction must be understood differently from what is required while expressing a prima facie view, asking the DG to conduct an investigation in terms of section 26(1) of the Competition Act. The former is a definite expression of the satisfaction recorded by the CCI upon due application of mind, while the latter is a direction *simpliciter* to the DG to investigate, akin to a department proceeding.

While the *SAIL* case did opine on the power of the CCI to issue interim relief only post the order passed by CCI under section 26(1) of the Competition Act in terms of the definition of inquiry provided under the General Regulations, in practicality, the purpose of interim relief has been withered away due to the time lag between the informant filing the information and its prayer for interim relief being heard since the CCI first has to make a determination under section 26(1) or section 26(2) of the Competition Act as to whether a prima facie case is being made out. In practice, the time lag between these two events would be around three to five months. This time lag creates challenges for the parties in order to get urgent interim relief to avoid irreparable injury.

The decisional practice of the CCI shows that CCI rarely exercises its power under section 33 of the Competition Act. This is because the conditions to grant interim relief are difficult to satisfy since the anti-competitive harm to the market, if any, is pending investigation.

[2] Conditions to Grant Interim Relief

In a case of interim relief, the Supreme Court in the *SAIL* case[65] noted that CCI should pass a reasoned order, which, *inter alia*, should satisfy the following three conditions: (i) record its satisfaction (which has to be of much higher degree than the formation of a prima facie view under section 26(1) of the Act) in clear terms that an act in contravention of the stated provisions has been committed and continues to be committed or is about to be committed; (ii) it is necessary to issue order of restraint,

63. *SAIL* case, para. 118.
64. *SAIL* case, paras 117, 118, 120, 122, 123.
65. *SAIL* case, para. 119.

and (iii) from the record before the CCI, there is every likelihood that the party to the *lis* would suffer irreparable and irretrievable damage, or there is definite apprehension that it would have adverse effect on competition in the market.

[a] Stronger Prima Facie Case

To fulfil the first condition, there must be a probability of the existence of a stronger prima facie violation of sections 3(1), 4(1) or 6(1) of the Competition Act. At the interim relief stage, the satisfaction of the CCI should be of a higher degree, depicting a definite expression recorded by the CCI that a strong case is made out and necessitating interim reliefs must be passed to protect the competition and competitors. Accordingly, at the interim relief stage, the evidence required to pass the threshold of the first condition is also higher than the prima facie view under section 26(1) of the Competition Act. In the *MMT-Go* case,[66] the CCI in its interim order held that the threshold for satisfaction for forming a prima facie view under section 26(1) is a tentative view at that stage, whereas to qualify the first condition for interim relief, a definite expression of the satisfaction of existence of a prima facie case needs to be recorded by the CCI. However, the threshold for satisfaction differs from case to case according to the availability of evidence. Suppose at the prima facie stage, evidence is high enough for the CCI to record its satisfaction with the interim order. Then, there may not be a requirement to raise the threshold of its 'satisfaction' for the interim relief.

Further, in *Fast Track Call Cab v. ANI Technologies*,[67] the CCI observed that an interim relief can't be granted just because of the existence of a strong prima facie case. The parties seeking interim relief have to show that the balance of convenience lies in their favour, and they will face irreparable loss or injury if interim relief is not granted.

[b] Necessary to Issue Interim Order or Balance of Convenience

The CCI has to compare the inconvenience between the competitor and all the stakeholders of the market on the one side and the alleged parties on the other side. In *Confederation of Real Estate Developer v. Department of Town and Country Planning*,[68] it was said that while considering the balance of convenience, the CCI has to contemplate whether justice would be best served by passing an interim order. In the *M/s Nuziveedu Seeds Limited & Ors. v. Mahyco Monsanto Biotech (India) Limited & Others*,[69] it was noted that, while granting interim relief, CCI needs to answer what will be the impact of the relief on the parties. If the interim relief is granted, then Monsanto will not face any major financial challenges, whereas if the relief isn't granted, then the risk to Nuziveedu Seeds Limited and the whole market ecosystem is imminent. So, the

66. Interim order dated 9 Mar. 2021, *MMT-Go* case, paras 91, 92.
67. Section 33 order in *Fast Track Call Cab v. ANI Technologies*, 2015 SCC OnLine CCI 141, para. 12.
68. Section 33 order in *Confederation of Real Estate Developer v. Department of Town and Country Planning*, Case No. 40 of 2017, para. 19.
69. Section 33 order in *M/s Nuziveedu Seeds Limited & Ors. v. Mahyco Monsanto Biotech (India) Limited & Others*, Case No. 107 of 2015, para. 25.

CCI analyses what would be the impact on both sides if the interim relief is granted. In this case, the CCI granted interim relief because if the CCI had not intervened at the interim stage, then neither can the extant position be restored *ex ante* at a later stage, nor the likely damage to the Informants be compensated.

Similarly, in *the MMT-Go* case,[70] the CCI, while deciding whether an interim order needs to be passed to grant access to FabHotels and Treebo on MakeMyTrip's online platform, the CCI found that the balance of convenience lies in favour of FabHotels and Treebo, and MMT-Go will not be put to much inconvenience by providing access to its online platform. Thus, for the second condition, the CCI does a balancing exercise, where the CCI weighs the inconveniences that would be felt by the competitors and all stakeholders of the market if the interim order isn't granted versus the inconvenience of the alleged parties if the interim relief is granted.

[c] Irreparable Harm

The third condition is divided into two sub-conditions, separated by an 'or', inferring any one of the sub-conditions is enough to fulfil the third condition. The first sub-condition considers the irreparable harm that is caused to the informant; however, the second sub-condition considers the irreparable harm to the competition in the market. Thus, the third condition will be fulfilled when there is a likelihood of irreparable harm to the informant or the competition in the market.

The determination of irreparable harm is based on factual circumstances. In the *M/s Nuziveedu Seeds Limited & Ors. v. Mahyco Monsanto Biotech (India) Limited & Others*,[71] the CCI observed that the destruction of the patented products would cause irreparable harm to the informant, the other stakeholder of the competition (i.e., farmers), and the ecosystem of cotton cultivation. Similarly, in the *Confederation of Real Estate Developer v. Department of Town and Country Planning*,[72] an interim order was granted to prevent irreparable harm to the informant and the buyers of the buildings (final consumers) by way of cancellation of licences and levying of penal interest.

Also, in the *MMT-Go* case,[73] irreparable harm would have been caused to FabHotels and Treebo, as well as the demand side of the market (i.e., hotel partners), if the CCI had not restrained MakeMyTrip from carrying on its anti-competitive practice. The anti-competitive practice has denied market access to FabHotels and Treebo, and therefore, they are not able to compete in the market. So, the CCI noted that the anti-competitive practice would irreversibly alter the competitive landscape by driving existing competitors from the market; hence, interim relief was passed directing MakeMyTrip to allow FabHotels and Treebo on its online platform.

70. Section 33 order in *MMT-Go* case, para. 106.
71. Section 33 order in the *M/s Nuziveedu Seeds Limited & Ors. v. Mahyco Monsanto Biotech (India) Limited & Others*, Case No. 107 of 2015, paras 24, 25.
72. Section 33 order in *Confederation of Real Estate Developer v. Department of Town and Country Planning*, Case No. 40 of 2017, para. 23.
73. Section 33 order in *MMT-Go* case, paras 108, 114, 117.

§1.04 COMPETITION LAW COMPLIANCE

The Competition Act is in its fourteenth year of existence. CCI has been extremely assertive in its enforcement outlook. According to the CCI Annual Report, 2022-23, the CCI has received more than 1,224 information alleging violations under sections 3 and 4 of the Competition Act and 1,015 merger filings under sections 5 and 6 of the Competition Act as of March 2023. The CCI has closed 699 matters against violation under sections 3 and 4, out of which 185 cases of contravention were found. Regarding the merger filings, CCI disposed of 1,007 merger filings.[74]

During 2022-23, a total of forty-eight final orders against contravention of sections 3 and 4 of the Competition Act were passed, and ninety-nine merger filings were disposed. As mentioned above, based on figures available in the public domain, the CCI has imposed an aggregate penalty of nearly INR 2672.48 crore.[75] Further, the CCI has imposed penalties on directors and officers-in-charge. Further, along with the monetary penalties, CCI imposes directions to modify the business practices or the structures of the companies for violating the Competition Act. Therefore, we see that the ramifications of not following the Competition Act are very severe.

In addition, the CCI also conducts numerous awareness programs. Due to the all-round efforts by CCI, a fair degree of awareness has been created among the companies with respect to the Competition Act.[76] The CCI also directs the companies to conduct events educating their respective members about the awareness of competition law and the consequent need for competition compliance.[77] Considering the ramifications of noncompliance with competition law, there is an urgent need for advocacy of competition law principles to Indian companies.

Every business model, operation or process shall be evaluated from the perspective of whether there is a risk of anti-competitive conduct therein. Steps must be taken to eliminate or minimize such risks. Companies should actively engage in such risk management activities, also known as Active Risk Management (ARM) initiatives. ARM is a function of the boards of companies. As any anti-competitive conduct would have disastrous consequences for the operations of the companies, the boards must be sensitive to 'red flags' in the operations of the company and monitor them. Non-compliance would bring in, besides fines, damages to reputation or brand value. Further, a positive determination of anti-competitive behaviour by a company would, in turn, lead to ripple regulatory effects; i.e., more governmental agencies may start investigations and start more intense scrutiny on the various business aspects of the company. The board should send an unequivocal message from top to bottom that business must be done in a compliant manner. Further, not only the companies but also each of the channel partners must act in a manner compliant with the competition law, and non-compliance by the channel partner may lead to termination of the

---

74. CCI Annual Report, 2022-23, Pg. xiv.
75. CCI Annual Report, 2022-23, p. Pg. xiv.
76. Organisation for Economic Co-operation and Development, Annual Report on Competition Policy Developments in India, 2018, para. 2.
77. *XYZ v. Tamil Film Producers Council*, Case No. 07 of 2018, para. 58.

agreement between the company and the channel partners. Furthermore, CCI considers that appointing common directors or partners among competing companies may increase the risk of anti-competitive practices. There are instances where the CCI had directed the companies to remove their common directors to prevent anti-competitive effect in the market.[78]

The CCI, in its advocacy booklets, has been advocating that every company must: (a) engage in ARM; (b) keep a record of all practices of the company and have it assessed for competition compatibility; and (c) provide periodic training to employees so that they are aware of the best antitrust practices. The CCI in its advocacy booklet sets out the following reasons in support of introducing a compliance programme:

(i) inculcates a culture of compliance throughout the organization which in turn can be a business enhancer offering positive benefits to business;
(ii) provides enterprises with a competitive advantage by enabling them to detect any violation at an early stage and take corrective measures to their advantage;
(iii) assists enterprises to enhance reputation and build goodwill;
(iv) enterprises that contravene the provisions of the Competition Act may suffer damage to their reputation, damaging years of careful marketing and brand development;
(v) obviates or reduces the costs and negative effects of litigation and regulatory intervention;
(vi) establishes enterprises as having social conscience, economic ethics and national interest at heart;
(vii) the existence of a strong Compliance Programme reflecting the eagerness of the management to comply may temper the severity of the punishment that may be meted out for violation;
(viii) companies must avoid appointing the same director or key managerial personnel on the boards of competing companies.

§1.05 APPEAL PROVISIONS

Right to appeal is a creation of a statute, and the legislature has to decide, for each statute, whether the right to appeal should be unconditional or conditional. Further, the statute can also expressly lay down what kinds of orders can be appealed to in higher forums.

The aspect of the right of appeal was discussed by the Supreme Court in the *SAIL* case.[79] The legislative intent that the framers never desired was that all orders, directions and decisions should be appealable to the NCLAT. Once the legislature has specified the direction or orders which would be appealable, the normal result

78. Canary Investments Limited, Link Investment Trust II, Intas Pharmaceuticals Limited, Dunearn Investments (Mauritius) PTE Limited, Crimson Investments Limited, Link Investment Trust. Combination Registration No. C-2020/04/741, 30 Apr. 2020, para. 15.
79. *SAIL* case, paras 41, 45, 48, 50, 51, 52, 58, 62-64.

would be that all other directions or orders are excluded from the operation of that provision. The presumption is in favour of the legislation because the legislature is deemed to be aware of all the laws in existence, and accordingly, the Competition Act has been enacted. Thereby, when other directions or orders have been excluded under the legislation from the scope of appellate jurisdiction, it will not be permissible to include such directions or orders by implication or with reference to other provisions by giving a liberal interpretation.

Also, if all directions or orders are allowed to be appealable, then it will give an opportunity to misuse the process of law by prolonging the process of litigation and thereby defeating the purpose of the Competition Act. No appeal lies against the prima facie order under section 26(1) of the Competition Act or the orders issuing directions for further investigation/inquiry under sections 26(7) and (8) of the Competition Act because these are mere administrative orders without affecting the rights of parties.

Hence, under section 53A of the Competition Act, only certain orders passed by the CCI can be appealed to NCLAT. Section 53A of the Competition Act provides that only the following kinds of orders passed by the CCI can be appealed to NCLAT.

[A] Appealable Orders

[1] Section 26(2) of the Competition Act

After receiving a reference or information under section 19(1) of the Competition Act, if the CCI is of the opinion that there exists no prima facie case, then the CCI shall pass an order for closure of the matter. In other words, the order passed by the CCI under section 26(2) of the Competition Act is a final order, as it puts an end to the proceedings initiated upon receiving the reference or information alleging contravention of the Competition Act. As this order deals with the rights and liabilities of parties by closing the case against another party, the Government Department or informant (as the case may be) has a right to appeal under section 53A of the Competition Act against such closure of the case.[80]

[2] Section 26(2A) of the Competition Act

The CCI can refuse an inquiry into any matter where the facts of the information or reference filed are the same or substantially the same, and the issues raised in the information or reference have already been decided.

[3] Section 26(6) of the Competition Act

After completing the investigation, if the DG finds no contravention, and post the objections/comments received from the parties, the CCI agrees with the DG's

80. *SAIL* case, paras 37, 38.

conclusion on finding no contravention, then the CCI closes its inquiry by passing an order under section 26(6) of the Competition Act. Thereafter, CCI communicates its order to the informant or government body. The informant/government body can file an appeal against this order because it is a final order, and it affects the rights of parties.[81]

[4] Section 26(9) of the Competition Act

After completion of further investigation or inquiry, the CCI shall hear the parties and accordingly pass an order closing the matter or pass an order under section 27 of the Competition Act. The CCI will also send a copy of its order to the parties.

[5] Sections 27, 28 and 31 of the Competition Act

The orders passed by the CCI where they have imposed penalty on the companies for violating the provisions of the Competition Act, or ordered a division of the dominant enterprise or passed an order with respect to the combination.

[6] Section 32 of the Competition Act

The CCI can enquire and pass appropriate order against the anti-competitive agreement, abuse of dominance and combination which are taking place outside India but have an anti-competitive effect on India. This order is also appealable under section 53A of the Competition Act.

[7] Section 33 of the Competition Act

Any interim relief passed by the CCI by issuing an order to temporarily restrict the anti-competitive activities, i.e., contravention of section 3(1), or 4(1) or 6(1) of the Competition Act.

[8] Section 38 of the Competition Act

With a view to rectifying any mistake apparent from the record, the CCI can amend any order passed by it under the provisions of this Competition Act.

[9] Section 39 of the Competition Act

In the event any person fails to pay a monetary penalty imposed on it under the provisions of the Competition Act, the CCI can take steps to recover the said penalty.

81. *SAIL* case, paras 24, 58.

[10] Sections 43, 43A, 44 and 45 of the Competition Act

The provisions of the Competition Act deal with any orders passed by the CCI on any person who does not cooperate with the investigation or furnishes false information to the CCI or the DG, as the case may be.

[11] Section 46 of the Competition Act

Orders passed by the CCI under the leniency regime (discussed in Chapter 2). While the Competition Act provides that only certain orders of the CCI (detailed above) can be appealed to the NCLAT, all orders or decisions passed by the NCLAT can be appealed to the Supreme Court under section 53T of the Competition Act.

[B] Pre-deposit of Penalty Amount for Appeal

Section 53B of the Competition Act provides the right to file an appeal and also lays down the rights of the parties. As an appeal is a statutory right, the parties have to file an application of appeal according to the prescribed procedure in the statute. As the appellate tribunal under the Competition Act is the NCLAT, the NCLAT Rules, 2016 will be followed. To curb frivolous appeals, the NCLAT has adopted the practice of directing each appellate to pre-deposit 10% of the penalty amount for admission of the appeal. The Supreme Court in *Ultra Tech Cement Ltd. v. Competition Commission of India and Others*[82] found that the erstwhile COMPAT was justified in directing the pre-deposition of 10% of the penalty amount from the appellant while granting a stay on the payment of the penalty. Further, in *Himmatlal Agrawal v. Competition Commission of India and Others,*[83] the Supreme Court dealt with the issue of whether appeal can be dismissed if the appellant fails to submit its pre-deposit amount. The Supreme Court held that section 53B of the Act does not impose any condition of pre-deposition for admitting the appeal. Therefore, the right to file the appeal and have the said appeal decided on merits is conferred by the statute. Hence, the Supreme Court held that the NCLAT can't just dismiss an appeal just because the appellate failed to pay the pre-deposit amount. However, for non-deposit of the amount, any interim order of stay may stand vacated, but appeal will be continued to be heard on merits.

The issue of the pre-deposit amount was incorporated in the statute after the Competition (Amendment) Act, 2023, amended section 53B of the Competition Act to mandate the appellate to deposit 25% of the penalty amount while filing an appeal.

82. *Ultra Tech Cement Ltd. v. Competition Commission of India and Others* [2018], (SC) (2018) 16 SCC 762, para. 7.
83. *Himmatlal Agrawal v. Competition Commission of India and Others* [2018], (SC) (2018) 17 SCC 421, para. 10.

§1.06 PRIVATE ACTION

The Competition Act also allows for private action/damages claims. Section 53N of the Competition Act provides that any person can file an application before the NCLAT for compensation that arises from the findings of the CCI, NCLAT, Supreme Court or an order of settlement. The NCLAT can pass an order for the recovery of compensation from any enterprise for any loss or damage shown to have been suffered by the Central Government or a State Government or a local authority or any enterprise or any person as a result of any contravention of the substantive provisions of the Competition Act (sections 3, 4, 5 and 6), having been committed by an enterprise or as a result of settlement order passed by the CCI. To date, there has not been one decided private action claim by the NCLAT; however, based on cause lists of NCLAT, there have been some cases which have been filed where compensation has been sought. Since the approach is unclear, it remains to be seen whether the Competition Appellate Tribunal will give compensation taking into account only actual loss or whether the compensation will also cover loss in profits. It must be apposite to note in this regard that while section 46 of the Competition Act provides for lesser penalty for leniency applicant in case of cartels, the risk of follow-on actions and compensation has to be borne by every cartel participant, even the leniency applicant.

§1.07 DUE PROCESS

Due Process, and in particular, conformity with the principles of natural justice, has been a key issue in matters that have been contested before the CCI. The right to cross-examine witnesses and the right to have access to information and documents relied upon by the CCI has been highly contested when the matters are taken up in higher forums like the High Court and NCLAT. While the scheme of the Competition Act does not provide for appeals to the High Court, however, the parties have approached the High Court on issues of due process and not substantive findings.

One of the earliest challenges on the nature of the CCI (whether it is a regulator or a tribunal) was made in the case of *Braham Dutt v. Union of India.*[84] In that case, the constitutional validity of Rule 3 of the Competition Commission of India (Selection of Chairperson and other Members of the Commission) Rules, 2003, was challenged. The principal point of contention was that the appointment of non-judicial person as Chairperson of the CCI violated the doctrine of separation of power, as enshrined in the Constitution of India. It was argued that the CCI, which was essentially a judicial body having adjudicatory powers on the questions of importance, should be headed by a retired Judge of the Supreme Court or a High Court. The Union of India contested the writ petition and pleaded that the CCI is a Regulatory Body which requires expertise in the field, and such expertise cannot be supplied by the members of the judiciary alone, and in any case, the power of judicial review is available with the High Courts and the

84. *Braham Dutt v. Union of India* [2005], (SC) (2005) 2 SCC 431, paras 3, 4, 5.

Supreme Court. During the pendency of the writ petition, two additional counter-affidavits were filed on behalf of the Union of India, in which it was submitted that the Government was proposing to make certain amendments so as to enable the Chairman and the Members to be selected by a Committee presided over by the Chief Justice of India or his nominee. The Supreme Court noticed the background in which the Competition Act was enacted, referred to the statements contained in the additional affidavits filed on behalf of the Union of India and observed:

> We find that the amendments which the Union of India proposes to introduce in Parliament would have a clear bearing on the question raised for decision in the writ petition essentially based on the separation of powers recognised by the Constitution. The challenge that there is usurpation of judicial power and conferment of the same on a non-judicial body is sought to be met by taking the stand that an Appellate Authority would be constituted and that body would essentially be a judicial body conforming to the concept of separation of judicial powers as recognised by this Court... We may observe that if an expert body is to be created as submitted on behalf of the Union of India consistent with what is said to be the international practice, it might be appropriate for the respondents to consider the creation of two separate bodies, one with expertise that is advisory and regulatory and the other adjudicatory. This followed up by an appellate body as contemplated by the proposed amendment, can go a long way in meeting the challenge sought to be raised in this writ petition based on the doctrine of separation of powers recognised by the Constitution.

While an affidavit was given in the Supreme Court by the Union of India to constitute the CCI with two bodies, one dealing with regulatory and advisory functions and the other dealing with adjudicatory functions, a half-hearted attempt was made in 2006 to denude the CCI of its adjudicatory functions by proposing addition of paragraphs 3(b) in the Competition (Amendment) Bill, 2006 to omit the provisions relating to adjudication of disputes between two or more parties. This is evident from the following extracts of the Bill presented before the Parliament:

> 3. The Competition (Amendment) Bill, 2006, *inter alia*, seeks to make the following amendments to the Competition Act so as to address various legal issues and to make the CCI fully operational on a sustainable basis, namely: (a) to provide the CCI would be an expert body which will function as a market regulator for preventing anticompetitive practices in the country and it would also have advisory and advocacy functions in its role as a regulator; (b) to omit the provisions relating to adjudication of disputes between two or more parties by the CCI and to provide for investigation through the Director General in case there exist a prima facie case relating to anti-competitive agreements or abuse of dominant position under the Competition Act, 2002 and conferring power upon the CCI to pass orders on completion of an inquiry and impose monetary penalties and in doing so the CCI would work as a collegium and its decisions would be based on simple majority.

However, when the amendments were finally made in the Competition Act, the Competition (Amendment) Act, 2007, most of the provisions relating to adjudicatory functions of the CCI were retained with minor modifications.

[A] Quorum of CCI

In furtherance to the earlier discussion by the Supreme Court in the case of *Braham Dutt v. Union of India*, a key issue, which was decided whether it is mandatory to have a person from the field of law in CCI's quorum, has been discussed in the following cases.

It has been clarified by the Delhi High Court that the absence of a judicial member would not stop the CCI from performing its functions. For instance, the Division Bench of the Delhi High Court in *Mahindra Electric Mobility Ltd. v. Competition Commission of India*[85] had to deal with the writ challenging the validity of two administrative orders of CCI which were passed without the presence of a judicial member in the quorum of the CCI. One of the principal points of contention in the writ petition before the Delhi High Court is that the CCI is not a mere regulator but a judicial tribunal. It has been argued that CCI is principally an authority that exercises judicial functions which have been conferred by the statute, has the trappings of a court and is a tribunal for the purposes of sections 3 and 4 of the Competition Act. It was further argued that CCI perceive itself as a judicial body and it predominantly engaged in adjudicatory functions. Thus, the writ petitioner submitted before the High Court that the presence of a judicial member should be made mandatory while passing an administrative order. However, the Delhi High Court held that CCI need not require a judiciary member while passing an administrative order. Then, it was held that CCI not only performs adjudicatory functions but also discharges administrative functions like directing DG to conduct investigations or further investigation. So, the Competition Act requires CCI to discharge multiple functions. Though the CCI's task as the primary regulator of the marketplace and watchdog of anti-competitive practices is undoubtedly required to adjudicate at a stage, it cannot be held that the CCI must necessarily comprise judicial members while carrying on all its functions. Just because the CCI discharges adjudicatory functions does not imply that the CCI is purely a judicial tribunal. Hence, the Court concluded that the CCI is a Tribunal, but it's not a judicial tribunal or mandatorily needs judiciary members. However, when the CCI passes an adjudicatory order which determines the rights and liabilities of parties, then the presence of at least one judicial member is necessary. Further, the High Court read section 8 of the Competition Act, which deals with the composition of CCI, to say that CCI should have a judicial member. Finally, the Delhi High Court directed to ensure the presence of a judicial member in the CCI, and the Government was directed to expeditiously appoint a judicial member in the CCI.

The Single Bench of the High Court of Delhi in *CADD Systems and Services Pvt. Ltd. v. Competition Commission of India*[86] validated the adjudicatory function or final order of the CCI that was passed in the absence of a judicial member. The Delhi High Court relied on the Supreme Court's judgment in *B.K. Srinivasan v. State of Karnataka*,

85. *Mahindra Electric Mobility Ltd. v. Competition Commission of India* [2019], (Delhi High Court) 2019 SCC OnLine Del 8032, paras 137, 138, 139, 142, 148, 150.
86. *CADD Systems and Services Pvt. Ltd. v. Competition Commission of India* [2019], (Delhi High Court) 2019 SCC OnLine Del 9252, paras 18, 19, 21.

wherein the so-called Ganga Clause was upheld, i.e., with the objective to put beyond challenge defects in the constitution of statutory bodies and defects of procedure which do not lead to any substantial prejudice. Section 15 of the Competition Act is used as a saving clause because it states that the proceedings of the CCI would not be invalidated due to vacancy or any defect in its constitution. Further, the Supreme Court's judgment in *K.R. Tamizhmani v. The State of Tamil Nadu* was also discussed by the Delhi High Court to say that till the time a judiciary member was selected, the existing tribunal would decide all the cases. Therefore, it was concluded that the final orders passed without a judicial member would not be invalidated by the CCI.

Similarly, the NCLAT in *Amazon.com NV Investment Holdings LLC v. Competition Commission of India*[87] held that no proceedings of the CCI will be invalid by reason of any vacancy in the quorum, and as per the legislative intent behind section 22(3) of the Competition Act, a judicial member does not interdict the functioning of CCI. After the Competition (Amendment) Act 2007, section 22(3) of the Competition Act requires at least three members for a valid quorum for discharging the functions of CCI, and the said provision does not mandate the presence of a judiciary member in the quorum. Thereafter, in *Pawan Jagetia v. Competition Commission of India,*[88] the NCLAT again held that the absence of a judicial member does not render the CCI order void. Furthermore, the NCLAT interpreted sections 8 and 9 of the Competition Act to show that nowhere has it been indicated that CCI must consist of a judicial member to decide the proceeding.

As per the proviso of section 22(3) of the Competition Act, the CCI's quorum requires three members to preside and cast votes. Between October 2022 and October 2023, the CCI had only two members on its board after the retirement of the Chairperson. This resulted in a lack of quorum at CCI. Due to a lack of quorum, CCI could not approve proposed combinations and could not perform its other adjudicatory duties. However, in order to discharge its adjudicatory role in terms of merger filings, the CCI adopted the doctrine of necessity and started passing orders in terms of combinations. Further, in relation to the adjudication of antitrust matters (sections 3 and 4 of the Act), the Delhi High Court in *Alliance of Digital India Foundation v. Competition Commission of India and Others*[89] held that any adjudicatory process wherein there is a vacancy on the CCI would not invalidate the proceedings of CCI. In this case, the CCI had passed a certain direction against Google for abusing its dominance in the app store market. However, due to the lack of a quorum, the CCI could not take action against Google on an application filed by the app developers, stating that Google is not complying with the CCI directions. Thereby, the petitioner filed a writ and submitted that even if CCI is not in quorum, it can still discharge its functions and entertain and adjudicate on the said application. Allowing the writ

87. *Amazon.com NV Investment Holdings LLC v. Competition Commission of India* [2022], (NCLAT) Competition Appeal (AT) No. 1 of 2022, paras 336-338.
88. *Pawan Jagetia v. Competition Commission of India* [2022], (NCLAT) Competition Appeal (AT) No. 16 of 2021, para. 31.
89. *Alliance of Digital India Foundation v. Competition Commission of India and Others* [2018], (Delhi High Court) (2023) SCC OnLine Del 2330, paras 67-75, 93.

petition, the Delhi High Court held that there is no provision in the Competition Act which prescribes a minimum number of members required to constitute a valid quorum of CCI for its adjudicatory functions. Thereby, the High Court directed the CCI to adjudicate the application filed under section 42 of the Competition Act.

[B] Principles of Natural Justice and Due Process of Law

The rule of law remains an important cornerstone of India's democratic setup, and principles of natural justice were required to be followed by CCI while passing an order which affected the rights of the parties. Reliance can be placed on a plethora of authorities across various courts in India and abroad who believe that denial of a right to a hearing constitutes a serious danger to the due process under the law as well as violates natural justice.

[1] Parties Must Be Heard Before the Final Order

Regarding the orders which affect the rights of the parties, the CCI must follow the due process of law and the principles of natural justice. The Gujarat High Court in *Casa2 Stays Private Limited v. Oravel Stays Private Limited ('OYO') and Another*[90] set aside the CCI's interim order by holding that OYO was not provided an equal opportunity of being heard before the interim order was passed. So, while granting interim relief under section 33 of the Competition Act, the CCI must follow principles of natural justice and fair play by providing all the parties with an opportunity to be heard. Further, in relation to final orders, the erstwhile COMPAT in *Board of Control for Cricket in India v. Competition Commission of India and Another*[91] emphasized that due process and the principles of natural justice are sacrosanct in final proceedings before the CCI. The erstwhile COMPAT has held that the CCI is obliged to comply with the various facets of the principles of natural justice and is required to comply with the rule of *audi alteram partem* and grant an effective opportunity of hearing to a person against whom a finding of contravention is likely to be recorded. In this background, the erstwhile COMPAT held that while the CCI did not *finally* agree with the findings recorded by its investigating arm, i.e., DG on the issue of the relevant market, it did not indicate anywhere that it did not agree with such findings and did not afford an opportunity to the party concerned an opportunity to contest the determination of the relevant market. Therefore, it was held that the finding of the CCI was in violation of the rule of *audi alteram partem*. Further, even the information relied upon by the CCI in its conclusion that the enterprise concerned (viz. Board of Control for Cricket in India) had abused its dominant position was not made available to the Board of Control of Cricket in India to refute and, therefore, the finding of the CCI was set aside.

90. *Casa2 Stays Private Limited v. Oravel Stays Private Limited ('OYO') and Another* [2021], (Gujarat High Court) R/Special Civil Application No. 5085 of 2021, paras 2,3.
91. *Board of Control for Cricket in India v. Competition Commission of India and Another* [2015], (COMPAT) Appeal No. 17 of 2013, paras 15, 24.

However, the party which is being investigated has no right to be heard at the stage of section 26(1) of the Competition Act because an order directing the DG to conduct investigation is required to be passed expeditiously and without spending undue time. Such an order is administrative in nature and does not entail any civil consequences. Thus, there is no need to follow the principle of *audi alteram partem.*[92]

[2] CCI Must Record Reasons in its Administrative Order as Well as Adjudicatory Order

The Supreme Court has also emphasized the due process and the need of the CCI and Appellate Tribunal to pass speaking orders. In the case of *Rangi International Limited v. Nova Scotia Bank and Others,*[93] a two-judge Bench of the Supreme Court considered the question of whether the CCI and the erstwhile COMPAT should record reasons in support of their orders. The Supreme Court observed that:

> The Competition Commission as well as the Competition Appellate Tribunal are exercising very important quasi judicial functions. The orders passed by the Commission and the Appellate Tribunal can have far-reaching consequences. Therefore, the minimum that is required of the Commission as well as the Appellate Tribunal is that the orders are supported by reasons, even briefly.

Though the CCI need not follow the principle of *audi alteram partem* in its administrative orders, it must record some reasoning while passing such orders. Because in the case of *Vardayani Offset v. Competition Commission of India and Other,*[94] the Gujarat High Court quashed the prima facie order for not recording reasons while passing the said order. Further, it was impossible for the parties to read the prima facie order because it was heavily redacted. So, the Gujarat High Court relied on the reasoning of the *SAIL* case to hold that CCI must record some or minimum reasons to show the existence of a prima facie case in the order passed under section 26(1) of the Competition Act, as the CCI failed to satisfy the basic requirement of fairness and natural justice by passing a prima facie order without reasoning. Also, in *WhatsApp LLC and Another v. Competition Commission of India and Another,*[95] the Delhi High Court observed that a prima facie order need not contain detailed reasons, but CCI must record all the material present at the stage before passing a prima facie order. It can be concluded that even though the CCI need not give an opportunity to hear the parties while passing a mere administrative order, it is expected of the CCI to record some reasoning while passing such orders.

92. *SAIL* case, para. 91; *J.K. Paper Ltd. v. Competition Commission of India* [2023], (Gujarat High Court) 2023 SCC OnLine Guj 1790, paras 15, 17.
93. *Rangi International Limited v. Nova Scotia Bank and others* [2013], (SC) (2013) 7 SCC 160, para. 3.
94. *Vardayani Offset v. Competition Commission of India and Other* [2020], (Gujarat High Court) MANU/GJ/1046/2020, paras 7, 10, 12, 17.
95. *WhatsApp LLC and Another v. Competition Commission of India and Another* [2022], (Delhi High Court) 2022 SCC OnLine Del 2582, para. 43.

[3] CCI Must Display Application of Its Mind and Follow Due Process of Law

In another case,[96] the erstwhile COMPAT has also deprecated the findings of the CCI where it mechanically approved the findings of the DG without examining the material on record. In doing so, the erstwhile COMPAT emphasized that being an adjudicatory body, the CCI is bound to act in accordance with the statute, the principles of natural justice and record reasons for its orders. Further, it held that such reasons should reflect and demonstrate the application of the mind. Similarly, the erstwhile COMPAT, in the case of *Dr. L.H. Hiranandani Hospital v. Competition Commission of India*[97] noted that CCI committed a failure because it 'did not independently examine the various factors enumerated in section 19(3), (5), (6) and (7) for deciding what constituted relevant market for the purpose of the present case.' The erstwhile COMPAT suggested that the CCI cannot merely rubber-stamp the analysis of DG and must, in appropriate circumstances, conduct its own examination/independent testing of allegations. Further, the erstwhile COMPAT noted that the DG and CCI cannot act on pure conjectures and must act on proper evidence.

Also, the NCLAT in *Hyundai Motor India Ltd. v. Competition Commission of India and Others*[98] noted that the DG's investigation report is merely an opinion primarily to assist the CCI in appreciating the evidence in arriving at a final decision during the inquiry. And therefore, the DG's investigation report is not binding on the CCI. It is expected of the CCI to analyse the evidence in conjunction with other evidence on record and then form its final opinion. Apart from the DG investigation report, the CCI gets evidence from the parties through submissions, applications, etc. Hence, to reach a conclusion, the CCI needs to provide opportunities to all the parties to adduce evidence supporting their side.

In another instance,[99] the erstwhile COMPAT reversed the CCI findings on failure to observe due process. In one of the cases, the appellants had argued before the CCI on due process violations by DG wherein DG had relied upon unverified documents and also did not provide an opportunity to cross-examine the witness and the documents. Further, the DG relied on his personal knowledge to find out a case of violation against the appellants. When the appellants had argued that the DG had not followed fair procedures and due process, the CCI only briefly mentioned the objections raised by the appellants and did not opine in detail on the fairness of the procedure and continued to opine on the merits of the case. When the matter went into appeal, the erstwhile COMPAT deprecated the approach taken by the CCI and ordered a fresh investigation to be done by the DG.

---

96. *Chemists and Druggist Association v. CCI and Another* [2015], (COMPAT) Appeal No. 21 of 2014, para. 51.
97. *Dr. L.H. Hiranandani Hospital v. Competition Commission of India* [2015], (COMPAT) [2015] Comp AT 1144, paras 30-35.
98. *Hyundai Motor India Ltd. v. Competition Commission of India and Others* [2018], (NCLAT) Competition Appeal No. 06 of 2017, para. 37.
99. *Himachal Pradesh Society of Chemist & Druggist Alliance & ors. v. Competition Commission of India* [2016], (COMPAT) Appeal No. 58 of 2015, paras 15, 17, 19.

[C] Problem of 'Revolving Door' Practice in CCI

In light of principles of natural justice, the CCI should not indulge in the practice of 'revolving door' and must follow the concept of 'who hears must decide'. Specifically for final orders, the CCI must ensure that, in all cases, the members who participate in the final hearings also decide the conclusion of the cases. To prevent the practice of the 'revolving door', the Delhi High Court in *Mahindra Electric Mobility Ltd v. Competition Commission of India,*[100] directed the CCI to frame guidelines with mandates that once final hearings in any matter or batch of matters begin, the constitution of the CCI should not vary. This direction was passed to prevent prejudice to the parties, but unfortunately, CCI is not following the direction of the Delhi High Court.

In *Balrampur Chini Mills Ltd. and Other v. Competition Commission of India and Others,*[101] the NCLAT set aside the order of the CCI by holding that the CCI failed to follow the principles of natural justice because five members of the CCI heard the final arguments, but only three members were present while passing the final orders. The NCLAT held that the 'coram' of CCI that heard the final arguments should remain the same till the time the necessary order is passed. To reach this conclusion, the NCLAT relied on the Delhi High Court's direction on the prohibition of 'revolving door' practice which was not followed by CCI in letter and spirit. NCLAT held that the CCI must follow the principle of one 'who hears must decide' to protect the spirit of natural justice and the principle of judicial procedure. Accordingly, the NCLAT remanded the matter to the CCI for the constitution of an appropriate 'coram' which would undertake a fresh hearing of this matter.

§1.08 JURISDICTIONAL BOUNDARY OF CCI

The CCI, as a competition watchdog, is empowered to promote competition and resolve competition law-related disputes. Section 18 of the Competition Act casts a special responsibility on the CCI to 'eliminate' anti-competitive practices and promote competition in the market. Further, section 61 of the Competition Act grants exclusive power to the CCI to exercise its jurisdiction in respect of any matter in which the Competition Act empowers the CCI. However, the jurisdiction of CCI has been challenged in numerous cases. The foundation of most jurisdictional challenges is the overlapping of jurisdictions and conflict with other regulatory authorities.

[A] CCI's Conflict and Co-existence with Other Regulatory Authorities

To know the limits of the judiciary boundary of the CCI, it is important to understand how the Supreme Court dealt with this issue of overlapping jurisdiction between the CCI and the Telecom Regulatory Authority of India (TRAI) in *Bharti Airtel* case.

100. *Mahindra Electric Mobility Ltd. v. Competition Commission of India* [2019], (Delhi High Court) 2019 SCC OnLine Del 8032, paras 163, 164, 169, 170, 177, 212.
101. *Balrampur Chini Mills Ltd. and Other v. Competition Commission of India and Others* (2023), (NCLAT) Competition Appeal (AT) No. 86 of 2018, paras 49, 59, 60, 67, 77, 78, 79.

In *Bharati Airtel* case,[102] Reliance Jio filed information against Airtel, Vodafone and Idea Cellular Ltd. ('Incumbent Dominant Operators' (IDOs)) for forming a cartel and denying Points of Interconnectivity to block the entry of Reliance Jio in the telecommunication market. CCI passed an order that there was a prima facie anti-competitive practice and accordingly directed DG to investigate the matter. Aggrieved by the order of CCI, IDOs filed a writ petition before the High Court challenging the jurisdiction of CCI. The High Court held that the CCI erred in passing such an order while the matter was pending before the TRAI. The CCI challenged the High Court's decision before the Supreme Court by contending that it has jurisdiction to adjudicate the said matter. Further, the CCI argued that the issue of whether the IDOs formed a cartel to block the entry of Reliance Jio is a competition law issue under section 3(3) of the Competition Act; however, the issue before TRAI was a violation of section 11 of the TRAI Act, 1997, in terms of fair competition among service providers, maintaining standards of Quality of Service, etc. So, it was submitted by CCI that both issues are different, and CCI only wants to look into the competition law issue without encroaching on the jurisdiction of TRAI. However, the Supreme Court held that the CCI has jurisdiction to deal with the anti-competitive agreement but only after the TRAI finds fault with the IDOs on the jurisdictional aspects. The TRAI was established to regulate the healthy growth of the telecom industry, protect the interests of consumers, ensure technical compatibility and effective inter-relationships between service providers, ensure compliance with licence conditions by telecom service providers (TSPs), resolve disputes between TSPs, and ensure fair competition in the telecom market. The TRAI has been constituted as an expert regulator of the telecom sector, hence, it is the most appropriate regulatory authority to adjudicate the issues. The Supreme Court held that the CCI should not initiate an inquiry into the matter until the time the TRAI adjudicates the issues under the TRAI Act, 1997, i.e., whether IDOs are under any obligation to provide Point of Interconnection (POIs),[103] whether the Reliance Jio is asking the POIs under reasonable terms, whether IDOs are denying the POIs to Reliance Jio as per licensing conditions, etc.

Interestingly, the Supreme Court in the *Bharati Airtel* case[104] further held that TRAI does not have the exclusive jurisdiction to deal with matters related to anti-competitive practices in the telecom sector. The TRAI is an expert in dealing with matters pertaining to telecom services, such as unfair conditions in the agreements of telecom operators and denial of the POIs. Whereas the CCI is an expert regulator of the market and overall economy. The CCI is better equipped to deal with the practices having appreciable adverse effects on the competition, to promote competition in the market, and protect the business users as well as the end customers. So, both regulators operate in different fields, and they can co-exist. But as the TRAI is the most appropriate regulator, first it needs to opine on the jurisdictional facts as to whether

---

102. *Bharti Airtel* case, paras 88, 90, 95, 99, 100, 101-105, 109, 110, 111, 112, 113, 114, 122.
103. POIs are points between two network operators which allow voice call originating from one operator (for instance, Airtel) to reach the network of other operator (for instance, Reliance Jio).
104. *Ibid.*

IDO were under any obligation to provide the POIs and quality issues during the testing period, then only the CCI can start the inquiry under section 26 of the Competition Act, and thereby decide whether the agreement between IDOs was anti-competitive in nature or not. The Supreme Court concluded by making the following observations:

> In a nutshell, that leads to the conclusion that the view taken by the High Court is perfectly justified. Even the argument of the learned ASG is that the exercise of jurisdiction by CCI to investigate an alleged cartel does not impinge upon TRAI's jurisdiction to regulate the industry in any way. It was submitted that the promotion of competition and prevention of competitive behaviour may not be high on the change of sectoral regulator which makes it prone to 'regulatory capture' and, therefore, CCI is competent to exercise its jurisdiction from the standpoint of the Competition Act. However, having taken note of the skilful exercise which TRAI is supposed to carry out, such a comment vis-à-vis TRAI may not be appropriate. No doubt, as commented by the Planning Commission in its report of February 2007, a sectoral regulator, may not have an overall view of the economy as a whole, which CCI is able to fathom. Therefore, our analysis does not bar the jurisdiction of CCI altogether but only pushes it to a later stage, after TRAI has undertaken necessary exercise in the first place, which it is more suitable to carry out.

Further, the Bombay High Court in *Star India Pvt. Ltd. v. Competition Commission of India*[105] set aside the CCI's prima facie order directing DG to investigate the conduct of Star India Pvt. Ltd. and Sony Pictures Network India Pvt. Ltd. causing refusal to deal with Noida Software Technology Park Ltd. The High Court of Bombay relied on the *Bharati Airtel* case and held that CCI has no jurisdiction to pass an order to investigate when the matter is pending before the Telecom Disputes Settlement and Appellant Tribunal. Similarly, in the *Trustees Association of India and Other v. Competition Commission of India and Other*,[106] a writ was filed before the Bombay High Court challenging the CCI's prima facie order. The writ petitioner argued that CCI is holding a separate investigation on the issue which is pending before the Securities and Exchange Board of India (SEBI). The Bombay High Court passed a stay order against the CCI's inquiry until SEBI concluded its enquiry and formed its prima facie view. The Bombay High Court also directed SEBI to complete its enquiry within sixty days and to form its prima facie opinion on the matter. Further, it was also directed to SEBI that if it concludes that there is no violation of the SEBI Act, 1992, and the matter should properly proceed before CCI, then whatever material SEBI has obtained shall be transmitted to CCI to save time in DG's investigation. The objective behind such directions is to prevent a scenario of conflicting orders due to parallel investigations by two different regulatory authorities into the same complaint.

105. *Star India Pvt. Ltd. v. Competition Commission of India* [2019], (Bombay High Court) 2019 SCC Online Bom 3038, para. 91.
106. *Trustees Association of India and Other v. Competition Commission of India and Other* [2022], (Bombay High Court) 2022 SCC OnLine Bom 10263, paras 4, 5, 7; *Trustees Association of India and Other v. Competition Commission of India and Other* [2022], (Bombay High Court) 2022 SCC OnLine Bom 10264, para. 4.

In *Telefonaktiebolaget LM Ericsson (Publ) and Others v. Competition Commission of India and Another,*[107] Ericsson filed a writ petition before the Delhi High Court challenging the prima facie orders of the CCI to investigate an abuse of dominance by Ericsson with regards to its Standard Essential Patents (SEPs). The facts of these cases have been discussed in detail in the chapter relating to Intellectual Property Rights (IPR) and competition law. The Single Bench dismissed the writ and allowed the CCI to continue with its inquiry. Against the Single Bench's judgement, Monsanto filed an appeal before the Division Bench. The issue before the Division Bench of the Delhi High Court was whether the CCI has jurisdiction to deal with the allegations against Ericsson for imposing unfair terms for licensing its SEPs because the Patent Act, 1970 shall have the exclusive jurisdiction to deal with patent-related issues. But the Division Bench of the Delhi High Court set aside the Single Bench's judgement and noted that if there is a conflict between two special laws, i.e., the Competition Act and the Patents Act, 1970, then the latest law would prevail over the prior law. After the Competition Act was enacted, the Patent Act had to go through an amendment in 2003. As per the rule of interpretation, the Patent Act, 1970 would prevail over the Competition Act for adjudicating disputes relating to patents. Hence, the CCI has no jurisdiction to investigate Ericsson for abusing its dominant position through its SEPs. However, it is important to note that an appeal is pending before the Supreme Court against the Division Bench's judgement.[108] It will be interesting to see the view which may be adopted by the Supreme Court if the matter were to go up in appeal because, unlike the *Bharti Airtel* case, there is no overlap between these two laws. Additionally, another point which one needs to bear in mind is that the proceedings under the Competition Act are in rem proceedings, whereas the proceedings under the Patents Act, 1970 are in personam proceedings.

Moving on to those case laws where no conflict exists between CCI and another regulator, hence the jurisdiction of CCI has not been restricted. In *Competition Commission of India v. State of Mizoram,*[109] the Supreme Court, allowing the CCI's jurisdiction into bid rigging matters in the lottery business, held that there is no conflict in the interplay between the Competition Act and the Lotteries (Regulation) Act 1998. The scope of CCI's jurisdiction is limited to examining issues of bid rigging or manipulation in the tendering process for the appointment of selling agents and distributors for the lottery business under section 3(3)(d) of the Competition Act. The Supreme Court held that lotteries may be a regulated commodity and may even be res extra commercium (i.e., a thing outside commerce), but it would not prevent CCI from exercising its jurisdiction as there is no conflict.

107. *Telefonaktiebolaget LM Ericsson (Publ) and Others v. Competition Commission of India and Another* [2023], (Delhi High Court) LPA 247 of 2016, paras 21, 27, 49-51.
108. *Competition Commission of India v. Monsanto Holdings Pvt Ltd. and Others,* (SC) SLP(C) No. 025026 of 2023.
109. *Competition Commission of India v. State of Mizoram* [2022], (SC) (2022) 7 SCC 73, paras 45, 46, 50, 60-64.

[B] Jurisdiction of CCI in Data Privacy and Data Management

Further, it is also important to note that the CCI exercises its jurisdiction to deal with anti-competitive practices in the digital communication market. In the context of competition in the digital communication market, the conflict is related to controlling, storing and sharing customers' data. In the era of data aggregation, the CCI has initiated a *suo motu* investigation against WhatsApp's exploitative conduct with respect to data collection and sharing it with its parent company (i.e., Meta).[110] As per the prima facie order, WhatsApp is abusing its dominant position by exploiting end-customers through its Privacy Policy 2021, where WhatsApp does not provide an 'opt-out' option to its end-customers from providing personal data. Challenging the order of CCI directing the DG to conduct a *suo motu* investigation, WhatsApp filed a writ petition before the Delhi High Court in *WhatsApp LLC and Another v. Competition Commission of India and Another.*[111] The primary contention of WhatsApp before the High Court was that a matter is pending against WhatsApp's Privacy Policy, 2021, before the Supreme Court. So, till the time the matter is sub judice, CCI should not pass any order. Further, WhatsApp argued that to avoid conflicting opinions, the CCI's suo motu investigation must be stopped. However, the High Court rejected such an argument by holding that the matter pending before the Supreme Court is the violation of the right to privacy under the Constitution of India, 1950, whereas the matter before the CCI is the abuse of dominance under section 4 of the Competition Act. Hence, there will be no conflict because the Supreme Court will not be dealing with the competition angle of WhatsApp's Privacy Policy. Therefore, in the absence of any irreconcilable repugnancy between the jurisdiction of the CCI and the Supreme Court, the CCI has the liberty to proceed with its investigation under section 26(1) of the Competition Act. Hence, the jurisdiction of CCI has not been ousted to deal with the policies on data collection under the ambit of the Competition Act.

At present, CCI is conducting inquiries against the policies and conduct of big tech companies, such as Apple,[112] Google,[113] Flipkart,[114] Amazon,[115] Swiggy[116] and Zomato.[117] In previous orders also,[118] the CCI has shown concern regarding the economic activity in relation to the collection, management, usage and sharing of data by big tech companies. In order to provide an efficient enforcement tool that will keep

110. *In Re: Updated Terms of Service and Privacy Policy for WhatsApp Users, Suo Moto* Case No. 01 of 2021.
111. *WhatsApp LLC and Another v. Competition Commission of India and Another* [2022], (Delhi High Court) 2022 SCC OnLine Del 2582, paras 30, 31, 32, 33.
112. *Together We Fight Society v. Apple Inc. and Anr.*, Case No. 24 of 2021.
113. *Digital News Publishers Association v. Alphabet Inc. and Ors.*, Case No. 41 of 2021.
114. *Delhi Vyapar Mahasangh v. Flipkart Internet Private Limited and Amazon Seller Services Private Limited,* Case No. 40 of 2019.
115. *Ibid.*
116. *National Restaurant Association of India v. Zomato Limited and Bundl Technologies Private Limited,* Case No. 16 of 2021.
117. *Ibid.*
118. *Umar Javeed v. Google LLC and Ors.*, Case No. 39 of 2018; *XYZ and Ors. v. Alphabet Inc. and Ors.*, Case Nos 07 of 2020, 14 of 2021 and 35 of 2021.

a check on these big tech companies, the legislation is also planning to introduce the Digital Competition Act, which will address the rising challenges in the field of competition law. These cases and concepts have been discussed in Chapter 6 of this Book.

It is also important to note that, after the enactment of the Digital Personal Data Protection Act, 2023, a Data Protection Board of India will be constituted under the said enactment. It would be interesting to see how the CCI and the Data Protection Board of India will coexist and coordinate with each other to parallelly enforce their respective laws.

[C] Contractual Remedies Can Simultaneously Co-exist with the Competition Act

The Supreme Court in the *SAIL* case[119] held that the legislature, while enacting the Competition Act, was aware of all the laws in existence and the consequences of the laws, including the Indian Contract Act, 1872 and Arbitration and Conciliation Act, 1996. Further, the legislature enacted the Competition Act with the intention to provide an additional remedy against the anti-competitive practices. Therefore, section 62 of the Competition Act states that the provisions of the Competition Act shall be in addition to, and not in derogation of, the provisions of any other law for the time being in force. It means the Competition Act clearly is not in derogation of the Indian Contract Act, 1872 and Arbitration and Conciliation Act, 1996, but in addition to them. The Delhi High Court, in *Union of India v. Competition Commission of India,*[120] said that the scope of inquiry before the CCI is entirely different from the scope of proceeding before a civil court or arbitration tribunal for breach of contract. A civil court may focus on the contractual obligations of the parties and would not go into the aspects of abuse of dominance by one of the contracting parties. However, the CCI is not concerned with the breach of contract or inter-party commercial disputes; its purpose is to prevent anti-competitive effects in the market due to violations of the provisions (sections 3 and 4) of the Competition Act. As the provisions of the Competition Act are in addition to the Contract Act, the party can approach both forums seeking relief.

Moreover, multiple remedies that arise from a set of facts would not prevent recourse to more than one proceeding. In *Uttrakhand Agricultural Produce Marketing Board ('UAPMB') and Others v. Competition Commission of India,*[121] a writ was filed by UAPMB challenging the prima facie order passed by the CCI. UAPMB argued that the Uttarakhand High Court had already considered this issue, so the CCI can't proceed against the UAPMB. However, the High Court rejected the argument because the issues before the Uttarakhand High Court and the CCI are materially different. It was noted that the allegations before the Uttarakhand High Court related to the arbitrary manner

---

119. *SAIL* case, (2010) 10 SCC 744, para. 41.
120. *Union of India v. Competition Commission of India* [2012], (Delhi High Court) 2012 SCC OnLine Del 1114, paras 6, 14-16.
121. *Uttrakhand Agricultural Produce Marketing Board ('UAPMB') and Others v. Competition Commission of India* [2017], (Delhi High Court) 2017 SCC OnLine Del 10906, paras 17-21.

in which the UAPMB was administering the procurement of liquor, whereas the proceedings before the CCI relate to whether there are any anti-competitive practices in the market. The Delhi High Court referred to section 62 of the Competition Act and held that even if other remedies are available under different laws, that would not prevent a party from availing of the remedies under the Competition Act. Thus, recourse to multiple proceedings on the same set of facts is not barred as per section 62 of the Competition Act.

Also, the parties which have already availed remedies from another forum are not barred from approaching the CCI on the same set of facts. In *Naveen Kataria v. Jaiprakash Associates Limited*,[122] where the informant had approached the Real Estate Regulatory Authority to complaint against the builder for the breach of contract, he filed an information under section 19(1) of the Competition Act alleging abuse of dominance against the builder. The CCI held that the informant is at liberty to approach other sectorial authorities because the provisions of the Competition Act are in addition to other laws. Hence, the informant is allowed to seek remedies from the Real Estate Regulatory Authority or any other forum along with the remedies from the CCI.

Though section 61 ousters the jurisdiction of the civil court in competition law matters, a party is still allowed to seek remedies from a civil court or arbitration tribunal regarding a monetary claim arising out of a contract. In *Nuziveedu Seeds Ltd and Others v. Mahyco Monsanto Biotec*,[123] a prima facie order was passed to investigate Monsanto for the contravention of sections 3(4) and 4 of the Competition Act in relation to the unfair terms of the Sub-License Agreement. Meanwhile, an arbitration proceeding also took place between the same parties under the Sub-License Agreement for monetary claims, and the arbitration tribunal was awarded in favour of Nuziveedu Seeds Ltd. and directed Monsanto to pay the amount. So, the issue before the Bombay High Court was whether section 61 of the Competition Act would oust the jurisdiction of the arbitration tribunal from entertaining monetary claim arising out of the Sub-License Agreement. The High Court held that the powers of the arbitration tribunal and the powers of the CCI are different and are not overlapping. In this case, the arbitration tribunal could not decide the issue relating to the breach of any of the provisions of the Competition Act. The High Court noted that the arbitration tribunal specifically dealt with the contractual obligation of Monsanto under the Indian Contract Act, 1872, and it had not touched upon the allegations of Monsanto's anti-competitive behaviour. On the expressive jurisdiction bar of civil courts or arbitration tribunals under section 61 of the Competition Act, the High Court held that if the subject matter of the pleadings falls outside the exclusive jurisdiction of the CCI or if the CCI is not well equipped to grant such relief, then the jurisdiction of a civil court or arbitration tribunal is not ousted. Thus, merely because Nuziveedu Seeds Ltd. had filed an information before the CCI, it would not oust the arbitration tribunal from deciding the monetary claims under any other commercial law.

---

122. *Naveen Kataria v. Jaiprakash Associates Limited,* Case No. 99 of 2014, para. 44.
123. *Nuziveedu Seeds Ltd and Others v. Mahyco Monsanto Biotec* [2020], (Bombay High Court) 2020 SCC OnLine Bom 816, paras 11, 12, 13, 17 245, 270, 272, 280, 282, 283, 285, 287, 288, 289, 293.

So, at the same time, the parties can approach CCI against the anti-competitive agreements as well as abuse of dominance, and the same parties can also approach a civil court or arbitration tribunal to seek enforcement of their contractual obligations for monetary claims. Both proceedings can be conducted parallelly and do not oust each other's jurisdiction in respect of the issues that can be exclusively decided by each of these forums.

§1.09 SCOPE OF JUDICIAL REVIEW UNDER ARTICLE 226 OF THE CONSTITUTION OF INDIA, 1950

The Competition Act nowhere provides jurisdiction to High Courts for adjudication of issues relating to competition law. However, relying on various decisions of the High Courts, it can be observed that the orders of the CCI are amenable to a writ under Article 226 of the Constitution of India, 1950. Article 226 of the Constitution of India, 1950, states that every High Court has the power to issue directions to quash the orders of regulatory authorities, and thus, a writ can also be filed to challenge an order of the CCI before the High Court.

Answering the question of maintainability of a writ petition or scope of writ jurisdiction against an order of CCI, the Delhi High Court in *Mahindra Electric Mobility Ltd. v. Competition Commission of India*,[124] held that CCI is amenable to judicial review under Article 226 of the Constitution of India, 1950, only for the procedural issues of the CCI. For instance, power under Article 226 can be invoked if it is shown that the CCI's prima facie order was passed without any reasoning, and then the prima facie orders can be corrected in writ proceedings. Similarly, regarding the conduct of proceedings at a later stage, CCI must ensure fair procedure and compliance with natural justice, or else the final order can be challenged before a writ court. Further, the Supreme Court in *the Bharati Airtel* case[125] upheld the High Court's direction which quashed the order of the CCI because it was related to the very jurisdiction of CCI. For such procedural error, the High Court was competent to exercise its power under Article 226 of the Constitution of India, 1950. Similarly, in the *Institute of Chartered Accounts of India ('ICAI') v. Competition Commission of India*,[126] the CCI arbitrarily used its power to investigate the Institute of Chartered Accounts of India (ICAI) (a regulatory authority) which was only discharging its regulatory functions. The Delhi High Court quashed the prima facie order of the CCI as it has no jurisdiction to investigate the decisions, policies, or the way ICAI discharges its functions.

It is interesting to note that, rather than quashing the prima facie order of the CCI, the High Court in *Google Inc. and Others v. Competition Commission of India and*

124. *Mahindra Electric Mobility Ltd. v. Competition Commission of India* [2019], (Delhi High Court) 2019 SCC OnLine Del 8032, para. 85.
125. *Bharti Airtel* case, paras 116, 118, 119.
126. *Institute of Chartered Accounts of India ('ICAI') v. Competition Commission of India* [2023], (Delhi High Court) 2023 SCC OnLine Del 3422, paras 52, 54, 64-67.

Another[127] directed the CCI to recall/review its prima facie order for violating the principles of natural justice. Thus, parties aggrieved by CCI's irregular inquiry can always seek a remedy by invoking the power of the High Court under Article 226. And if the High Court is convinced that some prejudice has been caused to the aggrieved party because due process of law has not been followed or principles of natural justice have been violated, then the High Court can provide an appropriate remedy.

However, the remedies of Article 226 of the Constitution of India, 1950 are only limited to procedural error and violation of principles of natural justice. Power under Article 226 of the Constitution of India, 1950, can't be invoked by the High Court to adjudge the validity of an order of CCI based on merits.[128] The Karnataka High Court in *Flipkart Interned Pvt. Ltd. and Others v. CCI and Others,*[129] while dealing with a writ against a prima facie order of CCI, held that a prima facie order is administrative in nature and the High Court would not be competent to adjudicate the validity of such an order on merits. In this case, the writ petitioner argued on the merits of the case, but the High Court dismissed the same by saying that the jurisdiction of a writ court is limited to the issue of prima facie order. Hence, all the grounds raised by Flipkart and Amazon on merits cannot be entertained in a writ petition.

§1.10 POWER OF RECALL

As discussed above, under the Competition Act, an investigation into an anti-competitive agreement or an abuse of a dominant position can be undertaken by the DG only if the CCI *first* finds a prima facie case under section 26(1). Therefore, upon the receipt of information under section 19 of the Competition Act, the CCI in a preliminary hearing determines whether a prima facie case has been made out by the informant. However, the enterprise against whom the information has been filed does not have a right of opportunity/hearing before the CCI when the prima facie order is passed.[130] It is up to the volition of the CCI to call the other party or not. Therefore, the prima facie order can be passed ex parte without the presence of the opposite party. Also, a prima facie order passed by the CCI is not appealable to the NCLAT,[131] and the parties are, therefore, required to participate in the investigation before the DG. This investigation, depending on the case and the volume of information, may last anywhere between a year and a few years. Therefore, during this period, the parties can either participate in the investigation proceedings before the DG for a few years or challenge the prima facie order under limited grounds before the High Courts in a writ petition under Article 226 of the Constitution of India, 1950.

127. *Google Inc. and Others v. Competition Commission of India and Another* [2015], (Delhi High Court) 2015, SCC OnLine 8992, paras 18(L), (M), 19-24.
128. *Bharati Airtel* case, para. 121.
129. *Flipkart Interned Pvt. Ltd. and Others v. Competition Commission India and Others* [2021], (Karnataka High Court) Writ Appeal No. 562 of 2021, para. 26.
130. *SAIL* case, para. 91.
131. Under s. 53A (1) (a) of the Competition Act only certain orders mentioned therein are appealable in the light of the dicta of the Supreme Court in *SAIL* case, para. 41.

Another option that is available to parties is to seek a recall of the prima facie order passed by the CCI. As noted above, the Delhi High Court in the case of *Google Inc. and others v. Competition Commission of India and Another*[132] has now held that the CCI has the power to recall its prima facie order. Although vide the Competition (Amendment) Act, 2007, the power relating to the review of the orders was stripped of the CCI, the High Court has held that the CCI has the power to recall its prima facie order and further held that there exists no specific bar in the Competition Act or any of the attendant regulations passed by the CCI to preclude the invocation of the inherent power to recall/review. The High Court has, however, held that the right of recall would be sparingly exercised and should be apparent on the face of the material before the CCI and without lengthy arguments and only if, without entering into any factual controversy, the CCI finds no merit in the information on which investigation has been ordered. This way it is possible for the parties to avoid the rigmarole of the complete investigation process before the DG by seeking a recall of the order. Further, even if the CCI were to reject the application seeking recall of the order, the right of the parties to approach the High Courts would still be available.

§1.11 SETTLEMENT OR COMMITMENT UNDER THE COMPETITION ACT

[A] Legal Framework for Settlement and Commitment

The Competition Act has a leniency mechanism to allow members in a cartel arrangement to come clean by filing a leniency application under section 46 of the Competition Act (discussed in Chapter 2). However, before the Competition (Amendment) Act, 2023, there was no separate provision in the Competition Act allowing for settlements/commitments to be accepted by the enterprises. The Competition (Amendment) Act, 2023, metamorphoses the enforcement mechanism of CCI by introducing 'settlement' or 'commitment'. These enforcement tools will expedite the inquiry, as they would enable the CCI to resolve disputes by closing an inquiry against the contravention of sections 3 and 4 of the Competition Act if an enterprise offers a settlement or a commitment, under the following terms:

- under section 48A of the Competition Act, an application for settlement (i.e., settlement amount) may be moved by the enterprise after the DG submits its report and before the final order under section 27 or 28 of the Competition Act is passed by the CCI; and

132. *Google Inc. and Others v. Competition Commission of India and Another* [2015], (Delhi High Court) 2015, SCC OnLine 8992, paras 18(L), (M), 19-24.

- under section 48B of the Competition Act, an application for commitment (i.e., behavioural and structural remedies) may be moved by the enterprise after the prima facie order under section 26(1) of the Competition Act is received by the enterprise and before receipt of the DG's investigation report under section 26(4) of the Competition Act.

Section 48C of the Competition Act also provides for revocation of the settlement/commitment order and penalty under three circumstances – *first*, if an enterprise fails to comply with the settlement/commitment order; *second*, if the enterprise has not made full and true disclosure; and *third*, if there has been a material change in the facts. However, while it has been expressly stipulated that no appeal shall lie to the NCLAT against an order for settlement/commitment under the Act, it has not been clarified whether an order revoking settlement/commitment will be appealable to the NCLAT. The absence of such a provision may lead to issues for enterprises, which may challenge this provision before the court of law.

Interestingly, settlement/commitment was impliedly read into the Competition Act even before their express introduction by way of the Competition (Amendment) Act, 2023. The Madras High Court, in the case of *the Tamil Nadu Film Exhibitors Association v. Competition Commission of India and Others,*[133] had identified that even without the existence of a specific provision enabling settlement/commitment, the scheme of the Competition Act allows for settlements and commitments to be reached between parties. The Madras High Court held that the CCI has residuary powers to pass orders which are wide in amplitude, and which empower the CCI to accept a settlement/commitment between parties. Further, it was observed that once a party agrees not to abuse its dominant position or continue with an anti-competitive agreement, the only question left for the CCI would be to deal with the question of imposition of penalty. However, the Madras High Court also struck a note of caution and held that CCI would be obliged to look into the settlement/commitment and check whether it was a cover-up to prevent an investigation being made into anti-competitive practices or abuse of dominant position. In doing so, the CCI would have to ensure that such settlements/commitments: (a) would not lead to the continuance of anti-competitive practices; (b) would not allow the abuse of the dominant position to continue; and (c) would not be prejudicial to the interest of consumers or to the freedom of trade. Further, competition law deals with the prevention of practices which cause or are likely to cause market distortion. A private settlement may settle a dispute between parties which may not remedy the entire market situation, which the CCI seeks to address.

133. *Tamil Nadu Film Exhibitors Association v. Competition Commission of India and Others* [2015], (Madras High Court) 2015 SCC OnLine Mad 7099, paras 33, 35, 41, 44, 45.

Nevertheless, the express introduction of settlement and commitment into the Competition Act will bring immense clarity and certainty into the system, therefore encouraging parties to opt for settlement and commitment. It may also be noted that an informant or aggrieved party has been permitted to file for compensation under section 53N of the Competition Act, even after a settlement has been offered by the enterprise. The mechanism is in tandem with the objective of 'ease of doing business in India' as well as in the interest of the stakeholders and, if implemented properly, could reduce litigation and allow easier resolution of a dispute relating to the Competition Act, ultimately benefitting the market.

[B] Procedure of Settlement and Commitment

Further, the CCI introduced the Competition Commission of India (Settlement) Regulations, 2023, and the Competition Commission of India (Commitment) Regulations, 2023, to specify the procedures for settlement and commitment, respectively. According to the said regulations, an enterprise has to file a written settlement/commitment application to the CCI with fees and certain details. A settlement application must be filed within forty-five days of receiving the DG's report, and a commitment application must be filed within forty-five days of receiving a prima facie order. A thirty-day extension may be given as per CCI's discretion. After receiving the settlement/commitment application, the CCI must hold a meeting within seven days. If the CCI is not prima facie satisfied, then it will ask the enterprise to revise its application within fifteen days. Once CCI is satisfied, the inquiry against the enterprise will be in abeyance until the final order. However, other parties shall be given an opportunity to raise objections against the settlement/commitment application. Finally, considering the factual scenario, application, and objections, the CCI may allow, reject, or direct the enterprise to revise (within fifteen days) its settlement/commitment application. After receiving the revised settlement/commitment application, the CCI will again decide whether to allow it or not. If the CCI is allowing settlement applications from the enterprise, then the enterprise must accept the same and deposit the settlement amount within thirty days. Whereas, if the commitment application gets approval, then the enterprise has to comply with the commitments. The entire timeline of a settlement application should be concluded within 120 days, whereas the entire timeline of a commitment application should be concluded within 90 days. However, the CCI can extend the timeline. The timeline of the entire settlement application and commitment application process has been described below.

A diagrammatic illustration of the timeline of an approved settlement application process is as follows:

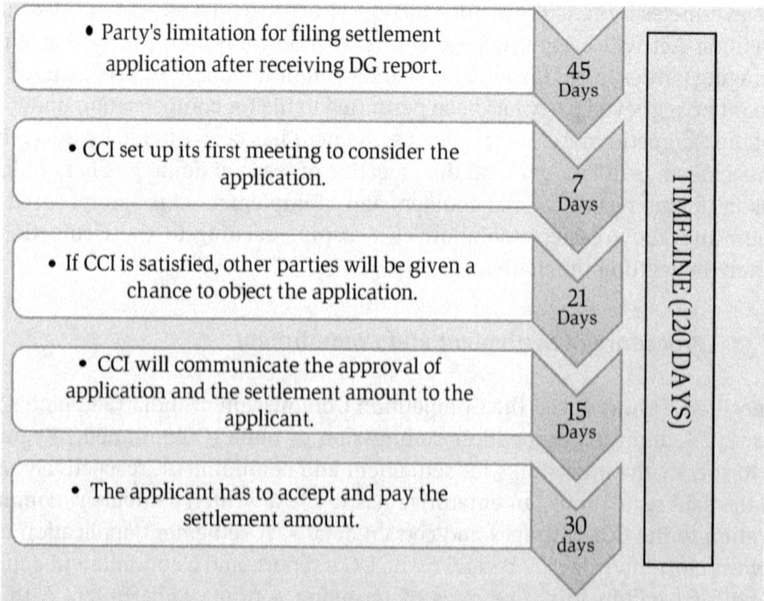

A diagrammatic illustration of timeline of a commitment application process is as under:

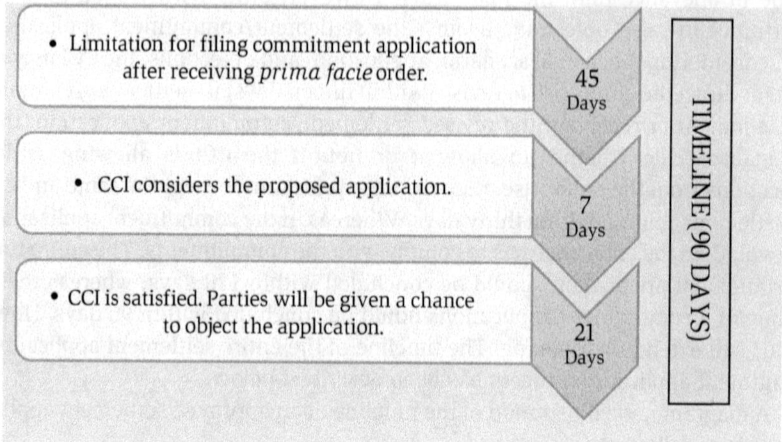

[C] The Challenges Ahead

It must be noted that neither the Competition Act nor the said regulations clarify whether a settlement/commitment may amount to an admission of guilt by an enterprise. The Standing Committee observed that[134] admission of guilt is not assumed in the settlement/commitment mechanism. Assuming that a settlement/commitment amounts to an admission of guilt, then the purpose of settlement/commitment will be lost since enterprises will be reluctant to file an application under section 48A or 48B of the Competition Act, even at the risk of prolonged litigation.

Further, there can be a scenario wherein only one party ('settlement/ commitment applicant') of a vertical anti-competitive agreement files a settlement/commitment application and agrees to change the concerning agreement, but the other party to the same vertical anti-competitive agreement has not participated in the said proceeding. In such a scenario, though the other party will get a chance to object to the settlement/commitment application, however, once the CCI approves the settlement/commitment application, then the commercial agreement between two private parties shall stand modified unilaterally based on the settlement/commitment offered only by the applicant without the consent of the other party. Thus, the CCI must take some steps to avoid unilateral novation/alteration of the contract in the garb of settlement/commitment proceedings by the applicant and prevent the applicant from taking any undue advantage of the same.

Finally, implementation of the settlements/commitments would be a great challenge for the CCI, so how the CCI would effectively monitor the compliance of settlement and commitment would be an interesting issue to watch out for in the future.

§1.12 SECTOR INQUIRY

The CCI regularly conducts market studies of different sectors or industries in order to understand the business structure and the problems of stakeholders. Such an exercise provides the CCI with better insights into the market, which would later help the CCI take action against the anti-competitive practices that are hindering the full pro-competitive potential of the market. The CCI interacts with market participants, end-customers, government agencies, academicians, etc., to collect data and have a deep understanding of the market and its practices. Also, some of the issues in specific circumstances may cause an anti-competitive effect on the competition in the market. Thus, after CCI recognizes existing anti-competitive practices, it can conduct a suo motu investigation and pass appropriate orders. Further, the CCI, through the findings of these market studies, also educates market participants to change their practices before they contravene the provisions of the Competition Act. Let's look at the market studies carried out by the CCI and the recommendations offered to the market participants.

134. Standing Committee on Finance, The Competition (Amendment) Bill, 2022, 52nd Report, p. 39.

[A] E-Commerce Market

The CCI has conducted a market study into the online markets to understand the practices of the e-commerce platforms and to realize the competitive force of the e-commerce market. The CCI noted major issues in the e-commerce market, such as platform neutrality, unfair contract terms of platforms, the imposition of price parity clauses to prevent business users from selling their goods at lower prices, exclusive agreements by online travel agencies, deep discounting, etc. After conducting the market study, the CCI noted that the marketplace platforms should adopt the following self-regulatory measures:

(i) the market participants must draft the search ranking parameters in simple language and display it in their Terms and Conditions;
(ii) the terms of collection, usage and sharing of the data with other market participants must be transparent;
(iii) user review and rating mechanism needs to be transparent, and fraudulent reviews or ratings must be prohibited;
(iv) modify the contractual terms and make them fair, reasonable and non-discriminatory towards business users;
(v) draft fair discount policies which include the basis of discount rates to show that there is no negative implication on the business users for not following the discount policy.

[B] Telecom Sector

The CCI research on the recent evolution of the telecom industry analysed challenges to the competition, identified the pro-competitive factors in the industry, and noted the competition between TSPs, etc. The CCI carried out the market study by collecting data from published reports, interviewing stakeholders, etc. The CCI noted that the telecom sector used to be a tightly controlled duopoly market due to high entry barriers. But now more participants are entering the market because the entry barrier has been relaxed, tariffs are subject to forbearance, and spectrum has been delinked from the license and is available in the secondary market. The erstwhile license regime of the telecom sector has been liberalized to keep pace with the market development. Further, the CCI noted that non-pricing-based competition is driving competition in the telecom industry. With respect to data privacy and competition issues, the CCI noted that the market participants must allow access and protect consumer privacy. Accordingly, the TSP must draft their privacy policies so that it may not exploit the consumer.

[C] Pharmaceutical Sector

In this market study, the CCI targeted the pharmaceutical sector. The CCI opined that it has come across various issues in branded generic drugs in India, such as competition in the generic drug market, drug prices, quality control of generic drugs, etc. CCI noted the price dispersion across different pharmaceutical companies, the market concentration, the leader of the market, trade association practices, etc. The CCI focused on demand-side and supply-side issues with respect to pharmaceutical distributors. The CCI also analysed the emerging competitive dynamics in online pharmacy. CCI said that there is huge growth in e-pharmacy after COVID-19 because e-pharmacy platforms provide an omnichannel experience, doorstep delivery, wide reach, etc. Finally, the CCI has made its key findings and observations at the end of the report:

(i) E-Pharmacies must adopt self-regulatory measures in relation to collecting, using and sharing data;
(ii) every stage of the pharmaceutical industry must be transparent;
(iii) there shall be uniformity in the quality standards across the sector, and steps need to be taken for effective implementation of existing quality standards;
(iv) organized drug testing to improve the quality of pharmaceutical products;
(v) building a national digital drug databank to bring information asymmetry across the sector.

[D] Cab Aggregators

The CCI published this report, which contains an economic analysis of a survey of drivers and riders, a controlled experiment, and stakeholder consultation. CCI collected data from two tier-I cities and two tier-II cities to get a diverse response on surge pricing in the cab aggregator market. Thereafter, the CCI studied the pricing behaviour of cab aggregators and found that the prices were not uniform across riders; hence, personalized pricing exists in the sector. The CCI also noted that the parameter that governs the pricing of fares is not transparent. Hence, the CCI recommended the following:

(i) There must be transparency regarding the break-down of the total fare.
(ii) The surge in pricing has not been perceived as counterproductive by the riders, however, the cab aggregators must put a cap on the pricing to prevent exploitative price situations.
(iii) Cab aggregators must maintain a basic level of transparency and information asymmetries on their platforms.

[E] Film Distribution Chain

The CCI conducted a market study on the film industry to understand the competition in the said industry. The CCI noted that the film industry is growing at a Compound Annual Growth Rate (CAGR) of 13.7% by 2023. The major factors behind the growth of the film industry are significant supply and demand, accessibility of smartphones, and inexpensive data. The CCI analysed previous competition law cases involving film associations and surveyed various stakeholders from different film industries. The CCI noted that the multiplex owners have a higher bargaining power than the film producers. Hence, considering the prevailing practices in deal-making between multiplexes and film producers, the CCI made the following recommendations:

(i) the standard form of contract must be avoided between multiplexes and film producers, and the contract must not be a unilateral, one-sided contract favouring the multiplexes;
(ii) multiplexes should provide fair terms to the film producers for their promotion of films;
(iii) multiplexes should not restrain the producers from releasing their films;
(iv) transparency in box office revenue collection by adopting a monitoring system;
(v) film associations must not facilitate anti-competitive practices in the industry.

§1.13 CONSUMER

One of the main objectives of the Competition Act is to promote economic efficiency by assisting in the creation of markets which are responsive to consumer preferences.[135] The prohibition of anti-competitive practices has direct or indirect benefits to the consumers who are at the end of the supply chain of the market. Therefore, the CCI enforces the principles of competition law to ensure that the consumer policies of the market players provide adequate and affordable choices for such consumers.[136] Along with enhancing the welfare of the supply side's consumers, the Competition Act also protects the demand-side or supply-side business users from being exploited or excluded from the market.[137]

Though the consumers can protect their rights by applying the consumer protection policies, i.e., the Consumer Protection Act, 2019, however, the Competition Act will be in addition to the remedies available under the Consumer Protection Act, 2019. As we discussed earlier, section 62 of the Competition Act says that the competition law is in addition to other laws. Similarly, section 100 of the Consumer Protection Act also says that the consumer protection law is in addition to other laws. Further, in accordance with this, the Supreme Court in the *Excel Crop* case,[138] said that the Competition Act will complement the Consumer Protection Act while holding that:

> Consumer welfare protection may be required in order to redress a perceived imbalance between the market power of consumers and producers. The imbalance between consumers and producers may stem from market failures such as

135. *SAIL* case, paras 6, 8, 125.
136. *Excel Crop* case, para. 21.
137. *Ibid.*
138. *Ibid.*

information asymmetries, the lack of bargaining position towards producers and high transaction costs. Competition policy may serve as a complement to consumer protection policies to address such market failures.

The CCI will provide a remedy to the consumer by rectifying the market failure. Whereas the Consumer Forums will protect consumers by directing the enterprise to compensate for the personal harm of the consumer. So, both laws prohibit unfair trade practices and protect the interests of consumers, but on different tangents. In *Shri Sunil Bansal v. M/s Jaiprakash Associates Ltd. and Ors.,*[139] a group of house owners filed information against the builder for abusing its dominance by imposing unfair terms on them. Challenging the jurisdiction of the CCI, the builder argued that the relevant product market is buildings which are immovable goods and CCI can't deal with immovable goods. Relying on a Supreme Court judgement on the Consumer Protection Act, the builder submitted that the activity of selling buildings amounts to the sale of immovable property and not 'goods' as 'goods' under the Competition Act, making reference to the Sale of Goods Act, 1930, which expressly excludes immovable property from its ambit. Thus, the buildings are also outside the scope of the CCI's jurisdiction. Finally, the builder submitted that this is a consumer law matter and that the Consumer Forum is the appropriate body to adjudicate the matter. However, the CCI rejected the contention of the builder because a Supreme Court's judgement on the Consumer Protection Act will not be applicable to a competition-related matter. The CCI held that the definitions of 'consumer' and 'service' under the Competition Act are wider than the definition of these terms provided in the Consumer Protection Act. Further, the CCI held that the purpose of the Competition Act allows the CCI to protect consumers from unfair practices. Finally, the CCI held that the availability of remedies before the Consumer Forum does not oust the jurisdiction of the CCI, as section 62 of the Competition Act says that the Consumer Protection Act is in addition to the remedies available under the Competition Act. Hence, CCI has jurisdiction to deal with the anti-competitive practices of the builder.

Furthermore, the definition of the word 'consumer' in the Competition Act is wider than the definition of 'consumer' in the Consumer Protection Act, 2019. The Competition Act has defined the meaning of the word 'consumer' under section 2(f) as any person who purchases goods or avails services for resale, commercial or personal purposes. The meaning of the word 'consumer' under the Competition Act is wider than the meaning that is given under the Consumer Protection Act, 2019. Section 2(7) of the Consumer Protection Act, 2019 defines the word 'consumer' as any person who buys or purchases goods or avails services for personal purposes, not commercial purposes, or to resale them further for profit.

Hence, from the definition given under the Competition Act, a consumer can be:

(i) the end-consumer, which purchases goods or avails services for personal use or consumption; or

139. *Shri Sunil Bansal v. M/s Jaiprakash Associates Ltd. and Ors.*, 2015 SCC OnLine CCI 180, paras 59, 63, 68, 69.

(ii) the business user who also purchases goods or avails services for commercial purposes or resale them.

The Competition Act protects a person who is involved in a business-to-business transaction because such a person will also fall within the definition of 'consumer'. While the Consumer Protection Act, 2019 is only concerned with the person who does not buy goods for commercial or business purposes, the Competition Act takes into account even intermediate consumers. The Consumer Protection Act, 2019 would not protect people who purchased goods or availed services for a 'commercial purpose'.

§1.14 ENTERPRISE

The word enterprise has been defined in a broad manner in the Competition Act. It is imperative to discuss the contours of the term enterprise because the scheme of the Competition Act allows the application of section 4 of the Competition Act to an enterprise or group and not every enterprise. Section 2(h) of the Competition Act defines the term 'enterprise' as a person or a Department of the Government which is engaged in any economic activity relating to the production, storage, supply, investment, etc., either directly or through one or more of its units or divisions or subsidiaries. However, the government bodies discharging sovereign functions, such as activity relating to atomic energy, currency, defence and space, will be excluded from the definition of 'enterprise'. Person has been defined in a broad manner to include any company, firm or juridical person.

From the definition of the 'enterprise', the following key points emerge:

(i) The statutory scheme of the Competition Act, the definition of enterprise and the decisional practice of the CCI with respect to enterprise have ensured that competitive neutrality is achieved in the present competition law dispensation. This means that state-owned and private businesses compete on a level playing field. Competitive neutrality requires that governments or state-owned enterprises should not misuse their powers to get an advantage over the private sector. Upon a bare perusal of the definition, it becomes clear that all the commercial activities of the government, excluding the sovereign one, come under the provisions of the Competition Act and that no anti-trust exemptions are applicable to state-owned enterprises. State-owned enterprises or public sector undertakings/enterprises (PSUs) are government majority-held companies, statutory corporations set up by an act of Parliament and fully owned by the government. Reading this with section 19(4)(g) of the Competition Act, the CCI can look into the activities of dominant enterprises, even if the dominant enterprise has acquired its dominance by way of statutory monopoly. In this regard, it is apposite to note that the CCI has looked into the activities of state-owned enterprises, details of which are provided in Chapter 3.

(ii) The definition explicitly excludes any function of the government that is relatable to sovereign functions that includes activity relating to energy, currency, defence and space. It has been observed by the Supreme Court that in a welfare state, functions of the state are not only the defence of the country or administration of justice or maintaining law and order but also extends to regulating and controlling the activities of people in almost every sphere, *inter alia,* educational, commercial, social, economic, political and even martial. In 2011, the Delhi High Court in *Union of India v. Competition Commission of India,*[140] explained the distinction between sovereign and non-sovereign functions with respect to the definition of enterprise under the Competition Act. The Delhi High Court noted that:

> Any welfare, commercial and economic functions are not sovereign functions and state while discharging such functions is as much amenable to the jurisdiction of CCI as any other private entity discharging such functions.

(iii) It must be kept in mind that the objective of the Competition Act is wide, and it seeks to prevent practices, having adverse effects on competition, promote and sustain competition in the market, protect the interests of consumers and ensure freedom of trade carried out by market participants. The Competition Act applies to all enterprises and persons based on the activity performed. Although the definition of the term 'enterprise' does exclude sovereign functions, it is to be noted that the Competition Act does not provide for exemption for enterprises from the purview of the Competition Act. Section 54 of the Competition Act provides that the Central Government may, by notification, exempt from the application of the Competition Act any enterprise which performs a sovereign function on behalf of the Central Government or the State Government. Thus, the scheme of the Competition Act provides that there must be an exemption which has to be granted by the Central Government under section 54 to state that the Competition Act is not applicable to such enterprises/class of enterprises.

(iv) It must be noted that the Supreme Court in *Coal India Ltd. v. CCI and Another,*[141] stated that Coal India Ltd., which is engaged in coal mining services, will fall under the definition of the word 'enterprise', as the definition includes any person or a Department of the Government which is engaged in an activity related to production, storage, supply, distribution, acquisition or control of articles or goods. Further, the legislature expressly includes even Departments of the Government separately within the ambit of the word 'enterprise'. Hence, government companies are not excluded from the definition of 'enterprise'. It's only the sovereign activity

140. *Union of India v. Competition Commission of India* [2012], (Delhi High Court) 2012 SCC OnLine Del 1114, para. 23.
141. *Coal India* case, paras 81, 82.

of the government bodies which is exempted. However, Coal India Ltd. is not discharging any sovereign function, so it will not be exempted. Similarly, the Delhi High Court in *Uttrakhand Agricultural Produce Marketing Board ('UAPMB') and Others v. Competition Commission of India*[142] said that the exemption under section 2(h) will not be applicable to the writ petitioners, which was a government body, charged with the function of supply and distribution of liquor.

(v) While the definition of enterprise is wide, it must be noted that for a person to be called an enterprise, it must perform a commercial activity. In *Mr. Umar Javeed and Others v. Google LLC and Another*,[143] the CCI held that even if Google is not charging anything for its general web service, it can still be considered commercial or economic activity. Through the general web service, Google was collecting user data and monetizing it through advertisements. Further, it must be noted that the CCI in some of the cases has held that trade association is not an enterprise since they do not perform any commercial function and earn revenue, although some anti-competitive decisions may be taken under the aegis of the trade association. Having said that, trade associations, which are not engaged in any commercial activity, will not fall under the exemption of enterprise because in some cases, the CCI has held in some other cases that trade associations are enterprises since they earn revenues from their decisions.[144] In the *Competition Commission of India v. Coordination Committee of Artistes & Technicians of W.B. Film & Television* ('*Coordination Committee* case'),[145] the Supreme Court held that a non-profit making entity may be considered an enterprise when it is engaged in some commercial or economic activities, even if it is operating in its charitable capacity at other times. If the activity of the trade association yields profits by selling goods or providing services, then the activity will be considered economic activity, and the entity will be constituted as an enterprise. The Supreme Court further noted that the members of the trade association were engaged in the production, distribution and exhibition of films/serials in West Bengal. The collective call to boycott the production of their competing members shows that the trade association takes decisions on the exhibition of films and serials, which is an economic activity. Hence, protection in the name of being a trade association goes against the object of the Competition Act. Therefore, the test is whether the person in question performs any commercial activity and earns a revenue stream. It is because of this reason that the CCI has not exercised jurisdiction over policy formulation functions of the government

142. *Uttrakhand Agricultural Produce Marketing Board ('UAPMB') and Others v. Competition Commission of India*, 2017 SCC OnLine Del 10906, para. 11.
143. *Mr. Umar Javeed and Others v. Google LLC and Another*, Case No. 39 of 2018, para. 210.
144. *M/s Shivam Enterprises v. Kiratpur Sahib Truck Operators Co-operative Transport Society Limited & Ors*, Case No. 43 of 2013, paras 13, 14.
145. *Competition Commission of India v. Coordination Committee of Artistes & Technicians of W.B. Film & Television* [2017], (SC) (2017) 5 SCC 17, paras 46, 47, 48.

because they cannot be considered to be 'commercial activities' and hence not an enterprise under section 2(h) of the Competition Act.[146] Therefore, a government body while formulating policy guidelines cannot be said to be indulging in policy decisions and hence cannot be termed as an enterprise and therefore section 4 will not be applicable to such entities.

§1.15 RELEVANT MARKET

Under the statutory scheme of the Competition Act, the definition of relevant market is of paramount importance. In an abuse of dominance analysis, an enterprise will be considered dominant only when the said enterprise holds a position of strength in the relevant market. Similarly, in a combination analysis, the CCI has to analyse whether the said combination will cause or is likely to cause an appreciable adverse effect in the relevant market in India. Also, in a vertical anti-competitive agreement analysis under section 3(4) of the Competition Act, although the Competition Act does not lay down expressly that the CCI has to define a relevant market, the decisional practice of the CCI (as elucidated in Chapter 2) would show that they have adopted the *de minimis* doctrine; i.e., parties with minimal market share entering into an agreement will not cause any appreciable adverse effect on competition (AAEC) in India.[147] The Supreme Court in the *Coordination Committee* case,[148] held that the first and foremost aspect that needs to be determined by the CCI is the relevant market in which the competition is affected due to the anti-competitive agreement. The Supreme Court interpreted the word 'market' in section 19(3) as 'relevant market' and held that it is important to determine the relevant market to identify the competitors of the concerned party, the boundaries of the competition, and the competitive constraints faced by market participants in order to examine the concentration of the market.

Similarly, the Supreme Court in the *Bharti Airtel* case[149] also noted the term 'market' in section 19(3) as 'relevant market'. However, later the Supreme Court, in the *Coordination Committee* case,[150] clarified that determination of 'relevant market' is not mandatorily determined for the violation of section 3(3) (cartel provisions) of the Competition Act. The Supreme Court clearly said that determining the relevant market is not a mandatory pre-condition in section 3(3) violations because of the statutory presumption contained in section 3(3) of the Competition Act. However, this clarification may not be applicable to vertical anti-competitive agreements because the *Coordination Committee case* specifically dealt with violation of section 3(3) of the Competition Act. Such statutory presumption is not present for violation of section 3(4) of the Competition Act, hence, it can be assumed that the Supreme Court never implied that delineation of relevant market is not mandatory for section 3(4). Although the

146. *Vineet Kumar v. Ministry of Civil Aviation*, Case No. 18/2013, paras 9, 10.
147. *Shri Ghanshyam Das Vij v. M/s Bajaj Corp Limited,* Case No. 68 of 2013, paras 77, 80.
148. *Coordination Committee* case, paras 14, 33-36.
149. *Bharti Airtel* case, para. 86.
150. Clarification order of *Coordination Committee* case, [2018], (SC) Miscellaneous Application No. 490 of 2017 in Civil Appeal No. 6691 of 2014.

legislative framework does not mandate the CCI to define a relevant market for a section 3(4) analysis, the final outcome of the analysis of the appreciable adverse effects on the competition may still require determining relevant market. Therefore, a broad understanding of the market contours has to be undertaken, even in section 3(4) analysis.

Relevant market is essentially a tool to identify and define the boundaries of competition between firms. The primary purpose of market definition is to identify the competitive constraints faced by enterprises.[151] In an abuse of dominance investigation, the main purpose behind identification of relevant market is to understand whether an enterprise has the position of strength to behave independently of the competitive forces. In a combination analysis, the CCI identifies the relevant market to see whether the combination would cause an AAEC in the relevant market. The mode of analysis in a combination analysis is whether the combination would create or strengthen market power in the relevant market. Generally, the CCI has approved combinations in the first phase itself because post-combination, the combined market share of the combining parties in the relevant market is minimal. Therefore, the objective of determining a relevant market is to identify those competitors of the enterprises involved that are capable of constraining the behaviour of the concerned enterprise and of preventing them from behaving independently of any effective competitive pressure. Further, regarding the scope of defining relevant market for combinations cases and abuse of dominance cases, the erstwhile COMPAT, in *National Stock Exchange of India Ltd. v. Competition Commission of India*,[152] observed that combination analysis is an *ex-ante* process of the proposed combination where CCI examines whether the proposed combination will adversely affect the competition of the market in the future. Thus, in combination cases, the CCI looks at the probabilities and likelihood of anti-competitive effects due to the combination. Therefore, it is natural that the determination of relevant market for combination cases becomes 'as narrow as possible' to evaluate the impact of combination in the future. However, such an analysis of a combination case is in sharp contra distinction with an abuse of dominance case, which is an *ex post* proceeding. In an abuse of dominance case, the CCI decides the past abusive conduct of an enterprise. Therefore, the analysis of abuse of dominance is an analysis of a past conduct. Thus, the mode of determination of relevant market in combination cases may differ from determination of relevant market in abuse of dominance cases.

Relevant market has been defined in section 2(r) of the Competition Act as the market which may be delineated according to the relevant product market and/or the relevant geographic market. Relevant market has been defined both in product terms as well as geographic terms. Relevant product market is defined in section 2(t) of the Competition Act to mean a market comprising the products or services which are regarded as interchangeable by the customer due to the characteristics of the products or services, their prices and use, or interchangeable by the supplier due to the ease of

151. *Bharti Airtel* case, para. 87.
152. *National Stock Exchange of India Ltd. v. Competition Commission of India* [2014], (COMPAT) MANU/TA/0016/2014, para. 54.

switching production without incurring any significant additional cost or risk. Therefore, the primary thrust of defining relevant product market is the interchangeability or substitutability of a given product in terms of price, characteristics, use and switching cost.

[A] Relevant Product Market

Section 19(7) of the Competition Act provides for the indices which have to be taken into account by the CCI, while determining the relevant product market.

While determining the relevant product market, the CCI shall consider all or any of the following factors, namely:

(a) physical characteristics, end-use of goods or the nature of services;
(b) price of goods or service;
(c) consumer preferences;
(d) exclusion of in-house production;
(e) existence of specialized producers;
(f) classification of industrial products;
(g) costs associated with switching demand or supply to other goods or services;
(h) categories of customers.

Thus, we see that demand side and supply side substitutability is the primary factor to be taken into account while determining relevant product market. Demand side substitutability assesses the extent to which customers could and would switch among substitute products in response to a change in relative prices or quality or availability or other features. It is to be noted that the relevant product market has to be defined by taking into account all those products or services which are regarded as interchangeable or substitutable by the consumer. So, two products which are not perfectly substitutable but functionally interchangeable would form part of the same relevant product market.

Apart from demand side substitutability, competition law authorities also look at supply side substitutability. Previously, the Competition Act only provided for consideration of demand side substitutability, and the CCI has also held in a few cases that it only considers demand side substitutability, and not supply side substitutability, which is to be considered for the purpose of determining the relevant market.[153] However, at the same time, in *JK Tyre & Industries Limited and J.K. Asia Pacific (S) Pte Ltd.*,[154] for the purpose of competition assessment in the tyre market, the CCI has also given due consideration to supply side substitutability.

Having said that, the Competition (Amendment) Act, 2023, amended the definition of relevant product market and also added a specific factor in section 19(7) of the

153. *Informant (Confidential) v. Grasim Industries Limited*, Case No. 51 of 2017, para. 20.
154. *JK Tyre, J.K. Asia Pacific (S) Pte Ltd., Cavendish Industries Ltd. and Kesoram Industries Ltd.*, Combination Registration No. C-2015/10/322, 18 Feb. 2016, para. 10.

Competition Act to introduce the concept of supply side substitutability. The wording of section 2(t) of the Competition Act states that relevant product market is that basket of products which are considered substitutable by the consumer or supplier. Therefore, the criteria for defining relevant product market under the Competition Act includes both demand side substitutability and supply side substitutability.

[B] Relevant Geographic Market

Section 2(s) of the Competition Act defines relevant geographic market as:

> market comprising the area in which the conditions of competition for supply of goods or provision of services or demand of goods or services are distinctly homogenous and can be distinguished from the conditions prevailing in the neighbouring areas.

Section 19(6) of the Competition Act further provides some factors which need to be taken into account by the CCI while determining relevant geographic market.

While determining the 'relevant geographic market', CCI shall have due regard to all or any of the following factors, namely: –

(a) regulatory trade barriers;
(b) local specification requirements;
(c) national procurement policies;
(d) adequate distribution facilities;
(e) transport costs;
(f) language;
(g) consumer preferences;
(h) need for secure or regular supplies or rapid after-sales services;
(i) characteristics of goods or nature of services;
(j) costs associated with switching supply or demand to other areas.

[C] Trends of the CCI

While the definitions and the approach of defining relevant market under the Competition Act are similar to other anti-trust jurisdictions, the important factor to note is the manner in which the CCI adopts the same in its analysis against vertical anti-competitive agreements, dominance investigation and merger control proceedings. Some of the key trends which can be seen are as follows:

[1] *Starting Point of Analysis*

As discussed earlier in the *Coordination Committee* case,[155] the first step of the analysis is the determination of the relevant market. It is only by defining the relevant market that a firm's market power can be assessed. The purpose of defining the relevant market is to identify which products and services operate as a competitive constraint on the behaviour of the suppliers of those respective products and services. The process of determining the relevant market starts by looking into a relatively narrow potential product market. Thereafter, the potential product market is expanded to include those substituted products which buyers or suppliers would still prefer, even after there is a price increase above the competitive price. Likewise, the relevant geographic market needs to be defined.

In fact, the Supreme Court in the *Bharti Airtel* case,[156] held that 'market' definition is a tool to identify the concentration of the market and the competition boundaries of the market participants. The relevant market is the key to determining which market participant holds the power over the market and the impact of the alleged conduct on the market. Thus, it is necessary to delineate the relevant product market and relevant geographical market to determine the market participant who has power over the market.

The CCI, in the *HT Media Ltd v. Super Cassettes Ltd.*,[157] has noted that '*since the allegation of the informant pertains to certain conduct of the opposite party in licensing its repertoire of songs to the informant, the market for licensing of music content (protect as intellectual property) is a good starting point for determination of the relevant market in this case*'. Therefore, the approach of the CCI in identifying relevant market starts from the relevant product or service of the alleged dominant enterprise, and then the substitutes of the said product are identified to determine the contours of the relevant market. Similarly, in a combination case, the CCI first identifies the overlaps between the parties in India as the starting point for relevant market determination.

[2] *Analysis in Multi-sided Markets Is from the Perspective of Affected Parties*

The tools of relevant market analysis remain the same, irrespective of how many 'sides' or user groups the enterprise in question may cater to. But in such situations, a question emerges as to from whose perspective will the relevant market be defined. This question was answered in the *MMT-Go* case.[158] In this case, the anti-competitive conduct of an online booking platform which connected users with various travel/tour-related service providers, such as hotels, airlines, trains, buses, was under consideration. The CCI held that since the alleged conduct under scrutiny was vis-à-vis hotels and franchise hotel service providers, assessment of dominance and relevant market

155. *Coordination Committee* case, paras 33-38.
156. *Bharti Airtel* case, para. 87.
157. *HT Media Ltd v. Super Cassettes Ltd.*, Case No. 40 of 2011, para. 134.
158. *MMT-Go* case, paras 190, 295.

delineation would have to be carried out from their perspective. To contextualize the discussion, the first thing to be considered here is who is this 'user' that should be the focus of assessment. When two distinct products/services are supplied, ascertaining substitutability only from the perspective of one user group may erroneously conflate the competitive constraints that exist separately and distinctly in relation to each user side. At the same time, the impact of such interactions on the substitutability has to be analysed primarily from the aggrieved user side.[159]

Hence, in the *MMT-Go* case, since the alleged conduct was related to the contractual arrangements between hotels and the online booking platform, the prime focus was the hotels' side of the market. Yet, the consumer side perspective (i.e., the other user group served by the platform) was not completely ignored and actually supplemented this understanding to account for the interdependencies between both sides of the market. The functioning of two-sided markets has been discussed in more detail in Chapter 6 on digital markets.

Thus, the principle emerges that the starting point for defining a relevant market is to first understand the service provided by the enterprise under scrutiny and then to identify alternate services that are substitutable in terms of price, characteristics and intended use from the perspective of the affected user group. Since market definition provides a tool to draw the boundaries within which to assess the anti-competitive harm alleged, the precise boundaries of markets will change depending on the context in which they are drawn. Therefore, even in two-sided markets, one needs to look at the alleged conduct and the affected party in question to define the relevant market.

[3] Relevant Geographic Market Can Only Be India

As explained in detail in Chapter 3, the dominant position has been defined under the Competition Act as position of strength enjoyed by an enterprise in the relevant market in India. Based on this technical reading of the provisions, it can be said that the Competition Act only allows that relevant geographic market can only be India or territories of India, and it can be interpreted that the scheme of the Competition Act does not allow for a worldwide definition of the relevant geographic market. In *Mr. Umar Javeed and Others v. Google LLC and Another,*[160] the CCI noted that even if general search services can be accessed by users anywhere in the world, the main general search services offer localized sites in different countries and in a variety of languages. The majority of users use the general web search in their local language; thus, India was considered the relevant geographic market for general web search because the conditions of competition are distinct and homogenous in India.

Similarly, in combination proceedings *of M/s Atos Worldline India Pvt. Ltd. v. M/s Verifone India Sales Pvt. Ltd. and Others,*[161] the CCI only looked at overlaps between the parties in India and the CCI determined the relevant geographical market to be the

159. *Ibid.*, paras 190-194.
160. *Mr. Umar Javeed and Others v. Google LLC and Another*, Case No. 39 of 2018, para. 219.
161. *M/s Atos Worldline India Pvt. Ltd. v. M/s Verifone India Sales Pvt. Ltd. and Others*, Case No. 56 of 2012, paras 6.12, 6.13.

whole of India because the condition of competition in the market of Point of Sale Terminals throughout India is similar.

In the *Automobile spare parts* case,[162] the CCI has taken the view that the relevant geographical market was pan India because the conditions of competition for the sale of spare parts and after-sale maintenance services are homogeneous for the authorized dealer and the independent repairers across the territory of India.

[4] Online Versus Offline Distribution Model

In the last decade, there has been massive growth in the online sector, and business enterprises as well as customers are preferring digital platforms over traditional offline markets. The market dynamics and character of the online market are different from those of the traditional offline market. However, earlier, the CCI did not delineate online and offline markets as separate product markets. In *Ashish Ahuja v. Snapdeal.com and Another*,[163] a seller of electronic products filed an information alleging that Snapdeal.com has abused its dominance by denying the sale of the informant's electronic product on its online e-commerce platform. The CCI passed an order under section 26(2) of the Competition Act, where it held that both offline and online markets were different in terms of shopping experience and discounts, and if the price in the online market increased, then consumers would shift to the offline markets and vice versa. Therefore, online and offline markets are substitutable; the CCI was of the view that offline and online markets were two different channels of distribution of the same product and were not two different relevant markets.

However, market definition, particularly in digital markets, is not a static concept, and the relevant market assessment must be done at each point in time based on the prevailing circumstances. Hence, CCI shifted from the narrow approach of painting online and offline channels with the same brush to thoroughly account for the challenges in digital markets and effectively enforce the Competition Act on online market players by delineating online markets as distinct relevant market. For instance, the CCI shifted its approach while delineating relevant market in *All India Online Vendors Association v. Flipkart India Pvt. Ltd.*[164] In this case, it was alleged that Flipkart was engaged in deep discounting, denied market access and leveraged its position to enter another market by extending discounts and manufacturing products under private labels. The CCI in its prima facie order under section 26(1) of the Competition Act, observed that Flipkart operates as a marketplace-based e-commerce platform, which facilitates trade between consumers and third-party sellers. Online platforms offer convenience for third-party sellers as well as consumers. The online marketplace provides a platform for third-party sellers to interact with a larger number of consumers, and it also benefits consumers by saving them time and commuting charges.

162. *Automobile spare parts* case, para. 20.5.26.
163. *Ashish Ahuja v. Snapdeal.com and Another*, Case No. 17 of 2014, para. 16.
164. *All India Online Vendors Association v. Flipkart India Pvt. Ltd.*, Case No. 20 of 2018, paras 21-25.

Hence, CCI determined the relevant product market as services provided by online marketplace platforms for selling goods.

Similarly, the CCI in *Delhi Vyapar Mahasangh v. Flipkart Internet Pvt. Ltd.,*[165] where it received information from a union of Micro, Small and Mini Enterprises engaged in the trade of mobile phones and other related accessories called Delhi Vyapar Mahasangh, against two big e-commerce platforms, Flipkart and Amazon, which are alleged to be engaged in vertical agreements under section 3(4) of the Competition Act, under which Flipkart and Amazon are preferring certain sellers. Further, it was also alleged that the e-commerce platforms contravene section 4 of the Competition Act by abusing their dominant position by engaging in predatory pricing and imposing unfair conditions. So, CCI passed a prima facie order, directing the DG to investigate the allegations. In this order, the CCI made a similar observation to the *Delhi Vyapar Mahasangh v. Flipkart Internet Pvt. Ltd*, and by saying that the online platform offers access to new markets to third-party sellers and increases consumers' choice of goods and services. An online platform ecosystem provides more benefits than a traditional brick-and-mortar set-up in terms of fixed costs and reach. Again, in *Lifestyle Equities C.V. v. Amazon Seller Services Pvt.*,[166] the CCI passed a dismissal order under section 26(2) of the Competition Act against the allegation against Amazon and Cloudtail. CCI reiterated the distinguishing characteristics of online platforms from offline platforms. CCI further noted that the digital sector is rapidly changing, and the delineation of the online platform cannot have a static approach. Hence, the relevant market should be delineated by considering the market reality and factual circumstances of each case.

Similarly, in *Matrimony.com Limited v. Google LLC and Others*,[167] the CCI distinguished between online and offline advertising services and found that neither of these markets is comparable. The CCI noted that online advertising is undertaken using the internet as a medium and, hence, it has a large coverage and wider reach. Similarly, online advertising is not substitutable for traditional offline advertisements, such as newspapers, radio or television, as mediums to advertise because traditional offline advertisements target fewer customers. Furthermore, online advertising also allows advertisers to accurately monitor the effectiveness of their advertisement, which is not possible for the advertiser who is using a newspaper or radio. Hence, the online advertisement market was held to be non-substitutable with the offline advertisement market. Similarly, in *the MMT-Go* case,[168] the CCI held that the online mode of booking service is not substitutable with offline mode of booking service. The CCI observed that end-consumer who is using online modes of payment would always prefer online channels to book hotels. And therefore, such end-consumers are considered distinct from those who prefer using traditional mode of booking by directing walk-ins to the hotels. Thus, CCI considered the online modes of booking services as a different relevant market.

165. *Delhi Vyapar Mahasangh v. Flipkart Internet Pvt. Ltd.*, Case No. 40 of 2019, para. 18.
166. *Lifestyle Equities C.V. v. Amazon Seller Services Pvt.*, Case No. 09 of 2020, para. 23.
167. Case Nos 07 and 30 of 2012, para. 97.
168. *MMT-Go* case, para. 198.

From the previous orders of the CCI, it can be concluded that both the seller side and buyer side perceive online platform differently than offline platform. Hence, the CCI has now taken a firm stance that online platform is neither substitutable nor interchangeable with traditional offline platforms. CCI's decisional practice and the trends in the delineation of online and offline forms of relevant markets have been analysed in more detail in Chapter 6 on digital markets.

[5] Aftermarket Versus Unified Systems Market

In the *Automobile spare parts* case[169] (discussed in Chapter 3), the DG concluded that the relevant market would be the aftermarket for spares of automobiles. The reason adopted by the DG was that once a customer purchases a car, he is locked in, and he is forced to buy the spare parts of the same brand since spare parts of one brand are not substitutable with spare parts of other brands. In such an aftermarket, each automobile manufacturer was dominant in respect of its respective spares since a customer who purchases a car cannot substitute spares of a different manufacturer and is locked into the aftermarket suppliers of the car manufacturer. This case best illustrates the concept of the relevant market being an aftermarket of a primary product. Consider the said example: a consumer wishes to buy a car. When he is exploring the options to buy a car, he has several options at each price segment, but once he has purchased the car, the consumer is 'locked in' and has to use the spare parts of that particular car manufacturer (for instance, a consumer who has bought a Maruti car cannot use spare parts of Toyota and or avail of the services of an authorized dealer of Hyundai). In such cases, there is a presence of two different markets: one a primary market and another, the aftermarket.

While determining whether the relevant market can be an aftermarket of a primary product, it has to be seen whether a consumer can shift the primary product when the prices of the spare parts of the said primary product go up without incurring substantial shifting costs. The CCI observed that consumers cannot change the car (i.e., Maruti to Toyota) if the prices of spare parts of Maruti go up exponentially. Further, due to the technical specifications and the complex engineering used to manufacture each brand of cars by the original equipment manufacturers ('car companies' / car manufacturers or 'OEMs'), the spare parts of one brand are not compatible with that of another brand, and therefore, the products in the secondary market for spare parts are not interchangeable with those of the primary market, and therefore they constitute distinct relevant product markets. Based on the above and actual economic evidence, the CCI came to the conclusion that the relevant market is the aftermarket for the supply of spare parts and technical designs for each car manufacturer separately.

It was argued by the car manufacturers that both the 'sale of primary product' as well as its aftermarket may be considered one unified systems market. In furtherance to this submission, it was argued that once the customer purchases a car, he is locked in to purchase the spare parts from the same car manufacturer. But this practice would

169. *Automobile spare parts* case, para. 20.5.54.

protect the reputation of the car manufacturers as well as benefit the customers as they would be well equipped with adequate information to make the right decisions while purchasing another car or spare parts. Further, the customers could ascertain the total cost that they would likely incur during the life cycle of the car. However, the unified systems market proposed by the car manufacturers was rejected, and CCI held that the car manufacturers were unable to provide any evidence to show the positive impact on consumers due to their lock-in practices. Additionally, the lock-in practices facilitated their ability to increase the cost of their products and exploit the consumers. Based on these parameters, the CCI concluded that manufacturers were unable to demonstrate that they could, or consumers could, bring about a pro-competitive effect and hence, rejected the systems market contention. Finally, the CCI held that the sale of primary products and aftermarket products can't be considered one unified market. The erstwhile COMPAT[170] also agreed with the CCI's reasoning in relation to the issue of whether the automobile and auto spare parts market constitutes a unified systems market. The erstwhile COMPAT looked at the practice of car manufacturers and held that car manufacturers failed to show any evidence to substantiate the claim of the positive impact on consumers. Finally, it was held that the choice of an Indian customer is driven by the mileage of the car, budget of the customer, and a broad understanding of the availability of 'good models' in the market. And therefore, the erstwhile COMPAT upheld the decision of CCI to separate the relevant markets for the sale of cars and the aftermarket (i.e., sale of spare parts and sale of repair services).

While in the *Automobile spare parts* case, the CCI did not agree with the unified systems market, in later cases, they agreed that a unified systems market may exist. In the case of *Trend Electronics v. Hewlett Packard Sales Pvt. Ltd.*[171] ('*HP* case'), it was argued by the informant that there were deficiencies in the after-sales services provided by Hewlett Packard (HP). The Informant has submitted that the laptop is the primary product in the instant case, and the market for repair, maintenance and after-sales services is the secondary market. While the order passed in the *HP* case is silent, it seems like the informant must have relied on the reasoning laid down by the CCI in the *Automobile spare parts* case. Having said that, the CCI, in the *HP* case, did not agree that there is a separate market for aftermarket in case of laptops. It noted that although the informant had submitted relevant market as the secondary market for repair, maintenance and after-sales services, no justification had been provided for considering the secondary market as a separate and distinct relevant market. Further, the CCI noted, based on information available/accessible in the public domain, that a consumer purchasing a laptop could reasonably ascertain the total cost that he is likely to incur during the life cycle of the laptop. Further, factors such as the high rate of obsoletion and low life span of laptops suggested that any unfair business strategy by the laptop manufacturers, in the after-sales services, is likely to affect the sales of the primary product. Further, the CCI noted that there are many options available to resell

170. *Automobile spare parts* case [2016], (COMPAT) 2016 SCC OnLine Comp AT 452, paras 69, 81.
171. *Trend Electronics v. Hewlett Packard Sales Pvt. Ltd.*, Case No. 92 of 2015, paras 14, 15.

used laptops, and the customers can switch to substitutable products without incurring substantial switching costs.

Based on the same, one can see that CCI will look at the particular sector and analyse the market dynamics to determine if an aftermarket exists in the first place.

[6] Lack of Scientific Sampling

The entire exercise of determination of relevant market is to identify the products/services which are considered substitutable and also identify the competitive constraints that the parties face. While the exercise is extremely pertinent in an abuse of dominance or a merger control investigation, the orders of the CCI are silent as to whether they conduct or appoint a third party to conduct a proper market survey of the sector in question. Further, the application of certain concepts like the Small but Significant and Non-Transitory Increase in Price (SSNIP) test is not uniform by the CCI. While in some cases, the CCI relies on the SSNIP test to determine the market,[172] in others, they do not adopt the said test.[173] The CCI must place more reliance on scientific sampling in its analysis. The CCI and DG should, in some cases, take assistance from independent third parties to conduct analysis in their investigations.

[7] Relevant Markets for Section 3(4) of the Competition Act Need Not Be Precisely Delineated

There is no need to go into precise relevant market determination for the cases against vertical anti-competitive agreements.[174] In *National Restaurant Association of India ('NRAI') v. Zomato Limited ('Zomato') & Others,*[175] the CCI held that for the contraventions under section 3(4) of the Competition Act, there is no need to precisely determine the relevant market. In this case, while passing an order under section 26(1) of the Competition Act, the CCI widely delineated the relevant market of Zomato and Swiggy as 'online food delivery platforms' and 'operate as online intermediaries for food ordering and delivery'.

Also, in the case of *Alleged anti-competitive conduct by Maruti Suzuki India Limited in implementing discount control policy vis-à-vis dealers,*[176] while holding Maruti Suzuki liable for imposing resale price maintenance on its dealers under section

172. *Belaire Owners' Association v. DLF Limited, HUDA & Ors.*, Case No. 19 of 2010. However, at the appellate stage, the erstwhile COMPAT held that there is no need to conduct any SSNIP test. *See, DLF Limited and Ors. v. Competition Commission of India and Ors.*, MANU /TA/0012/2014, para. 84.
173. *MCX Stock Exchange Ltd. v. National Stock Exchange of India Ltd. and Another*, Case No. 13 of 2009, para. 10.16. The CCI held that applicant of SSNIP test is unnecessary. The erstwhile COMPAT upheld the CCI's order in *the National Stock Exchange of India Ltd. v. Competition Commission of India* and Another [2014], (COMPAT) Appeal No. 15 of 2011.
174. *Hiveloop Technology Pvt. Ltd. v. Britannia Industries Ltd.*, Case No. 18 of 2021, para. 43.
175. *National Restaurant Association of India ('NRAI') v. Zomato Limited ('Zomato') & Others*, Case No. 16 of 2021, para. 34.
176. *Alleged anti-competitive conduct by Maruti Suzuki India Limited in implementing discount control policy vis-à-vis dealers*, Suo Motu Case No. 01 of 2019, para. 16.

3(4)(e) of the Competition Act, the CCI felt that there is no requirement of defining a precise relevant market for the assessment of a vertical anti-competitive agreement. The CCI held that Maruti is a manufacturer dealing in the upstream market with significant market power without precisely delineating the relevant market.

[8] No Static Approach to Relevant Market Analysis

In the case of *Federation of Hotel & Restaurant Association of India v. MakeMyTrip India Pvt. Ltd*,[177] the CCI has noted that in rapidly changing markets, market assessment cannot have a static approach and that market definition adopted in a previous combination approval involving the same parties, which happened two years before the assessment in that case, should not hold true as market dynamics change have changed due to the rapid evolution of the digital market. The CCI in that case noted that:

> Delineation of relevant market is based on *market realities as they exist at the time of assessment*. In rapidly changing markets in particular, market assessment cannot have a static approach. The Combination case cited by MMT-Go took place over two and a half years back. While this may not be a period sufficiently long for traditional markets to undergo perceptible change, *the pace of evolution of digital markets is significantly faster*. The intervening period has seen the online travel portals and the customised service that they provide to consumers on account of *big data analytics to have established a distinct and significantly more prominent position in the hotel reservation space in India*. In view of the increased popularity and use of OTAs by a large segment of consumers in India, *hotel operators now perceive them as a distinct mode of distribution which cannot be simply replaced or substituted by other offline modes or direct sale without losing out significantly on consumer reach*. Thus, on an overall consideration of the market realities and competition dynamics, the Commission finds it difficult to accept the assertion made by MMT-Go.

Similar attempts to rely on the previous case decided by CCI were made to object to the jurisdiction of the CCI to examine their present conduct by Amazon and Flipkart. The Karnataka High Court rejected the contention of Flipkart and noted that in a competitive market, various agreements are executed, new practices are adopted every day, and merely because some other issue has been looked into by the CCI earlier, it does not mean that on the ground of res judicata, the CCI cannot look into any information subsequently against the appellants. The Court further noted that the marketplace is by very nature a constantly evolving and dynamic space, that market forces can evolve in the course of few months, and that by no stretch of imagination, it can be held that enterprises shall be out of bound for all times and no action can be taken against them only because at some point of time the matter has been looked into by the CCI.

177. Case No. 14 of 2019.

§1.16 CONCLUSION

In the last fourteen years, the CCI has examined cases relating to anti-competitive agreements (discussed in Chapter 2 of this book), abuse of dominance (discussed in Chapter 3 of this book), and merger control (discussed in Chapter 4 of this book) from diverse sectors of the economy. According to the findings based on evidence, appropriate penalties and directions were imposed on the enterprises that were found to be engaged in anti-competitive practices. Also, India has emerged as the pioneer of the digital revolution all over the world. There is a steady rise in cases emanating from the digital markets (discussed in Chapter 6 of this book). To keep the regulatory vires abreast of the changing market dynamics, the CCI may need to develop its enforcement mechanisms so that market participants in digital markets do not evade the scrutiny of the CCI. Further, for the detection and enforcement of the Competition Act, a multidisciplinary approach needs to be taken by looking at both facts and law. Accordingly, amendments to the Competition Act and its Regulations may be made in order to enhance the enforcement of the principles of competition law.

CHAPTER 2

Anti-competitive Agreements and Competition Law

§2.01 LEGAL FRAMEWORK

Any agreement between persons or enterprises or association of enterprises or persons or association of persons, in respect of production, supply, distribution, storage, acquisition or control of goods or provisions of services, which causes an AAEC in India, is void under section 3(2) of the Competition Act, 2002 ('*Competition Act*'). The Competition Commission of India (CCI) has noted, in the case of *Shri Neeraj Malhotra v. Deutsche Post Bank Home Finance,*[1] that under the provisions of section 3, in an analysis of 'agreement', an agreement with an end consumer is not included.

It has been observed that an end consumer is not involved in any activities related to the supply side of the market and the word 'agreement' in section 3(1) refers to any agreement in respect of activities which are on the supply side. Thus, an 'agreement' for the purpose of section 3 analysis cannot be entered between a supplier and a consumer as consumer can never be involved in supply side activities.

For the purposes of section 3, first, the existence of an 'agreement' must be determined. The term 'agreement' normally refers to joint action or understanding by two or more parties and not unilateral action of one party.[2] As such, the term 'agreement' is construed in a very wide manner and includes any agreement or understanding or action in concert. The erstwhile COMPAT in *GlaxoSmithKline*

1. *Shri Neeraj Malhotra v. Deutsche Post Bank Home Finance,* Case No. 5 of 2009, para. 17.5. The erstwhile COMPAT in *GlaxoSmithKline Pharmaceuticals Limited & Anr. v. Competition Commission of India* [2016], (COMPAT) 2016 SCC OnLine Comp AT 400, para. 51, reiterated the reasoning of the *Shri Neeraj Malhotra v. Deutsche Bank* to hold that no case for collusive bidding was made out.
2. Section 2(b) of the Competition Act, 2002.

Pharmaceuticals Limited & Anr. v. Competition Commission of India[3] observed that the definition of 'agreement' in section 2(b) of the Act is inclusive in nature. An 'agreement' includes any arrangement or understanding or action in concert, whether such arrangement, understanding or action is formal or in writing or is intended to be enforceable by legal proceedings.

After the determination of an agreement, the effect of the agreement will have to be determined to see whether such an agreement causes, or is likely to cause, any AAEC in India. The AAEC analysis must be determined based on the parameters under section 19(3) of the Competition Act. It is the onus of the CCI to prove that an agreement causes or is likely to cause an AAEC in India. However, there are certain kinds of agreements which are mentioned under section 3(3) of the Act (i.e., cartel arrangements) which are presumed to have an AAEC in India. In such cases, the onus shifts on the parties to such an agreement to prove that the agreement will not cause or likely cause an AAEC in India based on parameters laid down in section 19(3) of the Competition Act.

Thus, there are certain categories of agreements which are mentioned under section 3(3) of the Act on presumptive rule approach, meaning that once the essential ingredients of an agreement are established, there is no further need to launch into an elaborate enquiry to find out the impact of such conduct on the market and that AAEC is presumed. In that situation, the burden shifts to the contravening parties to rebut the presumption by showing that their conduct does not result in AAEC in India.

§2.02 LEGAL FRAMEWORK OF CARTELS IN INDIA

Section 2(c) of the Competition Act defines a 'cartel' to include:

> an association of producers, sellers, distributors, traders or service providers who, by agreement amongst themselves, limit, control or attempt to control the production, distribution, sale or price of, or, trade in goods or provision of services.

As per the definition, the scope and ambit of the term 'cartel' is inclusive.[4] In the erstwhile regime, the term 'cartel' was not defined in the Monopolies and Restrictive Trade Practices Act, 1969. As such, through judicial pronouncement, the cartel was recognized as an agreement relating to restrictive trade practice. In *Union of India v. Hindustan Development Corporation*,[5] the Supreme Court relied on dictionaries and American jurisprudence to interpret the word 'cartel' as:

> ...The cartel therefore is an association of producers who by agreement among themselves attempt to control production, sale and prices of the product to obtain a monopoly in any particular industry or commodity. Analysing the object of formation of a cartel in other words, it amounts to an unfair trade practice which

---

3. *GlaxoSmithKline Pharmaceuticals Limited & Anr. v. Competition Commission of India*[2016], (COMPAT) 2016 SCC OnLine Comp AT 400, para. 48.
4. *GlaxoSmithKline Pharmaceuticals Limited & Anr. v. Competition Commission of India* [2016], (COMPAT) 2016 SCC OnLine Comp AT 400, para. 48.
5. *Union of India v. Hindustan Development Corpn.* [1993], (SC) (1993) 3 SCC 499, para. 14.

> is not in the public interest. The intention to acquire monopoly power can be spelt out from formation of such a cartel by some of the producers. However, the determination whether such agreement unreasonably restrains the trade depends on the nature of the agreement and on the surrounding circumstances that give rise to an inference that the parties intended to restrain the trade and monopolise the same...

It is apposite to note that the enforcement regime of the present competition law regime in India with respect to cartel enforcement is well established. Empirically, most of the decided cases on cartels deal with bid rigging in the government procurement sector.

Generally, the cartels are formed in secrecy to hamper free and fair competition by controlling or rigging the prices, products and customer/territorial allocation. Cartel members continue this concerted practice in secrecy to avoid the attention of the CCI. Thus, cartels are hard to trace and bust. So, to discourage cartelization, the statutory scheme under the Competition Act provides for a presumption wherein any agreement entered into between enterprises or associations of enterprises or persons or associations of persons or between any person and enterprise or practice carried on, or decision taken by, any association of enterprises or association of persons, including cartels, engaged in identical or similar trade of goods or provision of services, which: (a) directly or indirectly determines purchase or sale prices; (b) limits or controls production, supply, markets, technical development, investment or provision of services; (c) shares the market or source of production or provision of services by way of allocation of the geographical area of the market, or type of goods or services, or number of customers in the market or any other similar way; (d) directly or indirectly results in bid rigging or collusive bidding, shall be presumed to have an AAEC in India. Unlike in the case of dominance investigation, the provisions with respect to anti-competitive agreement are applicable to even an association of persons (like a trade association) and are not only limited to the unilateral conduct of an enterprise. Further, the ambit of section 3(3) also applies to a decision taken by an association of persons. The CCI has used the expanded ambit of section 3(3) of the Competition Act to include even decisions taken in a trade association meeting since a trade association is nothing but an association of enterprises or an association of persons.

§2.03 EXISTENCE OF AN AGREEMENT

It must be noted that to invoke the provisions of section 3 of the Competition Act, the existence of an 'agreement' is *sine qua non*. Such 'agreement' covered under section 3 of the Competition Act must be related to an economic activity, regardless of whether the activity intends to earn profit. Competition law frowns upon the activities of those enterprises or persons who, while undertaking their economic activities, indulge in practices which effect the competition adversely.[6]

6. *Competition Commission of India v. Coordination Committee Artistes & Technicians of W.B. Film & Television* [2017], (SC) (2017) 5 SCC 17, paras 44, 45.

The term 'agreement' has been defined in section 2(b) of the Competition Act. Section 2(b) of the Competition Act reads as:

> 'agreement' includes any arrangement or understanding or action in concert –
>
> (i) whether or not, such arrangement, understanding or action is formal or in writing; or
> (ii) whether or not such arrangement, understanding or action is intended to be enforceable by legal proceedings.

Based on the definition, we see that agreement has been defined in an extremely broad manner under the Competition Act to include any agreement, whether oral or written. The Supreme Court in *CCI v. Coordination Committee Artistes & Technicians of W.B. Film & Television ('Coordination Committee* case')[7] not only held that the definition of 'agreement' is inclusive and that the ambit of the agreement also includes any arrangement or understanding or even concerted practice. The CCI has, in fact, noted that the understanding between the competitors might be tacit, and the definition of the agreement includes situations where the parties act on the basis of a nod or a wink. It has been observed from the decisional practice of the CCI that there is rarely direct evidence of action in concert between the market participants. In the absence of such direct evidence, the CCI must determine, based on circumstantial evidence, whether the market participants are involved in any dealings and have some form of understanding which points to the fact as to whether they are acting in coordination with each other. It must be noted herein that section 36(2), read with section 41(2) of the Competition Act, confers on the CCI and DG all the powers of a Civil Court under the Code of Civil Procedure, 1908 which include summoning of a person and examining him on oath, requiring the discovery and production of documents, receiving evidence on affidavit, issuing commissions for the examination of witnesses or documents. In spite of being provided with vast sweeping powers of investigation, at times, it is very difficult to obtain direct evidence with respect to the existence of a cartel since cartels traditionally are always hatched in secrecy. In such a situation, the DG and CCI rely on circumstantial evidence. Circumstantial evidence includes evidence of communications among suspected cartel operators and economic evidence concerning the market and the conduct of those participating in it which suggests the existence of *consensus ad idem* among market participants as opposed to independent decision-making. Examples of circumstantial evidence can be receipts, visitor entry registers, credit card bills, travel details, email dumps, telephone/mobile bills, etc., which show that the market participants had interacted with each other on a regular basis to show some concerted action.

It would be seen that most of the analysis done by the DG and the CCI, while deciding cartel cases, is to analyse from direct communication and economic evidence whether there is an agreement between the market participants or whether the market participants were acting independently. The task of the DG and CCI becomes all the more onerous because most of the cartel investigations happen in an oligopolistic

7. *Ibid.*

industry where parallel behaviour is very common. The CCI must, therefore, differentiate between a case of an anti-competitive agreement among market participants and conscious parallelism among market participants. In this regard, the CCI has noted that the evidence of agreement has to be tested on the benchmark of 'preponderance of probabilities'.[8] In this regard, as observed by CCI in the case of *Alleged cartelization by steel producers,*[9] an order holding that there is no violation of section 3(3)(a) and (b) of the Competition Act:

> Since the prohibition on participating in anti-competitive agreements and the penalties which offenders may incur are well known, it is normal for the activities which those practices and those agreements entail to take place in a clandestine fashion, for meetings to be held in secret and for the associated documentation to be reduced to a minimum. Considering the remote possibility of getting direct evidence in the case of a cartel in many cases, the existence of an anti-competitive practice or agreement can also be inferred from the conduct of the colluding parties which may include a number of coincidences and indicia which, taken together, may, in the absence of any other plausible explanation, constitute evidence of the existence of an agreement. Thus, in case of agreements as listed in Section 3(3) of the Act, once it is established that such an agreement exists, it will be presumed that the agreement has an appreciable adverse effect on competition; the onus to rebut this presumption would lie upon the opposite party.

As mentioned above, agreement has been very widely defined in section 2(b) of the Competition Act. From the definition of agreement provided in the Competition Act, it can be seen that an agreement need not be in writing, nor necessarily has to be legally enforceable.[10] An arrangement or understanding is as good as a formal written agreement. The legislative intent is quite clear, and the definition encompasses both overt and tacit forms of agreements, and it is not required that it has to be an agreement as is understood in common parlance under the principles of contract law. Based on the wide definition provided under the Competition Act, the CCI has, in various decisions, noted that it is not the requirement under law to demand direct evidence of agreement in all cases and in the absence of direct evidence, existence of circumstantial evidence that tends to exclude the possibility of independent action would be sufficient to give rise to an inference of an agreement. In this regard, it is apposite to point out the observations of the CCI in the *Builders Association of India v. Cement Manufactures Association and Ors.*[11] ('*Cement cartel* case') that market participants often hatch anti-competitive conspiracies in secrecy. As the CCI would hardly find any direct evidence of the anti-competitive conduct, it has to look at the circumstantial or indirect evidence to establish the anti-competitive conduct. The word 'agreement' under the Competition Act has been given an inclusive definition, which is not restricted to

8. *In Re: Alleged cartelization by steel producers,* RTPE 09 of 2008, para. 111.
9. *Ibid.,* para. 112.
10. *In Re: Alleged anti-competitive conduct in the Beer Market in India,* Suo Motu Case No. 06 of 2017, para. 86. The CCI held that implementation of anti-competitive agreement under section 3(3) of the Competition Act or actual causing of AAEC is not a *sine qua non* for establishing contravention.
11. *Builders Association of India v. Cement Manufactures Association and Ors.,* Case No. 29 of 2010, para. 183.

written agreements, because market participants do not reveal their anti-competitive conduct to avoid being punished under the Competition Act. Hence, the CCI will consider all the circumstantial evidence before it concludes whether there is an anti-competitive agreement among the market participants.

The definition of agreement under the Competition Act also uses the term '*action in concert*'. The erstwhile COMPAT in *Indian Jute Mills Association, Royal Exchange and Others v. CCI and Others* ('*Jute Mill* case')[12] relied on the interpretation of similar terms from other laws, such as 'person acting in concert' in securities law. The erstwhile COMPAT cited *Daichi Sankyo Company Limited v. Jayaram Chigurupati*, where the phrase 'persons acting in concert' used in Regulation 2(1)(e)(1) of SEBI (Substantial Acquisition of Shares and Takeovers) Regulations, 1997, has been interpreted by the Supreme Court as a shared common objective between two or persons. There may be a direct or indirect agreement between such persons to share the common objective or purpose of acquisition or substantial acquisition of shares, etc., of the target company. Thus, the element of the shared common objective or purpose is the *sine qua non* for the relationship of persons acting in concert:

> ...There can be no 'persons acting in concert' unless there is a shared common objective or purpose between two or more persons of substantial acquisition of shares, etc. of the target company. For, dehors the element of the shared common objective or purpose the idea of 'person acting in concert' is as meaningless as a criminal conspiracy without any agreement to commit a criminal offence. The idea of 'persons acting in concert' is not about a fortuitous relationship coming into existence by accident or chance. The relationship can come into being only by design, by meeting of minds between two or more persons leading to the shared common objective or purpose of acquisition or substantial acquisition of shares, etc. of the target company. It is another matter that the common objective or purpose may be in pursuance of an agreement or an understanding, formal or informal; the acquisition of shares, etc. may be direct or indirect or the persons acting in concert may cooperate in actual acquisition of shares, etc. or they may agree to cooperate in such acquisition. Nonetheless, the element of the shared common objective or purpose is the sine qua non for the relationship of 'persons acting in concert' to come into being.

It has been seen that there are situations where competitors come together, either under the aegis of a trade association or otherwise, to carry out legitimate business activities, like industry lobbying, etc. The degree of cooperation among competitors can also be for the purposes of carrying out research and development activities. Thus, such agreements can be a means to share risk, save costs, increase investments, pool know-how, enhance product quality and facilitate invention. These agreements, therefore, can have pro-competitive benefits which are highly beneficial to the competitive structure of the market. Having said that, there can be situations wherein competitors enter into an agreement to maximize their own profits to the detriment of the consumers.

12. *Indian Jute Mills Association, Royal Exchange and Others v. CCI and Others* [2016], (COMPAT) 2016 SCC OnLine Comp AT 144, para. 96.

It must be observed that the operation of agreements can vary from cartels to conscious parallelism. It has been seen, from the decisional practice of the CCI, that the operation of cartels tends to be very complex, and it varies according to the number of participants involved and the nature of the market in question. The decisional practice (discussed *supra*) would show the way the CCI has relied on communication and economic evidence to identify whether the market participants have indulged in a cartel or not. Such analysis helps the CCI to conclude whether the parties have acted in furtherance of an anti-competitive agreement or unilaterally. It is the precise reason why concerted practice is caught under the provisions of the Competition Act. It is because, by its very nature, concerted practice does not have all the elements of a binding agreement but arises out of the behaviour of the parties concerned. The necessity to include any such arrangement or understanding within the ambit of an agreement caught under the prohibition of antitrust laws has been aptly described by Lord Denning in the case of *PRTA v. W.H.Smith and Sons Ltd.*, as quoted by the CCI in the *In Re: suo-motu case against LPG cylinder manufacturers* ('*LPG-I* case'),[13] namely:

> People who combine together to keep up prices do not shout it from the housetops. They keep it quiet. They make their own arrangements in the cellar where no one can see. They will not put anything into writing nor even into words. A nod or wink will do. Parliament as well is aware of this. So it included not only an 'agreement' properly so called, but any 'arrangement', however informal.

Further, as mentioned above, it is apposite to note that under the statutory scheme of the Competition Act, cartels are presumed to have an AAEC in India. With respect to the presumption stated, it has been mentioned by the Supreme Court of India that 'shall be presumed' is a presumption and not evidence in itself. In *Excel Crop Care Ltd. v. Competition Commission of India* ('*Excel Crop* case'),[14] the Supreme Court held that the kinds of agreements mentioned in section 3(3) of the Competition Act would be treated as *ipso facto* causing AAEC. If the CCI finds that the parties entered into an agreement covered under the categories of section 3(3) of the Competition Act, then the CCI need not undertake any further enquiry. Section 3(3) of the Competition Act shifts the onus on the parties entering into an agreement for one of the categories mentioned in section 3(3)(a) to section 3(3)(d) above to show, based on the indices mentioned under section 19(3) of the Competition Act, that such agreement does not cause an AAEC in India. The burden would shift upon such enterprises or persons to rebut the said presumption by providing adequate evidence.

Similarly, in *Uniglobe Mod Travels (P) Ltd v. Travel Agents Federation of India,*[15] while holding that the trade association had violated section 3(3) by collectively boycotting Singapore Airlines, the CCI explained the presumptive nature of section 3(3) of the Competition Act. The CCI said that once the existence of a horizontal

13. *In Re: suo-motu case against LPG cylinder manufacturers,* Suo-Moto Case No. 03 of 2011, para. 14.11.
14. *Excel Crop Care Ltd. v. Competition Commission of India* [2017], (SC) (2017) 8 SCC 47, paras 41.2, 49.
15. *Uniglobe Mod Travels (P) Ltd v. Travel Agents Federation of India,* Case No. 03 of 2009, para. 68.2.1.

anti-competitive agreement is established, the burden of proof shifts upon the parties who had entered into such agreement to prove that there is no anti-competitive effect from the said agreement.

Further, the Competition Act provides for an exception to the per se rule provided under section 3(3) of the Competition Act. The stated exception provides that the provision of section 3(3) shall not be applicable to an agreement entered into by way of joint venture arrangements which increase efficiency in terms of production, supply, distribution, storage, acquisition or control of goods or services.

§2.04 STANDARD OF PROOF

In order to establish the existence of a cartel, it is important to prove the existence of an agreement between market participants. As has been mentioned above, it has been observed from the decisional practice of the CCI that there is rarely direct evidence of action in concert between the market participants. In this regard, the CCI in the case of *GAIL (India) Limited v. PMP Infratech Private Ltd. and Another*[16] observed that the standard of proof required to prove an anti-competitive agreement would be based on 'preponderance of probabilities' and not 'beyond reasonable doubt'. Thus, in the absence of such direct evidence, the CCI has to determine, based on circumstantial evidence, whether the market participants are involved in any dealings and have some form of understanding which points to the fact as to whether they are acting in coordination with each other instead of acting unilaterally.

It would be seen that most of the analysis done by the DG and the CCI, while deciding cartel cases, is to analyse from communication and economic evidence whether there is an agreement between the market participants or not. While the competition authority was going through the transaction of Monopolies and Restrictive Trade Practices Act, 1969, regime to the present competition law regime, the DG investigated major steel manufacturers for colluding to raise the prices of steel products *In Re: Alleged cartelization by steel producers.*[17] From the investigation report, it was concluded that the steel manufacturers coordinated to raise their prices, and they also limited and controlled the production of steel products. However, the CCI made a note of flawed investigation since the CCI noted that multiple factors were the reason behind the price pattern moving in tandem, such as increase in landed import price, cost of production and the demand and supply analysis. Without any direct evidence to indicate the collusion, an anti-competitive agreement cannot be assumed. So, the standard of proof to establish the violation of section 3(3) required additional evidence or what is commonly referred to as 'plus factor', was not met in this case. A wide range of circumstantial evidence can be used to establish the additional evidence or plus factors.

16. *GAIL (India) Limited v. PMP Infratech Private Ltd. and Another*, Case No. 41 of 2019, para. 3; *In Re: Anti-competitive conduct in the paper manufacturing industry*, Suo Motu Case No. 05 of 2016, para. 153; *Mr. Rizwanul Haq Khan v. Mersen (India) Pvt. Ltd. and Another*, Reference Case No. 02 of 2016, para. 44.
17. *In Re: Alleged cartelization by steel producers*, RTPE 09 of 2008, paras 90, 101, 120, 121, 123.

It is imperative to note that conscious parallelism must be differentiated from cartel behaviour. Though parallel pricing or other parallel behaviour amounts to strong evidence, it does not justify the presence of cartel or anti-competitive agreement.[18] This means the CCI cannot shift the burden of proof by simply establishing parallel behaviour. In *A.R. Polymers Pvt. Ltd. and Others v. Competition Commission of India*,[19] the erstwhile COMPAT set aside the order of CCI where the opposite parties were held guilty for violating section 3(3)(a) and (d) of the Act by forming a bid rigging cartel to quote identical bids for the supply of Jungle Boots. The erstwhile COMPAT heavily relied on *Union of India v. Hindustan Development Corporation* because of the similarity in factual matrix to hold that mere quoting of identical tender offers by opposite parties does not mean a cartel has been formed. In that case, three manufacturers of steel bogies quoted identical prices to a tender notice issued by the Railway Board for the supply of cast steel bogies. The Tender Committee considered that the three manufacturers colluded and quoted a higher price. Thereafter, a counteroffer was given to the three manufacturers where the quotation was reduced. When the matter finally reached the Supreme Court, it was held that there was no cartel because '*a mere quotation of identical price and an offer of further reduction by themselves would not entitle them automatically to comer the entire market by way of monopoly since the final allotment of quantities vested in the authorities who in their discretion can distribute the same to all the manufacturers including these three big manufacturers on certain basis*'. Further, in the absence of a plus factor, the quoting of identical bids is not enough to infer as bid rigging under section 3(3)(d) of the Act.

This, thus, makes it clear that parallel behaviour neither shifts the burden of proof nor conclusively establishes a contravention under section 3(3) of the Competition Act. On similar lines, in the case of *Narendra Explosive v. Competition Commission of India*,[20] the erstwhile COMPAT ruled that CCI had erred in presuming the similar bid quotation of the opposite parties and they had been fixing the price of the CN Containers with disc. The Appellate Tribunal noted that DG did not collect any circumstantial evidence to conclude that the opposite parties communicated before submitting their bids or any consensus on the pricing of the product. The erstwhile COMPAT found the reasoning behind the similar quotation to be plausible because the concerned product was limited to three ordinance factories and was required to be manufactured as per specifications. The opposite parties' quotations were based on the last purchase price which was available in the public domain and acted as a guiding factor for the opposite parties. The quotations of the last purchase were available on the website of the ordinance factories; thus, the justification advanced by the opposite parties that the information available in the public domain behind the similar quotation

18. *Excel Corp* case, para. 52.
19. *A.R. Polymers Pvt. Ltd. and Others v. Competition Commission of India* [2016], (COMPAT) 2016 SCC OnLine Comp AT 240, paras 23, 35, 36, 39, 43.
20. *Narendra Explosive v. Competition Commission of India* [2016], (COMPAT) 2016 SCC OnLine Comp AT 422, paras 45, 47, 48, 52. The erstwhile COMPAT in *Deputy Chief Materials Manager, Rail Coach Factory, Kapurthala, Punjab v. Faiveley Transport India Ltd.*[2016], (COMPAT) Appeal No. 10 of 2016 set aside the order of CCI by holding that mere identity of price is not enough for holding that the opposite parties had indulged in bid rigging.

or parallel pricing was considered plausible by the Tribunal. Thus, the Courts have consistently held that mere parallel pricing will not suffice; one needs to demonstrate plus factors to conclusively demonstrate cartelization. Thus, if the parties under investigation can show business reasons for such parallel behaviour, they may not be held guilty of cartelization.

In Re: All India Tyre Dealers Federation v. Tyre Manufactures Association ('*Tyre* case'),[21] the case was initiated based on a complaint made by All India Tyre Dealers Association. Based on the complaint, the CCI undertook a detailed price-cost comparison of the tyre manufacturers to analyse whether the tyre companies have engaged in a cartel. Before analysing the communication and the economic evidence, the CCI noted that the industry is an oligopolistic market; it is extremely likely that each market participant is aware of the other participant's behaviour. In an oligopolistic market, interdependence between firms is an important characteristic of such a market which would mean that each firm in such a market considers the likely reactions of other firms while making independent decisions, particularly as regards prices and output. Though oligopolistic markets can lead to competitive outcomes, the outcomes may not always be market-driven but rather a result of concerted effort or collusion. Therefore, the parallel behaviour of competitors can be a result of intelligent market adaptation in an oligopolistic market or a case of anti-competitive agreement. So, the key factor of analysis to be done is whether there is an agreement between market participants to engage in cartelization or not.

Even the decisional practice of the CCI has recognized the aspect of parallel behaviour among enterprises, especially in an oligopolistic market. What the DG and CCI look for, in a cartel investigation, is whether there are any 'plus factors' which prove that there is an agreement among the market participants. Unlike contract law, the definition of 'agreement' under the competition law is much wider and includes both overt and tacit forms. In the *LPG-I* case,[22] an investigation was conducted by the CCI to analyse whether the manufactures of LPG cylinders had colluded and manipulated their bids for the supply of LPG cylinders to the Indian Oil Corporation Ltd. (IOCL). While conducting the said investigation, the CCI analysed the market in great detail and noted that the industry has structural characteristics which support cartelization. The DG noted that even though bid rigging can occur in any sector, there are some sectors in which it is more likely to occur due to particular features of the industry or of the product involved. The CCI held that there was a violation of section 3(3)(d) read with section 3(1) of the Competition Act. Post the decision of the CCI, the manufacturers preferred to go on appeal to the erstwhile COMPAT. On the basis of the facts mentioned above, the erstwhile COMPAT agreed with the observations made by the CCI and rejected the appeals made by the manufacturers. However, the said judgment of both the CCI and erstwhile COMPAT was set aside by the Supreme Court.

---

21. *In Re: All India Tyre Dealers Federation v. Tyre Manufactures Association*, MRTP Case: RTPE No. 20 of 2008, paras 86, 102.
22. Rajasthan Cylinders *and Containers Ltd. v. Competition Commission of India and Anr.* [2020], (SC) (2020) 16 SCC 615, paras 89-94, 105.

The Supreme Court noted that CCI and the erstwhile COMPAT erred in not considering the 'plus factors' by analysing the ground realities of the market. The way the tenders are floated indicated that IOCL was deciding the rate of the award and was in complete control over the tender process. The IOCL, through negotiation, set the final price which was less than the price quoted by the L-1 bidders. Furthermore, L-2 and L-3 bidders were also awarded the tender at the rate of L-1. The only difference was that an L-1 bidder received the order for larger quantities than L-2 and L-3. Similarly, an L-2 bidder received larger orders than an L-3. IOCL ensured that all the manufacturers got some orders.

Furthermore, in *the LPG-I* case, the CCI and the erstwhile COMPAT failed to consider the reasonable justification for the 'plus factors' by ignoring the fact that a few days before IOCL floated its tender, Bharat Petroleum Corporation Limited (BPCL) floated a tender for LPG cylinders. The BPCL tender acted as a guiding factor for the manufacturers while quoting their bids for the IOCL tender. The market conditions were not taken into account considering the fact that there were a small number of suppliers present in the market. The manufacturers quoted an identical price so that they could get some orders, or else they would be driven out of the market; hence, the argument that the manufacturers quoted an identical price despite varying costs loses its significance. Also, only nineteen manufacturers attended the meeting of the association. Also, there are twelve new entrants in the market, which is a significant number. Moreover, the market condition is described as an oligopsony where only a few buyers are present in the market, and they are controlling the market. In an oligopsony market, the Supreme Court noted that parallel pricing could not be concluded as a concerted practice, and further corroborative evidence is required to substantiate the presence of a cartel.

Setting aside the judgments of the CCI and erstwhile COMPAT, the Supreme Court held that IOCL was controlling the tender process. The Supreme Court noted that the CCI failed to carry out further analysis of the factors under section 19(3) of the Competition Act to hold that there was an adverse effect on the market. Finally, the CCI should have summoned IOCL before concluding that there was a violation of section 3(3)(d) of the Competition Act. Thus, by way of this case, the Supreme Court, while acknowledging the ill effects of cartelization, has created a defence for participants to the agreement to show that their arrangement does not cause AAEC in the market.

As mentioned in Chapter 1 of this book, the penalties on the cartel participants are huge under the Competition Act. Owing to such onerous fines, it will be very rare that one will find direct evidence, like minutes of meetings, etc., to conclude the existence of a cartel. It has to be seen whether a cartel exists or not from the totality of the circumstances. In the *Express Industry Council of India v. Jet Airways, Indigo, SpiceJet*[23] ('*Airline surcharge cartel* case'), the allegation was that certain domestic airlines introduced a Fuel Surcharge (FSC) for transporting cargo. This surcharge was fixed at a uniform rate of INR 5/kg. It was the case of the informant that, although the

23. *Express Industry Council of India v. Jet Airways, Indigo, SpiceJet,* Case No. 30 of 2013, paras 88, 93, 94, 106, 112, 113, 114.

levy of FSC was ostensibly introduced as being an extra charge linked to fuel prices, investigation showed that when such prices were reduced (as in the past), there had been no corresponding decrease in FSC. It was further stated that FSC has actually been increased by the airlines by acting in concert, and that too, by almost the same rate and from almost the same date. Likewise, FSC was uniformly increased in the past, even without a corresponding increase in fuel prices. Further, it was also averred that when fuel prices declined substantially, the airlines had, in concert, uniformly increased FSC. The CCI held that the market participants acted in a concerted manner in fixing the FSC rate. Regarding the definition of 'agreement', the CCI observed that the definition is inclusive and not exhaustive. As there is rarely any direct evidence, the CCI considers the situations as 'agreement' where the market participants are instructed based on nods or winks. Generally, the market participants engage in anti-competitive conduct in a clandestine manner, with secret meetings and hardly any explicit written documents exist. So, by taking together all the coincidences and indicia, the CCI had to reconstruct certain details by using the deduction method. In this case, the CCI unfolded the entire conspiracy by looking at the airlines' conduct, such as the issuance of circulars to increase FSC at a fixed price by different airlines. Further, CCI also noted that airlines had common agents through whom they were exchanging information. After a holistic appreciation of the evidence, the CCI could see that the airlines violated section 3(3)(a) of the Competition Act by entering into an anti-competitive agreement to fix the FSC.

Further, the statutory scheme provided under the Competition Act provides that the CCI has been conferred power to impose only civil fines, and it does not have criminal jurisdiction. Further, as described in the preceding chapter, under section 36 of the Competition Act, the CCI is vested with some powers of a Civil Court in the conduct of its enquiries. Therefore, based on the statutory scheme, the offences provided to in the Competition Act, including cartelization, not being criminal offences, the test of proof will be only 'balance' of probability' and 'liaison of intention' which can be established with the support of indirect or circumstantial evidence. This is in contradiction to a criminal offence where the offence has to be proved beyond reasonable doubt. In this regard, while upholding an order passed under section 27 of the Competition Act against a bid rigging cartel, the erstwhile COMPAT noted, in the case of *MDD Medical Systems India Pvt. Ltd. v. Foundation for Common Cause and Others*[24] and held that even though section 27 of the Competition Act speaks about penalty, the process against anti-competitive conduct under competition law is not similar to criminal offence where proof beyond reasonable doubt is required. Hence, in competition law jurisprudence, the test of probability would be a good test.

Based on the above, it can be seen that the CCI and DG can rely on both direct and circumstantial evidence. The key test in a cartel investigation, as had been laid down by the CCI, is analysis of the evidence which establishes that a particular set of acts and conduct of the market participants cannot be explained 'but for' some sort of

24. *MDD Medical Systems India Pvt. Ltd. v. Foundation for Common Cause and Others* [2013], (COMPAT) Appeal No. 93 Of 2012, para. 18.

anti-competitive agreement and action in concert among them. Consequently, the existence of an anti-competitive agreement can be inferred from the intention or conduct of the parties and may be established by circumstantial evidence alone in the absence of any alternate explanation.

In analysing whether there was a concerted action among the market participants, the CCI undertakes a detailed econometric analysis. In the backdrop of the legal position as delineated above, it becomes quite clear that in order to find contravention of section 3 of the Competition Act, it is not the requirement of law to demand direct evidence of agreement in all cases. In the absence of direct evidence, existence of circumstantial evidence that tends to exclude the possibility of independent action would be sufficient to give rise to an inference of existence of an agreement.

§2.05 DIRECT EVIDENCE

In a cartel case, it is very difficult to find direct evidence wherein there is a clearly formulated written agreement wherein the competitors have decided to engage in cartel behaviour. The Supreme Court in the *LPG-I* case[25] reproduced excerpts of the 'Organisation for Economic Co-operation and Development (OECD) Policy Roundtables Prosecuting Cartels without Direct Evidence 2006' to discuss the nature of evidence. The Supreme Court noted that direct evidence, such as documents or emails or any kind of communication describing the working of cartel, can rarely be found. However, in some of the cases, direct evidence is unearthed wherein members of a bid rigging cartel share their rate of the bid via email or a minute of the meeting which shows that the trade association in its meeting mandated the members to limit their production or dispatch to create an artificial demand.

As mentioned above, most of the cartel activities are hatched in secrecy; hence, direct evidence is very difficult to find. Although direct evidence is very hard to find, there have been instances of direct evidence which have been unearthed by the DG and CCI. For example, in cases relating to the entertainment industry, there have been instances wherein there have been minutes of the meeting of the trade association to show that the members decided to collectively boycott a non-member. In *M/s International Subscription Agency v. Federation of Publishers' and Booksellers' Associations in India (FPBAI)*,[26] the discount policy of the FPBAI explicitly stated that 'any of our associated companies shall not offer any discount on the publishers' price fixed for customers in India'. Further, FPBAI issued notice to its members for non-compliance with its discount policy. Based on this discount policy and the coercive action for non-compliance, the CCI held FPBAI for violating section 3(3)(a) and (b) of the Competition Act.

Even in *In Re: Cartelization by public sector insurance companies in rigging the bids submitted in response to the tenders floated by the Government of Kerala for*

25. *LPG-I* case, para. 82.
26. *M/s International Subscription Agency v. Federation of Publishers' and Booksellers' Associations in India (FPBAI)*, Case No. 33 of 2019, paras 18, 22.

selecting insurance service provider for Rashtriya Swasthya Bima Yojna. v. National Insurance Co. Ltd. and Others,[27] ('*Insurance cartel* case'), the case was initiated based on anonymous information which complained that four public sector insurance companies, namely National Insurance Co. Ltd., New India Assurance Co. Ltd., Oriental Insurance Co. Ltd. and United India Insurance Co. Ltd., had rigged the tender floated by the Government of Kerala for selecting an insurance service provider for implementation of the Rashtriya Swasthya Bima Yojna (RSBY) for the year 2010-2011. The information alleged that the insurance companies had formed a cartel and quoted higher premium rates in response to the tender. Further, by way of the 'Inter Company Coordination Committee' (ICCC) meeting attended by the officials of insurance companies, they had decided on an anti-competitive business sharing model to share the business.

In the *Insurance cartel* case,[28] the CCI relied on the investigation by the DG to note that the insurance companies had held a meeting under the aegis of the trade association with the sole agenda to discuss sharing of business and submission of quotation of a bid. The minutes of the meetings were considered direct evidence because they revealed that the decision to collude in terms of sharing of business and submission of quotation was taken by the insurance companies. Having said that, since the fines on cartels are huge, it will be very difficult in future cases once the companies are aware of the principles of competition law to find direct evidence of cartels.

The table below shows the decisional trends of the CCI in terms of analysis of direct evidence across multiple decisional cases.

S. No.	*Case Name (Citation)*	*Evidence (Paragraph No.)*	*Reasoning (Paragraph No.)*
1.	*In Re: Alleged Cartelisation in Supply of the LPG Cylinders Procured through Tenders by Hindustan Petroleum Corporation Ltd. (HPCL).* Suo Motu Case No. 1 of 2014	Direct evidence, such as emails were exchanged between bidders regarding price, business strategies, etc. (Paragraph 77)	The CCI held that the bidders discussed and shared sensitive and confidential information regarding the tender to manipulate the bidding process of tender no. 2. (Paragraphs 107, 111-113) In this case, the CCI found both direct and indirect evidence.

27. *In Re: Cartelization by public sector insurance companies in rigging the bids submitted in response to the tenders floated by the Government of Kerala for selecting insurance service provider for Rashtriya Swasthya Bima Yojna. v. National Insurance Co. Ltd. and Others,* Suo Motu Case No. 02 of 2014, para. 32.
28. *Ibid.*, paras 32, 33, 38, 39, 60.

S. No.	*Case Name (Citation)*	*Evidence (Paragraph No.)*	*Reasoning (Paragraph No.)*
2.	*Mr. Sajjan Khaitan v. Eastern India Motion Picture Association & Others*. Case No. 16 of 2011.	Coordination Committee passed a resolution and issued letters to the TV channels to stop the telecast of the dubbed version of the Mahabharata serial or face non-cooperation. (Paragraphs 5.4, 5.5, 7.1.4, 7.1.5) On 07 April 2011, Coordination Committee further threatened by demonstrating a strike against the TV Channels. (Paragraph 7.1.6)	The CCI held that the Coordination Committee imposed restrictions on the two TV Channels to prevent the telecast of a dubbed version of the serial 'Mahabharata'. (Paragraph 7.1.12)
3.	*Cement Cartel Case*. Case No. 29 of 2010.	Collection and exchange of retail prices of cement from different companies. (Paragraphs 212, 213)	The Rules and Regulations of the Cement Manufacturers Association show that it was used as a platform to share information among the cement manufacturers. (Paragraph 214) In this case, the CCI found both direct and indirect evidence.
4.	*In Re: Alleged anti-competitive conduct in the Beer Market in India*. Suo Motu Case No. 06 of 2017.	The beer manufacturers exchanged commercial information regarding MRP and Basic Prices through email and WhatsApp (Paragraphs 11(1)(iv) and (v), 18, 19, 20)	The information regarding Beer production, revenue details, targets, stock sold and stock held was exchanged to monitor each other's actual stock movement, and they can keep track of each other's market share. (Paragraphs 74, 78)

S. No.	*Case Name (Citation)*	*Evidence (Paragraph No.)*	*Reasoning (Paragraph No.)*
		The beer manufacturers agreed to share their periodical sales and sales data. (Paragraphs 56, 72, 73) The beer manufacturers decided to stop producing and restricted the supply of Beer. (Paragraphs 11(1)(vi), 67) The beer manufacturers exchanged emails regarding the purchase of second-hand bottles. (Paragraphs 11(1)(viii), 151) The beer manufacturers were able to hold discussions under the umbrella of the trade association. (Paragraphs 11(1)(ix), 163, 164)	Beer manufacturer decided to lower their production of beer to put pressure on the Excise Authorities to lower the Excise duty on Beer. Limiting supplies impacted the beer market because the price of beer increased. (Paragraphs 69, 70, 71) CCI found that the beer manufacturers shared information to decide the rate at which they would buy second-hand bottles. This resulted in limiting the supply of second-hand bottles. (Paragraphs 152, 153, 157) The CCI found that office bearers of beer manufacturers were holding discussions relating to anti-competitive practice under the aegis of the trade association. The trade association also arranged conference calls and facilitated discussions. (Paragraphs 164, 170). In this case, the CCI found both direct and indirect evidence.

S. No.	*Case Name (Citation)*	*Evidence (Paragraph No.)*	*Reasoning (Paragraph No.)*
5.	*Mr. Rakesh Khare v. Krishna Engineering Works and Others*. Reference Case No. 02 of 2020.	Physical meeting between cartel members in Hyderabad and Bombay to fix the quotes of the tenders. (Paragraph 80(i))	The cartel members exchanged commercial data either through physical meetings or virtual communication.
		Before submitting quotes, the cartel members were regularly communicating with each other via calls, messages, or mails. (Paragraph 100)	Exchange of commercial data, along with identical pricing or providing cover bids amounts to a violation of section 3(3)(d) of the Act. (Paragraph 95) In this case, the CCI found both direct and indirect evidence.
6.	*National Association of Container Freight Stations, Chennai Chapter v. Trailer Owners Association and Others*. Case No. 04 of 2018	DG noted that the trailer/truck trade associations restrict their members (i.e., operators of Inland Container Depots or Container Freight Stations) from plying more than twenty trailers. (Paragraph 4) The trade associations colluded to demand higher tariffs from the informant. (Paragraph 12) Hence, the price was fixed, and the output of the products was decided in various meetings of trade associations. (Paragraph 71)	The cartel members used the trade association as an instrument to fix price and restrict output. (Paragraphs 77, 78)

S. No.	*Case Name (Citation)*	*Evidence (Paragraph No.)*	*Reasoning (Paragraph No.)*
7.	*In Re: Cartelisation in the supply of Protective Tubes to Indian Railways*. Suo Motu Case No. 06 of 2020	The cartel members were continuously exchanging emails regarding the bidding process for the procurement of polyacetal protective tubes. (Paragraph 24)	The communication clearly shows the *modus operandi* of the cartel, which includes the bid allocation, revision of sharing pattern, induction of new members, calculation
			methods of the quotation, discussion on quotation, complaints regarding undercutting, and communication to withdraw offers. (Paragraph 25)
8.	*Chief Materials Manager, North Western Railway v. Moulded Fiberglass Products and Others*. Reference Case No. 03 of 2018	The CCI found that various e-mails and WhatsApp texts were exchanged between the cartel members. (Paragraph 37)	Cartel members were constantly exchanging information so that there would be a clear understanding of what their final bidding price and price breakdown would be (Basic Unit, Excise Rate, etc.). Similarly, geographical markets were also allocated for the cartel members. (Paragraphs 44-47)
9.	*In Re: Alleged anti-competitive conduct by various bidders in supply and installation of signages at specified locations of State Bank of India across India*. Suo Motu Case No. 02 of 2020.	Emails containing a summary of agreements, bidding sequence (categorization of the geographical market), and bidding amount were exchanged between the cartel members. (Paragraphs 29-33)	The bidding sequence and the bidding amount exactly matched. However, it is not necessary that the information exchanges need to be implemented to establish a violation

S. No.	*Case Name (Citation)*	*Evidence (Paragraph No.)*	*Reasoning (Paragraph No.)*
		The call records showed that the cartel members were engaged in telephonic conversations during the bidding process. (Paragraph 58)	under section 3(3) of the Competition Act. Mere presence of an agreement between competitors is enough to presume AAEC. (Paragraphs 34, 35)
10.	*In Re: Cartelisation by Shipping Lines in the matter of provision of Maritime Motor Vehicle Transport Services to the Original Equipment Manufacturers.* Suo Motu Case No. 10 of 2014	The cartel members regularly meet with each other to share commercially sensitive information with the objective of enforcement of the 'Respect Rule'. 'Respect Rule' is an understanding between the cartel members to maintain their established position within their main customer accounts and avoid competition. (Paragraphs 125, 173.7, 178.3, 207)	Instead of competing, the cartel members had a mutual understanding to avoid competition by fixing price, allocating marker and manipulating the bidding process. (Paragraph 207)
11.	*T.R. Chandran v. National Egg Co-ordination Committee (NECC).* Case Nos 09 and 36 of 2017.	Active communication (via WhatsApp texts, emails, meetings) between regional zones to fix and follow the price and production of eggs. (Paragraphs 154, 155, 192, 193)	Determination and implementation of price and production of eggs through coordination is a violation of section 3(3)(a) of the Act. (Paragraph 153)

S. No.	Case Name (Citation)	Evidence (Paragraph No.)	Reasoning (Paragraph No.)
12.	*In Re: Anti-competitive conduct in the paper manufacturing industry*. Suo Motu Case No. 05 of 2016.	From email exchanges and physical meetings, the cartel members were deciding to increase prices and monitor the implementation of their decisions. (Paragraphs 164, 197)	The CCI held that if rivals of a market are meeting to discuss the prices, then it is beyond any doubt that such conduct violates section 3(3)(a) of the Competition Act, as it is likely to cause AAEC. (Paragraph 204)
13.	*Mr. Rizwanul Haq Khan v. Mersen (India) Pvt. Ltd. and Another*. Reference Case No. 02 of 2016.	WhatsApp messages and emails were exchanged between cartel members to exchange the details regarding the various tenders for the Carbon Brushes. (Paragraphs 49, 50, 52)	Exchange of commercially sensitive information established that there was a 'meeting of minds' to manipulate the bidding process by pre-determining the quotation for tenders. (Paragraphs 51, 53)
14.	*Food Corporation of India v. Shivalik Agro Poly Products Ltd. and Others*. Case No. 07 of 2018	WhatsApp messages showed that the cartel members were coordinating. (Paragraphs 47, 48)	As per the evidence, the CCI concluded that there was a violation of section 3(3)(d) of the Competition Act. (Paragraph 63)
15.	*Eastern Railway, Kolkata v. M/s Chandra Brothers and Others*. Reference Case No. 02 of 2018.	The cartel members were frequently discussing commercially sensitive information through emails, telephone calls, and SMS. (Paragraphs 118, 119)	The cartel members were deciding the price bids through constant communication. (Paragraph 119)
16.	*XYZ v. Tamil Film Producers Council and Others*. Case No. 07 of 2018.	Circulars, letters, press releases and e-mails were issued by the trade	The CCI noted that the film associations called for a boycott so that they could have a better

S. No.	*Case Name (Citation)*	*Evidence (Paragraph No.)*	*Reasoning (Paragraph No.)*
		associations calling for a boycott against certain producers and theatre owners (Paragraphs 41-43)	bargaining position while negotiating the Virtual Print Fee charged by the Digital Cinema Service Providers/Digital Service Providers. (Paragraphs 43-45)
	M/s International Subscription Agency v. Federation of Publishers' and Booksellers' Associations in India. Case No. 33 of 2019.	The trade association directed its members not to provide any discount and issued advisories to its members. The trade association prohibited the members from participating in certain procurement advertisements. (Paragraph 24)	The conduct of the trade association limited the product and eliminated the quantum of discount. (Paragraphs 26, 39)
17.	*Chief Materials Manager, South Eastern Railway v. Hindustan Composites Limited.* Reference Case No. 03 of 2016.	Tender-related information was mailed to the cartel members. (Paragraph 34)	The CCI held that such mails are direct evidence to establish an arrangement to rig the bidding process. (Paragraph 35)
18.	*In Re: Cartelisation in Industrial and Automotive Bearings.* Case No. 05 of 2017.	Emails were exchanged between cartel members, and those emails contained price-sensitive information relating to the tender. Further, the cartel members made several telephonic calls during the tender processing period. (Paragraph 15)	A cartel was formed because price revision, along with minimum percentage of a price increase to be quoted, were discussed. (Paragraph 18)

S. No.	Case Name (Citation)	Evidence (Paragraph No.)	Reasoning (Paragraph No.)
19.	*M/s Suman Distributors, Murshidabad v. Bengal Chemists and Druggists Association and Others*. Case No. 36 of 2015	From letters and telephonic conversations, it was clear that Alkem was forcing stockists to obtain Stock Availability Information (SAI) from the Bengal Chemists and Druggists Association (BCDA) before Alkem commenced making supplies of drugs to them. (Paragraphs 20.2, 20.3, 21.9)	Alkem was in agreement with BCDA by issuing OLS to prospective stockists and was indulging in the practice of demanding SAI/Non-Objection Certificate/Approval Letter/Circulation Letter from BCDA before commencing supplies. This constitutes an anticompetitive agreement between Alkem and BCDA. (Paragraph 21.5)

§2.06 INDIRECT EVIDENCE: ROLE OF CIRCUMSTANTIAL EVIDENCE

The DG and CCI also look at the chain of circumstantial evidence to analyse whether the market participants entered into an anti-competitive agreement or not.

As mentioned above, the key area of analysing circumstantial evidence is to find out whether the particular set of acts and conduct of the market participants cannot be explained 'but for' some sort of anti-competitive agreement and action in concert among them.[29] The decisional practice of the CCI shows that most of the cartel investigations that have happened till now are in oligopolistic industries. As has been explained above, in an oligopolistic market, parallel behaviour is extremely common due to the interdependence of firms' conduct. The key chain of evidence must be seen whether such parallel behaviour is an action of conscious parallelism or an agreement to collude. The key thing that needs to be kept in mind is that the CCI looks at the totality of the evidence to come to a conclusion as to whether there is a case of cartelization. In this regard, it is to be noted that in most of the cartel cases, the market participants take a plea that their conduct is a case of parallel behaviour and not cartel behaviour. However, the CCI has noted that parallel behaviour, although common in an oligopolistic industry, may not carry on for a lengthy period of time unless there is a cartel arrangement between the market players. It is apposite to note the observations of the erstwhile COMPAT, where it was observed that:

> We do not think that this is a case of mere price parallelism. We have already made observation that price parallelism on one or two occasions though might raise

29. *Airline Surcharge Cartel* case, para. 39.

> strong suspicion, it may not be enough for drawing the inference of cartelization. We reiterate that observation. However, in this case it was not a sweet coincidence and in fact it is shown that this was not only a common pattern or practice, but this continued in case of tenders floated by other corporations. This consistent practice and common pattern when continues for a long time, there could be no other inference excepting that of cartelization.

There are two recognized forms of circumstantial evidence which are taken into account by the DG and the CCI in a cartel investigation: (a) communication evidence and (b) economic evidence. Communication evidence indicates that cartel operators met or otherwise communicated but does not describe the substance of their communications. It includes, for example, meetings at a trade association, records of telephone conversations among suspected cartel participants, their travel to a common destination, common hotel receipts, common entry in registers, and notes or records of meetings in which they participated. Economic evidence, however, can be categorized as either conduct or structural evidence. The former includes, most importantly, evidence of parallel conduct by suspected cartel members, e.g., simultaneous and identical price increases or suspicious bidding patterns in public tenders, lower capacity utilization, and high correlation on prices. The CCI has observed that among the set of circumstantial evidence, evidence of communication among the participants to an anti-competitive agreement may give an important clue for establishing any contravention. Communication evidence might prove that contravening parties met and communicated with each other to determine their future or present behaviour. Therefore, in terms of the weight of evidence, communication evidence is given more importance than economic evidence. The CCI in the *Cement cartel* case[30] considered various circumstantial evidence as plus factors to establish violation under section 3(3)(a) and (b) of the Competition Act. The CCI observed the plus factors, such as the exchange of price and production using the Cement Manufacturers Association (CMA) as a platform, lowering the capacity utilization, and lowering the supply of cement which resulted in price increases in the cement industry.

Further, it is to be noted that it is not necessary that cartel participants must raise prices at the same time, to be caught under the ambit of section 3(3) of the Competition Act. In fact, the CCI, in the *Airline surcharge cartel* case,[31] has noted that it is necessary to analyse the behaviour of the cartel participants, in entirety, to see whether they have engaged in a cartel. There may be situations wherein the market participants intentionally create artificial time gaps among themselves to increase the price, to show that it is a case of intelligent market adoption to the other competitors' action, but not a cartel. In this regard, it is apposite to note the observations of the CCI in the *Airline surcharge cartel* case:[32]

> The so-called time gap is just a matter of few days. It would be travesty of competition norms if such lag theory is countenanced by the Competition Agency. It is neither the requirement of law nor any other jurisprudence that cartels must

30. *Cement cartel* case, para. 232.
31. *Airline surcharge cartel* case, para. 79. (Order dated 7 Mar. 2018).
32. *Airline surcharge cartel* case, para. 114. (Order dated 17 Nov. 2015).

> originate symmetrically, progress symmetrically and culminate in a similar fashion. More often than not, the colluding parties would like to break the patterns through artificial gaps and arrangements so as to create a façade of competitive behaviour. In such a projected 'competitive landscape', it is the bounden duty of the Authority to pierce this artificial veil and to examine the real behaviour of the colluding parties. The present case perfectly fits such stratagem where artificial lags and gaps were sought to be passed off and projected to envision a competitive scenario when none existed. In fact, such justifications and explanations only complete the chain of the arrangement and understanding reached amongst the parties.

Now, we will discuss the manner in which the DG and CCI have looked at both communication and economic evidence in deciding cartel matters.

[A] Communication Evidence

Communication evidence is a type of indirect evidence consisting of proof that the cartel members attended a physical meeting or communicated virtually via telephone, WhatsApp, email, etc. As opposed to direct evidence, the substance of the communication may not be available in communication evidence.[33]

When an entity exchanges strategic information or price-related information with its competitors, who are accepting the information constitutes evidence, it will be presumed that the entity had accepted the information and implemented the information in line with the anti-competitive conduct. Information could be exchanged through mail, phone calls or meetings. Mere receiving calls or mails or attending meetings where some strategic information was passed would be enough to use it as evidence to establish an anti-competitive agreement. To avoid violation of section 3 of the Competition Act, the entity who received the information should object to the exchange of information.[34] The DG and the CCI, in any cartel investigation, investigate whether the market participants regularly meet, either under the aegis of a trade association or otherwise. Frequent meetings between competitors followed by similar market conduct have always been seen as a plus factor in a cartel investigation.

The following are some instances of communication evidence which has been relied upon by the CCI while deciding cartel cases.

[1] Frequent Meetings among Competitors

In the *LPG-I* case,[35] the CCI took note of the OECD's Document on detecting bid rigging in public procurement. The CCI noted that:

> The fact of agreement can be either communicated by words or conduct. Bidders need to know and communicate with each other to reach an agreement. Once

33. *LPG-I* case, para. 82. (SC).
34. *Ibid.*, para. 84. (SC).
35. *LPG-I* case, para. 14.17. (CCI).

> bidders know each other well enough to discuss bid rigging, they need a convenient location where they can talk. Of course, communications can occur by telephone, email, fax or letter, and they often do; however, many bid riggers believe that they are less likely to leave evidence of their communications if they have face-to-face meetings. These meetings occur most often at, or in association with trade association meetings, or other professional or social events. They are also likely to occur prior to the opening of the tender process.

In the *Cement cartel* case, the CCI noted that the cement companies participated in the meetings of the CMA. Further, under the aegis of CMA, the companies interacted on a regular basis on sensitive information like pricing, production details, dispatch details, etc. It was observed by the CCI that CMA, based on a governmental directive, collected retail prices and wholesale prices of the cement from different centres and transmitted them onwards to the government. It was observed by the CCI that the prices of cement for all the cement companies went up after two meetings of the CMA. One of the defences that was raised by the cement companies was that the prices of cement went up after two meetings of the Cement Manufactures Association and not all the meetings of the said trade association. However, the CCI noted that it is not required that prices of goods need to go up after each meeting, especially when the price of cement is already artificially inflated. This approach of the CCI to penalize cement companies when the prices went up after two meetings, and not all meetings show the assertive approach of the CCI. In this background, it is very important for companies to have proper document management systems and pricing policies to show, by way of contemporaneous documents, changes in prices of companies and reasons thereof so that during an investigation, such documents can be shown to justify the rationale for price change.

Even in the *Insurance cartel* case,[36] the CCI observed that the insurance companies held meetings under the aegis of the trade association to discuss the sharing of business and quotation for each bid. Such kind of communication evidence is taken by the CCI as evidence of cartel behaviour. Having said that, the CCI has also noted that just because the market participants have met in a trade association does not *ipso facto* mean that they indulged in an anti-competitive behaviour. For illustration, in the *Tyre* case, the CCI noted that the tyre industry had a trade association. However, on investigation, it was revealed that the trade association was used as a forum for lobbying for the welfare of the trade industry and making representations to governmental organizations, which cannot be viewed as anti-competitive. What the DG and CCI look at is whether the communication evidence so collected can be seen as a *plus factor*, i.e., whether such communication aims to formulate a cartel strategy. The CCI in *People's All India Anti-Corruption and Crime Prevention Society v. Usha International Ltd. and Others*,[37] from all the call data records obtained by the DG, noted that the

---

36. *Insurance cartel* case, paras 37, 38.
37. *People's All India Anti-Corruption and Crime Prevention Society v. Usha International Ltd. and Others*, Case No. 90 of 2016, paras 57-61, 63. Appeal against the CCO order was dismissed by NCLAT. *See, People's All India Anti-Corruption and Crime Prevention Society v. Usha Internationals* [2023], (NCLAT) Competition Appeal (AT) No. 46 of 2022.

competitors were frequently interacting with each other was considered a plus factor while proving a bid rigging cartel.

In fact, the erstwhile COMPAT has noted that the existence of a trade association gives an opportunity to the competitors to interact with each other and discuss trade problems. Further, it is not required to prove that any party actually discussed the prices by actively taking part in the meeting. If there is direct evidence to that effect, that is certainly a pointer towards the fact that such a party had a tacit agreement with its competitors. However, the existence of an association and further holding of the meetings just one or two days prior to the submitting bids, followed by quoting similar bid prices, gives a strong indication of collusive conduct.

[2] Publication of Price Bulletin

In two landmark cases decided by the CCI (such as the *Cement cartel* case), the CCI has noted that the practice of publishing price bulletins by a trade association is also a plus factor when deciding on a case for cartelization. In the *Cement cartel* case,[38] the CCI noted that the CMA collected wholesale and retail prices of cement. The retail prices collected from different centres are transmitted to the Department of Industrial Policy and Promotion (DIPP), while the wholesale prices are transmitted to the office of the Economic Advisor. The retail and wholesale prices are collected from all over the country. Although the mandate to collect the cement prices was given to the CMA, it was also observed that the CMA was nominating some representatives from each company to collect the prices for each region for all the companies operating in that region. Based on the same, it was noted by the CCI that the prices of all competing cement companies are being collected. In such a situation, when the cement companies nominated by CMA are collecting prices of other competing cement companies over telephones and e-mails, coordination on prices is easily facilitated. Based on the above, it was concluded by the CCI that when competitors are interacting using the platform of CMA, and they are in touch with each other over the phone and e-mails as regards prices - both retail and wholesale, it cannot be denied that there is always an opportunity to discuss the determination and fixation of prices for future, which is prohibited under the provisions of the Competition Act. The fact that it is being done under the instruction of DIPP (a wing of the Government of India) does not absolve CMA or the cement companies engaged in this exercise from running afoul of the provisions of the Competition Act. Further, the investigation showed that CMA had several publications, such as *Executive Summary-Cement Industry* and *Cement Statistics-Interregional Movement of Cement* which give details of the production and dispatch of each company and are circulated only among the members. Therefore, the cement companies not only get information on the prices of other cement companies but also receive details about the production and dispatch details of the other companies. The CCI noted that sharing such sensitive information makes coordination easier among cement companies and help them plan their future conduct. In light of the

38. *Cement cartel* case, paras 7(xlvii), 202, 247, 258.

above communication evidence, the CCI identified that there was information sharing among the competitors on prices, quantity and dispatch details, which in light of the economic evidence (discussed below) shows an agreement among the cement companies to cartelize.

Similarly, in *T.R. Chandran v. National Egg Co-ordination Committee (NECC)*,[39] the trade association (i.e., NECC) displayed daily egg prices, zone-wise, on its website and monitored the monthly/annual prices of eggs at various egg production and consumption centres. The CCI held that by mandating the farmers to follow the price fixed and by ensuring adherence to such fixed prices, the NECC has violated section 3(3)(a) of the Competition Act.

[3] Commonality of Key Business Personnel

In a bid rigging case, the investigation done by the DG and CCI had revealed that there was cross-ownership and common directors among the various bidders in the market. It was revealed that the companies involved in the bidding process are closely related, having common directors or different members of the same family at the helm of affairs. Having such a relationship indicated that out of the thirteen companies under investigation, the modus operandi of at least ten of these firms was governed by the principles of mutual understanding and benefit. This was seen as a plus factor since there is a chance of sharing commercially sensitive information among various companies, which will help in agreeing on future conduct.

Similarly, in the in *Re: Alleged cartelisation in supply of LPG Cylinders procured through tenders by Hindustan Petroleum Corporation Ltd. (HPCL)*, ('*LPG-II* case'),[40] and the *Airline surcharge cartel* case,[41] it was noted by the CCI that there were common agents that were appointed by market participants, which were seen to share commercial sensitive and future information of one company with another. Based on the same, it was noted that there was exchange of information between companies, which eventually led to collusion. Therefore, it is key that while appointing agents or other trading partners, a very strong non-disclosure agreement be signed with such entities that is scrupulously followed to ensure that there is no transmission of commercially sensitive information of one company to its competitors. Having said that, in the *Airline surcharge cartel* case, the airline companies said that there was the presence of common agents among airlines who could share commercially sensitive information among themselves. Although the agents are not allowed by the airline to disclose commercial information to other airlines, it cannot be ruled out that agents do share commercially sensitive information among airlines. Thus, while appointing agents,

39. *T.R. Chandran v. National Egg Co-ordination Committee (NECC)*, Case Nos 09 and 36 of 2017, paras 114, 153, 208, 209.
40. *Re: Alleged cartelisation in supply of LPG Cylinders procured through tenders by Hindustan Petroleum Corporation Ltd. (HPCL)*, Suo Motu Case No. 1 of 2014, paras 74, 109. The NCLAT upheld the order passes by the CCI by holding that the identical behaviours of the parties were a result of collusion. *See, Sahuwala Cylinders Pvt. Ltd. & Others v. Competition Commission of India and Another*[2022], (NCLAT) Competition Appeal (AT) No. 38 of 2019.
41. *Airline surcharge cartel* case, para. 106.

distributors or other trading partners, who are also the trading partners of their competitors, the companies must be extra cautious. Similarly, *In Re: Alleged bid-rigging in E-Tenders invited by the Department of Agriculture, Government of Uttar Pradesh for soil sample testing,*[42] some of the cartel members were family friends, and they submitted cover bids under the influence of friendship. The CCI noted this evidence as a plus factor to conclude the presence of a bid rigging cartel. Further, *In Re: Cartelization in Tender Nos 21 and 28 of 2013 of Pune Municipal Corporation for Solid Waste Processing,*[43] the CCI held that the bid rigging cartel was controlled by one person or family because the director of 2nd opposite party is a close friend of 1st opposite party. Further, the sole proprietor of 3rd opposite party and also the son of 4th opposite party's director.

[4] Other Evidence

The investigation pattern of the DG shows that they rely on other kinds of evidence to show that the market participants met before submitting a bid, like common visitor entries, common bank accounts or places used to submit bids, common agents, or hotel bills to show that the officers of companies met for a meal one day before the submission of a bid.

There are instances where bidders use common IP address to submit bids in order to manipulate the bidding process. CCI also considers other login details, including the user ID, username, login date and time, proximity of logout date and time and caller ID, to establish that the bids of all cartel members were filed by a common person.[44]

The table below shows the decisional trends of the CCI in terms of analysis of other types of communication evidence across multiple decisional cases.

S. No.	*Case Name (Citation)*	*Evidence (Paragraph No.)*	*Reasoning (Paragraph No.)*
1.	*In Re: Cartelisation in the supply of Protective Tubes to Indian Railways.* Suo Moto 06/2020	The cartel members used common IP address to submit their bids in twelve bidding processes. (Paragraph 20)	The CCI acknowledged the presence of a cartel because the cartel members filed their bids from common IP address. (Paragraph 29)

42. *In Re: Alleged bid-rigging in E-Tenders invited by the Department of Agriculture, Government of Uttar Pradesh for soil sample testing,* Suo Motu Case No. 01 of 2020, paras 30, 88.
43. *In Re: Cartelization in Tender Nos 21 and 28 of 2013 of Pune Municipal Corporation for Solid Waste Processing,* Suo Motu Case No. 03 of 2016, paras 5, 56-59.
44. *In Re: Chief Materials Manager, North Western Railway v. Molded Fiberglass Products and Others.* Case No. 03/2018, paras 34, 35.

S. No.	*Case Name (Citation)*	*Evidence (Paragraph No.)*	*Reasoning (Paragraph No.)*
2.	*In Re: Chief Materials Manager, North Western Railway v. Moulded Fibreglass Products and Others*. Case No. 03/2018	The cartel members used common IP address to submit bids in thirty-four tenders. (Paragraph 33) From other login details to conclude that all bids were submitted from a common IP address. (Paragraph 34)	The holistic evaluation of evidence showed that the cartel members colluded to fix prices, allocate markets, and rig the bidding process. (Paragraphs 58, 59)
3.	*GAIL (India) Limited v. PMP Infratech Private Ltd. and Another*. Case No. 41 of 2019.	The bids were submitted from a common IP address. Cartel members used the same office premises and systems to submit their bids for which they were competing. (Paragraph 43)	The CCI held that the cartel members were constantly communicating with each other to coordinate their actions, which shows the existence of anti-competitive activity. (Paragraph 39)
4.	*People's All India Anti-Corruption and Crime Prevention Society v. Usha International Ltd. and Others*. Case No. 90 of 2016.	The office bearer of one cartel member (designated bidder to win the tender) paid the Tender Charge on behalf of other cartel members who were providing only submitting cover bids. After the designated bidder won the tender, the other cartel members returned the refunded Tender Charge. (Paragraphs 47, 48)	All the evidence, i.e., usage of common IP address, call records, and close relationships between cartel members, has to be seen holistically to determine the existence of an agreement. (Paragraph 56)

S. No.	*Case Name (Citation)*	*Evidence (Paragraph No.)*	*Reasoning (Paragraph No.)*
		All the cartel members used a single IP address to submit their bids. (Paragraph 53)	

[B] Economic Evidence

Economic evidence is also analysed by the CCI on the touchstone of the test explained above. Economic evidence is the conduct of the market participants which is important to identify the presence of an anti-competitive. To analyse economic evidence in a cartel case, the DG and the CCI undertake elaborate analysis of data relating to demand trends of the product, production, production capacity, capacity utilization, cost analysis, price analysis, cost of sales/sales realization/margin; cost of production and final price movement for each market participant to see whether there is any agreement among the companies. Economic evidence includes the parallel behaviour of the market participants, the industrial performance of the market participants (huge profit margin, stable market shares, repetitive violators of competition law), and a market structure providing a suitable environment to form a cartel (characteristics of the market structure: high concentration, high entry barriers, high degree of vertical integration, homogenous product), etc.[45]

The investigation pattern suggests that the DG asks for data on price, costs, demand, capacity, etc., for a minimum of preceding three years. Such an exercise is done for each of the market participants which are being investigated to see whether there is a pattern undertaken by such market participants to indicate the existence of an agreement. For example, in the *Cement cartel* case,[46] the DG analysed the capacity utilization figures of 2010-2011 in comparison to the previous year to conclude that the cement companies had intentionally engaged in limiting the production of cement in order to raise the price of cement. This conclusion was reached because the CCI noted that the demand for cement is inelastic, and the demand for cement would more or less remain the same for a particular period of time every year. In light of the demand scenario, it was seen that the cement companies reduced their capacity utilization from 82% in 2009-2010 to 73% in 2010-2011 for the month of November, when there was a high demand for cement. Similar exercise was also done by the DG in the *Excel Crop* case,[47] where it was observed that the price of APT had increased exponentially in comparison to previous years, and it was also noted that the profit margin of the parties was also increased.

45. *LPG-I* case, (2018) 16 SCC 615, para. 82. (SC).
46. *Cement cartel case*, paras 239, 269, 276.
47. *Excel Crop case*, paras 3.17, 3.19. (CCI).

As mentioned above, parallel behaviour is extremely common in an oligopolistic market where each market participant considers the likely reactions of other firms while making independent decisions, particularly regarding prices and output. What must be analysed, from economic evidence, is whether the said action is a result of independent action or as a result of agreement. It is to be noted that economic evidence must be seen in the totality of the industry circumstances to see whether a case of cartel can be made out. There is no one-size-fits-all approach which can be taken in a cartel investigation. For example, in the Cement cartel case, the DG and the CCI found that cement companies indulged in limiting production by reducing their capacity utilization. Conversely, in the *Tyre* case,[48] it was found that while some of the tyre companies reduced their capacity utilization, it was not seen as evidence of cartelization since the overall production capacity had increased.

While economic evidence is seen and analysed by the company, it must be ensured that proper data on pricing and other sensitive information are properly maintained by the company. It was seen in the *Airline surcharge cartel* case[49] that all the airlines were giving the reason that the primary reason for charging a fuel surcharge was the rise in the aviation turbine fuel (ATF) price. However, upon investigation, it was found that none of the airlines could provide any contemporaneous documents to show how the rise in ATF prices had led to fixing and subsequent rises in fuel surcharge rates. In fact, on conducting a correlation analysis, it was found that at times, FSC rates were increased when ATF prices were falling. Due to lack of maintaining any pricing data by airlines, the CCI raised an adverse inference against them in a cartel investigation. This raised an important aspect of document retention policies wherein CCI hinted that companies should maintain proper contemporaneous documents to show that pricing decisions were taken unilaterally. The CCI took an adverse inference of not maintaining pricing data by airlines.

It must be noted that economic evidence is seen as an addition to communication evidence in a cartel investigation. Absence of economic evidence cannot be used as a defence to show that there is no cartelization. There has hardly been any cartel decision where the CCI has found an infringement of section 3(3) of the Competition Act only on the basis of economic evidence. Some of the key economic tests identified by the decisional practice of the CCI are detailed below.

[1] Analysis of Final Price in Comparison to the Input Price

Business prudence requires that the final price must account for the input price of the raw material and other overheads plus a markup to ensure that the business is profitable. Having said that, in a market where there are choices of market participants, each company undertakes to give the best possible price to have better revenue, more customers and more purchase orders. However, in a cartel case, the companies collude

48. *Tyre case*, para. 114.
49. *Airline surcharge cartel case*, paras 92, 93, 100, 106.

so that the prices of all companies are kept artificially high so that each one can earn supra-normal profits.

In light of the above, in most of the cartel cases, the DG analyses the final price increase of the product for each of the market participants during the period of investigation and compares such price increase with the price of input costs, during the same time, for producing the concerned product. During the same time, if it is seen that even the input price, i.e., the price of raw material, has gone up during the same point of time, an economic justification can be made for the price increase of the final product. In the absence of a price increase of the raw material, it can be concluded (based on various other additional factors) that the market participants colluded to keep the price levels high. In fact, in the *Cement cartel* case,[50] the CCI had noted that due to concreted practices, there was an increase in the cement price by all market participants, and the price was not increased due to a change in excise duty. Conversely, the CCI noted in the case of *Shubham Sanitarywares v. Hindustan Sanitaryware and Industries*[51] that the price of the product under question has not increased for the past three years. Such stagnant prices were taken by the CCI to indicate there was no cartel.

[2] *Price Correlation Exercise for All Market Participants*

In order to find out whether there is an agreement and concerted action among the market participants to raise prices in a consistent manner, the DG generally undertakes a price correlation exercise for each of the players; i.e., a correlation exercise is seen whether the prices of products for all market participants are similar and moving in the same direction. In the *Cement cartel* case,[52] it was seen by the DG, based on the data on market prices, that the correlation of change in prices or the movement of prices of all the companies is positive and very close to each other (more than 0.5%). Such a strong correlation between cement prices for all cement companies across regions in India gave a strong indication of price parallelism. Since the cost of production, transportation charges, etc., varies from company to company, economic prudence suggests that the price of individual companies should also vary. Therefore, the DG noted that the movement of prices of all the companies in the same range and in the same direction is not possible unless there is prior consultation and discussion about the prices among them. Based on analysis of correlations of absolute price, price change and percentage price change, it was concluded by the DG that the prices of the cement manufacturers show a positive correlation in every state of operation and hence was taken as evidence of cartelization. The observations of the DG were also agreed by the CCI in their final decision. Conversely, in the *Tyre* case,[53] the range between prices of tyres of different

50. *Cement cartel* case, para. 269.
51. *Shubham Sanitarywares v. Hindustan Sanitaryware and Industries*, Case No. 99 of 2013, para. 14. The CCI order was upheld by the erstwhile COMPAT in *Shubham Sanitarywares v. Competition Commission of India and Ors.*, Appeal No. 19 of 2016.
52. *Cement cartel* case, para. 7(xxv), 7(xxvii), 92, 223.
53. *Tyre* case, para. 320.

manufacturers was more than INR 1,000 for the period 2005-2009, and the range had come down to INR 600 in 2010. The CCI noted that the product under investigation, i.e., tyre, is homogeneous. For a homogenous product, a 6%-12% range of difference in prices implies that the prices are dissimilar and there is no parallelism in absolute prices. Further, with respect to price movement in percentage terms, it was noted that there were wide variations among various tyre manufactures. Such wide variations showed that there was no agreement among tyre companies.

Depending upon the facts and circumstances, the CCI considers whether the price parallelism by the competitors was due to the specific market condition or due to collusion before leading to an inference of cartelization.

This economic evidence is commonly found in bid rigging cases. One of the forms of bid rigging is Identical or Level bidding, where bidders coordinate to quote identical price of their bids. By publishing price lists, raising prices by a specific increment, fixing or removing discounts, or maintaining a decided price differentials based on quantity, type, or size of product, the bidders can manipulate the bidding process in their favour. For instance, in *Mr. Rakesh Khare v. Krishna Engineering Works and Others*,[54] the CCI held that there was a violation of section 3(3)(d) of the Competition Act because the bidders indulged in identical pricing in the bids in Eastern Railway tenders for the eight years. Similarly, in *People's All India Anti-Corruption and Crime Prevention Society v. Usha International Ltd. and Others*,[55] the CCI held that the prices quoted were similar; hence, the competitors were neither competitive nor independent.

[3] Production Capacity and Capacity Utilization

In all cartel investigations, the DG analyses the production capacity of the market participants during the period of investigation and also the capacity utilization during the same time frame. Further, the trend in the demand for said product under investigation is also seen during the same time frame. The reason for such an analysis is required to see whether the market participants have indulged in deliberately curtailing production in the face of rising demand, which will have the effect of an increase in the final price. For illustration, in the *Cement cartel* case,[56] the DG noted that the production capacity of cement had increased from 157 MMT in 2005-06 to 287 MMT by the end of March 2011. However, capacity utilization was on a continuous downward trend from 2008 to 2009. During the financial year 2010-2011, capacity utilization had come down to 73% from 82% in the previous years, in spite of a very high demand for cement. A lower capacity utilization by all cement manufacturers, in the absence of any justifiable reason, was taken by the CCI as a plus factor to prove the

54. *Mr. Rakesh Khare v. Krishna Engineering Works and Others*, Reference Case No. 02 of 2020, paras 85, 86, 95.
55. *People's All India Anti-Corruption and Crime Prevention Society v. Usha International Ltd. and Others*, Case No. 90 of 2016, paras 41, 43, 44.
56. *Cement cartel* case, paras 7(xxix), 7(xxxvi), 7(xxxix), 245, 246.

existence of an anti-competitive agreement among cement manufacturers to limit the production of cement, which in turn, increased the price of cement.

As such, the DG undertook a comparison of price index with capacity utilization index of each of the cement companies. It was noted that ever since 2006-2007, the capacity utilization and cement price index of cement companies have been moving in the opposite direction. While the capacity utilization has been declining, the price index has been increasing. It was also noted that the production capacity in total was increasing, and yet the capacity utilization of all cement companies was decreasing. The DG noted that the cement companies could not come up with any business rationale for the decrease in capacity utilization in spite of a surge in demand. Based on the same, the DG noted that this is a result of a deliberate attempt to reduce supply by not utilizing full capacity and thereby increasing the price of cement in the market. The DG also concluded that the cement companies are charging unreasonable and higher than competitive prices. The last quarter of the financial year 2010-2011 witnessed a price increase of 20%-50% throughout the country in comparison to prices in the third quarter of 2010-2011 which was a result of a reduction in capacity utilization and controlling the supply in the market. The observations of the DG were also endorsed by the CCI in the final decision.

Similarly, *In Re: Alleged anti-competitive conduct in the Beer Market in India*[57] ('*Beer cartel* case'), the CCI initiated a *suo motu* investigation pursuant to the receipt of a leniency application by Crown Beers India Private Limited and SABMillers India Limited under section 46 of the Competition Act read with Regulation 5 of the Competition Commission of India (Lesser Penalty) Regulations, 2009. From the evidence collected from the leniency application, the CCI prima facie noted that in several states and union territories, price fixation and implementation of price adjustment existed in the beer industry. After a holistic analysis of the evidence under the leniency application and the DG report, the CCI concluded the existence of a beer cartel in the ten states and union territories and found that the beer cartel violated section 3(3)(a), (b) and (c) of the Competition Act. The beer manufacturers reduced their beer production to create an artificial scarcity of their product in the market. The beer manufacturers were also sharing their commercial information, such as beer production, revenue details, targets, stock sold and stock held by the companies, and details of their stocks lying with the distributors. This was done to limit the production of beer in the market and put pressure on the government to lower the excise duty on beer. The CCI found both direct evidence and indirect evidence to hold such anti-competitive to be violative of section 3(3)(b) of the Competition Act.

57. *In Re: Alleged anti-competitive conduct in the Beer Market in India*, Suo Motu Case No. 06 of 2017, paras 71, 74. The NCLAT also upheld the CCI order in *Pawan Jagetia and Others v. CCI and Others* [2022], (NCLAT) Competition Appeal (AT) No. 16 of 2021. At present, at appeal is pending before the Supreme Court, Civil Appeal No. 000747 of 2023. The Supreme Court passed a stay on the CCI's recovery proceeding of the penalty, and the matter is *sub judice*.

[4] *Profit Margin of the Market Participants*

As a part of a cartel investigation, the DG analyses the profit margin of each of the market participants to see whether there is a trend which shows the existence of an agreement. In the *Cement cartel* case,[58] the CCI noted the cement manufacturing-wise trend in profit margins and net profit. Because of cartelization, cement manufacturers were able to make huge profits over the years by limiting and controlling supplies and by imposing a higher cost per cement bag. Furthermore, the net profit of the cement manufacturers shows that they were able to make a high net profit by eliminating competition and charging unreasonable prices.

[5] *Economic Evidence to Establish Bid Rigging*

[a] *Bid Price Versus Input Price*

In all the bid rigging cases, the DG makes an analysis of the final bid prices, the price of the inputs and other key indices of costs like freight, transportation, etc. This analysis is required to be done to see whether the price being quoted in a bid is an independent price of the market participants or if there is a case of bid rigging where the companies have colluded with each other during the process of bidding. In one of the bid rigging cases, it was noted that the bids quoted for the product by the manufacturers were the same and not based on cost and expected profit margins. It was noted, during the investigation, that though the source of procurement of raw material was the same for all the manufacturers, the cost incurred by each of the manufacturers for such procurement of raw material was not the same. The input cost was different for each company, yet all the companies submitted bids with the same price. Similarly, the CCI undertook a detailed analysis of the bidding pattern in the *Aluminium Phosphide* case, where it was seen that there was an identity in the rates quoted by the bidders even when the factories and the offices of these parties were not located in one and same state and they had to make supplies to locations far off from their factories located at different places. Therefore, in cases where in spite of a varying cost structure for companies, price bids submitted by companies have identical (to the last decimal) or similar bids have been held by the CCI, as a case of bid rigging. Therefore, to conduct a final price versus input analysis, the DG and CCI undertook a detailed costing analysis of each of the market participants and analysed the same in light of the final prices quoted by the concerned company.

Further, it is apposite to note the observations of the Supreme Court in the *Excel Crop* case.[59] One of the defences which are raised in every cartel matter is that it is a case of parallel pricing by the market participants, and such actions are not borne out due to any preconceived agreement. In this regard, the Supreme Court, in the context of bid rigging, had noted that identical pricing on one or two occasions, though it raises

58. *Cement cartel* case, paras 277, 283.
59. *Excel Crop* case, paras 48, 49. (SC).

strong suspicion, may not be enough to draw the inference of the concerted agreement, but when is repeated constantly with odd figures (same to the last decimal) and without any reasonable explanation for the same, would only draw an inference of a pre-concerted agreement.

In *Mr. Rakesh Khare v. Krishna Engineering Works and Others*,[60] the CCI observed the quotations of bidders and noted that despite differences in manufacturing, transportation, packaging, and insurance, the cartel members fixed their quotation at INR 17,800. Hence, this, coupled with other evidence, was held to be in violation of section 3(3)(d) of the Competition Act for manipulating the bidding process.

[b] Cover Bids

There have been instances wherein entities participate in the bidding process without any intention to compete but to create a façade of competition. Such entities have no technical qualification to participate in tenders because they might not be having proper equipment or experience certificate to fulfil the technical eligibility. Their sole purpose of participating in the bidding process is to support one of the entities to win the bid. Generally, the sister company or the entities have a good relationship with the designate winner who tends to submit bids so that the bid of the designate bidder will not be rejected due to insufficient number of bids,[61] thereby creating a mirage of competition, where none exists.

[c] Sub-contracting

In sub-contracting, the cartel member will suppress its bid or submit a losing bid so that in exchange it will get the sub-contract from the winner of the tender. This results in higher profits for both cartel members. Further, the cartel members can rotate their roles in subsequent tenders. The CCI in *Re: Surendra Prasad (MAHAGENCO's Tender for Coal Liaison service in Maharashtra)*[62] considered that the rivals working as sub-contractors for each other were used to establish the anti-competitive arrangement.

[d] Other Economic Evidence for Establishing Bid Rigging Cartel

There are also other types of economic evidence, such as collective withdrawal and common reason for withdrawal,[63] pattern of market allocation,[64] bogus expenses by

---

60. *Mr. Rakesh Khare v. Krishna Engineering Works and Others*, Reference Case No. 02 of 2020, paras 87, 88, 93.
61. *In Re: Alleged bid-rigging in E-Tenders invited by the Department of Agriculture, Government of Uttar Pradesh for soil sample testing*, Suo Motu No. 01 of 2020, paras 60, 97.
62. *Surendra Prasad v. Maharashtra State Power Generation Co. Ltd. & Others*, Case No. 61 of 2013, paras 41, 124, 125.
63. *In Re: Alleged Cartelisation in Supply of the LPG Cylinders Procured through Tenders by Hindustan Petroleum Corporation Ltd. (HPCL)*, Suo Motu Case No. 01 of 2014, paras 52-55.

the cartel members for showing losses,[65] etc., that can be considered a plus factor to establish a presence of bid rigging cartel.

The table below shows the decisional trends of the CCI in terms of analysis of communication and economic evidence across multiple decisional cases:

S. No.	*Case Name (Citation)*	*Evidence (Communication/Economic)*	*Reasoning*
1.	*Airline surcharge* case. Case No. 30 of 2013	The airline increased the FSC rate on the same date. (Paragraph 90) The airlines discussed the FSC rates in meetings. (Paragraph 106) The alleged airlines had hired common agents. (Paragraph 104)	The CCI held that the levy of FSC is at a fixed rate on per kilogram basis of the cargo weight. None of the airlines was able to furnish any data in support of the determination of FSC rates. Further, the airlines used common agents to exchange information among themselves. Hence, the airline acted in parallel to increase the FSC rates. (Paragraphs 84, 99, 106, 107)
2.	*People's All India Anti-Corruption and Crime Prevention Society v. Usha International Ltd. and Others.* Case No. 90 of 2016.	The call data record proved that the cartel members were constantly communicating during the tender proceeding. (Paragraphs 57-61) The rates quoted by the cartel members are very close, less than INR 30, despite the input cost and other conditions of the market. (Paragraph 41)	Frequent interaction among cartel members is considered a plus factor in proving a bid rigging cartel. (Paragraph 63) The CCI noted that the identical pricing shows that the cartel members are not competitive and independent. (Paragraphs 43, 44)

64. *In Re: Surendra Prasad (MAHAGENCO's Tender for Coal Liaison service in Maharashtra)*, Case No. 61 of 2013, paras 99-111.
65. *Ibid.*, paras 126, 127.

S. No.	Case Name (Citation)	Evidence (Communication/Economic)	Reasoning
3.	*Cement cartel* case (Case No. 29 of 2010)	Market is Oligopolistic because Cement, as a product, has only two or three categories. The monthly prices of cement of the cement manufacturers were moving in tandem. (Paragraph 229) The cement manufacturers were unable to provide any reasonable explanation for the determination of prices. (Paragraph 233) The cement manufacturers' overall capacity utilization reduced from 83% in 2009-10 to 73% in 2010-11. All the cement manufacturers reduced their production of cement in 2009 and 2010. Similarly, the cement manufacturers were colluding regarding the dispatch of cement. (Paragraphs 239, 245, 250-252, 257, 258, 260, 261) The price of cement per bag was increased by the cement manufacturers. Further, the sale, sale	The cement manufacturers were aware of the actions of each other and colluded in a manner which led to non-competitive outcomes. (Paragraph 220) There was price parallelism between different cement manufacturers because of the strong positive correlation in the prices. (Paragraphs 224, 232) The cement manufacturers were unable to corroborate the change in cement prices with the market dynamics. (Paragraph 238) After looking at the annual reports of the cement manufacturers, it was clarified that they were not utilizing the overall capacity. During 2009-10 and 2010-11, the production of cement has fallen drastically. The cement manufacturers similarly entered into an identical

S. No.	Case Name (Citation)	Evidence (Communication/Economic)	Reasoning
		realization and margin of cement manufacturers increased. Hence, the cement manufacturers earned huge profits. (Paragraphs 268, 280, 282)	behaviour relating to the dispatch of cement to control the supply of cement. (Paragraphs 252, 259, 263, 266) The cement manufacturer created an artificial demand by shortening production and, thereafter, increased the price of cement. Hence, the cement manufacturers deliberately reduced capacity utilization to manipulate and control the supply in the market and earned huge profits by increasing the prices. (Paragraphs 273, 275, 277, 283) The CCI found both direct and indirect evidence.
4.	*In Re: Alleged anti-competitive conduct in the Beer Market in India.* Suo Motu Case No. 06 of 2017	The beer manufacturers decided to stop producing and restricted the supply of Beer. (Paragraphs 11(1)(vi), 67)	The CCI held that exchange of commercially information competitors compromises the integrity of independent bidding process and was likely to stifle competition. (Paragraph 23)

S. No.	*Case Name (Citation)*	*Evidence (Communication/Economic)*	*Reasoning*
			Beer manufacturer decided to lower their production of beer to put pressure on the Excise Authorities to lower the Excise duty on Beer. Limiting supplies impacted the beer market because the price of beer increased. The CCI noted that the conduct of the beer manufacturer violated section 3(3)(b) of the Competition Act. (Paragraphs 69, 70, 71) In this case, CCI found both direct and indirect evidence.
5.	*LPG-II* case. Suo Motu Case No. 1 of 2014	Direct evidence, such as emails were exchanged between bidders regarding price, business strategies, etc. (Paragraph 77) The CCI also found certain indirect evidence, such as the bidders discussed and parallel acted in terms of: (a) quotation of bids (paragraph 48) (b) collective withdrawal of bids (paragraph 53)	The CCI held that the bidders discussed and shared sensitive and confidential information regarding the tender to manipulate the bidding process of tender no. 2. (Paragraphs 107, 111-113)

S. No.	*Case Name (Citation)*	*Evidence (Communication/Economic)*	*Reasoning*
		(c) common reason in withdrawal letters (paragraphs 54, 55) (d) common format of withdrawal letter (paragraph 60) (e) common IP address and agents (paragraphs 65, 74)	
6.	*In Re: Aluminium Phosphide Tablets Manufacturers.* Suo Motu No. 02 of 2011.	The bidders concerted to manipulate the bidding process by quoting identical rates even if their production costs were different. Also, they collectively abstained from bidding in certain tenders. (Paragraphs 3.14, 6.2)	The CCI said that the parallel behaviour of the bidders can be considered evidence of coordinated behaviour on the part of the three bidders regarding the tender. (Paragraph 6.29)
7.	*T.R. Chandran v. National Egg Co-ordination Committee (NECC).* Case Nos 09 and 36 of 2017.	The trade association (i.e., NECC) displayed daily egg prices, zone-wise, on its website and monitored the monthly/annual price of eggs at various egg production and consumption centres. (Paragraph 114)	Mandating the farmers to follow the price fixed by the NECC is a violation of section 3(3)(a) of the Competition Act. (Paragraphs 153, 208, 209)
8.	*In Re: Alleged bid-rigging in E-Tenders invited by the Department of Agriculture, Government of Uttar Pradesh for soil sample testing.* Suo Motu Case No. 01 of 2020	Some of the cartel members were family friends, and they submitted cover bids under the influence of friendship. (Paragraph 30)	The CCI used this evidence as a plus factor to conclude the presence of bid rigging cartel. (Paragraph 88)

S. No.	*Case Name (Citation)*	*Evidence (Communication/Economic)*	*Reasoning*
9.	*In Re: Cartelization in Tender Nos 21 and 28 of 2013 of Pune Municipal Corporation for Solid Waste Processing*. Suo Motu Case No. 03 of 2016	A director of a 2nd cartel member is the close friend of 1st cartel member, the sole proprietor of 3rd cartel member and the son of 4th cartel member's director. (Paragraphs 5, 56) Additionally, 2nd cartel member arranged the relevant documents, prepared demand drafts and authorization certificates, and uploaded the tender documents (common IP address) of all cartel members. (Paragraphs 57-58) 4th cartel member aided the 2nd cartel member in fulfilling the eligibility criteria for participation in the tenders. Even though the 4th cartel member was eligible to bid, it did not participate in the tender process and suppressed its bid. (Paragraph 60)	Even though the cartel members were separate legal entities and had bid as competitors, they were controlled by one person and had a commonplace for business. (Paragraphs 56-59) There is a meeting of mind among cartel members to rig the bidding process. Once an agreement on bid rigging is established, then it will be presumed to have an adverse effect. The onus to rebut the presumption is on the cartel members. (Paragraph 63)
10.	*Mr. Rakesh Khare v. Krishna Engineering Works and Others*. Reference Case No. 02 of 2020	The CCI took note of the identical pricing in the bids submitted by the cartel members in Eastern Railway tenders for the eight years 2012-19. (Paragraphs 85, 86)	By mutually deciding the prices to be quoted, the cartel members were manipulating the tenders. (Paragraph 95)

S. No.	*Case Name (Citation)*	*Evidence (Communication/Economic)*	*Reasoning*
		CCI took note of the quotations and found that despite differences in manufacturing, transportation, packaging, and insurance, the cartel members fixed their quotation at INR 17,800. (Paragraphs 87, 88)	The cartel members did not indicate the price break-down of their quotations as stipulated in the '*Instructions to Tenderers for Manual and E-Tender and General Tender Conditions for Open Tenders*' as issued by the procurement authority. This was done with the sole intention of keeping their bids identical. (Paragraph 93)
11.	*Food Corporation of India v. Shivalik Agro Poly Products Ltd. and Others.* Reference Case No. 07 of 2018.	From the depositions of the cartel members, it was clear that they had decided to quote an identical price. (Paragraphs 54, 59)	The CCI held that the cartel members indulged in bid rigging. (Paragraph 63)
12.	*In Re: Alleged bid-rigging in E-Tenders invited by the Department of Agriculture, Government of Uttar Pradesh for soil sample testing.* Suo Motu Case No. 01 of 2020	Cartel members submitted bids without prior experience in soil testing work and did not have any soil testing machine. (Paragraphs 10 (h), (j), (l)-(n).) One of the cartel members participated in the bidding process to support the designated bidder from being rejected due to insufficient number of bids. (Paragraph 60)	To help the designated bidder win, other cartel members indulged in submitting fake invoices and false certificates to act as cover bidders. (Paragraph 132)

S. No.	*Case Name (Citation)*	*Evidence (Communication/Economic)*	*Reasoning*
13.	*In Re: Surendra Prasad (MAHAGENCO's Tender for Coal Liaison service in Maharashtra).* Case No. 61 of 2013.	The previous record showed the cartel members worked as sub-contractors for each other in various contracts. (Paragraphs 41, 124)	Competitors working as sub-contractors for each other shows the anti-competitive arrangement. (Paragraph 125)

§2.07 SINGLE ECONOMIC ENTITY

It must be kept in mind that the provision, with respect to agreement, is only applicable in cases when there is an agreement between parties who are completely independent of each other and operate autonomously.

The CCI has noted and accepted the internationally accepted doctrine of single economic entity in its decisional practice.[66] It has been noted by the CCI and erstwhile COMPAT that agreements between enterprises which form part of the same group, owing to the fact that the sole control is exercised by one company, cannot be assessed under section 3 of the Competition Act. The rationale adopted by the CCI is that the agreement referred to under section 3 refers to agreement between two enterprises that are independent of each other and not between two enterprises which are part of the same group. The rationale is that enterprises within the same group are not autonomous in their operations since the decisive influence over such enterprises can be held by a single enterprise. In the *Exclusive Motors Private Limited v. Automobili Lamborghini S.P.A.* ('*Lamborghini* case'),[67] even when 'Volkswagen India' had a separate legal existence, the CCI and erstwhile COMPAT noted since it belonged to the same group as Automobili Lamborghini, they were considered a single economic entity and internal agreements between them were outside the scope of section 3. Further, in the said case, the erstwhile COMPAT looked in detail at the manner in which operations are carried out by Volkswagen India and Automobili Lamborghini. It was seen that the operations were totally controlled by a common parent entity, and hence, they formed a single economic entity. A note of caution must be struck herein that in the *Lamborghini* case, it was clear that the control was exercised by one entity. There can be situations, while interpreting the Competition Act, where one enterprise can form a part of two or more different groups. So, in such a case, agreements between enterprises may or may not form a part of the single economic entity. The concept of

66. *Exclsuive Motors Pvt. Ltd. v. Automobili Lamborghini S.P.A*, CCI order, Case No. 52 of 2012, para. 6. *Exclsuive Motors Pvt. Ltd. v. Automobili Lamborghini S.P.A and Another* [2016], (COMPAT) 2014 SCC OnLine Comp AT 1, paras 11, 14.
67. Luxury cars such as Audi, SEAT, Lamborghini, Volkswagen, Skoda, Bentley, Bugatti and Porsche – were all considered within the same group of Volkswagen.

single economic entity has to be seen on a de facto basis to see whether the parties to the agreement are acting in a manner which shows that they are in fact, a single unit.

The aspect of single economic entity was also discussed in the *Insurance cartel* case,[68] where section 27 order was passed against the cartelization by public sector insurance companies in rigging the bids submitted in response to the tenders floated by the Government of Kerala for selecting an insurance service provider for RSBY. The CCI was analysing whether the public sector insurance companies had engaged in bid rigging under the provisions of section 3(3)(d) of the Competition Act. A defence was raised by the insurance companies, stating that they constitute a single economic entity as all the insurance companies were owned by General Insurance Company. It was also submitted by the insurance companies that, pursuant to the enactment of the General Insurance Business (Nationalization) Amendment Act, 2002, the Government of India holds 100% shares of each of the insurance companies and controls the management and affairs of the insurance companies through Department of Financial Services (Insurance Division), Ministry of Finance.

However, the CCI did not accept the defence of single economic entity raised by the insurance companies. The CCI noted that although the public sector insurance companies are presently under the overall supervision of the Central Government, each of the insurance companies had placed a separate bid in response to the tenders issued by the Government of Kerala for the implementation of RSBY/CHIS schemes. Further, all decisions relating to the submission of bids, determination of bid amounts, business sharing arrangements, etc., were taken internally at the company level without any *ex ante* approval/directions from the Ministry of Finance. Even the decisions taken by the companies were not notified *ex post* to the Ministry. Based on the same, it was noted by the CCI that the insurance companies participated in the tenders independently, and the Ministry of Finance had no role to play. On this basis, the CCI held that the Ministry of Finance did not exercise any de facto (i.e., where an enterprise holds less than the majority of voting rights but in practice controls half of the votes) or de jure control (i.e., where an enterprise holds more than 50% of voting rights) over business decisions of insurance companies in submitting bids for impugned tenders and therefore, it was decided that insurance companies cannot be said to constitute a single economic unit.

The approach adopted by the CCI in the cases discussed above shows that the CCI will look into the manner in which the business decisions are carried out by enterprises and not limit itself to the shareholding pattern and board composition to check whether the actions of enterprises are independent of each other or not, to decide whether the enterprises form a single economic unit. To form a single economic entity, the CCI will look into both de jure control (control by way of shareholding, board of directors, etc.) and de facto control (the manner in which operations of a company are carried out).

68. *Insurance cartel* case, paras 22-26.

§2.08 DETERMINATION OF RELEVANT MARKET

The relevant market is the boundary within which all anti-competitive practices are analysed by the CCI. In the High Committee Report,[69] it is said that for horizontal agreement it is important to define relevant market. This will help to determine whether the concerned agreement between the parties is on substitutable products or not. It must be kept in mind that as per the statutory scheme provided under the Competition Act, there is no explicit requirement to construct a relevant market in an anti-competitive agreement investigation, like in an abuse of dominance investigation or a merger analysis. The decisional practice of the CCI clearly shows that there is no mandatory requirement under section 3(1) and section 3(3) of the Act as also under section 19(3) to determine and construct a relevant market. The CCI, in the *Cement cartel* case,[70] held that there is no need to determine relevant market for establishing an anti-competitive agreement because there is a distinction between 'market' as in section 3 and 'relevant market' defined in section 4 of the Competition Act.

However, in the case of the *Coordination Committee,*[71] the Supreme Court deviated from the decisional practice of CCI and observed that the first and foremost aspect that needs determination is the relevant market. In this judgment, the Supreme Court dealt with the substantive issue of contravening section 3(3)(b) by the members of the film and television artists trade union. The cartel members caused appreciable adverse effects by entering into agreements to prevent the telecast of the dubbed 'Mahabharat' serial on TV channels. Further, it was also held that the AAEC must be seen in the context of 'relevant market' as defined under section 2(r) of the Competition Act. However, if such an approach becomes the norm, it has the potential to have far-reaching implications, as it is likely to lead to an unnecessary pre-condition for analysing cartels. The CCI filed a clarification application to which the Supreme Court clarified that the determination of 'relevant market' is not a mandatory pre-condition for making assessment of cartels, particularly having regard to the statutory presumption contained in section 3 of the Competition Act itself.

§2.09 TYPES OF CARTEL

Section 3(3) of the Competition Act enlists specific types of agreements/arrangements among persons or enterprises or association of persons which are engaged in identical or similar trade of goods or provision of services which are considered per se anti-competitive. According to section 3(3) of the Competition Act, agreements, including cartels, which: (a) directly or indirectly determine purchase or sales prices;

69. High Level Committee on Competition Policy and Law, 2000, para. 4.3.4.
70. *Cement cartel* case, para. 6.5.44. However, the erstwhile COMPAT in *Lafarge India Limited and Others v. CCI and Another* [2015], (COMPAT) 2015 SCC OnLine Comp AT 1120, para. 137, remanded the matter back to the CCI because of the procedural errors and the principles of natural justice was not followed while passing the final order. Thereafter, on 31 Aug. 2016, the CCI passed the final order (para. 219) reiterating that there is no requirement of the Competition Act to determine a relevant market under the provisions of section 3.
71. *Coordination Committee* case, paras 14, 33.

(b) limit or control production, supply, markets, technical development, investment or the provision of services; (c) share the market or source of production or provision of services by way of allocation of the geographical area of the market, type of goods or services, or number of customers in the market or any other similar way; (d) directly or indirectly result in bid rigging or collusive bidding, are presumed to cause an AAEC in India.

The four kinds of horizontal agreements, recognized as cartels under section 3(3) of the Competition Act, are discussed herein below.

[A] Price Fixing

Section 3(3)(a) of the Competition Act provides that an agreement among enterprises at the same level of trade, which directly or indirectly determines purchase or sale prices, will be presumed to have an AAEC. The wording of the section is broad enough to cover not only the final price but also include other instances of terms of trade, like discounts, etc., which have an impact on the final price.

Fixing prices is a concerted activity between competitors to set their prices to buy or sell goods/services. For instance, *In Re: Anti-competitive conduct in the paper manufacturing industry*,[72] competitors of the paper manufacturing industry decide to coordinate to draw a road map for increasing the price of paper. The CCI found direct evidence in the form of emails where it was clearly written that the paper manufacturers were discussing to collude and increase the price of the product. The fear of competition was stopping them form increasing the price. However, the paper manufacturers found a way to dodge the prevailing competition in the market by colluding through participating in physical meetings or exchanging emails to share commercially sensitive information. Sharing commercial information between market participants takes away the freedom to decide the price of the goods as per the supply and demand of the market.

In *People for Animals (PFA) and Another v. National Egg Co-ordination Committee (NECC) and Other*,[73] the CCI decided that the National Egg Coordination Committee (NECC) had indulged in fixing and declaration of prices of eggs from 2009 to 2020. The NECC's zonal production centres coordinated with the zonal consumption centres as well as other production centres, and after conducting a thorough demand and supply analysis, declared daily prices for eggs to be followed by all farmers. It was also observed that NECC was strictly implementing its anti-competitive conduct on farmers in each zone by informing them not to sell at the fixed price and threatening to impose penalties in case of non-compliance. Apart from violating section 3(3)(a) of the Competition Act, NECC was also limiting the production and supply of eggs. Controlling production helped NECC to ensure that the farmers were selling eggs at fixed

72. *In Re: Anti-competitive conduct in the paper manufacturing industry*, Suo Motu Case No. 05 of 2016, paras 159, 160, 192.
73. *People for Animals (PFA) and Another v. National Egg Co-ordination Committee (NECC) and Other*, Case Nos 09 and 36 of 2017, paras 114, 116, 197, 198, 201. The NCLAT has upheld the order of *CCI in People of Animals v. CCI and Others*, Competition Appeal (AT) 25 of 2022.

prices. From a competition law standpoint, the price of the product should be based on the holistic assessment of demand and supply. Thus, it should not be subject to the vagaries of whimsical diktats of NECC or any of its members which would determine the pricing of a product. CCI found that NECC was trying to control prices by threatening the farmers by levying or threatening to levy penalties on them.

In terms of imposing other pricing conditions, such as discounts, CCI in *M/s International Subscription Agency v. Federation of Publishers' and Booksellers' Associations in India (FPBAI)*[74] held that FPBAI's discount policy prohibited all its members who deal in print journal and e-resources from offering any discount on the publishers' price to the Indian subscribers. FPBAI was a federation of publishers, subscription agents and booksellers, and it provided a platform for all its members to discuss their problems. FPBAI constituted a committee with the objective of maintaining uniformity in the supply of books and journals, ensuring fair margins to booksellers and providing efficient service to libraries. However, under the rules of the committee, the members of FPBAI were not allowed to offer discounts to Indian subscribers and were threatened with dire consequences for violating the rules of GOC. Therefore, FPBAI was held guilty of contravention of section 3(3)(a) and (b) of the Competition Act.

[B] Output Controls/Limiting Production

Section 3(3)(b) of the Competition Act provides that any agreement among enterprises at the same level of trade which limits or controls production, supply, markets, technical development, investment or provision of services will be presumed to have an AAEC. The decisional practice of the CCI would show that, among other factors, the CCI looks at demand analysis of the concerned product, production capacity and capacity utilization of the market participants to understand whether there is any trend/pattern wherein they limit the production. In addition, a demand analysis is also done for a period of time to see whether the market participants indulged in limiting production even when there was a high demand for the product under the investigation, which will, in turn, have a resultant impact on the rise in prices. Economic analysis would show that prices cannot be kept at elevated levels if market participants do not keep supply levels sufficiently low in relation to demand. Therefore, in order to ensure that production and supply are low, there is very little capacity addition over time by the market participants and in some cases, the companies may engage in a reduction of capacity. There may also be cases where the market participants are not operating at optimal capacity. Such an action will lead to a demand-supply mismatch and, thereby, an increase in price. The CCI has made detailed observations of this clause in cases relating to the cement industry, entertainment industry, and pharmaceutical industry, among others. The CCI has noted in the *Cement cartel* case[75] that the act of limiting and controlling supplies on the part of the cement companies over the

74. *M/s International Subscription Agency v. Federation of Publishers' and Booksellers' Associations in India (FPBAI)*, Case No. 33 of 2019, paras 18, 39.
75. *Cement cartel* case, paras 276, 277, 290.

years has been aimed at first creating shortages leading to built-up demand which, in turn, caused upward rise in prices in the wake of high demand of the product in the market. Since in some seasons, the demand is more, the cement companies restricted the supplies just before the peak demand which allowed the cement companies to sell cement at a higher price. Therefore, the act of limiting and controlling production and supplies in the market causes upward movement in the price of that product/service. Similarly, the deliberate act of shortage in production and supplies as a result of cartelization in a product/service which has inelastic demand, inevitably results in high prices. Similar observations were also made in the *NECC* case (*discussed supra*).

In the pharmaceutical industry too, the CCI has passed an order under section 27 of the Competition Act, holding the Chemist and Druggist Association liable for limiting and controlling supply[76] and restricting the ability of the enterprises to supply and sell drugs in the market. The CCI's order was a cease-and-desist order, along with certain directions to prohibit such anti-competitive practices. (as explained under the 'Trade Association' heading).

Similarly, in the entertainment industry, the CCI has taken note of the practices carried out by regional film association as being anti-competitive since such film associations frame rules and regulations to impose restrictions on the free and unrestricted distribution and exhibition of serials/films. Also, in the transportation industry, the CCI has observed that trade associations have violated section 3(3)(b) of the Competition Act by imposing restrictive terms for availing transportation services of their members. Such restrictions put the goods at indefinite halt and harm the business users and end users of the market. For instance, in *CJ Darcl Logistics Ltd. v. Dumper and Dumper Truck Union Lime Stone and Another*,[77] the Dumper Truck Union prevented the informant, which itself was a logistics company, from using its own vehicles to transport limestone. Further, threats were issued to force the informant to avail the service of the Dumper Truck Union and its association members. The concerted practice of the Dumper Truck Union resulted in limitation of transport services and helped all its members to fix a higher transportation rate.

[C] Market Sharing

Section 3(3)(c) of the Competition Act provides that any agreement among enterprises at the same level of trade, which shares the market or source of production or provision of services by way of allocation of the geographical area of the market, or type of goods or services, or number of customers in the market or any other similar way will be presumed to have an AAEC. Market sharing refers to agreements between competitors

76. *Varca Chemists and Druggists v. Chemists and Druggists Association*, Goa MRTPC 127/2009/DGIR4/28, para. 33; *Vedant Bio Sciences v. Chemists and Druggists Association of Baroda* C-87/2009/DGIR, paras 20.26, 20.27; *M/s Sandhya Drug Agency v. ADDA, BDDA, AIOCD, IDMA, OPPI*, Case No. 41 of 2011, para. 24; *Peeveear Medical Agencies v. AIOCD and Janssen* Case No. 30 of 2011, para. 18.
77. *CJ Darcl Logistics Ltd. v. Dumper and Dumper Truck Union Lime Stone and Another*, Case No. 31 of 2019, paras 34, 35; *National Association of Container Freight Stations, Chennai Chapter v. Trailer Owners Association and Others*, Case No. 04 of 2018, paras 79-81.

that divide up the market so that the market participants do not compete among themselves. Such market sharing can happen by way of geographical allocation or customer allocation. For instance, in the *Signages bidding* case,[78] the CCI found that the opposite parties formed a cartel and decided to split the geographically allocated market among themselves with regard to the tender floated by SBI Infra Management Solutions Private Limited for the supply and installation of signages of SBI. The cartel member categorized the geographical market into three to four categories:

(i) Type 1 (Bangalore, Chennai, Mumbai, Delhi): geographical presence and manufacturing presence.
(ii) Type 2 & 3 (Hyderabad, Lucknow, Bhopal, Patna, Jaipur): additional cost is required to transport signages.
(iii) Type 4 (Chandigarh, Kashmir, Kolkata, North East States): logistic constraints (remote areas).

Accordingly, the cartel members allocated the market and violated section 3(3)(c) and (d) by entering into an agreement to share the geographical circles they would want to be geographically allocated for the tender.

[D] Bid Rigging

Section 3(3)(d) of the Competition Act provides that any agreement among enterprises at the same level of trade, which directly or indirectly results in bid rigging or collusive bidding, will be presumed to have an AAEC. Bid rigging, defined in the explanation to section 3(3) of the Competition Act, means any agreement, between enterprises or persons engaged in identical or similar production or trading of goods or provision of services, which has the effect of eliminating or reducing competition for bids or adversely affecting or manipulating the process for bidding.

The Competition Act has explained 'bid rigging' as an agreement, between parties engaged in identical or similar production or trading of goods or provision of services, which has the effect of eliminating or reducing competition for bids or adversely affecting or manipulating the process for bidding. Since both bid rigging and collusive bidding are interchangeable, so the explanation is equally applicable to collusive bidding.[79]

The CCI has noted that collusive bidding or bid rigging may be of different kinds, namely, agreements to submit identical bids, agreements as to who shall submit the lowest bid, agreements for the submission of cover bids (voluntarily submit inflated bids), agreements not to bid against each other, agreements on common norms to

78. *Re: Alleged anti-competitive conduct by various bidders in supply and installation of signages at specified locations of State Bank of India across India*, Suo Motu Case No. 02 of 2020, paras 11.2, 39, 31, 37, 90, 91. The NCLAT upheld the decision of CCI in *Hith Impex Pvt. Ltd and Another v. CCI*, Competition App. (AT) Nos 21 and 65 of 2022; *Macromedia Digital Imaging Pvt Ltd. and Another v. CCI*, Competition App. (AT) Nos 24 and 26 of 2022.
79. *Excel Crop case*, paras 40-42, 46, 49, 56, 57. (SC).

calculate prices or terms of bids, agreements to squeeze out outside bidders, agreements designating bid winners in advance on a rotational basis, or on a geographical or customer allocation basis. There are various forms of collusive bidding or bid rigging, such as:

(i) Identical or Level bidding: Bidders coordinate to quote identical prices of their bids. Bidders can agree to adhere to publish price lists, raise prices by a specific increment, fix or eliminate discount, avoid advertisement of prices, or maintain specified price differentials based on quantity, type, or size of product.

(ii) Proxy or Cover bidding: Bidders artificially increase the price so that the bid will never be accepted or submit the bid without fulfilling the technical requirement.

(iii) Bid Suppression: Bidders refrain from bidding or withdrawing a previously submitted bid so that the designated bidder will win the tender.

(iv) Bid rotation: Bidders collude to take turns to win bids on different occasions.

(v) Bid allocation: Bidders share the geographical or product market and agree not to participate or compete for the tender.

The CCI has observed that in the event the tenders submitted are not a result of one's individual economic calculation but a result of consultation among several players submitting the tender, competition is said to be distorted in such a case. A case in this regard is the *Excel Crop* case[80] where all the firms set identical prices in their bids in spite of the firms having very distinct cost structures and sale prices. In all bid rigging cases, the DG and CCI make a detailed assessment of the cost structure of the company, a comparison of the input cost and final cost, production capacity and capacity utilization, etc., of each of the market participants to see whether there is any agreement among the market participants.

The Supreme Court, in the case of the *Excel Crop* case,[81] has indicated that collusive tendering or bid rigging is the practice whereby firms, which hold 100% market share, agree among themselves to collaborate on the response of a tender either by fixing the price or by boycotting the tender. The firms quoted identical bids for various tenders, even when the cost of production, geographical location and profit margins were different. Further, the firms disagreed with certain conditions given in the 2011 tender, so they acted in concert by boycotting the said tender floated by the procurement authority. The firms had the option to approach the procurement authority to seek clarification or amendment of such conditions. Rather than following the genuine path, the firms colluded among themselves to suppress their bids.[82] Bid rigging occurs when two or more enterprises (competing bidders or potential bidders) agree among themselves not to compete genuinely with each other for particular tenders which affects the prices they bid for, or they attempt to secretly influence the

80. *Ibid.*
81. *Ibid.*
82. *Ibid.*

outcome of a contract or series of contracts. This process allows one of the participants in the agreement to win the tender. Participants may fix prices, suppress, cover, rotate and allocate bids.

It is to be noted that the definition of bid rigging also includes any agreement among enterprises to manipulate the process of bidding. The entire process of bidding would entail the submission of technical and financial bids, negotiations with the counterparty, winning the bid, and the performance of the contract. In this regard, the erstwhile COMPAT has held, in the *Excel Crop* case, that bid rigging cases would encompass rigging in any or all of the processes involved in bidding, and not only limiting to first submission of technical and pricing bids.

The purpose of rigging the bid is to concert their bargaining power over the procurement authority and ultimately tilt the balance of negotiations towards their own favour to gain higher profit without worrying about the force of competition in the market and that they will be poached by competitors. Generally, in cartelization, cartels tend to artificially increase the bidding price or lower the quantity of goods or services.[83] Through collusion, the cartel members can use their bargaining power to get the upper hand during negotiations with the procurement authority.

As noted above, the decisional practice of the CCI shows that instances of bid rigging are very common in cases of government procurement. One of the common defences which are raised by cartel participants is that they are dealing with government, which is a strong counterparty, and hence, their practice of bid rigging does not cause any appreciable adverse effect. However, this defence has not been accepted by the CCI.

The CCI *In Re: Surendra Prasad (MAHAGENCO's Tender for Coal Liaison service in Maharashtra)* ('*Surendra Prasad order*'),[84] Maharashtra State Power Generation Co. Ltd. (MAHAGENCO) which was incorporated by the Government of Maharashtra for the generation of power in the State of Maharashtra invited tenders for coal liaisoning, and to supervise the quality and quantity of coal supplied. The opposite parties 2, 3 & 4 provided the service for coal liaisons, and they participated in the bidding process. The opposite parties 2 to 4 colluded to distribute the tenders among themselves. Ultimately, the opposite parties 2 to 4 got the bid. The CCI held the opposite parties guilty of section 3(3)(c) and (d) by establishing parallel conduct, sub-contracting and market allocation which was further corroborated with various corroborative evidence like purchasing the tender document on the same dates, communication between opposite parties, including details of financial information, etc.

Similarly, in *In Re: Cartelization in Tender Nos 21 and 28 of 2013 of Pune Municipal Corporation for Solid Waste Processing*[85] ('*Pune Municipal Corporate order*'), the CCI made an extensive analysis on whether the cartel members were engaged in identical business or not. In this case, the tender was floated for procurement of sewing

83. *Excel Crop* case, para. 41. (SC); *LPG-I* case, para. 78. (SC).
84. *In Re: Surendra Prasad (MAHAGENCO's Tender for Coal Liaison service in Maharashtra)*, Case No. 90 of 2016, paras 114, 122, 131.
85. *In Re: Cartelization in Tender Nos 21 and 28 of 2013 of Pune Municipal Corporation for Solid Waste Processing*, Suo Motu Case No. 03 of 2016, paras 44, 45, 46.

machines for distribution among the backward class people. The informant alleged that opposite parties colluded among themselves to rig the tendering process. The opposite *party* 1 was the seller of the sewing machine, the opposite parties 2, 3 and 4 were authorized dealers of opposite party 1, and the opposite party 5 was the government authority that floated the tender. Some opposite parties opposed the proceeding because they were engaged in a different business; hence, section 3(3)(d) would not apply to them. However, the CCI widely interpreted the term 'engaged in' to include all the opposite parties/cartel members in identical trade because they were participating in the same bidding process. This interpretation allows CCI to proceed against the proxy bidders & suppressive bidders. Such interpretation has only been applied to parties entering into an anti-competitive agreement to rig the bidding procedure, not to the other categories of anti-competitive agreements under section 3(3) of the Competition Act.

[1] Role of the Procurement Authority in Bid Rigging Inquiries

The decisional practice of the CCI has shown that most of the bid rigging case (if not all) happens in case of government procurement. In matters where there is an involvement of the Public Procurement Authority in facilitating the bid rigging cartel, then CCI uses the argument that the Public Procurement Authority and the bidders are not engaged in identical business. Thereby, Public Procurement Authority and bidders can never form a cartel. Further, in cases where there was an involvement of the Public Procurement Authority in facilitating the bid rigging cartel, there has been uncertainty regarding the collection of evidence from the Public Procurement Authority. For example, *in Surendra Prasad order,*[86] the CCI did not investigate the MAHAGENCO (the Public Procurement Authority) or examine the officials of MAHAGENCO.

The officers of the Public Procurement Authority provide important evidence in their deposition, so taking statements from them helps the CCI to reach a conclusion. In the *People's All India Anti-Corruption and Crime Prevention Society v. Usha International Ltd.*,[87] the DG investigated Pune Zilla Parishad and found evidence that helped CCI establish the agreement between bidders. Similarly, in the *LPG-II* case,[88] where CCI examined HPCL and considered the submissions made by HPCL to hold that certain bidders were not liable under section 3(3)(d) of the Competition Act. The facts of this case are similar to the *LPG-I* case. Unlike the *LPG-I* case, the fact of *the LPG-II* case shows that the tendering authority did not set the final price for the bids. The CCI initiated an inquiry against the cartelization to rig the bidding process of Tender No. 1 and Tender No. 2 floated by HPCL for 14.2 kg LPG cylinders. The tenders are for the supply of 14.2 kg LPG cylinders. The parties parallelly increased their quotation for procurement of the tenders, and HPCL suffered losses by placing orders at a higher

86. *Surendra Prasad order*, para. 89.
87. *People's All India Anti-Corruption and Crime Prevention Society v. Usha International Ltd.*, Case No. 90 of 2016, paras 19, 32, 33.
88. *LPG-II* case, paras 42, 43. The NCLAT upheld the order passes by the CCI by holding that the identical behaviours of the parties were a result of collusion.

rate. The CCI could not establish the violation of section 3(3)(d) for Tender No. 1. However, for Tender No. 2, sixty-six bidders were investigated and held liable for the contravention of section 3(3)(d) read with section 3(1) by manipulating the bidding process. Apart from certain bidders, fifty-one bidders were found to have indulged in bid suppression by withdrawing their bids from Tender No. 2.

However, the CCI in *Surendra Prasad order* failed to consider the procurement authority's consistent erring practice prevailing in the past to understand the involvement of the procurement authority in the manipulation of the bidding process. On 3 March 2005, MAHAGENCO had invited tenders for coal liaisoning. The four participants of the bidding process were B.S.N. Joshi & Sons Ltd. and all three opposite parties. B.S.N. Joshi was the L1 bidder, but MAHAGENCO did not award the contract to B.S.N. Joshi due to an ongoing litigation before the Bombay High Court (Nagpur Bench). B.S.N. Joshi appealed before the Supreme Court and the MAHAGENCO was ordered to consider the offer of B.S.N. Joshi. The order of the Supreme Court was disobeyed by MAHAGENCO. So, again, B.S.N. Joshi went to the Supreme Court to file a contempt petition against MAHAGENCO. In the contempt petition. In the contempt petition, the Supreme Court acknowledged that MAHAGENCO is favouring the cartelization among opposite parties 2 to 4[89] and said that:

> 17. We are distressed to see that MAHAGENCO had been encouraging the formation of a cartel and, thus, allowing the rate of transportation of coal to go high up. Unless a power generating company takes all measures to cut down such malpractices, the generation cost of electricity is bound to go higher and ultimately the same would be passed on to the consumers of electricity. We hope a public sector undertaking would take adequate and appropriate measures to meet the said contingency in future.

Then, MAHAGENCO rectified its conduct by awarding the contract to B.S.N. Joshi on 3 January 2009. However, on 12 September 2009, the contract was terminated by MAHAGENCO. After the termination, MAHAGENCO again awarded the contract to opposite parties 2 to 4. Moreover, since September 2009, MAHAGENCO has floated four tenders, but all four tenders were cancelled for various reasons. Due to cancellations, opposite parties 2-4 continued liaisoning coal to MAHAGENCO. The opposite parties 2-4 benefitted from this shot-gap arrangement.

Mr Surendra Prasad filed information under section 19(1) of the Competition Act. The informant alleged that MAHAGENCO was facilitating the formation of cartelization between opposite parties 2 to 4. The CCI, with a 5:1 majority, passed a section 26(2) order.[90] Then, the informant appealed before the erstwhile COMPAT and got a

89. *B.S.N. Joshi & Sons Ltd. v. Ajoy Mehta & Anr.* [2008], (SC) Contempt Petition 245 of 2007, para. 17.

90. *Surendra Prasad order*, Case No 61 of 2013. Justice (retire) S.N. Dhingra gave a dissenting order. Justice (retire) S.N. Dhingra held that there is a prima facie violation of section 3(3)(d) by opposite parties 2, 3 & 4. The procurement authority is facilitating the cartelization for bid rigging. Further, the procurement authority along with opposite parties 2 to 4 are violating section 3(4)(d). Also, the procurement authority abused its dominant position under section 4(2)(c).

favouring order.[91] The erstwhile COMPAT noted the observation of the Supreme Court and directed the DG to conduct an investigation, but in the said order, the DG was directed not to investigate the MAHAGENCO as it was a part of the cartel.

So, in the *Surendra Prasad order*, MAHAGENCO was not investigated, and it was held that:

> No doubt, the purport of the order of the Hon'ble Appellate Tribunal was to caution the DG not to proceed against MAHAGENCO upon the premise that it was part of the cartel. Hence, the DG, upon investigation, did not deem it appropriate to proceed against MAHAGENCO presumably because a cartel can be formed only by players who are engaged in the similar activities. In these circumstances, nothing would have turned up by even investigating MAHAGENCO in the present matter when the allegations of cartelisation could have been analyzed only against the bidders under the scheme of the Act as provided under Section 3(3) read with Section 3(1) of the Act.

Further, the Supreme Court, in the *LPG-I* case,[92] made an observation regarding the importance of examining Public Procurement Authority while investigating a bid rigging matter. The Supreme Court held that:

> we come to the conclusion that the inference drawn by the CCI on the basis of evidence collected by it are duly rebutted by the appellants and the appellants have been able to discharge the onus that shifted upon them on the basis of factors pointed out by the CCI. However, at that stage, CCI failed to carry the matter further by having required and necessary inquiry that as needed in the instant case... We are emphasising here that in such a watertight tender policy of IOCL which gave IOCL full control over the tendering process, it was necessary to summon IOCL. This would have cleared many aspects which are shrouded in mystery and the dust has not been cleared.

It is important to note that previously, the Supreme Court of India had also observed that there is an involvement of the Public Procurement Authority in encouraging and facilitating the bid rigging cartel. As noted above, the CCI in *People's All India Anti-Corruption and Crime Prevention Society v. Usha International Ltd.*[93] could not adjudicate Public Procurement Authority for facilitating the collusion because such conduct does not fall within the domain of current competition law.

With the amendment in competition law, through the Competition (Amendment) Act, 2023, the scope of anti-competitive agreements was widened which gives the power to the CCI to examine the conduct of enterprises which may not be at the same horizontal level but plays a key role is facilitating cartel (akin to hub-and-spoke issues). We can expect that the CCI would enforce competition law by including any facilitator of anti-competitive agreement under section 3(3) of the Competition Act. Hence, this amendment would also check the Public Procurement Authority from facilitating bid rigging under section 3(3)(d) of the Competition Act. This amendment would make the

---

91. *Shri Surendra Prasad v. CCI*, Appeal No. 43 of 2014, paras 26, 29.
92. *LPG-I* case, paras 102, 103. (SC).
93. *People's All India Anti-Corruption and Crime Prevention Society v. Usha International Ltd.*, Case No. 90 of 2016, paras 31, 32.

Act more comprehensive and effective by preventing Public Procurement Authority from escaping liability.

[E] Hub-and-Spoke Cartel

The ambit of section 3(1) of the Competition Act is wider, and it covers other anti-competitive agreements apart from the horizontal and vertical anti-competitive agreements. Moreover, the Competition (Amendment) Act, 2023, broadens the scope of anti-competitive agreements and would help the CCI to enforce competition law by including a party facilitating an anti-competitive horizontal agreement under section 3(3) of the Competition Act. After the said amendment, section 3(3) violation is applicable to those parties who may not be engaged in identical or similar trade. Hence, common agents, distributors and even Public Procurement Authority will now be amenable under violation of section 3 as third parties facilitating the existence of cartel. Though this amendment has not explicitly mentioned the term 'hub-and-spoke,' but the ultimate objective behind this amendment is to deal with such cartels. Previously, the CCI was hindered from enforcing competition law due to the absence of a specific provision for 'hub-and-spoke' cartel.

In the past, the allegations of a hub-and-spoke cartel have been expressly raised before the CCI in the *Fx Enterprise Solutions India Pvt. Ltd. v. Hyundai Motors* ('*Hyundai Motors* case')[94] and later in the *Samir Agrawal v. ANI Technologies Pvt. Ltd. and Others* ('*Cab Aggregators* case').[95] In both orders, the CCI did not find a reason to make a finding on the presence of a hub-and-spoke cartel. In the *Hyundai Motors* case, there is no finding on the existence of a hub-and-spoke cartel, however, in the Samir Agrawal order, the CCI elaborated on the following traditional circumstances for a hub-and-spoke cartel to exist:

(a) the spokes must use a third-party platform (or, the 'hub') to exchange sensitive information, including information on prices which can facilitate price fixing; and
(b) there needs to be a conspiracy to fix prices, which requires the existence of collusion.

The *Cab Aggregators* case[96] reached the Supreme Court, where the Supreme Court also explained the concept of hub-and-spoke arrangement by saying the spokes (i.e., competitors of a relevant market) require the hub (i.e., third-party platform) to facilitate cartelization by exchanging price-sensitive information which can facilitate price fixing. In the *Cab Aggregators* case, it was alleged that cab aggregators like Ola and Uber are facilitating cartelization among taxi drivers. However, the Supreme Court could not find that cab aggregators had a hub-and-spoke arrangement with the drivers.

94. *Fx Enterprise Solutions India Pvt. Ltd. v. Hyundai Motors,* Case Nos 36 and 82 of 2014, para. 7.
95. *Samir Agrawal v. ANI Technologies Pvt. Ltd. and Others,* Case No. 37 of 2018, para. 15. (CCI).
96. *Cab Aggregators* case [2021], (SC) (2021) 3 SCC 136, paras 4, 8. (SC).

§2.10 STRUCTURAL FACTORS AIDING CARTELIZATION

While cartelization can happen in any sector, the CCI has noted that there are certain industries which are more prone to cartelization than other industries due to certain inherent structural factors prevalent in those industries. For instance, there are numerous investigations in the pharmaceutical industry, film and entertainment industry, tyre industry, cement industry, paper industry, etc. Although the CCI has observed that just because such industry characteristics are present, it does not *ipso facto* mean that market participants have indulged in a cartel. In fact, there have been instances where the CCI has noted that although the industry has the structural characteristics that aid cartelization, the market participants have not indulged in cartelization (e.g., the *Tyre* case). However, as a part of economic analysis, the CCI does look at the industry characteristics in all cartel cases.

The CCI has, in its decisions, referred to the following structural factors in an industry which are prone to cartelization.

[A] Highly Concentrated/Oligopolistic Market

The CCI has noted that in an oligopolistic market, it is more likely that each market participant is aware of the other participants' behaviour. In an oligopolistic market, interdependence between firms is an important characteristic which would imply that each firm in such a market considers the likely reactions of other firms while making independent decisions particularly regarding prices and output. Though oligopolistic markets can lead to competitive outcomes, the outcomes may not always be market-driven but rather a result of concerted effort or collusion. Oligopoly markets are infamous for being recognized as the perfect market for cartels to thrive by charging higher prices at a supra-competitive level. The Supreme Court in the *LPG-I* case[97] and the NCLAT in the *LPG-II* case[98] discuss the 'Theory of Oligopolistic Interdependence' by saying that the oligopoly market itself facilitates cartels because the market players are interdependent, they are aware of each other's presence and follow each other's business strategies. Interdependency allows them to collude without any direct or indirect exchange of information, hence, creating a realm of conscious parallelism which lies outside the scope of competition law. In this regard, it is apposite to point out the observations of the CCI in the *Tyre* case:

> In a market which is oligopolistic in nature, it is more likely that each market player is aware of the actions of the other and influences each other's decisions. No doubt, interdependence between firms is an important characteristic of such a market which would mean that each firm in such a market takes into account the likely reactions of other firms while making independent decisions particularly as regards prices and output. Though oligopolistic markets can lead to competitive outcomes, the outcomes may not always be market driven but rather the result of concerted effort or collusion. The interdependence between firms can lead to

97. *LPG-I* case, para. 97. (SC).
98. *LPG-II* case, paras 33, 52. (NCLAT).

> collusion – both implicit as well as explicit. Thus, high concentration may provide a structural reasoning for collusive action resulting in parallelism (price or output), yet it is very important to differentiate between 'rational' conscious parallelism arising out of the interdependence of the firms' strategic choices and parallelism stemming from purely concerted action. Thus, inferring of cartels would require further evidences. Economic theory has demonstrated convincingly that 'conscious parallelism', is not uncommon in homogeneous oligopolistic markets. Competing firms are bound to be conscious of one another's activities in all phases, including marketing and pricing. Aware of such outcomes especially where there is little real difference in product the Commission is of the opinion that it is quite probable that in many such instances, conscious parallelism may be dictated solely by economic necessity. Avoidance of price wars is a common instance where this takes place.

Often, DG and CCI have observed that empirical studies have shown that bid rigging is more likely to occur in a concentrated market where only a small number of companies supply the goods or service and the suppliers are repetitive bidders.[99] Being limited in number, it becomes easier for them to coordinate and reach an agreement. Therefore, in a highly concentrated market, the market participants may engage in parallel behaviour, but the key area of analysis is to differentiate between rational conscious parallelism arising out of the interdependence of the firms' strategic choices and purely concerted action. However, under the garb of an oligopolistic market, an entity cannot justify its identical bidding as a general feature of a highly concentrated market. In case of the *Aluminium Phosphide* case, the Supreme Court rejected the defence of identical bidding in bid rigging cases because bids are quoted by considering the supply and demand of the product.[100] The said ratio of the Supreme Court has been applied by the CCI to reject the defence that identical price quotes for the tenders of sand and coal transportation is not anti-competitive because of the oligopolistic nature of the market. The CCI held that the defence of identical bidding being a general feature of an oligopolistic market cannot be used as a defence in bid rigging cases.[101]

[B] Demand and Supply Conditions

The CCI has noted that significant changes in demand or supply conditions tend to destabilize cartel arrangement (in that case, it was big rigging agreements), but a constant, predictable flow of demand, by way of frequent orders from the consumer, tends to increase the risk of collusion. Further, the CCI noted that if the demand for a product is seasonal and predictable, producers may take strategic decisions and tend to cartelize. However, if the demand for a product itself varies, because of strong substitutes in the market, or unpredictable sale conditions, or unpredictable bids being floated, strategic decisions cannot be taken, and cartelization may become difficult

---

99. *In Re: Shri Shamsher Kataria v. Honda Siel Cars India Ltd. & Others*, Case No. 03 of 2011, paras 14.14.2; *Director General (Supplies and Disposals) v. Puja Enterprises Basti and Others*, Case No. 1 of 2012, para. 5.
100. *Excel Crop* case, para. 49. (SC).
101. *Western Coalfields Limited v. SSV Coal Carriers Private Limited and Others*, Case No. 34 of 2015, paras 52, 58.

owing to the uncertain demand-supply conditions of the product itself.[102] The reason for that is that in an industry which has a stable and predictable flow of demand, the market participants can have an understanding among themselves as to who will 'win' the contract for a particular time and thereafter, if necessary, share the spoils with the other market participants. In a market which has a predictable demand (like in the case of frequent government procurement), the market participants can indulge in bid rigging as well as market sharing so that everyone can win a contract at an inflated rate and not a competitive rate.

[C] Homogeneous Product

The CCI, in various decisions, has noted that when the products or services offered by companies are identical or very similar, it is easier for them to reach an agreement on a common price structure. In the event the demand for the good is inelastic (like cement, LPG, etc.), firms intending to rig bids or engage in other cartel behaviour feel more secure, knowing that the purchaser has few, if any, good alternatives and thus their efforts to raise prices are more likely to be successful. In the *Cement cartel* case,[103] it was noted by the DG that cement has only two to three categories, i.e., Ordinary Portland Cement, Portland Pozzolana Cement and Portland Blast Furnace Slag Cement. This shows that the nature of cement is almost homogenous in nature. Market consisting of homogenous products allows the cement manufacturers to fix the prices at a huge profit margin.

[D] Active Trade Association

A famous quote by Adam Smith, which has even been mentioned in some of the decisions of the CCI, is that: '*People of the same trade seldom meet together, even for merriment and diversion, but the conversion ends in a conspiracy against the public, or some contrivance to raise prices.*'

Sometimes, trade associations or the members of trade associations collude together to form a cartel. In the *Coordination Committee* case,[104] two associations joined together in giving a call of boycott of the competing member. In such cases, the trade association cannot take the defence of the right of trade union to hide their anti-competitive practices under the cloak of the fundamental right of trade union under Article 19 of the Constitution of India, 1950.[105]

However, the mere formation of a trade association is not per se anti-competitive. The provisions of competition law would be applicable when that trade association transgress its legal contours and facilitates collusive or collective decision-making with the intention of fixing price, limiting or controlling the sale or production, or any other

102. *Tyres* case, para. 280.
103. *Cement cartel* case, para. 7(x).
104. *Coordination Committee* case, para. 47.
105. Article 19(1)(c) of the Constitution of India, 1950 guarantees to all the citizen of India the right to form associations and union or cooperative societies.

anti-competitive activities by its members, it violates the provisions of the Competition Act.[106] Trade associations can be used as legitimate forums for members of a business to promote standards, innovation and competition. In fact, trade associations are present in most industries with the primary objective of taking up and discussing industry issues, industry lobbying, resolving disputes between members, etc. The trade associations are forums for building consensus among its members on policy-related issues of the industry and safeguarding the interests of all the stakeholders. The stakeholders of an industry use trade associations as a platform to meet and discuss common issues. The CCI in *National Association of Container Freight Stations v. Trailer Owner Association and Others*[107] says if the member of a trade association uses this platform for legitimate purposes, then it would provide benefits, such as setting common technical standards for products or interfaces; setting the standards for admission to membership of a profession; arranging education and training for those wishing to join the industry; paying for and encouraging research into new techniques or developing a common response to changing government policy. Thus, mere membership or participation in a trade association may not amount to a violation of competition law.

But when the members misuse the facilities provided by a trade association to meet and enter into an anti-competitive agreement, then the members and trade association would fall under the violation of section 3(3) of the Competition Act. Internationally, as well as in India, trade associations remain vulnerable to stepping beyond the limits placed by competition law because, by definition, they involve meetings, discussions and cooperation among various, often virtually all competitors, in a particular line of business. As such, the decisional practice of the CCI would show that the CCI makes a detailed analysis of whether there is an active trade association in the industry concerned, and if yes, what are the roles and responsibilities of such a trade association and identify the nature of communication which happen in such trade association meetings. Trade association has been seen as a plus factor in most cartel cases decided by the CCI. It is apposite to note that even the CCI has realized the anti-competitive risks that may emerge from a trade association meeting and has passed a decision in an entertainment industry matter[108] mandating the concerned trade association to have, in place, a competition compliance manual and undertake effective competition law compliance training for all the office bearers of the trade association. This is an interesting advocacy-based initiative taken by the CCI, especially in the light of improving efficiency in the competition law enforcement.

---

106. *LPG-II* case, para. 46 (CCI); *Cj Darcl Logistics Ltd. v. Dumper and Dumper Truck Union Lime Stone and Another*, Case No. 31 of 2019, para. 35, where the trade association was limiting the transportation services by mandating stakeholders to only avail the services of members of the trade association. Further, rather than competing, all the members of trade association uniformly fixed a higher price for its service.

107. *National Association of Container Freight Stations v. Trailer Owner Association and Others*, Case No. 04 of 2018, para. 76; *Advertising Agencies Guild v. IBF & its Members*, Case No. 35 of 2013, para. 7.

108. *M/s Crown Theatre v. Kerala Film Exhibitors Federation*, Case No. 16 of 2014, para. 9(f).

§2.11 AAEC IN INDIA

As mentioned above, section 3(3) of the Competition Act envisages that once ingredients of section 3(3) are established, i.e., the market participants have entered into an agreement for price fixing, market allocation, limiting production/supply or bid rigging, there is no further need for the CCI to determine whether the factors mentioned in section 19(3) of the Act (described in details below) are met as there is a presumption in the Act that such agreements cause AAEC. The AAEC is presumed because the anti-competitive agreement covered under section 3(3) of the Competition Act is of the most pernicious nature, whereas the anti-competitive agreement mentioned under section 3(4) of the Competition Act must be seen with the factors under section 19(3) of the Competition Act because of they are less pernicious agreements.[109]

Thereafter, the statutory scheme of the Act is that the onus shifts on entities facing charges of a cartel to prove that there are pro-competitive effects of such agreements which outweigh the anti-competitive effects. The entities must rebut the said presumption by showing the positive factors contained in section 19(3)(d) to (f) of the Competition Act with adequate evidence. Once the entities lead adequate evidence, the CCI examines it from the prism of the 'rule of reason' by balancing the factors mentioned in section 19(3) of the Competition Act.[110] In the case of an investigation of an anti-competitive agreement, a balancing test has to be conducted of the pro-competitive effects of the agreement and the anti-competitive effects thereof. The balancing test needs to be done in light of any or all the factors enumerated in section 19(3) of the Competition Act. Clause (a) to (c) of section 19(3) deals with negative factors which restrict the competition in the market because of the anti-competitive effect of the agreement, whereas clause (d) to (f) of section 19(3) deals with positive factors which provides pro-competitive effects, such as, enhancing the efficiency of the distribution process and contributing to consumer welfare.[111] It is for the entities to prove the pro-competitive effects of their arrangement.[112]

It must be said, however, in a case of cartel investigation, once it has been proved that the market participants have engaged in a cartel, it is very difficult to show that such an arrangement has a pro-competitive element. The primary analysis done is whether there is any agreement among the market participants for fixing price, bid rigging or market allocation and if there is any agreement among them, the CCI has imposed orders under section 27 of the Competition Act. It is important to note that the Supreme Court in the *Coordination Committee* case[113] held that cartels have no defence since they are considered to have *ipso facto* AAEC. However, there was a change in trend after the Supreme Court in the *LPG-I* case[114] exonerated the bid rigging cartel because the entities were able to show pro-competitive effects in the market, such as

109. *FICCI v. United Producers and Others*, Case No. 01 of 2009, para. 23.6.
110. *LPG-II* case, paras 104, 105. (CCI).
111. *Cement cartel* case, Case No. 29 of 2010, para. 288.
112. *Vedanta Bio Sciences, Vadodara v. Chemists and Druggists Association of Baroda*, Case No. C-87/2009/DGIR, para. 96.
113. *Coordination Committee* case, para. 9.
114. *LPG-I* case, paras 71, 72, 75, 87, 91-92. (SC).

twelve new entrants in the market. It was found that the market was an oligopsony market with only three oil companies, and the price to determine the supply of cylinders to these oil companies had become an open secret for all market participants. Further, prior to the bidding process, another oil company floated a tender, and the rates of quotation were available publicly. Hence, the previous tender obviously became a guiding factor for bidders in the concerning bidding process. Even if the entities are from different regions having different production costs, they had to quote the same amount and also accept a lesser margin so that they could survive in the market.

The CCI interprets the ratio laid down in the *LPG-I* case to say entities need to rebut the presumption of appreciable adverse effect by showing positive effects under section 19(3)(d)-(f) emanating from the existence of such agreement.[115] However, by looking at previous case laws, where the Appellate Authority or the Supreme Court set aside the CCI order in cartel matter, it is because CCI failed to appreciate the evidence holistically.

Nonetheless, ignorance of the factors under section 19(3) of the Competition Act could be fatal, so it's always better to analyse the factors mentioned under section 19(3). A thorough analysis would lead to a well-reasoned order and would reduce the chances of being challenged and set aside by a higher judiciary body. For example, in *the Coordination Committee* case,[116] even after holding that there was an anti-competitive agreement between the film associations to control and limit the distribution and exhibition of dubbed serials, the CCI also analysed the factors under section 19(3) of the Competition Act. Based on the CCI's observation, the conduct of the film associations acted as an entry barrier to a new content into the market, and the bylaws of the film associations could not show any efficiency in terms of improvement of services or production.

While one of the defences that have been raised before the CCI is that the cartel participants were small and had minimal market share, and hence an agreement among them should not cause any AAEC in India, the CCI has noted that companies involved in a cartel may be having minuscule market shares individually; the CCI, however, is concerned about their ability to collectively affect the competition in the market. The CCI is concerned about the effect their action will have when seen in aggregation to the actions of their co-players in the market.

As such, the CCI, in the *LPG-I* case, *Coordination Committee* case and the *Cement cartel* case, undertook a brief analysis as to whether the agreement entered into between market participants has caused any AAEC in India. Based on the factors mentioned under section 19(3) of the Competition Act, the CCI noted the following:

---

115. *In Re: Cartelisation in the supply of Protective Tubes to Indian Railways*, Suo Motu Case No. 06 of 2020, para. 33. Also, *see Chief Materials Manager, North Western Railway v. Moulded Fibreglass Products*, Reference Case No. 03 of 2018, paras 55, 56.

116. *Coordination Committee* case, para. 48. *See*, CCI order of *Coordination Committee* case, Case No. 16 of 2011, para. 7.2.11.

[A] Creation of Barriers to Dissuade New Entrants/Existing Player to Expand in the Market

In the *Coordination Committee* case,[117] the film association acted in concert to create an entry barrier for the entry of dubbed content in the State of West Bengal. The concerted action of the film association limited the supply of dubbed serials in West Bengal, amounting to a violation of section 3(3)(b) of the Competition Act because the producer, distributor and exhibitor of dubbed serials and films were stopped from telecasting dubbed TV series. In *Maruti & Company v. Karnataka Chemists & Druggists Association & Others*,[118] the chemist and druggist association mandated non-objection certificates (NOC) from the association before the appointment of pharmaceutical stockiest. The CCI noted that seeking NOC amounts to the creation of entry barriers for the stockiest because it hinders the entry or growth of the stockiest in the market and restricts their freedom to do business with persons of their choice.

[B] Foreclosure of Competition by Hindering Entry into the Market

The Supreme Court in the *Coordination Committee* case upheld the observation of the CCI by holding that the film associations were harming the freedom of trade by hindering the entry of dubbed serials into the market. Such restrictive practice forecloses the business opportunities for the entities which were engaged in the production, distribution, and exhibition of dubbed serials.[119] Similarly, in *Mr. G. Krishnamurthy v. Karnataka Film Chamber of Commerce (KFCC) & Others* ('KFCC case'),[120] the KFCC and its members acted in concert to create entry barriers against the screening of dubbed cinemas. The film associations restored to threats and prevented the release of non-Kannada films dubbed in Kannada language, hence creating barriers to entry of new content in the market as well as causing foreclosure of competition.

[C] Accrual of Benefits to Consumers

In the *Cement cartel* case,[121] the CCI noted that the cement manufactures had intentionally acted to reduce production so that the prices could go up. Such concerted action resulted in an increase in cement prices which was detriment to the consumer. Similarly, in the *Coordination Committee* case,[122] it was observed that by restricting the dubbed series in the market, the film associations were depriving the consumers of

117. *Coordination Committee* case, para. 48.
118. *Maruti & Company v. Karnataka Chemists & Druggists Association & Others*, Case No. 71 of 2013, para. 5.36.
119. *Coordination Committee* case, paras 16, 18.
120. *Mr. G. Krishnamurthy v. Karnataka Film Chamber of Commerce (KFCC) and Others*, Case No. 42 of 2017, paras 107, 120. CCI order was upheld by NCLAT in *Karnataka Film Chamber of Commerce KFCC & Anr. v. Competition Commission of India and Ors.* [2018], (NCLAT) Competition Appeal (AT) No. 96 of 2018.
121. *Cement cartel* case, para. 289.
122. *Coordination Committee* case, para. 48. Also, *see* CCI order, Case No. 16 of 2011, para. 5.24.

watching programmes of their choice. Also, in the *KFCC* case,[123] the CCI could not perceive any benefits to consumers under section 19(3)(d) or has resulted in any improvement of production or distribution of goods or services under section 19(3)(e) of the Competition Act by preventing entry of dubbed cinemas. In bidding cases, fair competition in the bidding process would ensure benefit to the consumer, i.e., procurement authority and end consumer. In this regard, the CCI *In Re: Cartelisation in the supply of Protective Tubes to Indian Railways*[124] has noted that bidders cannot be allowed to fix any arbitrary price or limit the quantities. By manipulating the bidding process, the bidders are infringing the right of the procurement authority to make free choices as a consumer and ultimately harming the railway passengers. Furthermore, the CCI in the *People's All India Anti-Corruption and Crime Prevention Society v. Usha International Ltd.*[125] held that collusion to fix the price for the quotation would have an adverse effect on the fair price discovery process and the price paid by the public procurement authority.

[D] Improvements in Production or Distribution or Promotion of Technical, Scientific and Economic Development

The past orders of CCI show that a cartel has never been able to demonstrate the consumer benefits, improvement in product or promotion of innovation or economic development.[126] The previous decisions of CCI show that in cartel cases, there can't be any improvement in the production or distribution of goods or services, as provided under section 19(3)(e) of the Competition Act.[127] The CCI in *Uniglobe Mod Travels (P) Ltd v. Travel Agents Federation of India*[128] found a violation of section 3(3)(b) of the Competition Act by the travel associations for calling for a boycott of the sale of tickets of international airlines, i.e., Singapore Airlines. Both DG and CCI concluded that the boycott called by the associations does not promote the technical, scientific, and economic development of production or distribution of goods or services. In fact, it harmed the consumers because of the reduction in the availability of tickets.

---

123. *KFCC* case, paras 119, 120.
124. *In Re: Cartelisation in the supply of Protective Tubes to Indian Railways*, Suo Motu Case No. 06 of 2020, para. 37.
125. *People's All India Anti-Corruption and Crime Prevention Society v. Usha International Ltd*, Case No. 90 of 2016, para. 97.
126. *In Re: Alleged anti-competitive conduct by various bidders in supply and installation of signages at specified locations of State Bank of India across India*, Suo Motu Case No. 02 of 2020, para. 100; *In Re: Anti-competitive conduct in the paper manufacturing industry*, Suo Motu Case No. 05 of 2016, para. 202; *In Re: Cartelisation by Shipping Lines in the matter of provision of Maritime Motor Vehicle Transport Services to the Original Equipment Manufacturers*, Suo Motu Case No. 10 of 2014, para. 178; *In Re: Cartelisation in Industrial and Automotive Bearings*, Suo Motu Case No. 05 of 2017, para. 25.
127. *KFCC* case, para. 120.
128. *Uniglobe Mod Travels (P) Ltd v. Travel Agents Federation of India*, Case No. 03 of 2009, paras 46.7, 68.9.2. The travel associations appealed before the erstwhile COMPAT, but their appeals were rejected in *Travel Agents Association of India v. Uniglobe Mod Travels Pvt Ltd*, 2013 SCC OnLine Comp AT 101.

Although section 19(3) of the Competition Act provides for certain pro-competitive effects of any agreement which need to be seen, the CCI, in their decisional practice, has never appreciated any such defences in a cartel case. Having said that, the statutory scheme does provide that the market participants can show that the cartel arrangement will not cause an AAEC in India. One of the factors mentioned under section 19(3) of the Competition Act is to see whether the agreement results in accrual of benefits to consumers. Since the approach of the CCI and erstwhile COMPAT has mostly been consumer-driven, a cartel would, in most situations, result in price increases for consumers and hence would be seen as anti-competitive. It remains to be seen, however, in what cases the CCI will agree that a cartel arrangement has pro-competitive effects.

§2.12 TRADE ASSOCIATION

The establishment of a trade association can be for varied objectives such as industry lobbying and standard setting. However, in some cases, trade association can be seen as a conduit for conducting anti-competitive activities. If the trade association acted only as a trade unionist, then the provisions of competition law will not be applicable. However, if the trade association acts as a place to hatch a conspiracy against the competition of the market or uses it as an instrument by the members of the association to assert their collective bargaining over the non-members or the members who are challenging the trade association, then such trade associations would be held liable for violating the provisions of competition law.

The ambit of section 3(3) of the Competition Act is very wide, and it covers any agreement entered into between enterprises or associations of enterprises or persons or associations of persons or between any person and enterprise or practice carried on or 'decision' taken by, any association of enterprises or association of persons, including cartels. Thus, section 3(3) covers anti-competitive decisions taken by companies under the aegis of a trade association. Therefore, the CCI, in their decisional practice, imposes a twofold liability when companies engage in cartel behaviour under the aegis of a trade association: one, a liability on the company/constituent member of the trade association and second, on the trade association itself. For illustration, in the *Cement cartel* case,[129] the CCI imposed a liability on the cement companies as well as the association of cement manufacturers, i.e., CMA. In this regard, it is apposite to note the observations of the CCI, in one of its earlier decisions, in the case of *Uniglobe Mod Travels (P) Ltd v. Travel Agents Federation of India,*[130] wherein it was observed that:

> Trade association and their activities often tend to go beyond the terms of facilitation required by their members and thus attract scrutiny by competition authorities. Experiences in Canada, European Commission etc. has lead competition authorities to examine their activities from the lens of competition policy

129. *Cement cartel* case, paras 284, 292.
130. *Uniglobe Mod Travels (P) Ltd v. Travel Agents Federation of India,* Case No. 03 of 2009, para. 28.

> while dealing with trade association. A decision taken by a trade association which has the purpose of fixing prices, or limiting the output of members, or allocating the market among its members, will be prohibited under Section 3 of the Act as a form of anti-competitive co-ordination [emphasis supplied]. Similarly, the Act prohibits the individual members of a trade association from entering into an agreement or engaging in a concerted practice which limits output or allocates the markets. This will be the case regardless of whether the intention is to restrict competition or not.

Similarly, in case of the entertainment and pharmaceutical industry, it has been noticed that there are anti-competitive decisions taken by the trade association, which must be mandatorily followed by the members. Since section 3(3) of the Competition Act also covers anti-competitive decisions taken by the association of persons, such decisions of the trade associations are also covered under this clause. There have been multiple decisions where the CCI has imposed a penalty on the trade association. For example, in the *Cement cartel* case,[131] the CCI noted that cement companies were interacting using the platform of the CMA, and such interaction gave them an opportunity to determine and fix prices and limit production. The fact that it was being under the instruction of a governmental direction did not absolve them of any liability. The fact that CMA published statistics on production and dispatch of each company (factory-wise) and circulated information among its members; it facilitated the sharing of price, production and dispatch data which in turn made coordination among companies easier. Therefore, it is imperative that the companies who are a part of the trade association are cautious in their dealings with other companies while dealing under the aegis of the trade association. It must be noted, however, that trade association membership alone is not sufficient evidence of collusion or a conspiracy of anti-competitive practices. For considering whether any anti-competitive decisions were taken at the meeting of the trade association, sufficient evidence needs to be adduced to suggest that the trade association's members reached an actual explicit or tacit agreement which has an AAEC in India. Similarly, in the case of *Shri Ghanshyam Das Vij v. M/s Bajaj Corp Limited*[132] ('*Bajaj* case') decided by the CCI, it was noted that section 3(3) of the Competition Act covers not only agreements entered into between enterprises or associations of enterprises but also the practices carried on or decision taken by any association of enterprises engaged in identical or similar trade of goods or provision of services. Thus, all actions and practices of a trade association, including laying down provisions like imposing geographical restrictions on the dealers by the trade association or laying down criteria for carrying out business activities by the association, squarely fall within the ambit of the expression decision taken by an association of enterprises under section 3(3) of the Competition Act.

Few of the examples in the pharmaceutical Industry are worth noting herein wherein the CCI has held that the actions of the concerned trade associations were in violation of section 3(3) of the Competition Act. The CCI has come down heavily on the actions of the various Chemist and Druggist Association as being anti-competitive

131. *Cement cartel* case, para. 286.
132. *Shri Ghanshyam Das Vij v. M/s Bajaj Corp Limited*, Case No. 68 of 2013, paras 52, 53, 64.

under section 3 of the Competition Act. The CCI in *Varca Chemists and Druggists v. Chemists and Druggists Association, Goa,* has broadly held the following kinds of activities by Chemist and Druggist Association[133] to be anti-competitive:

(i) non-appointment of a stockiest or a wholesaler from among the non-members of the respective trade association;
(ii) requirement of an NOC from the association for appointment of a stockiest or wholesaler;
(iii) associations fixing trade margins below which the stockiest were not allowed to sell;
(iv) the distributors/retailers not allowed to give discounts to customers;
(v) compulsory approval from the trade association for the introduction of drugs in the market;
(vi) requirement for routing bids for the supply of drugs to the government and the hospitals through authorized stockiest only.

The CCI has held that the above terms and conditions amounted to restricting the ability of enterprises to supply and sell drugs in the market. Just to delve deep into the various activities of the chemist and druggist association, the CCI observed that members of the various chemist and druggists Associations of the districts/states have been seeking and enforcing fixed trade margins of 20% to retailer and 10% to distributor/stockist, in terms of the various Memorandum of Understanding (MOU) signed between three notable trade associations in the pharmaceutical industry: All India Organization of Chemists and Druggists (AIOCD) and the Organization of Pharmaceutical Producers of India (OPPI) and the Indian Drugs Manufacturers' Association (IDMA). The above fixed margins were possible only if drugs were sold at their respective MRP and the sellers did not indulge in undercutting by way of offering a discount to their customers. Even though the written MOU was rescinded, the practice of the sale of drugs only at MRP so as to ensure fixed trade margins to the retailers and the wholesalers was still being practised. Upon a detailed investigation by the DG, the following were noticed:

[A] Boycott

The minutes of the executive committee meetings of the trade association showed that organizational movements were proposed to be launched against chain stores that indulged in undercutting and home delivery service. It was also proposed that those who are not members of the trade association should not be serviced, and the wholesalers should stop the medicine supply to such a chain store. The minutes of the trade association also revealed that the areas where undercutting was rampant were

133. *Varca Chemists and Druggists v. Chemists and Druggists Association*, Goa MRTPC 127/2009/DGIR4/28, para. 33; *Vedant Bio Sciences v. Chemists and Druggists Association of Baroda* C-87/2009/DGIR, paras 20.26, 20.27; *M/s Sandhya Drug Agency v. ADDA, BDDA, AIOCD, IDMA, OPPI,* Case No. 41 of 2011, para. 24; *Peeveear Medical Agencies v. AIOCD and Janssen* Case No. 30 of 2011, para. 18.

identified, and action was taken against such stores. Also, in *Reliance Agency v. Chemists and Druggists Association of Baroda and Others,*[134] the CCI found an e-mail where the trade association was directing the stockiest from Gujarat not to purchase goods of AIMIL Pharmaceuticals (India) Ltd and calls were being made to boycott AIMIL. The trade association was interfering with the freedom of choice of a distributor of a pharmaceutical company by restricting it from choosing its business partner. Such interference not only disrupts the distribution chain but also results in limiting and controlling the supply of drugs in the market.

[B] No Objection Certificate

It was noticed in *Varca Chemists and Druggists v. Chemists and Druggists Association, Goa*[135] that the trade association mandated that a drug manufacturing company can appoint a stockiest only in consultation with the concerned State/District Chemists & Druggists Association. A NOC must be obtained for the appointment of a stockiest. Furthermore, where there is only one stockiest of the company in the district, the second stockiest can be appointed only in consultation with the concerned State/District Association, and even the second stockiest should be a bona fide member of the associations affiliated with the AIOCD. Upon investigation by the DG, it was observed that production of NOC or 'Letter of Consent/Cooperation' (LOC) from the respective District/State Chemists and Druggists Associations, affiliated to AIOCD, to the pharmaceutical companies by the prospective stockists are *sine qua non* for being appointed as a stockiest/wholesaler/distributor of pharmaceutical companies. The CCI took note of the practice and noted that the conduct of trade association in the matter of grant of NOC attracts the provisions section 3(3)(b) read with section 3(1) of the Competition Act as such actions create restraint on freedom of trade on account of NOC which has the effect of limiting or controlling the market or supply. In *M/s Suman Distributors, Murshidabad v. Bengal Chemists and Druggists Association and Others,*[136] it was clear that Alkem Laboratories Limited ('Alkem') was forcing stockiest to obtain SAI from BCDA before Alkem commenced making supplies of drugs to them. Alkem was in agreement with BCDA by issuing an Offer Letter for Stockiest to prospective stockiest and was indulging in the practice of demanding SAI/Non-Objection Certificate/Approval Letter/Circulation Letter from BCDA before commencing supplies. This constituted an anticompetitive agreement between Alkem and BCDA.

134. *Reliance Agency v. Chemists and Druggists Association of Baroda and Others,* Case No. 97 of 2013, paras 9, 31, 90.
135. *Varca Chemists and Druggists v. Chemists and Druggists Association, Goa,* MRTPC 127/2009/DGIR4/28, para. 27.27.
136. *M/s Suman Distributors, Murshidabad v. Bengal Chemists and Druggists Association and Others,* Case No. 36 of 2015, paras 20.2, 20.3, 21.9, 21.5; *Madhya Pradesh Chemists and Distributors Federation (MPCDF) v. Madhya Pradesh Chemists and Druggist Association (MPCDA) & Others,* Case No. 64 of 2014.

[C] PIS Approval

Upon an investigation by the DG, it was noted in *Varca Chemists and Druggists v. Chemists and Druggists Association, Goa*[137] that product information service (PIS) approval entails payment of prescribed charges for the purpose of publication of the product information in the PIS bulletin, which is published state wise. The PIS bulletin is a part of the magazine published at periodic intervals by the respective state chemists and druggist associations affiliated with AIOCD. The DG observed that pharmaceutical companies have to obtain PIS approval from the respective state chemists and druggists associations affiliated with AIOCD before they can introduce new products in the market. Further, the evidence collected by the DG revealed that the practice of PIS approval from the state chemists & druggist association on payment of the prescribed charges in the name of advertisement in the association bulletin is again a *sine qua non* in the absence of which new products are not allowed to be introduced in the distribution channel. The DG noted that the launch of a new product in the market being made contingent on PIS approval by the concerned association of Chemists & Druggists sometimes results in restraint of trade and leads to denial of market access/controlling of supply/market for any product of a company which can also deprive consumers of the benefits of such drugs. The evidence also revealed many instances where the association of chemists and druggists refused to grant PIS approval on a variety of factors, including asking for charges in excess of the prescribed charges. Based on further investigation, the CCI noted that the action of the trade association in delaying or withholding PIS approval on any ground is in violation of the provisions of section 3(3)(b) of the Competition Act.

[D] Fixing of Trade Margins

The investigation by the DG in *Varca Chemists and Druggists v. Chemists and Druggists Association, Goa*[138] revealed the fact that the trade margins had been decided for the wholesalers and retailers operating in the pharmaceutical market by way of an agreement between the trade and the industry. By way of this agreement, the DG noted that prices of drugs are directly or indirectly getting fixed and are not getting determined by the interplay of market forces. Therefore, it was observed that it implies that the manufacturer while deciding the MRP of the drugs cannot fix the prices without providing for the agreed minimum trade margins for the wholesalers and retailers of the entire Industry. The investigation further revealed that as the minimum trade margins are part of an agreement among the members of the trade and industry, there is hardly any occasion for price competition between one retailer and the other, resulting in drugs being generally sold on the MRP. The DG noted that, since the consumers have no choice, the retailers exploit the situation by not selling the drugs

137. *Varca Chemists and Druggists v. Chemists and Druggists Association, Goa*, MRTPC 127/2009/DGIR4/28), paras 10.2, 27.27, 27.43, 27.44.
138. *Ibid.*, para. 27.37.

below the MRP, wherein the trade margins of 20% on MRP are already built in as per the terms of their agreement. Based on the above, the CCI also observed that the practice of fixing trade margins is in violation of section 3(3)(a) of the Competition Act.

§2.13 JOINT VENTURE DEFENCE

The proviso to section 3(3) of the Competition Act provides for a defence to the joint ventures which increases efficiency in the market. The proviso states that the prohibition under section 3(3) of the Competition Act will not be applicable if the parties of the same level of production chain enter into an agreement by way of the joint venture to increase efficiency in production, supply, distribution, storage, acquisition or control of goods or provision of services.

However, the onus is on the parties to such an agreement, claiming joint venture defence to show such agreement will result in increasing efficiency which will outweigh the anti-competitive effects of such horizontal agreement. If the parties fail to satisfy the CCI that the horizontal agreement increased efficiency, then they can't avail of the protection under the proviso. For instance, in *FICCI Multiplex Association of India, New Delhi v. United Producers/Distributors Forum, Mumbai and Others,*[139] the film producers and distributors entered into a horizontal agreement to fix a high revenue sharing ratio from the multiplexes. The film producers and distributors enforced their unfair demands by refusing to release Hindi Motion Pictures for exhibitions in multiplexes. This resulted in contravention of section 3(3)(a) and (b) of the Competition Act. One of the defences taken by the film producers and distributors was that the horizontal agreement must be viewed in the nature of an efficiency-enhancing joint venture as per the proviso of section 3(3) of the Competition Act. However, rejecting the defence of joint venture, the CCI held that the proviso does not provide a blanket exemption. Further, the parties claiming the defence of joint venture first have to show how the horizontal agreement increased efficiency in the film industry. The CCI furthermore noted that rather than increasing efficiency, the horizontal agreement delayed the release of films and stopped the supply of films to the multiplexes. The CCI expressed an interesting observation against cartels by saying that the parties indulging in horizontal anti-competitive agreement can never increase efficiency in production, distribution, etc., benefit the consumer, or improve the technology. This is an interesting observation from the CCI since the statutory scheme does allow the parties to raise an efficiency defence. It would be really interesting to see in what situation the CCI does entertain the efficiency defence provided in the proviso of section 3(3) of the Act.

139. *FICCI Multiplex Association of India, New Delhi v. United Producers/Distributors Forum, Mumbai and Others,* Case No. 1 of 2009, paras 23.35-23.38, 23.52, 23.54. An appeal was filed before the erstwhile COMPAT, but it was dismissed. However, the defence of joint venture was not discussed before COMPAT. *See, Nandu Ahuja and Others v. CCI and Others* [2014], (COMPAT) Appeal No. 01 of 2012.

However, the CCI changed its stance in *Shri Yogesh Ganeshlaji Somani v. ZEE Turner Ltd. and Another,*[140] where the information was filed against two distributors of TV channels for entering into a joint venture and contravention of section 3(3)(a) and (b) of the Competition Act was alleged. The informant argued that the joint venture would not bring efficiency but cause anti-competitive effect on the market and deprive the consumers of the prices for the channels at competitive rates. But, after investigation, it was found that the objective clause of the joint venture agreement clearly shows that it would increase efficiency in the market by optimum utilization of resources and cost reduction, promote digitization and addressability, and curb piracy of TV channel signals. The CCI found no evidence to establish the violation of section 3(3)(a) and (b) of the Competition Act; hence, the joint venture had not resulted in fixing the price or limiting the production of TV channels. Similarly, in *Association of Third Party Administrators v. General Insurers' (Public Sector) Association of India and Others,*[141] information was filed against four insurance companies for entering into an anti-competitive agreement and collectively abusing their dominant position. These four insurance companies were set up as a joint venture company. Regarding the issue of whether the formation of the joint venture caused anti-competitive effect on the competition of the health insurance market, it was held that the joint venture brought efficiency enhancement in the insurance sector. The evidence collected with regard to the conduct of the insurance companies showed that there was no attempt to fix the prices or to restrict the supply of services in the market of health insurance. Furthermore, the decision to form a joint venture was found to be a commercial decision to bring efficiency by improving the level of service. In terms of services, the joint venture would ensure speedy cashless hospitalization for the end customers, cost-efficient services to the insurance companies and timely reimbursements for the hospitals. Thereafter, factors under section 19(3) were analysed, and it was held that the joint venture would bring pro-competitive efficiency to the market, and consumers would benefit because the quality and efficiency of service would improve.

It can be concluded that if parties to the horizontal agreement want to avail the defence of joint venture, then the objective of their joint venture agreement needs to align with the pro-competitive factors of section 19(3)(d)-(f) of the Competition Act. This would help them establish that the joint venture would generate efficiency in the market; hence, it falls outside the purview of section 3(3) of the Competition Act.

§2.14 LENIENCY REGIME

As discussed in the earlier parts of this chapter, it is very hard to detect cartels. For this reason, the leniency regime was introduced under the Competition Act, which acts as an incentive for the enterprise to come clean to the CCI by admitting their guilt for being

140. *Shri Yogesh Ganeshlaji Somani v. ZEE Turner Ltd. and Another,* Case No. 31 of 2011, paras 3.11, 3.12, 10, 12, 14.
141. *Association of Third Party Administrators v. General Insurers' (Public Sector) Association of India and Others,* Case No. 107 of 2013, paras 64, 67, 75, 78-81.

involved in cartelization.[142] Under section 46 of the Competition Act, the CCI is empowered to grant a reduction in the penalty of the enterprise in exchange for reporting a cartel and active cooperation during the investigation. Thus, leniency has been created as a tool to collect evidence which would help the CCI detect cartels.

[A] Legal Framework for Leniency Application

Section 46(1) of the Competition Act allows an enterprise to file a lesser penalty application by providing full and true disclosure of the cartel activity which would be considered vital disclosure with respect to its participation in a cartel. In the lesser penalty application, the applicant must provide all relevant information, documents and evidence which would help the CCI pass a prima facie order or final order. Apart from providing vital disclosure, the enterprise must offer complete and active cooperation during the investigation and inquiry process. The CCI will not grant lesser penalty after the DG completes its investigation and forwards a copy of its investigation report to the CCI.

Later, in 2023, the Competition Act was amended to allow the applicant to withdraw its application. This amendment also added sub-section (4) of section 46 of the Competition Act, which speaks about 'lesser penalty plus' regime. The objective behind introducing lesser penalty plus regime it to attract more vital disclosures regarding the cartels in the market by incentivizing a lesser penalty applicant to give vital disclosures about another cartel which is unknown to the CCI. For providing vital disclosures on the existence of another cartel, the applicant will not only get immunity for its participation in the other cartel but also an additional reduction (up to 30%) in its penalty for its participation in the cartel for which it had filed lesser penalty application.

The applicant must file the lesser penalty plus application before the DG completes its investigation on the cartel for which the applicant filed lesser penalty application and also before CCI forms a prima facie view regarding the other second (the +) cartel. The CCI has prescribed the process under section 46 of the Competition Act in the CCI (Lesser Penalty) Regulations, 2009 ('Lesser Penalty Regulations'). The Lesser Penalty Regulations govern the procedure and extent to which reduction of penalties could be granted by the CCI to lesser penalty/lesser penalty plus applicant.

[B] Process of Filing Lesser Penalty/Lesser Penalty Plus Application

The benefit of leniency will be granted to those applicants who have filed the lesser penalty application prior to the DG submitting its investigation report. The lesser penalty application must contain all material information as per Schedule I of the Lesser Penalty Regulations. After receiving the lesser penalty application, the CCI will record the date and time of receiving and mark the priority status of the applicant.

142. *Pawan Jagetia and Others v. Competition Commission of India and Others* [2022], (NCLAT), Competition Appeal (AT) No. 16 of 2021, para. 33.

Thereafter, the CCI will evaluate the lesser penalty application. Till the time the evaluation of an applicant is concluded, the lesser penalty application of the next applicant will not be considered. If CCI rejects the lesser penalty application of the first applicant, then the next applicant shall move up in order of priority for grant of priority status.

Along with a lesser penalty application, the applicant may further reduce its penalty by making vital disclosure about another cartel. In order to avail the benefit of up to 30% reduction (in addition to the reduction granted for the lesser penalty application), the lesser penalty applicant has to file a lesser penalty plus application containing all the information as specified in Schedule II of the Lesser Penalty Regulation. The lesser penalty plus application must be filed prior to the submission of DG's report regarding the first cartel (for which lesser penalty application was filed) and before CCI passes a prima facie order against the second (the +) cartel (for which lesser penalty plus application has been filed).

The CCI can reject a lesser penalty/lesser penalty plus application if the applicant fails to comply with the conditions to vital disclosure of the information as referred to and described in Schedule I or Schedule II of the Lesser Penalty Regulations, then the CCI may reject the application. Also, if the applicant, who had not filed the written application as per Schedule I or II while submitting material information to CCI, fails to file the application in the format of Schedule I or II within fifteen days, the applicant forfeits its claim for the benefit of grant of lesser penalty/lesser penalty plus. In addition to these two conditions for dismissing an application, Regulation 11 of the Lesser Penalty Regulations provides three more conditions for forfeiture of the benefit under the leniency regime. Regulation 11 says if the CCI finds that the applicant has failed to:

(i) comply with the conditions on which the benefit of lesser penalty was granted;
(ii) adduced false evidence or failed to submit any material information knowing it to be material; or
(iii) the disclosure made is not vital.

For any of these abovementioned conditions, a lesser penalty/lesser penalty plus application can be dismissed, and the applicant will not be immune to the monetary penalty imposed under section 27 of the Competition Act. Hence, the lesser penalty/lesser penalty plus application made to the CCI must be extremely granular so that they can protect their priority status and also make vital disclosure to ensure that the grant of the reduction in monetary penalty.

[C] Priority Status of the Lesser Penalty Applicant and Lesser Penalty Plus Applicant

The Lesser Penalty Regulations provide that only after receiving an application in the format of Schedule I or II can the CCI mark the applicant's priority status. Hence, an applicant should file an application for lesser penalty/lesser penalty plus containing all material information as specified in Schedule I or Schedule II to the CCI for furnishing the vital disclosures relating to the existence of the cartel. On the receipt of the application, the CCI shall there upon mark the priority status of the applicant which will be intimated to the applicant.

And thereafter, the CCI determines priority status by looking at when the application was filed, the evidence in possession of the CCI during the stage when the lesser penalty/lesser penalty plus application was filed, whether the evidence provided through that application significantly added value to the investigation/inquiry, fulfilment of the essential conditions given in Regulation 3 of the Lesser Penalty Regulations, and the entire factual scenario of the case.

Depending upon the priority status, the CCI grants the leniency and decides the quantum of reduction. Further, the same priority status will also be applicable to the office-in-charge of the applicant because the CCI allows the same quantum of reduction in penalty under section 48 of the Competition Act.

A diagrammatic illustration of priority status for the reduction of penalty is as follows:

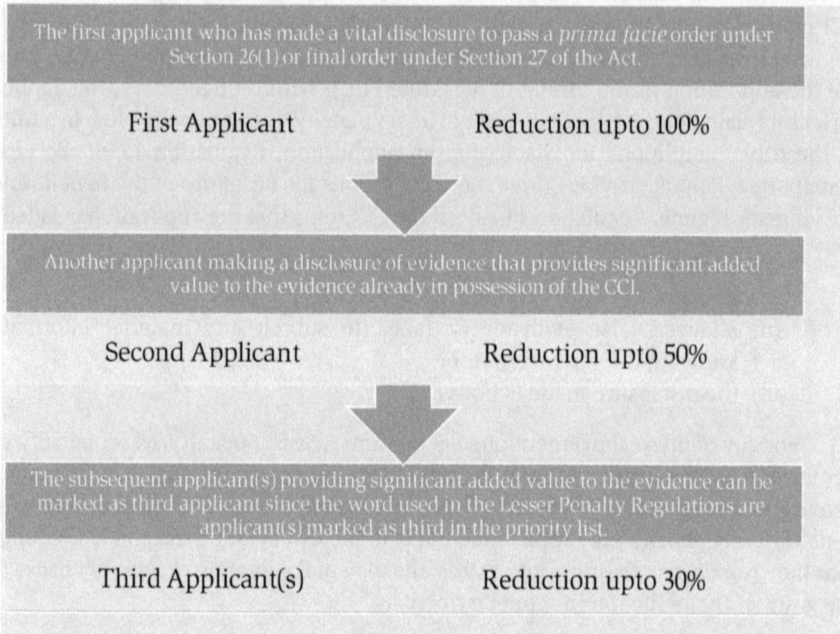

For the first lesser penalty applicant, the CCI can grant up to a 100% reduction of penalty. To get a 100% reduction, the applicant must be the first to make a vital disclosure by submitting evidence which would help the CCI to pass an order under section 26(1) of the Competition Act or make a vital disclosure at an early stage of the investigation to help CCI in finding the contravention of the Competition Act. Further, the applicant must actively cooperate in the investigation and inquiry.

The second lesser penalty applicant can also benefit from a reduction in penalty of up to or equal to 50% upon making a disclosure of evidence that provides significant added value to the evidence already in possession of the DG/CCI. After the second applicant, there can be more than one applicant which can be marked as third lesser penalty applicant since the word used in the Lesser Penalty Regulations is applicant(s) marked as third in the priority list. The third lesser penalty applicant(s) may be granted a reduction of penalty up to 30% of the full penalty leviable. Along with providing significant added value, the applicant must cooperate during the investigation and help CCI establish the complete trail of anti-competitive conduct.

Further, if the lesser penalty applicant makes vital disclosure of a second cartel unknown to the CCI, then the CCI may grant an additional reduction in penalty up to 30% of the penalty imposed with regard to lesser penalty plus application.

[D] Evaluation of Lesser Penalty/Lesser Penalty Plus Application

[1] Vital Disclosure to Establish the Cartel

Moreover, the applicant who files a lesser penalty/lesser penalty plus application must make vital disclosure by submitting all the evidence that would materially contribute to passing a prima facie view or establishing the existence of the cartel.[143] Vital disclosure has been defined under Regulation 2(j) of the Lesser Penalty Regulations as full and true disclosure of information by the applicant to the CCI, which would satisfy the CCI in forming a prima facie view about the existence of a cartel under section 3 of the Competition Act. The ambit of vital disclosure is extremely specific, and it should assist the CCI in forming a prima facie view that there exists a cartel; based on such disclosure provided by the applicant, the CCI will direct the offices of the DG to investigate the matter.

Therefore, the lesser penalty/lesser penalty plus application to the CCI has to be extremely specific and granular, seeking leniency under the Lesser Penalty Regulations, and such application must contain all material information and evidence relating to the establishment or existence of a cartel.[144] Further, the applicant must be very

143. The CCI can also use its inherent power to grant lesser penalty even without a leniency application. *M/s. Federation of Gujarat State Chemists & Druggists Associations and Others*, Case Nos 65, 71, 72 of 2014 & 68 of 2015, paras 190, 191. The CCI remitted 40% penalty amount on Hetero Healthcare Ltd. even without a leniency application. The CCI considered the mitigating factors such as the admission of the Hetero Healthcare Ltd. regarding the violation of the Competition Act and active cooperation with CCI during inquiry.

144. However, admission of presence of cartel through leniency application does not always lead to finding on violation of section 3 of the Competition Act. *In Re: Alleged Cartelisation in Flashlights Market in India*, Suo Motu Case No. 01 of 2017, paras 99, 100, 101, leniency application was filed by Eveready revealing instances of exchange of commercially sensitive information between competitors through the Association. Subsequently, Panasonic also filed an application disclosing information exchange between competitors in the flashlights market. Based on which investigation was also carried out by the DG, however it was found that emails were exchanged to monitor the market of flashlight but could not establish the presence of cartelization under section 3 of the Competition Act.

careful before filing such an application because the CCI and DG can still use the evidence from the application even after the applicant withdraws it.

[2] Other Conditions to Evaluate a Lesser Penalty/Lesser Penalty Plus Application

Furthermore, the applicant must actively cooperate with the CCI till the completion of the inquiry. If the applicant fails to comply with the condition on which the lesser penalty/lesser penalty plus was granted, or provides false evidence in its application, or provides evidence which is not vital, then the CCI will not lessen the penalty amount. The Regulation 3 of the Lesser Penalty Regulations stipulate the following essential conditions that the CCI must take into account before reducing the penalties:

(i) The applicant should not have any further participation in the cartel after filing lesser penalty/lesser penalty plus application, unless CCI directs otherwise.
(ii) The information provided should be a 'vital disclosure', as mentioned under Regulation 2(j) of the Lesser Penalty Regulations.
(iii) The applicant should cooperate to the best of its ability with the CCI, *inter alia*, by providing all relevant information, documents and evidence as required.
(iv) The applicant should cooperate genuinely, fully, continuously and expeditiously throughout the investigation and other proceedings before the CCI.
(v) Relevant evidence should not be concealed, destroyed, manipulated or removed by the applicant.
(vi) Names of all the office bearers of the enterprise which is involved in cartelization shall be provided by the applicant.

[E] Trend of CCI in Adjudicating Lesser Penalty Applications

While the lesser penalty plus can be granted to only one applicant, the CCI can grant lesser penalty to more than one applicant. Provided that such information in the lesser penalty application significantly adds value and helps the DG/CCI reach a conclusion about the existence of a cartel. The term 'significant added value' has been defined as the extent to which the evidence provided enhances the ability of the DG/CCI to establish the existence of a cartel under section 3 of the Competition Act. In this regard, the applicant(s) generally contends that the investigation report of the DG has remained incomplete, and the disclosure via application added value to the investigation/inquiry.[145] In *Nagrik Chetna Manch v. Fortified Security Solutions and Others*,[146] the CCI granted 50% leniency to the first applicant for making a good value addition to the ongoing investigation, and its evidence provided a clearer picture of the

145. *Nagrik Chetna Manch v. Fortified Security Solutions and Others*, Case No. 50 of 2015, para. 77.
146. Case No. 50 of 2015, paras 104 and 105.

modus operandi of the cartel. But, the first applicant did not get 100% leniency because he did not file the application before CCI formed its prima facie view or at the very beginning of the investigation.

It is to be noted that the imposition of penalty is discretionary under the provisions of the Competition Act and the Lesser Penalty Regulations. The discretion of the CCI in regard to reduction in monetary penalty will be exercised with due regard to the stage at which the lesser penalty applicant comes forward with the disclosure, the evidence already in possession of the DG/CCI, the quality of the information provided by the applicant and the entire facts and circumstances of the case. *In Re: Cartelization in respect of tenders floated by Indian Railways for supply of Brushless DC Fans and other electrical items,*[147] was the order where CCI for the first time granted leniency, and in this order, the CCI granted leniency by reducing 75% in the monetary penalty. Thought the applicant disclosed vital information relating to the existence of the cartel; however, 100% leniency was not granted because the application was not made at an early stage of the investigation. When the application was submitted, the CCI already had e-mail exchanges which satisfied it to direct an investigation for cartelization in tenders for the Indian Railway's Brushless DC Fans.

While dealing with a leniency application, the CCI considers a few factors, as mentioned in Regulation 3 of the Lesser Penalty Regulations. Taking into account all these factors, the CCI decided to grant 100% leniency to Panasonic Energy, *In Re: Cartelisation in respect of zinc carbon dry cell batteries market in India.*[148] The CCI noted that the evidence and cooperation provided by Panasonic Energy were crucial to initiate the investigation and helped during the investigation to seize direct evidence, such as email exchanges, handwritten notes, and other documents. However, the CCI decided to grant a 30% lesser penalty to Eveready Industries and a 20% lesser penalty to Indo National. Though the leniency application provided by Eveready Industries and Indo National actively cooperated during the investigation, however, their applications could not provide any 'significant value addition' because almost all evidence was already available with the CCI.

Let's see how the CCI has exercised its powers under section 46 read with the Lesser Penalty Regulations. The orders where the CCI has granted leniency to the cartel members have been tabulated below:

147. *In Re: Cartelization in respect of tenders floated by Indian Railways for supply of Brushless DC Fans and other electrical items,* Suo Motu Case No. 03 of 2014, paras 7.7, 7.8, 7.10, 7.11.
148. *In Re: Cartelisation in respect of zinc carbon dry cell batteries market in India,* Suo Motu Case No. 02 of 2016, paras 10.2, 10.3, 10.4.

Sl. No.	Case (Citation)	Priority Status	Vital Disclosure	Lesser Penalty (%)
1.	*Cartelization in tenders for the supply of Brushless DC Fans.* Suo Motu Case No. 03 of 2014. (18.01.2017)	*1st: Pyramid Electronics* Application was filed after CCI directed the DG to start investigation.	The details submitted by the applicant helped the CCI to connect the dots to reveal the matching of prices among the bidders.	75%
2.	*Cartelisation in zinc carbon dry cell batteries market.* Suo Motu Case No. 02 of 2016. (19.04.2018)	*1st: Panasonic* The CCI directed the DG to start an investigation based on the application of Panasonic. Further, the application also helped to establish the presence of cartel.	Cartelization to control the price and limit the production of zinc-carbon dry cell batteries was proved due to the leniency application.	100%
		2nd: Eveready Application was filed after three days of initiating investigation.	Provided active cooperation during investigation.	30%
		3rd: Indo National Application was filed after three weeks of initiating investigation.	Provided active cooperation during investigation.	20%
3.	*Nagrik Chetna Manch v. Fortified Security Solutions and Others.* Case No. 50 of 2015 (01.05.2018)	*1st: Mahalaxmi Steels* Application was filed after investigation was initiated.	First to admit the existence of cartel and cooperated during investigation and inquiry.	50%
		2nd: Sanjay Agency Application was filed after investigation was initiated.	Disclosed roles of other persons and provided copies of email exchanges.	40%

Sl. No.	*Case (Citation)*	*Priority Status*	*Vital Disclosure*	*Lesser Penalty (%)*
		3rd: Lahs Green Application was filed after investigation was initiated.	Copies of email exchanges and active cooperation during investigation and inquiry.	50%[149]
		4th: Ecoman Enviro Solutions Application was filed after investigation was initiated.	Admitted the presence of cartel and co-operated throughout the investigation and inquiry.	25%
4.	*Cartelisation by broadcasting service providers by rigging the bids submitted in tenders floated by Sports Broadcasters.* Suo Motu Case No. 02 of 2013. (11.07.2018)	*1st: Globecast* Application enabled to form prima facie opinion to pass an order directing DG to investigate.	Submitted vital evidence, such as the details of sporting events in which bid rigging took place, the role of ex-employees, email exchanges for sharing commercially sensitive information, etc. Also, cooperated during investigation.	100%
		2nd: ESCL Filed application after receiving notice from the DG.	Provided corroborative evidence and additional evidence to the ongoing investigation.	30%

149. *Nagrik Chetna Manch v. Fortified Security Solutions and Others*, Case No. 50 of 2015, para. 119. The quantum of reduction of penalty is more for Lahs Green, than Sanjay Agency. It is because, though Lahs Green was marked as 3rd in the priority status in the case, but Lahs Green got 1st priority status with respect to disclosure of a different tender for the first time.

Sl. No.	Case (Citation)	Priority Status	Vital Disclosure	Lesser Penalty (%)
5.	*Anticompetitive conduct in the Dry-Cell Batteries Market in India*. Suo Motu Case No. 02 of 2017. (30.08.2018)	*1st: Panasonic* Pursuant to the application of Panasonic, the CCI was able to form prima facie opinion and directed the DG to investigate.	Provided vital evidence, such as Product Supply Agreement and email exchanges which helped to disclose the modus operandi of the Cartel. Also, the applicant actively cooperated during investigation.	100%
6.	*Anticompetitive conduct in the Dry-Cell Batteries Market in India*. Suo Motu Case No. 03 of 2017. (15.01.019)	*1st: Panasonic* The Application helped the CCI to pass an order to initiate investigation.	Provided vital evidence to form prima facie opinion and contravention of section 3, and the applicant actively cooperated during investigation.	100%
7.	*Cartelisation in the supply of Electric Power Steering Systems*. Suo Motu Case No. 07 (01) of 2014. (09.08.2019)	*1st: NSK Limited* Based on the application, the CCI initiated investigation.	NSK provided vital disclosures by submitting evidence of the cartel.	100%
		2nd: JTEKT Corporation The application was filed during pendency of investigation.	JTEKT provided significant added value to the evidence already in possession of the CCI and actively cooperated with the investigation and inquiry.	50%

Sl. No.	*Case (Citation)*	*Priority Status*	*Vital Disclosure*	*Lesser Penalty (%)*
8.	*In Re: Alleged anti-competitive conduct in the Beer Market in India.* Suo Motu Case No. 06 of 2017.[150] (24.09.2021)	*1st: SABMiller India Limited* Based on the application, the CCI initiated investigation.	When SABMiller India Limited filed, the CCI and DG had no evidence. The application explained the nature and *modus operandi* of the beer cartel and explained the market structure of the Beer industry. Further, active cooperation helped during the investigation and inquiry.	100%
		2nd: United Breweries Limited The application was filed during pendency of investigation. However, the application was filed before the dawn raid took place.	The United Breweries Limited provided additional evidence on coordination in respect of premium institutions in Bengaluru, Karnataka and with respect to the purchase of old/used bottles. Further, OP1 helped DG and CCI in mapping price parallelism.	40%
		3rd: Carlsberg Application filed during the investigation and after the DG conducted the search and seizure operations.	Carlsberg helped in forming the complete trail of anti-competitive conduct of the beer cartel.	20%

150. Also, it is important to note that, in *Pawan Jagetia and Others v. CCI and Others* [2022], (NCLAT) Competition Appeal (AT) No. 16 of 2021. paras 33-37, NCLAT held that once the

Sl. No.	*Case (Citation)*	*Priority Status*	*Vital Disclosure*	*Lesser Penalty (%)*
9.	*Anti-competitive conduct in the paper manufacturing industry*. Suo Motu Case No. 05 of 2016. (17.11.2021)	*1st: Trident Limited* Application filed during the investigation.	Admitted that the applicant had formed a cartel and supported with vital disclosure. The applicant also actively cooperated during the investigation.	100%
10.	*Cartelisation by Shipping Lines in the matter of provision of Maritime Motor Vehicle Transport Services*. Suo Motu Case No. 10 of 2014. (20.01.2022)	*1st: Nippon* Based on the application, the CCI initiated investigation.	Full and true disclosures and continuous cooperation provided by Nippon enabled the CCI to order an investigation but helped establish contravention.	100%
		2nd: Mitsui Joint application[151] was filed after the commencement of investigation.	Application added value and the applicant cooperated during investigation.	50%
		3rd: Nissan Motors Joint application was filed after the commencement of investigation.	Application added value and the applicant cooperated during investigation.	30%

applicant files an application under section 46 of the Act, and lesser penalty or lesser penalty plus is granted, then the applicant cannot contest on the merit of the case.

151. *In Re: Cartelisation by Shipping Lines in the matter of provision of Maritime Motor Vehicle Transport Services*, Suo Motu Case No 10 of 2014, para. 230, the parties have not been able to show any provision in the Competition Act or the Regulations which enable the parties to file joint lesser penalty application.

Sl. No.	*Case (Citation)*	*Priority Status*	*Vital Disclosure*	*Lesser Penalty (%)*
11.	*Chief Materials Manager, North Western Railway v. Moulded Fibreglass Products and Others*. Case No. 03 of 2018. (04.04.2022)	*1st: Black Burn* Joint application was filed after the commencement of investigation.	Made full and true disclosures of information and continuous co-operation during investigation.	80%
		2nd: Moulded Fibreglass Joint application was filed after the commencement of investigation.	Could not provide much additional value but made full disclosures and continuously co-operated during investigation.	40%
		3rd: Jai Polypan Joint application was filed after the commencement of investigation.	Provided value addition which was used by the CCI to form a complete trail evidencing anti-competitive conduct.	30%
		4th: Quadrant EPP Joint application was filed after the commencement of investigation.	Provided value addition which was used by the CCI to form a complete trail evidencing anti-competitive conduct.	20%
12.	*Cartelisation in the supply of Protective Tubes to Indian Railways*. Suo Motu Case No. 06 of 2020. (09.06.2022)	*1st: Jai Polypan* Based on the application, the CCI initiated investigation.	Prima facie order for investigation was passed due to the application. Further, full and true disclosures of evidence and continuous cooperation helped the CCI establish the cartel.	100%

The essential factors under Regulation 3 of the Lesser Penalty Regulations, based on which CCI exercise its discretionary power to allow a lesser penalty application, vary on a case-by-case basis. Consequently, the reduction of monetary penalty also varies; thus, the trend of CCI in relation to adjudication of the lesser penalty application is not consistent. Therefore, as noted above, the key thing in any application is that such application must be extremely granular with all relevant details so that the CCI can take help from such evidence to establish a contravention under section 3 of the Competition Act. In addition to providing evidence which was not in possession by the offices of DG/CCI or which the previous applicant did not give, the applicant must actively cooperate with the DG/CCI during the investigation or inquiry proceeding.

Importantly, any information and document submitted under the Lesser Penalty Regulations are treated as confidential (including in respect of the identity of the applicant) unless such information is already in the public domain or is required to be disclosed by law. Further, the application made under the Lesser Penalty Regulations is kept confidential, so there is no chance for the future applicant to know that the contents of the information are already available to the authorities. It can be a tricky situation if a lesser penalty/lesser penalty plus application is made without any vital or added disclosure since the applicant has already confessed to being involved in a cartel and may not still get any immunity. Similarly, an applicant can withdraw its lesser penalty/lesser penalty plus application, but under Regulation 10, the DG/CCI will be at liberty to use the evidence submitted by the applicant except for its admission.

Finally, it is to be noted that under the statutory scheme of the Competition Act, the CCI, in its discretion, can grant lesser penalty/lesser penalty plus. However, the risk of such an applicant being sued for compensation under section 53 of the Competition Act is not taken away.

§2.15 LEGAL FRAMEWORK FOR VERTICAL AGREEMENT

Vertical agreement means the agreement/arrangement/understanding between enterprises that are at different stages or levels of the production chain and, therefore, in different markets. Section 3(4) of the Competition Act enlists a non-exhaustive list of vertical agreements which would be treated as void agreements if they cause or are likely to cause AAEC.[152] Unlike certain kinds of horizontal anti-competitive agreements (i.e., cartel arrangements discussed *supra*), vertical agreements are not pre-se anti-competitive, and the CCI assess these vertical agreements under the rule of reason analysis. The concept of rule of reason stated that the vertical agreement would fall foul of section 3(4) of the Competition Act only if such agreement has caused or has the

152. *Federation of Hotel & Restaurant Associations of India (FHRAI) and Others v. MakeMyTrip India Pvt. Ltd. (MMT) and Others*, Case No. 14 of 2019 and Case No. 01 of 2020, para. 291. Also, *see M/s ESYS Information Technologies Pvt. Ltd. v. Intel Corporation (Intel Inc.) & Ors.*, Case No. 48 of 2011, paras 8.3.3, 8.3.6.

potential to cause AAEC as per the factors laid down in section 19(3) of the Competition Act.[153]

For assessing vertical anti-competitive agreements, the rule of reason is applicable because such agreements are concluded between entities operating at different stages of the production chain and are not between competitors of the same market. So, for the operation of business, these entities enter into several commercial agreements, many of which enhance efficiency with sound economic justification. As these entities are not competitors, their incentives are generally aligned with that for the benefit of the customers. Hence, such vertical agreements may not necessarily cause AAEC of the market, and treating such vertical agreements as per se anti-competitive might result in restraining pro-competitive commercial agreements.[154]

The High Level Committee on Competition Policy and Law, 2000 ('*High Level Committee*')[155] had noted that:

> generally, vertical agreements are treated more leniently than horizontal agreements as, prima facie, a horizontal agreement is more likely to reduce competition than an agreement between firms in a buyer-seller relationship... In the past, the U.S. anti-trust laws had treated vertical restraints, like tie-in arrangements quite harshly. This thinking has changed in recent times, and, under the rule of reason, vertical agreements are generally treated more leniently than horizontal agreements. This is because vertical agreements can often perform pro-competitive functions. Such agreements are generally considered anti-competitive if one or more of the firms that are party to the agreement have market power. In such a situation, the agreement is, in any case, likely to attract the provisions of the law relating to abuse of dominance.

In light of the aforesaid, the CCI adjudicates the allegation of vertical agreement under the rule of reason to see whether the vertical agreement caused or is likely to cause an adverse effect. Looking at the steps taken by CCI while deciding the matters related to vertical anti-competitive agreements suggests that CCI follows an 'effect-based analysis' through the rule of reason framework. Thus, to determine the violation of section 3(4) of the Competition Act, the CCI follows the following steps, i.e., *first*, nature of the vertical agreement under inquiry; *second*, delineation of relevant markets; *third*, significant market power of the party; and *fourth*, effect-based analysis to determine AAEC.

§2.16 TYPES OF VERTICAL AGREEMENTS

Section 3(4) of the Competition Act provides an inclusive list of vertical agreements. There can be other forms of vertical agreements, however, all vertical agreements must be analysed under the rule of reason analysis. It is noteworthy that vertical agreements are often analysed by the CCI on a joint investigation of section 3(4) read with section

153. *Jasper Infotech Private Limited (Snapdeal) v. KAFF Appliances (India) Pvt. Ltd. (Kaff)*, Case No. 61 of 2014, paras 48, 51.
154. *Ibid.*, para. 48.
155. High Level Committee on Competition Policy and Law, 2000, paras 4.4.0, 4.3.1.

4 of the Competition Act, since a vertical agreement entered into by an undertaking with insignificant market power will generally not cause any AAEC in India.

We will now discuss the various kinds of vertical agreements mentioned under section 3(4) of the Competition Act below.

[A] Tie-In Arrangement

Explanation (a) of section 3(4) defines tie-in arrangement or tying arrangement as an agreement imposing a condition on a customer to purchase the goods or services in order to purchase some other goods or services. In a tie-in arrangement, the seller ties two distinct or separate products or services with each other so that the customer is forced to purchase the tied product or service along with the tying product or service. The product or service that the customer wants to purchase is called tying product, and the product or service which is forced upon the customer is called tied product or service.

For example, the product that the buyer wants to purchase is called the tying product (Product X), and the product which is required to be purchased to get Product X is called tied product (Product Y). The producer of Product X imposes a condition on the buyers that in order to purchase Product X, they have to purchase Product Y.

Also, for a better understanding of tie-in arrangement, it is important to distinguish tie-in arrangement from bundling arrangement. The CCI made detailed observations on the difference between tie-in and bundling in the *Sonam Sharma v. Apple* ('*Apple* case').[156] In this case, the DG found that Apple locked its iPhone with the cellular services of Airtel or Vodafone. It was a case of 'contractual tying', which means a buyer can only purchase an iPhone by subscribing to the cellular services of Airtel or Vodafone. However, looking at the minuscule market share of the tying party, the CCI held that the said tie-in arrangement was not an anti-competitive agreement between Apple and cellular service providers. Enough evidence was not adduced to prove that the tie-in arrangement foreclosed the market or created entry barriers for new entrants.

Though 'tie-in' and 'bundling' are used interchangeably in common market parlance, the CCI explained the difference between both the terms by saying that 'tie-in arrangement' and 'bundling' are strategies to sell products and services, and both the strategies are used for different purpose. A producer uses a 'tie-in arrangement' as a strategy when it does not want to specify to the customer that the two products are fixed at the time of purchase, whereas a 'bundling' strategy is used when the products are sold in fixed proportions. The CCI in the *Apple* case further noted that '*a tying arrangement occurs when, through a contractual or technological requirement, a seller conditions the sale or lease of one product or service on the customer's agreement to take a second product or service. In other words, a firm selling products X and Y makes the purchase of product X conditional to the purchase of product Y. Product Y can be purchased freely on the market, but product X can only be purchased together with product Y.*'

156. *Sonam Sharma v. Apple*, Case No. 24 of 2011, paras 19, 65-71.

Thereafter, the CCI in the *Apple* case,[157] explained the term 'tie-in arrangement' by providing examples of the tied sales of machines with maintenance services or complementary products. Also, producers force the buyers to purchase two or more products because all these products are compatible with each other. More often, tying is a sales strategy usually adopted by producers to promote/introduce a slow-selling or unknown product when it has in its portfolio a fast-selling or well-known product over which it has certain market power (in this example, Product X). The aspect of tie-in is also seen, while deciding abuse of dominance investigation, under the abuse of leveraging (discussed in the chapter on abuse of dominance).

However, 'bundling' or 'package tie-in' is a strategy used by the producer to make the buyer purchase more goods. Further, the CCI held that '*price bundling is a strategy whereby a seller bundles together many different goods/items for sale and offers the entire bundle at a single price. There are two forms of price bundling – pure bundling, where the seller does not offer buyers the option of buying the items separately, and mixed bundling, where the seller offers the items separately at higher individual prices*'.[158] Mixed bundling is usually preferable to pure bundling because the reference price effect makes it appear even more attractive to buyers, and there are fewer laws forbidding mixed bundling.

The CCI has noted that there can be pro-competitive rationale behind tie-in arrangements like assembly benefits (economies of scale and scope), quality improvement and addressing pricing inefficiencies. The following conditions are required to be analysed to see whether a tie-in arrangement is anti-competitive for a section 3(1) analysis:[159]

(i) Presence of two separate products or services capable of being tied.
    Tie-in arrangements must consist of two products where the seller forces the buyer to purchase one product (i.e., tied product – Product X) if the buyer purchases another product (i.e., tying product – Product Y).
(ii) The seller must have significant market power in the market of the tying product to appreciably restrain free competition in the market of the tied product.
    To establish the presence of tying arrangements, the sufficient market power of the seller in the tying market to leverage into the market of tied product must be presence. Thereafter, it has to be shown that the seller has used its market power to force the buyers to purchase the tied product along with the tied product.
(iii) The tying arrangement must have a substantial effect on the commerce.
    Considering the area of analysis is whether an agreement causes or is likely to cause an AAEC, tie-in arrangements are generally not perceived as being anti-competitive when a substantial portion of the market is not affected.

157. *Apple* case, Case No. 24 of 2011, para. 66.
158. *Apple* case, para. 67.
159. *Ibid.*, para. 69.

Similarly, in *Arshiya Rail Infrastructure Ltd. (ARIL) v. Ministry of Railway (MoR) & Others*,[160] the CCI held that tie-in arrangement is used by an entity which has a dominant position in one product/service (i.e., transportation services – tying service) and ties it with a laggard product (i.e., maintenance of container – tied service) to promote the laggard product. However, there was no tie-in arrangement in the said case because none of the entities were in the business of maintenance services. As per the facts, MoR granted a licence and concessionaire agreement entered with fifteen private operators to move container trains on the railway lines on a licence basis. The informants, who were private operators, alleged that MoR, Indian Railway and Container Corporation of India, had indulged in abusive conduct as a group or a single economic entity in the market for the transport of freight via railways. One of the allegations was on violation of section 3(4)(a) of the Competition Act because MoR insisted that maintenance of container trains can only be sourced from it. However, the CCI dismissed this allegation by saying that the supplementary condition to obtain a fitness certificate of train from MoR does not amount to a tie-in arrangement in terms of section 3(4)(a) of the Competition Act. The CCI observed that MoR imposed such conditions to maintain railway operation and protect the overall safety of passengers.

[B] Exclusive Dealing Agreement

Explanation (b) to section 3(4) of the Competition Act defines an exclusive dealing agreement as an exclusive agreement imposed by the seller which restricts the buyer from purchasing any goods or services other than those of the seller. Exclusive dealing agreement also covers the vertical restraint imposed by the buyer on the seller from dealing with other buyers. The seller who is accepting this restrictive term has no option but to supply its product or service to the designated purchaser as per the condition. For example, Manufacturer A entered into an exclusive dealing agreement with all the retailers to buy only the product of Manufacturer A or the authorized dealers of Manufacturer A.

Prior to the Competition (Amendment) Act, 2023, this explanation was called an 'exclusive supply agreement', and it used to cover only the vertical agreement where restraint was exclusively imposed on the buyer by the seller. So, the Competition Act was amended to recognize the imposition of the exclusive agreement from both the seller side and the buyer side.[161]

The issue of exclusive dealing agreement (supply-side) was discussed in the *Shri Shamsher Kataria* v. *Honda Siel Cars India Ltd. and Others* ('*Automobile spare parts* case'),[162] where both the CCI and the erstwhile COMPAT held that the authorized dealers were prohibited from sourcing spare parts from any other enterprise, apart

160. *Arshiya Rail Infrastructure Ltd. (ARIL) v. Ministry of Railway (MoR) & Others*, Case No. 64 of 2010, para. 21.
161. Report of Competition Law Review Committee, 2019, paras 5.5-5.7.
162. *Shri Shamsher Kataria v. Honda Siel Cars India Ltd. and Others*, Case No. 03 of 2011, para. 20.6.4; Also, *see Toyota Kirloskar Motor Private Limited and Others v. CCI* [2016], (COMPAT) 2016 SCC OnLine Comp AT 452, para. 125.

from the OEMs. These exclusive agreements imposed restrictions on the buyer side of the market to buy and sell the spare parts exclusively; hence, section 3(4)(b) of the Competition Act was violated. In another case, the CCI in *M/s ESYS Information Technologies Pvt. Ltd. v. Intel Corporation and Others*[163] held that exclusive agreement means that the agreement by the seller restricts the distributors from dealing with any competitors of the seller. In the absence of any evidence, the CCI was unable to show that the concerned agreement with Intel exclusively imposed a restriction on the distributors to deal with Intel. Also, there was evidence which showed that Intel allowed the distributors to deal with other sellers.

[C] Exclusive Distribution Agreement

Explanation (c) to section 3(4) of the Competition Act defines exclusive distribution agreement as an exclusive agreement to limit, restrict or withhold the output or supply of any goods or services or allocate any area or market for the disposal or sale of the goods or services. Such an exclusive agreement restricts the distribution side of the market. For example, a supplier entered into an exclusive distribution agreement with the manufacturer to specifically distribute the product with authorized dealers, and not any independent dealers.

The aspect of exclusive distribution agreement was discussed in the *Bajaj* case.[164] The CCI discussed the anti-competitive effects which can flow from an exclusive distribution agreement. The CCI observed that exclusive distribution agreement is when a supplier enters into an agreement with the distributor, wherein the distributor sells the product within a particular group or area. Such an agreement limits the distribution, creates entry bars and harms the intra-brand competition.

While assessing the violation under section 3(4)(c) of the Competition Act, the CCI considers whether the distributor is restricted to deal in the products of other brands in or outside the particular customer or region that caused any harm to the intra-brand or inter-brand competition. In *M/s Karni Communication Private Ltd. & Other v. Haicheng Vivo Mobile (India) Private Ltd. and Others*,[165] it was alleged that Vivo imposed a clause in the distribution agreement to restrict smartphone distributors from selling Vivo smartphones via online platforms to customers, hence, violated section 3(4)(c) of the Competition Act. This allegation was dismissed because Vivo had allowed the distributors to sell Vivo's products online on various e-commerce portals like www.Flipkart.com, www.Amazon.in, www.Snapdeal.com, etc. The CCI held that there was no exclusive distribution agreement. Further, the CCI said that Vivo never directly restricted the distribution of its products, and consumers had options to buy Vivo products from various sources. Similarly, in *M/s K.C. Marketing v. OPPO Mobiles*

163. *M/s ESYS Information Technologies Pvt. Ltd. v. Intel Corporation and Others*, Case No. 48 of 2011, para. 8.3.7.
164. *Bajaj* case, para. 75.
165. *M/s Karni Communication Private Ltd. & Other v. Haicheng Vivo Mobile (India) Private Ltd. & Others*, Case No. 35 of 2018, para. 27.

MU Private Limited,[166] the CCI held that to protect the interests of all distributors who have made an investment in the product, the producer can designate specific sale regions to distributors and restrict the distributors from selling outside their specified regions. Such exclusive distribution agreement causes no AAEC because there is no bar for the customers of one region to purchase the product from a distributor in another sales region. Further, there is no restriction on the distributor to deal in the products of other producers in or outside the sales region. Thus, in effect, the CCI has accepted that there can be certain restrictions which may be imposed in a vertical agreement to prevent free-riding (this was specifically highlighted in the *Bajaj* case), however, the parties who are in market power must keep in mind the factors mentioned under section 19(3) of the Act prior to imposing such vertical restraints.

In the *Automobile spare parts* case,[167] it was found that the OEMs and their authorized dealers entered into agreements/arrangements pursuant to which the authorized dealers of the OEMs sell cars and provide after-sales services to the consumers of the OEMs. Further, there are agreements entered into between OEMs and the original equipment suppliers (OESs). Further, apart from the agreement between OEM with their dealers, there were agreements between OEMs with the OESs prohibiting them from selling the spare parts manufactured by them for OEMs in the open market. The CCI concluded by saying that OEMs violated section 3(4)(b), (c) and (d) of the Competition Act. OEMs entered into exclusive agreement and refusal to deal to restrict the access of spare parts and diagnostic tools directly to the Indian aftermarket; the arrangement between OEMs and authorized dealers violated section 3(4) of the Competition Act. The OEMs increased the risk of consumer safety because their restrictive conduct led to a rise in the use of fake spare parts and prevented independent repairers from using effective diagnostic tools. After identifying the various kinds of agreements, the CCI analysed that the said network of agreements created foreclosure effects and barriers to entry into the market. Based on the same, the CCI identified AAEC in terms of the factors mentioned under section 19(3) of the Competition Act.

[D] Refusal to Deal

Explanation (d) of section 3(4) of the Competition Act defines refusal to deal as an agreement which restricts or is likely to restrict their business partners in terms of dealing with the competitors of the enterprise which is imposing such restriction. It must be noted that refusal to deal has mostly been dealt with under an abuse of dominance investigation. An example of refusal to deal is when an E-Commerce Platform – 'B' enters into an agreement with a smartphone retailer prohibiting it from listing its smartphones on the E-Commerce Platform – 'A' and E-Commerce Platform – 'C'.

---

166. *M/s K.C. Marketing v. OPPO Mobiles MU Private Limited*, Case No. 34 of 2018, paras 30, 31.
167. *Automobile spare parts* case, para. 20.6.29. The erstwhile COMPAT in *Toyota Kirloskar Motor Private Limited and Others v. CCI* [2016], (COMPAT) 2016 SCC OnLine Comp AT 452, upheld the order of CCI.

The issue of refusal of deal will depend upon the facts and circumstances of each case. Interestingly, in *Hiveloop Technology Pvt. Ltd. v. Britannia Industries Ltd.,*[168] while passing an order under section 26(2) of the Competition Act, the CCI held that no distributor can ask for an absolute right to deal from a manufacturer to deal with them. In this case, Hiveloop Technology alleged that Britannia refused to deal directly with it, and there is a vertical agreement between Britannia and its distributors to restrict Hiveloop Technology from dealing with certain brands and biscuits of Britannia. Britannia argued that it has not imposed any such restrictions on its distributors, and it has commercial freedom to choose its business partners in the vertical chain. CCI accepted the argument of Britannia and held that an enterprise can refuse to choose their trading partners as long as there is fair functioning of the markets. The CCI recognized that Britannia has commercial right when it comes to choosing its business partners, and CCI can't interfere with such right.

In two cases with similar facts concerning non-dealing of a goods provider with a distributor, the CCI expounded the position that every enterprise, including a dominant enterprise, has the freedom to choose its business partners.[169] The crux of the allegations in both cases was that the goods provider (i.e., Britannia (discussed *supra*) and Parle, respectively) was not providing its biscuits, which were regarded as a 'must stock item' to the distributor (i.e., Hiveloop Technologies/Udaan). The CCI noted that this matter required a resolution of two competing rights: the informant's right to do business with Britannia/Parle with respect to certain products versus Britannia/Parle's right not to engage with the informant since it had the freedom of choice as to whom to contract within the vertical chain as well as its level of engagement. In this case, CCI noted that both Britannia and Parle had their own commercial justifications for refusing engagement with the informant, viz., the capacity and quality of service provided and that no foreclosure had arisen in the market. As a result, the CCI held that manufacturers have some autonomy available to deal with their goods the way they want, in alignment with their business requirements. If this were not the case, then it has a consequence of replacing the business/commercial prudence of an entity by taking away the autonomy of such undertaking/entity. Hence, the type and nature of distributors a manufacturer desires to partner with is part and parcel of its business autonomy, and the CCI cannot ipso facto substitute its regulatory wisdom for that of the commercial wisdom of the businesses unless the commercial wisdom is palpably in the face of the provisions of the Competition Act and 'the criteria laid down are ex facie unfair and/or discriminatory and designed with a view to exclude/eliminate competition on merits'.[170]

Thus, nobody can ask for an absolute right to deal with a particular business. Similarly, there is no absolute right of refusal. This will depend upon the facts and

168. *Hiveloop Technology Pvt. Ltd. v. Britannia Industries Ltd.*, Case No. 18 of 2021, paras 45, 46, 49, 51, 55.
169. *Hiveloop Technology Pvt. Ltd. v. Britannia Industries Ltd.*, Case No. 18 of 2021; *Hiveloop Technology Pvt. Ltd. v. Parle Products Private Limited*, Case No. 28 of 2021.
170. *Hiveloop Technology Pvt. Ltd. v. Parle Products Private Limited*, Case No. 28 of 2021, para. 33.

circumstances of each case; even a dominant entity, at times, has the freedom to refuse to conclude contracts based on objective justifications.

Further, refusal to deal need not be absolute and ought to be seen in the context of the factual setting coupled with the factors under section 19(3) of the Competition Act. A refusal, either total or partial, could also have underlying valid justifications with commercial consideration, especially in the backdrop that it makes little economic sense for businesses to take a restrictive approach when it comes to expanding their horizon and reach. Consequently, though refusal to deal may be, inter se, two or more parties, its anti-competitive effect would have to be seen in the context of the overall market conditions. Hence, a manufacturer cannot be forced to onboard any person/entity in the chain merely on asking because distribution networks are built and strengthened over a period of time with sound underlying commercial considerations. Thus, the question to be asked in business decisions to engage or not to engage with a downstream entity from a competition perspective is whether such a decision is likely to cause AAEC should the upstream entity choose not to deal with the downstream entity.

Thus, the takeaway is that firms have an autonomy to choose their trading partners as long as the exercise of such autonomy does not affect the fair functioning of the markets because, depending upon the market power commanded by such firms, their conduct may cause foreclosure of the market for other players.

The CCI, in the *Bajaj* case,[171] where it was alleged that Bajaj exercised its market power to impose restrictions on its distributors from supplying Bajaj's products to retailers which were from other territories, the distributor had no other option but to accept such restrictive conditions. The CCI noted that competition law issues with respect to refusal to deal/supply will arise when an enterprise, generally with stronger market power, refuses to deal with its customers or suppliers. The effect in such a scenario is that the downstream market gets affected due to such refusal. However, the CCI held that though there were vertical restraints on the distributors, there was no violation of section 3(4)(d) due to the lack of sufficient evidence to satisfy the presence of entry barriers, foreclosure of the market, or harm to the end consumers.

Also, in a case relating to the automobile sector, the CCI found that there was no exclusive agreement or refusal to deal between the car manufacturers and their distributors in the *Hyundai Motors* case[172] because the prohibition to deal with other car companies was never mandated on the distributors. Mere requirements of prior written permission of Hyundai do not impose any exclusivity or cannot be concluded as refusal to deal under section 3(4) of the Competition Act. Additionally, it was found that there were distributors who were dealing with other car companies without seeking permission from Hyundai, and despite the knowledge of such parallel dealerships, no action was taken against such distributors.

Though generally vertical anti-competitive agreements are imposed as vertical restraints where one party has no other option than accepting the condition of the other

---

171. *Bajaj* case, paras 69, 76, 81.
172. *Hyundai Motors* case, paras 71, 72, 74, 75.

party, however, it could also be a mutually agreed condition to eliminate their competitors. The CCI in its most prominent decision on refusal to deal in the *Federation of Hotel & Restaurant Associations of India and Others v. MakeMyTrip India Pvt. Ltd. and Others* ('*MMT* case'),[173] passed an order against MakeMyTrip (MMT - an online travel agency) and Oravel Stay Ltd. (OYO - franchisee service provider to independent hotels) for their anti-competitive practices, including MMT's refusal to deal and delisting of the competitors of OYO. The CCI observed that section 3(4) is neither exhaustive in nature nor does it require that the restriction is in the form of an imposition. So, the CCI can also look into the restrictive agreement which was mutually agreed by both parties to harm the competitors or competition in the market. In this case, MMT agreed to delist OYO's competitors, i.e., Fabhotels and Treebo, whereas OYO agreed not to list its inventories on the platforms of MMT's competitors, i.e., Yatra, Cleartrip, PayTM, etc. Such a mutually agreed clause between MMT and OYO was held to be anti-competitive because it foreclosed both markets and took away the opportunity for the competitors to get a fair chance to compete. Further, refusal to list Fabhotels and Treebo on MMT's platform would not only reduce consumer choices but also stifle the innovation in the market. MMT was a dominant player, and OYO enjoyed a significant market position in their respective markets, and entering into a vertical anti-competitive agreement caused AAEC to create entry barriers and harm the competitors.

Similarly, while passing an order under section 26(1) of the Competition Act, the CCI in *Delhi Vyapar Mahasangh v. Flipkart Internet Private Limited and Another*[174] identified online platform services as fulcrum of the commercial success of the sellers to reach customers. If such platforms refuse to deal with sellers, then it would create a major hindrance for the sellers to sell their products to the customers. In this case, a group of sellers filed information alleging that Flipkart and Amazon entered into exclusive agreements and tie-ups with their preferred sellers. Through these vertical exclusive agreements, Flipkart and Amazon are exclusively launching mobile phones of the preferred sellers on their e-commerce platforms, selling the products of preferred sellers at a heavily discounted price and providing preferential listing/promotion of private labels. This leads to other sellers being excluded and foreclosed from the market because they are not allowed to compete equally on the said e-commerce platforms. By considering all these allegations against two e-commerce platforms, which hold significant market power in the relevant market, CCI directed the DG to investigate the said vertical agreements.

173. *Federation of Hotel & Restaurant Associations of India and Others v. MakeMyTrip India Pvt. Ltd. and Others*, Case No. 14 of 2019 and Case No. 01 of 2020, paras 289, 291, 292, 293, 295, 298, 300, 301.

174. *Delhi Vyapar Mahasangh v. Flipkart Internet Private Limited and Another*, Case No. 40 of 2019, paras 6, 7, 11, 18, 20, 23, 25.

[E] Resale Price Maintenance

Explanation (e) to section 3(4) defines resale price maintenance. Resale price maintenance means any agreement to sell goods or services where the prices to be charged on the resale by the purchaser shall be stipulated by the seller unless it is clearly stated that prices lower than those prices may be charged. The Competition (Amendment) Act, 2023 modified the said explanation to include indirect restrictions on the pricing condition, such as threats and imposition of sanctions if the seller fails to maintain the resale price or promotional offers to the seller for maintaining the resale price. Like in other jurisdictions across the globe, resale price maintenance remains one of the most vexed areas of antitrust enforcement. Contrary to some international authorities, in India, an arrangement for resale price maintenance is only void if it causes an AAEC in India. In fact, the High Level Committee[175] noted that 'in a number of countries, RPM is presumed to be per se anti-competitive. The majority of the Members of the Committee also felt that RPM should be treated as presumed to be illegal. However, after considerable discussions, in order to arrive at a consensus, it was decided not to treat it as presumed to be illegal. It will be judged under the "rule of reason"'.

It has been alleged in many cases, that the object of vertical price restraints is primarily restriction on price competition between enterprises operating in the market. Resale price maintenance implies a direct or indirect object to fix or enforce a minimum resale price to be observed by the distributors or any downstream resellers of the manufacturer's products. The CCI, in *M/s ESYS Information Technologies Pvt. Ltd. v. M/s ESYS Information Technologies Pvt. Ltd. and Others*,[176] explained section 3(4)(e) of the Competition Act by saying resale price maintenance includes the agreement to sell goods on the condition that the resale price shall be fixed by sellers unless it is clearly stated that prices were lower than those prices may be charged. In this case, the CCI found that resale prices were not stipulated by Intel, and the distribution agreement allowed the distributors to fix their own resale price. On the allegation that Intel was monitoring the downstream price, the CCI held that such conduct can't be termed anti-competitive.

The CCI has witnessed various developments with regard to the treatment of vertical agreements having conditions of resale price maintenance, especially in the online distribution sector. Disputes on the competition law have been brewing in India between e-tailers and brick-and-mortar businesses for a long time now, with the emergence of strong e-tailers in the market. The strategy of the e-tailers in tying up exclusive launches and offering significant discounts for various products being sold on their respective platforms has left an impact on the businesses of conventional brick-and-mortar retailers. The brick-and-mortar outlets have stated that they are going out of business due to the actions of the strong e-tailers, and the companies are also facing a difficult time in managing their distribution chain in the process. An emerging issue in the area of vertical agreements is the maintenance of resale price maintenance

175. High Level Committee on Competition Policy and Law, 2000, para. 4.4.1.
176. *M/s ESYS Information Technologies Pvt. Ltd. v. M/s ESYS Information Technologies Pvt. Ltd. and Others*, Case No. 48 of 2011, para. 8.3.8.

both in the context of online and offline markets. Issues of resale price maintenance pertain to the effort on the part of companies to ensure a price of their product to ensure parity between online and offline sellers, thereby preventing free-riding by offline agents so as to protect the interest of dealers who maintain brick-and-mortar stores. This issue was first decided by the CCI in the case of *Mr. Mohit Manglani v. M/s Flipkart India Private Limited and Others,*[177] in the context of the sale of a book of a famous Indian author, (Chetan Bhagat's book, 'Half Girlfriend') which was exclusively available on Flipkart's website. Allegations were raised that such arrangements slowly destroy players in the brick-and-mortar space and tend to create product-specific monopoly, leading to manipulation of price, control of production and supply, imposition of terms and conditions detrimental to the interests of consumers and distortion of fair competition in the marketplace. However, CCI did not agree with these allegations and held that such exclusive arrangements do not create any entry barriers for new entrants as the products (such as mobile phones, tablets, books, cameras, etc.) sold through the exclusive platforms face competitive constraints and are neither dominant nor hold a monopoly status. Further, the introduction of the e-platforms brought pro-competitive effectiveness to the market.

Similarly, in *Jasper Infotech (Snapdeal) v. KAFF Appliances,*[178] the online retailers have also instituted an information against companies who imposed restrictions on the manner in which online distribution is to be done by the e-tailers. Jasper (the company which owns and operates snapdeal.com) instituted an information against a manufacturer which had placed restrictions on its dealers in dealing with e-tailers. In the said case, the CCI has directed the DG to investigate the allegation pertaining to minimum resale price maintenance imposed by KAFF Appliances (India) Pvt. Ltd. (KAFF). Snapdeal is an online marketplace which provides a medium for buyers and sellers to meet and transact. It was alleged that KAFF, being aggrieved by the sale of its products at discounted prices on Snapdeal, started imposing resale price maintenance and adduced an email exchange between KAFF and Snapdeal to the effect that KAFF will not allow the sales of its products on Snapdeal if the Minimum Operating Price (MOP) is not maintained. However, the DG's main investigation report and supplementary investigation report could not find any evidence showing imposition of resale price maintenance by KAFF. With regard to the email exchange between the parties, the CCI accepted the justification of the KAFF that the email was to safeguard the goodwill and protect the right of KAFF to choose the most efficient distribution channel. Finally, the conduct of KAFF was not sufficient to cause AAEC.

In another case, though, the NCLAT set aside the CCI order in the *Hyundai Motors* case[179] because the CCI and DG failed to delineate the relevant markets and no proper inquiry was carried out by the CCI, and appeal against the NCLAT order is pending before the Supreme Court. Nevertheless, the reasoning of the CCI on resale price

177. *Mr. Mohit Manglani v. M/s Flipkart India Private Limited and Others,* Case No. 80 of 2014, para. 17.

178. *Jasper Infotech (Snapdeal) v. KAFF Appliances,* Case No. 61 of 2013, paras 55, 63, 67, 70.

179. *Hyundai Motors* case, paras 79, 81, 85, 88-92, 116; *See*, NCLAT order *Hyundai Motor India Ltd. v. CCI and Others* [2018], (NCLAT) Competition Appeal No. 06 of 2017, paras 40, 41.

maintenance is important for academic purposes. Here, in a claim pertaining to resale price maintenance, CCI found that Hyundai placed restrictions on its dealers on the maximum permissible discount that may be given by a dealer to the end-consumer, coupled with the practice of price monitoring put in place by Hyundai wherein the dealers were penalized on account of any deviation. After considering the DG report, the CCI held that Hyundai contravened section 3(4)(e) of the Competition Act by imposing resale price on its distributors and monitoring the maximum permissible discount level through the Discount Control Mechanism. Under the Discount Control Mechanism (DCP), Hyundai maintains the maximum discount which a distributor can provide to the end consumers, and Hyundai monitors its enforcement by regularly conducting meetings with its distributors to discuss the change in price and discount. As per the DCP, the distributors can't offer a higher discount which is above the authorized discount. The CCI held that resale price maintenance can prevent competition at both the intra-brand and inter-brand levels. Not allowing to offer a higher discount harms the end customers because they have to pay a higher price. Resale price maintenance reduces the intra-brand competition which results in reduction of the pressure on the competing car manufacturers to sell their product at a competing price. In addition to resale price maintenance, the CCI also ruled that Hyundai entered into a tie-in arrangement by tying the sale of its car only with the purchase of recommended lubricants and oils. The conduct of Hyundai caused AAEC because the cost of cars increased which is a case of consumer harm.

In the case of *Alleged anti-competitive conduct by Maruti Suzuki India Limited in implementing discount control policy vis-à-vis dealers* ('*Maruti Suzuki* case'),[180] the CCI passed an order under section 27 of the Competition Act against Maruti Suzuki for enforcing maximum discount limits on its distributors through the DCP comes within the ambit of resale price maintenance. Further, it was found that failure to comply with the DCP by offering extra discount, the distributors were threatened with penalty and suspension of supplies. There were many instances where the distributors had to pay a penalty amount for violating DCP. Hence, it was established that the resale price maintenance was enforced on distributors. Thereafter, the CCI analysed the factors under section 19(3) and held that the resale price maintenance prevented intra-brand competition and inter-brand competition by not allowing the distributors to decrease the cost of the vehicles. This facilitated all the distributors from selling the vehicles at higher prices because there was no price competition. On the other hand, the customers had to pay higher prices to buy the vehicles. Hence, the CCI held that Maruti Suzuki violated section 3(4)(e) of the Competition Act and harmed both the competition and the stakeholders of the market.

180. *Alleged anti-competitive conduct by Maruti Suzuki India Limited in implementing discount control policy vis-à-vis dealers* Suo Motu Case No. 01 of 2019, paras 18, 21, 34, 39, 42, 45, 46, 48-50.

Another important observation on resale price maintenance was made in the case of *Shubham Sanitarywares v. Hindustan Sanitarywares and Industries Ltd and others*,[181] where the opposite party was offering higher discounts to bulk builders and less discounts to retail customers. The CCI passed an order under section 26(2) by holding that offering different discounts to different customers does not violate section 3(4)(e) of the Competition Act. However, it was also noted that forcing the dealers to implement specific discounts on different customers may be construed as a violation of section 3(4)(e) of the Competition Act. Further, the CCI held that the discount policy in that case did not seem to have any AAEC in India and dismissed the case.

§2.17 ESSENTIAL CONDITIONS NECESSARY TO ESTABLISH VERTICAL ANTI-COMPETITIVE AGREEMENT

As a part of effect-based analysis, the CCI examines two key conditions, i.e., (a) the relevant markets of the parties to the agreement; and (b) their market power in the relevant market. So, before analysing the factors under section 19(3) of the Competition Act (discussed in the subsequent part), the CCI essentially requires delineating the relevant market. Then, in the context of the delineated relevant market, the CCI analyse the market presence of the party and its position of strength. It is important to know the market concentration and which enterprise holds the significant market position because the vertical anti-competitive agreements imposed by an enterprise having significant market strengths generally have a foreclosure effect, would create entry barriers, cause harm to the customers or drive the existing competitors out of the market. In some cases, the CCI delineates relevant markets and determines the market strength of both parties to the vertical anti-competitive agreement, especially in cases where it was alleged that both parties mutually agreed to the vertical anti-competitive agreement.[182] For example, in the MMT case, the CCI identified two markets: both upstream and downstream markets where MMT and OYO (the parties to the said exclusive agreement) and then came to the conclusion that MMT and OYO were respectively holding market power in their respective markets.

[A] Delineation of Relevant Markets of the Parties

The decisional practice of the CCI shows that delineation of relevant market of the alleged parties must take place as a pre-requisite condition to analyse AAEC in the market. Thus, as a first and foremost step to analyse the AAEC, the CCI should correctly delineate the relevant market according to the factors enumerated in section 19(5), (6) and (7) of the Competition Act.

The issue relating to tie-in arrangement between Hiranandani Hospital and Cryobanks was found to be in contravention of section 3(4) of the Competition Act in

181. *Shubham Sanitarywares v. Hindustan Sanitarywares and Industries Ltd and others*, Case No. 99 of 2013, para. 11.
182. *MMT* case, paras 22, 23, 291, 292, 297; *Apple* case, para. 33.

the market of stem cell banking in *Mr. Ramakant Kini v. Dr. L.H. Hiranandani Hospital* ('*Hiranandani* case').[183] Mrs Jain entered into an agreement with M/s Life Cell India Pvt. Ltd. (Life Cell) to avail its services for banking of stem cells. Mrs Jain was registered with Hiranandani Hospital for maternity-related services and for the delivery of her child. As the time of delivery of the child drew near, Mrs Jain requested Hiranandani Hospital to allow Life Cell to collect the stem cell blood. Hiranandani Hospital refused to accede to the request of Mrs Jain on the grounds that she could avail the services of Cryobank and not any other stem cell banking service provider. The CCI held that the Hiranandani Hospital had an exclusive agreement with Cryobank under section 3(4) of the Competition Act. The CCI also said that for the purpose of section 3, there is no requirement to identify the relevant market but must see if the agreement has an anti-competitive effect in the market of the product/service of any party of the agreement. However, at the appellate stage, section 3 was read with section 19(3), (5), (6) and (7) of the Competition Act to set aside the order of CCI by the erstwhile COMPAT.[184] It was held that CCI failed to independently analyse factors of section 19(3), (5), (6) and (7) of the Competition Act to determine a violation of section 3(4) of the Competition Act. Further, the CCI erred in delineating the relevant market as the market of maternity services, ignoring that the whole dispute revolves around the agreement on stem cell bank services. It was also noted that CCI overlooked that the agreement entered between Hiranandani Hospital and Cryobanks did not restrict the choice of the service provider in the market for stem cell bank services. To understand the importance of the delineation of relevant market for analysing the factors of section 19(3), the erstwhile COMPAT largely relied on the *Apple* case, where tying-arraignment was not established because there was no foreclosure in either of the relevant markets of tying parties. Thus, previously decided cases show that relevant market was delineated to analyse the appreciable effect of alleged vertical anti-competitive agreements on the market, the other players of the market and the end consumer.

Without delineation of the relevant product markets and relevant geographical markets, the inquiry against the vertical anti-competitive agreement would be considered incomplete. In the *Hyundai Motors* case,[185] the NCLAT set aside the order of CCI because CCI failed to delineate the relevant product market and the relevant geographical market while deciding the violation of section 3(4)(a) and (e) of the Competition Act. In the *Hyundai Motors* case, an information was filed by an authorized dealer of Hyundai, engaged in the business of reselling and servicing vehicles and spare parts. The business activities of an authorized dealer comprised of sales of vehicles, spare parts, accessories, and other related activities. The CCI held that the conduct of Hyundai contravened section 3(4)(a) and (e), however, the NCLAT set aside the CCI's order by holding that the CCI's inquiry under section 26 was incomplete because the relevant market has not been taken into consideration by the CCI. The finding of the

183. *Mr. Ramakant Kini v. Dr. L.H. Hiranandani Hospital,* Case No. 39 of 2012, para. 25.
184. *Dr. L.H. Hiranandani Hospital v. CCI and Another* [2015], (COMPAT) [2015] Comp AT 1144, paras 29, 30, 32, 33(70), 34.
185. *Hyundai Motor* case, paras 40, 50. (NCLAT).

NCLAT was based on the reasoning provided by the Supreme Court in the *Coordination Committee* case, where the Supreme Court held that CCI should delineate the relevant market in which the competition is affected due to the anti-competitive agreement. The Supreme Court interpreted the word 'market' in section 19(3) as 'relevant market' and held that it is important to determine the relevant market to identify the competitors of the concerned party, the boundaries of the competition, and the competitive constraints faced by market participants in order to examine the concentration of the market. The concentration of the market is key to determining which market participant holds the power over the market and whether its anti-competitive conduct would appreciably affect the market. Thus, it is necessary to delineate the relevant market to determine the market participant who has power over the market while analysing whether its conduct has an anti-competitive effect.

However, unlike merger control and abuse of dominance cases, the statute is silent, and it may be argued that for the cases under section 3(4) of the Competition Act (at least at the *prima facie stage)*, there is no need to go into precise relevant market delineation.[186] For instance, in *National Restaurant Association of India ('NRAI') v. Zomato Limited ('Zomato') & Others,*[187] the CCI held while passing a prima facie order directing the DG to conduct an investigation against Swiggy and Zomato for the alleged contravention of section 3(4) of the Competition Act, the relevant market need not be delineated precisely in vertical anti-competitive agreement cases. In furtherance to this observation, the CCI delineated the relevant market of Zomato and Swiggy as online food delivery platforms and operate as online intermediaries for food ordering and delivery. Also, while holding Maruti Suzuki liable for imposing resale price maintenance in the *Maruti Suzuki* case,[188] the CCI did not precisely delineate the relevant market. CCI held that Maruti is a manufacturer dealing in the upstream market.

[B] Significant Market Power in the Relevant Market

The decisional practice of CCI shows that the market share or market power of the party to the vertical agreement is a pre-requisite requirement for establishing violation of section 3(4) read with section 3(1) of the Competition Act.[189] So, for the proper analysis of the anti-competitive effect, the CCI must look at the market shares of the parties entering into such an agreement, and also the market shares of other market

186. *Hiveloop Technology Pvt. Ltd. v. Britannia Industries Ltd.*, Case No. 18 of 2021, para. 43.
187. *National Restaurant Association of India ('NRAI') v. Zomato Limited ('Zomato') & Others*, Case No. 16 of 2021, para. 34.
188. *Maruti Suzuki* case, para. 16.
189. *Arshiya Rail Infrastructure Ltd. (ARIL) v. Ministry of Railway ('MoR') & Others*, Case No. 64 of 2010, para. 21; *Tamil Nadu Consumer Products Distributors Association v. Fangs Technology Private Limited & Other*, Case No. 15 of 2018, para. 23, the CCI observed that the market share of the opposite party 1 has declined from 14.4% to 12.1% during 2017-18, and the turnover was also lower than its competitors. So, the CCI passed an order under section 26(2) of the Competition Act by holding that the opposite party-1 does not hold significant market power to violate section 3(4)(e) of the Competition Act.

players.[190] The market share of the party is compared with that of other market players to analyse whether vertical restraint by the concerned party would cause or is likely to cause adverse effects on the competition. Also, it is implicit that the vertical agreement between two insignificant players will not affect a substantial portion of the market.[191] For instance, *In Re: Accessories World Car Audio Private Limited v. Sony India Private Limited & Other*,[192] while rejecting the allegation of vertical anti-competitive agreement, the CCI held that the market of car audio products consisted of a large number of players and there was no player who possesses significant market share. The CCI was of the opinion that if the market had been fragmented with the presence of a large number of players exerting competitive constraints on each other, then the vertical agreement couldn't cause any AAEC.

Also, in *Automobiles Dealers Association, Hathras, UP v. Global Automobiles Ltd. & Ors.*,[193] the informant alleged that clause 3 of the letter of intent and statement of Global Automobiles shows that there was an exclusive distribution agreement with its dealers for the sale of two-wheeler vehicles. Clause 3 of the letter of intent restricts the dealers from dealing with the competitors of Global Automobile without their permission. However, due to the non-significant market share of both parties, Global Automobile was a new entrant in the two-wheeler manufacturing industry. So, even if there was a restrictive vertical agreement, the presence of adverse effects on competition was not established.

To consider a vertical agreement as an anti-competitive agreement under section 3(4), the enterprises who are a part of the vertical agreement must have a significant market share, the absence of which is unlikely to create any AAEC in the market. For instance, in the *Apple* case,[194] the CCI examined the 'share of market' to assess whether there is anti-competitive effect due to the tie-in arrangement between Apple and mobile network service providers (i.e., Vodafone and Airtel) to limit the market for iPhone in India. As per the available data, the CCI observed that Apple at that relevant point in time had a market share of less than 3% in the smartphone market, and no market participant in the mobile network services market had a market share of more than 30%. Thus, due to insignificant market shares of the parties involved in their relevant market, the CCI observed that none of the parties to the vertical agreement has the strength to adversely affect the market outcome in terms of creating entry barriers, market foreclosure, etc.

This principle was also followed in the case of *Shri Dhanraj Pillay v. M/s Hockey India*,[195] where the CCI approving its earlier *Apple* case held that for an agreement to

190. *M/s Karni Communication Private Ltd. & Other v. Haicheng Vivo Mobile (India)*, Case No. 35 of 2018, para. 25.
191. *Re: Accessories World Car Audio Private Limited v. Sony India Private Limited & Other*, Case No. 03 of 2020, paras 22, 23.
192. *In Re: Accessories World Car Audio Private Limited v. Sony India Private Limited & Other*, Case No. 03 of 2020, paras 22, 23.
193. *Automobiles Dealers Association, Hathras, UP v. Global Automobiles Ltd. & Ors.*, Case No. 33 of 2011, paras 12.2, 12.5, 12.11, 12.12, 12.13.
194. *Apple* case, paras 73, 74, 78.
195. *Dhanraj Pillay and others v. Hockey India*, Case No. 73/2011, paras 10.13.2, 10.13.3.

have an AAEC in India, the person imposing the vertical restriction should be in a dominant position, and the intent behind the restriction should be foreclosure without any obvious efficiency justifications. Further, in an order passed by the CCI in the *Bajaj* case,[196] the CCI invoked the doctrine of *de minimis* (i.e., where the agreements of the enterprises will have an insignificant effect on the market) to oppose the submission against a vertical agreement to have an AAEC in India. The CCI observed that such an agreement can't harm the market where the position of the party to the agreement is weak. As Bajaj Corp. Ltd. does not hold a strong position in the relevant market of the hair oil segment, the restriction imposed by Bajaj Corp. Ltd. would not cause any negative effect on the inter-brand competition.

Conversely, if an agreement has been entered into by an enterprise having a strong market power, it is more likely that such an agreement will cause or likely to cause AAEC in India. The CCI has noted that when an enterprise with strong market power enters into an agreement, the CCI will place greater reliance on the anti-competitive factors mentioned in section 19(3) of the Competition Act which are entry barriers and foreclosure effects. In this regard, it is apposite to note the observations of the CCI in the *Automobile spare parts* case,[197] where it relied on EU jurisprudence and noted that the European Court of Justice (ECJ) in its judgment of *Nederlandsche Banden-Industrie Michelin (Michelin) v. Commission* explained that a dominant player holds a special responsibility to prevent distortion of competition. Hence, the law forbids a market player holding significant market strength from entering into a vertical agreement. Once the market player crosses the threshold of becoming a significant market player, then entering into a vertical anti-competitive agreement would cause an adverse effect on the market.

Nevertheless, the stance of the CCI is that one of the parties in the agreement must have a sizeable market presence and may not enjoy a dominant position, as mentioned under section 4 of the Competition Act, to have any anti-competitive concerns.[198] The key area of analysis that has to be seen under an agreement analysis under section 3 is that the agreement must cause or likely to cause an AAEC in India. Therefore, for an agreement to be void, it must distort the competitive structure of the market appreciably. It must be noted that the CCI has noted that an agreement having insignificant effects will not be a void agreement under section 3 of the Competition Act. To be void, such anti-competitive effects in the agreement must cause AAEC. While there are no straight jacket formulae given under the Competition Act to conclude when an enterprise will have a market power amenable to section 3(4) of the Act, it may be presumed at least on a prima facie basis that any enterprise having a market share of 30% or more will be deemed to be an enterprise having a strong market power, and hence any vertical restrictions so imposed by the enterprise must take into account the factors mentioned under section 19(3) of the Competition Act.

The market participant must have significant market power in its relevant market to restrain the free competition in the downstream or upstream market, create an entry

196. *Bajaj* case, paras 77, 80.
197. *Automobile spare parts* case, paras 20.6.31. 20.6.32, 20.6.35, 20.6.38.
198. *Hiranandani* case, paras 29, 30.

barrier, drive the existing market participants out of the market, or affect the market outcome by deterring entry. Hence, the market power of the parties to the vertical agreement needs to be looked at while assessing the factors to the AAEC under section 19(3) of the Competition Act.

§2.18 FACTORS TO DETERMINE AAEC IN INDIA

As mentioned above, an agreement will be void under section 3(2) of the Competition Act if it causes or is likely to cause an AAEC in India. It would be pertinent to note that for all agreements (other than those agreements mentioned under section 3(3) of the Competition Act), whether at the horizontal level, vertical level or pure commercial agreements,[199] the burden of proof would be on the CCI to demonstrate that the agreement causes or is likely to cause an AAEC in the market in India. The CCI undertakes an effect-based analysis based on the factors to determine AAEC as provided under section 19(3) of the Competition Act. It is worthwhile to note that section 19(3) contains a checklist of both negative factors and positive factors. The negative factors bring anti-competitive effects, such as the creation of barriers to new entrants, likely to drive the existing competitors and the potential to foreclose the competition or harm consumers. The positive factors bring pro-competitive effects, such as improvement in production/distribution, scientific/economic development, or benefit to consumers.

The CCI have to consider all or any of the following factors while determining whether the vertical agreement has caused or is likely to cause AAEC. The negative factors indicate that there is an AAEC, whereas the absence of these negative factors would normally indicate that there is no AAEC. The positive factors are shown by the enterprise to justify efficiency of their agreement; thus, the presence of these positive factors indicates there is no AAEC.[200]

Though there is no straight jacket formula as everything depends on a case-by-case basis, so, for a complete analysis of the net impact of the vertical anti-competitive agreement, all the factors under section 19(3) need to be examined while assessing.

[A] Negative Factors

The negative factors due to vertical agreements disrupt healthy and fair competition in the market. The negative factors result in anti-competitive effects which might foreclose other suppliers/distributors by raising barriers to entry, drive out the existing competitors to reduce intra-brand or inter-brand competition, exploit the end-consumer of the market to earn more profit or create entry barriers to lock the

199. The CCI in the *Hiranandani* case, Case No. 39 of 12, para. 11, found an independent violation under section 3(1) which was not a violation of section 3(3) or 3(4) of the Competition Act. Although the *Hiranandani case* was overturned in appeal on market issues, the point of law that there can be a separate violation of section 3(1) is stated herein.

200. *Automobiles Dealers Association, Hathras, UP v. Global Automobiles and Others,* Case No. 33 of 2011, para. 12.9.

consumers by depriving them of better choices. In the *MMT* case,[201] where MMT was an online travel agency providing travel and tourism-related services, it entered into an agreement with OYO which was providing franchising services to budget hotels, to delist Fabhotels and Treebo (competitors of OYO). The CCI noted that the agreement between MMT and OYO had foreclosed an important online channel of distribution for the Fabhotels and Treebo in the form of denial of market access. Moreover, the agreement created entry and expansion barriers which made it difficult for a new player to enter the market and impossible for existing players to survive. Driving out Fabhotel and Treebo from the market adversely effected the budget hotels in the downstream market because this agreement limited the options of budget hotels while seeking franchise services. The CCI noted that for both franchisors and budget hotels, MMT was the key access route to reach the end consumers. So, this foreclosure had a significant impact on their business in terms of visibility, and thus, they were not getting a fair chance and had no opportunity to compete on merits.

More than the harm to the competitors, the CCI is more concerned about the harm to the competitive process. Thereby, along with anti-competitive effects on the competitors, the CCI also looks at the harm caused to the end consumers due to the vertical restraints. In the *Maruti Suzuki* case,[202] it was observed that the vertical restraint did not result in accrual of any consumer benefits; rather, it resulted in the denial of benefits to consumers as they were made to pay high prices. The vertical restraint in the form of resale price maintenance eliminated the price competition between the dealers and thereby did not incentivize the dealers to pass on the benefit of extra margin to the end consumers by providing better services. Similarly, in the *MMT* case,[203] the CCI observed that the vertical anti-competitive agreement harmed the consumers side by depriving the end-consumers of a wide range of choices, better schemes and policies, technological developments and other benefits of a competitive market.

The CCI should examine all vertical agreements which were entered between vertical parties in order to look into the totality of all the factors mentioned in section 19(3). In this regard, it is noteworthy to look at the observations of the CCI in the *Automobile spare parts* case.[204] The CCI analysed all the agreements entered between OEMs and their dealers and OEMs and their suppliers. The OEMs had entered into a selective distribution system, and they had prohibited their dealers from sourcing any spare parts from any third party apart from OEMs or their authorized vendors. Further, it was also observed that the conduct of the OEMs acts as an entry barrier for independent repairers because the authorized dealers were also prohibited from selling the spare parts to the independent repairers over the counter. The CCI looked into the totality of the agreements to see whether there was a case of anti-competitive behaviour that could be made out. The CCI emphasized the point that efficiencies claimed by the OEMs cannot allow the creation of entry barriers to eliminate the

201. *MMT* case, paras 297, 298, 299 304, 306, 308.
202. *Maruti Suzuki* case, paras 48, 50, 55.
203. *MMT* case, para. 298.
204. *Automobile spare parts* case, paras 20.6.31. 20.6.32, 20.6.33, 20.6.38.

competitive force in the market. For the sake of efficiency gains, the CCI can't ignore the negative effect of the said agreement on the consumers and the market stakeholders. Hence, it was held that short-term efficiency gains must not outweigh the long-term negative effects stemming from the elimination of competition in the market. Understanding the nature of competitive constrain is necessary while analysing AAEC under section 19(3) of the Competition Act. The CCI relied upon the General Court's order in *GlaxoSmithKline Services Unlimited v. Commission*, wherein it was held that an analysis of the effect of the concerned agreement can be done by balancing the negative factors and positive factors of the agreement. However, the negative factors will be prioritized to prevent the market player from indulging in anti-competitive behaviour. The CCI held that even if one or two of the vertical agreements do not violate the competition law and bring efficiency, they may still be held to be anti-competitive if the holistic analysis of all the vertical agreements shows long-term anti-competitive effects to the market by creating entry barrier, driving out existing players, foreclosing the market, and charging exploitative prices from end-customers.

[B] Positive Factors

Factors mentioned in sub-clause (d)-(f) of section 19(3) deal with the pro-competitive effects to the competition in the market. These factors enhance the efficiency of the distribution process and contribute to consumer welfare; hence, they are called positive factors. To determine whether the vertical agreement caused AAEC or not, the CCI should always balance the effect of both positive and negative factors because such an agreement which creates barriers to entry may also induce improvements in the promotion or distribution of goods.[205] For instance, in *Mr. Mohit Manglani v. M/s Flipkart India Private Limited and Others*,[206] where the CCI dismissed the allegation against e-tailers for causing appreciable adverse effects through their vertical restraint in terms of purchase and price of goods in their e-platforms. To reach its conclusion, the CCI analysed the pro-competitive effect of the agreement on the touchstone of factors elucidated under section 19(3) and held that there was no violation under section 3(4) of the Competition Act. It was found that e-tailers increased competition and provided a mechanism for price comparison and comparison of other pros and cons of the products. Hence, it was found that the agreement did not result in an AAEC in the Indian market. The CCI pointed out that the online distribution system had, in fact, shown considerable consumer efficiencies by providing the option of doorstep delivery to consumers which was more convenient than the delivery service provided by brick-and-mortar retail outlets.

Thus, while balancing the anti-competitive effect and pro-competitive effect due to the agreement under section 3, the CCI generally take note of the importance of competition in the market. In a competitive market, the market players are under

205. *Bajaj* case, para. 81.
206. *Mr. Mohit Manglani v. M/s Flipkart India Private Limited and Others*, Case No. 80 of 2014, para. 17.

continuous pressure to improve their capacity and product efficiency to favour customers' welfare. Also, the consumer will benefit because the price of the product will reduce. Further, to survive in the market, market players would be innovative and develop new technologies.[207]

[1] Business Justifications or Rationales

Apart from the positive factors mentioned in section 19(3) of the Competition Act, the CCI can dismiss the allegation of section 3(4) of the Competition Act by considering the business purpose or rationale behind the vertical restraints. In fact, the CCI in the *Bajaj* case[208] has noted that business purpose or rationale of agreements must be looked into and even acknowledged that vertical arrangements can be justified on certain grounds like protection from free riding, efficient management of sales of products, economic efficiency, etc. The business rationales which were considered by the CCI in its previous orders include:

- (i) the objective of the requirement of written permission for the dealers from the entity before dealing with the competitors of the entity is to ensure no one is free-riding on facilities and services provided by the entity and monitor the financial activity of the dealers;[209]
- (ii) exclusive distribution agreement can be used as protection from free riding, efficient management of sales of products, and economic efficiency;[210]
- (iii) exclusively selling the product through its authorized distributors to protect the brand image and goodwill;[211]
- (iv) to protect the interest of all distributors, an exclusive distribution agreement can designate specific sale regions to distributors and restrict the distributors from encroaching on each other's sale regions;[212]
- (v) monitoring the resale price of its own products cannot by itself be said to be anti-competitive;[213] and
- (vi) agreement to sell products exclusively on online platforms results in benefiting the consumers in terms of providing opportunity to the consumers to compare the prices and better delivery services.[214]

Hence, the CCI also looks at the business rationale behind the agreement along with the pro-competitive effects like consumer benefits, improvement in production/distribution, or technological/economic development to hold section 3(4) of the Competition Act is not applicable to such agreements.

207. *Hiranandani* case, para. 18.
208. *Bajaj* case, para. 75.
209. *Hyundai Motor* case, Case Nos 36 and 82 of 2014, para. 70. (CCI).
210. *Bajaj* case, para. 75.
211. *Ashish Ahuja v. Snapdeal.com & Ors.*, Case No. 17 of 2014, para. 19.
212. *M/s K.C. Marketing v. OPPO Mobiles MU Private Limited*, Case No. 34 of 2018, paras 30, 31.
213. *M/s. ESYS Information Technologies Pvt. Ltd. v. Intel Corporation and Others*, Case No. 48 of 2011, para. 8.3.8.
214. *Mr. Mohit Mangslani v. M/s Flipkart India Private Limited & Ors.*, Case No. 80 of 2014, para. 17.

§2.19 EXEMPTION UNDER SECTION 3 OF THE COMPETITION ACT

Section 3(5) of the Competition Act provides for two exemptions, which are intellectual property exemption and export exemption.

Section 3(5)(i) of the Competition Act provides for the intellectual property exemption. The Competition (Amendment) Act, 2023, widens the scope of section 3(5)(i) of the Competition Act by making this provision more inclusive. The inclusive list of IPRs includes: the Copyright Act, 1957; the Patents Act, 1970; the Trade Marks Act, 1999; the Geographical Indications of Goods (Registration and Protection) Act, 1999; the Designs Act, 2000; the Semi-conductor Integrated Circuits Layout-Design Act, 2000; and any other intellectual property law.

The Competition Act provides a limited defence to agreements under section 3 relating to IPR, wherein a person has the right to restrain any infringement of or impose reasonable conditions, as may be necessary, for protecting any rights conferred under IPR legislation. The CCI has observed, in certain decisions, the ambit of the exemption provided under this section. The ambit of the said clause has been discussed in detail in Chapter 5 on IPR and competition law.

Section 3(5)(ii) provides for an exemption in cases of an agreement, for the purposes of section 3, which relates primarily to exports. Section 3 of the Competition Act provides that any agreement which causes or is likely to cause any AAEC in India is void. Therefore, section 3 only covers agreements which have an effect in India. In this backdrop, section 3(5)(ii) provides for an export exemption. Section 3(5)(ii) of the Competition Act provides a safe harbour for the enterprise to enter into an anti-competitive agreement relating to the export of goods from India.

Therefore, the Competition Act exempts export cartels, i.e., a cartel between enterprises located in India which intend to cartelize in markets outside India, as opposed to import cartels, i.e., a cartel between enterprises located outside India with the aim of cartelizing in a relevant market within India. Similarly, any vertical agreement which has the sole purpose of exporting goods outside India will not be covered under section 3 of the Competition Act. In *Shri Nirmal Kumar Manshani v. M/s Ruchi Soya and Others,*[215] the parties to the horizontal anti-competitive agreement pleaded that the agreement pertained to export sales, and therefore, export cartels would be exempted under section 3(5)(ii) because such an agreement had no effects on the markets in India. But, the CCI rejected the plea because neither the Parties were exporters, nor was the agreement exclusively related to exports. Merely because the end product was being exported by the millers and the processors would not immunize the contravention of section 3 of the Competition Act.

The exemption under section 3(5)(ii) of the Competition Act can only be granted to enterprises which are actual exporters of goods from India. *In Re: Cartelisation by Shipping Lines in the matter of provision of Maritime Motor Vehicle Transport Services to the Original Equipment Manufacturers v. Nippon Yusen Kabushiki Kaisha and*

215. *Shri Nirmal Kumar Manshani v. M/s Ruchi Soya and Others*, Case No. 76 of 2012, para. 99.

Others,[216] the CCI rejected the plea for the exemption under section 3(5)(ii) because the opposite parties were not the exporters *as per* the provision but were merely providing maritime transport services to the OEMs who were actually exporters. It was further noted that the exemption under section 3(5)(ii) would not be allowed merely because the end product was being exported out of India. To claim such an exemption, the enterprises must have entered into an anti-competitive agreement exclusively for the supply distribution or control of any exported goods or services.

There are not many orders on the exemption under section 3(5)(ii) of the Competition Act. Thus, the jurisprudence on exemption from the anti-competitive agreements pertaining to the export of products has not been developed. In the coming years, we can expect the CCI to apply and analyse this exemption in a detailed manner.

§2.20 CONCLUSION

Over the past year, the CCI has dealt with various cases involving anti-competitive agreements. Through active enforcement of the Competition Act, the market is protected from the ill effects of anti-competitive agreements. This chapter discussed past case laws and how anti-competitive agreements are treated under competition law. Looking forward, we can expect stronger enforcement and a stricter stance towards cartels and vertical restraints. Along with these two traditional anti-competitive agreements, CCI will also deal with 'hub-and-spoke cartels'. Also, on the side of enforcement, it would be interesting to see how CCI is going to use 'leniency plus' to detect more cartels. Thus, competition law is expecting a huge development in its jurisprudence.

216. *In Re: Cartelisation by Shipping Lines in the matter of provision of Maritime Motor Vehicle Transport Services to the Original Equipment Manufacturers v. Nippon Yusen Kabushiki Kaisha and Others,* Suo Motu Case No. 10 of 2014, para. 37.2.

CHAPTER 3

Abuse of Dominance and Competition Law

§3.01 LEGISLATIVE FRAMEWORK

Section 4 of the Competition Act provides that no 'enterprise' or 'group' will abuse its dominant position. The said section deals with unilateral conduct. Dominant position has been defined under the Competition Act as 'position of strength, enjoyed by an enterprise, in the relevant market, in India, which enables it to (i) operate independently of competitive forces prevailing in the relevant market; or (ii) affect its competitors or consumers or the relevant market, in its favour'.[1]

In India, the determination of 'dominance' is based on a qualitative assessment of the prevalent market dynamics and the relative position of strength enjoyed by the market participants. Section 4 of the Competition Act stipulates specific practices, i.e., imposition of unfair or discriminatory conditions on price in purchase or sale (including predatory pricing), limiting or restricting the production of goods, denial of market access, and leveraging market position in one relevant market to enter into another relevant market, by dominant enterprises shall amount to abuse of dominance.

[A] Textual Interpretation of Section 4 of the Competition Act

Decisional practice suggests that the key analysis that is done by the CCI, the erstwhile COMPAT and the NCLAT, to date, in analysing dominance cases is whether the enterprise under investigation has a 'position of strength'. Such 'position of strength' so enjoyed by the enterprise should enable it to affect the competitors or consumers and the market dynamics in its favour.

There have been various indices (provided under section 19(4)) which have been given under the Competition Act for determining whether the concerned enterprise, under inquiry, is dominant. In light of the factors mentioned, the CCI looks at the

1. Competition Act, section 4 (2) a – Explanation.

market dynamics and behaviour of the enterprise under inquiry to analyse whether the concerned enterprise is dominant or not. Akin to the position in foreign antitrust jurisdictions, it must be noted that merely having a position of dominance is not bad under the provisions of the Competition Act, but it must be proved that the dominant enterprise has also 'abused' its dominance. This is a marked departure from the earlier legislative framework under the previous regime under the Monopolies and Restrictive Trade Practices Act, 1969, wherein emphasis was placed on the size of the concerned player, rather than the actual abusive practice by, or conduct of such a player.

[B] Dominance Per Se Is Not Illegal

In a marked departure from the earlier regime, as discussed at the beginning of this chapter, the Competition Act does not prohibit dominance, only its abuse. Thus, dominance per se is not illegal, rather, it is the abuse of dominance that is prohibited.

Several complaints have been filed before the CCI seeking intervention in cases of mergers which are likely to create dominant enterprises with the capacity to abuse this dominance.[2] However, CCI has consistently held that 'the mere existence of dominance bereft of any abusive conduct under the provisions of Section 4 of the Act, cannot be held to be the basis to order an investigation'.[3] However, 'post-facto, if any matter of abusive conduct under Section 4 of the Act is brought to the notice of the Commission, the same may be looked into at that stage in terms of the provisions of the Act'. Similarly, in *Satyen Narendra Bajaj v. PayU Payments Private Limited*,[4] it was alleged that pursuant to the combination between PayU and Wibmo, the Combined Entity would attempt to monopolize the e-payment gateway market in India, which was likely to have exploitative as well as exclusionary effects in the market of e-payment processing gateways. However, the CCI held that the same was insufficient to give rise to proceedings for abuse of dominance. It observed that:

> ...while the Act prohibits an abuse of dominant position by an enterprise, mere existence of dominant position, without any prima facie evidence of its abuse, is not recognised as an anti-competitive conduct in the scheme of the Act. In order to establish a prima facie case for intervention, an abuse of a dominant position cannot be based on a mere existence or potential to achieve dominance in the market.

Therefore, a mere apprehension of abuse of dominance is not enough to initiate an investigation under the Competition Act because dominance per se is not anti-competitive and only abusive conduct is if the same falls within the provisions of section 4 of the Competition Act.

2. *Consumer Unity & Trust Society v. PVR Limited and INOX Leisure Limited*, Case No. 29 of 2022; *Vikas Verma v. Adani Ports and Special Economic Zone Ltd. & Others*, Case No. 02 of 2021; *Satyen Narendra Bajaj v. PayU Payments Private Limited*, Case No. 23 of 2019.
3. *Vikas Verma v. Adani Ports and Special Economic Zone Ltd. & Others*, Case No. 02 of 2021.
4. *Satyen Narendra Bajaj v. PayU Payments Private Limited*, Case No. 23 of 2019.

[C] Procedure Adopted in an Abuse of Dominance Investigation

Based on the definition of dominance and the scheme of the Competition Act, it is to be noted that in every dominance investigation, there are three key elements which are analysed by the CCI:

(A) definition of relevant market;
(B) to analyse whether the entity under investigation is 'dominant' in the relevant market;
(C) if the entity is found to be dominant, whether the dominant entity has engaged in any actions which can be considered an abuse of the dominant position under section 4 of the Competition Act.

Every investigation of abuse of dominance proceeds as per this structure, and the analysis will be incomplete without a detailed analysis of each of these elements. We have dealt with, in detail, the concepts of 'enterprise' and 'relevant market' in an earlier chapter and the same is not repeated here for the sake of brevity.

As such, practically, it must be noted that most of the decisions depend on the definition of relevant market, and it is for this reason a substantial amount of analysis is done in every dominance investigation on the definition of relevant market to be adopted. Unless an enterprise enjoys a dominant position in the relevant market, its conduct cannot be subjected to an abuse inquiry. Hence, it is a pre-condition for applying section 4 of the Competition Act, which decrees a set of standards of conduct which are applicable to dominant firms and not to non-dominant firms. This is because what may be commercially justified for the latter may become exploitative and exclusionary when practised by the former. A particular conduct when exhibited by a non-dominant player may not be violative of section 4, but the same conduct by a dominant player could be a contravention.[5] The entire Competition Act is predicated on the fact that there are certain activities which done by a dominant player will cause market distortion due to its sheer size, and thus, such activities cannot be allowed. This is why dominant players cannot defend their conduct on the basis of the fact that other industry players also follow the same conduct. On this point, it is relevant to note the analysis of the CCI in *Belaire Owner's Association v. DLF Limited*[6] ('*DLF* case').[7] While refuting the competition law concerns emanating from the agreements between builders and buyers, DLF argued that such one-sided agreements are standard industry practices and all the players in the market follow such practices. The CCI, however, did not give importance to the defence because it noted that DLF is a market leader and a trendsetter, and it is not bound by practices of other players, and in any case, the practice itself is anti-competitive and abusive (as has been discussed later in the chapter). As such, after observing the market practice of DLF, the other players have aped the practice of executing one-sided agreements because they do not have the competitive might of the dominant enterprise. In fact, if DLF were to modify its

5. *Umar Javeed and Ors. v. Google LLC and Anr.*, Case No. 39 of 2018, para. 572.
6. *Belaire Owner's Association v. DLF Limited*, Case No. 19 of 2010.
7. *Ibid.*, para. 12.20.

agreement to make it more buyer-friendly, it would be able to put sufficient pressure on its competitors to follow suit. Accordingly, the CCI concluded that DLF has acted in a manner which has affected competitor and consumer behaviour, to its advantage.

Hence, the above sequential exercise must be necessarily followed while determining an allegation of contravention of section 4 of the Competition Act.[8]

§3.02 POSITION OF STRENGTH

The decisional practice of the CCI, erstwhile COMPAT and NCLAT would show that they undertake a holistic analysis to understand whether the entity under investigation enjoys a position of strength to influence the competitive forces prevalent in the market to its advantage.[9] In the case of *MCX Stock Exchange Ltd. v. NSE India Ltd*[10] ('*NSE* case'), a 'position of strength' was analysed by CCI on the basis of the comparative advantages enjoyed by NSE over its competitors in terms of financial resources, technical capabilities, brand value, historical legacy, etc., and whether an as efficient competitor would be able to engage in the same conduct as NSE.[11] The reason is that such an enterprise can force its competitors to act in a certain manner which would make the market and consumers respond or react such that it is beneficial to the dominant enterprise but detrimental to the competitors. In addition, the analysis is whether such advantages allow the enterprise to undertake certain activities (like low pricing) which the competitors would find difficult to follow on a sustained basis. By virtue of the said observation and approach taken by the CCI in the *NSE* case, it seems to have adopted the efficient competitor test for dominance investigations. This means that whether a certain conduct is exclusionary or abusive depends on whether a competitor, which is as efficient as the dominant enterprise, would be able to sacrifice profits in the same manner in the long run as the dominant enterprise. Herein, it was found that NSE's competitors, i.e., MCX, would not be able to sustain the below-cost pricing adopted by NSE, and hence, NSE was held to be in a dominant position.

This approach of the CCI for determining a 'position of strength' was reaffirmed in *XYZ and Ors v. Alphabet Inc. and Ors*[12] ('*Play Store* case'). In the said case, it was alleged that Google was abusing its control over the Play Store and Android Operating System (OS) in the markets for licensable mobile OS for smart mobile devices and app stores for Android OS in violation of the provisions of section 4 of the Competition Act. This was facilitated through, *inter alia*, mandating app developers to use Google's proprietary Google Play Billing System (GPBS) for in-app purchases and paid apps on the Play Store and advantaging Google Pay, an United Payment Interface (UPI) over competing UPI apps. On the aspect of position of strength, the CCI observed that the moment there is any imposition of any unfair or discriminatory condition by a

8. *Coal India Limited, West Bengal v. Competition Commission of India* [2017], CompLR 0447 (CompAT), para. 20.2-20.4.
9. *RKG Hospitalities Pvt. Ltd. v. Oravel Stays Pvt. Ltd.*, Case No. 03 of 2019, para. 43.
10. *MCX Stock Exchange Ltd. v. NSE India Ltd*, Case No. 13 of 2009, para. 10.36.
11. *Ibid.*, para. 10.38-10.49.
12. *XYZ and Ors v. Alphabet Inc. and Ors.*, Case Nos 07 of 2020, 12 of 2021 and 35 of 2021.

dominant player, the statutory prohibitions shall trigger for all instances of abuse enshrined under section 4(2) of the Competition Act. In this case, Google enjoyed unparalleled competitive advantages which even its nearest rivals were unable to match.[13]

It is to be noted that the aspect of position of strength is not to be viewed in a snapshot manner at a point in time, but the assessment of position of strength must be made over a period of time. The CCI has noted that an enterprise takes years to acquire a position of strength, and therefore, its conduct must be examined over a period of time while undertaking dominance investigations. The CCI has opined in the *DLF* case that an examination of the dominant enterprise needs to be done over a period of time to examine whether a case of abuse under section 4(2) of the Competition Act is made out. The relevant portion of the order is as follows:

> It should be noted that dominance is neither acquired nor asserted in a transient moment in time. It takes years for an enterprise to acquire a position of strength and its conduct has to be examined over a period of time in most cases to ascertain whether it constituted abuse. Use of snapshot data of market shares or market presence based on current active stock figures would give a false picture that, if applied in the context of the Act, may even cause avoidable harm to the market [emphasis supplied]. Therefore, our assessment of dominant position is by looking at the profile, presence and achievements of DLF Ltd. over the years as well as its conduct, particularly in relation to consumers, over a period of time.

At the same time, it must be borne in mind that markets by their very nature are dynamic and keep changing with time. Hence, while analysing dominance, an important factor that needs to be taken into consideration is the time-period during which the contravention of the provisions of the Competition Act is alleged. For instance, after the *DLF* case, when similar allegations were once again raised for identical conduct by DLF two years later in *Amit Mittal v. DLF Limited*,[14] it was found that the market scenario had changed, and DLF was no longer dominant and consequently, no case of abuse can be made out. This also highlights that precedents may not always be valuable in competition law cases as all analysis is based on the effect of market forces.

Similarly, in *Fast Track Call Cab Pvt. Ltd. and Meru Travel Solutions Pvt. Ltd. v. ANI Technologies Pvt. Ltd.* (*Ola* case),[15] an objection was taken that the period of investigation of Ola's conduct was stretched to September 2015 instead of January 2015, when the first order for investigation was passed by the CCI. The CCI clarified that '*though the allegations highlighted in the information serve as a starting point for investigation, the same does not determine its scope in entirety. Moreover, the purpose of investigation in the said markets is not limited to visualizing the static nature of competition, but to have an overall examination of the dynamic aspects*'. Further, the proceedings before CCI are in rem, not in personam. Hence, this brings us to the point

13. *Ibid.*, para. 81.
14. *Amit Mittal v. DLF Limited*, Case No. 73 of 2014, para. 33.
15. *Fast Track Call Cab Pvt. Ltd. and Meru Travel Solutions Pvt. Ltd. v. ANI Technologies Pvt. Ltd.*, Case Nos 6 & 74 of 2015.

that it is not necessary for the period of assessment of dominance to be strictly restricted to the information filed, especially if it's a continuing conduct.

[A] Parameters of Dominance under the Competition Act

To determine position of strength, the definition of dominance under the Competition Act provides for two broad parameters which the CCI needs to look into to identify whether the enterprise in question enjoys a position of strength. The enterprise must:

(1) operate independently of competitive forces prevailing in the relevant market;
(2) affect its competitors or consumers or the relevant market in its favour.

[1] Operate Independently of Competitive Forces Prevailing in the Relevant Market

A market operates where there is an interplay of market forces of demand and supply. Further, a market participant is constrained in its behaviour because of various competitive forces prevalent in the market, like other efficient competitors, strong buyers, market structure, market entry, or any other relevant factors in the concerned market. A market participant may also be constrained by other factors like strict government regulations. Therefore, for the purpose of ascertaining dominance, it is important to examine the ability of an enterprise to operate independently of such competitive forces prevalent in the market, especially competitive forces generated by its rivals. However, this does not mean that the analysis is only limited to direct competitors since the word used is '*competitive forces*'.

Further, an enterprise cannot behave in a manner which is totally lopsided in its favour without keeping into account the concerns of the other market participants, unless the entity in question has an appreciable position of strength. As elaborated earlier, the CCI, erstwhile COMPAT and NCLAT, in their decisional practice, have always given emphasis on whether the enterprise has a position of strength, which can be derived from its market share, financial muscle, regulatory barriers, structural barriers emanating from the operations of dominant enterprise and other operational barriers which have become entry barriers for new players in the market. In this regard, it is apposite to note the approach of the CCI in the *DLF* case. The CCI reviewed the agreements entered into between DLF and the buyers in great detail. We have already discussed how the CCI rejected DLF's defence that such one-sided agreements are standard industry practices on account of DLF's position as a dominant enterprise. Further, the CCI also noted that, under normal competitive market conditions, having such one-sided agreements in place should result in loss of customers since the consumers will shift to some other real estate builder, but such events were not happening. This clearly amplifies the point that DLF is operating independently of the competitive forces. The relevant observations of the CCI in this regard are as follows:

> ... The moot point in this case and indeed the competition concern is that a dominant builder/developer is in a position to impose such blatantly unfair conditions in its 'agreement' with its customers and bind them in such one-sided contractual obligation. In a competitive scenario, where the enterprise indulges in such anti-consumer conduct, there is sufficient competition in the market to provide easy alternatives for the consumer. *The competitive forces would ensure that the builder/developer would soon face loss of customers, which would force it to become more consumer-friendly.* [emphasis supplied] However, only when a dominant enterprise indulges in such conduct is there little hope for the consumers because not only that enterprise indulges in such behaviour with impunity but smaller competitors would want to enjoy as much advantage by following the leader. Since a weaker competitor is not in a position to take on the competitive might of the dominant enterprise, it would rather emulate the dominant enterprise and take similar advantage of the consumers.
>
> If an enterprise has the ability to influence its competitors or the consumers in a relevant market, as demonstrated above, there could be little doubt in its ability to influence the market itself in its favour. An announcement of several large projects by DLF Ltd. at one go could make its competitors react by holding some of their own projects to avoid market saturation. Similarly, prospective consumers may defer their demand in expectation of availability of projects to be offered by the market leader. Thus, DLF Ltd. would be able to influence both the supply and demand of projects in the relevant market. These possibilities indicate that DLF Ltd. has a position of strength as envisaged in Explanation (a)(ii) to section 4 of the Act...

[2] Affect Its Competitors or Consumers or the Relevant Market in Its Favour

This is the second limb in the definition of dominance. The language used in the provision is '... operate independently of competitive forces prevailing in the relevant market or affect its competitors or consumers or the relevant market, in its favour'. Hence, dominance can be established by proving either limb of this definition. As seen in *M/s Kansan News Pvt. Ltd. v. M/s Fastway Transmission Pvt. Ltd. & Ors.*,[16] the CCI observed that the large subscriber base of the multi-system operators (MSOs), which carried the channels offered by broadcasters, meant that every broadcaster was dependent on their network. In such a situation, the MSOs were found to be in a position to affect the market in their favour.

It is critical to find out whether the entity can operate independently of other competitive forces emanating from competitors and consumers. This limb of the definition deals with the link between the position of strength held by the enterprise concerned and the competitive process, i.e., the way in which the concerned enterprise and other relevant stakeholders interact in the market. Dominance is the ability to prevent effective competition from being maintained on the market and to act to an appreciable extent independently of other players. A non-dominant firm cannot

16. *M/s Kansan News Pvt. Ltd. v. M/s Fastway Transmission Pvt. Ltd. & Ors.*, Case No. 36/2011, para. 6.4.10.

operate independently of competitive forces, and hence, regulatory intervention in the commercial decisions of such enterprises is neither warranted nor desired. The credible threat of availability of alternative suppliers and power of the consumer to exercise choice operate as forces to deter exploitation. However, in the case of a dominant enterprise, consumers cannot check exploitation as their choices are constrained, and hence, statutory prohibition and, consequently, timely intervention are required to prevent abuse of dominance. Thus, abuse cannot be looked into in isolation of the market position of the enterprise because an unfair condition constitutes an 'abuse' or offence only for a dominant enterprise.[17]

Generally, in a competitive market, any behaviour of a market participant will have a corresponding response from other players in the relevant market. For example, if a market participant increased the price of its good or imposed unreasonable conditions to the detriment of the counterparty, the consumer would choose the product of the competitor of such market participant. Further, an increase in price will also result in lowering of sales if there is a substitute good available in the relevant market. However, when such behaviour is being imposed by the dominant enterprise, the consumers have no option but to abide by the conditions imposed by such a dominant undertaking. They are faced with a Hobson's choice/'*take it or leave it*' proposition by such an enterprise. Similarly, in the event the dominant undertaking starts undercutting the price of its product, the other players in the market have no option but to follow suit just to remain competitive in the market. An enterprise which is capable of substantially increasing prices above the competitive level for a significant period of time is generally in a position of strength and possesses the requisite ability to act to an appreciable extent independently of competitors, customers and consumers. Further, unlike enterprises in a market characterized by effective competitive constraints, a dominant enterprise is able to price above the competitive level and earn supra-normal profits in the process. In addition, dominant enterprise can also maintain supra-normal profits by reducing output and, hence, escalating demand for the product. The key point is whether the enterprise can conduct its business operations irrespective of the behaviour of the competitors, its customers and consumers. If the answer is yes, then the enterprise/group will be considered to be in a position of strength.

As was the situation in the *NSE* case, the competitors of NSE had no option but to follow the practice of transaction waivers given by NSE just to remain competitive in the market. In the process, apart from NSE, all the other competitors incurred heavy losses, some in fact, exited the market. Therefore, the key analysis to be done is whether the enterprise under investigation can affect the behaviour of consumers or competitors to its advantage. On this aspect, the CCI in the *DLF* case, observed that an enterprise may have the capability to not only operate independently of competitive forces but also influence its competitors or consumers or the relevant market itself in its favour. This is a higher degree of strength which allows the enterprise to freely adopt

17. *Coal India Limited, West Bengal v. Competition Commission of India* [2017], CompLR 0447 (CompAT), para. 20.3.

price or non-price strategies to overcome downward pressures on its profit from its competitors, capture or bind consumers or create a market environment that would deter newer competition, both in terms of competing enterprises or rival products.[18]

This aspect of acting independently was also discussed in the case of *Shamsher Kataria v. Honda Siel Cars India Limited & Ors.*[19] ('*Automobile Spare Parts* case'). The CCI, in this case, observed that the underlying principle in the definition of a dominant position is linked to the concept of market power which allows an enterprise to act independently of competitive constraints prevalent in the market. Such independence affords such an enterprise the capacity to affect the conditions in the relevant market, in its favour, and to the economic detriment of its competitors and consumers. The notion of independence, which is the special feature of dominance, is related to the level of competitive constraint facing the enterprise/group under investigation. For dominance to exist, the enterprise or the group concerned must not be subject to effective competitive constraints. In other words, it thus must have substantial market power. Market power is generally noted in matured antitrust jurisdictions as the power to influence market prices, output, innovation, the variety or quality of goods and services, or other parameters of competition on the market for a significant period of time.

In the *Automobile Spare Parts* case, the CCI relied on the jurisprudence of the EU to analyse the aspect of independence from the competitive forces. It found that as per the EU Guidance on the Commission's Enforcement Priorities in Applying Article 82 EC Treaty to Abusive Exclusionary Conduct by Dominant Undertakings, '*the capacity of an enterprise to operate independently of competitive forces*' is related to the degree of competitive constraints that are exerted on the concerned enterprise. Dominance implies that such competitive constraints are not sufficiently effective, and as a result, the enterprise is able to enjoy substantial market power over time. Hence, the notion of independence means that an enterprise's actions are largely insensitive to the actions and reactions of competitors, customers and, ultimately, the consumers in the market.

It is pertinent to note that the term independence does not mean that there is an absence of any other competitor in the relevant market. It implies that the enterprise in question does not face substantial competitive constraints from the other competitors in the market, and thereby, the enterprise has the market power to change the market dynamics in its favour.

The CCI as well as the erstwhile COMPAT have also made their observations on this point in the *NSE* case. In this case, the NSE started giving repeated transaction fee waivers for transactions done in the currency derivative segment. It must be noted that a stock exchange cannot determine the price at which a particular scrip will be sold in the market. A stock exchange just provides a platform on which scrip can be traded, and it gets a transaction fee for each transaction done on its exchange. Based on the same, it is apposite to note that for a stock exchange, transaction fee is the single most important source of revenue. However, since NSE was providing transaction fee

18. *DLF* case, para. 12.47.
19. *Shamsher Kataria v. Honda Siel Cars India Limited & Ors.*, Case No. 03 of 2011, para. 20.5.59.

waivers for transactions done in the Currency Derivative Segment, MCX-SX and other players which offered services only in the Currency Derivatives had no other option but to follow suit and provide waivers in the Currency Derivative Segment. In the process, the other players, including MCX-SX incurred huge financial losses and depletion in their financial resources. However, NSE continued to make supra-normal profits because it had the licence to operate in other segments (equity, futures/options and wholesale debt market) from the securities regulator which MCX-SX did not have. Thus, in the process, MCX had to adopt the policy to sustain itself in the market for the CD segment. In this factual background, the erstwhile COMPAT noted the following with respect to the behavioural conduct of NSE while establishing dominance:

> The most relevant question was as to whether the NSE could continue with its no transaction fee policy, as compared to its competitor MCX-SX. It is absolutely clear that while NSE could continue because of its relative strength in other segments, MCX-SX could not have continued with that policy and per force it had to adopt the same policy of no transaction fees, as otherwise it could not have even entered the market, forget about its sustenance in that market.

[B] Special Responsibility of a Dominant Player

Dominant enterprises are under a special responsibility to prevent their conduct from impairing genuine undistorted competition.

In the *DLF* case, the erstwhile COMPAT observed that being the market leader, DLF had a special duty to be within the four corners of the law. On this basis, it refused to reduce the penalty imposed on DLF since its fight with the allottees was not a fight among equals. It was observed that 'we cannot be unmindful of the fact that the individual allottees even if they come from the highest strata of the society, either collectively or individually, were pitted against a mighty company, which brand itself to be the biggest real-estate developer. We also cannot ignore the fact that the DLF was a market leader and it was stressed before us by the counsel appearing for the allottees that the other real estate company have also adopted almost the same language in the agreements, which is used by the Appellant with their allottees.'

The special responsibility becomes even more important when a dominant player is in the position of a gatekeeper and guarding the entry of a market. For instance, in *Matrimony.com Limited v. Google LLC* ('*Matrimony* case'),[20] the CCI observed that since 'Google is the gateway to the internet for a vast majority of internet users,' it is obligated to discharge its special responsibility. 'As Google has the ability and the incentive to abuse its dominant position, its "special responsibility" is critical in ensuring not only the fairness of the online web search and search advertising markets, but also the fairness of all online markets given that these are primarily accessed through search engines.'

20. *Matrimony.com Limited v. Google LLC*, Case Nos 07 and 30 of 2021.

In the *Umar Javeed v. Google LLC* ('*Google Android* case'),[21] the CCI opined that markets should be allowed to compete on merits and the onus is on the dominant players (in the present case, Google) to ensure that its conduct does not impinge this competition on merits. Hence, Google was clothed with a special responsibility to not indulge in the conducts enumerated under section 4(2) of the Competition Act and to be mindful of the exclusionary implications of the restrictions imposed by it on OEMs. Google's special responsibility as a dominant player obligated it to use more competition-friendly alternatives so as to not take unfair advantage of its position and ensure fairness and reasonableness in its conduct.

Further, even in the *Play Store* case, in the market for UPI apps, the CCI found that Google was applying different technological standards on its own Google Pay UPI app and competing UPI apps. The CCI held that Google, being a dominant player in the app store for Android OS, has a special responsibility to ensure that access to its platform is available on non-discriminatory terms for all trading partners. Simply because the Google Pay UPI app is in-house, it does not grant Google any right to self-preference and offer dissimilar treatment to other competing UPI apps. This discrimination was not explained or justified by Google on any objective and rational basis, such as any technical constraints limiting seamless integration of third-party apps (TPAP). Hence, it had no reason to escape its special responsibility.

[C] Collective Dominance

Now that we have analysed the two limbs of the definition of a dominant position, it is pertinent to take note that the CCI has observed in the case of *Unitech*[22] that there can only be one enterprise that is dominant in a relevant market. In the said case, the CCI held that because DLF was already dominant in the relevant market, no other entity could be held to be in a dominant position. Further, the language of section 4 of the Competition Act is very different from Article 102 of the Treaty on the Functioning of the European Union (TFEU; in the light of which the Courts in Europe have held that there is a collective dominant position that can be exercised by undertakings in Europe). In fact, the CCI has also consistently observed that section 4 also does not permit a collective dominant position,[23] and there is no concept of 'collective dominance' or 'joint dominance' in the Competition Act.[24] Therefore, as the law stands

21. *Umar Javeed and Ors. v. Google LLC and Anr.*, Case No. 39 of 2018, paras 495, 557.
22. *Jagmohan Chhabra v. Unitech Ltd*, Case No. 21 of 2011, para. 11.
23. *Indian Sugar Mills Association v. Indian Jute Mills Association*, Case No. 38 of 2011; *Brickwork Ratings India Pvt. Ltd v. CRISIL Ltd.*, Case No. 47 of 2019, para. 33; also take note that in the Competition (Amendment) Bill, 2012 wanted to amend section 4 to include abuse either jointly or singly but this bill was not passed.
24. *Builders Association of India v. Cement Manufacturers' Association and Ors.*, Case No. 29 of 2010, para. 177; *Dwarikesh Sugar Industries Limited v. Wave Distilleries & Breweries Ltd. and Ors.*, Case No. 47 of 2014, para. 47; *Delhi Vyapar Mahasangh v. Flipkart Internet Private Limited and its affiliated entities and Anr.*, Case No. 40 of 2019, para. 15; *Mr. Arjun v. Vaicom 18 and Ors.*, Case No. 57 of 2017, para. 10.

today, the CCI will hold that there can neither be more than one enterprise that is dominant in a relevant market nor can there be a collective dominant position.

This position was clarified in detail in the *Ola* case, wherein it was argued that Uber and Ola could both be held dominant simultaneously in the relevant market. The CCI refuted this argument and held that there cannot be more than one dominant enterprise in the relevant market at a particular point in time. This is on the basis of the following factors:[25]

(i) Provisions of section 4(2) of the Competition Act clearly stipulate that dominant position can be held by only one enterprise or one group. 'There shall be *an* abuse of dominant position, if *an* enterprise or *a* group –.' The term 'a'/'an' used evidently states the singular form, which shows that the intention of the legislature was never to hold more than one enterprise to be in a dominant position unless they are part of the group within the meaning of section 5 of the Competition Act.

(ii) The explanation (a) to section 4 uses the phrase 'operate independently' which clearly shows that the concept of 'dominance' is meant to be ascribed to only one entity. The whole essence of section 4 lies in proscribing unilateral conduct exercised by a single entity or group independent of its competitors or consumers. In the presence of more than one dominant entity, none of those entities would be able to act independently of one another.

(iii) If there was any scope for more than one entity being envisaged by the Competition Act, factors like 'size and resources of competitors', 'economic power of the enterprise including commercial advantages over competitors', etc., would not have found place under section 19(4) of the Competition Act.

(iv) Section 28 of the Competition Act, which specifically deals with the division of enterprises enjoying dominant position, the usage of the words unambiguously indicates that the Competition Act does not provide for more than one enterprise to be dominant in the relevant market.

(v) Clause 4 of the Competition (Amendment) Bill, 2012 (Bill No. 136 of 2012) which lapsed due to the dissolution of Lok Sabha, stated as follows:

> In section 4 of the principal Act, in sub-section (1), after the words 'or group', the words 'jointly or singly' shall be inserted. (emphasis supplied)

Hence, the aforesaid proposed amendment further reinforces the proposition that there is no scope in the present scheme of the Competition Act, either expressly or by implication, to contemplate the presence of two independent entities as dominant at the same time in the relevant market, else this amendment would not have been required.

25. *Ola* case, paras 106-116.

Further, the fact that collective dominance was not included in subsequent legislative discussions on the Competition Act, i.e., the Draft Competition (Amendment) Bill, 2020 and Competition (Amendment) Act, 2023, clearly highlights that legislative intention runs contrary to the inclusion of 'collective dominance' in the legal regime.

Having said that, in a real-world marketplace, there are several examples where one will notice that in an oligopolistic marketplace, there are two big competitors, and the other players are small players in the market. Some common examples are Pepsi & Coca-Cola, Boeing & Airbus, Visa & Master Card, Nestle & Hindustan Unilever, P&G & Hindustan Unilever, etc. The Competition Act does not deal in a vacuum but in the manner in which the enterprises operate in the market. Thus, the practical realities and impact faced in the market should also be considered under the Competition Act.[26] Therefore, in these markets, it is possible that each of the entities faces competition from one another, and to say that neither would be dominant in a relevant market would not take into account the market dynamics since all the other stakeholders in the market are completely dependent on the said entities. It is very likely that the two enterprises are above the rest of the competitors, and the latter is unable to compete with the two competitors, and their market conduct is dependent on the behaviour of the bigger players. The question of whether two enterprises can be dominant in the same market is pending before the Supreme Court in the *Ola* case.

In any event, the conduct of two enterprises which have market power in the same market is amenable to investigation under section 3(4) of the Competition Act, which deals with vertical arrangements between upstream and downstream players. For instance, investigations are currently pending in the case of *All India Vendors Association v. Flipkart*[27] (where Amazon and Flipkart operate in the same market) and *National Restaurant Association of India v. Zomato Limited*[28] (where Swiggy and Zomato operate in the same market). Reference may be made to the discussion on section 3(4) in earlier chapters.

§3.03 EXAMINING POSITION OF STRENGTH BY CONDUCT OF THE ENTERPRISE

The CCI, erstwhile COMPAT and NCLAT have examined the conduct of the enterprise under investigation to analyse whether the enterprise enjoys a position of strength. In the process, the authorities assess whether the enterprise can operate independently of the market forces. The CCI has further observed that the market leader enjoys a unique position in the market; it has the ability to influence the market, and it often lays down the rules of the game. Generally, such market power naturally tends to be exercised by such enterprises to the detriment of the interest of its competitors and consumers.

---

26. It would also be relevant to note that under section 19(4)(j) the market structure is also a factor that has to be considered while determining dominant position.
27. *All India Vendors Association v. Flipkart*, Case No. 20 of 2018.
28. *National Restaurant Association of India v. Zomato Limited*, Case No. 16 of 2021.

It is pointed out that one of the aspects which are considered in an *ex post* analysis is whether the conduct itself shows that the enterprise in question is dominant, i.e., could the enterprise have engaged in such conduct had it not been dominant. This logic is a circular fallacy, however, it is a sensible approach in practice because in an *ex post* conduct analysis, the conduct has already happened. This is unlike merger analysis, where conduct is always analysed *ex ante*.

[A] *NSE* Case

Both the CCI and erstwhile COMPAT have examined the aspect of position of strength in detail in the *NSE* case, which emanated from the information filed by MCX-SX relating to an allegation of predatory pricing by NSE by using its overwhelmingly dominant position in the market for stock exchange services in India. NSE was providing complete transaction waiver (zero pricing) in the currency derivative segment. It was also alleged that NSE engaged in exclusionary behaviour by providing a substantial reduction in admission and trade-related fee structure in the currency derivative segment which was aimed at: (i) eliminating competition from the currency derivative segment, (ii) discouraging potential entrants from entering the relevant market for stock exchange services, and (iii) achieving the foreclosure of all competition in the market for stock exchange services.

NSE was given the regulatory licence by the Indian securities regulator to operate in all segments of the stock exchange, i.e., equity segment, futures and options segment, wholesale debt segment and currency derivative segment. However, MCX-SX had licence to operate only in the currency derivative segment. It was also alleged that NSE's strategy of providing transaction fee waivers, admission fee and data fee waivers and the low level of deposit requirements were only in its currency derivative segment and were completely at variance with its conduct in other segments. Such conduct of zero pricing followed by the NSE was aimed at eliminating competition from the currency derivative segment. The other competitors in the currency derivative segment, including MCX-SX, had no option but to follow the pricing policy of the NSE and provide transaction waivers and other benefits like low deposit requirements to merely sustain in the market, let alone remain competitive. In providing such repeated waivers, MCX-SX and the other competitors incurred huge financial losses to the extent of leaving the market. We will deal with the findings on dominance and abuse of dominance by the CCI and erstwhile COMPAT later in the chapter.

For examining position of strength, both the CCI and erstwhile COMPAT raised the following questions to deliberate on the position of strength enjoyed by NSE.[29]

29. *NSE* case, para. 10.38-10.49.

[1] Can NSE Sustain Zero Pricing Policy in the Relevant Market Long Enough to Outlive Effective Competition?

The CCI looked at the financial statements of NSE and observed, on the basis of the reserves, surplus and profits after tax on the balance sheet that NSE has the capacity to defer profits from the currency derivate segment since they were earning supra normal profits from the other segments. Further, based on the financial statements of NSE and MCX-SX, the CCI also observed that the long-term risk of possible market failure in the currency derivative segment of NSE was lesser compared to MCX-SX.

[2] Does the Policy of NSE to Provide Complete Transaction Waivers Make Any Commercial Sense?

Based on the financial strength of NSE and its market conduct in the entire stock exchange market, it was observed by the CCI and erstwhile COMPAT that the policy of NSE to provide such waivers, only in the currency derivative segment, did not make any commercial sense. The only logic for deliberately incurring losses in the currency derivative segment and providing such continuous and repeated waivers for more than two years of operation was to eliminate competition in the currency derivative segment. The CCI noted that the NSE was fully aware of its financial powers and noted that in spite of providing transaction waivers only in the currency derivative segment, it was recording a profit in excess of INR 300 crores. However, MCX-SX which was operating only in the currency derivative segment was incurring huge losses and financial depletion. The CCI observed that it is:

> unthinkable that a professionally managed modern enterprise can afford such financial complacency in the face of competition unless it is part of a bigger strategy of waiting for the competition to die out. This complacence can only point to awareness of its own strength and the realization that sooner or later, it would be possible to start generating profits from the business, once the competition is sufficiently reduced.

[3] Would the NSE Be in a Position to Provide Complete Transaction Waivers Endlessly Had It Not Have Such Financial Muscle?

The CCI examined the market conduct and analysed the financial muscle that NSE possessed. It opined that NSE had undeniable advantages over its competitors, and it was in a position to continue with its conduct because of such strengths vis-à-vis competitors. It was this financial strength which allowed the NSE to continue with its conduct and affect the competitors in its favour. Based on the above parameters, the CCI noted that NSE was in a position of strength.

Thus, one can see that CCI looks at the conduct of the enterprise under investigation to determine whether they are in a position of strength. It is worthwhile to note that while the Competition Act does provide for indices of dominance, the CCI makes a holistic assessment to find out whether the entity in question is operating independently of the competitive forces. As such, the CCI, in the *DLF* case, had also made an observation that it can look at the factors outside the relevant market to analyse whether the entity in question is operating independently and, thus, enjoys a position of strength. Thus, there may be situations in which the relevant market is defined as Market X, but the CCI can look into their past behaviour in Market Y and also the financial muscle of the enterprise or its group holistically to conclude that the concerned enterprise enjoys a dominant position.

§3.04 INDICES OF DOMINANCE: 'ALL OR ANY FACTOR'

As mentioned above, dominance is a position of strength enjoyed by an enterprise/group which enables it to prevent effective competition from being maintained in the relevant market by behaving to an appreciable extent independently of its competitors and consumers. Section 19(4) of the Competition Act provides for certain indices which the CCI can take into account while determining whether the entity, under investigation, enjoys a dominant position or not. The CCI, in its advocacy booklet on abuse of dominance, has noted that 'It is the ability of the enterprise to behave/act independently of the market forces that determines its dominant position. In a perfectly competitive market no enterprise has control over the market, especially in the determination of price of the product. However, perfect market conditions are more of an economic "ideal" than reality. Keeping this in view, the Act specifies a number of factors that should be taken into account while determining whether an enterprise is dominant or not'. It is to be noted that in conducting a dominance analysis, it is relevant to consider the market position of the alleged dominant enterprise, market position of the competitors, barriers to entry and expansion, regulatory norms and buyer power. The existence of dominant position may be derived from several factors which, taken separately, may not necessarily be determinative.

While the Competition Act provides for the indices for determining dominant position under section 19(4), these are not exhaustive, and the CCI makes a holistic assessment to understand whether the entity under investigation enjoys a position of strength unique to its own facts and market under consideration.[30] As mentioned above, it can look at market situations in different relevant markets too, to determine whether the entity under investigation enjoys dominant position.[31] The erstwhile COMPAT has also observed that there is no tick-the-box approach while determining whether an entity enjoys a dominant position. Further, it must also be noted that in rapidly changing markets such as digital markets and platform markets, market assessment cannot have a static approach, and hence, competitive assessments are based on market realities as they exist at the time of assessment.[32]

---

30. *Fast Track Call Cab Pvt. Ltd. and Meru Travel Solutions Pvt. Ltd. v. ANI Technologies Pvt. Ltd.*, Case Nos 6 & 74 of 2015, para. 71.
31. *DLF* case, para. 12.61.
32. *Lifestyle Equities C.V. and Anr. v. Amazon Seller Services Private Limited and Anr.*, Case No. 09 of 2020, para. 27.

The Supreme Court has also observed that section 19(4) empowers the CCI to have regard to 'all' or 'any' of the factors to arrive at the finding of whether or not an enterprise enjoys a dominant position. Hence, even a single factor being 'any' factor may form the foundation to find whether an enterprise enjoys dominance.[33] No priority is given to any factor enlisted under section 19(4) of the Competition Act while determining dominance.

Now, we look at each factor mentioned in the said section for determining dominance.

[A] Market Share

The analysis of the market position of the allegedly dominant enterprise vis-à-vis its competitors provides insight into the degree of actual competition prevalent in the relevant market. As a rule of thumb, as a first step, the CCI analyses the market share of the enterprise under investigation to determine whether it has a dominant position or not. In this regard, the CCI has relied on the jurisprudence of the EU in the *Automobile Spare Parts* case and has opined that market share provides a useful first indication of the market structure and of the relevant importance of the other competitors active in the market.[34]

In the event the enterprise under investigation has a high market share compared to other competitors present in the relevant market, it will be noted by the CCI as an indication of dominance, provided that such market share has been held for some length of time.[35] Hence, for a firm to be dominant, it should be able to sustain its market share for a reasonable period of time. While there is no arithmetic guidance provided as to the minimum level of market share which an enterprise must command to determine whether an entity is in a dominant position or not, it has been generally seen that a market share of more than 50% gives a guidance that the entity is dominant.[36] It is also pointed out that uniform market share thresholds and a standard time period to assess the durability of market share cannot be applied in the same manner to all sectors due to variance across industries.[37] The CCI and the DG have generally relied on industry reports, consumer surveys, internal records of companies and other reports to determine the market share of the players in the relevant market. For calculating market share, the CCI looks into both volume and value sales.[38]

33. *Coal India Limited and Anr. v. Competition Commission of India and Anr.* [2023], (SC) Civil Appeal No. 2845 of 2017, para. 86.
34. Reliance was placed on *Hilti v. Commission* [1991] ECR II-1439, paras 90, 91 and 92; Case T-340/03 *France Télécom v. Commission* [2007] ECR II-107, para. 100.
35. *Informant (Confidential) v. Grasim Industries Limited*, Case Nos 51, 54 & 56 of 2017; *JSW Paints Private Limited v. Asian Paints Limited*, Case Nos 36 of 2019 & 17 of 2021, para. 48.
36. *Automotive Tyres Manufacturers Association v. General Insurance Corporation of India*, Case No. 21 of 2020, para. 15; *Indian National Shipowners' Association v. Oil and Natural Gas Corporation Limited*, Case No. 01 of 2018, para. 122.
37. *Fast Track Call Cab Pvt. Ltd. and Meru Travel Solutions Pvt. Ltd. v. ANI Technologies Pvt. Ltd.*, Case Nos 6 & 74 of 2015, para. 84.
38. *DLF Limited v. Competition Commission of India*, [2014] Comp AT 12.

In the *Google Android* case, Google was found to command a stable, consistent and significant market share of more than 90% based on the investigation of the DG in each of the following markets:

(i) market for licensable OS for smart mobile devices in India;[39]
(ii) market for app stores for Android smart mobile OS;[40]
(iii) market for general web search in India;[41]
(iv) market for non-OS specific web browsers in India;[42]
(v) market for online video hosting platforms in India.[43]

In the *Play Store* case also, market share was the first factor for determining dominance, and the CCI reaffirmed Google's overwhelmingly high market share of more than 95% in the market for licensable OS for smart mobile devices in India and market for app stores for android OS (as discussed above).

[1] Market Share Is Not the Sole Criterion for Determining Dominance

The primary reason for calculating market share is to determine the real market position of the entity under investigation. While the CCI has always analysed the market share in a dominance investigation, it has observed in numerous decisions (like the *NSE* case and the *DLF* case) that it looks into other factors under section 19(4) of the Competition Act and does not limit itself only to market shares to determine whether the entity enjoys a position of strength. Even in the case of *Ramakant Kini v. Dr L H Hiranandani Hospital, Powai,*[44] the CCI, while assessing the dominance of the Hiranandani hospital in the relevant market for provision of maternity services by super speciality and high-end hospitals within a distance of 12 km from the Hiranandani Hospital, held that the market share of an entity is '*only one of the factors that decides whether an enterprise is dominant or not, but that factor alone cannot be decisive proof of dominance*'. This position of the CCI has been reiterated in a slew of other cases as well.[45]

While the CCI has noted that market share provides a first indicator of the market success of the concerned enterprise in comparison to its competitors, it is not the sole criterion for determining dominance. In the *Automobile Spare Parts* case,[46] the CCI has noted that market shares are the initial indications which are to be put in perspective

39. *Google Android case*, paras 95-104.3.
40. *Ibid.*, paras 156-162.
41. *Ibid.*, paras 222-229.
42. *Ibid.*, paras 284-289.
43. *Ibid.*, paras 308-316.
44. *Ramakant Kini v. Dr L H Hiranandani Hospital, Powai,* Case No. 39 of 2012.
45. *Biocon Limited and Anr. v. F. Hoffmann-La Roche AG and Ors.* Case No. 68 of 2016, para. 54; *Fast Track Call Cab Pvt. Ltd. and Meru Travel Solutions Pvt. Ltd. v. ANI Technologies Pvt. Ltd.*, Case Nos 6 & 74 of 2015, para. 104; *Federation of Hotel & Restaurant Associations of India and another v. MakeMyTrip India Pvt. Ltd. and others with Rubtub Solutions Pvt. Ltd. v. MakeMyTrip India Pvt. Ltd. and others*, Case 14 of 2019 & 01 of 2020, para. 229; *Indian National Shipowners' Association v. Oil and Natural Gas Corporation Limited*, Case No. 01 of 2018, para. 123.
46. *Automobile Spare Parts* case, para. 20.5.65-20.5.68.

in light of the other factors mentioned under section 19(4) to make an overall assessment of the market power of the firm under investigation. Even in the *DLF* case,[47] the CCI has noted that the provisions of section 19(4) make it evident that market share *need not necessarily be the single predominant factor,* and often, a host of other factors have to be considered.

It is pointed out that if sufficient and undisputed data is not available to determine market share in a credible manner, it becomes even more important to draw on other corroborating data and analyse the other factors in greater depth to off-set the difficulties in working out specified market shares on account of data constraints, and/or to complement the market share when margins between competitors are not wide enough in determining the strength of the enterprise in terms of affecting market forces as set out in the Explanation (a) to section 4.

Further, it is to be noted that high market share (of say more than 50%) assumes greater dominance in a market which has a low level of concentration than in a relatively concentrated but equally divided market. In this regard, it is apt to point out the observation of the Report of the High Level Committee on Competition Law, 2000, which noted that:

> But then, this ambiguity has a justification having regard to the fact that even a firm with a low market share of just 20% with the remaining 80% diffusedly held by a large number of competitors may be in a position to abuse its dominance, while a firm with say 60% market share with the remaining 40% held by a competitor may not be in a position to abuse its dominance because of the key rivalry in the market. [emphasis supplied]

This was seen in the *Ola* case,[48] wherein it was held that a market share of more than 50% could not lead to a presumption of dominance, especially when the scheme of the Competition Act does not specify any numerical threshold. Competition and competition law is not about counting the number of firms in a particular relevant market to determine whether or not that market is competitive. Every market is unique, with a unique number of players that are determined organically by competitive forces. In appeal, the NCLAT noted that there was a significant rising trend in the assessment period, whereafter Ola's market share plateaued or witnessed a gradual decline. Hence, there can be markets which may not be competitive even with a large number of players and equally possibly there can be markets which can work perfectly well with fewer players, constraining the conduct of each other (in this case, Uber constrained the conduct of Ola as shall be discussed under abuse). What is significant is that the existing firms are effective enough to constrain the behaviour of one another so as to dissuade independent abusive conduct by any of them.[49]

47. *DLF* case, para. 12.54.
48. *Ola* case, para. 84.
49. *Meru Travel Solutions Pvt. Ltd. v. Uber India Systems Pvt. Ltd. and Ors.*, Case No. 96 of 2015.

[B] Strength of the Enterprise Vis-à-Vis the Competitors

To determine dominance, it is essential for the CCI to analyse whether the enterprise can operate independently and affect the competitors in its favour. For this, the CCI analyses the competitive strengths of the enterprise under investigation vis-à-vis the other competitors. The CCI, in the *DLF* case, has clearly mentioned that it is critical to evaluate the relative position of strength in terms of the size and resources of the enterprise vis-à-vis the competitors in a dominance investigation. CCI also takes into account financial parameters like profit after tax, net income, sales, capital employed, etc. The CCI made a very interesting observation in the *DLF* case[50] that the relative strength of the dominant enterprise vis-à-vis other competitors need not be confined only to the relevant market as that would defeat the very purpose of the parameters under sections 19(4)(a), (b) and (c) of the Competition Act, limiting the analysis to a specific product or market alone. Rather, the overall size and resources of the enterprise and competitors in question can also be considered to arrive at a comparative position of strength. In the *DLF* case, while the market was defined to be limited to Gurgaon, the CCI actually looked into the financial reserves of the entire DLF group as a whole.

In appeal, the erstwhile COMPAT also held that the size and resources of DLF, its capital employed, and its total business were nowhere comparable to its competitors. It also observed that while comparing the size and strength of the companies, *inter se*, all the factors have to be taken into consideration as to whether the size and resources of a particular company make it dominant or not.[51]

The CCI also discussed in detail the issue of competitive strengths of the enterprise vis-à-vis its competitors in the case of *HT Media Ltd v. Super Cassettes Ltd*[52] ('*Super Cassettes* case'). The *Super Cassettes case* was initiated due to information filed by HT Media Ltd which ran an FM radio channel, alleging that Super Cassettes had abused their dominant position by: (a) charging excessive amount as licence fees/royalty in licensing its copyright of 'Bollywood' movie songs; (b) imposing a minimum commitment charge irrespective of actual needle hour; and (c) making conclusion of licensing arrangement subject to acceptance of excessive licence fees and minimum commitment charge.

While determining the issue of whether Super Cassettes were dominant in the relevant market, the CCI took note of the industry in question and made the following comparisons between Super Cassettes and other competitors to determine the competitive strength of Super Cassettes:[53]

(1) income of Super Cassettes vis-à-vis its competitors;

50. *DLF* case, para. 12.60.
51. *DLF Limited v. Competition Commission of India*, [2014] Comp AT 12, para. 93.
52. *HT Media Ltd v. Super Cassettes Ltd*, Case No. 40 of 2011.
53. *Ibid.*, paras 179-180.

(2) purchase of rights by Super Cassettes (forty-eight Bollywood films in 2010 and 2011) compared to its closest competitors (like Sony) which could not even purchase more than ten to eleven films per year;
(3) purchase of rights by Super Cassettes of all movies which had bankable stars, i.e., top Bollywood stars. In this regard, the CCI observed that Super Cassettes has purchased a number of films with 'bankable' stars, and while the purchase of music rights of films which have 'bankable' stars does not guarantee that the music is a hit, the presence of 'bankable' star is likely to generate much more interest in such movies than a normal film without superstars, and therefore, the likelihood of its success is more than a film which has lesser known actors.

Therefore, the CCI observed that the superior financial strength in the market coupled with superior resources, as in this case, is an important indicator of dominance of an enterprise.

Keeping these factors in mind, the CCI noted that Super Cassettes had a superior market position vis-à-vis its competitors. However, the strength of an enterprise cannot always lead to a presumption of dominance and, instead, may be attributed to competitive efficiency and innovation. For instance, in the *Ola* case, the informant suggested relying on the ability of Ola to engage in predatory pricing as a factor of its dominance. In this case, Ola and Uber were aggressively competing by engaging in below-cost pricing (discussed in more detail in the abuse part). The CCI held that most firms, dominant or not, can engage in practices, such as exclusive dealing, below-cost pricing, loyalty discounts, etc., especially new entrants, so as to gain a toehold in the market. Hence, holding them dominant on this basis can have a chilling effect on competition as an entrant armed with a new idea, a superior product or a technological solution that challenges the status quo in a market and shifts a large consumer base in its favour would have to be erroneously held dominant. This brings us to the point that market power is a matter of degree. In most markets, every enterprise will have some degree of market power, by virtue of which they can affect consumers or competitors in its favour to some extent. The key consideration is to determine dominance.

The NCLAT[54] elaborated on this and noted that the end-to-end provision of service from booking to alighting from the taxi with tracking system of the taxi – all provide a high degree of reliability and assurance of availability of taxis anywhere, including security to riders and enough demand to drivers. This is a new way of doing business and Ola could translate this concept into reality by employing technology in a more effective and enabling fashion to provide services which previous radio taxi operators were not able to. Before the advent of technology-leveraged, network-based aggregator models, taxi services such as Meru, Fast Track, Easy Cab, Taxi For Sure, etc., also leveraged technology to provide ease of booking and taxi rides, yet Ola's model differed from them. Also, Ola offered customer discounts and drivers' incentives

54. *Meru Travels Solutions Pvt. Ltd. and Anr. v. Competition Commission of India* [2017], (NCLAT) Competition Appeal (AT) No. 19 of 2017, paras 21-24.

in conjunction with these facilities and conveniences to attract riders and create and reinforce a brand image over a period of time. This helped Ola to grab a big chunk of the market. Further, Uber's presence in the market around the same time provided competition to Ola, and it had to calibrate and change its market strategy, including pricing, to respond to Uber's competition. Thus, in effect, the NCLAT held that innovation should not be stifled. It is an acknowledgement of the fact that robust market players can also emerge as a result of pro-competitive and legitimate business practices by offering superior products and adopting innovative and disruptive technologies through investment in research, development and infrastructure. Hence, competitive efficiency and innovation do not always lead to a presumption of dominance but can be an indicator of healthy competition in the market.

Conversely, in the *Play Store* case[55] and *Google Android* case,[56] Google argued that it faced competitive constraints from Apple's iOS, which itself had access to significant resources equivalent to Google's scale. However, the CCI rejected this on the grounds that app stores are OS specific, and an OEM cannot change the app store once the device has been manufactured with a specific OS. Hence, the CCI held that Apple (iOS) is not substitutable with Google (Android). Similarly, app developers making apps for iOS cannot automatically port them to Android as they are based on different source codes, and users cannot download an app from the Google Play Store for their iOS devices. Android and iOS cater to a distinct set of customers and are complementary rather than substitutable distribution channels. Hence, Apple's App Store is not an option at all and thus cannot be considered a substitute. This brings us to the point that in considering the strength of competitors, it is first necessary that they should belong in the same relevant market and offer substitutable goods or services, as opposed to being a complementary distribution channel. Non-substitutable products or services cannot pose effective constraints.

[C] Economic Power of the Enterprise Including Commercial Advantages over Competitors

In the *DLF* case,[57] the CCI created a lucid picture of the comparative strengths of DLF as opposed to its nearest competitors. It noted that DLF had started its business way back in 1946, and apart from the residential sector, it had leading positions in commercial, retail and office space sectors as well, which was clear from its Red Hearing Prospectus. In fact, DLF started bookings in its projects despite not having the necessary clearances. This itself indicated the position of strength enjoyed by DLF in the eyes of consumers since they bought the properties even without any clearances. Hence, DLF was held to be dominant on the basis of its profile, presence and achievements over the years, as well as its conduct, particularly in relation to

55. *Play Store* case, paras 103-1110.
56. *Google Android* case, paras 75-84.
57. *DLF* case, para. 12.69-12.76.

consumers, over a period of time. This detailed treatment was also upheld by the erstwhile COMPAT in appeal.

[1] Network Effects

Network effects refer to a phenomenon where the value of a platform increases as more people use it. For instance, a social media platform will become more valuable to users with an increase in the number of users they can connect with. Generally, the strength of the network varies with the number of users; i.e., more users make the network more valuable and this keeps reinforcing the strength of the network once it reaches a critical mass of users.

In two-sided markets, network effects may enable a large platform/network to become dominant and insulate itself from potential competition, as entrants may find it difficult to challenge the large incumbent. The strength of network effects thus becomes a key factor in the determination of dominance in such markets.[58] Network effect in turn ensures that customers do not switch to other platforms easily unless there is a new competitor entering the market with an altogether disruptive technology.[59]

In CCI's decisional practice, it has observed that digital markets such as online search,[60] digital advertising,[61] e-commerce,[62] etc., are characterised by network effects which operate as entry barriers as new players are unable to match the scale of operations and users enjoyed by the incumbent platform, which reinforces its dominant position. This has been discussed in more detail in Chapter 6 on digital markets.

In Re: Updated Terms of Service and Privacy Policy for WhatsApp Users ('*WhatsApp* case'),[63] the CCI, in their order directing investigation, found WhatsApp to be dominant in the relevant market for over the top (OTT) messaging apps through smartphones in India, *inter alia,* on the basis that WhatsApp's pronounced network effects make it difficult for the users to switch apps and force users to stay locked into its network:

> In India, the network effects have indubitably set in for WhatsApp, which undergird its position of strength and limit its substitutability with other functionally similar apps/platforms. This, in turn, causes a strong lock-in effect for users, switching to another platform for whom gets difficult and meaningless until all or most of their social contacts also switch to the same other platform. Users wishing to switch would have to convince their contacts to switch and these contacts would have to persuade their other contacts to switch. Thus, while it may be

58. *Fast Track Call Cab Pvt. Ltd. and Meru Travel Solutions Pvt. Ltd. v. ANI Technologies Pvt. Ltd.*, Case Nos 6 & 74 of 2015, paras 90-92; *Vijay Gopal v. Big Tree Entertainment Pvt. Ltd. and Ors.*, Case No. 46 of 2021, para. 31.
59. *Harshita Chawla v. WhatsApp Inc. and Facebook Inc.*, Case No. 15 of 2020, para. 84.
60. *Umar Javeed and Ors. v. Google LLC and Anr.*, Case No. 39 of 2018, para. 252.
61. *Digital News Publishers Association v. Alphabet Inc and Ors.*, Case No. 41 of 2021, paras 19, 291.
62. *All India Online Vendors Association v. Flipkart India Private Limited and Anr.*, Case No. 20 of 2018, para. 28.
63. *In Re: Updated Terms of Service and Privacy Policy for WhatsApp Users*, Suo Moto Case No. 01 of 2021.

technically feasible to switch, the pronounced network effects of WhatsApp significantly circumscribe the usefulness of the same.

In the *Play Store* case,[64] the CCI observed that OS exhibits indirect network effects; i.e., the benefit to users of an OS increases with the volume and quality of native apps they can access on that OS, and similarly, the benefit to app developers increases with the number of users they can access on an OS. This is likely to act as a barrier to new entry and expansion as it creates a 'chicken and egg' problem, i.e., an OS needs a critical mass of users to attract app developers but also needs a critical mass of app developers to attract users. In the *Google Android* case, CCI explained this proposition of network effects with the following figure:[65]

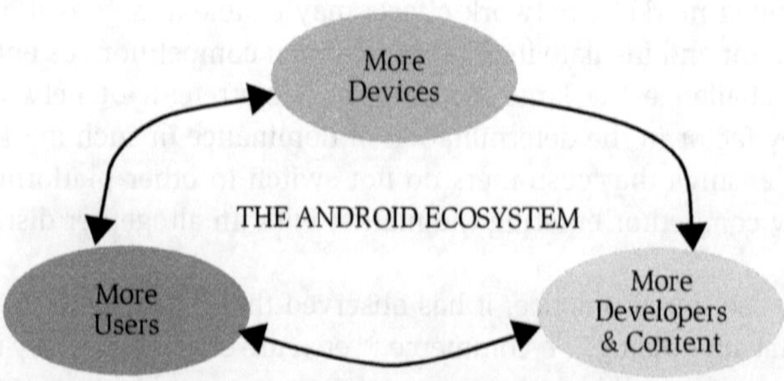

Thus, more app developers creating apps for an OS increases the value of the OS in the eyes of the users, leading to an increase in the number of users, which means more devices based on the said OS are sold. This is a positive feedback loop which feeds into itself thereby increasing the value of the Android ecosystem at large.

In *Federation of Hotel & Restaurant Associations of India and another v. MakeMyTrip India Pvt. Ltd. and others* ('*MMT* case'),[66] the CCI held that positive indirect network effects operate in the market in that both hotels and consumers positively value the presence of more users on the other side of the platform, as it creates higher visibility and potential sales (for hotels) and wider variety and options (for consumers).

However, it is not always the case that network effects are seen as an impregnable barrier to entry to expansion. For example, in the *Ola* case,[67] it was found that both Ola and Uber were aggressively competing with each other to attract participants, i.e., drivers and riders, on both sides of their platforms. However, despite Ola having the largest network, the network effect was not strong enough to deter entry and rapid expansion of Uber. Thus, the consideration of whether network effects act as a barrier to entry and expansion in the market requires a case-by-case analysis. While network

64. *Play Store* case, para. 102.
65. *Google Android* case, paras 111,112.
66. *Federation of Hotel & Restaurant Associations of India and another v. MakeMyTrip India Pvt. Ltd. and others with Rubtub Solutions Pvt. Ltd. v. MakeMyTrip India Pvt. Ltd. and others*, Case 14 of 2019 & 01 of 2020, para. 226.
67. *Ola* case, paras 90-93.

effects undoubtedly play a significant role in digital markets (as shall be discussed in detail in Chapter 6), it is essential to assess the extent of such barriers to fully understand their implications on the market. This requires an analysis of the unique characteristics of each market and the strategies employed by the market participants.

[D] Consumer Dependence

The dependence of consumers on an enterprise also strengthens its position. One of the important aspects to note herein is the identification of the consumers in a particular case. In *Biocon Limited v. F. Hoffman-La Roche AG*[68] ('*Roche* case'), the CCI ordered an investigation into Roche for alleged anti-competitive conduct with respect to its biological cancer drug, Trastuzumab. The issues of CCI's jurisdiction to decide competition issues arising out of patents have been discussed in Chapter 5 on IPR. In assessing Roche's dominance, the CCI observed that the introduction of Trastuzumab gave its innovator Roche, a significant edge over its competitors. Further, existing patients who were already undergoing treatment based on the reference biological drug did not switch to its substitutes, as the doctors might not have prescribed an alternative medicine during ongoing treatment, especially considering the nature of the disease. Hence, consumer dependence on Trastuzumab increased Roche's position of strength.

In the *MMT* case,[69] the CCI, while delineating the relevant product market, highlighted the non-substitutability of MMT with other forms of booking options which creates dependence of hotels on online travel aggregators (OTAs) like MMT. Given that MakeMyTrip, Goibibo ('MMT-Go') was the biggest OTA, having the highest market share during the period under investigation, the dependence of the hotel side on MMT-Go for their survival and growth, was evident.

In the *Google Android* case,[70] theoretically, Google claimed to make the source code of Android available for free via the Android Open-Source Project and under an open-source licence known as 'Apache licence'. However, in reality, this was not a substitute for Google Android because unlike the open-source licence, each version of Android introduced new APIs, bug fixes and security fixes that brought new features to the OEMs. This was perpetuated through Google's application programming interface (APIs) which were contingent on OEMs signing Google's agreements. Further, even access to critical and 'must have' apps like the Google Play Store (which was the largest app store across all mobile OSs in India) was dependent on signing these agreements. Without access to Google Play Services, a smart device would not be commercially viable or at least the OEM offering these devices would be competitively disadvantaged. Further, OEMs were also dependent on Google because it owns the IPRs related to Android OS, and even the 'Android' name and the Android logo are property of Google and not part of the assets available through the Android Open-Source Project.

68. *Biocon Limited v. F. Hoffman-La Roche AG,* Case No. 68 of 2016, para. 56.
69. *MMT* case, para. 231.
70. *Google Android* case, paras 25-49.

This conduct along with the abuse emanating out of the same has been discussed in Chapter 6 on digital markets.

The CCI on the basis of the investigation report of the DG noted that though Android OS theoretically is an open-source project, it was actually controlled by Google. It found that in order to have access to the proprietary apps of Google, including Play Store, Play Services, Google Search, etc., as well as the trademarks related to Android, OEMs have to sign multiple agreements with Google such as Mobile Application Distribution Agreement (MADA), Anti-fragmentation Agreement (AFA), Android Compatibility Commitment Agreement (ACC) and Revenue Sharing Agreement (RSA). The cumulative effect of these agreements has been described in the following flowchart:

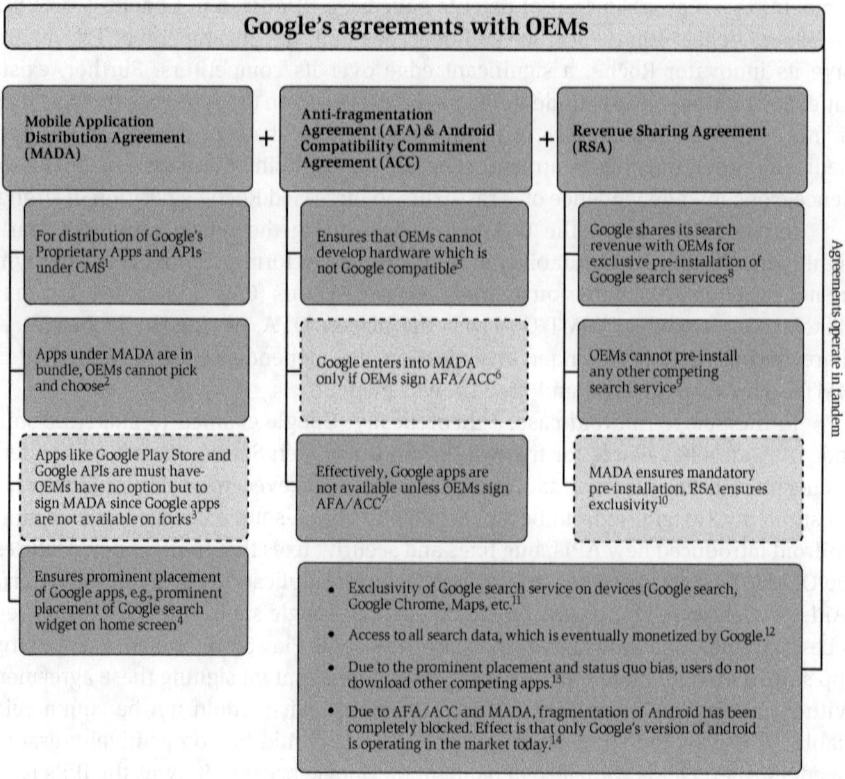

Hence, due to the compatibility obligations of OEMs following these agreements, they were restrained from manufacturing and selling devices incorporating the forked version[71] of Android OS. Therefore, any OEM who wants to offer these 'must have' services to its customers must sign and accept the restrictions laid down in MADA,

71. an operating system that is a modified, competing version of Android OS based on the Android source code.

AFA/ACC and, thereafter, RSAs to maximize the revenue. Hence, competing general search service providers were not in a position to nullify the competitive edge that Google secured for itself through pre-installation as well as premium placement under MADA. This meant that Google had manufactured unyielding consumer dependence in its favour. The anti-competitive effects of these agreements, as has been elaborated by the CCI, have been discussed under abuse.

Herein, it is pointed out that in appeal, Google argued before NCLAT that all three agreements (MADA, AFA/ACC, RSA) should be separately looked into. However, the NCLAT rejected this on the premise that when all three agreements are signed by an OEM, its consequence has to be conjointly looked into. This implies that when the subject of all three agreements relate to Android open source and are interrelated, they have to be read conjointly to examine their cumulative effect to examine the dependence of consumers and the extent of network effects as a barrier to entry.

[E] Entry Barriers

The CCI in its decisional practice of abuse of dominance, has always looked into entry barriers while determining whether an entity is dominant or not. It has been noted that low barriers to entry or expansion by actual or potential competitors can deter a company from raising prices if expansion or entry would be likely, timely and sufficient. Having said that, expansion or entry must be immediate and of sufficient scope and magnitude to constitute an efficient, competitive constraint on the enterprise concerned.

Barriers to entry can include not only legal barriers but also advantages peculiar to the dominant company. They include all those behaviour patterns which a new entrant will have to follow in order to be sustainable in the market. Such patterns may be a result of the dominant incumbent. The CCI also considers the behaviour of the dominant undertaking, which may in turn become a market barrier for other enterprises in the market. For example, in the *NSE* case, NSE started providing transaction waivers only in the currency derivative market. In such a situation where the rules of the game are set by the dominant incumbent, a new player has no option but to match the behaviour of the dominant enterprise, in this case, which was providing transaction waivers to start with to enter the said market, leave alone being competitive.

Entry analysis provides information on the significance of potential competitors for competition in the market concerned and thus about market power and its durability – to the extent such power is found. The relevant question to be asked here is whether entry or expansion will pose a credible competitive constraint on the incumbent. The CCI analyses whether the potential entrant, if any, will dilute the strength of the dominant incumbent. If the potential entry does not dilute the strength, then entry barriers are too high in the market, and that entry shall not be swift to constrain the behaviour of the dominant enterprise. To determine whether a firm's market power is durable, the CCI takes into account whether the potential entrant is sufficient to preclude the exercise of market power.[72] Expansion or entry must also be sufficient to defeat the exercise of market power, i.e., it must be large enough, and of a character, to constrain the behaviour of a firm alleged to be dominant or in possession of substantial market power to a sufficient extent. Further, the entry must be swift and within a short time frame to pose an effective competitive constraint on the dominant incumbent.

[1] Legal Barriers to Entry

Barriers to entry include legal barriers to entry (like applicable governmental rules and regulations on the number of players in the market or any entry fees). For example, laws/governmental regulations which limit the number of market participants (like the *Adani* case discussed below), such as by granting special or exclusive rights in the shape of concessions, licences or IPR. Legislative measures that grant a single enterprise, including public bodies, the exclusive right to perform a certain activity exclude rivals and may lead to such an enterprise having a statutory monopoly in a relevant market.[73] Further, regulatory approvals that may be required to be obtained for the development, manufacturing/import and marketing of a product also constitute a legal barrier to entry, such as in the pharmaceutical sector where significant regulatory approvals are required for releasing a drug in the market.[74]

[2] Strategic Barriers to Entry

As mentioned above, barriers to entry include not only legal barriers but also strategic barriers which the potential entrant has to overcome to provide an effective competitive constraint on the behaviour of the dominant incumbent. Such strategic barriers will include barriers like high sunk costs, time, expertise, resources, advertising and promotional expenses, distribution and supply network, vertical integration, innovation, research and development, and inflow of huge capital which confers a competitive advantage on the dominant incumbent, which makes it difficult for the other

72. *Amit Mittal v. DLF Limited*, Case No. 73 of 2014, para. 31.
73. *Central Organisation for Railway Electrification v. M/s PPS International*, Ref. Case No. 05 of 2018, para. 14; *Confederation of Indian Alcoholic Beverage Companies and Anr. v. Kerala State Beverages (Manufacturing and Marketing) Corporation Ltd.*, Case No. 10 of 2021, para. 58; *Confederation of Real Estate Developers Association of India v. Greater Noida Industrial Development Authority* and *Confederation of Real Estate Developers Association of India v. New Okhla Industrial Development Authority* and *Supertech Limited v. Greater Noida Industrial Development Authority*, Case Nos 34, 37 & 38 of 2020, para. 49; *Department of Sports v. Athletics Federation of India*, Ref. Case No. 01 of 2015, paras 42-44; *Dhanraj Pillay and Others v. M/s Hockey India*, Case No. 73 of 2011, para. 10.10.2; *Hemant Sharma and Ors. v. All India Chess Federation*, Case No. 79 of 2011, paras 41-44; *HPCL-Mittal Pipelines Limited v. Gujarat Energy Transmission Corporation Limited and Ors.*, Case No. 39 of 2017, para. 61; *Mr. Shravan Yadav and Ors. v. Volleyball Federation of India and Anr.*, Case No. 1 of 2019, para. 30; *Starlight Bruchem Ltd. v. Flora and Fauna Housing & Land*, Case No. 53 of 2017, para. 97.
74. *Biocon Limited and Anr. v. F. Hoffmann-La Roche AG and Ors.*, Case No. 68 of 2016, para. 57.

enterprises to enter the market and compete effectively with the alleged dominant enterprise.[75]

The CCI analysed the issue of such barriers in the *Automobile Spare Parts* case and the *Super Cassettes* case. The *Automobile Spare Parts* case[76] revolved around the issue of non-availability of spare parts in the aftermarket. The CCI analysed the market and noted that the technical compatibility of a consumable secondary product (aftermarket, i.e., spare parts) is intrinsically linked to the durable primary product (the car). The owner of the primary product is locked in and has to necessarily use the spare parts/diagnostic tools compatible with the car. Such technical compatibility requirement is itself an entry barrier for other competitors to enter the relevant market for aftermarket since they would need to procure the relevant parts which are technically compatible with the primary product to service the consumer.

Further, the CCI also noted that by way of agreements entered into with suppliers, the OEMs (i.e., manufacturers of the primary products) have put in place restrictions to ensure that independent repairers do not have access to such spare parts. The independent repairers require spare parts and diagnostic tools to effectively compete with the authorized dealers in the aftermarket of repairs and maintenance for each brand of cars manufactured by the OEMs. By virtue of a network of agreements, it was observed in the market that suppliers of spare parts were prohibited by OEMs from supplying the spare parts in the open market which can then be readily procured by independent repairers or players who want to enter into the market of repair and maintenance. However, in the given market situation, independent repairers and new entrants will have to rely on authorized dealers for spare parts and diagnostic tools. In sum and substance, the CCI noted that by virtue of such agreements, the entire market across the value chain was locked, which in turn, led to consumer loss in terms of increased prices.

Even in the *Super Cassettes* case, the CCI noted there are significant strategic barriers to entry in the market.[77] It was noted that to be successful in the business of licensing music, music rights have to be purchased (the purchase price can go up to INR 10 crores), and massive investments, in the form of sunk costs and acquisition costs, are required for promotion of the music and, to establish an efficient distribution network. Further, a new player, to be an efficient competitor to the dominant incumbent, has to build a repertoire of music which takes a considerable amount of time and requires significant investments. The CCI further analysed that, for a new entrant to act as an effective competitive constraint on the behaviour of the dominant enterprise, such entry must be done within a quick time span. Based on the above, the CCI, in the *Super Cassettes* case, noted that there are high barriers to entry.

75. *Biocon Limited and Anr. v. F. Hoffmann-La Roche AG and Ors.*, Case No. 68 of 2016, para. 57; *Department of Agriculture, Cooperation & Farmers v. M/s Mahyco Monsanto Biotech (India) Limited and M/s Nuziveedu Seeds Limited (NSL) v. Mahyco Monsanto Biotech (India) Limited (MMBL) & Ors*, Reference Case No. 2 of 2015 & Case No. 107 of 2015, para. 38; *East India Petroleum Pvt. Ltd. v. South Asia LPG Company Pvt. Ltd.*, Case No. 76 of 2011, para. 46.
76. *Automobile Spare Parts* case, para. 20.5.66, 20.5.67.
77. *Super Cassettes* case, paras 183, 184.

In the *Matrimony* case,[78] the CCI observed that Google has an insurmountable scale advantage and given that only market participants in the online general web search market can compete in the search advertising market, the barriers in the one market also effectively restrict entry into the second market.

In the *Play Store* case,[79] the CCI found that there were significant barriers to entry in the form of financial and human capital and investment in research and development, along with overcoming the problem of ensuring wider acceptability of the new OS among the OEMs (since commercial success of an OS depends on the willingness of OEMs to sell devices based on that OS), app developers and specially users. Google's restrictions on the use of Android due to its agreements with OEMs and interoperability also foreclose the entry of new entrants as they give financial incentives for pre-installation of certain Google apps and, thus, work as significant barriers to entry in the relevant market. The fact that no new OS developer has been able to enter the market of licensable OS in the last five years and existing players like Windows Phone OS have left the market was also taken as evidence of the existence of entry barriers. These same barriers exist in the context of app stores as well, which require significant investment for development, marketing and updates. In addition, prominent placement given to Google's app results in a status-quo bias of consumers. Further, many of the pre-installed apps could also not be deleted due to the operation of the agreements entered into between Google and OEMs. This, in the view of the CCI, also operated as an entry barrier.

In the *Google Android* case,[80] the lack of availability of compatible application programming interfaces ('APIs' are a software layer working in the background of Android that is used to update Google apps and other apps from the Google Play Store) operated as an entry barrier. This is because without this access, OEMs could not update Google services, fix bugs, etc., and if they operated without access to Google's proprietary apps, they would be at a competitive disadvantage as the most popular Google services like Google Maps, Google Search, etc., rely on these interfaces to function. The 'forked' OS based on the open-source licence-based OSs do not stand any chance before Google and, thus, are not in a position to constrain Google in any manner as they lack the whole gamut of functionalities offered by Google.

[F] Countervailing Buyer Power

One of the factors mentioned under section 19(4) of the Competition Act is the dependence of consumers on the enterprise. Buyer power is an essential factor to consider in case of dominance investigations. A firm with a high market share may not be able to raise price or wield market power if the counterparty is a large and effective buyer. Buyer power has been identified as the ability of the buyer to influence the terms and conditions on which it purchases goods. The buyer can switch to competing

78. *Matrimony* case, para. 122.
79. *Play Store* case, paras 92-102.
80. *Google Android* case, paras 534-536.

suppliers, promote new entry or vertically integrate into the upstream market, thus deterring a firm with a high market share from specifying exploitative conditions. The key factors to be taken into account while determining buyer power are the size and resources of the buyer, switching costs and the presence of an effective substitute.[81]

As elaborated earlier (while deliberating on entry barriers), the CCI had noted, in the *Automobile Spare Parts* case, that there is limited interchangeability of spare parts between the automobiles manufactured by various OEMs because of differences in technical features between cars manufactured by each OEM. In light of the fact that there is no technical compatibility between spare parts manufactured by each OEM, each consumer of an OEM is completely dependent upon the concerned OEM. Further, the OEMs, through a network of contracts with their suppliers, have ensured that they are the sole supplier of the spare parts and diagnostic tools used to repair their brand of automobiles in the aftermarket. Therefore, the independent repairers, who are consumers of the OEMs in the aftermarket for spare parts and diagnostic tools, are also solely dependent upon such enterprises.

Similarly, in the *DLF* case,[82] the CCI noted that the consumers have very little or no countervailing buying power. The CCI further noted that there are very few developers/builders of luxury, high-end apartments and thousands of prospective buyers. Such market conditions would ensure that consumers will be the price takers and would have no option but to accept any conditions that are imposed upon them by the developer. In such a market, any seller in a position of strength would have no need to sacrifice its producer's surplus to meet competition. In fact, the market followers would find it advantageous to adopt similar price and non-price strategies as the market leader since in such a market, the consumer does not possess much market power.

Also, in the *Super Cassettes* case, the CCI noted that there is no effective buyer in the said market, keeping in mind the following factors:

(1) Based on the available statistics of Top 100 and Top 20 songs/music broadcast on radio, Super Cassettes owned a majority of the music labels, and it has a 58% share of the top 100 songs played on private FM channels. Apart from market share, the CCI noted the vast repertoire of Super Cassettes, which comprised Bollywood music, is extremely popular with listeners and consequently popular with advertisers. Due to such popular content, Super Cassettes commanded a position of strength. Given such market dynamics, the CCI noted that the customers of Super Cassettes are heavily dependent on the music content of Super Cassettes.

(2) Further, as discussed above, the CCI noted that Super Cassettes imposed a minimum commitment charge ranging from 30%–50% of play out which radio stations are required to pay irrespective of whether they play that amount of music on the FM stations or not. Apart from Super Cassettes, no

81. *Harshita Chawla v. WhatsApp Inc. and Facebook Inc.*, Case No. 15 of 2020, para. 87.
82. *DLF* case, para. 12.75.

other music provider imposed a charge like the minimum commitment charge. Further, the evidence on record suggested that the radio stations had shown a strong resistance initially to the imposition of minimum commitment charge by Super Cassettes. In spite of such resistance, Super Cassettes continued to impose the same on the radio operators. As such, one of the radio stations, Radio City, terminated its contract with Super Cassettes due to the imposition of such unfair conditions as the minimum commitment charge. After lapse of sometime post the termination, it entered into a fresh contract with Super Cassettes having the same earlier clause of imposition of minimum commitment charge, which incidentally was the reason why the earlier contract was terminated. The CCI noted the statements made by Radio City to the DG, during the investigation process, and observed that the business of Radio City was hampered post the termination of their agreement with Super Cassettes. Radio City was not able to broadcast a huge repertoire of music owned by Super Cassettes. Further, during that relevant period when Radio City was not broadcasting the music of Super Cassettes, the other radio stations were performing considerably better than Radio City in terms of revenues as Radio City did not have the licence to play the music of Super Cassettes. Radio City's response is also evidence of the fact that the radio station could not effectively compete without playing the music of Super Cassettes.

Dependence of consumers and disparity in size and resources are crucial factors in determining the presence or absence of countervailing buyer power.[83] The case of *Kapoor Glass Private Limited v. Schott Glass India Private Limited* ('*Schott Glass* case')[84] concerned glass tubes manufactured by Schott Glass which were then sold to the manufacturers of glass ampoules, vials, cartridges and syringes, etc., which were in turn sold to pharmaceutical companies for storing drugs. Thus, the market of borosilicate glass tubes was the upstream market, whereas the market of ampoules, vials, cartridges, syringes, etc., was the downstream market. To vertically integrate its operations with the downstream manufacturing business, Schott Glass entered into a joint venture agreement with a downstream manufacturer Kaisha Manufacturers Pvt Ltd to form Schott Kaisha Private Ltd (Schott Kaisha). The CCI found that all other convertors except Scott Kaisha lacked the requisite size or financial strength to exercise countervailing buying power and were dependent on Schott for their supplies. Hence, the CCI held that Schott was dominant in the upstream market and Schott Kaisha was dominant in the downstream market. It is pointed out that ultimately, the erstwhile COMPAT[85] held in appeal that the discriminatory treatment met out to other convertors on account of the fact that they did not have the capacity to require the same quantity

83. *Matrimony.com Limited v. Google LLC*, Case Nos 07 and 30 of 2021, para. 124.
84. *Kapoor Glass Private Limited v. Schott Glass India Private Limited*, Case No. 22 of 2010, para. 9.2.22-9.2.26.
85. *Schott Glass India Pvt. Ltd v. Competition Commission of India*, [2014] Comp AT 1, para. 42.

was justified, and hence, no case of abuse made out on this count. This has been discussed in detail in the abuse part.

The CCI in the *Play Store* case,[86] on the basis of the investigation report of the DG, found that OEMs lack sufficient countervailing buyer power vis-à-vis Google. The large established user base of Android devices, contributing to strong network effects, makes the ecosystem attractive to OEMs and App developers. Given the fact that Android OS enjoys significant consumer demand in India, OEMs are not able to develop/identify alternatives to compete with Android OS. Rather, they have to comply with Google's agreements.

There has been a series of information filed against Coal India,[87] and CCI has opined on each of the cases. Collectively, the cases are referred here as the *Coal India* case. In the *Coal India* case, when Coal India challenged its dominance before the COMPAT, it argued that there existed countervailing buyer power. However, the erstwhile COMPAT negated this argument by elaborating on the lack of substitutes or alternative suppliers. It held that there was no effective countervailing buyer power since there were virtually no alternative suppliers in view of the market structure and regulatory barriers which prevented the buyers from sponsoring new entry or entering the supply market themselves.

[G] Statutory Monopoly

The Competition Act provides that the CCI can analyse the behaviour of enterprises that have acquired their dominant position because of a statute or a governmental policy/regulation. These are enterprises where dominance is acquired as a result of the policy of the government.[88]

The inclusion of statutory monopolies within the ambit of competition law can be traced to the High-Level Committee Report which had recommended that except for government entities engaged in sovereign functions, there is no valid justification to exclude any other entity, including government enterprises, from the ambit of the law. Competition law should extend to all consumers, regardless of the purpose for which they purchase goods or services. Hence, State monopolies, government procurement and foreign companies - are all subject to competition law.[89]

In fact, the CCI has analysed the behaviour of Coal India in a vast number of cases. Coal India is a public sector undertaking which has a monopoly due to a policy of the government. In the *Coal India* case, it was noted by the CCI that the dominant position of Coal India was acquired as a result of the policy of the Government of India by creating a public sector undertaking in the name of Coal India Limited and vesting

86. *Play Store* case, paras 103-113.
87. For instance, *M/s Maharashtra State Power Generation Company Ltd. v. Coal India and Ors.*, Case Nos 03 of 2012, 11 of 2012 and 59 of 2012; *Madhya Pradesh Power Generating Company Limited. v. Coal India Ltd. and Ors.*, Case Nos 05 of 2013, 07 of 2013 and 44 of 2013; *M/s West Bengal Power Development Corporation Ltd. v. M/s Coal India limited & Ors.*, Case No. 37 of 2013; *M/s GHCL Limited v. M/s Coal India Limited & Ors.*, Case No. 08 of 2014.
88. *Beach Mineral Producers Association v. IREL (India) Ltd.*, Case No. 26 of 2022, paras 46, 47.
89. High Level Committee Report, para. 4.8.8.

the ownership of the private mines in it. Coal India's dominance was affirmed by the erstwhile COMPAT in an appeal which noted that 'dominance, even if created statutorily is within the purview of the Act and subject to prohibitory regime under Section 4 …'.[90] Further, the Supreme Court in subsequent appeal also observed that 'a monopoly, undoubtedly, stood created by the Nationalisation Act' and a monopoly/dominant position, whether acquired as a result of statute/being a government company/public sector undertaking, is a relevant factor[91] and that such a statutory monopoly is amenable to the jurisdiction of the CCI.

Further, the CCI also noted the conduct of Coal India and held that they are a dominant entity, not only because of their status of a statutory monopoly but also because of their conduct towards their customers. While analysing the market dynamics in the case, the CCI noted that the National Coal Distribution Policy had laid down that the power sector is to be supplied 100% of its normative requirement. In spite of this mandate, Coal India had been able to decide the quantity of coal to be supplied based on its commercial feasibility and entering into one-sided Fuel Supply Agreements and MOUs with its buyers, where Coal India was eligible for incentives even if their supplies were below 100% requirement (as mandated under the National Coal Distribution Policy). Such factors showed that Coal India was dominant. We will deal with the abuse, as discussed by the CCI, erstwhile COMPAT and Supreme Court in the Coal India case, in the later parts of the chapter.

Similarly, the issue of a monopoly created because of a government regulation was discussed in the case of *Faridabad Industries Association v. Adani Gas Limited*[92] ('*Adani Gas* case'). The *Adani Gas* case was initiated due to an information filed by Faridabad Industries Association. It was alleged that Adani Gas Limited, being the dominant player in the market of supply and distribution of natural gas in the region of Faridabad, had put unconscionable terms and conditions in the Gas Sales Agreement. Such terms made the Gas Sales Agreement totally unilateral, lopsided and heavily tilted in favour of Adani Gas Limited. It was further alleged that Adani Gas Limited, in the garb of executing the said Gas Sales Agreement, had imposed its diktat upon the buyers of natural gas, who are members of Faridabad Industries Association. Further, it was also pointed out that the Gas Sales Agreement had been drafted unilaterally by Adani Gas Limited without leaving any scope for the members of the association, who are buyers of gas and are solely dependent on supplies from Adani Gas Limited.

Based on the industry in question, the CCI noted that Adani Gas Limited has a 100% market share since it is the only entity which is authorized under the relevant law and government regulations (the regulations framed under the Petroleum and Natural Gas Regulatory Board Act, 2006 gave twenty-five years exclusivity) to set up, expand and operate a city gas distribution system in the city of Faridabad.

90. *Coal India Limited, West Bengal v. Competition Commission of India*, [2017] CompLR 0447 (CompAT).
91. *Coal India Limited and Anr. v. Competition Commission of India and Anr.* [2023], (SC) Civil Appeal No. 2845 of 2017.
92. *Faridabad Industries Association v. Adani Gas Limited*, Case No. 71 of 2012.

Subsequently, the NCLAT also supported the CCI's finding on the dominant position of Adani Gas Limited.[93] It reiterated that all the buyers of natural gas were solely dependent upon supplies of natural gas by Adani Gas Limited, which was the only supplier in the market. The NCLAT specifically observed that the fact that the pipeline infrastructure setup by Adani Gas Limited can subsequently be used now by any other competitor to distribute natural gas does not create any dent in the aforesaid finding. Hence, even if there are subsequent pro-competitive changes in the nature of a monopolized service, that would not have a retrospective effect in assessing dominance and abuse. We will deal with the abuse part, as discussed by the CCI and NCLAT in the *Adani Gas* case, in the later portions of the chapter.

In *Air Works India (Engineering) Private Limited v. GMR Hyderabad International Airport Limited (GMR)*[94] ('*GMR* case') also, the concept of statutory monopoly or state-conferred dominant position was discussed. In this case, GMR which was the manager and operator of the Rajiv Gandhi International Airport Hyderabad (RGIA), entered into a license agreement with the informant, which was a provider of third-party services to airlines and general aviation, namely the Line Maintenance Services and the Base Maintenance Services. Licensees such as the informant were dependent on GMR to grant the necessary license to operate from the Airport for the provision of its services to various airlines, and it was an understanding among all licensees who are operating at RGIA for the technical support services that as long as they are carrying on their operations, the license would continue to be granted. However, GMR owing to its sole control over RGIA, abused its dominance in order to protect and promote its own group entity, which was a competitor of the informant in the downstream market for provision of Line Maintenance Services at the RGIA, by terminating the license of the informant. The aspect of abuse has been discussed in the subsequent parts of this chapter. On the question of dominance, the CCI observed that in the case of airports, there has been an emerging trend where the ownership and management of the airport is undertaken in a public-private partnership. In the case of RGIA, a concession agreement was signed between GMR and the Government of India for thirty years which effectively made GMR the exclusive operator and manager of RGIA. The conferment of this exclusive privilege on GMR undoubtedly turned it into a monopoly:[95]

In *International Spirits and Wines Association of India v. Uttarakhand Agricultural Produce Marketing Board*,[96] alcoholic beverage manufacturers were entirely dependent on the opposite parties for access to retailers and in turn, the end-consumers in the State of Uttarakhand. This was because a dominant position was bestowed upon them owing to the Excise Policy and the Liquor Wholesale Order in place, making the

93. *M/s Adani Gas Limited v. Competition Commission of India and Anr* [2020], TA (AT) (Competition) No. 33 of 2017.
94. *Air Works India (Engineering) Private Limited v. GMR Hyderabad International Airport Limited (GMR)*,Case No. 30/2019.
95. *Ibid.*, paras 39,40.
96. *International Spirits and Wines Association of India v. Uttarakhand Agricultural Produce Marketing Board*, Case No. 02 of 2016.

opposite parties the exclusive procurement agency and sole distributors of Indian-made foreign liquor, and no alternate access route to the market was available. The CCI held that the 'State of Uttarakhand, like other states in the country, has created monopolies by canalising liquor procurement.' Hence, such regulatory exclusion of competition virtually allowed the opposite parties to enjoy a monopoly in their respective functions.

[H] Using the Regulatory Power to Enter Commercial Activities

The CCI has grappled with the issue of a regulator entering commercial space. Such overlap has been found by the CCI largely in the sports sector, which operates in a pyramid structure, i.e., a single national sport association per sport and Member State, which operates under the umbrella of a single continental/national Federation and a single worldwide Federation, which is at the top of the pyramid. This means that only one apex body is responsible for the management of the sport at the national level, thereby conferring it with a monopoly status. Competition cases relating to sports associations/federations usually arise due to the conflict between their regulatory functions and their economic activities.[97] In such cases, by using their dominance by virtue of being a regulator, they enter into commercial activities like granting franchisee rights, media rights, etc. For instance, the CCI held that the Board for Control of Cricket in India had abused its dominant position.[98] When the matter went up in appeal, as discussed in Chapter 1, the erstwhile COMPAT remanded the matter back on the issue of due process and the legal value of the evidence relied on by the CCI while deciding the case.[99] The aspects of due process and natural justice were highlighted in Chapter 1. Accordingly, the CCI ordered the DG to conduct a further investigation into the matter in accordance with the directions contained in the above order of COMPAT. The CCI considered the Supplementary Investigation Report and found that the regulator was intruding into commercial activities. It observed that Board of Cricket Control in India (BCCI) historical evolution enabled it to attain a monopoly status in the organization of cricket events in India such that it had now become the de facto regulator of the sport. This was on account of the pyramidical structure of sports governance and endorsement from International Cricket Council (ICC), the national body for cricket in India which vested power into its members like BCCI to decide on any matter relating to the sport by declaring it as the 'custodian' of cricket in the concerned territory. Section 32 of the ICC Manual made BCCI the exclusive authority to sanction/approve cricket events in India, and any tournament/match not approved by it was regarded as 'disapproved cricket' in India.

A similar situation transpired with regards to Hockey India (HI), a national association for hockey in India which was vested with certain rights by the Federation of Indian Hockey (FIH), prime among them being the right to sanction/approve hockey

97. *Department of Sports v. Athletics Federation of India*, Ref. Case No. 01 of 2015; *Hemant Sharma and Ors. v. All India Chess Federation*, Case No. 79 of 2011, paras 41-44.
98. *Surinder Singh Barmi v. Board for Control of Cricket in India*, Case No. 61 of 2010.
99. *Board of Cricket Control v. Competition Commission of India*, [2015] CompLR 0548.

events in India. The CCI found that the most significant source of dominance of HI is its regulatory powers, which empower it along with FIH to create entry barriers for other rival (i.e., private) leagues by requiring them to obtain sanctions for their tournament and requiring players to obtain *NOCs from HI to participate in rival tournaments*. The aspects of granting sanctions for a league and giving NOCs for participation are regulatory in nature but are in a clear position to impact the market for organizing events and are a vital source of dominance. The CCI also held that HI's dominance stems from its role as an organizer of international hockey events, which allows it to control a pool of players by entering into agreements with them for playing in such events. Since players are a vital input to the organization of any sport, the ability to control top players leads to dominance of HI. In doing so, the CCI considered the cases settled in other jurisdictions in this aspect and noted the observations in the *ELPA* case, where the Court on the issue of dominance of sports association insisted that '... *a system of undistorted competition, such as that provided for by the treaty, can be guaranteed only if equality of opportunity is secured between the various economic operators. To entrust a legal person such as ELPA, the National Association for Motorcycling in Greece, which itself organizes and commercially exploits motorcycling events, the task of giving the competent administration its consent to applications for authorization to organize such events, is tantamount de facto to conferring upon it the power to designate the persons authorized to organize those events and to set the conditions in which those events are organized, thereby placing that entity at an obvious advantage over its competitors. Such a right may therefore lead the undertaking which possesses it to deny other operators access to the relevant market.*'

Another example of regulatory dominance can be seen in the case involving the Confederation of Professional Baseball Softball Clubs,[100] which is the apex institution for organising baseball events and selecting players for national and international tournaments. It operates in a similar pyramidal structure with like powers and relevant international affiliations as the HI and the Board of Cricket Control. As a result, the CCI held its regulatory powers, including sanctioning/disapproving proposals for the organization of baseball events and subjecting players to disciplinary action, were found to make it the predominant controller of the services provided by baseball players who have less bargaining power. The CCI also found that 'there are high regulatory barriers in the sport of baseball since Association of Basketball Federation of India is the only body recognized by Ministry of Youth Affairs & Sports, Government of India, International Baseball Federation and Indian Olympic Association' thereby solidifying its dominant position.

[I] Other Factors

In the *Coal India* case, Coal India argued that it was subject to social obligations and social costs in terms of section 19(4)(k), and its work constituted contribution to economic development as under section 19(4)(l) of the Competition Act. However, the

100. Case No. 03 of 2021.

erstwhile COMPAT noted that Coal India failed to demonstrate '*any social obligations or social costs or developmental objectives permeating its functioning in determining the conditions of sale so as to impact its market power*'.

As mentioned earlier, the Competition Act provides the CCI with the flexibility to look into factors that are not covered explicitly in section 19(4) but are relevant for determining dominance in the relevant market. The objective is to identify the ability of the enterprise concerned to operate independently of the competitive forces prevailing in the relevant market or to affect its competitors or consumers or the relevant market in its favour. The importance attached to various factors would differ depending on the facts of each case, the specificity of each piece of information and the sector of economic activity involved.[101]

For instance, the investigation of the DG highlighted a few important findings regarding Google's control over Android OS in the *Play Store* case[102] which was held to be an important factor in concluding the dominance of Google:

(i) Even though the source code for the Android mobile OS is released by Google for free under an open-source license, the Android-based OEMs are highly dependent on Google. Google as the sponsor of the Android platform enforces platform rules through a combination of compatibility provisions, contracts, and trademark licenses. This includes seeking Google's final written approval for using the licence, even though technically it is available for free if they want to use a suite of proprietary apps known as Google Mobile Services (GMS) which includes a variety of Google apps, such as Google Maps, YouTube, Google Play, and Google Search.

(ii) Google owns the IPRs of Android OS. Further, the use of 'Android' which is a trademark of Google, is restricted to Android-compatible devices only and is subject to the OEMs' compliance with separate contractual and technical obligations (collectively referred to as 'Android Compatibility Program'). This compliance has to be undertaken every time Google releases a new version of Android OS.

In addition, Google argued before the CCI that OEMs can customize and modify Android OS to build differentiated versions, thereby offering competition to Android OS. However, the CCI found that this is irrelevant to determining Google's dominance since even these customizations have to comply with the Android Compatibility Program in order to pre-install GMS. Consequently, such customised OEMs do not pose any competitive constraints on Google. On this basis, the CCI held that although Android is ostensibly open-source, Google holds a significant, unparalleled and incontrovertible influence in its development.

Some other factors which are increasingly considered in the analysis of dominance in digital markets have been discussed in detail in Chapter 6 on digital markets.

---

101. *Air Cargo Agents Association of India v. International Air Transport Association*, Case No. 79 of 2012.

102. *Play Store* case, paras 78-81.

The above factors clearly demonstrate the factors which the CCI takes into account while determining dominance. While the factors laid down under section 19(4) of the Competition Act are indicative, the CCI looks into all factors, including the behaviour of the dominant undertaking to determine whether the entity derives a position of strength.

§3.05 ABUSE OF DOMINANCE

It must be noted that the Competition Act provides that only abuse of dominance is in violation of the provisions of the Competition Act. An enterprise merely holding a dominant position is not a violation of the Competition Act.

The CCI has held that the types of abuses identified under section 4(2) of the Competition Act are exhaustive and not illustrative. However, considering the language, structure and the overall purpose of the Competition Act, it may be argued in an appropriate case, the kinds of abusive conduct mentioned in section 4(2) are only specific instances of abuses and not exhaustive of all the abusive conducts covered under section 4.

[A] Statutory Scheme

The substantive contravention of abuse of a dominant position is covered under section 4(1) which reads – '*No enterprise or group shall abuse its dominant position*'. It would be interesting to note that the statutory scheme under sections 3(1), 4(1) and 6(1) are the same:

- Section 3 (1) – '*No enterprise* ... *shall* enter into *any agreement* ... which causes or is likely to cause an appreciable adverse effect on competition in India'.
- Section 4 (1) – '*No enterprise* or group *shall abuse its dominant position* '.
- Section 6 (1) – '*No* person or *enterprise shall* enter into a *combination* which causes or is likely to cause an appreciable adverse effect on competition in India.'

The language of the three provisions is uniform and similar, and a perusal of these provisions would demonstrate that the substantive obligations are covered under sections 3(1), 4(1) and 6(1). The provision stipulates that the enterprises should not enter into any agreement causing or likely to cause an AAEC in India or abuse its dominant position or enter into a combination causing or likely to cause and AAEC in India. This is also further demonstrated by section 19(1) of the Competition Act which states, 'The Commission may inquire into any alleged contravention of the provisions contained in sub-section (1) of Section 3 or *sub-section (1) of Section 4* ...'. Therefore, the Competition Act supports the view that the contravention that the CCI will inquire into is a contravention under section 4(1). Therefore, the scheme of the statute clearly provides that the substantive obligation is enshrined in section 4(1).

The CCI has also correctly held in the *Hiranandani* case (discussed in Chapter 2) that section 3(1) is the genus, and agreements covered under sections 3(3) and 3(4) are but particular species of agreements that will otherwise be covered under section 3(1) and that agreements not falling within section 3(3) and 3(4) will still fall under section 3(1).[103] This logic should equally apply in the case of section 4.

Section 4 provides the substantive obligation that an enterprise cannot abuse its dominant position. Section 4(2) identifies certain conduct as abusive in nature for the purposes of section 4(1). It reads – 'There shall be an abuse of dominant position under sub-section (1), if an enterprise or group' undertakes any of the actions mentioned therein. Section 4(2) independently does not exhaustively identify all the abusive conduct under section 4(1); it only states that the specific conducts identified in section 4(2) are considered to be an abuse of dominant position. Therefore, conduct that is abusive in nature will still be covered under section 4(1) as the emphasis is on 'abuse'. The natural meaning of the term 'abuse' would be applicable. If it were to be held that section 4(2) is exhaustive, then it would result in holding section 4(1) nugatory and otiose. It has been held by the Supreme Court in a large number of cases that interpretation will be adopted which would give meaning to a provision rather than to hold it nugatory. Therefore, the statutory scheme of section 4 and the legislative scheme of the Competition Act would demonstrate that the abusive conduct mentioned in section 4(2) is not exhaustive but is merely illustrative of certain kinds of abusive conduct.

§3.06 TYPES OF ABUSE

We will deal with the abuses mentioned under each of the sub-sections of section 4 and the manner in which the CCI, the erstwhile COMPAT and the NCLAT have analysed the various headings of abuse mentioned in this section. It is important to note that the section is applicable to both enterprise and group.

[A] Unfair Terms and Conditions

Section 4(2)(a)(i) of the Competition Act states that there shall be an abuse of dominant position if an enterprise or a group imposes unfair or discriminatory condition in purchase or sale of goods or service. It must be noted that the approach of the CCI is to see whether the dominant undertaking, being in a position of strength, is using its muscle power to force the counterparties into agreements which are one-sided and commercially beneficial only for the dominant undertaking, without any business justification. Unless there is an imposition of unfair or discriminatory condition or price, as the case may be, there will be no breach of section 4(2)(a)(i) or 4(2)(a)(ii) of the Competition Act. There can be no dispute that the moment there is imposition of such a condition, the mischief of section 4 will be attracted.[104]

103. *Hiranandani* case, para. 15.
104. *DLF Limited v. Competition Commission of India*, [2014] Comp AT 12, para. 56.

The CCI has taken an approach to see whether the condition, so imposed by the dominant undertaking because of its power, is unfair qua the counterparty. What is unfair and fair would depend on the facts and circumstances of each case. As such, the essence of any contract is *consensus ad idem*. Conversely, there can be situations wherein a counterparty executes a contract with a dominant undertaking, they have no option but to follow and sign the contract which is heavily in favour of the dominant undertaking. Such a contract would be considered by the CCI as unfair since there is no *consensus ad idem*. In this regard, it is apposite to note the observations made in the dissent order passed by the CCI in the case of *Sunil Bansal v. M/s Jaiprakash Associates Ltd. & Others:*[105]

> It is to be noted that the dictionary meaning of the word "impose" is force on someone, or take advantage of someone by demanding their attention or commitment. The meaning of unfair is "not based on, or behaving according to the principles of equality and justice". Thus, imposing unfair conditions would mean that one of the *party who enjoys a higher bargaining power is in a position to dictate terms to the weak party who is not in a position to negotiate* [emphasis supplied].

Based on the above, the CCI analyses the conduct of the dominant undertaking to determine whether they have imposed any unfair terms and conditions. The factors that are generally kept in mind are whether the rights and obligations of the parties to the agreements are one-sided or mutual. For example, if an agreement is entered into by parties for sale and purchase of any good, any delay on the part of the supplier to supply goods and the purchaser to provide timely instalments must give rise to a penalty including interest. However, if the penalty is only levied on one party (as occurred in the *DLF* case, *Coal India* case and the *Adani Gas* case) and not on the dominant enterprise (like no penalty on Coal India for non-supply of graded coal on time), CCI would view such clauses to be unfair and hence a case of abuse of dominant position would be made out.[106]

Unfair terms are often in the nature of mandatory acceptance of the dominant firm's policies, even if they are harmful. CCI's decisional practice indicates that contractual terms that are one-sided with no option besides acceptance are unfair.[107] For instance, in the *WhatsApp* case, WhatsApp updated its Terms of Service and Privacy Policy for users to the effect that consent to sharing and integration of user data with other Facebook Companies for a range of purposes, including marketing and advertising, was made a precondition for availing WhatsApp service. There was also opacity, vagueness and open-endedness about the nature, kind and extent of data sharing that the user was being compelled to consent to. There was also no option to opt out of the said Policy update, and the users now have to mandatorily agree if they want to continue using WhatsApp Messenger. On this basis, the CCI ordered an investigation into WhatsApp's conduct for imposing unfair terms by propagating a

105. Case No. 72/2011.
106. *Naveen Kataria v. Jaiprakash Associates Limited*, Case No. 99 of 2014.
107. *Madhya Pradesh Power Generating Company Limited v. South Eastern Coalfields Ltd. and Anr.*, Case Nos 05, 07, 37 & 44 of 2013; *Neha Gupta v. Tata Motors Ltd. and Ors.*, Case No. 21 of 2019 and Case No. 16 of 2020, paras 121, 122.

take-it-or-leave-it' policy. Subsequently, WhatsApp challenged the jurisdiction of CCI to pass such an order before the Delhi High Court owing to potentially conflicting opinions when the Supreme Court was already looking into whether the Policy was violative of the right to privacy under Article 21 of the Constitution. However, the Delhi High Court clarified that the investigation by the CCI is confined to whether the Policy furthers the dominant position occupied by WhatsApp and institutes anti-competitive practices. The Supreme Court is not analysing the Policy through the prism of competition law. The spheres of operation of both are vastly different. Hence, it allowed the investigation to proceed.[108] The Delhi High also affirmed the prima facie findings of CCI that WhatsApp's dominance due to lack of/restricted interoperability between platforms, its ability to engage in data concentration and the opacity, vagueness, open-endedness and incomplete disclosures in the Policy have the potential to undermine the competitive processes and create further barriers to market entry.

A key concept of unfair conduct is exclusionary conduct, was seen in the *Google Android* case. The complex, self-reinforcing and pervasive nature of Google's agreements have been described earlier. The collective unfair impositions under these agreements, as elaborated by the CCI, have been described in the following diagram:

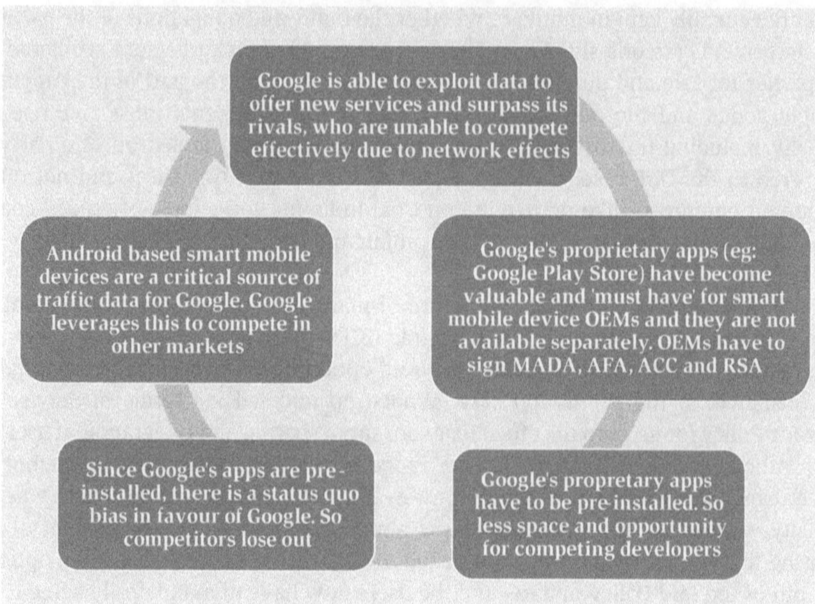

By virtue of the agreements discussed above, Google ensured that users continued to use its search services on mobile devices which facilitated uninterrupted growth

108. *WhatsApp LLC v. Competition Commission of India*, Delhi High Court LPA 163/2021&LPA 164/2021; *WhatsApp LLC v. Competition Commission of India*, Delhi High Court W.P.(C) 4378/2021 & CM 13336/2021.

of advertisement revenue for Google. Further, it also helped Google to further invest and improve its services to the exclusion of others. Thus, the underlying objective of Google in imposing various restrictions via MADA, AFA/ACC and RSAs was to protect and strengthen its dominant position in general search services and, thus, its revenues via search advertisements.

Per the CCI, Google's agreements, i.e., MADA, AFA, ACC and RSA, collectively manifested the following exclusionary conducts:

(i) MADA requires non-exclusive preinstallation of Google Search, Search Widget, and Google Chrome (with Google Search as default) on all Android devices. Further, Google also secures exclusivity for its search services on all the OEMs' devices through RSAs. However, the competing search service providers, due to Google's preinstallation through MADA, cannot secure exclusivity even on devices not covered by RSAs. At most, these rivals can achieve pre-installation along with Google, that too at an inferior position since Google demands default home screen placement which itself is premium real estate with limited availability (since it would get users hooked, as explained below).

(ii) Similarly, in the case of search services, Android devices have Google Search, Search Widget, and Google Chrome (with Google Search as default) preinstalled on the default home screen. These three Search Access Points generate a significant volume of search queries (which, again, Google monetizes in its other verticals). Given the mandatory presence of Google search services on the home screen, the OEMs may not like to pre-install another search widget/search app on the home screen itself to avoid any bad user experience, limited system memory/space, etc.

(iii) Through Google's prominent presence on the default home screen of the device, the user is more likely to use Google on the home screen as compared to rival services on the second or third screen. This 'status quo bias' cannot be overcome by rivals. Given the preference for Google's services by users (which are also created out of perpetuating these obligations), the OEM cannot afford to offer devices without Google's apps (which are only available through MADA, etc.). These default positions for search queries are also true for mobile web browsers and desktop/PCs (Google Chrome with Google Search set as default).

(iv) Google offers a bouquet of services and with their increased usage, it is in an unassailable position to exploit economies of scale and scope with enormous data generated by all these apps together. The competitors being unable to offer these services and being placed at an inferior position in the Android ecosystem are at a competitive disadvantage. Google, with additional data that feeds into its search-advertising business model, increase its competitive advantage over other rivals.

Hence, these agreements prohibit alternative vendors from outcompeting Google's apps on merits and foreclose competition even in the adjacent markets by creating impenetrable walls. Google's rivals can neither compete by creating forked OS (due to AFA/ACC) nor by offering their services to OEMs because even if they do manage to enter into pre-installation arrangements with OEMs, a significant volume of search queries will be diverted to Google due to the operation of MADA and RSA. There is also no option but to sign these agreements and accept all the contained restrictions due to the 'must have' nature of Google's services which makes them commercially necessary. Thus, the mandatory pre-installation of the entire GMS suite (with no option to un-install the same) and their prominent placement amounts to imposition of an unfair condition on the device manufacturers and thereby in contravention of the provisions of section 4(2)(a)(i). Subsequently, the NCLAT in appeal also upheld that pre-installation of the entire GMS Suite amounts to imposing unfair conditions on OEMs which is an abuse of dominant position by Google. It added that this is because there is an element of compulsion and OEMs have no negotiation power, and they have to accept the terms and conditions offered by Google which compel them to enter into such one-sided agreements for commercial viability.

Herein, it is appropriate to mention Google's contention before the NCLAT that no OEM complained against the unfairness of MADA, which was the counterparty in the agreement. Google cited CCI's own previous decisions to argue that unfairness must be judged from the testimonies of the counterparty, in this case, the OEMs and not any other third party. It was strenuously argued by Google that OEMs were happy with the Google bouquet of must-have apps which they were offering as a bundle. However, the NCLAT held that competition law being a public law, is concerned with the effect on the entire market. Hence, the regulator (i.e., CCI) which is obliged to discharge its statutory function cannot confine its analysis and decision only on the basis of evidence of countervailing parties and competitors.[109] Ultimately, NCLAT ruled that the action of Google of tying their apps together is in violation of the Competition Act.

As a result, CCI ordered several remedies, *inter alia,* including that Google shall not impose anti-fragmentation obligations on OEMs, licensing of Google Play Services to OEMs shall not be linked with the requirement of pre-installing any other application of Google, etc. It also specifically directed Google not to enforce the anti-competitive clauses identified in the respective agreements (MADA, AFA/ACC and RSAs).

On the point of exploitative conduct constituting an unfair condition under section 4(2)(a)(i) of the Competition Act, it is relevant to mention that examination of exploitative conduct which involves imposition of unfair conditions by a dominant enterprise in a business to business transaction is essentially to undertake a fairness or reasonability test, which requires examining both how the condition affects the trading partners of the dominant enterprise as well as whether there is any legitimate and objective necessity for the enterprise to impose such condition.[110] Appreciation of the context and rationale becomes even more important in the cases of buyer power;

109. *Google LLC and Anr. v. Competition Commission of India and Ors.* [2023], (NCLAT) Competition Appeal (AT) No. 01 of 2023, paras 81, 82.
110. *Indian National Shipowners' Association v. Oil and Natural Gas Corporation Limited*, Case No. 01 of 2018.

otherwise, large players may be penalized in the mere attempt of negotiating competitive terms.

[1] Discriminatory Conditions

Apart from unfair conditions, discriminatory conditions are also held to be an abuse of dominant position.[111] Similar to the aspect of discriminatory pricing, if the dominant undertaking makes any conditions which are discriminatory in nature among similar set of consumers without any rational business justification, such discriminatory clauses would be covered under the heading of abuse. This also includes preferential treatment granted to certain users over others.[112]

For instance, in the *Schott Glass* case, the CCI observed that the increased quantity supplied to Schott Kaisha could result in lower overall cost for Schott which can be passed on to the consumers in the form of a more favourable discount. Schott was also giving favourable conditions to Schott Kaisha, such as in its target discounts (based on quantity purchased) and functional discounts (which imposed additional conditions on the convertors to promote Schott's products). On this basis, the CCI found Schott to be in violation of sections 4(2)(a)(i) and (ii) of the Competition Act on account of discriminatory treatment between Schott Kaisha and other convertors purchasing from Schott.[113] However, the CCI minority opinion held that for a discount policy to be held as 'discriminatory', two conditions should be met: (i) dissimilar treatment to equivalent transactions; and (ii) harm to competition or is likely harm to competition such that the buyers suffer a competitive disadvantage in the downstream market.

In an appeal before the COMPAT,[114] Schott argued that CCI misunderstood the concept of 'discriminatory pricing' and ignored the basic principle that the prices could be called 'discriminatory' only if they were for equivalent transactions, meaning thereby that if a different price was charged for the same quantity of the same product, only then would the pricing would have been discriminatory. Here, the facts were that the quantity purchased by Schott Kaisha far exceeded the purchases of any other converter, and no other convertor had the capacity to require the same quantity. The prices with the convertors were also negotiated on a one-to-one basis based on the quantity purchased. Therefore, the cost differential in inputs caused by the discount scheme of Schott did not affect the end price of the final products. Discount scheme of Schott did not harm the competitive ability of the customers and competition in the downstream relevant markets. The erstwhile COMPAT relied on the observations of the minority order which alluded to the EU and American jurisprudence, which provided that *discrimination in prices between different purchasers of the same products*

111. *Clear Media (India) Private Limited v. Prasar Bharti*, Case No. 19 of 2017, para. 16.
112. *Confederation of Indian Alcoholic Beverage Companies and Anr. v. Kerala State Beverages (Manufacturing and Marketing) Corporation Ltd.*, Case No. 10 of 2021, para. 65.
113. *Schott Glass* case, para. 9.83-9.87.
114. *Schott Glass India Pvt. Ltd v. Competition Commission of India*, [2014] Comp AT 1, paras 43-45.1.

is condemned, where the effect of such discrimination may be to substantially lessen competition. Hence, in an application of the two conditions mentioned above, it was deduced that the discount in this case was given on a slab basis, and the same rate of discount was applicable to transactions falling in the same quantity slab. Hence, (i) transactions of different volumes of tubes could not be inferred as equivalent transactions warranting equivalent treatment from the seller, and (ii) Schott's conduct did not affect downstream competition since prices of final products charged by Schott Kaisha to the pharmaceutical companies were same or in some instances higher as compared to the prices charged by the other players. In fact, if any other converter matched the quantity purchased by Schott Kaisha, they were entitled to the same kind of discount. Further, this functional discount policy had been applied uniformly to all the converters at the same flat rate since its inception in a non-discriminatory manner. Therefore, such a policy could not be deemed to be discriminatory in terms of price differentiation. The erstwhile COMPAT affirmed this position and also added that there would have to be some reasonable discretion in the manufacturer for conducting business. Hence, the findings of the CCI were overturned.

This position has also been followed in other cases.[115] Hence, this brings us to the concept of equality among equals: a dominant enterprise is obligated to treat only similar entities equally since businesses operating under similar circumstances have the freedom to develop and implement their own marketing and discounting strategies based on their unique objectives, market conditions, and customer preferences. Consequently, the aspect of discriminatory pricing cannot impede the ability of a dominant enterprise to have an objective-based discounting and marketing policy, as the aim of competition law is to maintain a balance between promoting fair competition and allowing businesses, including dominant ones, to operate effectively and innovatively. This is an extension of the principle of rational business justification, which means that if dominant enterprises have a rational justification to justify their business practice, then the same cannot be termed as anti-competitive.

Further, in the *Play Store* case, the CCI concluded that Google's various conducts and policies in relation to the Play Store were in violation of section 4(2)(a)(i) of the Competition Act. These are as follows:

(i) Making access to the Play Store for app developers, dependent on mandatory usage of GPBS for paid apps and in-app purchases, constitutes an imposition of unfair condition on app developers.

(ii) Google has gradually increased the scope of the mandatory requirement to use its own billing system by explicit additions in the policy. This has to be agreed to by all app developers who want to list their app on the Play Store without any scope for changes/negotiations. Since Android is the most widely used smart device ecosystem in the country, Google acts as the gatekeeper between the app store and the smart device user. As a result of

115. *TAM Media Research Private Limited v. Prasar Bharati (Broadcasting Corporation of India)*, Case No. 70 of 2012, para. 9.4., 9.5; *Rajendra Khare v. Information Systems Audit and Control Association*, Case No. 42 of 2021, para. 32.

its financial might and its control over the entire ecosystem, Google undoubtedly has a much stronger bargaining position vis-à-vis app developers, who are forced to accept Google's unilateral terms that deter legitimate competition and increase their costs of operation.

(iii) Google also restricts the ability of app developers to inform consumers within an app of the ability to purchase in-app content elsewhere, such as on a website ('Anti-steering Provisions'). Thus, app developers do not have the freedom to choose their communication channel to interact with their users. This is an unfair imposition as it impedes the ability of app developers to increase their usage/membership, and they are prohibited from using third-party payment processors that may offer greater benefits and innovative features to the app users.

(iv) Google is following discriminatory practices by not using GPBS for its own applications, i.e., YouTube. This also amounts to imposition of discriminatory conditions as well as pricing, as YouTube is not paying the service fee as being imposed on other apps covered in the GPBS requirements.

(v) Google was also found to have access to a significant volume of user data which it did not share with the app developers, affecting their ability to improve their services and compete effectively. However, this confiscated data was then exploited by Google which is particularly exacerbating since Google itself admitted that it considers app developers to be its competitors. Data as a factor of abuse of dominance has been discussed in more detail in the Chapter on Digital Markets.

(vi) Google takes significantly more time for settlement of payment to app developers, i.e., fifteen to forty-five days from the transaction, as opposed to the settlement period followed by other payment processors which take only one to three days to remit the payment to app developers. Google receives the payments within a shorter and stricter deadline from the payment aggregators. However, it fails to observe such a strict timeline when it comes to making payments to app developers. This unjust enrichment on the part of Google is unfair to the app developers, especially small app developers who require regular and prompt cash flows.

(vii) Service fee is imposed by Google on apps offering digital content, but the distinction between physical and digital content is ambiguous, without adequate transparency or justification for the differential treatment accorded to apps by Google, leaving it susceptible to discrimination.

It is pointed out that Google argued that there is no violation of section 4(2)(a)(i) of the Competition Act because Google's Payments Policy is fair, and the use of standard terms reduces the potential for discrimination. Further, that Google's policies – including the requirement that apps use GPBS for IAPs of digital goods – apply to all apps on Google Play, including Google's own app. However, the CCI found that the service fee imposed on apps that compete with Google's proprietary apps disadvantages Google's rivals and distorts the competition dynamic in the apps market. For instance, the fee charged to ShareChat, a video distribution app, was not made applicable to YouTube, which was Google's own app. Google, thus, sets out rules for the Play Store that may implicitly exclude or discriminate against downstream competition. In the build-up to the network effects, Google required app developers to develop apps that would attract consumers to the app stores. The CCI observed that once Google also started developing these competing apps and entered into these 'complementor' markets, its incentives changed. This meant that Google lost its incentives to compete on and ensure fair terms on its platform upon entering into the downstream market of app distribution: now, instead of just being the owner of the platform, i.e., the Play Store, Google started competing with its customers on the platform, i.e., the app developers. The CCI also noted that Google admits that some of the app developers are its competitors.

Non-disclosure of essential and competitively relevant information is also an unfair imposition.[116] For instance, in *Digital News Publishers Association v. Alphabet Inc. and Ors.*,[117] the CCI ordered an investigation into Google's conduct, resulting in denial of fair share in the digital advertising revenue to news publishers and disclosure of inadequate information to reach a fair settlement. There ostensibly existed opacity on critical aspects like data and audience management practices, generation and sharing of revenue with publishers, etc. Information asymmetry, i.e., lack of transparency with respect to these aspects was prima facie prejudicial to the interest of publishers, by in turn affecting the quality of their services and innovation, thereby causing consumer detriment. Hence, such policies of Google constituted imposition of unfair conditions and price in violation of section 4(2)(a) and thus merited an investigation. The investigation of the same is pending.

[2] Analysis of Specific Unfair Terms and Conditions

In its decisional practice, the CCI has examined abusive conduct having regard to the terms of the contract, out of which it emanates from the standpoint of the provisions of the Competition Act.

The *DLF* case was the first major case on the issue of a dominant enterprise imposing unfair terms and conditions on the counterparty. DLF, a real estate player, was imposing one-sided terms on the buyers. The CCI went into great depth and analysed the clause of the Apartment Buyers Agreement. It is to be noted that when the matter was heard at COMPAT, it did not analyse the issue of the said agreements because they were entered into prior to 20 May 2009 (the date when section 4 of the Competition Act was notified). However, the erstwhile COMPAT did hold DLF guilty of abuse of dominant position through imposition of one-sided or unfair conditions through the Apartment Buyers Agreement. It observed that prior to the enactment of the Competition Act, the element of dominance was absent from the statute book, and hence, it cannot be argued that one-sided agreements which were 'imposed' on the allottees (rather, they were voluntarily executed) is contrary to the law since sections

116. *Matrimony.com Limited v. Google LLC,* Case Nos 07 and 30 of 2021.
117. *Digital News Publishers Association v. Alphabet Inc and Ors.*, Case No. 41 of 2021.

3 and 4 were not available when the agreements were executed. Consequently, it rejected CCI's approach of examining all the clauses of the Apartment Buyers Agreement. Conversely, when the matter was initially heard at CCI, it took great pains to identify the specific clauses of the Agreement and the conduct of DLF towards its buyers, based on which it ultimately held that DLF was guilty of abuse of dominant position.

While the erstwhile COMPAT did not analyse the specific clauses of the buyer agreement like the CCI did (although it specifically noted that '*it was only because of the question of retrospectivity that we did not go into the merits of the analysis of various clauses of the ABA*'), it is noteworthy to see the approach of the CCI. The relevant clauses under the Apartment Buyers Agreement which were held to be abuse of dominant position by the CCI were broadly as under:[118]

(1) Unilateral changes in agreement and supersession of terms by DLF without any discussion or even informing the allottees, such as changing the layout plan, inter se areas earmarked for different uses like residential, commercial, etc., increasing/decreasing the super area, zoning plans, usage patterns, carpet area and the like. The allottees had no option but to accept the sweeping changes, even if made without assigning reasons, and were not allowed to raise any objections. This was after the allottees were compelled to pay almost 95% of the consideration amount within twenty-seven months of booking. Hence, the buyer got locked in with DLF, having paid a substantial amount with no free exit option to go to other real estate service providers.
(2) Additional charges for preferential location determined at the discretion of DLF were to be paid upfront, but if the allottee did not get the location, he would only get the refund at the time of the last instalment, that too without any interest. DLF also retained total discretion regarding the arrangement for power supply and rates levied for the same, even if it exceeded the rate charged by other power suppliers. DLF's exit clause gave them full discretion, including abandoning the project, without any penalty. However, the allottees had no exit option except when DLF fails to deliver possession within the agreed time. Even in that event, they get their money refunded without interest only after the sale of said apartment by DLF to someone else.
(3) DLF continued to enjoy full rights on the community buildings/sites/ recreational and sporting activities, including maintenance, but allottees did not. In fact, third-party rights were also created without the allottee's consent. For instance, even if the buyer has paid the full amount, the builder can raise a subordinate mortgage on the property for financing its own purposes, and the consumers would be subjected to this mortgage. Further, high punitive penalty was imposed for default by allottees along with excessive interest (@15% per annum and for all periods of delay exceeding the first ninety days after the due date an additional penal interest @3% per annum) and

118. *DLF* case, para. 12.90-12.103.

insignificant penalty for DLF's default (in the event of delay, the builder would pay compensation at INR 5 per square foot per month for delays beyond three years).

Based on these practices, the allottees become captured consumers who were subject to abuse by DLF through imposition of unfair conditions contained in the agreement. DLF's conduct also revealed that such abuse was not a one-time practice but continued (and often aggravated) throughout the period of construction. Thus, the CCI held that by conduct and by the provisions of the agreement, DLF was guilty of abuse of dominant position.

These are some of the clauses that show how heavily loaded the buyers' agreement is in favour of DLF Ltd. and against the buyer. Under a normal market scenario, a seller would be wary of including such one-sided and biased clauses in its agreements with consumers. The CCI held that the impunity with which these clauses have been imposed, the brutal disregard for consumer rights that has been displayed in its action of cancelling allotments and forfeiting deposits and the deliberate strategy of obfuscating the terms and keeping buyers in the dark about the eventual shape, size, location, etc., of the apartment cannot be termed as fair. The course the progress of the project has taken again indicates that DLF Ltd. beguiled and entrapped buyers through false solicitations and promises contrary to consumer interest. The person who chooses a particular apartment does so after considering factors such as floor area ratio, availability of bigger common areas, common facilities, etc. If the number of apartments in a project is substantially increased, as in this case, there is considerable reduction in consumer welfare. *For example, if a hundred residents are supposed to share one swimming pool, their satisfaction from that common pool would be far less if suddenly the builder tells them they have to share the pool with 200 residents. In economics, 'value' is based on the perceived utility of any product or service. Consumers pay according to this perception. If something is done that drastically or substantially reduces that perceived value, it can only be termed as an unfair conduct by the seller. Under Competition Act, such unfair conduct by a dominant enterprise is contravention of the provisions of the Act.*

In the *DLF* case, the erstwhile COMPAT also observed that CCI confining itself to only the one-sided nature of the agreement was not the be-all and end-all of the matter, and it had to be seen whether DLF's actions contravened section 4 of the Competition Act. This primarily included non-disclosure of the additional construction and then proceeding with the construction. It was the element of secrecy and uncertainty with which DLF conducted its business which made it a tainted condition. In this regard, *inter alia,* the erstwhile COMPAT held:[119]

(i) Increasing the number of floors without increasing the number of lifts and thus, a lift which was to be shared with a hundred persons would now have to be shared with five hundred persons, which would add to day-to-day woes and all this without giving the faintest idea to the allottees as to how

119. *DLF Limited v. Competition Commission of India,* [2014] Comp AT 12, paras 74, 99-121.

many floors were to be actually constructed and applied for. This mysterious vagueness amounts to imposition of an unfair condition since it left the allottees in the continued position of a trapped customer as they have no idea how far the DLF could go higher and how many floors it could add to each building.

(ii) DLF argued that the original allottees were given an assurance that instead of their previously selected apartment, they could select an apartment out of the added floor. However, this meant the allottees had to forego their claims on the improvements made in the originally selected apartment, the special features, etc. Further, DLF was very vague in its offer, as it could accept moving some allottees while rejecting others. This offer itself amounts to an imposition of discriminatory condition since where a provision could enable an authority to discriminate, such provision itself is bad.

(iii) DLF tried to argue that the modifications were accepted by the authorities and, hence, were free of fault. However, erstwhile COMPAT categorically held that it was not concerned with the '*the legality or validity of the construction*', but '*the impact that it made on the allottees, who did not have even a ghost of idea, as to how many persons they would have to share lifts with or their common area, or for that matter their swimming pool and gymnasium*'. This highlighted the sinister unfairness on the part of DLF, which still had a duty to disclose the action.

(iv) The allottees were allured by DLF's promise of luxury facilities, without which the apartments could not be termed 'luxury apartments'. Hence, DLF was duty-bound to let the allottees know about the proposed increase and obtain their consent.

(v) If the allottee did not concur with the increase of INR 5 to INR 10 in case of holding charges, he would not be entitled to compensation on account of delay in construction. This is nothing but a ruse to avoid the payment of compensation on account of delayed construction. Such a unilateral increase in the holding charges and the threatened consequence amounted to abuse of dominance by DLF.

(vi) The CCI also failed to consider that what was being offered to the allottees was a piece of illegal and unauthorized construction, which amounts to imposing unfair conditions against the wishes of the consumer. '*We cannot imagine as to what would have happened had the approvals not come in the year 2009 by which time, the 29 floors of Belaire residential housing scheme was already over*'.

Based on the *DLF* case, it was noted that the approach of the CCI is to see whether the consumer has any bargaining choice vis-à-vis DLF or if they are subject to continuous abusive tactics of the DLF. Similarly, the CCI dealt with the similar issue of unfair terms and conditions imposed by Coal India on thermal and non-thermal power producers. The *Coal India* case[120] revolved around imposition of unfair and discriminatory terms in the Fuel Supply Agreement entered into between Coal India and the buyers. Further, there were certain existing Fuel Supply Agreements which were already in place with some power plants and some new Fuel Supply Agreements were signed with new power plants/buyers. Before delving deep into the issue of unfair and discriminatory terms and conditions contained in the Fuel Supply Agreement and identifying the unfair clauses as such, the CCI analysed the repercussions of having unfair terms under the Fuel Supply Agreement.

It was noted by the CCI that a Fuel Supply Agreement is a long-term agreement between a buyer and Coal India which has to be differentiated from other ordinary long-term agreements due to the cascading and systemic effects which may flow from its terms, conditions and their execution. The consumer in a Fuel Supply Agreement is a power generating company, however, the effect has consequences further down the value chain, given that the cost of electricity constitutes between 60% and 70% of the tariff paid by the end consumer. Further, CCI noted that while the obligations and responsibility of supply of coal by Coal India stop at the level of the Fuel Supply Agreements, the obligations and responsibilities of the power generating companies extend beyond the power sector in as much as any inefficiency and anti-competitive conduct in one segment of the value chain would have the effect of creating and causing a systemic risk in the entire economy. Based on the same, CCI noted that it is imperative that a Fuel Supply Agreement address the issue of mutual obligations and responsibilities holistically rather than merely from a perspective of ordinary contractual obligations. Accordingly, the CCI was of the view that assessment of the obligations and responsibilities enshrined within the Fuel Supply Agreement calls for an integrated and holistic approach that considers not only the anti-competitive effects on power-generating companies but also on the entire power sector as a whole.

Based on the above rationale of having an efficient Fuel Supply Agreement in the interest of the power sector and the end consumer, the CCI noted[121] that the Fuel Supply Agreement must guarantee commercial and operational viability for both sellers and buyers of coal by consisting of three essential characteristics – quality, quantity and deliver schedules/timelines. The sellers must supply good quality coal at pre-agreed prices in a timely manner, and the buyers must pay promptly and intimate their requirements in advance, with penalties for non-fulfilment of these obligations. Any price/supply shocks should be mutually resolved between the parties. Since the outcome of Fuel Supply Agreements (FSA) is directly related to the Power Purchase Agreement (PPA) signed between power generators and distributors, any mismatch between FSA and PPA results in a cascading effect affecting the tariffs to consumers.

Considering the above, the CCI looked into, in great detail, each of the clauses of the Fuel Supply Agreements and found the following terms and conditions unfair and discriminatory:

120. *Coal India* case, Case Nos 03, 11 & 59 of 2012, paras 155-259.
121. *Ibid.*, para. 158.

(a) The unilateral drafting of the Fuel Supply Agreement:[122] The terms and conditions of a commercial contract should be negotiated by the buyer and seller. However, the Fuel Supply Agreement was unilaterally drafted by Coal India without even consulting the buyers of the coal. A process of discussion on the drafting of the fuel supply agreements did happen, but these were commercial discussions limited to the Ministry of Power, which was not the key stakeholder as far as the Fuel Supply Agreement was concerned. The investigation and evidence on record revealed that the inputs of the power utilities, who were the buyers, were not considered. Based on this unilateral approach of Coal India, the CCI highlighted that under *certain market conditions, some contracts become unconscionable especially when the markets are not functioning in a competitive manner. In such a scenario, the party with superior bargaining power is able to dictate terms that are overwhelmingly one-sided. Then, the other party is confronted with the 'take it or leave it' proposition* [emphasis supplied].

(b) Issue of supply of coal through MOUs:[123] Coal India had been insisting on the buyers to execute additional MOUs in addition to the Fuel Supply Agreements, which became integral to the contract. These MOUs, *inter alia*, provided that the quantum of coal supply will be decided by Coal India but shall not exceed 50% of the annual contracted quantity. Also, for the calculation of compensation for short-supply or short-lifting, the annual contracted quantity under the Fuel Supply Agreement shall be reduced by 50%. Hence, they diluted the supply obligations of Coal India. The CCI noted that the MOUs were framed in such a manner which not only reduced the obligation of Coal India to supply the necessary quantity but also reduced the compensation payable in case of a short supply. Further, the purchasers had no option but to accept such one-sided terms and conditions as there was no scope for negotiation, giving an upper hand to Coal India. Hence, the CCI observed that the MOU constituted imposition of unfair terms.

(c) Procedure for sample collection for assessment of quality of coal:[124] An examination of the Fuel Supply Agreements executed between Coal India and the new power producers, existing power producers and public sector undertakings revealed that there were different methods adopted for sample collection. For existing public sector undertaking power producers, there was a provision for automatic mechanical sampling for coal, whereas, for existing private producers and new private power producers, it was manual till 2012 when the words '*or any suitable mechanical arrangement*' were inserted in the agreements. These changes were themselves found to be abstract and ambiguous, besides having the potential to cause a conflict of interest. Based on the same, the CCI was of the opinion that that the provisions for sampling of coal are *ex facie* discriminatory between public sector undertakings and

122. *Ibid.*, paras 151-160.
123. *Ibid.*, paras 242-249.
124. *Ibid.*, paras 172-190.

private producers. The CCI noted that in an appropriate case, the distinction based on two consumers may have some rational justification, but presently, it was not readily inferred as to how a distinction in the matter between the various buyers (be it existing power producers, new power producers or public sector undertakings) relating to sample collection may have any justification, leave alone a justification which may satisfy the requirements of law. Thus, the order of the CCI showed that an artificial distinction among consumers would not be accepted as a defence for discriminatory pricing. To differentiate among various kinds of consumers, the undertaking must have a rational business justification. What is rational would depend on market situations, the obligation of the dominant undertaking and the facts and circumstances of each case.

(d) Sampling of coal at loading and unloading points:[125] The sampling was done at both ends, i.e., loading and unloading points, by an independent party. However, Coal India made unilateral changes in the sampling procedure. A comparison between the sampling procedure adopted by the other players in the market revealed that the latter provided for sampling at the loading end only. However, there was a provision for analysis by both parties at their respective labs, and for this purpose, three sets of samples (one each for seller, buyer and referee) were taken. Thus, the buyers have been given opportunity to test the sample to their satisfaction. Hence, compared with another player in the relevant market, the procedure of sample collection and analysis adopted by Coal India was heavily tilted in their favour. Thus, these terms and conditions regarding the commitment of Coal India to ensure the quality of coal were held to be unfair and prejudicial towards consumers.

(e) Supply of ungraded coal:[126] When the price of coal is based on the grade/quality, the buyer has the right to get the grade for which he is paying the price. However, the Fuel Supply Agreement did not impose a strict liability upon Coal India and its subsidiaries to supply only the agreed grades but only mentioned making adequate arrangements to assess the quality and for providing monitoring mechanism to prevent loading of ungraded coal. It merely provided that Coal India need only *try* that the ungraded coal is not loaded, however, if the ungraded coal was loaded and transported, there was no provision for compensation. Further, even in case of supply of ungraded coal which was in breach of the agreed quality under the Fuel Supply Agreement, the buyer was saddled with all the expenses on transportation, royalty, taxes, etc., without any justification. However, other players in the market reimbursed the freight costs borne by the buyer in case of supply of ungraded coal. The CCI did note that the ungraded coal may have some value and Coal India may be able to sell such ungraded coal in the open market to the willing buyer. However, forcing the buyer who has specifically contracted

125. *Ibid.*, paras 191-194.
126. *Ibid.*, paras 195-199.

for supply of graded coal to pay for such goods transported by default was not fair in any circumstances. The CCI held that Coal India cannot absolve itself of the responsibility of supplying only graded coal. In this regard, it is apposite to note the observations of the CCI:

> the consumers cannot be forced to pay the cost of ungraded coal. Such condition not only gives an upper hand to the seller but also reduces its commitment to supply right quality of coal. *The conduct of the seller is guided by the FSA and if there is no obligation on the seller to assure the supply of only graded coal, the coal companies are not bound to do the same.* [emphasis supplied] It is not out of place to mention that such provisions also result in misappropriation or mishandling of the limited resources of railways in supply of rake to the coal industry as well as of the buyer. The ultimate sufferer is the end user of power on whom the increased cost is passed on. Thus, the terms and conditions in FSA regarding supply of quality coal should be guided by the strict adherence to the desired quality and the measures relating to grading, sampling and testing of the coal needs to be incorporated in the agreement to the satisfaction of both the parties.

(f) Compensation for supply of oversized, wet and sticky coal:[127] In the process of supply of coal, there are chances of dispatch of oversized, wet and sticky coal along with stones. For any Fuel Supply Agreement to have a semblance of fairness, it must necessarily provide for payment of compensation in such an event and operate in a non-discriminatory manner among all classes of buyers. However, the compensation under the Fuel Supply Agreement for new power producers was capped at 0.75% of the total quantity of coal, whereas there was no cap on compensation for existing power producers. Hence, the CCI held that the same is *ex facie* unfair since the cap was not based on actual quantity or any other reasonable basis besides discrimination between the two classes of buyers.

(g) Unilateral termination of agreement: The CCI noted that Coal India enjoys a situation of statutory monopoly, and the buyers are heavily dependent upon Coal India. In light of the same, insertion of a clause reserving the right to unilaterally terminate the agreement without having scope for review by any independent agency is not fair under the extant regulatory framework operating in the coal sector.[128]

The erstwhile COMPAT reaffirmed the findings of the CCI that Coal India abused its dominant position in contravention of section 4(2)(a)(i) of the Competition Act. Certain relevant observations of the erstwhile COMPAT and their analysis in addition to the findings of the CCI have been stated below:[129]

(i) Clause 9 stipulated that the bid of successful buyers would be forfeited if they failed to lift the coal within the specified period. However, there was

127. *Ibid.*, paras 200-208.
128. *Ibid.*, para. 228.
129. *Ibid.*, para. 22.

no corresponding clause to provide compensation to successful bidders if Coal India failed to supply the coal. In fact, Coal India itself admitted that during the period of assessment, it defaulted in 701 instances in providing coal to the successful bidders, and no compensation was paid for such defaults.

(ii) Coal India was also unable to rebut the assertion of the buyers that its failure to supply coal to the successful bidders affected them financially (since they lost interest on the money deposited) while Coal India enjoyed this credit free of cost. Such clauses are one-sided and disturb the normal contractual equilibrium, and the uneven obligations were a result of the market power exercised by Coal India. The fact that buyers agreed to such unequal terms despite adverse financial effects made it apparent that there was no competitive pressure on Coal India.

(iii) Coal India's argument that such forfeiture clauses without compensation were standard industry practice was rejected because of its failure to prove that the entities issuing such notices were dominant in their relevant markets. This once again brings us to the point that unfair conditions require intervention by the CCI only if the enterprise is dominant.

The *Coal India* case is currently pending an appeal before the Supreme Court to be decided on merits. However, in its interim observations, the Supreme Court has held that even if Coal India were to fall within the description of the state, it will not absolve Coal India of its liability under the Competition Act. The Supreme Court has noted that Coal India '*act with caprice, or unfairly or treat otherwise similarly situated persons or things with discrimination... We may only add that in judicial review the appellants would be held to the standard of fairness as also the duty not to discriminate.*'[130] As also discussed earlier, to treat the classes of buyers differently, Coal India ought to have had a rational business justification which could rationalise dissimilar treatment. However, per CCI, it did not have any reasonable basis to treat similarly placed buyers in a discriminatory manner.

Similar to the *Coal India* case where Coal India had an absolute monopoly and thereby had the power to impose such unfair and discriminatory conditions, the CCI and the DG undertook a detailed exercise of analysing the various provisions of the Gas Sales Agreement and also the industry in question in the *Adani Gas* case. The industry dynamics involved in the present case was that Adani Gas Limited was not the producer of natural gas, but it was a supplier of natural gas. The natural gas was sourced by Adani Gas Limited from GAIL (India) Limited by entering into multiple upstream contracts with GAIL (India) Limited. This fact was taken into account by CCI while reviewing the clauses of the Gas Sales Agreement to see whether Adani Gas Limited was acting unilaterally and unfairly.[131] The NCLAT supported the finding that Adani Gas Limited abused its dominant position qua the Industrial Customers by

130. *Coal India Limited and Anr. v. Competition Commission of India and Anr.* [2023], (SC) Civil Appeal No. 2845 of 2017, pp. 99, 100.
131. *Adani Gas* case, paras 78-104.

imposing unfair, lopsided, unilateral and harsh conditions that were detrimental to the interests of the consumers under the Gas Sales Agreement. It also remarked that even Adani Gas Limited must have been conscious of such conditions being unfair to consumers and abusive of its dominant position which is clearly inferable from its conduct in substituting the original Gas Sales Agreement with a revised one modifying the contravening terms and conditions.[132]

The aspect of unfair conditions was also discussed in the *Super Cassettes* case. It was alleged that Super Cassettes was imposing minimum commitment charges per month irrespective of actual needle hour (each aggregate of sixty minutes of actual broadcast of sound recordings by FM radio station excluding commercials, advertisements, voice-over, anchor time, etc.) of broadcast of the music content of Super Cassettes by the radio station. The CCI, relying on the investigation report of the DG, found that no other competitor of Super Cassettes was levying a minimum commitment charge. Further, a minimum commitment charge was required to be paid by the radio operators irrespective of the actual number of needle hours of the music of Super Cassettes that is broadcast on the radio channel. On a review of the agreements for granting licenses to the radio operators containing the provision for minimum commitment charge, it was observed that the minimum committed needle hours for the playoff of the songs of Super Cassettes imposed by it are as high as 50%. This was done to ensure that the business share of Super Cassettes in the relevant market and that if half of the total songs played by the FM stations have been fixed by Super Cassettes, the other music companies will be left with only 50% of the total market share of the relevant market. Further, the investigation had revealed that the condition of minimum commitment charge is distorting the competition in the relevant market. On the one hand, it increases the cost of music for FM radio stations as they are forced to pay extra money even if they are not playing songs of Super Cassettes, and on the other hand, it also forces FM stations to play at least the minimum guaranteed needle hour even though there is no demand of such songs from the listeners.

The CCI agreed with the report of the DG and noted that minimum commitment charge is exploitative and exclusionary in nature. It is exploitative as it forces the customers to pay for music that they may not play. Exclusionary conduct is characterized by improper strengthening of market power by the dominant enterprise. The CCI thereby observed that the imposition of minimum commitment charge by Super Cassettes has an anti-competitive effect on the market as it forecloses other competitors from a substantial share of the market. Since the private radio station is contractually bound to pay Super Cassettes a minimum guarantee, they are likely to broadcast the amount of music that they have already paid for. Therefore, a certain amount of music that plays out on private FM radio stations is already fixed for Super Cassettes. This results in the competitors of Super Cassettes not being able to compete for and being foreclosed from broadcasting their music on this prefixed play out of 50% reserved for Super Cassettes.

132. *M/s Adani Gas Limited v. Competition Commission of India and Anr*, TA (AT) (Competition) No. 33 of 2017, para. 29.

In the *MMT* case, an information against MMT-Go and Oravel Stays Private Limited (OYO) alleging an abuse of dominant position by indulging in predatory pricing, exorbitant commissions, etc. MMT-Go held a dominant position in the relevant market for online intermediation services for booking hotels in India. MMT imposed parity obligations through Across Platform Parity Agreements which are stipulations where the sellers guarantee online selling platform terms that are at least as favourable as those granted to any other platform, thus ensuring the former a competitive advantage over its competitors. MMT-Go imposed rate parity obligations (i.e., that a hotel will not be able to supply its room night to any other OTA at a price lesser than the price offered to MMT-Go) in conjunction with room parity obligations (i.e., at any given point of time, the hotels rooms offered for sale at MMT-Go would not be lesser than any other OTA), deep discounting strategies and exclusivity conditions. The effect of these parity obligations has been explained through the following example: Consider that Hotel A is listed on all OTAs and decides to supply a room night to MMT-Go at INR 1,000 per night. Now, Hotel A will not be able to supply the room night at a price lower than INR 1,000 per night to any other OTA. Considering that MMT-Go charges a commission of 20% from Hotel A on every room night sold through MMT-Go's portal, Hotel A will get INR 800 per room night sold while MMT-Go will keep INR 200 per night. The same logic applies to room parity obligations as well.

Based on an in-depth assessment, the CCI found that the collective operation of deep discounts (discussed under predatory pricing), exclusivity condition and parity conditions by MMT-Go created a self-reinforcing ecosystem that reinforces MMT-Go's dominant position in the relevant market. As a result, the parity obligations increase the distribution cost for hotels and prohibit them from delisting from MMT-Go without losing considerable sales and visibility due to the following reasons: First, it helps MMT-Go to retain and further increase its network of users/travellers, who would increasingly use the platform for availing the best deals. Second, it impedes the competitive process between OTAs by limiting the competitive levers/instruments at the disposal of other portals that, for instance, cannot get better prices from hotels by offering lower commission rates. The hotels were so dependent on MMT-Go that they had no option but to accept the onerous terms. Third, the consequent adverse effect on sale of rooms through other platforms/channels and their user bases further accentuates the dependence of hotels on MMT-Go as well as the bargaining power imbalance that already exists between MMT-Go and its hotel partners. Fourth, the increased sales through MMT-Go may lead to unilaterally determined higher commissions charged by it, giving it the ability to also pass on discounts which are admittedly funded through these commissions, which may adversely impact the prices at which the hotel rooms are being offered to end consumers. The conduct of MMT-Go was, thus, found to be in contravention of section 4(2)(a)(i) of the Competition Act.[133]

Based on the above, we see that the approach of the CCI, while deciding whether a clause is unfair or not, is to see whether the counterparty has any choice but to accept the onerous and one-sided terms imposed by the dominant undertaking as well as its

133. *MMT* case, paras 248-266.

collective impact on the market. In doing so, the analysis of the clause may not be limited to the counterparty who chooses whether to complain or not but the entire market, as the aim of competition law is to protect competition in the market. This aspect was clarified by the NCLAT in the *Google Android* case[134] discussed earlier, wherein Google had argued that since there was no complaint made by any OEM regarding abuse of dominance by Google, the CCI could not have analysed the impositions to which they were subjected. However, the NCLAT confirmed that CCI is statutorily obliged to promote and sustain competition, protect the interests of consumers and ensure freedom of trade for all market participants. Hence, its analysis cannot be confined only to the evidence led by countervailing parties and competitors but also extends to any conduct or arrangement concerning the interests of consumers.

[B] Unfair and Discriminatory Pricing

Section 4(2)(a)(ii) of the Competition Act provides that there shall be an abuse of dominant position if an enterprise or a group imposes unfair or discriminatory pricing in the purchase or sale (including predatory pricing) of goods or service. It is to be noted that there are two sets of pricing abuses: unfair and discriminatory. Unfair pricing is one where the pricing conduct of the dominant player is unfair qua the other stakeholders in the market, be it the consumers or other competitors. What is unfair or fair would depend on the facts and circumstances of each case.

The CCI found on the basis of the investigation of the DG in the *Play Store* case, that Google has not subjected its own app to the conditions and service fee as being forced upon the other apps in violation of section 4(2)(a)(ii) of the Competition Act. These discriminatory practices are exploitative, resulting in a competitive disadvantage and harming competitors of Google in the downstream market, i.e., app developers, by increasing their cost. The app developers have two choices: either absorb this increased cost or pass on the increased cost to the end users of their apps.[135]

The decisional practice indicates looking at the harm the pricing behaviour of the dominant enterprise causes to the ultimate consumer. Even while undertaking a dominance investigation in the case of intermediate goods which are not consumed by the final consumer, the CCI undertakes a value chain analysis and sees whether the unfair price, so charged, will have any impact on the final consumer. This kind of value chain analysis was also done by the CCI in the *Coal India* case.[136]

Having said that, it must be noted that the CCI looks into the aspect of unfair pricing only to see whether there is an abuse of dominant position and not to see whether any individual players are getting excluded from the market on the grounds of their own inefficiency.

The wording of the section is unfair pricing, and it would cover all instances of pricing abuses like fidelity discounts, margin squeezes, etc. The CCI, in the *NSE* case

134. *Google Android* case, paras 81, 82.
135. *Play Store* case, para. 273.
136. *Coal India* case, paras 158, 271.

has alluded to the efficient competitor test.[137] The efficient competitor is the test where the CCI will analyse, for price-based alleged abuses, whether a competitor, which is as efficient as the dominant company, can compete against the pricing behaviour of the dominant company. The question is whether the dominant company itself would be able to survive the exclusionary conduct in the event that it would be the target.

The CCI noted in the *Super Cassettes* case that price abuses may be 'exclusionary', i.e., pricing strategies adopted by dominant firms to foreclose competitors.[138] Such strategies include a wide variety of measures, such as predatory pricing, price squeezes, loyalty rebates, etc. Pricing abuses may also be 'exploitative', i.e., which cover instances where a dominant firm is accused of exploiting its customers by setting excessive prices. Evidently, a dominant firm, under the Competition Act, abuses its dominance if it charges 'unfair prices' to its customers, which includes both unfairly high or excessive price and unfairly low or predatory price.

Further, the clause also provides that discriminatory pricing is also an abuse. As the name suggests, discriminatory prices are instances wherein the dominant enterprise imposes different pricing parameters for a similarly situated class of consumers without any intelligible differentia or rational business justification.

Furthermore, section 4 provides that no enterprise or group will engage in any unfair pricing. Therefore, there may be situations of margin squeeze where two enterprises belonging to the same group engage in unfair tactics to remove their competitors in the downstream market, which have no upstream presence. The key part to be analysed is whether the pricing strategy adopted by the dominant enterprise, or its group, is unfair qua the competitors and consumers. The decisional practice indicates undertaking an analysis of whether the dominant enterprise, due to its position of strength, is engaged in practice where the counterparties/competitors have no option but to follow the diktat of the dominant enterprise. In the process, the market operates in the favour of the dominant enterprise.

We will now discuss the practices which have been identified by the CCI, COMPAT/NCLAT as well as the Supreme Court as instances of unfair pricing.

[1] Excessive Pricing

The CCI, in the *Automobile Spare Parts* case and the *Super Cassettes* case, discussed the issue of excessive pricing in great detail. It relied on the jurisprudence of excessive pricing as laid down by the EC while analysing the test of excessive pricing under Article 102 (earlier 82) of the EC treaty. The CCI, in the Super Cassettes case and the *Automobile Spare Parts* case, relied on the *United Brand* case decided by the ECJ[139] which held that a price charged is excessive if it has no reasonable relation to the economic value of the product supplied. It was noted by the CCI that the ECJ, in *United Brands,* proposed a cost-based test to assess the relationship between the economic

137. *NSE* case, para. 28.2.
138. *Super Cassettes* case, paras 196, 197.
139. *United Brands Co v. Commission of the European Union* [1978] ECR 207.

value of the product/service and the price charged for it by a dominant undertaking. Based on international jurisprudence, the CCI observed that the key issue to be determined in an investigation of excessive pricing is whether *the difference between the costs actually incurred and the price actually charged is excessive and, if the answer to this question is in the affirmative, whether a price has been imposed which is either unfair in itself or when compared to competing products*. The CCI, relying on the *United Brands* case, noted that the test for a claim under excessive pricing is two-fold: the first stage aims to identify the profit margin of the dominant enterprise, and the second stage is to identify whether the said profit margin is 'excessive'. If it is, the second stage is to consider whether the excessive price is unfairly high and consequently abusive. The first stage of the test for exploitative pricing involves calculating the difference between the production cost and the price of the product/service in order to identify the profit earned by the dominant enterprise.

Although the legal test adopted by the ECJ in the *United Brands* case was adopted by the CCI, it noted in the *Automobile Spare Parts* case the practical difficulties while analysing the cost benchmarks and allocating costs. CCI noted that analysis of costs is difficult *considering an enterprise may have diverse production techniques and market operations which incur various categories of costs, and working out production costs may raise great difficulties, especially determining what costs should be taken into account cost price ratio to show that price charged exceeds the costs incurred*. Further, practical difficulty in ascertaining costs would include an apportionment of the indirect costs and general expenditure which may vary significantly according to the size of the enterprise under investigation, its object, the group structure, including its relationship with its subsidiaries, its territorial area of operations and whether it is a single product or a multi-product firm. A multi-product enterprise will have common and joint costs, and how to allocate such costs to each area of operations is an area of concern. The problem gets further compounded if multiple businesses are housed under a single enterprise instead of multiple enterprises in the same group.

As elaborated earlier, the *Automobile Spare Parts* case dealt with the aspect of the non-availability of spare parts in the open market by OEMs and substantial price markup on spare parts by OEMs. The CCI undertook a detailed cost-price comparison in this case. The methodology adopted by the CCI, to determine whether there exists an abuse of excessive pricing in this case, was as follows:

(a) *Cost incurred by the OEMs to manufacture/source the spare parts:*[140] Based on the investigation by the DG, the CCI noted that the OEMs source their components/spare parts to be used for the assembly line requirements as well as aftermarket requirements primarily from the local OESs. Several components assembled in the car are also imported from overseas suppliers. Therefore, the cost of production of a spare part for an OEM is the price at which the spare part is sourced from the OESs or overseas suppliers. Since the OEMs source a majority of their spare parts, both for assembly line and

140. *Automobile Spare Parts* case, para. 20.5.87.

aftermarket requirements from OESs or other overseas suppliers, a starting point for the cost price analysis used by the CCI was the price at which the spare parts are sourced by OEMs from the OESs' and other suppliers.

(b) *Price charged by OEMs to analyse markup:*[141] In order to analyse the mark up from the point of the OEM to the final customer, the CCI undertook an analysis of the price difference between the price at which the spare parts are sourced by the OEMs to the price charged by OEMs to the final customer. It was noticed by the CCI, based on the investigation report of the DG, that the OEMs were charging an average mark up of 100% and in some cases, the markup was as high as 5,000%.

The entire objective of the price-cost analysis is to establish the profit margin of the enterprise under investigation. As such, an enterprise merely having a profit margin does not itself indicate that the price is excessive. Every enterprise will charge a markup to ensure that their business is profitable. At this point in time, such profit margin becomes a case of excessive pricing, and thereby, unfairness will be dependent on the facts and circumstances of each case. It is very difficult to put down an arithmetic test as to what percentage of the markup will be considered excessive.

Section 4(2)(a)(ii) does not prohibit profit margins but prohibits unfair pricing. For instance, initial high prices can be attributable to being the reward for innovation as innovators may have invested huge sums in research and development on product development.[142] Similarly, the fact that a particular company is making more profits than the others can never be a competition consideration unless the company taking advantage of its dominant position starts abusing its dominance.[143]

Having said that, where it has been established that a price substantially exceeds the cost of production, it is necessary to assess whether the difference is so great as to be 'excessive', triggering a review of the fairness of the ultimate price so charged. In the *Automobile Spare Parts* case, the CCI noted that the '*concept of unfairness of a price is related to the notion that such price is unrelated to the "economic value" of the product and that such price are being charged by the enterprise because of its capacity to use its market power or position of strength in that relevant market to affect its competitors or consumers in its favour* [emphasis supplied]'. The CCI noted that markups of an average of 100% and in some cases, markups as high as 5,000% are disproportionate to the economic value of the products supplied by OEMs. Further, the CCI noted that a case of unfair pricing has been made out, considering the following characteristics of the industry:

(a) *Procurement of spare parts is necessary, irrespective of the price:* The CCI noted that the actual cost of procuring the spare parts is much lower than the price at which they are being sold to the ultimate consumer. In spite of this, the value of such spare parts to the consumer is great because without such spare

141. *Ibid.*, para. 20.5.88-20.5.90.
142. *Biocon Limited and Anr. v. F. Hoffmann-La Roche AG and Ors,* Case No. 68 of 2016, para. 80.
143. *Schott Glass India Pvt. Ltd v. Competition Commission of India*, [2014] Comp AT 1, para. 57.

parts, the owner will not be able to effectively repair his automobile. The locked-in consumer is forced to purchase spare parts in order to effectively render the much more expensive primary market equipment, i.e., the automobile itself, in a workable condition. In a way, it can be said that when the demand for the goods is inelastic and, therefore, the manufacture of those goods charges a high price and earns supra normal profits in the process, such manufacturer can be said to be engaged in unfair pricing.[144]

(b) *Lack of effective competition in the aftermarket:* The CCI noted that all the OEMs have entered into agreements with their overseas suppliers, and most of the local OESs contractually prohibit the suppliers from selling spare parts directly in the open market. Therefore, the OEMs are the only source of genuine spare parts available in the aftermarket. The OEMs require their authorized dealers to source the spare parts only from the authorized dealers of the OEMs and further restrict the over-the-counter sale of spare parts and diagnostic tools to independent repairers. Such restrictions had a twin-fold effect: (i) they created entry barriers for the OES who could produce matching quality spare parts by eliminating direct access by OES to supplying genuine spare parts of an OEM in the aftermarket. In the process, OEMs were foreclosing competition in the supply of genuine spare parts and diagnostic tools for the various models of automobiles manufactured by the OEMs; and (ii) the independent repairers were foreclosed from having genuine spare parts from the market to effectively repair the automobile. By having such a restriction, the independent repairers failed to pose an effective competitive restraint on the OEMs and their dealers in the market for repair and maintenance.[145]

(c) *Reaping trading benefits that would not have been available in a competitive market:* Based on these industry dynamics, the CCI opined that in order to analyse the unfairness of the prices charged by the OEMs, what has to be ascertained is whether the dominant firms have leveraged the opportunities arising out of their dominant position to reap trading benefits, i.e., economic advantages, that would otherwise have been beyond their reach in a normal and sufficiently competitive market. Further, as mentioned above, the CCI noted the fact that the OEMs are the only source of supplying spare parts for its brand of automobiles in the aftermarkets. This factor was key in analysing the enterprise's degree and intent of exploitative pricing. In this regard, the CCI relied on the observations of the ECJ in the case of *General Motors Continental NV v. Commission,*[146] where it was observed that the holder of *the exclusive position may abuse the market by fixing a price – for a service which it is alone in a position to provide*. Even in this industry dynamic, OEMs were the sole provider of the service of repair and maintenance due to such restrictive clauses in the agreement between OEMs and the suppliers. Based

144. *Automobile Spare Parts* case, para. 20.5.94.
145. *Ibid.*, para. 20.5.96.
146. *General Motors Continental NV v. Commission* [1975] ECR 1376.

on these facts, the CCI noted that the OEMs are the only source of genuine spare parts compatible with its brand of automobiles in the aftermarket which allows such OEMs to use the opportunities arising out of its dominant position to reap trading benefits which it would not have reaped if there had effective competition in the relevant market.[147]

(d) *No consumer benefits:* As elaborated earlier, the consumers of the original equipment manufacturers (OEMS) are completely dependent on the OEMs for their spare parts requirements. Apart from the lack of alternate suppliers of spare parts, the CCI noted that there are efficiencies enjoyed by the OEMs, in the form of cost savings, in having its distribution channel not passed on to the customer in the form of low prices of spare parts. On the contrary, the spare parts are being sold at a very high markup.[148]

In appeal, the COMPAT[149] observed that the DG's investigation adopted a relatively simplistic approach to assessing the price of the spare parts charged by the OEMs. Unfairness need not necessarily come from the price being excessive. It could also come from the special circumstances of a given situation when a monopoly has been proved and consumers have nowhere else to go. In such cases, significantly higher prices can also operate as unfair prices. In this case, there was exculpatory evidence to suggest that the prices that were charged were abnormally high. In fact, a sizable 55% of the total profits from the business were generated from the sale of spare parts alone, while the OEMs incurred losses on the sale of cars. This was possible because the margins from spare parts business exceeded the margin from car business substantially since the OEMs were able to mark up the price of spare parts without any competitive constraints.

Another key point analysed by the erstwhile COMPAT was the OEMs' attempt to justify the restrictions on account of protecting their IPR and preventing spurious/counterfeit spare parts in the market. However, the erstwhile COMPAT rejected this argument, stating that the primary reason for the large availability of counterfeit spare parts was the significantly high price of the original spare parts. If the OEMs were to make genuine spare parts available in the market at reasonable prices without any artificial constraints, then consumers will automatically be incentivized to purchase the original spare parts, thereby increasing competition in the market.[150]

The aspect of excessive pricing was also discussed in the *Super Cassettes* case. In that case, CCI did not find a case of excessive pricing made out because of the practical difficulty in apportioning the cost. The CCI noticed that the price charged by Super Cassettes was higher than that charged by its competitors. Having said that, CCI said that a claim of excessive pricing cannot be made solely because the price charged by Super Cassettes is more than its competitors. This observation of the CCI is very

147. *Automobile Spare Parts* case, para. 20.5.97.
148. *Ibid.*
149. *Toyota Kirloskar Motor Private Limited and Ors. v. Competition Commission of India and Ors.*, Competition Appeal Nos 60, 61 and 62 of 2014, paras 90-92.
150. *Ibid.*, paras 113, 119, 156, 157.

pertinent because it shows that even after a thorough investigation by the DG and a review process by the CCI, they could not apportion the actual cost required for an excessive pricing investigation.

In the *Play Store* case, it was alleged that Google engaged in excessive pricing by charging 15%-30% commission in the name of service fee on each transaction of in-app purchases and paid apps; this was also corroborated by the DG in the investigation report. Google, *inter alia*, claimed that the CCI could not act as a price-setting regulator and decide what Google Play's service fee model ought to be. The CCI observed that Google's monetization model is based on cross-subsidization, where 3% of the apps offering paid apps or IAPs are made to bear the entire cost of the Play Store, even though all the apps are using similar services of the Play Store. Further, Google has other revenue streams from the 'free apps' listed on Play Store, in the form of advertisement-related revenue earned by Google from the apps hosted on Play Store. These revenue streams are also contributing towards recoupment of the costs associated with Play Store and Android ecosystem, in addition to the service fee. However, the CCI declined to give any finding on excessive pricing due to lack of sufficient information on Google's monetization model. Yet, it did lay down that 'In general, any conditions (including price related conditions) imposed on business users, by the gatekeepers or platform operators, should be fair, reasonable and non-discriminatory.'

[a] The CCI Is Not a Price Regulator

In its decisional practice, the CCI has observed that it is not a price regulator, and hence, it cannot set or control the prices in the market. Its purpose is to ensure a competitive market structure where prices are determined by market forces and fair competition among businesses. Price regulation can lead to incorrect prices and distort market outcomes. For instance, in *Vijay Gopal v. Big Tree Entertainment Pvt. Ltd. (BookMyShow) and Others,*[151] it was alleged that BookMyShow was charging high convenience fee from consumers for using its ticketing portal through exclusivity agreements with cinema owners. The CCI opined that it cannot act as a price regulator to determine the correct fee. Nevertheless, it also observed that exclusivity arrangements by BookMyShow may result in the softening of competition and, therefore, bolster the market power of BookMyShow without any incentive for it to lower such fees in future. Hence, it is the impact on the competitive process and its ability to decide a fair price that has to be assessed.

In *Manjit Singh Sachdeva v. Director General*[152] also, the CCI declined to address the issue of excessive airline ticket prices by laying down a MRP on tickets. The CCI observed that it can '*neither go into the issue of MRP i.e., what should be the MRP for any product or service and fix the MRP, nor the Commission can give direction to the Government of India that it should fix MRP of a service being provided by private*

151. *Vijay Gopal v. Big Tree Entertainment Pvt. Ltd. (BookMyShow) and Others,* Case No. 46 of 2021, para. 35.
152. *Manjit Singh Sachdeva v. Director General,* Case No. 68 of 2012, para. 3.

entrepreneur.' It held that air fares should be determined by the market forces of demand and supply and fixing the price would be contrary to the spirit of competition law.

The Supreme Court in *Rajasthan Cylinders v. Union of India*[153] has also clarified that the CCI should not serve as a price regulator. 'Competition authorities should not be price regulators; they should be the guardians of the competitive process.' It noted that as a matter of policy, direct regulation of price should be a remedy of last resort.

Price controls are by definition designed to suspend the operation of the market mechanism and introduce artificial intervention in the working of the free markets. Therefore, price determination by market forces of demand and supply encourages players to innovate and compete according to the conditions of competition in a free market. It was perhaps the idea behind the CCI not interfering in the pricing % in the *Play Store* case wherein the CCI had to enter into a price adjudication issue; rather, the CCI held that options must be made available to app developers to use the third-party payment processors of their choice and consequently, the CCI ensured that the market remains competitive.

[2] Predatory Pricing

Given the definition of predatory pricing as enshrined under explanation (b) to section 4 of the Competition Act, the major elements involved in the determination of predatory behaviour are:

(a) pricing below cost for the relevant product in the relevant market by the dominant enterprise;
(b) such low pricing is done with the intention of reducing competition or eliminating competitors. This is traditionally known as the predatory intent test.

For determination of 'Cost', the CCI passed the CCI (Determination of Cost of Production) Regulations, 2009, (hereinafter referred to as 'Cost Regulations'). Further, the Cost Regulations provide for a proxy cost benchmark which will be used as a benchmark for predatory price investigations and shall generally be the average variable cost. Regulation 3 of the Cost Regulations provides that.

[3] Determination of Cost

(1) 'Cost' in the Explanation to section 4 of the Act shall, generally, be taken as an average variable cost, as a proxy for marginal cost:

> Provided that in specific cases, for reasons to be recorded in writing, the Commission may, depending on the nature of the industry, market and

153. *Rajasthan Cylinders v. Union of India*, [2019] (4) SCJ 247, para. 97.

technology used, consider any other relevant cost concept such as avoidable cost, long run average incremental cost, market value.

Based on Regulation 3(1) of Cost Regulations, 'Cost' in the Explanation to section 4 of the Act shall, generally, be taken as an average variable cost as a proxy for marginal cost. Having said that, the Cost Regulations give the Competition Commission of India the flexibility to adopt any other cost methods, such as average avoidable cost, long-run average incremental cost or market value, depending on the concerned industry. Regulation 2(c) of the Cost Regulations provides a definition of the various cost benchmarks which may be followed in a predatory pricing investigation:

(a) 'total cost' means the actual cost of production, including items, such as cost of material consumed, direct wages and salaries, direct expenses, work overheads, quality control cost, research and development cost, packaging cost, finance and administrative overheads attributable to the product during the referred period;

(b) 'total variable cost' means the total cost minus the fixed cost and share of fixed overheads, if any, during the referred period;

(c) 'total avoidable cost' means the cost that could have been avoided if the enterprise had not produced the quantity of extra output during the referred period;

(d) 'average avoidable cost' is the total avoidable cost divided by the total output considered for estimating 'total avoidable cost';

(e) 'long run average incremental cost' is the increment to long-run average cost on account of an additional unit of product, where long-run cost includes both capital and operating costs;

(f) 'market value' means the consideration which the customer pays or agrees to pay for a product which is sold or provided or can be sold or provided, as the case may be.

(2) In arriving at the cost figures, the Commission/Director General may take the help of suitable experts.

However, the Cost Regulations provide that CCI, depending on the industry in question, may adopt an alternate definition of costing to appropriately define the cost benchmark while determining a case of predatory pricing. There has only been one decided case by the CCI and erstwhile COMPAT on predatory pricing, which was the *NSE* case. Therein, they did not delve into actual cost benchmark because NSE was providing complete transaction waivers for transactions in the currency derivative segment. Thus, it was a case of zero pricing being charged by the NSE. Therefore, the approach adopted by both the CCI and erstwhile COMPAT was that zero pricing is a case of unfair pricing without identifying any cost benchmark. Such an approach was taken because zero pricing would be lesser than any cost benchmark, be it average variable cost, average avoidable cost or long-run incremental cost.

The relevant facts on the pricing abuse were that NSE, being the super dominant enterprise, was providing complete transaction waivers, i.e., zero pricing on trading done in the currency derivative segment. It is to be noted that NSE has been given the licence by the Indian stock market regulator to operate on all segments of the stock exchange, i.e., the equity segment, futures and options segment, wholesale debt market segment and the currency derivative segment. It is to be noted that the key revenue stream of the stock exchange is the transaction fee. Having said that, since NSE was giving complete waivers on any transaction done in the currency derivative segment, MCX-SX and other competitors, who had the licence to operate in the currency derivative segment only, had no option but to follow suit and provide complete waivers to remain competitive in the market. Further, such waivers were also coupled with other exclusionary tactics like low deposit fees, etc. In the process, MCX-SX faced huge losses to the point of great financial depletion which would have caused MCX-SX to exit the market. During the deliberations of the same before the CCI and COMPAT, the NSE took the argument that it does not incur any variable cost in operating in the currency derivative segment and hence zero pricing is not below cost. The erstwhile COMPAT did not agree with the fact that NSE did incur any variable cost, looking into the investigation report prepared by the DG. Based on the same, the erstwhile COMPAT noted that the action of providing complete transaction waivers by the NSE was below cost. Both the CCI and the erstwhile COMPAT observed that it is not required (in light of the facts of the *NSE* case) to delve into the appropriate cost benchmark since zero pricing will be below any cost benchmark adopted. It is apposite to note that the approach of both the CCI and erstwhile COMPAT was to show how the behaviour of NSE was a case of broader abuse of unfair pricing without going into too many technical details of cost benchmark to be adopted, as required for a predatory pricing claim.

The CCI opined on when a price charged by a dominant enterprise can be regarded as unfair. By way of their approach, the CCI seems to have relied on the efficient competitor test. The CCI noted that the behaviour by NSE of providing complete transaction waivers was a case of unfair pricing, an abuse under section 4(2)(a)(ii) of the Competition Act because the act was unfair qua its competitors. The CCI noted that the term 'unfair' mentioned in section 4(2) of the Competition Act is to be examined either in the context of unfairness in relation to a customer or in relation to a competitor. The test that was adopted was whether the dominant company itself would be able to survive the exclusionary conduct in the event that it would be the target. Relying on the report prepared by the DG, the CCI noted that NSE has deep pockets which allowed it to carry on giving transaction fee waivers over a prolonged period of time in the currency derivative segment. In fact, the CCI noted that, even after providing transaction waivers, NSE was earning supra-normal profits because of its operations in other segments, whereas MCX-SX are incurring huge losses by giving such waivers. Based on the same, it was observed that zero pricing by NSE was a clear case of unfair pricing. The relevant observations of the CCI are as follows:

> As discussed above, NSE has a position of strength which has enabled it to resort to zero pricing since August, 2008. MCX-SX does not have such strength or deep

> pockets. There is practically no justifiable reason for NSE to continue offering its services free of charge for such a long duration when it is paying for manpower and other resources for running the business. It is also a fact that no enterprise would have the intention to engage in a profit-less venture for eternity. MCS-SX, which operates only in the CD segment, has no other source of income. This is a major constraint. In these circumstances, the zero price policy of NSE cannot be termed as anything but unfair. If this Commission were to treat it as fair, it would go against the grain of the Competition Act and betray the economic philosophy behind it. If even zero pricing by dominant player cannot be interpreted as unfair, while its competitor is slowly bleeding to death, then this Commission would ever be able to prevent any form of unfair pricing including predatory pricing in future. Had NSE and MCX-SX been on equal footing in terms of resources directly available, spectrum and scale of operation, nationwide presence, length of existence etc. perhaps perception of unfairness would not have been so blatant and impossible to ignore, but in this case, the sense of the two being equal or even almost equal does not exist. Therefore, this Commission concludes that the zero price policy of NSE in the relevant market is unfair. In this case, the conduct of zero pricing by the NSE is beyond the parameters of promotional or penetrative pricing. It can, in fact, be termed as annihilating or destructive pricing.

When the matter went up in appeal, the erstwhile COMPAT upheld the reasoning of the CCI and also ruled that NSE engaged in unfair pricing, considering the position of strength that NSE derived in the relevant market. NSE offered no justification to continue with the predatory pricing except the inference that it intended to eliminate MCX-SX from the market. NSE attempted to draw a distinction between zero-pricing, as a facet of unfairly low price versus predatory pricing. However, the erstwhile COMPAT observed that for unfairly low price also, there has to be some price somewhere, which is certainly more than zero. In other words, even if NSE was offering its services free of charge, that does not mean that these services did not have any cost. Hence, NSE's conduct was a clear-cut example of predatory pricing, and its policy was well-intentioned to oust the competitors from the market.[154]

In the *Ola* case, investigation was initiated because of information filed by Fast Track Call Cab Private Limited which alleged that Ola cabs, being the dominant player in the city of Bangalore, was engaging in predatory pricing. Materials were placed on record to show how Ola Cabs was giving unrealistic invectives to drivers and very low fares to consumers. However, Ola was not found to be dominant on account of competitive constraints posed by Uber, which was engaging in the same strategy of below-cost pricing. Yet, CCI analysed the conduct of unfair pricing prevalent in the relevant market and expressed its hesitation to interfere in the market that was at a nascent stage and yet to evolve. Some relevant observations are as follows:[155]

(i) Ola did not initiate the strategy of aggressive pricing, and its negative indexed margin since June 2014 seems more to be a reactive strategy to Uber's aggressive pricing. Further, Uber's loss in the relevant market has remained substantially higher than Ola's loss except for a brief period from

154. *NSE* case, paras 92-96.
155. *Ola* case, paras 101, 122-123.

December 2014 to January 2015. Moreover, Ola's response to the aggressive pricing strategy of Uber in the relevant market since June 2014 is indicative of the competitive constraint posed to it by Uber.

(ii) 'The Commission does not fully disagree with the Informants that the low prices of OP are not because of cost efficiency, but because of the funding it has received from the private equity funds.' However, there was no evidence that access to such funding was inequitable, not competitive and had aberrations. Moreover, it was their penetrative pricing strategy that facilitated them to garner high market shares in a short span of time as well as develop the networks to a size that could provide sufficient positive externalities to the participants of the network.

(iii) The long-term impact of this pricing strategy is difficult to determine at this stage as the market is yet to mature. 'Without going into the legitimacy of OP's pricing strategy, suffice to say that besides statutory compulsion of non-intervention in the present case, as OP is not dominant in the relevant market, the Commission is hesitant to interfere in a market, which is yet to fully evolve'.

It is an interesting proposition whether CCI would have intervened to stop the predatory pricing if the market was not at a nascent stage. In almost an extension to the CCI's reasoning, the NCLAT observed that although it was clear that the major discounts and incentives offered by Ola coincided with its rapid spurts in market share, it essentially engaged in a practice of increasing supply to meet the demand to create a win-win situation for riders and drivers. Ola first expanded its market share by generating demand through customer discounts, and once there was a good increase in demand, it started offering drivers incentives. Thus, Ola's pricing strategy was in response to market conditions, helped by a heavy infusion of funding. Further, Uber was a significant competitor in the relevant market, and Ola was found to be responding to the pricing actions of Uber while trying to establish itself as a relatively new entrant in the market. On this basis, the NCLAT concluded that OLA's conduct to establish/consolidate its brand in the market and increase its market share simultaneously was not below-cost pricing for any sustained period of time which could be labelled as predatory pricing and abuse of its dominant position.[156] Rather, it was to establish itself as an effective and reliable brand in the market and also open up a latent market to its advantage through awareness generation about its brand and network/platform through promotional initiatives like discounts and incentives, attracting new customers and gaining riders' confidence. Thus, the CCI and NCLAT have in effect, observed that it may be an effective and legitimate business strategy to engage in predation to create a market.

Similarly, an investigation was ordered against Uber for prima facie engaging in predatory pricing because Uber was losing INR 204 per trip in respect of every trip made by the cars of the fleet owners due to the fidelity discounts offered to the drivers

156. *Meru Travels Solutions Pvt. Ltd. and Anr. v. Competition Commission of India and Anr.* [2022], (NCLAT) Competition Appeal (AT) No. 19 of 2017. para. 39.

to keep them attached to Uber's network, which does not make any economic sense other than pointing to Uber's intent to eliminate competition in the market during the period of assessment.[157] Though the CCI had found that Uber was not dominant, the erstwhile COMPAT directed the DG to cause an investigation on the basis that there were good reasons for a prima facie case. Uber challenged the order of the erstwhile COMPAT before the Supreme Court, which dismissed the challenge. Although eventually, Uber was not found to be guilty of predatory pricing because it was not found to be dominant in the market owing to the highly fluctuating market shares of Uber and Ola,[158] the observations of the Supreme Court on predatory pricing are relevant.[159] It noted that if, in fact, a loss is made for trips made, section 4(2)(a)(ii) 'would prima facie be attracted inasmuch as this would certainly affect the appellant's competitors in the appellant's favour or the relevant market in its favour. Insofar as "abuse" of dominant position is concerned, under section 4(2)(a), so long as this dominant position, whether directly or indirectly, imposes an unfair price in purchase or sale including predatory price of services, abuse of dominant position also gets attracted. Explanation (b) which defines "predatory price" means sale of services at a price which is below cost.' It must be noted herein that the NCLAT has interpreted the observation of the Supreme Court in the *Uber* case as a qualifier for a view for conducting an investigation; however, as a final conclusion, NCLAT has ruled that engaging in pricing below cost may have some rational business justification.

It is to be noted that there are two limbs to the definition of predatory pricing under the Competition Act: (a) pricing below cost, as determined under the Cost Regulations; and (b) the pricing below cost was undertaken with a view to reduce competition or eliminate the competitors. There are two distinct expressions which are used in the second limb of the definition, i.e., reduce competition or eliminate the competitors. While the former refers to reduction in the degree of competitive pressure exerted by competitors, the latter refers to exit of competitors.

Further, the use of the terms 'with a view' used in the definition of predatory pricing contemplates an objective standard that any rational business undertaking would view, given the circumstances. The Indian Parliament, while selecting the words of law, is well aware of its consequences and the term 'with a view' does not contemplate the degree of proof of intent followed in criminal law. Therefore, the CCI has to undertake an intention analysis to see whether the action of the dominant enterprise to price their goods below cost was with a view to eliminating competition.

The key questions that need to be asked while deriving intention would be:

(a) whether the pricing behaviour only makes commercial sense or is it a part of a predatory strategy or;

157. *Meru Travels Solutions Private Limited v. Competition Commission of India*, (COMPAT) Competition Appeal No. 31 of 2016.

158. *Meru Travel Solutions Pvt. Ltd. v. Uber India Systems Pvt. Ltd. and Others*, Case No. 96 of 2015.

159. *Uber India Systems Pvt. Ltd. v. Competition Commission of India and Ors.* [2019], (SC) Civil Appeal No. 641 of 2017.

(b) are there also other reasonable explanations? Is there an actual or likely exclusionary effect, the scale, duration and continuity of such low pricing?

Thus, providing free or below-cost services cannot by itself raise competition concerns unless the same is offered by a dominant enterprise and shown to be tainted with an anti-competitive objective of excluding competition/competitors.[160] The aspect of intention was also deliberated in detail in the *NSE* case, both by the CCI and erstwhile COMPAT, that the strategy of NSE in adopting transaction fee waivers only in the currency derivative segment was specifically targeting reducing the competitive pressures exerted by MCX-SX and other competitors. Based on the same, NSE was found to be engaging in unfair pricing. The relevant observations made by both authorities while analysing the conduct of NSE are as follows:

(a) It was argued by NSE that their action of providing transaction fee waivers was to promote the new currency derivative segment and penetrate the new market. However, this contention was rejected. It was noted by the CCI that zeal or foresight for the development of a new product market can definitely lead to initiatives such as promotional or penetrative pricing. However, such practice of promotional pricing can be understandable for a period of a few months or even a year and not for a continued prolonged period of more than three years. The CCI noted that the continuance of such pricing practice well into the third year of existence of a market can only be seen as an instance of astute strategy for market capture or extreme commercial self-interest. Further, the erstwhile COMPAT also relied on the investigation report of the DG, which noted that for the other segments, NSE did not follow such a policy of promotional pricing when those segments were first introduced. Therefore, it was observed that NSE does not have a policy of providing transaction fees to develop the market, but they selectively gave repeated waivers in the currency derivative segment for a prolonged period of time with the intention of eliminating competition from the market.
(b) The erstwhile COMPAT also noticed that the NSE was giving opaque and repeated waivers of transaction fees. As stated earlier, transaction fees are the major source of revenue stream for any stock exchange. NSE was giving repeated waivers, and MCX-SX had no option but to follow suit and in the process incur huge losses. The erstwhile COMPAT observed that as *on 20 May 2009* (date when section 4 of the Competition Act came into effect), there were only two major players: NSE and MCX-SX. NSE knew that MCX-SX only operated in the currency derivatives segment, making them direct competitors, even if we only consider the relevant market to be currency derivatives. NSE offered zero transaction fees, and it was clear that if they continued with this, MCX-SX would have no choice but to follow suit, which is exactly what happened. MCX-SX had to maintain zero transaction fees to stay competitive.

160. *Bharti Airtel Limited v. Reliance Industries Limited and Anr.*, Case No. 03 of 2017, para. 22.

> Consequently, in the first year, MCX-SX suffered significant losses of INR 29.81 crores, while NSE made a profit of INR 515.54 crores. It was well-known worldwide that MCX-SX only had a license to operate in the CD segment, so if they stuck with zero transaction fees, which was a direct result of NSE's policy, they would face severe financial difficulties. Even though they managed to survive, this was not a justification for NSE's conduct. NSE ignored section 4 of the Competition Act and continued with its policy of zero transaction fees even after the provision came into effect. Analysing this situation, it was evident that MCX-SX couldn't effectively compete with NSE due to NSE's pricing strategy. Hence, there was substantial evidence that proved that NSE's prices had the potential to push out MCX-SX, their only competitor at the time, as well as any other competitors without NSE's resources. This shows that NSE had the intent of predation, and hence, it was found to be in violation of section 4(2)(a)(ii) of the Competition Act.

In the *MMT* case, it was alleged that MMT-Go offered deep discounts on hotel rooms and provided rooms at prices which are impossible for the hotels to themselves offer, thereby eliminating competition as well as tarnishing the reputation of the hotels. During the investigation, the DG found that the average room revenue was less than the average variable cost during the period under investigation, and MMT-Go was found to have incurred a net variable loss on per room night basis. On this basis, the DG concluded that MMT-Go engaged in deep discounting and predatory pricing. However, CCI concluded that platforms often incur lack of profitability to build network effects through continuous investment to attract both sides of the platform to interact and, thus, create value/demand for other users to join the platform. Other OTAs were also incurring losses or facing heavy competition as they invested in the growing market. But, such lack of profitability does not necessarily imply predatory pricing. Thus, the CCI held that a finding of predation based on simple cost categorization is not substantiated by the data and evidence presented in the Investigation Report.[161]

Therefore, an analysis of CCI's decisional practice reveals that CCI has always exercised restraint in concluding whether a certain price is unfair or not to avoid being perceived as a price regulator. Its main goal is to eliminate any bottlenecks in the market, free up the market and in the process, facilitate healthy competition which can allow the market to naturally influence prices.

[4] Differential Pricing

As mentioned above, section 4(2)(a)(ii) provides for two prohibited pricing practices: unfair and discriminatory pricing. Unfair pricing would cover all kinds of pricing abuses like predatory pricing, excessive pricing, etc. Differential, as the name suggests, would mean differentiating among similar kinds of customers on pricing without any intelligible differentia.

161. *MMT* case, paras 273, 274.

In *Asianet Digital Network (P) Ltd. v. Star India Private Limited and Ors,*[162] the CCI considered the price discrimination practised by Star India Private Limited (SIPL). The informant was a MSO who received broadcasting signals from SIPL for monetary consideration for supplying the channels of SIPL to customers. The relevant regulatory framework provided that the subscription fee for the same would be determined strictly according to the Interconnection Regulations 2017, no extra benefits will be offered to any MSO and the maximum permissible discount is capped at 35% (a minimum of 20% distribution fee and other marketing discounts of maximum 15%). However, the informant started losing subscribers to Kerala Communicators Cable Limited (KCCL) as the latter was able to offer low prices to subscribers. This was because KCCL was getting the channels at about 30% of the MRP with about 70% discount (special discounts of up to 50% added with a distribution fee of 20%). The resultant impact was that the informant was constrained to price its channels higher than KCCL and ultimately paid the price by losing consumers consistently, whereas KCCL gained new consumers. Thus, SIPL was found to have been providing a bouquet of channels to the competitor of the informant at lesser prices, resulting in a denial of market access and also amounting to unfair/discriminatory pricing.

Hence, it can be said that by offering different subscription and distribution fees to similarly placed cable operators, SIPL discriminated between the two. The result of that discrimination could be quantified in the increased prices which the informant had to pass on to the consumer, thereby losing its subscriber base. The adverse impact of differential pricing can, therefore, be seen on the entire market: consumers (who have to bear high prices or poor services at the same price and end up dropping such service providers), the competitor (who is resultantly forced to leave the market) and the market (which loses on healthy competition and choice of service providers).

[a] Meeting Competition Defence

It must be noted that the statutory scheme of the Competition Act provides for meeting competition defence on the part of the dominant enterprise. The meeting competition law defence can be availed by the dominant enterprise in both unfair pricing investigation and unfair terms investigation, discussed in detail earlier. Explanation to section 4(2)(a) reads as:

> For the purposes of this clause, the unfair or discriminatory condition in purchase or sale of goods or service referred to in sub-clause (i) and unfair or discriminatory price in purchase or sale of goods (including predatory price) or service referred to in sub-clause (ii) shall not include such condition or price[163] which may be adopted to meet the competition.

Previously, section 4(2)(a) allowed dominant enterprises to engage in 'discriminatory' pricing if such discriminatory pricing has been adopted to meet the competition

162. *Asianet Digital Network (P) Ltd. v. Star India Private Limited and Ors.,* Case No. 09 of 2022.
163. The words 'discriminatory condition or price' were substituted by the words 'condition or price' via the Competition (Amendment) Act, 2023.

in the market. This limited the scope of the defence and suggested that dominant enterprises are free to use only discriminatory condition or price to meet competition. It did not allow the dominant enterprise to adopt unfair pricing as a part of the meeting competition defence. So, in determining the pricing of its product, a dominant enterprise could not engage in pricing below cost just because a competitor was pricing its product below cost. This was modified by way of the Competition (Amendment) Act, 2023, by extending it to unfair price as well, besides discriminatory prices.

Meeting competition has not yet been argued in any of the cases before the CCI to date. As such, the Act provides for an inherent right which is given to dominant undertakings to take any action to protect their own commercial interest. However, the defence of meeting competition ought to be given a very strict interpretation and action by the dominant enterprise must be strictly proportionate to the legitimate commercial objective being pursued. This is especially so considering the special responsibility of a dominant player to prevent their conduct from impairing genuine undistorted competition. It must be noted that even the dominant enterprise must have the right to defend its own commercial and economic interest in the face of action taken by certain competitors. In other words, to minimize the short-run losses resulting directly from competitors' actions can be a legitimate aim. This automatically implies that an objective justification is not possible if the dominant company is not able to show that its conduct is only a response to differential pricing by others or if the CCI demonstrates that the objective aim of the conduct is to foreclose competitors directly. In order to fulfil the proportionality test, the dominant company must in the first-place show that the chosen conduct is a suitable way to achieve the legitimate aim of meeting competition.

Suffice it to say, as noted by the CCI in the *Ola* case,[164] wherein a case of unfair pricing was not found due to severe competition among the players in the market, regulatory intervention is not warranted to either protect the existing players or to increase the number of players in the market when the conditions of competition are fair. Therefore, competition is not an end in itself; it is a means towards a greater end which presumes that competition in or for the market, *inter alia,* leads to desirable outcomes for the consumers, ensuring a wide variety of quality products/services at the best possible prices.

[C] Limiting or Restricting Production and Technical Development

The Competition Act provides that there shall be an abuse of dominant position if the dominant player limits or restricts the production of goods or provision of services. Although this provision was not specifically discussed in the *Automobile Spare Parts* case, it could have been argued that OEMs, by entering into restrictive agreements with the suppliers and prohibiting the supply of spare parts to the independent repairers, are limiting the provision of repair services. This clause is worded in a very broad manner, and it would include all practices, whether by way of entering into restrictive

164. *Ola* case, para. 98.

covenants with channel partners or other commercial partners, which limit the production of goods or provision of services.

The aspect of limiting technical development was also discussed in the Google Android case. In the *Google Android* case, Google imposed anti-fragmentation obligations, i.e., the OEMs were prohibited from taking any actions and/or allowing/encouraging any third party to take any action that may cause or result in the fragmentation of Android. Thus, for example, OEMs using alternative OS could lose their access to Google's proprietary apps because this could be viewed by Google as a fragmentation of Android.[165] This resulted in reducing the incentives of market participants to develop Android forks, providing smart mobile devices with distinctive features and additional functionalities, i.e., reduced consumer choice. Moreover, Android fork developers would have an incentive to set up credible and efficient systems to ensure the correct functioning of apps on devices running their Android fork, leading to a wider pool of apps. However, the obligations imposed by Google which extended to the entire portfolio of the devices, restricted technical and scientific development of smart device OSs by thwarting potential development attempts of OEMs that could have borne fruits and added to the variety of OSs in the market. Hence, the restrictions imposed by Google deprive the market of the fruits of fair competition in contravention of section 4(2)(b)(ii) of the Competition Act.[166]

Google was also found to be in violation of the provisions of section 4(2)(b)(ii) of the Competition Act in the *Play Store* case because the CCI held that mandatory imposition of GPBS. Through this policy, Google forced all app developers on its platform to exclusively process all app and in-app purchases on the Play Store through its proprietary billing system GPBS. For this, Google also charged a commission of 15%-30% on each transaction. As a result, competing payment processors were no longer allowed to offer their services and app developers were denied the benefits of free competition, such as competition on reducing the commission fee, better services, etc. The CCI found that GPBS disturbs innovation incentives and the ability of both the payment processors and app developers to undertake technical development and innovate, thus limiting technical development in the market for in-app payment processing services.[167]

[D] Denial of Market Access

Denial of market access under section 4(2)(c) requires that there should be a conduct and, second, that the conduct should have resulted in a denial of market access, i.e., anti-competitive effect/distortion in the market in which denial has taken place.[168]

In its decisional practice, the CCI has also clarified that though free entry is one of the necessary conditions for competition to flourish, in view of the specificities of certain sectors, entry may be subject to regulatory conditions. However, such denial

165. *Google Android* case, paras 34, 120.
166. *Ibid.*, paras 504-583.
167. *Play Store* case, para. 313.
168. *XYZ v. REC Power Distribution Company Ltd*, Case No. 33 of 2014.

must be evaluated on a case-by-case basis by considering the legitimate regulatory goals, such as quality, safety, orderly growth of the sector, etc., to ensure that there is no anti-competitive conduct without a plausible regulatory rationale.[169]

In *East India Petroleum Pvt. Ltd. v. South Asia LPG Company Pvt. Ltd.*,[170] issues were raised regarding access to LPG terminal infrastructure at Vishakhapatnam Port, which was owned by South Asia LPG Company Pvt. Ltd. (SALPG). SALPG required users to necessarily use the cavern and pay higher charges. Basis the investigation of the DG, the CCI found that the restrictions levied by SALPG constituted an unfair imposition in the provision of terminalling services and were likely to discourage imports and restrict the services otherwise offered by the informant, i.e., East India Petroleum Pvt. Ltd. (EIPL), which was also a provider of terminalling services. Because of these restrictions, SALPG did not allow EIPL to connect its apparatus to SALPG's infrastructure or allow the use of its infrastructure on a standalone basis. This prevented EIPL from receiving its cargo, thereby causing foreclosure. SALPG argued that the restrictions on access to terminalling infrastructure were justified as they ensured the safety and technical feasibility of the entire apparatus and created business efficiencies. However, these efficiency justifications advanced by SALPG were held to be unfounded since they ignored the inefficiencies/losses resulting from the prohibition of bypass of cavern and the resultant foreclosure of competition. Since the bypass restrictions were found to have restricted the business volumes of the EIPL without any reasonable grounds, it was also held to be a denial of market access in contravention of section 4(2)(c) of the Competition Act. Subsequently, the NCLAT also upheld the reasoning of the CCI and noted that SALPG's plea that the services offered by other players are less efficient was an afterthought, and the restrictions were imposed by it primarily to protect its commercial interest at the cost of competition.[171]

[1] Freedom to Choose Trading Partners

In the *GMR* case, while analysing the abuse of dominance by GMR in giving preference to its group entity GAT in the downstream market over the informant, the CCI made a general observation regarding the ability of every entity, including a dominant player, to choose trading partners of their choice. Accordingly, the CCI observed that:

> As a general principle, every entity, dominant or otherwise, has freedom to choose its trading partners. It is a basic and fundamental right to decide with whom an enterprise wishes to deal and as such refusal to deal is not per se sufficient to conclude contravention of the provisions of the Act. However, there is no dearth of literature and decided case laws to provide guidance on when a refusal to deal by a dominant enterprise/undertaking constitutes an abuse.

169. *Surinder Singh Barmi v. Board for Control of Cricket in India*, Case No. 61 of 2010.
170. *East India Petroleum Pvt. Ltd. v. South Asia LPG Company Pvt. Ltd.*, Case No. 76 of 2011.
171. *Hindustan Petroleum Corporation Ltd. v. Competition Commission of India & Ors.*, Competition Appeal (AT) No. 69 of 2018.

'Para 76 of the Guidance on the Commission's enforcement priorities in applying Article 82 of the EC Treaty (now Article 102 TFEU) to abusive exclusionary conduct by dominant undertakings [2009] OJ C 045/7 provides the following:

> 'Typically, competition problems arise when the dominant undertaking competes on the "downstream" market with the buyer whom it refuses to supply. The term "downstream market" is used to refer to the market for which the refused input is needed in order to manufacture a product or provide a service.'

However, every refusal to deal by a dominant enterprise may not amount to a contravention of the Competition Act. For instance, a manufacturer can protect the sanctity of its distribution channel and goodwill in relation to the goods/services offered under its brand names, i.e., it has no legal obligation to warrant genuineness of products/services *outside* its distribution channel, and any insistence that the same be bought from its authorized distributors in itself cannot prima facie be considered abusive/exclusionary. Hence, there is no inherent right for third parties to become an authorized distributor in such a case.[172] Dominant firms also have the autonomy to choose their trading partners as long as the exercise of such autonomy does not affect the fair functioning of the markets as based on their market power, their conduct on refusal to deal may lead to foreclosure of market for other players.[173] A refusal, either total or partial, could also have underlying valid justifications with commercial consideration. Hence, the CCI cannot substitute its regulatory wisdom for that of the commercial wisdom of the businesses unless the conduct is ex facie unfair and/or discriminatory and designed with a view to exclude/eliminate competition on merits.[174] The key point is assessing whether the refusal to deal has an anti-competitive effect on the entire market. As with other abusive conduct, competition law is concerned with the impact on the entire market as opposed to a few players exiting the market, especially because of their own inefficiencies.

At the same time, this freedom to choose trading partners is not unrestrained. This brings us to the concept of essential facilities doctrine. The language used in the provision is 'denial of market *access*' and not *entry*, which means that the concern is not mere entry into the market but also accessibility of the market. This distinction is crucial because it shifts the focus from the mere act of entering a market to the broader issue of whether market participants can readily and fairly access that market. In practical terms, this means that it's not just about being able to set up shop in a market but also about being able to operate, compete, and access the necessary facilities or resources to do so. Hence, the doctrine may not be applicable with the same force in the Indian scenario.

172. *Hexa Communications Private Limited v. Atos India Private Limited*, Case No. 07 of 2022, para. 52.
173. *Hiveloop Technology Pvt. Ltd. v. Britannia Industries Ltd.*, Case No. 18 of 2021; *Mr. Dushyant v. National Accreditation Board for Testing and Calibration Laboratories*, Case No. 48 of 2021, para. 18.
174. *Hiveloop Technology Pvt. Ltd. v. Parle Products Private Limited*, Case No. 28 of 2021.

[2] Essential Facilities Doctrine

By way of section 4(2)(c), the legislature wanted to introduce the aspect of essential facilities into the Indian context. The CCI came out with an advisory booklet on the issue of denial of market access and essential facilities doctrine. The CCI, in the booklet, observed that the presence of entry barriers preventing new businesses from entering a specific market poses a significant challenge to promoting healthy competition. In situations where a dominant enterprise controls an infrastructure or facility necessary for accessing the market, and this infrastructure is not easily replicable at a reasonable cost in the short term and can't be substituted with other products or services, that enterprise should generally share this facility with its competitors at a fair cost unless there are valid justifications to do otherwise. This principle is known as the essential facilities doctrine.

In the *GMR* case, the CCI found that the informant was essentially a 'buyer' (a customer) of GMR for availing access to the location/space at RGIA which seems to be a necessary 'input' for providing Line Maintenance Services. Although the CCI took note of the freedom of all enterprises including dominant players to choose their own trading partners, it highlighted that a dominant player cannot refuse access to an input if it is indispensable or non-substitutable and cannot be obtained through an alternative source. This brings us to three guiding conditions for deciding if a refusal to deal by a dominant entity constitutes a contravention of the Competition Act: (i) first, the refused input is indispensable for an entity in order to compete on the downstream market; (ii) second, refusal shall most likely eliminate competition on the downstream market; and (iii) third, refusal shall most likely damage consumers. This is a simplified consideration of essential facilities doctrine. In the *GMR* case, the CCI held on the basis of existing jurisprudence of essential facilities doctrine that an asset is considered to be essential facility if it fulfils certain main economic conditions. These conditions and GMR's corresponding fulfilment of the same have been mentioned below:

(a) *The dominant entity controls access to an essential facility* – RGIA was an essential facility since it is not possible for the Line Maintenance Service provider to station itself outside the airport premises as the service is required between the landing and take-off of the aircraft.
(b) *The facility cannot reasonably be duplicated by the competitor* – The level of competition in the downstream market is low since apart from the informant, other dedicated service provider of Line Maintenance Services is GMR's own group company, GAT. The informant and GAT were the most significant players in the downstream market, posing competitive constraints on each other. The remaining players are either small or provide such services only for captive consumption so as not to provide any effective competitive constraint in the downstream market.
(c) *The dominant entity denies access to the competitor* – Given that physical presence at the airport premises is indispensable to provide Line Maintenance Services, non-renewal of the informant's license by GMR prima facie seems to

amount to the Informant's exclusion from the downstream market, which may skew the market in favour of GAT. The informant also alleged that GMR had made attempts to poach its technically skilled employees and disabled its electricity supply, apart from finally locking the said premises.

(d) *There should be no alternative means of entering the relevant market at a reasonable cost without having access to the essential facility* – For providing Line Maintenance Services, the service provider needs to be located at the airport since the services are rendered during the intermittent interval between the arrival of an aircraft and its next take-off, requiring the service provider to be physically present at the airport to attend to such aircraft on an immediate basis.

(e) *There must be spare capacity on the facility in question* – The provision of Line Maintenance Services was always undertaken through licenses with third parties, and airlines could choose their service provider. However, GMR terminated the license to refuse access to the facility, even though spare capacity existed.

Consequently, the CCI found a prima facie case of denial of market access since all the conditions for refusal to deal, i.e., indispensable nature of input, elimination of competitors and damage to consumers, were made out.

In the *Google Android* case, it was found that Google restricted access to its application programming interfaces, i.e., its proprietary software which is essential for the functionality of apps in the Google Play Store as well as other core Android services. Accordingly, the CCI directed Google to provide access to the same to its competitors, app developers and OEMs without going through necessary technical and commercial engagement with Google. However, the NCLAT subsequently set aside this direction on the grounds that such proprietary software must fetch value for Google and, therefore, remain an incentive for a technological company to further carry out such development and monetize it through its commercial use. This has been discussed in more detail in Chapter 5.

In *Informant (Confidential) v. Grasim Industries Limited*,[175] the CCI, while dealing with access to VSF yarn which was an indispensable input in the VSF spinning industry, noted that dominant enterprises have a special responsibility with respect to the supply in the market. This is because if dominant firms deny access to an indispensable input, players may be driven out of the market/marginalized and hence, such conduct would amount to exclusionary abuse and refusal to deal.

[3] 'In Any Manner': Expression of Wide Import

The CCI, by way of its booklets and decisional practice, wanted to interpret this provision in an extremely broad manner to cover all practices wherein the dominant

175. *Informant (Confidential) v. Grasim Industries Limited*, Case Nos 51, 54 & 56 of 2017, paras 32, 33.

enterprise refuses to share the essential facility, not only with its competitors but also indulges in practice which results in denial in market access for any the downstream markets. However, the erstwhile COMPAT in the case of *M/s Fast way transmission Pvt. Ltd. v. Kansan News Pvt. Ltd.*,[176] attempted to reduce the ambit of the interpretation adopted by the CCI for this section by holding that section 4(2)(c) would only apply in case of denial of access to a competitor. The logic given was that if two players are not competing with each other in equivalent products, transactions or services, then they could not engage in denial of market to the other.

However, the Supreme Court reversed the findings of the erstwhile COMPAT on this interpretation of denial of market access.[177] The words '*in* any *manner*' in section 4(a)(c) are of wide import, so the logic of the erstwhile COMPAT that broadcasters and MSOs cannot be in competition with each other is incorrect. This means that it is not necessary for the players in the market to be dealing in equivalent or identical products, transactions or services to cause denial of market access to the other. Once an enterprise has been held to be dominant, it is irrelevant who it is in competition with. The Supreme Court found that dominant position under section 4 was clearly made out on account of 85% market share, and this dominance was abused by causing denial of market access to a broadcaster. At the same time, it set aside the penalty levied by the CCI on the ground that the reason for termination given by the respondents was otherwise justifiable. The observations of the Supreme Court on the denial of market access are as follows:

> The words 'in any manner' are words of wide import and must be given their natural meaning. This being the case, *it is difficult to appreciate the reasoning of the Appellate Tribunal that, as the broadcaster and MSOs are not in competition with one another, the provisions of Sections 3 and 4 do not get attracted*. As has been held by us, the 'dominant position' held by the respondent MSOs is clearly established for the purpose of Section 4 in the present case, and the Commission finding in that behalf is also not set aside by the Appellate Tribunal. If this be so, then *once a dominant position is made out on facts, whether a broadcaster is in competition with MSOs is a factor that is irrelevant for the purpose of application of Section 4(2)(c) which, as has been found by us, becomes applicable for the simple reason that the broadcaster is denied market access due to an unlawful termination of the agreement between the said broadcaster and the respondents 1-4.*

Hence, any denial of market access, partial or complete, will amount to contravention under section 4(2)(c), and it is not necessary that such contravention has to be by a competitor qua another. In *International Spirits and Wines Association of India (ISWAI) v. Uttarakhand Agricultural Produce Marketing Board*[178] also, the CCI held that it is not necessary for the alleged conduct to have caused an 'absolute denial of market access' to invoke the prohibition of section 4(2)(c). The phrase 'in any manner'

176. *M/s Fast way transmission Pvt. Ltd. v. Kansan News Pvt. Ltd.*, (COMPAT) Appeal No. 116 of 2012.
177. *Competition Commission of India v. M/s Fast Way Transmission Pvt Ltd and Ors*. [2018], (SC) Civil Appeal No. 7215 of 2014, paras 13-16.
178. *International Spirits and Wines Association of India (ISWAI) v. Uttarakhand Agricultural Produce Marketing Board*, Case No. 02 of 2016, para. 129.

depicts the presence of wide scope, and any denial of market access, partial or complete, will amount to contravention under section 4(2)(c) of the Competition Act. Similarly, in the *Roche* case,[179] the CCI held that a partial denial of market access would also hurt the ability of a competitor to effectively compete on merits in the relevant market.

It must be noted that the words in any manner in this clause were added by way of an amendment in 2007. The intent of this amendment was to include all strategies which may be carried out by the dominant enterprise to deter entry or defer potential competition. The said clause seeks to cover all instances wherein dominant undertaking by its actions is creating insurmountable barriers to entry for new entrants to come into the market. This interpretation has been reiterated in subsequent decisions of the CCI, such as the *Play Store* case wherein it was observed that denial of market access 'in any manner' would fall under the ambit of section 4(2)(c) of the Competition Act, regardless of whether it is a denial of access to competitors or denial of access to players in vertically affected markets.

In the *Play Store* case, the various policies of Google were found to be in violation of section 4(2)(c) of the Competition Act. Through mandatory and exclusive imposition of GPBS, app developers were forced to only use GPBS for payment processing of paid apps and in-app purchases on the Play Store. As a result, app developers were prevented from conducting business with payment processors of their choice and correspondingly, payment processors were prohibited from offering their services to app developers listed on the Play Store. The analysis of the CCI has been described below:

(i) Mandatory imposition of GPBS by Google results in denial of market access for payment aggregators as well as app developers. By virtue of imposition of GPBS, the app developers would be mandated to use Google's services for payment processing. Further, the anti-steering provisions of Google forbid app developers from re-directing users to websites for payment outside the app. In the absence of these stipulations, the app developers could have negotiated better terms and conditions with other payment service providers in a competitive market. Hence, app developers are deprived of commercial freedom.

(ii) This also forecloses the opportunity for other payment processing service providers to serve the app developers. This would also discourage app developers from developing their own in-app payment processor. With the mandatory imposition of GPBS, another payment processor will lose out on the market collectively valued over USD 3 billion, impacting their ability to carry out any innovations and product improvements, which can be catastrophic in such network-effect-driven markets.

Further, payment processors were placed vertically with Google in relation to providing Play Store services to app developers and app users. Google's practices of

179. *Roche* case, para. 77.

prohibiting app developers from using any other payment processors caused denial of market access to the payment processors in the vertically affected market. Google had argued that there was no violation of section 4(2)(c) of the Competition Act because Google was not itself active in the alleged payment processing market and, as such, could not have abused that position to deny payment processors access to that market. In India, the CCI noted that Google subcontracts with third parties to conduct the payment processing for payments made through Google Play. Google also argued that the DG had not defined the relevant market in which the denial was alleged in order to assess whether there had been any anti-competitive effect. In this regard, the CCI noted that there is no legal requirement to precisely define a separate relevant market where the impact of the abusive conduct takes place. Accordingly, the CCI found that Google abused its dominant position in the app store market to cause denial to payment processors in general. This is sufficient to give a finding under section 4(2)(c) of the Competition Act.[180]

In the *Automobile Spare Parts* case, the CCI noticed that there had been restrictions imposed by the OEMs on the spare parts suppliers not to sell the spare parts in the open market. In the process, the independent repairers were not able to procure the spare parts over the counter and had no other option but to procure the spare parts from the authorized dealers. Through a network of agreements between OEMs and suppliers, it was ensured that the OEMs were the only source of supply of spare parts in the aftermarket. Based on the facts, the CCI concluded that the OEMs are engaging in practices which amount to denial of market access, and hence an abuse under section 4(2)(c) of the Competition Act.

The CCI noted that a dominant enterprise is engaging in an abuse when it itself competes in both the upstream and downstream markets and is in effective control of a product/service in the upstream market which is required by the enterprises in the downstream market to effectively carry out their economic activity, as this amounts to engaging in practices which may exclude a competitor from such downstream market. Such exclusion may be occasioned by refusing to supply such products/services to enterprises in the downstream market. The CCI relied on the investigation report of the DG, wherein the OEMs had submitted that the spare parts, diagnostic tools and workshop manuals are their proprietary materials and, therefore, accessible only to the authorized dealer network of each OEM.

Further, the CCI observed that the make of each brand of car is unique, and the independent service providers require the spare parts and diagnostic tools compatible with the various models of automobiles manufactured by the various OEMs to carry out their economic activity of providing repair and maintenance services in the Indian automobile aftermarket. However, it was noted that each OEM, which is already a dominant player in the aftermarket for the supply of spare parts and diagnostic tools through their own or related network of authorized distributors, also operates in the aftermarket for after-sale repair and maintenance services of their own brand of cars as the sole supplier of their spare parts and diagnostic tools. Each OEM has two types of

180. *Play Store* case, para. 315.

customers: (a) car owners who purchase the automobiles manufactured by the OEMs in the primary market, and (b) independent service providers in the aftermarket. An owner of a car cannot fit the spare parts into the machine by himself and requires the services of a specialized technician. Therefore, the owners of automobiles not only operate in the aftermarket as purchasers of spare parts but also require the service of firms engaged in maintenance and repair work. The independent repairers, who are not part of the official dealer network of the OEMs, do purchase the spare parts of the automobiles manufactured by the OEMs from the OEMs. Therefore, the independent service providers are customers of the OEMs in the aftermarket and further compete with the OEMs in the repairs and maintenance service aftermarket. Also, it was noticed by the CCI that even the authorized dealers of the OEMs are forbidden to supply spare parts to independent repairers over the counter. Based on these collective facts, the CCI observed that OEMs have effectively denied access to spare parts to these independent repairers by entering into agreements with the suppliers forbidding the suppliers to sell the spare parts in the open market. It concluded that such practice of preventing the independent repairers from competing with the authorized dealers of the OEMs amounted to denial of market access under section 4(2)(c) of the Competition Act.

The CCI also relied on the jurisprudence of the EC[181] that such behaviour cannot be countenanced if its 'actual purpose is to strengthen this dominant position and abuse it'. Hence, denial of market access aimed at excluding a competitor from the market by means other than legitimate competition allows the OEMs to further strengthen their dominant position and abuse it.

The CCI also touched upon briefly on the issue of denial of market access in the *NSE* case. It was alleged that NSE had taken a stake of about 26% in Omnesys, which is a technology vendor providing software for financial and securities market. The product of Omnesys, known as 'NOW' was made, which was a substitute for software called 'ODIN'. ODIN was developed by FTIL, the promoter of MCX-SX and the market leader in the brokerage solutions sector. It was alleged that after taking an equity stake in Omnesys, DotEx intentionally wrote individually to the members/brokers of NSE, offering them NOW free of cost for the next three years. NSE also simultaneously refused to share its currency derivative segment Application Programme Interface Code (APIC) with FTIL, thus disabling the ODIN users (who constituted about 85% of the stock brokers/traders) from connecting to the currency derivative segment of the NSE from trading platform through their preferred mode, ODIN. The product thus thrust upon everyone (consumers) desirous of accessing the currency derivative segment of NSE was the product 'NOW' developed by Omnesys in place of ODIN. Further, it was alleged that NSE had put 'ODIN' on the watch list across all its segments, thereby deterring its members and their constituents from using 'ODIN' as their front-end solution. Based on the investigation, the CCI noted that ODIN and NOW are competing software and such software is an essential facility without which trading cannot be done. Relying on jurisprudence from matured anti-trust jurisdictions, it was noted by the CCI that the: (i) action of NSE of placing FTIL, the developer of ODIN (and one of

181. *United Brands Co v. Commission of the European Union*, Case 27/76 [1978] ECR 207, para. 189.

the promoters of MCX-SX) on its watch list; and (ii) denying APIC for interface between its own software NOW and ODIN for the currency derivative segment, prevents the clients of the NSE, most of who use ODIN for all other segments, from choosing ODIN for the CD segment trade on NSE. The CCI noted that the said action is anti-competitive in the aftermarket of trading software for the currency derivative segment of the NSE. The CCI noted that if the APIC had been provided to ODIN, there would have been healthy competition between the two software platforms, ODIN and NOW, for clients. This competitive environment would have driven advancements in the technical development of all such trading software, benefiting the market.

Based on this discussion, the CCI concluded that NSE/DotEX's actions in denying APIC to ODIN and placing FTIL on a watch list amounted to exclusionary practice as they hindered competition both in the aftermarket for trading software on NSE and in the relevant market.

[a] Denial of Market Access Includes Non-price Parameters Also

The aspect of denial of market access in any manner is very wide, and it includes all strategies adopted by the dominant enterprise to deter or defer competition. This also includes non-price strategies adopted by dominant firms to unlawfully raise their rivals' costs or exclude them from the market. An investigation was ordered, where it is alleged that the dominant enterprise has engaged in denial of market access by engaging in bad faith litigation and abusing the judicial process. The prima facie case made in this regard is against JCB India in the case of *M/s Bull Machines Pvt Ltd. v. JCB India and Ors.*[182] (*JCB* case). The *JCB* case was initiated based on information filed by Bull Machines. Bull Machines was engaged in the manufacturing of low-cost backhoe loaders, called 'Bull Smart', a light construction equipment. It was alleged that during the formal launch of 'Bull Smart' at the 'Excon 2011 Exhibition', Bull Machines was served with an ex parte interim injunction order granted by the High Court of Delhi by JCB wherein it was alleged that Bull Machines had infringed the design registrations/copyright of JCB in developing the backhoe loader 'Bull Smart'. The said order of the Delhi High Court restrained Bull Machines and its dealers 'from making, selling, offering for sale, dispatch, advertising, directly or indirectly dealing in/launching backhoe loaders in any manner'. It is in the case of the Bull Machines that JCB obtained the ex parte ad interim injunction order based on misrepresentation of images/design registration number/documents and bogus numbers, suppression of its pre-existing UK patent, misrepresentation by comparing the wrong angle of the images in the application and reliance upon fraudulent design registrations which were pre-existing in the public domain. It is further alleged that JCB, armed with the ex parte order of the Hon'ble Delhi High Court, forced Bull Machines to remove the backhoe loader 'Bull Smart' from 'Excon 2011 Exhibition' in front of a huge crowd of dealers, existing and potential customers, end customers, financing company officials, bankers, suppliers, foreign delegates and peers in the industry and media.

182. *M/s Bull Machines Pvt Ltd. v. JCB India and Ors*, Case No. 105 of 2013.

Post the order by the Delhi High Court, Bull Machines filed an application for vacation of the ex parte interim stay order and submitted all the evidence required to show that there is no similarity in the design of the backhoe loader 'Bull Smart' developed by it and the designs registered by JCB. Bull Machines also submitted evidence to the High Court showing that JCB misrepresented the images and the design registration numbers/documents and misled the Delhi High Court to secure an ad interim ex parte injunction order in its favour.

It was averred by Bull Machines that after nearly ten months from the filing of the said suit, JCB voluntarily withdrew its application for ex parte interim injunction without submitting any inspection report or reply. In view of the above, the Delhi High Court dismissed the petition and the ex parte interim order procured by JCB by misrepresenting facts before the Delhi High Court was vacated. However, the case of Bull Machines was that huge irreparable damages had already been caused to Bull Machines, and in the process, JCB's objective of deferring the entry of Bull Machines was achieved. The entire case of abuse made by Bull Machines is based upon the alleged bad faith litigation by JCB before the Hon'ble High Court of Delhi, which itself was based on designs and copyrights obtained fraudulently by JCB. It alleged that the bad faith litigation initiated by JCB against it alleging infringement of its design rights was totally false and that the said legal proceedings before the Delhi High Court were only initiated to harass it and prevent the launch of 'Bull Smart', which in effect would have competed with backhoe loaders of JCB in the relevant market. Based on the evidence on record, the CCI passed a prima facie view and asked the DG to investigate whether JCB has denied market access and foreclosed the entry of 'Bull Smart' by engaging itself in bad faith litigation. This was premised on its preliminary finding that predation through abuse of judicial processes presents an increasing threat to competition, owing to its relatively low anti-trust visibility.

In contrast, in the *Roche* case, a case for denial or market access on account of vexatious litigation was not made out. The CCI noted that abusive strategies include rendering rivals' products incompatible without adding any technical improvement to the replaced product; indulging in vexatious litigation purely aimed at harassing rivals; influencing government or regulatory procedures; and impeding the entry of generics/biosimilars by denigrating or disparaging rivals' products. In this case, it was alleged that Roche indulged in vexatious civil litigation as a tactic to exhaust smaller rivals' resources and delay or prevent their entry into the relevant market. The CCI observed that to cause denial of market access by engaging in legal action, such legal action should be aimed at harassing the competitor respondent without any objective basis and be conceived with an anti-competitive intent/plan to eliminate competition. However, in the *Roche* case, it could not be proved that the litigations filed by Roche were baseless or tainted with ulterior motives. Yet, a prima facie case for denial of market access was made out on the ground that Roche tried to influence regulatory authorities in its favour by misrepresenting the status of approvals granted to the informant's drug.[183] Further, when Roche was not successful in evading entry, it also

183. *Roche* case, para. 74.

approached doctors, hospitals, tender authorities, etc., to influence their perception of the efficacy and safety of the informants' products. The latter behaviour crossed the line of puffery aimed at promoting one's own product and actually amounted to maligning the image of the informant, thereby causing competitive advantages to them and consequent harm to the informant and the market as a whole.

The abovementioned cases are a testament to the fact that the import of the expression 'denial of market access *in any manner*' is very wide and encompasses both price and non-price conduct.

[E] Imposing Supplementary Obligations

Section 4(2)(d) of the Competition Act provides that there shall be an abuse of dominant position if the dominant enterprise or group makes the conclusion of contracts subject to acceptance of supplementary obligations by other parties which, by their nature or according to commercial usage, have no connection with the subject of such contracts. This includes instances of tying and bundling. Tying instances would include cases of technical tying, contractual tying, tying of products with services, etc. It is to be noted that the practice of adopting tying practices, in itself, will not constitute a breach of the provisions of the Competition Act. As such, tying is a legitimate business practice, and an enterprise can make considerable savings in production, distribution and transaction costs. Based on international jurisprudence, the following needs to be addressed for an abuse of dominance of tying to be made out:

(i) the enterprise has a dominant position regarding the tying product;
(ii) the tied product is a distinct product from the tying product;
(iii) element of coercion;
(iv) anti-competitive foreclosure.

In *Harshita Chawla v. WhatsApp Inc.*,[184] the CCI clarified that while 'tying' refers to a practice where the seller of a product or service ('tying product') requires the buyers to also purchase another separate product or service ('tied product'); 'bundling' typically means that the two products are sold by the seller in a fixed proportion as a bundled package at a particular price. Based on economic literature, the CCI laid down four conditions, as described above, to assess whether WhatsApp was tying its messaging services with its UPI enabled Digital Payments App: (i) the tying and tied products are two separate products (WhatsApp Messenger and WhatsApp Pay are two distinct products with different functionalities operating in different markets); (ii) the entity concerned is dominant in the market for the tying product (WhatsApp is prima facie dominant in the relevant market, i.e., 'market for OTT messaging apps through smartphones in India'); (iii) the customers do not have a choice to only obtain the tying product without the tied product (Installation of the WhatsApp messenger *does not* appear to explicitly mandate/coerce the user to use WhatsApp Pay exclusively); and (iv) the tying is capable of restricting/foreclosing competition in the market (UPI digital

184. *Harshita Chawla v. WhatsApp Inc. and Facebook Inc.*, Case No. 15 of 2020.

payments market is very competitive and consists of various established players so WhatsApp Pay will not automatically gain market share due to pre-installation). Thus, since the elements of coercion and foreclosure were absent, the allegation of tying against WhatsApp was not made out.

Even if one of the above elements is missing, then a case for tying would not be made out. For instance, in *Baglekar Akash Kumar v. Google LLC*,[185] it was alleged that Google had tied its video-conferencing app Google Meet with its email service, i.e., Gmail. However, the CCI found that Google Meet is also available as an independent app outside the Gmail ecosystem, and users have the choice to use either of the apps with all their functionalities without necessarily having to use the other. Hence, no case for tying is made out since there is no coercion.

Tying cases can be covered under both section 4(2)(d) and section 4(2)(e), which deals with leveraging. It can also include practices where an IPR holder licences its IPR only on some additional condition. This has been covered in the chapter on IPR and competition law.

In the *Google Android* case,[186] as discussed earlier, Google had a dominant position in the market of licensable OS, i.e., Android, as well as the supply of each of the services offered under GMS, i.e., Search, YouTube, Chrome and Play Store. Further, we have also discussed how the OEMs had weak countervailing power with respect to Google since each of Google's services was a 'must have', and the OEMs had no option except to agree to Google's terms in order to access these services. Since Android-based applications are written to work with Google Play Services, a smart device without them would not be commercially viable or at least the OEM offering these devices would be competitively disadvantaged because the customers also would not find such a smart device attractive. Google did not negotiate on key terms of the MADA, which were found to result in anti-competitive conduct: pre-installation of the entire suit of GMS as well as prominent placement thereof. By foreclosing the market for rivals, MADA also reduced the potential choice for users. Based on the investigation, the CCI also concluded that Google Play and other apps of Google covered under GMS have different functionalities and thus, there is no technical necessity to offer these services together. Hence, the CCI found the obligations under MADA, RSA, AFA and ACC to be in the nature of supplementary obligations imposed by Google on OEMs since if they wish to pre-install even a single app of Google, they had to agree to the pre-installation requirements of the entire bouquet of Google's apps. Additionally, the said Google apps were to be prominently placed on the mobile; thus, it was a case of both pre-installation and primary placement. Thus, Google's conduct was held to be in contravention of section 4(2)(d) of the Competition Act. Subsequently, the NCLAT[187] upheld the findings of the CCI in light of Google's anti-competitive requirements under MADA regarding prominent placement, pre-installation and other conditions applied to OEMs. It noted that:

185. *Baglekar Akash Kumar v. Google LLC*, Case No. 39 of 2020.
186. *Google Android* case, paras 345-373.
187. *Google LLC and Anr. v. Competition Commission of India and Ors.* [2023], (NCLAT) Competition Appeal (AT) No. 01 of 2023, paras 94-98.

> Clause 4.4 of MADA enjoins upon the OEM to – (i) distribute all Core Applications, (ii) distribute on the Default Home Screen a Google – provided widget, Google Play Store icon; and an icon that provides direct access to Core Applications which is labelled as 'Google', and among other conditions also stipulates that any Google Application that is not a Core Application is placed no more than one level below the Default Home Screen. There is also a condition that the OEM shall implement the "Home button animation" as per Google's guidelines if Google Assistant is enable on the Android device and also implement Google Hotword, if it is supported by the device.

On this basis, the NCLAT concluded that the conditions which are applied on OEMs through MADA which essentially provides Google Applications, are in the form of 'supplementary obligations' attracting section 4(2)(d).

[F] Leveraging of Dominant Position

Section 4(2)(e) of the Competition Act provides that there shall be an abuse of dominant position when the dominant undertaking uses its dominant position in one relevant market to enter into or protect another relevant market. The Competition Act has expressly included the aspect of leveraging as an abuse of dominant position. A contravention of section 4(2)(e) requires two markets to be identified, the first relevant market in which the erring entity is alleged to be dominant and the second market in which the said entity is entering or protecting its position, directly or indirectly, by virtue of dominance in the first relevant market.

The key point of consideration is that there must be an exploitation of market power by the dominant player in the market in which the enterprise is dominant to enter into or protect its position in the market in which such player is not dominant. There are situations, especially in a multi-product company or group, where there are a lot of joint costs and cross-subsidization. When cross-subsidization becomes an issue of leveraging depends on the facts and circumstances of each case:

(a) The CCI has examined the provision relating to leveraging in the *NSE* case and the *Automobile Spare Parts* case. The CCI has noted that the dominant enterprise in the first market need not possess a dominant market position in the second market where it makes attempts to leverage its market power. The aspect of leveraging deals with a situation where an enterprise in dominant position in any delineable relevant market uses its strength therein to enter or protect any other delineable relevant market. The Competition Act does not provide that there has to be a high degree of associational link between the two markets (the market in which the enterprise is dominant and the second market which it intends to enter or protect) being considered for the abuse of leveraging. The CCI, in the *NSE* case observed that:

> The Indian Competition Act recognizes leveraging as an act by an enterprise or group that "uses by its dominant position in one relevant market to enter into, or protect, other relevant market." Nowhere does the Act indicate that there has to be a high degree of associational link between the two markets

being considered for this sub section. This is so because competition concerns are much higher in India than in more mature jurisdictions because of the historical lack of competition laws. In India, if an enterprise dominant in the market of audio-visual (AV) equipment enters into the market of say, computers, it is possible for it to use its strength in terms of finances, technological expertise, sales network etc. in the AV market to muscle its way into and protect its position in the computer market, even though the two markets are not at all connected. That is why the Act does not indicate any requirement of associational link.

(b) As observed in the *NSE* case, the section uses the term 'relevant market' and other relevant market. Hence, it is incorrect to argue that the whole of section 4 pivots around determination of only one 'relevant market'. There can be a second relevant market which may also be treated as the 'other market' for the purpose of section 4(2)(e). The Competition Act recognizes the fact that an enterprise may be multi-product and may be operating in two (or more) markets. In case of multi-product enterprises, such enterprises can use their position of strength derived in one market to leverage their position and gain an unfair advantage over their competitors in the other market. While its conduct in the second market has to be separately examined for abuse if and after it acquires a dominant position in the second market, the fact that it has used the strengths from the first market to wrongfully enter into or to protect the second market is itself an abuse under the Competition Act. It is to be further noted that in the event such an enterprise, after entering the other relevant market through such leveraging and thereafter acquires dominant position in the other market, commits further acts of abuse in that relevant market, then there would be a separate violation of section 4(2)(a)–(d) of the Competition Act. The 'relevant market' of the explanation (a) applies equally in intent for sections 4(1) and (2), but the relevant market in respect of clauses (a) to (d) of section 4(2) can be different than the relevant market for the purpose of clause (e). The CCI observed in the *NSE* case as follows:

> To further clarify, if an enterprise merely uses its dominant position in any 'relevant market' to enter or protect some other "relevant market" wrongfully, it can only be held guilty of contravening section 4(2)(e). But if the enterprise, after entering the other relevant market through such leveraging and acquiring dominant position there, commits further acts of abuse (such as unfair pricing) in that relevant market, then there would be a separate violation of section 4(2)(a).
>
> It is worthwhile to observe here that the language of section 4(2)(e) does not exclude the possibility that the enterprise is dominant in both, the "relevant market" as well as the 'other relevant market'. An enterprise can be dominant in one market and can enter another market, acquire position of strength there and then commit acts to protect its position.

Based on the above approach, the CCI noted that NSE, a super dominant entity in the non-currency derivative market, leveraged its dominant position by using its strength in the non-currency derivative segment to enter into and protect its position in the currency derivative segment. The CCI observed that they could issue periodical waivers in the transaction fees in the currency derivative segment and yet earn profits in the process, while the others earned huge losses because of their strength in the non-currency derivative segment. It is noteworthy to point out that when the matter went up in appeal before the erstwhile COMPAT, it disagreed with the definition of the relevant market adopted by the CCI. The CCI had identified two markets: a market for currency derivative and a market for non-currency derivative segment. After defining the market, the CCI observed that the NSE is using its dominance in the non-currency derivate segment market to protect its position in the currency derivate segment market. However, the erstwhile COMPAT held that there is only one definition of relevant market, that is, the market for stock exchange services market where NSE is committing the abuse of unfair pricing (discussed above).[188] Since there was only one definition of relevant market adopted by erstwhile COMPAT, it held that NSE could not have been guilty of breaching section 4(2)(e) of the Competition Act. Having said that, NSE was found to be guilty of section 4(2)(a) of the Competition Act for unfair pricing.

Increasingly, there is a focus on cross-leveraging by digital platforms which are able to exploit user data and create functional entry barriers in the market by entrenching themselves in neighbouring or even in unrelated markets.[189] The aspect of data as a tool for abuse has been discussed in Chapter 6.

In the *Google Android* case,[190] it was found that Google engaged in tying (through pre-installation) and leveraging by using its dominant position in one market to enter and protect the other market. Google engaged in tying conduct in several ways – it tied access to Play Store with its services of Search, Chrome as well as YouTube through imposition of MADA which required pre-installation of the entire bouquet of Google's apps even if the OEMs wanted to access only one app. Google's different services constituted different markets in each case and Google was found to be dominant in both. The NCLAT[191] affirmed the findings of the CCI that tying between Play Store and Search, Chrome and YouTube was used to achieve and perpetuate dominance by Google in the markets of the latter services, thereby causing anti-competitive effects such as foreclosure and denial of consumer choice.

Similarly, in the *Play Store* case, the CCI held Google to be guilty of leveraging its dominance in markets other than the relevant markets delineated by it. It was found that the practices followed by Google resulted in leveraging its dominance in the: (i) market for licensable mobile OS and app stores for Android OS to protect its position in the downstream markets; and (ii) market for app stores for Android OS to protect its position in the market for apps facilitating payments through UPI in India, in violation of the provisions of section 4(2)(e) of the Competition Act.[192]

In *Digital News Publishers Association v. Alphabet Inc and Ors.*, Google was found to prima facie occupy a significant position in the relevant markets: Online

188. *National Stock Exchange of India Ltd. v. CCI*, [2014] Comp AT 129, paras 116-121.
189. *WhatsApp* case.
190. *Google Android* case, paras 374-465.
191. Paragraphs 136-143.
192. *Play Store* case, paras 317, 358.

General Web Search Services, Online Search Advertising Services, and the market for Online Digital Advertising Services. It was observed that Google was using its dominant position in the relevant markets to enter/protect its position in the market for news aggregation services in violation of section 4(2)(e) of the Competition Act.

The issue of leveraging was also discussed in detail in the *Automobile Spare Parts* case. As has been discussed at length above, it was noted by the CCI that the OEMs have a dominant position in the market for spare parts and diagnostic tools because of the limited inter-brand interchangeability of spare parts. Further, the OEMs, pursuant to a network of restrictive contracts and commercial practices, became the sole supplier of genuine spare parts and diagnostic tools in the aftermarket. Additionally, the OEMs are also active in the market for repair and maintenance through their network of authorized dealers. The CCI noted that there are interlinkages between the repair/service markets and the spare parts/diagnostic tools market, and the OEMs have a commercial incentive to leverage their dominance from the relevant market of spare parts/diagnostic tools to that of repairs and maintenance services. The CCI noted that OEMs (acting through their authorized dealer network) deny 94.99% of the total service providers active in the Indian automobile aftermarket (consisting of multi-brand retailers, semi-organized service stations and unorganized garage workshops), effective access to the Indian aftermarket on competitive terms.

It was noted that the OEMs typically provide after-sale services and repair of their brand of automobiles through a network of authorized dealers. These authorized distributors are also the source of supply of genuine spare parts for various models of automobiles manufactured by an OEM. As discussed above, the OEMs restrict the ability of independent repairers to obtain spare parts from authorized dealers. Further, the OEMs restrict the suppliers from supplying spare parts in the open market. In addition, the OEMs had also imposed a warranty condition on the consumers that their warranty would be denied if the cars were serviced by an independent repairer or other multi-brand service repairers. The CCI also noted that in the limited instances where spare parts are available to the actual owners, the owners have to buy such spare parts at the MRP and then avail the services of the independent repairers at additional costs, whereas the authorized dealers are able to provide such services at cheaper rates since the applicable spare parts are available to the authorized dealers at a discount over the MRP. Therefore, in practice, in most cases, the owners of various brands of automobiles are completely dependent on the authorized dealer network of the OEMs and are not in a position to exercise the option of availing services of independent repairers. Therefore, the users of cars wanting to purchase the spare parts have to necessarily avail the services of the authorized dealers of the OEM. Based on these facts, the CCI held that the OEMs are leveraging their dominant position in the market for the supply of spare parts to protect their market of maintenance of cars.

§3.07 OBJECTIVE JUSTIFICATION

Dominant enterprises often seek to justify their conduct that may appear anti-competitive on the surface based on business efficiencies. The legitimacy of such objective justifications is based on a determination of the facts and circumstances. At the outset, it is clarified that such a justification must be able to stand on its own legs without itself being illegal. For instance, in the *DLF* case, DLF argued that the (abusive) terms of its agreements with the buyers were a standard 'industry practice'. However, the CCI observed that '*even without taking into account the fact that being an industry practice cannot be a defence for anti-competitive practices/conduct, DLF for one certainly cannot claim the defence of having adopted an industry practice for practices which are found to be anti-competitive and/or abusive.*'

As discussed earlier, the CCI, in their decisional practice, has adopted the effects test. The effect test implies that unilateral conduct may escape the prohibition of section 4 of the Competition Act in case the dominant enterprise can provide an objective justification for its behaviour or it can demonstrate that its conduct produces efficiencies which outweigh the negative effect on competition. The burden of proof for such an objective justification or efficiency defence will be on the dominant enterprise. The possible types of objective justification would be in cases where it can be shown that dominant enterprise can show that the otherwise abusive conduct is actually necessary conduct on the basis of objective business rationale. The NSE also raised multiple business rationales for engaging in fee waivers in the currency derivative segment to promote the currency derivative. NSE raised the point of promotional/penetrative pricing.[193] It is to be noted that although these defences were not held to be valid by the CCI and erstwhile COMPAT, yet they heard the matter on objective justification at great length. Their approach implies that the CCI will take into account objective justification as a defence. In this background, it becomes all the more necessary for companies, that have a high market share, to adopt proper documentation of their business processes and decisions which can be used in defence in an abuse of dominance investigation.

The CCI has also held that protection of commercial interest by a dominant enterprise, at the cost of competition, is contrary to its responsibility cast under the Competition Act. Effective competition does not necessarily mean prevalence of the most efficient to the exclusion of relatively less efficient choices to consumers. In any case, there is no justification for imposing restrictions on competition by a dominant enterprise to protect its commercial interest.[194]

In the *Google Android* case,[195] Google had argued that users and OEMs prefer Google's services due to their superior nature. In fact, this may be a common argument taken by any dominant enterprise that the reason for their success is the strength of their product. However, it is pointed out that if that is the case, then the market has to be the judge, and this 'preference' cannot be forced on users. On similar lines, the CCI observed that:

> If Google is of the view that the presence of its applications provides a great out-of-the-box experience, then the user or the OEM would itself decide to use its

193. *NSE* case, para. 10.57.
194. *East India Petroleum Pvt. Ltd. v. South Asia LPG Company Pvt. Ltd.*, Case No. 76 of 2011.
195. *Google Android* case, para. 489.

> application. There does not appear to be any necessity to impose restrictions through MADA, RSAs and AFA/ACC, to achieve the same. The market forces would itself take care of that.

In the *MMT* case,[196] MMT-Go claimed that its parity obligations were an industry practice, particularly to address the problem of free-riding – i.e., to prevent hotels from benefitting from the investment of the OTA in advertisement and promotion of the hotel for free. However, the CCI rejected this since the effect and implications of a conduct indulged in by a dominant platform on its users and competition in the relevant market is fundamentally different from when a smaller insignificant player does it. Comparing the combined effect that deep discounting and parity together have, when imposed by a dominant platform that has already reaped the benefits of network effects in its favour, with that of the parity conditions of other platforms is not a like-to-like comparison. Further, the aspect of the special responsibility of a dominant player like MMT-Go was also brought into the picture due to the potential adverse effects that it may have on competition as well as hotels.

[A] Effects Doctrine

The agreements or combinations having or likely to have an AAEC in India are declared void under sections 3(2) and 6(1) of the Competition Act, respectively. However, section 4 does not have any such similar provision. Sections 3 and 6 are concerned with the 'effects' of an agreement or a combination. In contrast, under section 4, because of the dominant position enjoyed by an enterprise, the legislature in its wisdom has decided that an 'enterprise' shall not 'abuse' such a position. The emphasis under section 4(1) is on 'abuse' and the word 'abuse' has not been defined under the Competition Act; hence, the presumption was that the legislature has wisely left it open to be decided on a case-by-case basis because the 'nature and type of abuse' may differ with time and depending upon the market in question. However, this position has now been clarified by the NCLAT which has held that the effects doctrine is applicable to section 4 as well, as shall be discussed below.

While the wording of the Competition Act may show that the principle of strict liability is laid down and no effects have to be seen (an 'unlawful per se' approach), the CCI has incorporated the effects doctrine in its analysis of dominance investigations, in line with global practice. In this regard, it is apposite to note the observations of the CCI in the case of *Dhanraj Pillai v. Hockey India,* wherein the CCI looked into the effects of the restrictive conditions imposed and noted that the conditions did not amount to abuse of dominance as they were intrinsic and proportionate to the objectives of the organization:[197]

> Commission opines that proportionality of the regulations can only be decided by considering the *manner in which regulations are applied* [emphasis supplied]. It is

196. *MMT* case, paras 264-266.
197. *Dhanraj Pillai v. Hockey India,* Case No. 73 of 2011.

the manner of applying regulations that raise competition concerns as it may be used as a tool for foreclosing new entrants.

Similarly, in the *Schott Glass* case, the erstwhile COMPAT found that unlawful price discrimination required a showing of both '(i) dissimilar treatment to equivalent transactions; and (ii) harm to competition or likely harm to competition in the sense that the buyers suffer a competitive disadvantage against each other leading to competitive injury in the downstream market.' The erstwhile COMPAT found the CCI had wrongly ignored the second limb and that the evidence showed there was no effect on the downstream market and the ultimate consumer did not suffer as a result of the alleged conduct. In this case, not only was an effects-based analysis undertaken, but also the objective justifications raised by the parties to justify their conduct were considered.

The NCLAT made elaborate observations on applicability of the effects doctrine to section 4 in the *Google Android* case and laid down the test as follows: *For proving abuse of dominance under section 4, effect analysis is required to be done, and the test to be employed in the effect analysis is whether the abusive conduct is anti-competitive or not.*[198] For this, the NCLAT undertook a detailed analysis, which has been summarised below:

(i) The legislative intent is clear in respect of the expression 'AAEC' being only present in sections 3 and 6, and not section 4. But what needs to be examined is whether, even if the AAEC test is not attracted in section 4, any analysis of the conduct of an enterprise or group of anti-competitive has to be looked into or not? The answer is yes.

(ii) The 2009 Guidance to Article 102 of the Treaty on the Functioning of the EU noted that for exclusionary abuses in Article 102, the European Commission (EC) will intervene if there is any likelihood of anticompetitive foreclosure. Even in its recent case laws, the EC has adopted an effects-based approach while analysing exclusionary abuse. However, such an effects-based approach is not mandated for exploitative abuses under Article 102.

(iii) In *Intel v. Commission*,[199] the General Court continued to adopt a strict per se approach to exclusivity rebates, which it said were illegal unless the dominant firm could show an objective justification for granting them. However, there was an increasing intellectual consensus against the application of per se rules to unilateral behaviour, and the judgment of the General Court in Intel attracted particular hostility because of its formalistic approach. This has been confirmed in recent decisions such as in *Paroxetine*[200] ['*...having regard to all relevant facts, conduct may be characterised as abusive only if it is capable of restricting competition and, in particular,*

198. *Google LLC and Anr. v. Competition Commission of India and Ors.* [2023], (NCLAT) Competition Appeal (AT) No. 01 of 2023.
199. *Intel Corp. v. European Commission*, Case C-413/14 P.
200. *Generics (UK) Ltd and Others v. Competition and Markets Authority*, Case C-307/18, para. 154.

> *producing exclusionary effects*.'] and *TeliaSonera*[201] [*in order to establish whether (a margin squeeze) is abusive, that practice must have an anti-competitive effect on the market*.] Further, in its decisional practice, it has sought to produce evidence of anti-competitive effects.

Importantly, the NCLAT relied on the findings of the Report of the High Level Committee on Competition Law, which preceded the Competition Act, and noted that the dominance investigations should be undertaken based on the effects doctrine. The key issue that needs to be analysed is whether the conduct of the dominant enterprise is harming the competitive process prevalent in the relevant market. The relevant observations of the report are as follows:

> Discriminatory behaviour and any other exercise of market power leading to the prevention, restriction or distortion of competition would obviously be included. We probably need to clarify that there is a fine distinction between defending one's market position or market share which is perfectly legal and legitimate and may involve certain level of aggressive competitive behaviour and exclusionary and anti-competitive behaviour.
>
> Key questions for adjudication on abuse of dominance could include:
>
> - *How will the practice harm competition?*
> - Will it deter or prevent entry?
> - Will it reduce incentives of the firm and its rivals to compete aggressively?
> - Will it provide the dominant firm with an additional capacity to raise prices?
> - Will it prevent investments in research and innovation?
> - Do consumers benefit from lower prices and/or greater product and service availability?
>
> In order to understand the aim of the provision, the discussion on abuse in the Raghavan Committee Report was perused. The Committee took note that this report indicates that an effects based approach was contemplated to establish abuse of dominance under Section 4.
>
> ... Based on the above, the Committee discussed that the CCI has interpreted Section 4(2) keeping in mind that one of the key aims of the Act is to prevent practices which adversely affect competition in India. It has therefore, wherever appropriate, analysed the effects of alleged abusive conduct by dominant entities before passing orders regarding such conduct. The CCI has relied on the effects built into some of the clauses of Section 4(2) to support its approach, e.g. 'denial of market access in any manner' in Section 4(2)(c).
>
> After conducting an analysis of the CCI's orders, the Committee came to the conclusion that the current text of Section 4(2) has not proven to be a hindrance to the CCI's ability to assess effects in abuse of dominance disputes. It was agreed that since it may not be necessary to undertake an effects analysis in all kinds of abuse, e.g. exploitative abuse, it may not be appropriate to mandate an effects analysis in Section 4(2). Therefore, it was concluded that no legislative amendment is required in this regard. [emphasis supplied]

This approach taken by the Report of the High Level Committee on Competition Law suggests that conduct in question must in the first place have the capability, by its

201. *Konkurrensverket v. TeliaSonera Sverige AB*, Case C-52/09, para. 68.

nature, to distort competition or foreclose competitors from the market. To establish such capability, it is in general sufficient to investigate the form and nature of the conduct in question. Second, it implies that, in the specific market context, a likely market-distorting foreclosure effect must be established. The competition law concern is to prevent exclusionary conduct of the dominant firm[202] which is likely to limit the remaining competitive constraints on the dominant company, including the entry of newcomers, so as to avoid consumers being harmed. This means that it is competition, and not competitors as such, that is to be protected. By foreclosure, it means that actual or potential competitors are completely or partially denied profitable access to a market. Foreclosure may discourage the entry or expansion of rivals or encourage their exit. Foreclosure thus can be found even if the foreclosed rivals are not forced to exit the market: it is sufficient that the rivals are disadvantaged and consequently led to compete less aggressively.

[B] IPR as a Defence

Protection of IPRs has been separately included as a defence to anti-competitive conduct under section 3(5) of the Competition Act. However, this defence is only limited to anti-competitive agreements. There have been several discussions to extend the benefit of this defence to abuse of dominance as well. In fact, the Parliamentary Standing Committee Report, 2022 also recommended the inclusion of a defence allowing reasonable conditions and restrictions for protecting IPR may be provided in cases of abuse of dominance on the lines with the international jurisdictions, that is, the EU, the US and the UK which provide for such exemption. However, the Parliament rejected the same, and so far, the provision has not found its way into the Competition Act due to concerns in the era of the new age economy that mention of IPR defence explicitly may allow a dominant player to abuse its position of dominance.

However, it is apposite to note that the NCLAT, in its decisional practice, seems to have upheld the use of IPR as a defence by dominant enterprises in the *Google Android* case.[203] The CCI had directed Google not to deny access to its APIs to OEMS, app developers and existing or potential app developers. Google argued that it cannot be asked to share APIs as it constitutes the IPR of Google. The NCLAT upheld this argument and set aside the direction of CCI to allow open access to Google's APIs by observing that Google's APIs constitute its proprietary software, into which Google has made investments for scientific and technical development. Thus, the same should fetch value to Google and allowing open access to such proprietary software will decrease the incentive for technological companies to continue innovation.

202. *Bharti Airtel Limited v. Reliance Industries Limited and Anr*, Case No. 03 of 2017.
203. *Google Android case*, paras 188-190.

§3.08 CONCLUSION

The decisional practice and statutory regime of abuse of dominance indicates a holistic consideration of all facts and circumstances to hold an entity guilty of abuse. It is not a static consideration but gives scope for commercial justifications and business efficiencies. At the same time, dominant players have to be cautious about employing business practices in line with their special responsibility to prevent genuine and undistorted growth of competition in the market. The idea is to strike a balance – to ensure a competitive and level playing field for all market participants and prevent monopolistic practices that may harm consumers and hinder economic growth and, at the same time, prevent excessive curbs on dominant enterprises and avoid hindering innovation in the market.

CHAPTER 4

Mergers and Competition Law

§4.01 INTRODUCTION

It is imperative to have an effective merger control regime to ensure that corporate reorganizations do not distort the competitive structure of the market. Considering combinations create permanent and lasting changes to the market, it is necessary to ensure timely intervention in case the combination causes or is likely to cause any AAEC. At the same time, interventions should not be so strict so as to deter combinations and ease of doing business in the economy. The Indian merger control regime, which comprises the Competition Act and the attendant CCI (Procedure in regard to the transaction of business relating to Combinations) Regulations, 2011 ('Combination Regulations'), has attempted to strike a balance between these two goals.

In this chapter, CCI's approach to regulation of combinations, viz. the procedure followed, factors considered, obligations of the parties, remedies issued and penalties imposed have been discussed. To date, in its decisional practice, the CCI has not refused approval for any combination. They have imposed both behavioural and structural commitments. In this background, the chapter also highlights the emerging trends in the Indian merger control regime.

§4.02 THRESHOLD LIMITS

Section 5 of the Competition Act characterizes combinations under four broad categories:

(a) acquisition of shares, voting rights, control or assets of an enterprise;
(b) acquisition of control of an enterprise by an enterprise engaged in a similar line of business; and
(c) mergers or amalgamation;

(d) deal value threshold.[1]

The Indian merger control regime provides for mandatory notification in case the prescribed thresholds under the Competition Act of assets or turnover are met. At the outset, it is also clarified that for the purpose of determining notifiability under the Competition Act, the value of assets and turnover of the acquirer along with the target must be considered. This is clear from the language of section 5(a) which lists the thresholds applicable to the control, shares, assets or voting rights of the parties to the combination 'jointly'.[2]

A tabular snapshot of the present threshold limit for assets and turnover is as below.

[A] Parties to the Combination

Situation	*Entity*	*Assets*		*Turnover*
In India	Acquirer and Target	> INR 2,000 crores[3]	Or	> INR 6,000 crores
		OR		
Worldwide	Acquirer and Target	> USD 1 billion	Or	> USD 3 billion
	Of which in India	INR 1,000 crores		INR 3,000 crores

[B] Group Thresholds

Scenario	*Entity*	*Assets*		*Turnover*
In India	Group and Target	> INR 8,000 crores	Or	> INR 24,000 crores
		OR		
Worldwide	Group and Target	> USD 4 billion	Or	> USD 12 billion
	Of which in India	INR 1,000 crores		INR 3,000 crores

Section 20(3) of the Competition Act provides that the Central Government, in consultation with the CCI, can enhance or reduce, or keep at the same level,[4] the

1. Yet to be notified in the official Gazette.
2. Section 43A Order against Diasys Diagnostics Systems GmbH, 31 Aug. 2016, para. 14.
3. 1 crore = 10 million.
4. Competition (Amendment) Act 2023, section 20.

threshold limits of the value of assets and turnover mentioned under section 5 of the Competition Act. The enhancement will be based on the wholesale price index on fluctuation in the exchange rate of the rupee or foreign currencies or other such factors deemed relevant by the Central Government.

[C] Deal Value Thresholds

The Competition (Amendment) Act, 2023 amended section 5 to introduce a new deal value threshold to cover those combinations where the value of the transaction in connection with the acquisition of any control, shares, voting rights or assets of an enterprise, merger or amalgamation exceeds INR 2,000 crores and, the target has substantial business operations in India. Noticeably, the *de minimis* or target exemption (as discussed in the subsequent parts of this chapter) will not be available to a transaction if the deal value thresholds are met, and thus, the transaction will necessarily be notifiable.

The objective of the amendment is to cover 'killer acquisitions', a term used to refer to combinations in technology and digital markets where big entities acquire smaller rivals, i.e., kill their competitors by acquiring them. Since such firms generate returns over time, often operating on zero or even negative revenue in their initial years, these transactions tend to escape antitrust scrutiny. Some commentators across the globe, including in India, felt that the absence of such deal value thresholds was one of the major reasons why such acquisitions could not be checked in an *ex ante* framework. This was a significant loophole as several transactions involving industry leaders, such as Facebook/WhatsApp, Flipkart/Myntra, etc., escaped competition assessment by the CCI since the asset and turnover thresholds were not triggered.

Further, the Competition Commission of India (Combinations) Regulations, 2023 ('Draft Regulations') clarify that 'value of the transaction' refers to '*every valuable consideration, whether direct or indirect, immediate or deferred, cash or otherwise*' and shall include non-compete fees as well as, consideration attributable to interconnected transactions, incidental commercial arrangements entered into within two years of the closing of the notifiable transaction (such as technology assistance agreements, licensing of IPR and supply of materials), options and securities on an as-converted basis and contingencies. In case the transaction value is not specified in the transaction documents, then the value approved by the board of directors or other approving authority of the notifying party shall be considered. If the precise transaction value cannot be determined with certainty, then there is a presumption that the deal value threshold has been met.

A target enterprise will be deemed to have substantial business operations in India if at least 10% or more of its global:

(i) users, subscribers, customers, or visitors in the twelve months preceding the deal execution date were in India or;
(ii) gross merchandise value, for the twelve months preceding the deal execution date was from India or;

(iii) turnover for the preceding financial year was in India.

All the thresholds prescribed under section 5 are sector-agnostic, which means that they are applicable to all industries regardless of the nature of their operation. Further, the criteria for determining substantial business operations look beyond mere asset and turnover by accounting for factors like users, subscribers, etc. Hence, the deal value threshold is proposed to be a catch-all provision to prevent firms, especially those operating in digital markets, from escaping CCI's scrutiny.

§4.03 TARGET LEVEL/*DE MINIMIS* EXEMPTION

The *de minimis* or target exemption was introduced by way of a notification issued by the Ministry of Corporate Affairs, Government of India (MCA Circular) in March 2011 in exercise of the powers under section 54 of the Competition Act.[5] It exempts any transaction from notification requirement where the:

(i) value of assets being acquired, taken control of, merged or amalgamated is less than INR 350 crores in India or;
(ii) turnover is less than INR 1,000 crores in India.

These thresholds were increased from INR 250 crores to INR 350 crores and INR 750 crores to INR 1,000 crores, respectively, in March 2016.[6] Subsequently, the MCA issued another notification in March 2017 to expand the scope of the target exemption, which was earlier available to only certain types of combinations resulting from acquisitions, to combinations resulting from mergers, amalgamations and acquisition of control transactions.[7] Originally, the *de minimis* exemption was valid for a period of five years till March 2022, but it was subsequently extended till March 2027.[8] Through the Competition (Amendment) Act, 2023, the *de minimis* exemption which was provided through the MCA Circular has been formally included in the Competition Act itself. As mentioned earlier, the target exemption is not available to combinations notifiable on the basis of the deal value threshold.

Thus, transactions which do meet the target exemption are not notifiable because ordinarily, such transactions do not cause or are not likely to cause AAEC. However, not making it available to a transaction which triggers the deal value threshold implies that legislative intent is to lend greater scrutiny to combinations involving digital and technology companies since their distortionary impact on the market is not immediately seen.

5. MCA Notification S.O. 482(E), published in Gazette dated 4 Mar. 2011.
6. MCA Notification S.O. 674(E), published in Gazette dated 4 Mar. 2016.
7. MCA Notification S.O. 988(E), published in Gazette dated 27 Mar. 2017.
8. MCA Notification S.O. 1192(E), published in Gazette dated 16 Feb. 2022.

[A] Asset and Turnover Details

As discussed above and based on the decisional practice of CCI, a transaction involving the acquisition of a target enterprise which meets the prescribed thresholds will be exempt from merger control filing requirements. It is to be noted that for the de minimis exemption to be applicable, either the asset or turnover requirement has to be met. For the sake of clarity, if the target enterprise has assets of more than INR 350 crores but a turnover of less than INR 1,000 crores, the target exemption will be applicable, and no merger notification will be required to be made.

[1] Scope of De Minimis *Exemption*

CCI's earlier approach was that even if only certain assets of an enterprise are being acquired, the entire assets and turnover of the enterprise, on a consolidated basis are to be taken into account for determining notifiability.[9] Therefore, such assets, though seemingly not relevant to the transaction in terms of impacting any competitive structure, would still have to be notified. However, this position has undergone a change, as discussed below.

In the acquisition of 'Savlon' and 'Shower to Shower' trademarks along with other related assets from Johnson & Johnson by ITC Limited, i.e., the acquirer, notice was not filed with the CCI.[10] It was argued that acquisition of mere trademarks of an enterprise does not amount to acquisition of 'assets'. However, the CCI observed that trademarks constitute an asset since they provide economic value to their owners. Further, explanation (e) to section 5 of the Competition Act also includes trademarks and similar other commercial rights provided under various laws within the ambit of 'value of assets'. Thus, acquisition of trademarks is an acquisition of assets in terms of section 5(a) of the Competition Act and is a combination if the jurisdictional thresholds are met. Further, the CCI also observed that acquisition of immovable properties or manufacturing facilities is not a pre-requisite for attracting section 5 of the Act, as assets include not only tangible assets but also intangible assets, in the form of IPRs, viz. trademarks.

The second limb of CCI's reasoning was rather contentious. In assessing the applicability of the *de minimis* exemption threshold, the CCI held that where the sale involved a part, a division or business of the selling entity, the assets/turnover figures of the entire seller entity, rather than those of the part, etc., being transferred, should be taken into account. Basis this approach, the exemption was not available and ITC should have notified the acquisition. Accordingly, a penalty was imposed on ITC. Upon appeal, the NCLAT set aside the penalty imposed by CCI by holding that only the

9. G&K Baby Care Pvt. Ltd. and Danone Asia Pacific Holidays 11/Adyay, Combination Registration No. C-2011/08/03, 24 Aug. 2011; AICA Kogyo Company Limited and Aica Laminates Indian Private Limited, Combination Registration No. C-2011/09/04, 30 Sep. 2011; NHK Automotive Components India Pvt. Ltd. and NHK Spring Co. Ltd., Combination Registration No. C-2011/10/05, 4 Nov. 2011.
10. Section 43 Order against ITC Limited, 11 Dec. 2017, paras 10, 11.

assets/turnover attributable to the portion, division or business being transferred should be counted for the target.[11] Another aspect to note is that at the time of notification, the value of the asset or turnover of the target in India had to be below INR 250 crores and INR 750 crores, respectively. During the pendency of the appeal, the thresholds were increased to INR 350 crores and INR 1,000 crores, respectively. As a result, the NCLAT also held that the notification was clarificatory in nature and applied with retrospective effect. As a result, the relevant turnover of the target fell below the threshold, and the *de minimis* exemption was available for the transaction.

Therefore, the NCLAT propounded the legal position by clarifying that the assets and turnover of only the relevant portion of the target's business have to be calculated to determine the applicability of the *de minimis* exemption. If the entire assets and turnover were considered, then the target exemption would be rendered meaningless because several transactions would have to be notified, even if the actual value of the transaction (i.e., in terms of the relevant business undergoing combination) is much lower than the prescribed threshold.

It appears obvious that an extension of the principle that the assets/turnover of only the relevant portion of the target's business has to be considered for availing the *de minimis* exemption would mean that the assets/turnover of the parent company (if a subsidiary is being acquired) would be excluded. However, the CCI rejected this argument in the acquisition of Novartis Animal Health India (target) by Eli Lilly.[12] Eli Lilly did not file a notice of the acquisition by relying on the *de minimis* exemption because the target's turnover and assets fell well below the prescribed levels. However, the CCI observed that since the target was an unincorporated entity, it was not a '*person or enterprise*' for the purpose of *de minimis exemption*, so the thresholds should apply to the target's parent company, i.e., Novartis India. The logic was that a business division of an enterprise does not have a distinct legal personality from that of the enterprise which houses the business division/segment. Since the value of assets and turnover of Novartis India exceeded the thresholds, the *de minimis* exemption was not applicable to it. The CCI reasoned that the *de minimis* exemption applies only to the 'enterprise', whose assets, control, shares, voting rights or assets are being acquired not of the value of assets and turnover of the segment/particular business being acquired (i.e., the target in the present case). This position was subsequently followed by the CCI in other cases as well.[13]

The NCLAT in appeal, reversed the finding of the CCI.[14] It was clarified that the *de minimis* exemption is applicable to a 'person' or 'enterprise', and the term 'enterprise' also included unincorporated businesses, as per the definition under section 2(h) of the Competition Act. More importantly, the NCLAT held that for the *purpose of calculation of assets and turnover, what is being acquired is relevant, as the*

11. *ITC Limited v. Competition Commission of India* [2023], (NCLAT) Competition Appeal (AT) No. 11 of 2018.
12. Section 43A Order against Eli Lilly and Company, 14 Jul. 2016, paras 13.1-13.7.
13. Section 43A Order against Reydel Automotive Holdings B.V., 2 Feb. 2017, para. 11.3; Section 43A Order against SRF Ltd, 16 Aug. 2016, para. 8.
14. *M/s. Eli Lilly and Company v. Competition Commission of India* [2020], (NCLAT) TA (AT) (Competition) No. 03 of 2017, paras 25-31.

assets/turnover of what is left over with the sellers after the acquisition will have no role to play in the context of the business conducted by the purchaser post-acquisition. In the present case, Eli Lily acquired only the business of 'animal health,' i.e., Novartis Animal Health India and not the entire business of Novartis India Limited, which included both human health and animal health. Hence, since the turnover and assets attributable to the target were below the threshold, the target exemption was available, and the acquisition was not liable to be notified.

Herein, it is relevant to note that after the CCI passed its order penalizing Eli Lily in 2016, before the matter was finally decided by the NCLAT, the MCA issued a fresh notification under 2017 which clarified that the value of assets or turnover shall be limited to only such portion/division/business of the enterprise as is being acquired/taken control of/merged/amalgamated with another enterprise.[15]

Therefore, it is now clear that to avail the *de minimis* exemption, the assets and turnover of only the 'true target' (i.e., business division/subsidiary being acquired) have to be considered. This will prevent unnecessary burden on the CCI since more entities will be able to avail the target exemption as the value of assets and turnover of a subsidiary is usually likely to be lesser than that of the parent company.

Further, the issue of whether intra-group revenue is to be included in assessing the thresholds of the *de minimis* exemption was raised in *Avago Technologies Limited/Broadcom Corporation*,[16] where the acquirer Avago did not notify the transaction on the assumption that target exemption was available because after excluding the revenue generated from the intra-group sales of the target, the target thresholds were not met. However, the CCI clarified that the statutory definition of turnover under the Competition Act does not provide that goods or services provided to group-entities are to be excluded. The value of turnover is taken as provided in the books of accounts of the enterprise concerned. In this case, the books of accounts of the targets' group companies also did not distinguish between the revenue generated through intra-group sales or through sales to third parties.

Thus, it is clear that the entire value of the turnover of the target and its group companies has to be considered as it is in assessing the applicability of the *de minimis* exemption without drawing a distinction between internal and external sales of the target.

[2] Proof of AAEC Is Necessary to Investigate a Combination Which Has Availed the Target Exemption

In its decisional practice, the CCI has also held that if a transaction was exempt from the notification requirement on account of the *de minimis* exemption, such transaction cannot be investigated without actual proof of anticompetitive effects on the market.[17] The merger of PVR and INOX, which were among the largest players in the film

15. MCA Notification S.0. 988(E), published in Gazette dated 27 Mar. 2017.
16. Section 43A Order against Avago Technologies Limited, 7 Jun. 2017, paras 8.4-8.6.
17. *Vikas Verma v. Adani Ports and Special Economic Zone Ltd. & Others*, Case No. 02 of 2021; *Satyen Narendra Bajaj v. PayU Payments Private Limited & Another*, Case No. 23 of 2019.

exhibition industry in India, was not notified because it qualified for the *de minimis* exemption since the turnover of INOX was less than INR 1,000 crores. An information was filed on the apprehension that the combined entity would be dominant in the relevant market and the proposed agreements will result in short and long-term consumer harm.[18] It was contended that the combined entity would become the largest player in the relevant market in terms of market share, thereby leading to consolidation of market power and AAEC as it was likely to reduce consumer choice, adversely impact consumers in terms of high prices and deterioration in food and service quality, prevent other cinemas from accessing movies from distributors and advertising content, high bargaining power of the combined entity, etc. However, the CCI observed[19] that first, no entity, much less a dominant entity, was in existence for assessment of conduct in the present case. Second, even if the proposed transaction was concluded, dominance per se is not anti-competitive, and only conduct is if the same falls within the provisions of section 4 of the Competition Act. The CCI held that '*apprehension of likelihood of AAEC by an entity which is yet to take form cannot be a subject matter of inquiry/investigation under Section 3 or 4*'. Further, section 3 of the Competition Act examines the likelihood of AAEC arising out of conduct qua an agreement and not a likelihood of conduct itself. Such assessment is *ex ante*. Hence, CCI found no prima facie violation and observed that if any violation was made *post facto*, it could then be examined in terms of the provisions of the Competition Act.

In appeal, the NCLAT affirmed CCI's view by holding that at the outset, the very filing of information alleging a violation of section 3 of the Competition Act without any agreement existing in terms of section 3(1) was not in accordance with the law.[20] In any case, the words '*likely to cause an AAEC in India*' under section 3(1) were of no consequence because in the present case, the parties did not enter into any anti-competitive agreement but only merged with each other. Further, the NCLAT also affirmed CCI's findings with reference to section 4 and added that liberty existed to examine any abusive conduct *post facto*, but without any prima facie abusive conduct, no action could be taken.

Thus, if an enterprise qualifies for the *de minimis* exemption, it cannot be forced to notify a transaction merely on the likelihood of AAEC. Since the assessment of combinations is an *ex ante* analysis that takes place before the combination is actually given effect, antitrust scrutiny is warranted only if the jurisdictional thresholds are triggered and not otherwise. The mere likelihood of dominance or causing AAEC in the future is, therefore, insufficient for initiating an investigation into a proposed combination.

18. *Consumer Unity & Trust Society v. PVR Limited and INOX Leisure Limited*, Case No. 29 of 2022.
19. *Consumer Unity & Trust Society v. PVR Limited and INOX Leisure Limited*, Case No. 29 of 2022, paras 15-17.
20. *Consumer Unity & Trust Society v. CCI and Others* [2023], (NCLAT) Competition Appeal (AT) No. 61 of 2022, paras 16-18.

[B] Calculation on a Consolidated Basis

The threshold limit of assets and turnover for the target enterprise mentioned in the MCA Circular is calculated on a consolidated basis. The calculation of the threshold limits will be aggregated to include the assets and turnover of the target company along with all of the downstream companies which such target company has control over. For example, an acquirer is acquiring shares or control of Company A. Company A has two subsidiaries operating in India, Company B and Company C. Since Company A is the target company, the calculation of assets and turnover of Company A has to be analysed to see if the *de minimis* exemption can be availed for such transaction. For the said calculation to analyse whether the *de minimis* exemption would be applicable, the calculation will be aggregated to include the assets and turnover of Company B and Company C, along with Company A.

A diagrammatic illustration of the same is as follows:

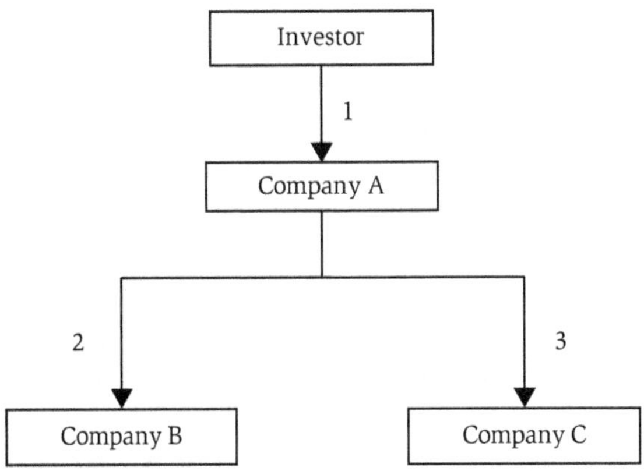

Notes to the graphic illustration:
Note 1: Investor acquires shares of the Company A.
Note 2: Company A has a 51% shareholding in Company B.
Note 3: Company A has 51% shareholding in Company C.
Thus, Company B and Company C are subsidiaries of Company A. To ascertain whether the target exemption will be available, the assets and turnover of Company B and Company C will be clubbed together with Company A.

In *Allcargo/GATI*,[21] Allcargo acquired 46.86% of the equity share capital of GATI without filing a notice with the CCI. Upon examination, the CCI found that Allcargo had considered the assets and turnover of only the target on a standalone basis and not the target 'group', i.e., the turnover of the target consolidated with its subsidiaries. Once the latter were considered, the thresholds of the target exemption were met, and the

21. Section 43A Order against Allcargo Logistics Limited, 2002, 2 May 2022, paras 4, 5.

exemption was no longer available. Thus, the position is well-settled that the acquirer must take into account the consolidated financials of the target, i.e., an aggregate of the target's group entities and not merely the financials of the target on a standalone basis.

In the *Investcorp* case,[22] the CCI held that pooled investment schemes generally envisage demutualization of investment management and ownership, wherein the subscribers give authority to the investment managers to conduct the operations of the fund. Accordingly, in case of the acquisition of any investment management businesses, the value of assets and turnover of the controlled portfolio entities would also be relevant for the purpose of computing threshold for the purpose of section 5 of the Competition Act. In the present case, including the assets and turnover of the portfolio entities of the target in the calculation process exceeded the *de minimis* threshold, so the target exemption was not available. Thus, this case is another example of the principle that calculation has to be done on a consolidated basis because the assets and turnover of the target have to be considered on a comprehensive basis.

[C] Regulation 5(9)

Post the MCA Circular, the CCI amended the Combination Regulations by adding Regulation 5(9),[23] which, in effect, diluted the *de minimis* exemption. Regulation 5(9) reads as:

> Where, in a series of steps or individual transactions that are related to each other, assets are being transferred to an enterprise for the purpose of such enterprise entering into an agreement relating to an acquisition or merger or amalgamation with another person or enterprise, for the purpose of section 5 of the Act, the value of assets and turnover of the enterprise whose assets are being transferred shall also be attributed to the value of assets and turnover of the enterprise to which the assets are being transferred.

By way of this amendment, the CCI clarified that in cases where assets/business units or division of an enterprise is transferred to an enterprise and, subsequently, the transferee enterprise enters into an acquisition/combination with a third enterprise, the entire value of assets and turnover of the transferor enterprise (as opposed to only the assets and turnover of the divisions being transferred to the transferee enterprise), will be clubbed with the assets and turnover of the transferee enterprise for the purposes of calculating the threshold limits provided under section 5 of the Competition Act. The two transactions must be an interrelated transaction for it to be applicable. This is called the principle of aggregation or the principle of attributability because the value of assets and turnover of the parent entity is 'aggregated' with the joint venture and becomes attributable to the joint venture.[24]

22. Paragraph 16.
23. Vide Competition Commission of India (Procedure in regard to the Transaction of Business relating to Combinations) Amendment Regulations, 2012.
24. Etihad Airways PJSC, Jet Privilege Private Limited and Jet Airways (India) Limited., Combination Registration No. C-2013/12/144, 5 Feb. 2014, para. 4.

A diagrammatic illustration of the principle of aggregation is as follows:

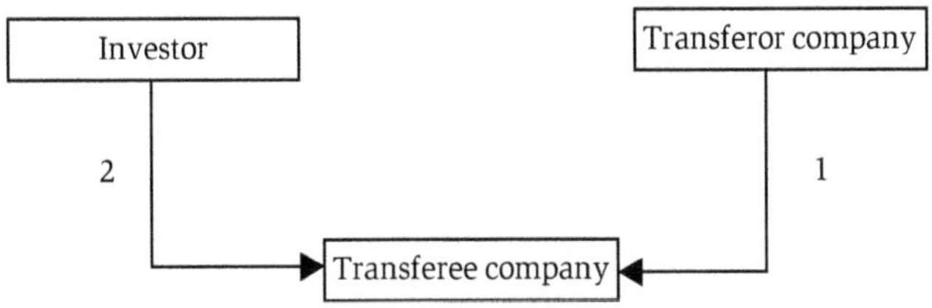

Note to the illustration:
Note 1: Transferor company transfers assets to the Transferee company.
Note 2: Post the transfer, the Investor invests in the Transferee company.

The principle of aggregation laid down by the insertion of Regulation 5(9) has, in effect, diluted the *de minimis* exemption laid down by the MCA Circular. It is to be noted that because of the principle of aggregation and the outlook of the CCI to look at substance over form, structuring deals to avoid merger notification has been done away with. Thus, CCI is extending its powers to monitor more transactions than what was initially envisaged in 2011, when the Combination Regulations came into force.

However, as mentioned earlier, the MCA Circular of March 2017 has clarified that the value of assets and turnover of only the 'true target' has to be considered, i.e., only the portion/division/business that is being acquired.[25] This has significantly diluted the ambit of Regulation 5(9) because now only the value of the relevant assets being transferred by the parent(s) and the turnover generated by such relevant assets will be considered.

In the past, the CCI has used Regulation 5(9) of the Combination Regulations to expand their ambit to newly created joint ventures by attributing the assets/turnover of the transferring parent to such joint ventures.[26] Thus, post the MCA Circular of March 2017, where there is no transfer of assets and merely a transfer of capital by the parent entities, target exemption will generally be available as such joint ventures are unlikely to meet the prescribed thresholds. Even where assets are transferred to create a joint venture, only the value of such assets as are attributable to the joint venture, and not that of the transferor, will be considered for determining the applicability of the target exemption.

§4.04 SHARES

Section 5 is applicable to acquisition of shares, control, voting rights or assets. Shares have been defined under section 2(v) of the Competition Act to mean the shares in the

25. MCA Notification S.O. 988(E), published in Gazette dated 27 Mar. 2017.
26. Andhra Pradesh Gas Distribution Corporation Limited, GDF Suez Energy International Global Developments B.V., Shell Gas B.V. and GAIL (India) Limited, Combination Registration No. C-2015/10/333, 4 Feb. 2016, paras 2-4; Fujitsu Limited, Panasonic Corporation and Development Bank of Japan Inc., Combination Case No. C-2014/09/206, 27 Oct. 2014.

share capital of a company carrying voting rights and includes any security which entitles the holder to receive shares with voting rights, as well as stocks except where a distinction between stock and share is expressed or implied.

Based on the definition, non-voting instruments like preference shares and non-convertible debentures will not be considered 'shares' for the purposes of the Competition Act. However, convertible instruments will be considered shares because they entitle the holder to receive shares with voting rights at a future date. It is very common in the structuring of a transaction to issue convertibles (i.e., instruments which will be converted into equity shares at a later point in time at a given conversion price) to the acquirer. Therefore, any convertible instruments which are normally issued to the acquirer (like warrants, convertible debentures, convertible preference shares) will be counted as 'shares' for the purposes of the Competition Act and the Combination Regulations. It is apposite in this regard to note the merger approval decision of the CCI in the notice for acquisition of Independent Media Trust,[27] where Independent Media Trust was acquiring zero coupon optionally convertible debentures (i.e., debentures which can be converted into equity shares carrying voting rights, at the open of the debenture holder) of the target company. The CCI noted that the optionally convertible debentures were shares for the purposes of section 2(v)(i) of the Competition Act since the conversion option entitled the holder to receive equity shares of the target companies.

Similarly, in the acquisition of 26% equity share capital of Mangalore Fertilizers and Chemicals Limited by SCM Soilfert Limited ('*SCM Soilfert* case'),[28] in the transaction constituting acquisition of 0.8% equity share capital of Mangalore Chemicals and Fertilizers Limited (MCFL) through open market transactions, it was not disputed that the shares carried voting rights with them. Hence, despite the subsequent decision of the acquirers to not exercise the voting rights associated with such shares, the acquired shares nevertheless were 'shares' within the meaning of the Competition Act.

Thus, in determining what constitutes shares, whether the option to convert the shares into equity shares or the right to vote is actually exercised does not matter, and the key aspect is the conferment of the holder with the right to vote.

§4.05 GROUP

As mentioned in the threshold table, the threshold limits of assets and turnover are applicable on both enterprise level as well as group level. Section 5 explanation (b) of the Competition Act defines group as follows:

> (b) 'group' means two or more enterprises which, directly or indirectly, are in position to –

27. Independent Media Trust, RB Media Soft Pvt Ltd., RRB Media Soft Pvt Ltd., RB Media Holdings Pvt Ltd., Adventure Marketing Pvt Ltd., Watermark Infratech Pvt Ltd., and Colorful Media Pvt Ltd., Combination Registration No. C-2012/03/47, 24 May 2012, para. 14.
28. Section 43A Order against SCM Soilfert Limited and Deepak Fertilizers and Petrochemicals Corporation Limited, 10 Feb. 2015, para. 10.2.

(i) exercise twenty-six per cent or more of the voting rights in the other enterprise; or
(ii) appoint more than fifty per cent of the members of the board of directors in the other enterprise; or
(iii) control the management or affairs of the other enterprise.

Thereafter, the MCA, by a notification, exempted the 'group' exercising less than 50% of voting rights in another enterprise from section 5 of the Competition Act for a period of five years.[29] Thus, from the definition, in the event: (i) an enterprise holds more than 50% of voting rights in another enterprise, directly or indirectly, or (ii) the enterprise has the right to appoint more than 50% of the directors in another enterprise, or (iii) an enterprise controls the management or affairs of another enterprise, then both the enterprises would be considered to be part of the same group.

A diagrammatic representation of group is as follows:

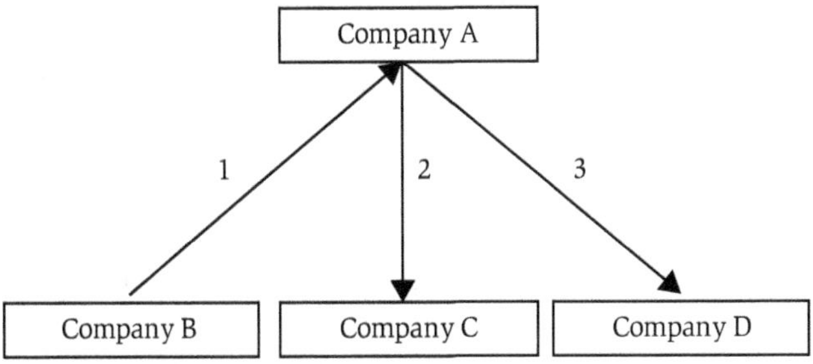

Note to the diagrammatic representation:
Note 1: Company A holds 51% equity shareholding in Company B.
Note 2: Company A can appoint three out of five directors on the board of Company C.
Note 3: Company A exercises control over Company D.

Based on the above diagrammatic representation, Company A, Company B, Company C and Company D all form part of the group of Company A.

Further, it is also to be noted that for the purposes of the Competition Act and the attendant Combination Regulations, one company can be a part of two different groups. For the sake of clarity, let us analyse the following diagrammatic representation.

29. The said notification came into effect on 4 Mar. 2011.

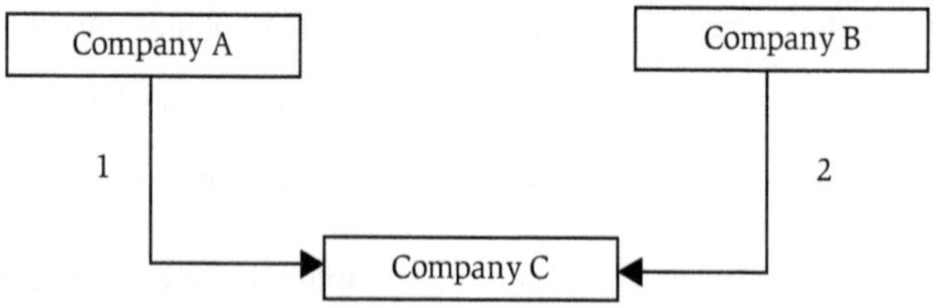

Note to the diagrammatic representation:
Note 1: Company A holds 51% shareholding in Company C.
Note 2: Company B exercises control over the operations of Company C by having affirmative vote items (as discussed below under the heading of control).
In such a situation, Company C forms part of the group of both Company A and Company B.

It is relevant to mention that 'family' constitutes 'group' for the purposes of the Competition Act. In the combination related to the transfer of business, assets and operations of Jaiprakash Associates Limited to UltraTech Cement Limited[30] ('*UltraTech* case'), while filing the notice, UltraTech had reported that it was a subsidiary of Grasim Industries Limited which in turn was a flagship company of Aditya Birla Group. However, UltraTech did not provide any details in respect of shareholding/control of Kumar Mangalam Birla and his family and the companies owned/controlled by them in Century and Kesoram (which were also involved in the cement business). UltraTech argued that the definition of 'group' did not include the members of a 'family' within its ambit and that 'family' has not been defined in the Competition Act. In this regard, the CCI held that *what is of the essence here is collective common control of certain individuals and enterprises over an enterprise; the individuals may or may not comprise a family.* The assessment of common control has been an integral part of the decisional practice of the CCI.[31] Consequently, the shareholding of the family member was a relevant disclosure for the purposes of the combination that ought to have been made in as much as it constituted part of the same group of companies as UltraTech.

Thus, it can be said that determination of what constitutes 'group' essentially hinges on what constitutes control. If control is being exercised by one enterprise over another, then irrespective of whether such enterprises belong to the same family or even different groups, they fall within the same group for the purposes of competition assessment. The concept of control has been discussed in more detail below.

§4.06 CONTROL

Section 5, Explanation (a) of the Competition Act defines control as follows:

30. Section 44 Order against UltraTech Cement Limited, 12 Mar. 2018, paras 4, 5, 12.2-12.5.
31. Nirma Limited, Banihal Holdings Private Limited, Kargil Holdings Private Limited, Combination Registration No. C-2014/11/221, 28 Jan. 2015; Zuari Fertilisers and Chemicals Limited and Zuari Agro Chemicals Limited, Combination Registration No. C-2014/06/181, 4 Sep. 2014.

(a) 'control' means the ability to exercise material influence, in any manner whatsoever, over the management or affairs or strategic commercial decisions by –
   (i) one or more enterprises, either jointly or singly, over another enterprise or group; or
   (ii) one or more groups, either jointly or singly, over another group or enterprise

The definition of control has far-reaching implications under the merger control regime in India since it is not only required to ascertain the threshold on a group level but also to assess whether the exemptions mentioned in Schedule I of the Combination Regulations (discussed subsequently in this chapter) can be availed by the parties to the combination or its group.

[A] Meaning of Control

Generally, in various investment structures, control is normally exercised by the majority shareholder in the target enterprise. However, there may be situations where the de facto control is exercised by another person along with the majority shareholder (like grant of quorum rights, contractual minority affirmative rights under a shareholders agreement, etc.). The CCI, in its decisional practice, has reviewed the investment structure and the management structure to analyse the issue of control. As mentioned above, there can be situations under the Competition Act where the same target enterprise is controlled by two separate enterprises.

In *Century Tokyo Leasing Corporation/Tata Capital Financial Services Limited*, the CCI held that affirmative rights relating to the following items would be considered 'control' for the purposes of the Competition Act:[32]

(i) annual budget;
(ii) annual business plan;
(iii) exit and entry into lines of business;
(iv) appointment of management;
(v) determination of their remuneration; or
(vi) strategic business decisions (no materiality threshold specified).

Further, in one of the merger approval orders passed by the CCI in the Notice given by Caladium Investment Pte Ltd.,[33] the following affirmative rights were held to be controlled for the purposes of notification:

(i) creation of or entering into or termination of joint ventures or partnerships and/or creation or sale/liquidation of its significant strategic investments, direct/indirect joint ventures or its subsidiaries; and

32. Century Tokyo Leasing Corporation and Tata Capital Financial Services, Combination Registration Number C-2012/09/78, 4 Oct. 2012.
33. Caladium Investment Pte. Ltd., Combination Registration No. C-2015/05/278, 25 Jun. 2015, para. 7.

(ii) reorganization or change in the nature of its current business or activities or launch of any new line of business(es).

It is appropriate to note that the word control has been used in various statutes in India. With respect to any transaction, there can be multiple regulatory overlaps between the securities market regulator in India, the SEBI and the provisions of the Competition Act and the attendant Combination Regulations. In case of an acquisition of control over a listed company by an acquirer (along with persons acting in concert), a requirement of a mandatory open order is required to be made under the provisions of the Securities and Exchange Board of India Act, 1992 and the SEBI (Substantial Acquisition of Shares and Takeovers) Regulations, 2011 ('Takeover Code'). Similarly, as discussed above, in case of acquisition of control of a target enterprise which meets the thresholds under the Competition Act, it will require a filing to be made before the CCI for approval. Having said that, the definition of control under the Takeover Code and the Competition Act and the regulatory outlook on control by SEBI and CCI are very different. The threshold of control under the Competition Act is much lower than that of other prevalent regimes in India.

As mentioned above, under the provisions of the Competition Act, 'control' has been defined in a circular manner to include 'controlling the affairs or management of one or more enterprises or group, either jointly or singly'. However, the definition of control under the Takeover Code provides that:

> Control includes the right to appoint a majority of directors, or to control the management or policy decisions exercisable by a person or persons acting individually or in concert, directly or indirectly, including by virtue of their shareholding or management rights or shareholders agreements or voting agreements or in any other manner.

A case in point is the merger approval decision of the CCI in the acquisition of 24% equity stake and certain other rights in Jet Airways (India) Limited by Etihad Airways PJSC ('*Jet/Etihad* case') and the treatment given to it by under regulators in India, namely the Foreign Investment Promotion Board and the SEBI. The CCI noted, in its approval, that Etihad had acquired control over the assets of Jet Airways.[34] Based on the same set of agreements, investment structure and board structure, the Foreign Investment Promotion Board held that Etihad had not acquired control over Jet Airways. Post the observation of the CCI on control, SEBI investigated the *Jet/Etihad* case in order to determine if the requirement to make an open offer had been triggered by the transaction under the provisions of the Takeover Code. In this regard, SEBI passed an order holding that Etihad had not acquired control over Jet Airways and hence there was no requirement to make an open offer by Etihad Airways. While passing the order, SEBI compared the definition of control under the Foreign Direct Investment Policy, the Competition Act and the Takeover Code, finding that the same are *pari materia* under the Foreign Direct Investment Policy and the Takeover Code.

34. Etihad Airways and Jet Airways, Combination Registration No. C-2013/05/122, 12 Nov. 2013, paras 14-16.

However, it noted that the definition under the Competition Act, which deals with 'controlling the affairs and management', is of much wider import than that under the Takeover Code, which includes the right 'to appoint majority of the directors' or controlling 'the management or policy decisions'. Accordingly, the decision of CCI would not be the guiding factor for SEBI in determining if control has been acquired under the Takeover Code.

[1] Control Includes the Ability to Exercise Material Influence

Previously, the CCI's interpretation of the definition of control oscillated between the 'material influence'[35] standard and the 'decisive influence'[36] standard in determining control.

Under the decisive influence standard, the ability of a firm to exercise decisive influence over the management or affairs of a target enterprise through majority shareholding, veto rights, or contractual covenants was considered in order to determine control. In contrast, the material influence standard is a lower threshold, wherein the ability of a firm to influence affairs and management of the other enterprise through factors such as shareholding, special rights, status and expertise of an enterprise/person, board representation, and structural/financial arrangements is considered to determine control. Thus, in simple terms, under the material influence standard, a firm will be said to be in control if it exercises a significant level of influence over the decisions of the target, even if such influence is not absolute or decisive in nature.

In September 2022, CCI revised its 'Frequently Asked Questions' on combinations which brought certainty to CCI's interpretation of control as unequivocally adopting the threshold of material influence. Thus, material influence as a factor of control was evolved through CCI's decisional practice, as discussed below and subsequently added to the statute through the Competition (Amendment) Act, 2023.

In the *UltraTech* case,[37] the CCI observed in competition law practice, control is considered a matter of degree. In particular, if the three limbs of the definition of 'group' as under explanation (b) to section 5 of the Competition Act are 'either/or' tests and fulfilment of even a single limb would confer control: i.e., the first test of the two enterprises belonging to the same group is the ability to exercise 50% or more voting rights; the second test is in terms of ability to control majority of composition of Board of Directors; and the third test, which is most dynamic, is in terms of ability to control or manage the affairs of the other enterprise. For example, if a particular enterprise does not hold 50% shares in the other enterprise, it may still have the ability to control if it has majority on the Board of Directors. Similarly, in the event an enterprise does not have requisite shareholding nor the ability to control the majority composition of the

35. UltraTech Cement Limited and Jaiprakash Associates Limited, Combination Registration No. C-2015/02/246, 12 Mar. 2018.
36. Aditya Birla Chemicals Limited and Grasim Industries Limited, Combination Registration No. C-2015/03/256, 31 Aug. 2015.
37. Section 44 Order against UltraTech Cement Limited, 12 Mar. 2018, paras 12.8-12.11.

Board of Directors, it is possible to infer control by virtue of ability to control and manage the affairs of the other enterprise.

The international jurisprudence considers 'material influence' as the lowest form of control with other higher forms such as de facto control (implies a situation where an enterprise holds less than majority of the voting rights but in practice controls over more than half of the votes actually cast at a meeting) and de jure control or controlling interest (a shareholding conferring more than 50% of the voting rights of an enterprise) in that order. As stated earlier, material influence, the lowest level of control, implies the presence of factors which give an enterprise ability to influence affairs and management of the other enterprise, including factors such as shareholding, special rights/veto rights, status and expertise of an enterprise or person, Board representation, structural/financial arrangements, etc. It may be noted that only one enterprise can have a controlling interest in the other enterprise, but more than one enterprise can control the other enterprise (situation of joint control). Likewise, there are other terms which are used to express control, such as negative control (by virtue of ability to block special resolutions) or operational control (by virtue of commercial cooperation agreements (CCAs) with or without involving equity). Thus, while examining the third limb of the definition of group, regard needs to be given to the likelihood of the aforesaid degrees of control and not just the special rights as considered by the Acquirer.

The CCI, in their FAQs has defined the standard of control in the following manner:

> Material influence – the lowest level of control – implies the presence of factors that give an enterprise/person the ability to influence the affairs and management of the other enterprise, including factors such as shareholding, special rights, status and expertise of an enterprise or person, board representation, structural/financial arrangements, etc. De facto control implies a situation where an enterprise holds less than majority of the voting rights but, in practice, controls over half of the votes actually cast at a meeting. Further, the factors relevant for material influence are relevant for ascertaining de facto control as well. It may be noted that the concepts of material influence and de facto control are very significant in competition law as there can be situations where commercial realities can be more telling than formal agreements and structures. Controlling interest, or de jure control, means a shareholding conferring more than fifty per cent (50%) of the voting rights of an enterprise. It may be noted that only one enterprise can have a controlling interest in the other enterprise, but more than one enterprise can control the other enterprise (situation of joint control). Likewise, there are other terms which are used to express control, such as negative control (by virtue of ability to block special resolutions) or operational control (by virtue of commercial cooperation agreements with or without involving equity).

Further, it is relevant to note that whether any right provides material influence over the management or affairs or strategic commercial decisions or not depends upon its nexus with the likely economic behaviour of the target. There may be acquisition of control, including material influence, even if it is not the declared intention of the parties. Control is the possibility of exercising material influence rather than its actual exercise.[38] For instance, the ability to participate in the board meetings by a representative of the acquirer not only provides access to commercially sensitive information but also provides ability to influence strategic commercial decisions of the target. The extent of influence exerted in such situations depends upon several factors, such as the extent of industry knowledge, length of experience, recognition in the business world, length of association with the enterprise, dependence of the target for funding, supply of inputs or sale of product and services, etc.

Another emerging concern on CCI's radar is common ownership of the acquirer in competitors in the same industry. For instance, the combination involving 3% investment by ChrysCapital in Intas Pharmaceuticals, was approved by the CCI on the condition that ChrysCapital would remove its nominee director in a competing portfolio investment (other pharmaceutical companies like Intas Pharmaceuticals) and agree not to exercise veto rights over certain strategic corporate actions. The nature of rights enjoyed by ChrysCapital in its portfolio companies did not enable it to unilaterally undertake or stall any corporate action but allowed it to materially influence the strategic affairs of the said entities. The proposed investment allowed ChrysCapital to gain a similar position pursuant to its investment in Intas. Hence, the CCI observed that in such combinations, the Acquirer's ability to access non-public information as well as materially influence the strategic affairs of the competitors, whether by veto or consultation or advisory right or by way of representation on the board such as director or observer, merit examination of the impact of combination on the competition between them.[39] This approach of the CCI is interesting because it was merely a minority acquisition. Yet, it appears to be consistent with CCI's decisional practice,[40] wherein it has addressed the issue of common ownership through practical remedies such as preventing the acquirer from appointing common directors in its competing portfolio companies, accessing non-public information related to the competitors and adopting information firewalls. This indicates a trend of greater scrutiny for acquisitions involving common shareholdings based on the ability of the acquirer to materially influence the affairs of the competing entities in its portfolio.

Therefore, the standard of control has been significantly diluted over the years, thereby covering more transactions within its ambit and reducing the scope of availing exemptions (as discussed later in this chapter) since material influence is triggered at a much lower threshold.

It is now clear that material influence includes within its ambit de facto control as well as de jure control and, based on how the ability to influence the affairs and management of the other enterprise is exercised, it may be classified as negative control, positive control, sole control or joint control. Each of these classifications has been discussed subsequently.

38. Section 43A Order against Bharti Airtel Limited and Lion Meadow Investment Limited, 23 Aug. 2023, paras 37-40.
39. Canary Investment Limited and Link Investment Trust II, Combination Registration No. C-2020/04/741, 30 Apr. 2020, paras 10, 11.
40. Northern TK Venture Pte. Ltd., Combination Registration No. C-2018/09/601, 29 Oct. 2018; General Atlantic Singapore ACK Pte. Ltd., Combination Registration No. C-2023/04/1017, 6 Jun. 2017.

[2] *Beneficial Ownership Is not Necessary to Establish Control*

CCI's decisional practice indicates that beneficial ownership is not necessary to establish control.[41] For instance, in acquisition of real estate fund management and private equity fund management businesses of IDFC Alternatives Limited by Investcorp India Asset Managers Private Limited ('*Investcorp* case'),[42] the CCI observed that in acquisitions of mutual fund companies, the beneficial interest in these assets lies with the unitholders and the investment manager does not enjoy ownership or controlling rights over the assets of any of the funds. However, these investment structures envisage demutualization of investment management and ownership, wherein subscribers give authority to the investment managers to conduct the operations of the fund. Consequently, although the beneficial ownership of these categories of funds lies with unitholders, the control over the operations and management of the fund is entrusted to the investment manager. Funds have varying degrees of interest, such as sole control, joint control, mere financial interest, etc., in their portfolio entities. The investment manager of the fund, being the authority to exercise and protect such interest, would invariably enjoy control over the portfolio entity where the shareholding and/or contractual rights of the fund are such as to enable material influence or a higher degree of control over the given portfolio entity. Needless to say, when the fund management business of such a fund is acquired, the acquirer would also gain control over such portfolio entities of the fund.

This again lowers the threshold of control since it becomes immaterial whether beneficial interest or ownership over the portfolio entities is being acquired or not, thereby necessarily triggering notifiability of the transaction.

[B] Indices of Control

As discussed above, the CCI has clarified that control includes positive and negative control, such as quorum rights and veto rights with respect to decision-making relating to the appointment of management personnel, annual business plan, annual budget plan, commencement or ceasing of a business activity, operating in new location, etc.

Acquisition of positive control includes an acquisition of an affirmative vote items such as the veto right of decision-making relating to changes/amendments to the memorandum and/or articles of association, changes in the capital structure, including through new issues of equity or equity-linked securities, buyback, rights issue, bonus issue, stock/share split, sweat equity shares, redemption of securities, capital reductions, etc., significant changes to the incentive structure of the senior management and appointment or removal of any member of the senior management, reorganization or change in the nature of current business or launch of any new business, appointment

41. Section 43A Order against Global Infrastructure Partners India Private Limited, 30 Aug. 2022, para. 11.
42. Section 43A Order against India Asset Managers Private Limited, 17 Dec. 2021, paras 10-12.

or removal of any nominee director, changes to dividend policy,[43] annual business plan, annual budget plan, commencement or ceasing of a business activity, operating in new location[44] and other strategic business decisions.[45]

The CCI has also clarified in its decisional practice that negative control amounts to control for the purposes of the Competition Act.

For instance, the CCI approved an increase in the voting rights percentage of Canada Pension Plan Investment Board (CPPIB) in ReNew Energy Global plc (ReNew) pursuant to a buyback programme announced by ReNew.[46] Ordinarily, a buyback of shares is not notifiable unless it leads to acquisition of control, in lieu of the exemption provided by Item 6 of Schedule I read with Regulation 4 of the Combination Regulations. In this case, the voting rights acquired by CPPIB on the completion of buyback were likely to exceed 25%, thereby conferring it with the ability to block any special resolution in ReNew. Hence, the exemption was not available to CPPIB because it would acquire negative control. Subsequently, the principle that acquisition of shares exceeding 25% amounts to negative control due to the ability to block a special resolution has been upheld in other cases as well.[47]

Thus, 'control' has a very wide ambit in competition law since negative control, which does not amount to control for the purposes of SEBI, requires notification to the CCI.

In *MSM India/SPE Holdings/SPE Mauritius*, the CCI has effectively concluded that the right to block special resolutions (by way of a more than 26% equity stake) amounts to 'negative control', which is 'control' for the purposes of the Competition Act.[48] In the said case, the acquirers collectively held 62% of equity shares in MSM India along with the right to nominate three directors on the Board. Grandway and Atlas, collectively, held 32.39% of equity shares and had the right to nominate two directors on the Board. The Shareholders Agreement provided that certain actions of MSM India could be undertaken only with the prior approval of the shareholders, representing 75% of the total shareholder interest. These actions included *certain strategic commercial decisions of MSM India* beyond *mere investor protection rights*, such as MSM India engaging in any new business or opening locations in cities other than Mumbai, Delhi, Bangalore and Chennai and the hiring or termination of the chief executive officer, chief financial officer, head of marketing, head of programming and general counsel or other counsel of MSM India or any other employee whose salary was

43. Caladium Investment Pte. Ltd. Combination Registration No. C-2015/01/243, 5 Mar. 2015.
44. Century Tokyo Leasing Corporation and Tata Capital Financial Services, Combination Registration No. C-2012/09/78, 4 Oct. 2012.
45. SPE Investments and SPE Holdings, Combination Registration No. C-2012/06/63, 9 Aug. 2012.
46. Canada Pension Plan Investment Board, Combination Registration No. C-2022/06/936, 15 Jul. 2022, paras 4, 5.
47. Section 43A Order against Telenor ASA, Telenor (India) Communications Private Limited and Telenor South Asia Investments Pte Limited, 3 Jul. 2018, para. 17.
48. SPE Investments and SPE Holdings, Combination Registration No. C-2012/06/63, 9 Aug. 2012 – This form of 'negative control' is considered to be 'control' within the meaning of the Competition Act. However, *Securities Appellate Tribunal (SAT) in SEBI v. Subhkam Ventures (I) Pvt Ltd.* (2011) has opined that such 'negative control' would not amount to control under SEBI's regime.

or was proposed to be greater than USD 30,000 per year and the material terms of the employment of such officers and material terms of employee benefit plans applicable to employees of MSM India. Further, MSM India could not undertake certain actions without the consent of both the Acquirers and Sellers, i.e., Grandway and Atlas. In other words, the Acquirers and Sellers had to agree with each other to make MSM India undertake certain actions in the Shareholders Agreement. Importantly, the collective shareholding of the sellers of 32.39% was sufficient to block/veto any action that required special resolution under the provisions of the Companies Act, 1956. Considering the collective shareholding and the rights of Grandway and Atlas pursuant to such shareholding (including those pursuant to the Shareholders Agreement), it was observed that the facts and circumstances of the case envisaged joint control by the Acquirers and Sellers over MSM India. The aspect of joint control has been discussed in more detail in the next section.

[C] Joint Versus Sole Control

The definition of control, as provided under the Competition Act, provides for both sole and joint control. Sole control exists when only one entity controls the target enterprise, i.e., only it can determine the *strategic commercial decisions* of the target enterprise. Such control can be exercised in cases where there is a majority shareholding held by one enterprise over the target enterprise or by a voting arrangement among the shareholders to evidence that only the enterprise has control over the target enterprise.

Joint control is deemed to exist in a situation when two enterprises exercise decisive influence over the target enterprise. Unlike sole control which confers a single entity to determine the strategic decisions in the target enterprise, joint control is characterized by the possibility of a deadlock situation resulting from the power of two or more enterprises to reject proposed strategic decisions. Joint control does not require two enterprises to have equal rights or equal degree of control in the other enterprise. A constraining presence on the decision-making process or affairs or management of an enterprise by a person suffices control.[49]

As also discussed above in the context of negative control, joint control existed with the sellers in the *MSM India* case since they had the ability to block special resolutions in MSM India. Therein, the CCI held that:[50]

> joint control over an enterprise implies control over the strategic commercial operations of the enterprise by two or more persons. In such a case, each of the persons in joint control would have the right to veto/block the strategic commercial decision(s) of the enterprise which could result in a dead lock situation [emphasis supplied]. Joint control over an enterprise may arise as a result of shareholding or through contractual arrangements between the shareholders. However, careful scrutiny is required to differentiate mere investor protection

49. Section 43A Order against Bharti Airtel Limited and Lion Meadow Investment Limited, 23 Aug. 2023, para. 40.
50. SPE Investments and SPE Holdings, Combination Registration No. C-2012/06/63, 9 Aug. 2012.

> rights from those rights which result in a situation of joint control. The assessment of joint control over an enterprise would depend on the facts and circumstances of each case with due consideration of relevant factors such as statutory and contractual rights of the shareholders.

The issue of control was also discussed in the *Jet/Etihad* case,[51] where the CCI opined the following based on the equity shareholding, presence of director of investors on board and the manner of future functioning of the target company after consummation of the transaction proposed by the parties to the combination:

> 14. In the instant case, both the Parties are engaged in the business of providing international air transportation services. The background of the IA pursuant to which 24 percent equity interest in Jet is proposed to be acquired categorically states that the Parties wish to enhance their airline business through a number of joint initiatives. In such a case, Etihad's acquisition of twenty-four (24) percent equity stake and the right to nominate two (2) directors, out of the six (6) shareholder directors, including the Vice Chairman, in the Board of Directors of Jet, is considered significant in terms of Etihad's ability to participate in the managerial affairs of Jet.
>
> 15. With a view to achieve the purported objective of enhancing their airline business through joint initiatives, the Parties have also entered into the CCA. Under the CCA, the Parties have *inter alia* agreed that: (A) they would frame co-operative procedure in relation to (i) joint route and schedule coordination; (ii) joint pricing; (iii) joint marketing, distribution, sales representation and cooperation; (iv) joint/reciprocal airport representation and handling; (v) joint/reciprocal technical handling and belly-hold cargo and dedicated freight capacity on services (into and out of Abu Dhabi and India and beyond); (B) the Parties intend to establish centres of excellence either in India or Abu Dhabi; (C) Etihad would recommend candidates for the senior management of Jet; (D) Jet would use Abu Dhabi as its exclusive hub for scheduled services to and from Africa, North and South America and UAE; and (E) Jet would refrain from entering into any code sharing agreement with any other airline that has the effect of: (i) bypassing Abu Dhabi as the hub for traffic to and from the above said locations, or (ii) is detrimental to the co-operation contemplated by the CCA.
>
> 16. It is observed that the Parties have entered into a composite combination comprising *inter alia* the IA, SHA and the CCA, with the common/ultimate objective of enhancing their airline business through joint initiatives. The effect of these agreements including the governance structure envisaged in the CCA establishes Etihad's joint control over Jet, more particularly over the assets and operations of Jet.

The key aspect to note herein is that the CCI did not only limit itself to look at the board or the shareholder composition to determine control but also analysed all the transaction agreements to understand whether the acquirer will have any strategic influence over the operations of the target company, post the acquisition. It was noted that apart from acquiring shares in Jet, Etihad will have its nominee directors on the board of Jet, and also, both Etihad and Jet will conduct their operations jointly, as elucidated in the CCA entered into between Jet and Etihad. Hence, the key ingredient

---

51. *Jet/Etihad case.*

of control is that the enterprise must show that it has the possibility to exercise influence on the target enterprise with respect to its '*strategic business decisions*'.

Therefore, exercise of control depends on a number of elements and all of these elements have to be assessed comprehensively. For instance, control may be exercised in the following ways: (i) through acquisition of majority shareholding or (ii) through contractually holding rights, including those rights mentioned in the vote sharing agreement, commercial cooperation and technology collaboration agreements, affirmative vote items contained in the investment agreements, shareholder's agreements, etc. Based on the above approach, the key aspect to be noticed is that the CCI analyses the facts and circumstances of each case, chooses substance over form approach and sees whether control has been acquired by an acquirer. However, purely investor protection rights awarded to financial investors may not be regarded as control.[52] A case-by-case analysis has to be seen even for investor protection rights to see whether such a bucket of rights provided to the investor would amount to control or not.

§4.07 CALCULATION OF ASSET VALUE

At the outset, it is relevant to mention that correctly calculating the turnover/assets of the parties is essential to determine whether the notification thresholds stipulated under the Competition Act and Combination Regulations are met.[53]

Asset value has been defined under Explanation (e) of section 5[54] of the Competition Act as:

> the value of assets shall be determined by taking the book value of the assets as shown, in the audited books of account of the enterprise, in the financial year immediately preceding the financial year in which the date of proposed merger falls and if such financial statement has not yet become due to be filed with the Registrar under the Companies Act, 2013 then as per the statutory auditor's report made on the basis of the last available audited accounts of the company in the financial year immediately preceding the financial year in which the notice is filed under sub-section (2) or sub-section (4) of section 6, as reduced by any depreciation, and the value of assets shall include the brand value, value of goodwill, or value of copyright, patent, permitted use, collective mark, registered proprietor, registered trade mark, registered user, homonymous geographical indication, geographical indications, design or layout- design or similar other commercial rights, if any, referred to in sub-section (5) of section 3.

Based on the definition, to calculate the asset value, one has to look at the book value of the assets as shown in the audited financial statements of the companies in the preceding year. The financial statements of a company will have a column on asset value, which includes both fixed and current assets.[55] Under the definition of asset

52. Aalok Dilip Shanghvi & Others, Combination Registration No. C-2015/03/254, 29 Apr. 2015.
53. Deli CMF, Combination Registration No. C-2019/02/640, 22 Mar. 2019.
54. Introduced via Competition (Amendment) Act, 2023.
55. For illustration, even if a company has hived off substantial assets during the course of the year and then entered into a transaction, the hived off assets will also become a part of the asset value for the purposes of section 5 of the Competition Act.

value under the Competition Act, only depreciation can be reduced from the asset value as shown in the balance sheet. There is no netting off of current liabilities or encumbrances or provisions or the like permitted under the Competition Act for calculation of the asset value.

A sample balance sheet of a company has been taken for illustration and described in the following table:

Particulars	*Value*
Assets	
Non-current assets	
- Fixed assets - Goodwill - Non-current investments - Deferred tax assets - Long-Term loans and advances	A B C D E
Gross non-current assets (GNCA)	
Depreciation	A + B + C + D + E F
Current assets	
- Current investments - Inventories - Trade receivables - Cash and bank balances - Short-term loans and advances - Other current assets	G H I J K L
Gross current assets (GCA)	G + H + I + J + K + L
Asset value for calculation under section 5 of the Competition Act	[GNCA + GCA] - F

The Competition Act does not provide for adjustments made in the calculation of an asset value, post the date of the annual audited books, to represent permanent changes in the economic reality of the concerned company.

For calculating asset value for a group, the consolidated financial statements of the preceding years are taken (as opposed to standalone financial statements). Use of such consolidated financial statements eliminates double counting which may arise when combining asset value from various standalone financial statements of enterprises falling with the same group.

§4.08 CALCULATION OF TURNOVER

The Competition (Amendment) Act, 2023 brings certainty to the term 'turnover' by defining it under explanation (c) of section 5 as meaning the turnover certified by the statutory auditor on the basis of the last available audited accounts of the company in the financial year immediately preceding the financial year in which notice is filed with the CCI. Specifically, such turnover shall exclude (i) intra-group sales, (ii) indirect taxes, (iii) trade discounts and (iv) all amounts generated through assets or business from customers outside India. It is pointed out that some of these exclusions, such as indirect taxes, income from ancillary operations, and intra-group sales, have already been clarified by the CCI through FAQs on its website. However, uncertainty still prevailed. Thus, the amendment consolidates the legal position by providing much-needed certainty to parties by specifying these exclusions in the Competition Act itself.

Further, it is also relevant to mention that any income generated from the securities held by a mutual fund company is considered turnover, irrespective of whether holding those securities confers control to the mutual fund company or not.[56]

§4.09 KEY ISSUES IN ACCOUNTING

The parties have to undertake an accounting assessment on their own to analyse whether the transaction crosses the threshold limits provided under the Competition Act. If yes, the parties will have to notify the CCI for approval unless the transaction qualifies for the *de minimis* exemption (as explained earlier in the chapter) or falls within one of the exemptions/exclusions mentioned under the Competition Act or Schedule I of the Combination Regulations (discussed subsequently).

There are certain key decisional accounting practices which have been followed by the CCI, in its merger approval decisions, which have to be borne in mind. The most pertinent is the approach regarding revenues from exports.

The CCI has clarified that even if an Indian enterprise derives turnover largely from exports, revenue figures provided in the consolidated financial statements of the Indian enterprise will be treated as '*Indian turnover*,' making the jurisdictional threshold applicable to it.[57] As long as an enterprise is located or registered in India and notes its global turnover in its Indian books of account, such turnover shall have to be taken into account for the purposes of calculating turnover threshold for the purpose of merger notification, even if they are derived from exported goods/services or those generated by other group companies which have a market presence outside India. This approach adopted by the CCI is likely to have an impact on industries, especially in the information technology, business process outsourcing and pharmaceutical sectors. In such industries, the revenues will primarily be export revenue. In this regard, the Indian approach differs substantially from the models prevailing in other jurisdictions. For illustration, in the EU, turnover for merger jurisdiction is computed based on the

56. Section 43A Order against Massachusetts Mutual Life Insurance Company, 7 Aug. 2023.
57. Mylan Inc., Combination Registration No. C-2013/04/116, 20 Jun. 2013.

allocated turnover which in turn depends on the geography where the service is provided and where the consumers are located. The Indian approach of calculating turnover, though simplistic in terms of accounts' maintenance, inevitably broadens the scope of coverage of the merger jurisdiction and may include notification of several transactions even when they have a negligible impact on competition *in India*. Further, there was an erstwhile exemption in Schedule I which gave the parties the option not to notify a combination which had an insignificant local nexus in India, which has hitherto been deleted. This implies that the jurisdiction of the CCI has been enlarged to cover purely offshore combinations. Although a pure offshore combination will be cleared by the CCI since such a transaction will not cause AAEC in India, nevertheless, a notification to the CCI for approval has to be made. Failure to file a notification will attract penalties, which are discussed in the subsequent parts of the chapter.

§4.10 OBLIGATION TO NOTIFY A COMBINATION

At the outset, it is relevant to mention that the rationale behind requiring notification of instances of acquisition of assets is that mergers and acquisitions may lead to a situation where economic advantages are conferred upon the parties involved, thereby giving them an ability to influence the competition dynamics of a market. Such economic benefits can be received by acquiring shares, voting rights or control of an enterprise or by acquiring assets of an enterprise, and there is no distinction between any of these in as much as they lead to economic advantages. Accordingly, acquisition of assets is required to be notified, just like acquisition of shares, voting rights and control. In doing so, two things are important:[58]

(i) the economic significance or competitive significance is the primary consideration behind requiring asset acquisitions to be notified for merger review purposes. For instance, in case of mergers and acquisitions in the telecom industry, spectrum is a resource which is a 'must have' as that is essential to provide telecommunication services.
(ii) whether the concerned asset constitutes a business or whether market turnover can be attributed to it. However, their absence does not diminish the economic significance of the asset on a standalone basis.

The Competition Act and the Combination Regulation provide for a mandatory suspensory regime. Section 6(2) of the Competition Act provides that a merger notification will have to be filed with the CCI for approval of an acquisition, merger or amalgamation which meets the threshold limits mentioned above. Further, section 6(2A) of the Competition Act provides that the combination will not come into effect until the earlier of: (i) 210 days[59] have passed from the date the merger control

58. Reliance Jio Infocomm Limited and Reliance Communications Limited, Combination Registration No. C-2017/06/516, 11 May 2018, paras 11-19; Bharti Airtel Limited and Bharti Hexacom Limited, Combination Registration No. C-2017/05/510, 11 May 2018, paras 18-24.
59. 210 days has been substituted for 150 days by the Competition (Amendment) Act, 2023 but the provision is yet to be notified.

notification was filed with the CCI or (ii) the CCI approves the combination under section 31 of the Competition Act.

From the above, it is apparent that a person or enterprise proposing to enter into a combination needs to give notice to the CCI unless the requirement has been dispensed with. After notice to the CCI, parties to the combination are required to observe a standstill obligation for 210 days from the date of notice to the CCI or the date of approval of the combination by the CCI, whichever is earlier.

In this backdrop, we will now discuss certain key procedural steps and issues, which need to be kept in mind while filing a notification with the CCI.

[A] Pre-filing Consultation

In accordance with international best practices, the CCI allows for informal and verbal consultation with its staff/case team prior to the filing of notice for a proposed combination in terms of section 6(2) of the Competition Act. Such pre-filing consultations (PFC) aim to help the parties identify the information required to file a correct and complete Form I/II/III.

The Draft Regulations have codified PFC from what used to be an informal mechanism by amending the law. However, the Draft Regulations reiterate the principle from CCI's decisional practice that the guidance provided through such PFC is not binding on the CCI. This means that if parties fail/make erroneous notification filing even after seeking PFC, then that is not a ground to absolve the parties from their error.

For instance, in the merger involving Akira Marketing Private Limited, Mama Catering Private Limited, Claridges Hospitality Private Limited and Azure Hospitality Private Limited,[60] the parties claimed that they became aware of CCI's opinion that the transaction was notifiable only after seeking a PFC and consequently, they filed a notice subsequent to their consultation. However, the CCI observed that the option for seeking PFC was always open to the parties. Thus, it can be concluded that the PFC is only a clarificatory mechanism made available to the parties to understand if their transaction is notifiable, but it does not dispense with the obligation to notify the CCI. Hence, seeking a PFC belatedly, i.e., after consummating a transaction, does not make the parties immune from the notification requirement.

[B] Responsibility to File the Merger Notification

As mentioned earlier, the Indian merger control regime is mandatory and suspensory in nature. This means that if a transaction meets the thresholds prescribed under section 5 of the Competition Act and is not exempt under the Combination Regulations or through government notifications such as the MCA circular, then it has to be

60. Akira Marketing Private Limited, Mama Catering Private Limited, Claridges Hospitality Private Limited and Azure Hospitality Private Limited, (Combination Registration No. C-2017/05/508, 24 Jan. 2018, paras 7-8.

mandatorily notified to the CCI. Further, the consummation of the transaction shall remain suspended, and there is an obligation on the parties to 'stand still' till the completion of 210 days from the date of notification or till CCI approves the combination.

Regulation 9 of the Combination Regulations provides that the obligation to file the merger notification with the CCI falls on the acquirer in case of acquisition of shares, control and assets.[61] In cases of a merger or an amalgamation, the obligation to notify is on both parties to the combination.[62] The obligation to file a notice has been illustrated below:

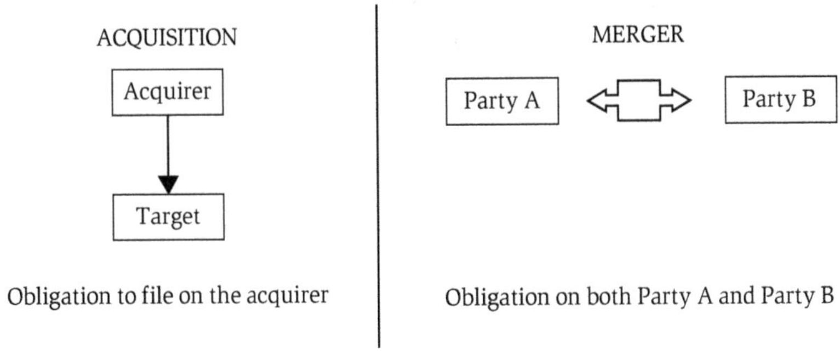

In section 43A proceedings against Zulia Investments Pte Limited and Kinder Investments Pte Limited,[63] the CCI had observed that '*it is expected that the parties must demonstrate a high sense of responsibility in filing combination notifications within the prescribed time limit, after effective and bonafide due diligence*'. This is especially important because section 20(1) of the Competition Act precludes the CCI from initiating any inquiry after the expiry of one year from the date on which a combination, which has not been notified, takes effect. Therefore, there is a real possibility in such situations that a combination which may actually cause AAEC, can end up escaping the scrutiny of the CCI if the mandatory notification is not filed. Even if notice is filed belatedly before the expiry of this one year, '*there could be problems in case the combination has been consummated, since restoring the original position may be as difficult as unscrambling an omelette.*'

In the acquisition by Twin Star Technologies Limited (Twin Star) of several companies in the Videocon Group, the notification was filed pursuant to a Resolution Plan submitted by Twin Star under the Corporate Insolvency Resolution Process of the target companies.[64] Twin Star was part of a group headed by Volcan Investments Limited (the acquirer group), and the competition analysis was undertaken on this

61. To be filed in Form I or Form II, as the case may and in accordance with Regulation 11 of the Combination Regulations.
62. *Ibid.*
63. Section 43A Order against Zulia Investments Pte. Ltd. and Kinder Investments Pte. Ltd., 1 Aug. 2013, paras 15, 16.
64. Twin Star Technologies Limited, Combination Registration No. C-2020/11/786, 8 Dec. 2020.

basis. At the time, Twin Star had submitted that the ultimate acquiring entity had not been finalized, so it was unclear who would actually be the eventual acquirer. In this regard, the CCI held that under the Combination Regulations, a proposed intimation of amendment of the notification to specify a different acquirer is not possible after the making of the order. This is because if the different acquiring entity was jointly controlled, this would require a competition analysis taking account of the joint controller not forming part of the acquirer group. In any case, the CCI clarified that notification by one enterprise and actual acquisition by another was not envisaged by the Combination Regulations, so the clearance order was limited to acquisition by Twin Star.

Thus, in effect, this means that any new acquirer, even if it is a part of the same transaction which has already been approved, would have to file a fresh notification since, depending on the identity and nature of the acquirer, it may be necessary to undertake a new and different competition analysis.

[1] Triggering Events

In case of acquisitions, the trigger for notifying the transaction to the CCI is the execution of any binding agreement or other such document for the acquisition of control/shares/voting rights/assets/control under section 5 of the Competition Act.

The aspect of '*binding document*' was first deliberated by the CCI in one of its decisions in 2012.[65] The proposed combination related to the acquisition of the Pantaloons Format Business of Pantaloon Retail (India) Limited by Aditya Birla Nuvo Limited (ABNL) through its wholly owned subsidiary Peter England Fashions and Retail Limited by way of a demerger and merger of Future Value Fashion Retail Limited into Peter England Fashions and Retail Limited, pursuant to a scheme of demerger and merger under sections 391-394 of the Companies Act, 1956 ('Scheme of Arrangement') ('*ABNL* case'). The parties had entered into a binding MOU. The MOU contemplated a series of other transactions to be consummated alongside the Scheme of Arrangement, including making a voluntary open offer in accordance with the Takeover Code. Further, a wholly owned subsidiary of ABNL would invest an amount of INR 800 crores in Pantaloon Retails India Limited by subscribing to optionally fully convertible debentures. The parties filed the merger notification with the CCI based on the binding MOU being signed between the parties. They were of the opinion that a binding MOU would constitute a binding document for the purposes of Regulation 5(8) of the Combination Regulations and, hence, will trigger the notification norms under the Competition Act and the Combination Regulations. At the time of the filing of the notice with the CCI, the terms of the Scheme of Arrangement were still under finalization and were yet to be approved by the Board of Directors of the parties. Further, at the stage of the execution of the binding MOU, certain key commercials, like the share entitlement ratio, were still under negotiation.

65. Aditya Birla Nuvo Retail and Ors., Combination Registration No. C-2012/07/69, 14 Aug. 2012.

The CCI rejected the merger approval notice filed by the parties as premature and held that signing the MOU (even though binding) cannot be the trigger for notification. The reason adopted by the CCI was that signing of the MOU was only the first step towards negotiations between the parties in relation to the finalization of the scheme, valuation, exact scope of the assets to be acquired, share entitlement ratio and also the approval of the same by the Board of Directors of the respective parties. It was noted by the CCI that the binding MOU is only an 'interim' arrangement and cannot be considered 'binding agreement' for the purposes of the trigger as the MOU will be terminated upon execution of the definitive agreement and the Scheme of Arrangement.

Further, Regulation 5(8) also provides that: (1) in cases where the acquisition is without the consent of the target enterprise, any document executed by the acquirer conveying a decision to acquire control, shares or voting rights shall be the 'other document,' and (2) where such a document has not been executed but the intention to acquire is communicated to a Statutory Authority, the date of such communication shall be deemed to be the date of execution of the other document for acquisition. It must be pointed out that Regulation 5(8) as mentioned above has undergone two sets of amendments: one on 3 July 2015 and a second amendment on 7 January 2016. Earlier, the Regulation 5(8) of the Combination read as:

> Provided further that where such a document has not been executed but the intention to acquire is communicated to the Central Government or State Government or a Statutory Authority, the date of such communication shall be deemed to be the date of execution of the other document for acquisition.

Post the amendment on 3 July 2015, the relevant part of Regulation 5(8) reads as:

> Provided further that where such a document has not been executed but the intention to acquire is communicated to the Central Government or State Government or a Statutory Authority, the date of such communication shall be deemed to be the date of execution of the other document for acquisition.

Prior to the amendment on 3 July 2015 in the Combination Regulations, the CCI also discussed the issue of binding document in 2014.[66] The proposed combination is related to the acquisition of 50% of the issued and paid-up equity share capital of Trent Hypermarket Limited (THL) by Tesco Overseas Investments Limited (TOIL). The notice was given by TOIL, pursuant to the execution of the Joint Venture Agreement and Share Purchase Agreement (SPA) between TOIL, THL and Trent Limited (Trent) on 21 March 2014.

TOIL had filed an application dated 17 December 2013 ('Application') and sought the approval of the DIPP, Ministry of Commerce & Industry and Foreign Investment and Promotion Board, Ministry of Finance (FIPB) for the acquisition of 50% of the issued and paid-up equity share capital of THL.

66. Trent Hypermarket Limited/Tesco Overseas Investments Limited, Combination Registration No. C-2014/03/162, 27 May 2014.

It was argued by TOIL that had they filed the merger notification for approval within thirty days of the Application, at such a preliminary stage, full details of the proposed combination would not have been available, and the notice would have been incomplete and without relevant and detailed information, necessary for a review by the CCI. Reference was made by TOIL to the *ABNL* case, discussed above. It was noted by TOIL that CCI had held in the ABNL case that merger notification was premature as the discussions with respect to the terms of the combination were still underway, being subject to definitive agreements. Hence, the preliminary document executed by the parties was an interim arrangement and did not trigger the requirement to file a merger control notification. The CCI, however, disagreed with the contention of TOIL. CCI made a difference between *ABNL* case and this case and noted that the *ABNL* case involved a scheme of merger/demerger and did not involve intimation of such proposal to the Central Government or State Government or any Statutory Authority. Thus, CCI noted that TOIL was required to give notice to it within thirty days of its application to the DIPP and the FIPB, i.e., by 16 January 2014. However, the notice was given by TOIL on 31 March 2014, with a delay of around seventy-three days.

The second set of amendments came on 7 January 2016 which added a proviso to Regulation 5(8) of the Combination Regulations which states that a public announcement has been made in terms of Takeover Code for acquisition of shares, voting rights or control, such public announcement shall be deemed to be the 'other document'. Hence, that other document would only mean public announcements made to SEBI in terms of the Takeover Code. Thus, together with the amendment on 3 July 2015, the amendment on 7 January 2016 has now further provided that the communication with a Statutory Authority is no longer a trigger to filing a combination notice with the CCI.

Pursuant to the Competition (Amendment) Act, 2023, 'other document' is now defined in the explanation of section 6 of the Competition Act and has been removed from Regulation 5 under the Draft Regulations. This is *pari materia* to the amendment of 7 January 2016, as discussed above, and formalizes the legal position in the Competition Act itself that where acquisition is without the consent of the target, the public announcement made to the SEBI under the Takeover Code shall be the trigger for notification to CCI.

The latest position on trigger documents can be seen from the following cases – on the point of what constitutes a binding document for the purpose of notification. The CCI penalized an acquirer, Baxalta Incorporated (Baxalta), under section 43A of the Competition Act for failure to file notice.[67] In this case, the notice was filed by Baxalta within thirty days of signing a Global Separation and Distribution Agreement (GSDA) for the transfer of Baxter's Indian bioscience business and related assets (target business) to a newly created wholly owned subsidiary of Baxter, viz. Baxalta Bio-Science (India) Private Limited (Baxalta India) after taking a PFC from the CCI. Thereafter, the ownership and control of Baxalta India was to be transferred to Baxalta (implementation of the India leg of the combination). Baxalta did not file a notice prior to the PFC because notification because the India leg of the transaction was to be

67. Section 43A Order against Baxalta Incorporated, 8 Mar. 2016, para. 10.3-10.6.

effected through a separate local implementation agreement. In this regard, the CCI held that the GSDA was the binding document executed between Baxter and Baxalta, which satisfied section 6(2) of the Competition Act. Thus, the argument of the acquirer that the trigger event for the merger notification in India would be the local implementation agreement for the India Separation was not valid. The CCI further reasoned that if the parties to the combination notify the combination only upon the execution of a local agreement and not after execution of the global agreement, in spite of meeting jurisdictional thresholds prescribed under section 5 of the Competition Act, then there is the possibility that the combination would be consummated at the global level even before the CCI has assessed the same (as had happened in the instant case). In such a situation, the independent market behaviour of the parties to the combination has already ceased even before the CCI carried out its assessment of the combination, which would defeat the purpose of the suspensory regime of regulation of combinations.

Thus, the position is that the obligation to notify a transaction to the CCI arises upon the execution of the global agreement itself and not the local agreement pursuant to the transaction, if the former is executed prior.[68] Hence, the global agreement is the trigger for notification of the combination.

Further, in case of interconnected transactions, the notification requirement is triggered upon the execution of the first binding document. This was clarified in section 43A proceedings initiated against Cairnhill CIPEF Limited and Cairnhill CGPE Limited in their acquisition of 11% equity shares in Mankind Pharma Limited (target).[69] This is pursuant to the principle of interconnected transactions (as discussed subsequently in this chapter) as given under Regulation 9(4) of the Combination Regulations which provides that '*where the ultimate intended effect of a business is achieved by way of a series of steps or smaller individual transactions which are inter-connected, one or more of which may amount to a combination, a single notice, covering all these transactions, shall be filed by the parties to the combination*'.

In this regard, in its decisional practice, the CCI has also observed that an interconnected part of the combination cannot escape notification on the technical pretext that binding agreement has not been entered into for such inter-connected transaction. If one agrees otherwise, then notification of a connected transaction can be avoided by just postponing the execution of the binding document for the interconnected part.[70]

Thus, while it is true that the notification requirement commences upon the execution of the first binding document and not necessarily the first document, in case of interconnected transactions, since the steps to the transaction are interdependent upon each other to achieve a single, final objective – the obligation to notify is triggered

68. Section 43A Order against Schulke & Mayr GmbH, 13 Jan. 2017, para. 8.3.
69. Section 43A Order against Cairnhill CIPEF Limited and Cairnhill CGPE Limited, 13 Apr. 2017, paras 4-8.
70. Section 43A Order against Canada Pension Plan Investment Board and ReNew Power Limited, 21 Nov. 2019, para. 18.

upon the execution of the first relevant agreement in such series of interconnected transactions.

In this regard, it is apposite to note the findings of the CCI in the proposed acquisition of shares of Telewings Communications Services Private Limited (Telenor India) by Lakshdeep Investments & Finance Private Limited (Lakshdeep). The transaction involved four steps for which a combined notice was filed pursuant to the execution of a Share Subscription and Shareholders' Agreement (SSHA) between Telenor South Asia Investment Pte Limited (Telenor South Asia), an indirect wholly owned subsidiary of Telenor ASA (Telenor, the ultimate holding company of Telenor Group), Lakshdeep and Telenor India.[71] Essentially, (i) Telenor India was to acquire 2G spectrum and requisite licenses for telecommunication operations in India, then (ii) Lakshdeep was to acquire 51% shares in Telenor India followed by (iii) acquisition of Unitech Wireless (Tamil Nadu) Private Limited's business on a going concern basis by Telenor India and finally, (iv) after the approval of FIPB, Telenor was to increase its shareholding in Telenor India to 74% by purchasing shares from Lakshdeep, leaving the latter with 26% share in Telenor India. Despite different parties acting as acquirers in the entire transaction, only Lakshdeep filed a notice before the CCI as the acquirer in step (ii). The CCI held that in terms of Regulation 9(1) and Regulation 9(3) of the Combination Regulations respectively, in case of an acquisition or acquiring of control of enterprise(s), the acquirer is required to file the notice and in case of a merger or an amalgamation, parties to the combination are required to jointly file the notice, accordingly, for inter-connected transactions, all the acquirers/parties are required to jointly file the notice. Lakshdeep could not have raised the issue on steps (iii) and (iv) which could have been raised only by Telenor India separately. In order to subject the entire transaction for assessment in terms of Regulation 9(4), the notice must have been filed by all the concerned parties together. Thus, the fact that all the four steps were disclosed did not absolve the parties of their respective obligations to file separate notices or to file a composite notice jointly by each of the relevant parties. This is because the competition assessment of the entire transaction, i.e., including all the parties, has to be undertaken together to assess the impact on the market. Therefore, the takeaway is that parties cannot absolve themselves of their responsibility to file a notice merely because another party has filed a notice for the same transaction(s) unless such notice is jointly filed.

One of the only few cases where penalty was not imposed under section 43A was when Sundaram Finance Limited (SFL) filed an application to Reserve Bank of India (RBI) seeking its approval to increase its stake in Royal Sundaram (target) from 49.9% to 75.9% on a unilateral basis without the prior knowledge or consent of the selling shareholder (RSA) or the target.[72] The application neither contained any details about the contemplated acquisition nor any authorization in the form of a board resolution or otherwise. The issue was whether the communication of the intention to acquire to a statutory authority triggered a notice under section 6(2) of the Competition Act. The

71. Section 43A Order against Telenor ASA, Telenor (India) Communications Private Limited and Telenor South Asia Investments Pte Limited, 3 Jul. 2018, para. 21.
72. Section 43A Order against Sundaram Finance Limited, 12 Jul. 2016, paras 4-9.

CCI observed that the application filed to the RBI could not be termed as a binding document triggering notification. Regulation 31(b) of the Combination Regulations stipulates that the trigger for notification is the date of execution of any agreement or other binding document for acquisition. In the present case, the application to RBI did not reflect any intention or understanding whatsoever between the parties towards the acquisition. Rather, it was merely an application by SFL to seek permission to be put on the same level field as other potential buyers of the shares from the RSA so that it was not handicapped from making an offer, should the opportunity present itself since NBFCs like SFL require prior permission of the RBI to have higher equity in an insurance venture. Thus, the application to RBI was neither an agreement for acquisition nor a binding document for acquisition. Consequently, it was held that SFL was not required to give notice within thirty days of its application to the RBI.

Therefore, the crux of the responsibility to file a notification is that it is triggered when the first binding document is executed between the parties, except in cases of interconnected transactions wherein the first step of the combination becomes the trigger point for notifying the combination.

[C] Single Notice in Case of an Interconnected Transaction

As discussed briefly in the previous section, Regulation 9(4) of the Combination Regulations provides that the parties can file a single notice in case of multiple business transactions which are interrelated and interconnected to each other.

The parties to the combination have to analyse whether the transactions are interdependent or interconnected to each other by analysing the 'economic realities' of the transaction. In the event that the multiple transactions have a condition that none of the transactions would take place without the other, such multiple transactions can be said to be inter-connected or inter-dependent.

In this regard, it is apt to note CCI's Order with respect to the merger approval notice given by Relay B.V., an indirect wholly owned subsidiary of Diageo Plc. (Diageo) (Both Relay B.V. and Diageo are jointly referred to as the 'Acquirer'), and United Spirits Limited (USL),[73] for the proposed acquisition of shares and control of USL.

The transaction postulated the following situations:

(1) Relay B.V. agreed to subscribe to the new equity shares of USL ('preferential shares'), representing 10% of USL's post-issue enlarged share capital, by way of preferential allotment, on terms and subject to the conditions as provided in the Preferential Allotment Agreement (PAA).
(2) Further, Relay B.V. agreed to purchase equity shares of USL from certain existing shareholders of USL, including United Breweries (Holdings) Limited (UBHL) and Kingfisher Finvest India Limited (KFinvest), by entering into a

73. United Spirits Limited by Relay B.V. (Diageo), Combination Registration No. C-2012/12/97, 26 Feb. 2013.

SPA, amounting to around 17.4% of USL's enlarged share capital (i.e., sale shares). Further, the merger notice provided that as per the terms of the SPA, in certain circumstances, where: (i) the preferential allotment is not completed, and (ii) Relay B.V. holds less than 25.1% of the equity shares in USL after taking into account the sale shares acquired under the SPA, the shares acquired pursuant to the mandatory open offer under the Takeover Code or the shares acquired in any other manner, then UBHL and KFinvest will sell and Relay B.V. will acquire, such number of additional equity shares in USL which will take Relay B.V.'s shareholding in USL to 25.1%. Such number of shares of USL which UBHL and KFinvest would require to sell to Relay B.V., under the aforesaid conditions, was termed as 'additional shares'. In this regard, it has also been stated that if the preferential shares representing 10% of USL's post-issue enlarged capital are subscribed to by Relay B.V., then no additional shares would be required to be sold to Relay B. V.

(3) The execution of the SPA and the PAA triggered an obligation on the part of Relay B.V. to make a mandatory tender offer to the public shareholders of USL under the Takeover Code. Accordingly, on 9 November 2012, Relay B.V. announced its intention to launch a mandatory tender offer under the Takeover Code (MTO) to acquire the equity shares from the public shareholders of USL which represent up to a maximum of 26% of USL's enlarged share capital (i.e., the offer shares). It was stated in the notice that on acquisition of the sale shares, preferential shares and the offer shares (if the MTO is fully subscribed), Relay B.V. would hold 53.4% of the USL's enlarged equity share capital.

(4) Further, the agreements provided that Relay B.V., or an affiliate of Relay B.V., may also, at any time and from time to time, acquire other shares in USL in order to obtain an aggregate shareholding of at least 50.1% of USL's equity share capital (i.e., the other shares). It was provided under the Shareholders Agreement (SHA) that if either of UBHL or KFinvest, or any of their controlled affiliates, transfer all or part of their shares in USL to any third party, it shall first offer such shares exclusively to Relay B.V. On receipt of such an offer, Relay B.V. would have the right to elect to acquire all or, in some cases, part of such offered shares (i.e., the ROFO shares) by giving a notice to UBHL or KFinvest, or as the case may be, within a specified period, in terms of the SHA.

The CCI, based on the market structure, gave a blanket approval for a period of five years to the Acquirer to acquire shares of up to 53.4% USL. From a competition law analysis, the CCI viewed the entire transaction as interrelated and undertook the competition law analysis based on the entire transaction.

The scope of Regulation 9(4) of the Combination Regulations, where the parties have the liberty to file a single notice in relation to inter-connected or inter-dependent transactions, was discussed in a decision by the erstwhile COMPAT in the case of

Thomas Cook (India) Ltd. & Ors. v. CCI.[74] erstwhile COMPAT overturned the penalty imposed by the CCI on parties (Thomas Cook India (TCIL), its subsidiary (TCISIL) and Sterling Holiday Resort (SHRIL)) operating in the travel and hotel related services in and from India. The parties had entered into a composite two-step scheme of demerger of SHRIL wherein its shares would be transferred to TCISIL, followed by the amalgamation of its remaining business into TCIL and issuing of certain equity shares of TCIL to SHRIL's shareholders. The penalty was imposed on account of failure to furnish information and consummation of certain market purchases wherein transfer of equity shares of SHRIL by TCISIL was made. The transaction has been described in the following diagram:

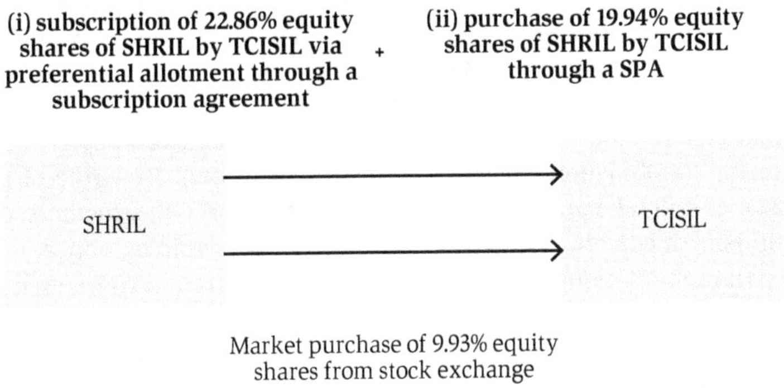

Notes to the diagram:
i. The obligation to make an open offer under Takeover Code was triggered pursuant to steps (i) and (ii) above. This can be considered step (iii).
ii. The above transactions were in lieu of the demerger/amalgamation.
iii. TCISIL notified the equity shares purchased via the SPA and preferential allotment through the subscription agreement under steps (i) and (ii) but did not notify the market purchase prior to its consummation.

On the one hand, the parties maintained the plea that market purchases had nothing to do with the demerger/amalgamation scheme, and more so because it was an exempted transaction because of the MCA Circular; the CCI, on the other hand, concluded that market purchases were intrinsically connected with the two-stage scheme and was thus required to be notified under section 6(2) of the Competition Act.

It must be borne in mind that the two-stage scheme and market purchases were authorized in the same meeting, followed by a joint press release. It also remained an agreed fact that the market purchases were entitled to an exemption under the MCA Circular, as agreed by the CCI as well. However, the CCI declined to give the benefit of this exemption to the parties mainly on the grounds that the market purchases were intrinsically connected with other transactions. The erstwhile COMPAT criticized this

74. *Thomas Cook (India) Limited & Ors v. Competition Commission of India* [2015], (COMPAT) Appeal No. 48 of 2014.

approach of the CCI and stated that the latter failed to take cognizance of the fact that the implementation of the two-stage scheme for demerger/amalgamation was not dependent on the market purchase of equity shares of SHRIL. Therefore, the mere fact that various transactions were executed in close proximity to the market purchases of the equity shares of SHRIL by TCISIL would not be sufficient to deny the benefit of the MCA exemption notification to the parties. Further, the erstwhile COMPAT went on to interpret the scope of the exemption in the context of Regulation 9(4) of the Combination Regulations and concluded that the notification is not riddled with any condition. Therefore, if the transaction involving market purchases of equity shares of SHRIL was covered under the exemption notification, the same was not required to be notified under section 6(2) of the Competition Act. It also noted the good faith of the parties who disclosed each and every transaction, including the market purchase of equity shares at the time of notification, even though separate or composite notice was not filed in relation to the market purchases.

Though not discussed in the decision of the erstwhile COMPAT, it must be borne in mind that post the order of the CCI in the *Thomas Cook* case, Regulation 9(5) was inserted in the Combinations Regulation (discussed below). By virtue of Regulation 9(5), substance will take precedence over form and transaction structures, or transactions comprising a combination which has the effect of avoiding notice in respect of whole or part of the combination would be disregarded and still considered notifiable. As a result, a takeaway for companies from the Thomas Cook decisions and Regulation 9(5) of the Combination Regulations would be to avail maximum benefits of various exemptions under the framework of the statute and notifications even in case of inter-connected transactions where a composite notice is being filed. However, if the sole purpose of such structuring, especially by way of performing an inter-connected transaction, is to evade notice, the same may be penalized for non-notification.

Subsequently, the Supreme Court also reiterated CCI's findings.[75] It recognized that although the market purchases were not mentioned in the other transaction documents, they were consummated only after almost finalizing the composite combination. This clearly suggested that market purchases would not have taken place in the absence of the demerger scheme and the other acquisitions. When a series of transactions is envisaged to accomplish a combination, all the transactions have to be taken into consideration by the CCI, not an isolated transaction. While it is open for the parties to structure their transactions in a particular way, the substance of the transactions would be more relevant to assess the effect on competition irrespective of whether such transactions are pursued through one or more steps/transactions. Structuring of transactions cannot be permitted in such a manner so as to avoid compliance with the mandatory provisions of the Competition Act. Further, Regulation 9(4) envisages the possibility that a business transaction may be achieved by a combination of inter-connected or inter-dependent steps/transactions. Thus, since market purchases were not independent and could not be used in isolation for the

75. *Competition Commission of India v. Thomas Cook (India) Ltd. & Anr.* [2018], (SC) Civil Appeal No. 13578 of 2015, paras 27-31.

purpose of any exemption, a single composite notice had to be filed for the combination. As a result, the Supreme Court held that the market purchases did not qualify as a combination in view of the target exemption notification.

Therefore, the implication of the collective decisions above ('*Thomas Cook* case') is that parties may avail of the exemption notification even in case of an inter-connected transaction where a composite notice is filed. Furthermore, the test of inter-connected transaction is the dependence of one transaction on the other. What is key is the substance of the transaction, which should not be structured to achieve the effect of avoiding notice for the whole or part of the combination. Thus, the applicability of the exemption is determined by the entire composite combination together.

The above-discussed understanding of Regulation 9(5) has also been affirmed by CCI in its decisional practice. A landmark case where CCI heavily penalized the failure to disclose inter-connected transactions was Amazon's failure to notify the details of a shareholders' agreement requiring Amazon's prior written consent for Future Coupons Private Limited (FCPL) to decide any matter relating to FRL, as part of Amazon's acquisition of FCPL. On a holistic appreciation of the facts, it was found that the commercial agreement and acquisition of shares in FCPL to secure shareholding and rights over FRL had been inter-connected to each other and were conceived, contemplated, negotiated and consummated as part of one composite combination (i.e., to ultimately acquire certain rights over FRL).[76] Therefore, Amazon failed to give a single notice covering all the inter-connected steps of the combination, as required in Regulation 9(4), read with Regulations 9(5) of the Combination Regulations and section 6(2) of the Competition Act. This has been discussed in more detail under the heading on failure to furnish material information.

Another limb to determining the interconnected nature of transactions comes by way of the European Commission's Consolidated Jurisdictional Notice, which provides that '*If two or more transactions (each of them bringing about an acquisition of control) take place within a two-year period between the same persons or undertakings, they shall be qualified as a single concentration, irrespective of whether or not those transactions relate to parts of the same business or concern the same sector ... It is sufficient if the transactions, although not carried out between the same companies, are carried out between companies belonging to the same respective groups*'. This approach, that multiple acquisitions between the same enterprises within a two-year period would be considered inter-related transactions, has also been affirmed by the CCI.[77]

In an interesting first, the CCI penalized CPPIB together under both section 43A and section 44 of the Competition Act because while it notified the first acquisition in ReNew (Transaction I), it did not notify ReNew's acquisition of Ostro which was another energy company (Transaction II).[78] This order is consistent with its decisional practice of mandating a single, composite notification in case of inter-connected

76. Sections 43A, 44 and 45 Order against Amazon.com NV Investment Holdings LLC, 14 Dec. 2021, paras 52-67.
77. Section 43A Order against Piramal Enterprises Limited, 2 May 2016, para. 7.
78. Section 43A Order against Canada Pension Plan Investment Board and ReNew Power Limited, 21 Nov. 2019, paras 12.6, 18 and 27.

transactions.[79] The primary question to determine the inter-connectedness of Transactions I and II was whether the Primary Acquisition in Transaction I was pursued to support Ostro Acquisition. The CCI relied on the observations of the Supreme Court in the *Thomas Cook* case that the guiding factor for determining the scope of notification to CCI would be the substance of a combination and technical interpretations to isolate two different steps of transactions of a composite combination would be against the spirit and provisions of the Competition Act. Consequently, no part of a composite combination can be seen in isolation for the purpose of any exemption, as also clarified by the Supreme Court in the *Thomas Cook* case. In concluding that the transactions were inter-connected, the CCI went beyond the transaction documents and scrutinized the press releases issued by the parties as well as internal documents such as e-mail correspondence between the parties.

Thus, this order highlights the need for parties to maintain consistency in their internal and external communication with respect to past, current and future transactions that might be inter-connected with the proposed transaction to ensure that there is complete disclosure, inclusive of any potential intent in the future, at the time of notifying the proposed transaction. In such cases, a single, composite notice of all the interconnected transactions must be filed.

[D] Substance over Form

Regulation 9(5) of the Combination Regulations clarifies that the requirement for the filing of a merger notification will be determined by the substance/intent of the transaction. It provides:

> The requirement of filing notice under regulation 5 of these regulations shall be determined with respect to the substance of the transaction and any structure of the transaction(s), comprising a combination, that has the effect of avoiding notice in respect of the whole or a part of the combination shall be disregarded.

The form of the transaction is rendered moot with respect to filing the merger notification. Regulation 9(5) seeks to ensure that the parties to a combination do not avoid the mandatory CCI filing by adopting innovative structuring to their transactions. It is akin to piercing the veil and analysing the actual substance of the transaction to see whether the transaction in itself would require the approval of the CCI.

Read together with the aspect of filing a single notice for an inter-related transaction, it becomes clear that as long as the proposed combination exceeds the applicable thresholds and does not qualify for any of the exemptions mentioned under the Competition Act and the Combination Regulations, the parties will need to take prior approval from the CCI, before consummating the transaction. So, there may be situations where there are a number of intermediate transactions which are consummated by the parties which may not be notifiable, but if the entire set of transactions is

79. Section 43A Order against Telenor ASA, Telenor (India) Communications Private Limited and Telenor South Asia Investments Pte Limited, 3 Jul. 2018; Section 43A Order against Bharti Airtel Limited and Lion Meadow Investment Limited, 23 Aug. 2023.

viewed as one composite transaction, such transaction will be notifiable. In such cases, the CCI will disregard multiple transactions and mandate the parties to file the merger control notification. While such an interpretation is adopted by the CCI to regard substance over form, the trigger date becomes an issue. To exercise abundant caution, it is better to file for notification before the CCI prior to consummating the first series of transactions.

[E] Form of Filing

Regulation 5(2) provides that generally the parties to the combination will file Form I (a short form) as specified in the Combination Regulations. However, Regulation 5(3) of the Combination Regulations provides that parties may, at the discretion, file Form II (a detailed lengthy form) preferably in cases where: (i) the parties to the combination are engaged in production, supply, distribution, storage, sale or trade of similar or identical or substitutable goods or provision of similar or identical or substitutable services and the combined market share of the parties to the combination after such combination is more than 15% in the relevant market or (ii) the parties to the combination are engaged at different stages or levels of the production chain in different markets, in respect of production, supply, distribution, storage, sale or trade in goods or provision of services, and their individual or combined market share is more than 25% in the relevant market. Further, in cases where the parties to the combination have filed notice in Form I and the CCI requires information in Form II to form its prima facie opinion whether the combination is likely to cause or has caused AAEC within the relevant market in India, it shall direct the parties to the combination to file notice in Form II (the lengthy form).

[F] Green Channel

Vide notification dated 13 August 2019, the CCI amended the Combination Regulations and introduced an automatic system of approval for combinations through a 'Green Channel' route. Under this process, subject to certain safeguards, combinations would be deemed to be approved where the criteria prescribed under Schedule III of the Combination Regulations are satisfied, i.e., where parties have no horizontal overlaps, no vertical relationships and no complementary businesses. The objective of the green channel is to facilitate faster clearance of the combinations that do not have such overlaps. The green channel is essentially a trust based system created by the CCI that in case the parties affirm that there is no overlap between the parties, then the form can be filed under the green channel route.

For availing the green channel benefit, the pertinent question that should be asked is whether the parties to the transaction, their respective group entities and/or any entity in which they, directly or indirectly, hold shares and/or control, exhibit horizontal overlap, vertical overlaps or complementarity, considering all plausible alternative market definitions. If the answer to the question is yes, then the transaction cannot avail the benefit of the green channel approval facility.[80]

Under the green channel approval facility, a proposed combination is deemed to have been approved by the CCI under section 31(1) of the Competition Act upon filing of a notice under Regulation 5A(1) of the Combination Regulations and acknowledgement thereof. The green channel approval facility does not envisage a detailed assessment of the likely effect of a combination on competition in India that is otherwise undertaken for all other combinations. If any overlap exists between the parties to the combination, their respective group entities and/or any entity in which they, directly or indirectly, hold shares and/or control, then the case requires a detailed assessment of the likely effect of the combination on competition in India and accordingly is not eligible for the benefit of the green channel approval facility.

Further, the first proviso to Regulations 5A(2) of the Combination Regulations provides that where the CCI finds that the combination does not fall under Schedule III and/or the declaration filed pursuant to sub-regulation (1) is incorrect, the notice given and the approval granted under this regulation shall be void ab initio and the CCI shall deal with the combination in accordance with the provisions contained in the Competition Act. This means that if an incorrect green channel notice has been filed, then a penalty can be imposed by CCI if the transaction has already been consummated.[81]

The green channel facility rests on a trust-based mechanism based on self-assessment and correct declaration. Thus, it is incumbent upon the person seeking to avail this route to it is incumbent upon the person choosing to avail the green channel approval facility to observe *uberrima fides* (utmost good faith) in availing the same and should subject only the eligible combinations for this channel. Needless to say, any deviation from the prescribed eligibility criteria or misuse of this privilege constitutes a breach of trust, warranting repercussions. Accordingly, the CCI has started penalizing enterprises for abusing the green channel route.[82]

The Competition (Amendment) Act has formalized the green channel route by introducing it within the Competition Act. This is a positive step as it provides formal recognition of the green channel route, which has become a popular mechanism to notify non-problematic transactions, i.e., transactions that are unlikely to cause AAEC due to the absence of horizontal overlaps, vertical or complementary relationships – in a hassle-free and less cumbersome manner than through normal filing procedure.

§4.11 PENALTY FOR NON-FILING

The Competition Act read with the attendant Combination Regulations provides for a mandatory notification of the transaction to the CCI. The Competition Act provides for a suspensory regime; i.e., the parties cannot consummate a combination (for which

80. Section 43A Order against Platinum Jasmine A 2018, 18 Aug. 2023, paras 27-29.
81. Section 43A Order against Platinum Jasmine A 2018, 18 Aug. 2023, para. 31.
82. Section 43A Order against Platinum Jasmine A 2018, 18 Aug. 2023, para. 38.

approval of the CCI is required) without obtaining the approval of the CCI. The penalty exposure for non-notification of a combination or consummation of the combination without obtaining the approval of the CCI is huge and exposes the parties to a penalty which may be up to 1% of the total turnover or assets or the value of the transaction, whichever is higher, of such a combination.

Further, an approval of a combination under section 31 neither obliterates nor condones the contravention, for which a penalty is to be imposed under section 43A of the Competition Act. The proceedings under both provisions operate in two different fields.[83] This is why, to date, although several orders have been passed under section 43A of the Competition Act,[84] not a single combination has been denied approval on filing the correct notice. This highlights that CCI's objective is not to affect the commercial freedom of parties to enter into combinations in furtherance of their business interest but only to ensure that the exercise of such freedom does not distort competition since if combinations are not appropriately notified, they are likely to escape CCI's scrutiny and if consummated, may cause irreversible harm to the market.

For instance, in its acquisition of stake in CSC e-Governance Services India Limited, Axis Bank did not file a notice to the CCI on the premise that it had made a bona fide error in assessing the applicability of the *de minimis exemption* due to incorrect calculation of turnover.[85] However, the CCI held that it is immaterial whether failure to give notice under section 6(2) of the Competition Act was '*bona fide or mala fide; or it was inadvertent or intentional*'. In this case, both the assets and turnover of CSC e-Governance were higher than the threshold prescribed in the *de minimis* exemption. Thus, even if an error was made in assessing the applicability of the *de minimis* exemption, that did not negate the fact that the transaction was not eligible for the exemption in the first place. The CCI held that the argument of error was not a relevant argument for determining whether section 43A of the Competition Act gets attracted or not.[86]

Hence, the position emerges that parties cannot claim to be absolved of their duty to notify a transaction under the Competition Act merely on the grounds of an error. Even after a penalty has been levied for non-filing of notice under section 43A, there is an obligation to notify the concerned combination section 6(2) of the Competition Act.

[A] Gun Jumping

'Jumping the gun' (or 'gun-jumping') refers to the practice of consummating a transaction before receiving the statutory clearance from the relevant competition regulator or illegal coordination between the merging parties prior to closing. CCI in its decisional practice has imposed a penalty upon the parties for jumping the gun under

83. *SCM Soilfert and Deepak Fertilizers and Petrochemicals v. Competition Commission of India* [2016], (COMPAT) Appeal No. 59 of 2015; Section 43A Order against Intellect Design Arena Limited, 7 May 2018, para. 10.2.
84. Section 43A Order against Clariant Chemicals India Limited, 16 Aug. 2016, para. 7.
85. Section 43A Order against Axis Bank Limited, 9 Aug. 2023.
86. *Ibid.*, paras 20, 21.

section 43A of the Competition Act since India follows a mandatory and suspensory merger control regime.

The basic objective of standstill obligations contained in section 6(2A) of the Competition Act is to ensure that the parties to a combination transaction compete as they were competing before the initiation of the combination process till the time the transaction is reviewed for any AAEC and is approved by the CCI. Hence, the standstill obligations essentially require that the parties maintain the independence and autonomy of the target in the interim stage between notifying and approval of the combination. Accordingly, the basis of examination of a gun-jumping contravention is whether the parties have ceased to compete as they were competing earlier or whether they have ceased to act independently.[87]

While a notional date may be indeed required to ensure certainty in respect of the valuation of a business and further to ensure that the value of the business is preserved, the acquirer of a business may also be permitted to impose customary standstill and interim arrangements on the target. The CCI has clarified that it is incumbent on the acquirer to ensure that the form and scope of the aforesaid customary arrangements imposed by it on the target is inherent and proportionate to the objective of ensuring certainty in business valuation and preservation of the same (inherence proportionality test).[88] As laid down in section 43 A, proceedings against Bharti Airtel ('*Airtel* decision') (discussed in more detail in the next section), the inherence proportionality test seeks to balance the concerns of any potential competition distortions. It is only fair that the onus to prove and ensure that the action/agreement under review is inherent and proportionate to the legitimate business objectives, such as ensuring the preservation of economic valuation, is on the parties to a combination.

Based on the above decisional practice of the CCI, it is imperative that enterprises do not fall foul of the merger control norms and indulge in gun-jumping. The CCI acknowledged that certain exchanges of information between parties are inherent to the very process of mergers and acquisitions; however, this legitimate objective of the parties can raise gun-jumping concerns.

Earlier, procedural gun-jumping was a ground for penalizing parties, i.e., where notice was not filed before the CCI within thirty days of execution of a binding document pursuant to section 6(2) of the Competition Act. However, procedural gun-jumping is no longer a ground for violation by way of exemption granted by the Central Government to parties from filing a prior notification to the CCI within a mandatory period of thirty days.[89] Thus, now the principal ground for penalizing parties for gun-jumping is a case of substantive gun-jumping wherein it entails an improper pre-closing integration of the parties to a transaction, for example, sharing of commercially sensitive information, allocating customers, and undertaking joint marketing efforts during the waiting period.

87. Section 43A Order against Bharti Airtel Limited, 27 Aug. 2018, para. 8; *UltraTech* case, para. 13.5.
88. Section 43A Order against Bharti Airtel Limited, 27 Aug. 2018, paras 10, 36.
89. MCA Notification S.0. 2039(E), published in Gazette dated 29 Jun. 2017.

The first seminal case of substantive gun-jumping was found by the CCI in the *Jet/Etihad* case.[90] Etihad, the acquirer, on 1 May 2013, had notified CCI of its proposed acquisition of a 24% equity stake in Jet Airways. The transaction was approved by CCI on 12 November 2013. However, by a separate order under section 43A of the Competition Act, the CCI observed that: (i) certain provisions of the CCA entered into between Etihad and Jet had already been implemented prior to obtaining the approval of the CCI; and (ii) sale of certain landing/take-off slots of Jet at the London Heathrow Airport (LHR Transaction), had not been notified to the CCI for approval and the transaction of sale and lease back of airport slots had been completed. Based on the same, CCI levied a penalty of INR 10 million on Etihad for gun-jumping.

In another case, the CCI received a merger notification from Zuari Fertilisers and Chemicals Limited (ZFCL) and Zuari Agro Chemicals Limited (ZACL) (collectively referred to as the Acquirers) pursuant to a shareholders agreement dated 12 May 2014, entered into between the Acquirers, and the UB group comprising UBHL, Kingfisher Finvest India Limited and McDowell Holdings Limited for an acquisition of up to 3,08,13,939 equity shares of MCFL (representing additional 26% stake in MCFL) ('*Zuari* case'). The CCI held that during the continuation of the tranche agreements, transactions amounting to approximately 16.43% in the equity share capital of MCFL were consummated prior to giving the merger approval notice to the CCI. The CCI noted that the parties had not provided adequate evidence to show that said acquisition qualifies for an exemption under Entry 1, Schedule 1 of the Combinations Regulations (discussed in detail below). Furthermore, the CCI relied on a television interview of the head of the Acquirer's company in which the then-Chairman of MCFL and promoter of UB group, i.e., Mr Mallya, wanted to operate MCFL as a joint venture between Zuari and UB group that affirmed the intent of the parties to consummate the transaction to some extent. Based on the above facts, the CCI imposed a penalty of INR 3 crores.

In the *Adani Green Energy Limited/S.B. Energy Holding Limited* combination, the transaction was notified to the CCI after the execution of SPAs by and between the acquirer, i.e., Adani Green Energy and Softbank.[91] The CCI found that the SPA, particularly the clause which, *inter alia*, allowed the parties to discuss the ongoing business and operations of the target and its subsidiaries, allowed the acquirer to provide inputs on the business of the target, which the target had to take into account in furtherance of its best interests. When tested on the pedestal of the inherence-proportionality framework as laid down in the *Airtel* decision, the CCI found that even if the intent of the acquirer was to monitor and preserve the economic value of the target (inherence), it was not proportional to this objective since it explicitly included discussions on business and operations in its scope in addition to specific provisions relating to monitoring and preserving the economic value of the target.

Further, although in this case the SPA provided for a 'clean team' protocol, it was only a lip service.[92] While on the one hand, the clause stated that information will be disclosed only to duly constituted clean teams which shall be ring-fenced from

90. *Jet/Etihad* case.
91. Section 43A Order against Adani Green Energy Limited, 9 Mar. 2022.
92. *Ibid.*, paras 45-48.

management, on the other hand, the inputs were to be taken into account in the best interests of the target, which necessarily implied that information was to be shared with the management to act on the given inputs. Hence, the CCI held that the execution of the SPA amounted to gun-jumping before approval of the CCI prior to the expiry of the timelines contained in section 6(2A) of the Competition Act.[93]

Another noteworthy aspect is that although the inputs were non-binding in this case, the CCI adopted a hard stance in that the issue of concern in such cases is access to information and the decisions being based on a wider pool of information, including the inputs of a competitor who is in the process of acquiring the business. Under such circumstances, the eventual result may be a coordinated outcome regardless of whether the inputs are binding or otherwise.[94]

This marked the first case where the agreement between the parties in broad terms facilitated the exchange of information and discussion on the ongoing business operations of the target, agreeing that the target will take such inputs into account after the execution of definitive agreements before the transaction was approved by the CCI. Further, if clean team protocols are being adopted to mitigate the risk of disclosure of sensitive information, it must be commensurate with the scope and likely effect of the clause. The clause itself is not sufficient to absolve the parties of their standstill obligations.

Basis the above, from a plain reading of the Competition Act, it would appear that it does not contemplate imposition of penalties for gun-jumping (and only covers a 'failure to file'), however, the CCI in its decisional practice has levied penalties on parties under section 43A for gun-jumping, as constituting a breach of the standstill obligation under section 6(2) of the Competition Act.

In this regard, it is also relevant to mention that for the imposition of penalty under section 43A, the action may not be mala fide in case there is a breach of the statutory provisions of the civil law, penalty is attracted simply on its violation. The Supreme Court has noted that there is also no requirement of mens rea or intentional breach as an essential element for levying a penalty under section 43A.[95] The Supreme Court noted that:

> *"There was no requirement of mens rea under section 43A or an intentional breach as an essential element for levy of penalty. The Act does not use the expression "the failure has to be willful or mala fide" for the purpose of imposition of penalty. The breach of the provisions of the Act is punishable and considering the nature of the breach, it is discretionary to impose the extent of penalty. Mens rea is important to adjudge criminal or quasicriminal liability, not in case of violation of the civil statutory provision".* In *Hindustan Steel Ltd. v. State of Orissa* AIR 1970 SC 253, with respect to the failure to comply with the civil obligation this Court has laid down thus:

93. *Ibid.*, paras 27-44.
94. *Ibid.*, para. 55.
95. *Competition Commission of India v. Thomas Cook (India) Limited* [2018], (SC) Civil Appeal No. 13578 of 2015, para. 32; Section 43A Order against Veolia Environnement S.A., 17 May 2022, para. 33; *SCM Solifert Limited & Anr v. Competition Commission of India* [2018], (SC) Civil Appeal No. 10678 of 2016, para. 23.

> *In our opinion, mens rea is not an essential ingredient for contravention of the provision of a civil Act. In our view, the penalty is attracted as soon as a contravention of the statutory obligations as contemplated by the Act is established and, therefore, the intention of the parties committing such violation becomes immaterial. In other words, the breach of a civil obligation which attracts penalty under the provisions of an Act would immediately attract the levy of penalty irrespective of the fact whether the contravention was made by the defaulter with any guilty intention or not. This apart that unless the language of the statute indicates the need to establish the element of mens rea. It is generally sufficient to prove that a default in complying with the statute has occurred.* The penalty has to follow and only the quantum of penalty is discretionary. *In our considered opinion, the penalty is attracted as soon as the contravention of the statutory obligation as contemplated by the Act and the Regulation is established and hence intention of the parties committing such violation becomes wholly irrelevant.*

We also further hold that unless the language of the statute indicates the need to establish the presence of men's rea, it is wholly unnecessary to ascertain whether such a violation was intentional or not. On a careful perusal of section 15(D) (b) and section 15E of the Act, there is nothing which requires that *mens rea* must be proved before a penalty can be imposed under these provisions. Hence once the contravention is established then the penalty is to follow:

> The imposition of penalty under section 43A is on account of breach of a civil obligation, and the proceedings are neither criminal nor quasi-criminal. Thus, a penalty has to follow.

This implies that even if parties jump the gun unintentionally, that would not be grounds to absolve them of their liability.

Therefore, any kind of arrangement between the parties to the transaction that allows collusion, irrespective of the manner of collusion and if and whether such collusion actually materializes, can be said to constitute gun-jumping. The CCI in its decisional practice has identified some arrangements specifically as amounting to gun-jumping. These have been discussed below.

[1] Part/pre-payment of Consideration

In its decisional practice, the CCI has held that depositing of advance consideration prior to the CCI's approval amounts to gun-jumping.[96]

The seminal case in this regard is that of Hindustan Colas Private Limited (acquirer), which had made payment in the form of a refundable deposit pursuant to the SPA.[97] This was held to amount to gun-jumping because the CCI reasoned that while the distinction between refundable and non-refundable may have some merit in assessing the likelihood of reversion to the status quo ante in form, it may not be

96. Section 43A Order against LT Foods Limited and LT Foods Middle East DMCC, 11 May 2018, para. 8.
97. Section 43A Order against Hindustan Colas Private Limited, 14 Sep. 2016, para. 6.

relevant from the perspective of potential competition distortions. The pre-payment of price (whether refundable/nonrefundable) may have a number of competition-distorting effects viz., (i) it may lead to a strategic advantage for the acquirer; (ii) it may reduce the incentive and will of 'target' to compete; and (iii) it may become a reason/basis to access the confidential information of the 'target'. On an overall basis, it may be said that pre-payment of consideration may have the impact of creating a tacit collusion which may cause an adverse effect on competition even before consummation of the combination. Thus, the CCI held that what is important is pre-payment of consideration, and solely the fact of the same being refundable or otherwise is not relevant. The Competition Act mandates *ex ante* examination of combinations, and therefore the issues such as whether the parties actually benefitted or not from the impugned conduct or whether there were any commercial exigencies behind a particular conduct are not relevant for a determination under section 6(2) and 6(2A) of the Competition Act.

The aforesaid observations on the need and rationale behind the standstill obligations and the concerns in terms of potential competition distortions are not merely abstract generalizations. By implication, the same brings out the test conditions for determining when a combination can be deemed to have come into effect. As has been brought out, the impugned conduct/arrangement, etc., needs to be examined in terms of: (i) reduction in competition intensity test; (ii) infringement with ordinary course of activities test; and (iii) likelihood of causing potential competition distortions, for deciding on the aspect of when a combination can be said to have 'come into effect'.

This view of the CCI that if the merger is not consummated and the advance paid is indeed refunded, the fact of such payment may have already led to the two parties not acting independently, and subsequent refund cannot restore the loss of competition in the interim period, was also upheld in the *Airtel* decision.[98]

In the *UltraTech* case, the acquirer UltraTech had advanced a corporate guarantee worth INR 500 crores to the target JAL as part of the acquisition.[99] It was argued that since the corporate guarantee was repayable, it did not amount to consummation of the combination so as to constitute gun-jumping. In its assessment, the CCI noted that the sole purpose of extending the corporate guarantee along with disbursement of a short-term loan was for the combination. Hence, the extension of corporate guarantee was not in the ordinary course of business or an independent transaction, but it was in fact pursuant to the combination. Thus, the extension of corporate guarantee by UltraTech in favour of JAL amounted to pre-payment of consideration and consummating a part of the combination before the approval of the same by the CCI. The CCI, in line with the position in the above-discussed cases, held that even if the loan amount is repayable, the same does not mitigate violation of the standstill obligations.

The key issue is that such an arrangement may result in the parties to the combination not acting independently as they are required to do till the combination is approved by a competition authority. In the event a transaction is not consummated

98. Paragraphs 18-23.
99. Paragraphs 13-17.

and such arrangement is restored, the competition would have still been harmed in the interim time period. It may be noted that pre-payment of consideration is considered significant as such an arrangement is potentially likely to facilitate tacit collusion which is considered to be the worst form of collusion and therefore cannot be allowed.

In the combination involving Adani Transmission Limited,[100] the acquirer advanced loans to the seller of the target asset. The circumstances were that a creditor had proposed to acquire assets of the debtor/seller, and the consideration payable for the acquisition was adjustable with the loan advanced. The CCI held that this was also in violation of the standstill obligations under section 6(2A) of the Competition Act because the advancement of the loan was in the nature of advance consideration.

Another aspect to note in pre-payment/advance payment of consideration is that the substantive issue involved is that of the conduct of the parties to a combination and not only that of timing of conduct. If only the timing of conduct was material, then it would imply that parties, during the stage of negotiations, may enter into cooperation on any commercial/financial/marketing aspects leading to integration of their operations and yet claim that the conduct cannot amount to gun-jumping, as it occurred prior to the execution of definitive agreements or filing of notice. Hence, what is critical in such cases is determination of the fact whether the alleged conduct is pursuant to the combination and has the effect of consummating a part of a combination and not the timing of the same.[101]

Therefore, the consistent position now is that irrespective of whether any payment is returnable/non-returnable or refundable/non-refundable, any such payment made in advance or as a form of pre-payment towards the combination amounts to gun-jumping because it inherently violates the principle of maintaining independence between the target and the acquirer till the combination has been approved. Hence, CCI's observations regarding *ex ante* notification requirement and standstill obligations apply both to consummation of a proposed combination or any part thereof.

[2] Escrow Arrangements

Escrow arrangements are an ordinary feature of public market transactions. In simple terms, they refer to those arrangements where the acquirer is not entitled to exercise control over such shares pending completion of the open offer. In its decisional practice, the CCI has observed that escrow arrangements amount to gun-jumping for the purposes of combination assessment.

The leading case in this regard is the *SCM Soilfert* case,[102] where the acquirers entered into an escrow agreement, whereby the shares acquired were credited into a specifically designated escrow account, which was to be maintained till approval of the acquisition by the CCI. The escrow agreement, *inter alia*, provided that SCM shall not

100. Section 43A Order against Adani Transmission Limited, 30 Jul. 2018, para. 9.
101. *UltraTech* case, para. 7; Section 43A Order against Chhatwal Group Trust, Shrem Infraventure Private Limited and Shrem Roadways Private Limited, 8 Aug. 2018, para. 12.
102. Paragraphs 9, 10.

exercise its legal and beneficial rights accruing upon the acquisition of shares by way of the Second Acquisition (acquisition of shares of 0.8% equity shares of MCFL) till such time the shares are held in the escrow account. The CCI held that since the Second Acquisition was a part of the proposed combination, the decision to keep the acquired shares in an escrow account maintained with the escrow agent and to not exercise any beneficial interest, including voting rights, was that of the acquirers and not due to any statutory requirement in this regard. Further, the Competition Act and Combination Regulations do not exempt a situation wherein a buyer acquires shares but decides not to exercise legal/beneficial rights in them from the purview of the provisions of the Competition Act in general and section 43A of the Act, in particular. Therefore, the keeping of shares in an escrow account amounted to gun-jumping, even if the acquirers were not entitled to exercise any legal or beneficial rights over them till approvals from regulatory bodies were obtained.

In appeal, the erstwhile COMPAT upheld CCI's findings that the creation of an escrow account accompanied by a covenant on the acquirer's own volition to abstain from exercising the voting rights does not eliminate the statutory requirement of prior notice since notification under section 6(2) of the Competition Act has to be *ex ante*.[103]

Subsequently, the Supreme Court also affirmed the findings of the CCI and erstwhile COMPAT that it was irrelevant whether the acquirers could exercise or not exercise beneficial rights over the shares till the proposed combination was approved by the CCI.[104] It held that the legislative scheme under section 6(2A) of the Competition Act which prescribes a standstill obligation together with the notice requirement 'prior to' entering into a combination under section 6(2) lays down that notification has to be made before entering into the combination. Ex post facto notice has not been contemplated under the legal regime. The intent of the Competition Act is that the CCI has to permit the combination to be formed after it has had an opportunity to assess the ability of the proposed combination to cause AAEC in the market. If notification is made ex post facto, it would defeat the legislative intention of *ex ante* notification.

This position that the acquisition of shares via escrow mechanism cannot be permitted without prior approval of the CCI in an *ex ante* merger review regime has been consistently upheld by the CCI in other cases as well.[105]

Thus, the conclusion is that the argument that notification was not required by keeping the shares in escrow account is incorrect because it amounts to consummation of the transaction and if such transactions are notified ex post facto (i.e., after the escrow arrangement has already been made – like in *SCM Soilfert* case), then the legislative intention to assess the combination prior to giving it effect will be defeated.

103. *SCM Soilfert Limited and Deepak Fertilizers and Petrochemical Ltd. v. Competition Commission of India* [2016], (COMPAT) Appeal No. 59 of 2015.
104. *SCM Soilfert and Anr. v. Competition Commission of India* [2018], (SC) Civil Appeal No. 10678 of 2016, paras 17-21.
105. Section 43A Order against Hindustan Colas Private Limited, 14 Sep. 2016, para. 6.10; Section 43A Order against SABIC International Holdings B.V., 19 Jul. 2022, paras 25-36.

[3] *Interim Conditions*

Another form of gun-jumping is through imposition of interim conditions while the combination approval is still pending with the CCI. For instance, in LT Food's proposed acquisition of the business of processing raw material for rice, marketing, distribution, export and sale of various types of rice, including trademarks and associated goodwill from Hindustan Unilever Limited (HUL),[106] the Framework Agreement executed between the parties required certain measures to be undertaken by HUL as a condition precedent to the combination or an obligation post execution of the Framework Agreement. These conditions included requirement to handover certain inventories to the acquirers, acquirer's introduction and interaction with the suppliers of the seller, restriction on promotional spending, etc. The CCI held that imposing interim conditions prior to CCI's approval of the combination amounted to a violation of the standstill obligations under sections 6(2) and 6(2A) of the Competition Act.[107]

Thus, any kind of interim conditions in relation to the combination cannot be enforced prior to CCI's approval, irrespective of whether such conditions are preparatory in nature or if they actually amount to giving effect to the combination.

[B] Importance of Mitigating Factors

Section 43A of the Act empowers the CCI to impose a penalty on such person or enterprise which may extend to 1% of the total turnover or the assets, whichever is higher, of such a combination. While arriving at an appropriate amount of penalty in a case, the CCI may consider the factors such as the conduct of the parties during the proceedings, circumstances of the case, etc.[108]

For instance, in the section 43A proceedings against Dewan Housing Finance Corporation Limited, the acquirer had submitted copies of legal advice/opinion that no filing was required to be made to the CCI for a merger between a parent company and its subsidiary as they would together constitute one single entity. The CCI held that delay in filing notice on account of incorrect legal advice may be regarded as a mitigating factor in levying penalty.[109]

However, the various mitigating factors submitted by the parties have to be assessed against the backdrop of the seriousness of the violation itself. Thus, the failure to file cannot be treated as a routine compliance default, as it could potentially have the grave consequence of defeating the very purpose of providing for regulation of combinations. It is, therefore, imperative for the companies to understand and appreciate the full extent of their responsibility for complying with the requirement of timely filing of the notifications regarding proposed combinations.[110]

106. Section 43A Order against LT Foods Limited and LT Foods Middle East DMCC, 11 May 2018.
107. *Ibid.*, para. 8.8.
108. Section 43A Order against Cummins Inc., 11 Aug. 2023.
109. Section 43A Order against Dewan Housing Finance Corporation Limited, 3 Jan. 2013, paras 4-9.
110. Section 43A Order against Zulia Investments Pte Limited and Kinder Investments Pte Limited, 1 Aug. 2013, para. 16.

§4.12 EXCLUSIONS AND EXEMPTION

The Competition Act and the Combination Regulations provide for certain exclusions and exemptions from filing merger control notification. Additionally, the Central Government may also exempt certain enterprises from the notification requirement (such as the MCA Circular discussed above) by issuing an official notification. These exemptions and exclusions are discussed herein below.

[A] Acquisition by Public Financial Institution, Foreign Portfolio Investor, Bank or Category I Alternative Investment Fund

Section 6(9)[111] of the Competition Act provides that the obligation to notify a combination to the CCI for approval is not applicable to a share subscription or financing facility or any acquisition by a public financial institution, foreign portfolio investor, bank or Category I alternative investment fund, pursuant to any covenant of a loan agreement or investment agreement.

The CCI, in its analysis of erstwhile section 6(4) of the Competition Act, which was applicable to public financial institution, foreign institutional investor, bank or venture capital fund, has held that public financial institution, foreign institutional investor, bank or venture capital fund acquiring shares directly on the floor of a stock exchange (by way of execution of contract note) which is not pursuant to a loan agreement or investment agreement are not entitled to exemption under section 6(4) of the Competition Act. Thus, such transactions are required to file a notice and seek approval from the CCI for approval. The CCI held that a contract note cannot be considered an investment agreement for the purposes of section 6(4) of the Competition Act because the contract note issued by the stockbroker is in the nature of a receipt and the contract note is issued subsequent to the execution of the trade on the stock exchange.

In light of the stance adopted by the CCI that a contract note will not amount to an investment agreement, there have been instances in the past where a foreign institutional investor has approached the CCI for pre-clearance of its trades (by asking for approval for an acquisition in a target entity in tranches within a definite time-period) and not file a post facto intimation under the provisions of section 6(4) of the Competition Act.[112]

[B] Exempt Transactions

Regulation 4 of the Combination Regulations, read with Schedule 1 of the Combination Regulations, provides for certain exempted transactions, i.e., transactions which will not require a merger control filing before the CCI.

---

111. Substituted by section 6(9) by the Competition (Amendment) Act, 2023.
112. KKR Mauritius Direct Investments I. Ltd., Mauritius and Magma fincorp Ltd., Combination Registration No. C-2011/11/10, 13 Dec. 2011.

The wording of the exemption has to be given due importance by the practitioners. There can be situations where a pure technical filing has to be made, which would be expeditiously cleared by the CCI. The exemptions and the manner in which the CCI have analysed the exemptions are discussed herein below:

[1] Schedule I Item 1

> An acquisition of shares or voting rights, referred to in sub-clause (i) or sub-clause (ii) of clause (a) of section 5 of the Act, solely as an investment or in the ordinary course of business in so far as the total shares or voting rights held by the acquirer directly or indirectly, does not entitle the acquirer to hold twenty five per cent (25%) or more of the total shares or voting rights of the company, of which shares or voting rights are being acquired, directly or indirectly or in accordance with the execution of any document including a shareholders agreement or articles of association, not leading to acquisition of control of the enterprise whose shares or voting rights are being acquired.

The explanation to Item I states that the acquisition of less than 10% of the total shares or voting rights of an enterprise shall be treated solely as an investment and provides the conditions for the same. This has been discussed subsequently in this section.

Earlier, the threshold provided in Schedule I Item I was 15% which was increased by way of an amendment to 25%. The amendment aligned the Combination Regulations with the Takeover Code by increasing the limit of exempted shareholding from 15% to 25% so long as such shareholding was acquired as an investment or in the ordinary course of business and did not result in an acquisition of control of the target enterprise. A case-by-case analysis will have to be undertaken to assess whether the acquirer is acquiring control over the target enterprise, in which case, a merger notification will have to be made even if the acquisition is less than 25%.

A diagrammatic illustration of the exemption is as follows:

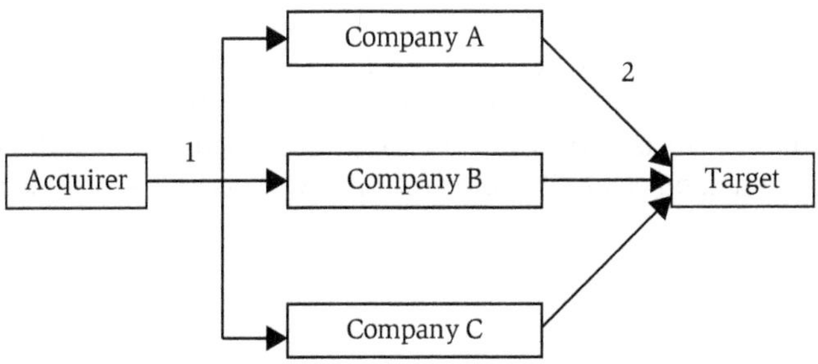

Notes to the diagrammatic representation:

Note 1: Acquirer holds 100% shareholding in each of Company A, Company B and Company C.

Note 2: Company A, Company B and Company C plan to invest in shares representing 10% shares of the Target.

It must be noted that the exemption is worded to include cases where acquirer acquires the shares directly or indirectly. In this case, the acquirer plans to invest 30% shares of Target indirectly through its subsidiaries, Company A, Company B and Company C. Therefore, this series of transactions will not be able to avail of the exemption. Further, as mentioned above, even if the investment is less than 25% in the target company, it has to be seen whether the acquirer, directly or indirectly, will exercise control over the operations of the target enterprise.

As delineated above, the manner in which control has been interpreted by the CCI is different from other Indian regulators. Therefore, while structuring any private equity transactions, a private equity investor will have certain affirmative vote items. Such vote items can be construed to mean control, for the purposes of the Competition Act, in which case, a notification will be required to be made. There have been many cases where private equity funds have made merger filings because of the affirmative vote items which are proposed to be held by them post the consummation of the transaction.

Further, the exemption is only available to acquisitions solely as an investment or in the ordinary course of business. Based on the same, strategic investment will not be covered by this exemption because strategic investments are not in the 'ordinary course of business' or 'solely as an investment'. In the early years of the merger control regime, the CCI had made an observation in the combination decision of SAAB and Pipavav[113] that strategic investments are not entitled to an exemption. In this case, the proposed acquisition was in the nature of a strategic technology partnership between SAAB and Pipavav and also provided certain affirmative rights, including the right to nominate one director on the Board of Pipavav to enable it to preserve the value of its investment in the company and prevent misuse of IPRs with respect to the projects. The CCI held that such rights precluded the acquisition from being an acquisition in the ordinary course of business or solely for the purpose of investment.

The objective of this provision is to distinguish between instances of ordinary shareholding and strategic shareholding, falling short of the position of acquisition of control.

In a subsequent merger approval order, the CCI has also observed that an acquisition of shares or voting rights, even if it is of less than 25%, may raise competition concerns if the acquirer and the target are either engaged in the business of substitutable products/services or are engaged in activities at different stages or levels of the production chain. Based on the observations of the CCI, the following key points emerge:

113. SAAB AB (Publ.) and Pipavav Defence and Offshore Engineering Company Limited, Combination Registration No. C-2012/11/95, 1 Jan. 2013.

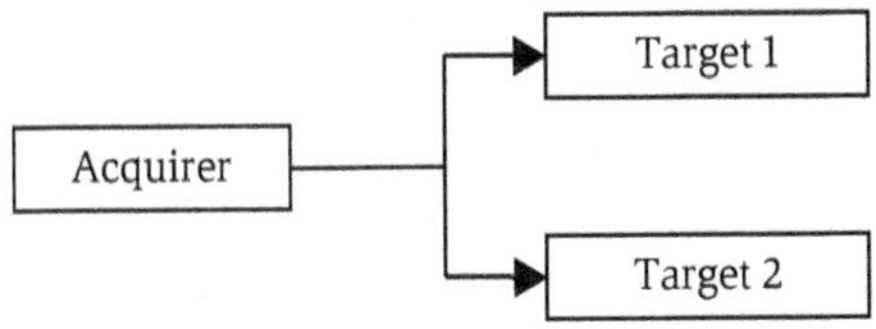

In the above diagram, the Acquirer is engaged in the manufacture of electronic goods. Target 1 is also involved in the manufacture of electronic goods, and Target 2 is involved in the distribution of electronic goods. In such a case, an investment by the acquirer in either Target 1 of Target 2, even if non-controlling and less than 25%, would necessitate an approval of the CCI. Such acquisitions will not be considered by the CCI as an acquisition made solely as an investment or in the ordinary course of business and thus would require a merger filing.[114]

Item 1 Provision comprises three conditions, i.e., acquisition of less than 25% of shares or voting rights, acquisition done 'solely as an investment' or in the 'ordinary course of business' and acquisition not leading to control. Even if one of the three conditions prescribed under this item is not satisfied, the benefit of Item 1 Provision is not available. These conditions have been discussed in more detail below.

[a] 'Solely as an Investment'

Item 1 Schedule I was amended to add a proviso to explain what is considered an acquisition 'solely as an investment'. Explanation to Item 1 of Schedule I of the Combination Regulations treats the acquisition to be 'solely as an investment' if the acquirer:

(i) acquires less than 10% shareholding;
(ii) has the ability to exercise only such rights that are exercisable by the ordinary shareholders of the enterprise whose shares or voting rights are being acquired to the extent of their respective shareholding and;
(iii) is not a member of the board of directors of the enterprise whose shares or voting rights are being acquired and;
(iv) does not have a right or intention to nominate a director on the board of directors of the enterprise whose shares or voting rights are being acquired and;
(v) does not intend to participate in the affairs or management of the enterprise whose shares or voting rights are being acquired.

All of these conditions must be simultaneously fulfilled to obtain the benefit of the Explanation to Item 1, Schedule 1. It is necessary to note that private equity investors investing in companies in India will have their nominee on the board and will participate in the affairs of the investee company, even if their shareholding is less than

114. New Moon B.V., Combination Registration No. C-2014/08/202, 10 Nov. 2014.

10%. Therefore, such investments will not be regarded as acquisitions made solely as an investment and, thus, will require notification.

CCI has clarified that the phrase 'solely as an investment' indicates 'passive investment' as against a 'strategic investment'.[115] Thus, to qualify for Item 1 exemption, '*an acquisition must not have been made with an intention of participating in the formulation, determination or direction of the basic business decisions of the target or likely to cause or result in the same*' by means of voting rights, agreements, representation on the board of the target or its affiliate companies, affirmative/veto rights in the target, etc.[116]

In the combination involving PI Opportunities Fund, the CCI examined the different conditions that must be met in order for a combination to be considered 'solely as an investment':[117]

(i) The first condition under proviso (B) to Item 1 prescribes that there should be no representation of the acquirer on the board of directors of the enterprise whose shares or voting rights are being acquired. In this case, there was no existing Board seat held by the acquirers in the target, and accordingly, this condition was met.

(ii) The second condition of the same proviso requires that there should not be a right or intention to nominate a director on the Board of directors of the enterprise whose shares or voting rights are being acquired, and there should not be any intention on the part of the acquirer to participate in the affairs or management of the enterprise whose shares or voting rights are being acquired. In this case, the CCI noted that the acquirers and sellers executed a SPA, pursuant to which they acquired a shareholding in target. At the time of execution of the SPA, the acquirers were aware that the seller had a Board seat on the target. This Board seat was offered to the acquirers by the target, and subsequently, the acquirers appointed one Board member. Based on the foregoing, the intention of the acquirers to participate in the affairs and management of the target could not be ruled out.

Herein, in the context of the appointment of the board member, the CCI drew a distinction between 'right' and 'intention' in consideration of the intent and purpose of the Item I Provision. The CCI observed:

> *The reference to 'right', i.e., an existing right captured in the transaction documents, and 'intention', i.e., a futuristic right or position, is meant to ensure that the regulatory framework is consistent with the core principle of 'substance over form'.* Accordingly, whether the proposal to appoint a director on the board of target was moved by the target or whether the parties first acquired only shares and subsequently negotiated/agreed for board representation or participation in management in related or unrelated developments to the transaction, or where such an

115. Section 43A Order against Zuari Fertilisers and Chemicals Limited and Zuari Agro Chemicals Limited, 10 Feb. 2015, para. 8.
116. *SCM Soilfert* case, para. 8.3.
117. Section 43A Order against PI Opportunities Fund – I and Pioneer Investment Fund, 30 Sep. 2022, paras 32-39.

> arrangement forms intrinsic part of the transaction ab initio, *the substance in each case is the parties gaining the ability to participate in management or affairs and, in that context, the mechanism leading up to it is just a question of form.* If the Acquirers' contentions regarding these differences are accepted, this would imply that parties to a combination can structure their transactions separating the acquisition of shares and acquisition of rights/board seat, etc., and claim the benefit of Item I Provision. Clearly, this would defeat the intent and purpose of the Act, which is to ensure that the competitive dynamics are not influenced, as the same can be influenced not only by active decisions but also by way of broad understanding or awareness of competitively sensitive information. *The end result in each case is sufficient to lead to coordinated outcomes, frustrating the process of competition.*

Hence, the combination did not satisfy the conditions of the Explanation to Item 1 Provision, and hence, it was not 'solely as an investment'. Although CCI did not examine proviso (A) to Item 1, which requires the investor to have the same rights in the target as an ordinary shareholder, it is clear upon analysis that no ordinary shareholder has the right to appoint members on the Board of the target. This analysis was confirmed in the section 43A proceedings against Trian Partners AM Holdco, Ltd. and Trian Fund Management, L.P ('*Trian* case'), where CCI proceeded to add a third limb to the determination undertaken in the combination involving PI Opportunities Fund, as discussed above.[118] Herein, the CCI, after finding that the conditions of proviso (B) to explanation of Item 1 Provision were not met, proceeded to analyse proviso (A). It was noted that if the acquirer wants to avail the exemption, it should only have the ability to exercise rights that are exercisable by the ordinary shareholder of the enterprise whose shares or voting rights are being acquired to the extent of their respective shareholding. The Item 1 Provision covers the transactions not amounting to the acquisition of control and, accordingly, does not differentiate between various rights, viz., investor protection rights, informational rights, etc. In this case, Trian acquired two Board seats in a matter of less than two months from the date of the closing of the transaction. Such rights are not available to ordinary shareholders. Thus, it was held that the acquirers clearly had the intention to participate in the affairs and management of the target, so Item 1 exemption was not applicable to the case.

Hence, based on the above discussion, it can be concluded that the intention to participate in the affairs and management of the target has to be determined after examination of both the conditions, i.e., proviso (A) and (B) to explanation of Item 1 Provision.

In the *Axis Bank/CSC e-Governance* acquisition,[119] Axis Bank did not notify its acquisition of a 9.91% stake in CSC e-Governance Services India Limited (CSC) on the premise that the benefit of the Item 1, Schedule I of the Combination Regulations was available to the transaction. It was found that Axis Bank proposed the nomination of a director on the board of directors, had both representation and intention to have representation on the board of directors of CSC and to participate in its management or

118. Section 43A Order against Trian Partners AM Holdco, Ltd. and Trian Fund Management, L.P., 30 Sep. 2022, paras 39-42.
119. Section 43A Order against Axis Bank Limited, 9 Aug. 2023, paras 22-24.

affairs. Consequently, the transaction could not be regarded as 'solely as an investment' and the exemption was not allowed.

Thus, the CCI has focused on the acquirer's ability to control the management or affairs of the target enterprise, such as through the right or intention to appoint members to the board of directors or otherwise. In its decisional practice, CCI has held that such transactions cannot be termed as being solely an investment.[120]

Based on the above discussion, it can be concluded that the intention of the Item 1 provision is to exempt cases of ordinary shareholding and not strategic shareholding. Both the conditions under the proviso to Explanation to Item 1 provision have to be simultaneously fulfilled in order to claim exemption because if even a single condition is violated, the transaction could no longer be said to be solely for the purpose of investment. This implies that wherever there is an attempt in substance to exercise control through an investment, no matter how that control is exercised (the different types of control have been discussed earlier in this chapter), such transaction will no longer remain 'solely as an investment' but would trigger notifiability of the transaction.

[b] 'In the Ordinary Course of Business'

Over time, CCI has started treating 'solely as an investment' and 'ordinary course of business' as two separate and distinct limbs of Item 1, Schedule 1 exemption, instead of painting them with the same brush in the same condition.

In the combination involving PI Opportunities Fund, the core issue was whether the combination, i.e., acquisition of 6.03% shareholding in FRL (target) through on-market purchases as a block deal and subsequent appointment of directors on the Board of the target was covered under Item 1 exemption. The findings of the CCI have been analysed and explained below:[121]

(i) The first test for examining a transaction for being in the ordinary course of business is whether the same is a revenue transaction or a capital transaction. In its decisional practice,[122] the CCI has held that the term 'ordinary course of business' is meant to refer to transactions which are frequent, routine and usual. Thus, it corresponds to revenue transactions, which are those transactions which are short term and constitute income and expenditure and are accordingly reflected in the profit and loss account or income statement of the enterprise. Capital transactions, however, are those which affect non-current items, such as fixed assets, long-term debt, etc., and affect the position statement of an enterprise. Hence, transactions in the

120. Kedaara Capital Fund II, Combination Registration No. C-2019/06/666, 20 Jun. 2019; Section 44 Order in the *UltraTech* case, para. 12.16; Section 43A Order against SABIC International Holdings B.V., 15 Jul. 2022, paras 27, 28.

121. Section 43A Order against PI Opportunities Fund – I and Pioneer Investment Fund, 30 Sep. 2022, para. 40.

122. Bharti Airtel Limited and Bharti Hexacom Limited, Combination Registration No. C-2017/05/509, 11 May 2018.

ordinary course of sale and purchase of securities are done solely with the intent to benefit from the short-term price movement of securities which re-emphasizes the underlying aspects of frequency, duration of holding, intent, etc.

(ii) What constitutes a revenue or capital transaction varies from business to business, i.e., a capital transaction for one business may be a revenue transaction for the other. In this case, the acquirers contended that their investments in the target were inextricably connected with the objective of constituting and operating the investment fund and such investments are considered to be routine and in the ordinary course of business of the investment funds. For example, for a seller of plant and machinery, sale of plant and machinery may be an activity in the ordinary course of business as the same constitutes its regular trade, while for any player who was using a machine to produce goods for sale, sale of such machine would be a capital transaction. In fact, the same item may also have a different classification. For example, furniture held for sale by a furniture seller would be a current asset, and the sale proceeds of the same would be revenue receipts, but for the same business, the stock of furniture held for use in office furnishings, etc., would be a non-current asset and the expenditure incurred on purchasing the same would be capital expenditure and receipts from the sale of such furniture would be a capital receipt.[123] However, in this case, the acquirers contended that their investments in the target were inextricably connected with the objective of constituting and operating the investment fund and that such investments are considered to be routine and in the ordinary course of business of the investment funds.

(iii) While revenue transactions mean and imply items of income and expenditure, an 'investment' by its very definition constitutes a capital transaction being an item of 'asset' for the investing firm. Thus, the key consideration for the 'ordinary course of business' test is that the activity in question should not even be an 'investment'.

(iv) The moment it is concluded that the activity in question is an 'investment', the question for the determination of notifiability is whether the same is 'solely as an investment', i.e., the nature of the investment is such which is not likely to impact the competition dynamics or otherwise. Going by the same, once the activity is held to be an 'investment', even if it does satisfy 'solely as an investment' test, it cannot be considered to be in the 'ordinary course of business' by implication.

This position was also subsequently upheld in the *Trian* case,[124] where the CCI reiterated the above findings and observed that going by the above reasoning, the key

123. Reliance Jio Infocomm Limited and Reliance Communications Limited, Combination Registration No. C-2017/06/516, 11 May 2018, paras 25-28; Bharti Airtel Limited and Videocon, Combination Registration No. C-2017/05/509, 11 May 2018, paras 28-30.

124. *Trian* case, paras 41-47.

consideration for the 'ordinary course of business' test is that the activity in question should not even be an 'investment'.

The key takeaway from the above case is that an investment, being a capital transaction, can never be in the ordinary course of business. This reasoning significantly dilutes the 'ordinary course of business' test because it is contradictory to the first limb of Item 1 Provision which exempts transactions solely made as an investment. As a result, it is almost impossible to rely on the ordinary course of business limb because 'investments' of all kinds are excluded from its ambit, even though the very purpose of Item 1 Provision was to exempt ordinary investments that are not strategic in nature. Therefore, this interpretation of 'ordinary course of business' is likely to render this limb of the exemption as a dead letter because it cannot be practically utilized by parties entering into an 'investment'.

This position has been reiterated in the decisional practice of CCI. For instance, access to knowledge and expertise in the financial inclusion sector by Axis Bank in its acquisition of stake in CSC was found to fall outside the scope of the ordinary course of business because it was deemed to have a strategic intention.[125] Thus, only transactions which are undertaken solely to benefit from the short-term price movement of securities can be considered to be done in the ordinary course of business. Therefore, long-term investments made with the strategic intent to participate in the decision-making process or gain access to sensitive information cannot obtain the benefit of Item 1, Schedule 1 exemption.

[2] Schedule I Item 1A

> An acquisition of additional shares or voting rights of an enterprise by the acquirer or its group where the acquirer or its group, prior to acquisition, already holds twenty five per cent (25%) or more shares or voting rights of the enterprise, but does not hold fifty per cent (50%) or more of the shares or voting rights of the enterprise, either prior to or after such acquisition:
>
> Provided that such acquisition does not result in acquisition of sole or joint control of such enterprise by the acquirer or its group.

The CCI amended this exemption in January 2016. Prior to the exemption, the exemption allowed for a creeping acquisition of 5% every financial year by the acquirer or its group in an enterprise wherein the acquirer or its group already holds 25% or more share or voting rights in the target enterprise but less than 50%. This exemption was linked to the concept of 'creeping acquisition' provisions of the Takeover Code. However, there were many technical filings made where investors increased their shareholding from 26% to 49% post the relaxation of the foreign direct investment regime in India. Such transactions required the approval of the CCI even though there was no change in control. Post this amendment, an investor who holds between 25% and 50% of the equity share capital or voting rights of the target enterprise would be

125. Section 43A Order against Axis Bank Limited, 9 Aug. 2023, paras 24-26.

allowed to increase the shareholding below 50% without the approval of the CCI, provided such acquisition does not result in acquisition of sole or joint control.

[3] Schedule I Item 2

> An acquisition of shares or voting rights, referred to in sub-clause (i) or sub-clause (ii) of clause (a) of section 5 of the Act, where the acquirer, prior to acquisition, has fifty percent (50%) or more shares or voting rights in the enterprise whose shares or voting rights are being acquired, except in the cases where the transaction results in transfer from joint control to sole control.

The exemption is applicable to further acquisitions in the target enterprise where the acquirer already has more than 50% in the said target enterprise. It is to be noted that on a technical reading of the exemption, the acquirer has to hold more than 50% in the target enterprise for the exemption to be applicable and not acquirer with its group. Further, the exemption will not be applicable when such further acquisition results in a transfer from joint control to sole control. We have discussed the concept of joint and sole control in the earlier parts of the chapter. From a plain reading of the Item 2 Provision, it is clear that the benefit of this provision is not available in instances where the transaction results in a transfer from joint control to sole control.

A diagrammatic representation of the exemption is as follows:

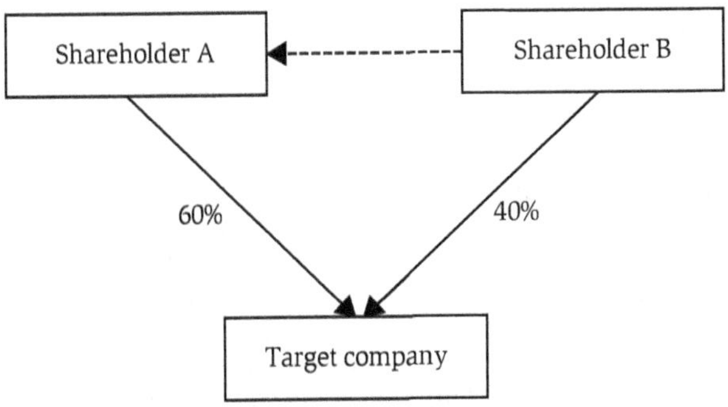

Shareholder A holds 60% of equity shareholding in the Target company and Shareholder B holds 40% equity shareholding in the Target company. By way of SPA, Shareholder B will transfer its 40% shareholding in Target company to Shareholder A. Such SPA will not avail of the exemption because the transaction will result in a transfer from joint control of Shareholder A and B in the Target company to sole control of Shareholder A. The CCI dealt with this exemption in the *MSM* case (discussed above while discussing control), where the largest shareholder (holding approximately 67% of the shareholding) purchased the shares from the other existing shareholders. The existing shareholders held approximately 33% of the target enterprise which was purchased by the largest shareholders. The CCI held that the transaction resulted from joint control to sole control, and hence, the exemption was not available.

In the proceedings against Bharti Airtel Limited (Bharti) and Warburg Pincus affiliate Lion Meadow Investment Limited (Lion Meadow), Bharti's acquisition of Lion Meadow's 20% shareholding in Bharti Telemedia Limited (BTL) and Lion Meadows' subsequent acquisition of a 0.664% shareholding in Bharti was not notified to the CCI because the parties asserted that Item 2, Schedule 1 exemption was applicable.[126] They argued that Lion Meadow did not have control of BTL before the transaction, and instead, BTL continued to retain sole control as exercised prior to the transaction. The CCI held that when determining the applicability of benefit of Item 2 Provision, 'joint control' and 'sole control' should be read to include the ability to exercise material influence over the management or affairs or strategic commercial decisions of the target. Further, veto on the matter of economic or commercial significance to the target is always considered conferring control in terms of and for the purposes of section 5 of the Act. In this case, LMIL held a bundle of rights in the target along with its shareholding, including affirmative veto rights in certain matters, information rights, right to appoint a non-executive director on the board of the target, etc. Thus, it had the ability to exert material influence over management or affairs or strategic commercial decisions of the target. These rights were transferred to BTL after the transaction. Hence, the benefit of Item 2 exemption was not available to the transaction since there was a transfer from joint to sole control from BTL to LMIL.

Therefore, the key question for determining the applicability of Item 2, Schedule 1 exemption, is whether there was a transfer from joint control to sole control. Here, control is to be assessed as per the decisional practice of CCI under section 5, which has been discussed earlier in this chapter.

[4] Schedule I Item 3

> An acquisition of assets, referred to in sub- clause (i) or sub-clause (ii) of clause (a) of section 5 of the Act, not directly related to the business activity of the party acquiring the asset or made solely as an investment or in the ordinary course of business, not leading to control of the enterprise whose assets are being acquired except where the assets being acquired represent substantial business operations in a particular location or for a particular product or service of the enterprise, of which assets are being acquired, irrespective of whether such assets are organized as a separate legal entity or not.

The exemption is only available in cases of acquisition of assets solely as an investment or in the ordinary course of business. Based on the interpretation adopted by the CCI for exemption outlined in point (1) above, the exemption will not be applicable for strategic investments and where such acquisition leads to acquisition of control.

The scope of this exemption was discussed by the CCI in the *Jet/Etihad* case.[127] Etihad and Jet Airways had entered into an agreement regarding the sale of three

126. Section 43A Order against Bharti Airtel Limited and Lion Meadow Investment Limited, 23 Aug. 2023, paras 41-48.
127. *Jet/Etihad* case, para. 6.

landing/take-off slots of Jet Airways at London Heathrow Airport to Etihad and the lease of the same slots back to Jet Airways (LHR Transaction). Etihad did not file a merger notification for the LHR transaction, contending that the LHR Transaction was an exempted transaction under Item 3 of Schedule I to the Combination Regulations as it was pursued in the ordinary course of business. Further, it was also contended by Etihad that the three slots acquired did not represent Jet's substantial business operations in/from London on account of the fact that slots merely represent the landing rights enjoyed by Jet at LHR Airport, whereas Jet's actual revenue and business operations comprised of ticket sales from its flight to/from London. It was argued that the book value (depreciated) of the three pairs of slots was only a fraction of Jet's worldwide assets.

However, the CCI did not agree with the contention of Etihad. It noted that the sale/purchase of landing/take-off slots may generally be treated as a transaction in the ordinary course of business. However, in the instant case, the slots sale was coupled with another agreement to lease back the same slots to the seller, followed by acquisition of equity stake in Jet by Etihad and a wide-ranging commercial co-operation agreement between the Parties. Further, Item 3 to Schedule I categorically excludes acquisition of assets that represent the substantial business operations of the target enterprise in a particular location or for a particular product or service. Here, only the three landing/take-off slots of Jet Airways at LHR formed the basis of Jet's entire business operation between India and London and considering that Jet had no other take-off/landing slots in London, the three slots formed the basis for Jet's entire services between India and London; absent these slots, Jet would have no business operation nor would have earned any revenue in the said sector. Etihad's contention that the value of the slots sold was a fraction of Jet's worldwide assets was also not tenable as the relevant yardstick for comparison was Jet's business operations between India and London. Therefore, the subject matter of acquisition effectively represented the 'entire operations' of Jet between India and London and, hence, could not avail the Item 3, Schedule I exemption.

In two combinations involving the acquisition of the right to use spectrum, the CCI identified the key conditions for applicability of Item 3, Schedule I exemption.[128] The issue was whether acquisition of the right to use spectrum (Spectrum Transaction) in certain licensed areas was covered under Item 3 of Schedule I of the Combination Regulations. The CCI noted that there are two essential conditions to this exemption: (i) acquisition of assets not directly related to the business activity of the acquirer; or (ii) acquisition of assets made solely as an investment or in the ordinary course of business. In this case, the acquirers were TSPs; hence, the asset in question, i.e., spectrum, was directly related to their business, so condition (i) is not met. As far as being in the ordinary course of business is concerned, the activities must be revenue transactions (which are short term and only impact the existing state of operations and do not change the operating potential) and not capital transactions (which are long

128. Reliance Jio Infocomm Limited and Reliance Communications Limited, Combination Registration No. C-2017/06/516, 11 May 2018, paras 24-29; Bharti Airtel Limited and Videocon, Combination Registration No. C-2017/05/509, 11 May 2018, paras 27-32.

term and impact the ability of a business to carry out revenue transactions). For example, the installation of a new production unit (capital expenditure) would be expected to lead to an increase in production which in turn would be expected to lead to greater sales revenue. This difference has already been discussed in the context of Item 1, Schedule 1 exemption, so it has not been repeated here. What is important is that the activities for which the business is established would be the activities in ordinary course and the activities which are meant to help the business carry on its ordinary activities efficiently would be the strategic capital transactions. In the facts of the case, the main revenue activities of a TSP constituting an 'ordinary course of business for a TSP' are activities relating to the provision of mobile telephony services. Hence, the activities relating to acquisition/transfer of resources, such as spectrum which are used to render such services, are strategic capital transactions and cannot be equated to ordinary revenue activities.

The acquirers' contention that spectrum is basic and essential to the business of a TSP was rejected because all assets are basic and essential to the end business revenue activities. Thus, the implication of such logic would be that none of the instances of acquisition of assets would be covered under the merger review process, which is incorrect. Another factor to consider is that the results of ordinary activities of a business are depicted in the profit and loss account in the financial statement, while the position of assets and liabilities is contained in the balance sheet. The acquires had duly recognized spectrum as an intangible asset, i.e., a non-current asset in its balance sheet and not as an asset held for sale which would have been reflected as a current asset. Considering the totality of these factors, Item 3 exemption was not made available to spectrum transactions.

Therefore, the key takeaway is that in order to claim Item 3, Schedule I exemption, the acquisition must be solely as an investment or in the ordinary course of business, which in turn means that the acquisition should be a revenue transaction and should not be strategic in nature.

[5] Schedule I Item 4

> An amended or renewed tender offer where a notice to the Commission has been filed by the party making the offer, prior to such amendment or renewal of the offer: Provided that the compliance with Regulation 16 relating to intimation of any change is duly made.

[6] Schedule I Item 5

> An acquisition of stock-in-trade, raw materials, stores and spares, trade receivables and other similar current assets in the ordinary course of business.

[7] Schedule I Item 6

An acquisition of shares or voting rights pursuant to a bonus issue or stock splits or consolidation of face value of shares or buy back of shares or subscription to rights issue of shares, not leading to acquisition of control.

[8] Schedule I Item 7

Any acquisition of shares or voting rights by a person acting as a securities underwriter or a registered stock broker of a stock exchange on behalf of its clients, in the ordinary course of its business and in the process of underwriting or stock broking, as the case may be.

[9] Schedule I Item 8

An acquisition of shares or voting rights or assets, by one person or enterprise, of another person or enterprise within the same group, except in cases where the acquired enterprise is jointly controlled by enterprises that are not part of the same group.

The exemption provides for intra-group acquisition. As such, the intra-group acquisition exemption is not an absolute exemption under the Combination Regulations. The diagrammatic representation of the exemption is as follows:

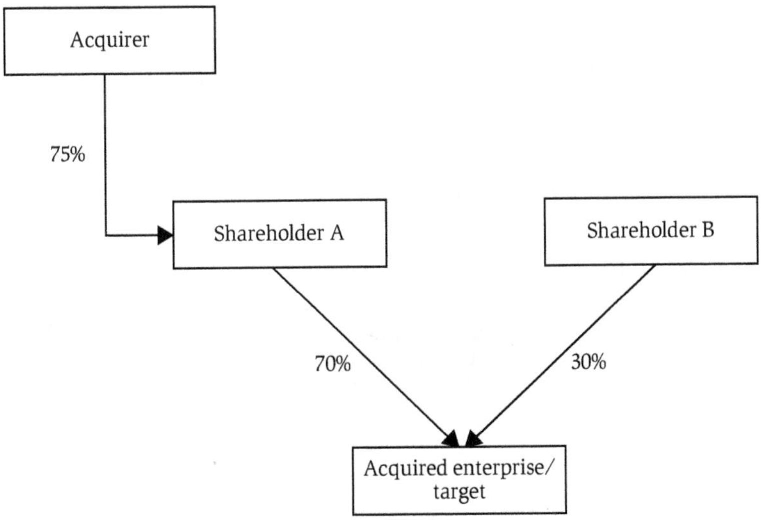

The Acquirer holds 75% shareholding in Shareholder A. Further, Shareholder A holds 70% in the Acquired Enterprise. Therefore, the Acquirer, Shareholder A and the Acquired enterprise are a part of the same group.

Shareholder B holds 30% in the Acquired enterprise and hence exercises control over the Acquired enterprise. Therefore, the Acquired Enterprise falls into two groups: the group to which Shareholder A belongs and the group of Shareholder B. As a part of the transaction, Shareholder A wants to transfer its 70% shareholding to the Acquirer. While such a transaction would be an intra-group transaction, it will not be able to claim an intra-group exemption since the acquired enterprise is jointly held by companies falling into two different groups. Based on the same, such a transaction would require the approval of the CCI. As mentioned above, it will be a mere technical filing since such transactions generally will not cause any AAEC.

In the acquisition of shares of Telenor (India) Communications Private Limited (Telenor India) by Lakshdeep Investments & Finance Private Limited (Lakshdeep), the steps of the combination were as follows: (i) Telenor India to participate in 2G spectrum auction and acquire necessary spectrum; (ii) Upon Telenor India being declared successful, Lakshdeep to acquire 51% of share of Telenor India; (iii) Telenor India to acquire business of Unitech Wireless (Tamil Nadu) Private Limited (Uninor) on a going concern basis (iv) Telenor (Parent of Telenor India) to increase its shareholding in Telenor India to 74% and consequently, Lakshdeep to hold 26% in Telenor India (tranche 1). It was submitted that Steps (iii) and (iv) are intra-group asset transfer and intra-group acquisition of shares, respectively, under Item 8, Schedule I of Combination Regulations and hence, need not be notified to CCI. This has been described in the following diagram:

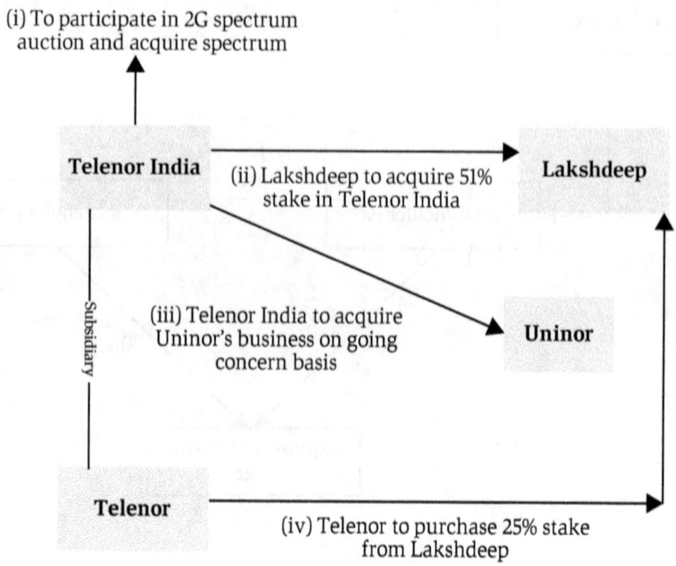

While CCI assessed and approved Step (i) on a standalone basis,[129] it observed that as Lakshdeep would hold shares in Telenor India to the extent of 51%, transfer of business from Uninor to Telenor India and increase in stake of Telenor in Telenor India from 49% to 74% cannot be considered intra-group transactions and therefore Item 8 of Schedule I is not applicable. Subsequently, CCI received a notice under section 6(2) of the Act by Bharti Airtel Limited and Telenor India for the proposed transfer of 100% shares of Telenor India to Airtel.[130] While reviewing the same, CCI observed that Telenor had already consummated Steps (iii) and (iv) above and also increased its shareholding from 74% to 100% ('*tranche 2*') without notifying the same. Since Lakshdeep had 26% stake in Telenor India after tranche 1, CCI observed that Lakshdeep still had joint control over Telenor India, and therefore, the transfer of the same had the effect of changing control of Telenor India from joint control of Lakshdeep and Telenor to sole control of Telenor. Consequently, tranche 2 was also held to not be an intra-group transaction and, hence, not covered under Item 8, Schedule I. Relying on Ultratech Cement Limited,[131] CCI observed that Lakshdeep would have decreased its shareholding to 49% if Telenor did not get the requisite approvals and; to 26% in case, it did. Consequently, in both cases, the minimum shareholding of Lakshdeep would have been 26%, which, with or without any affirmative voting rights, confers the ability under the Companies Act to block special resolutions on Lakshdeep by virtue of its shareholding itself and exert negative control over the management and affairs of Telenor India. Hence, Telenor would not have had the ability to exercise sole control over Telenor India and Uninor.

It can be said that the change of control (different aspects of control have already been discussed earlier in the chapter), as well as the change in independence of the merging entities, has a key role to play in availing the Item 8 exemption.[132]

[10] Schedule I Item 9

> A merger or amalgamation of two enterprises where one of the enterprises has more than fifty per cent (50%) shares or voting rights of the other enterprise, and/or merger or amalgamation of enterprises in which more than fifty per cent (50%) shares or voting rights in each of such enterprises are held by enterprise(s) within the same group.
>
> Provided that the transaction does not result in transfer from joint control to sole control.

129. Lakshdeep Investments and Finance Private Limited, Combination Registration No. C-2012/10/87, 29 Nov. 2012.
130. Bharti Airtel Limited, India and Telenor (India) Communications Private Limited, India, Combination Registration No. C- 2017-04-494, 30 May 2017.
131. UltraTech Cement Limited, Combination Registration No. C-2015-02-246, 10 Apr. 2015.
132. Section 43A Order against Sarva Haryana Gramin Bank and Punjab National Bank, 14 Feb. 2017; Taurus Ventures Limited and Capricorn Ventures Limited, Combination Registration No. C-2015/02/251, 26 Mar. 2015.

The exemption provides for intra-group merger exemption. As such, like the intra-group acquisition exemption, the intra-group merger exemption is not an absolute exemption under the Combination Regulations. The diagrammatic representation of the exemption is as follows:

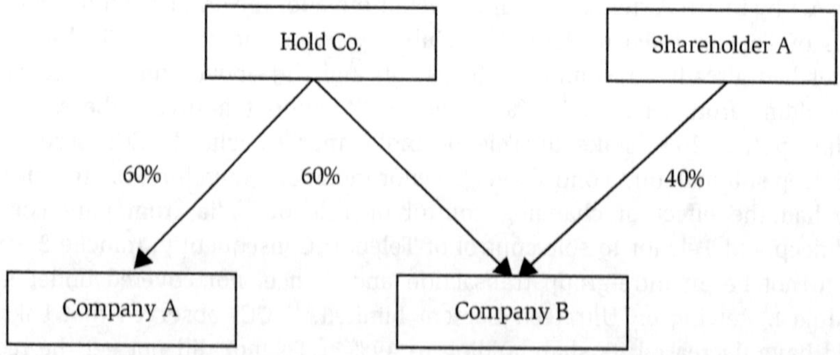

In the above diagrammatic representation, Hold Co. holds 60% in Company A and Company B. Based on the same, Hold Co., Company A and Company B fall within the same group. Shareholder A also holds 40% in Company B; thus, Company B is a part of two groups. Company A and Company B enter into a scheme of arrangement under the Companies Act for merger. This merger, although within the same group, will not be able to avail of the exemption because it is a case of transfer of joint to sole control.

[11] Schedule I, Item 10

> Acquisition of shares, control, voting rights or assets by a purchaser approved by the Commission pursuant to and in accordance with its order under section 31 of the Act.

This exemption covers situations wherein the CCI has imposed a structural commitment on the parties to the combination to divest some assets. Upon some divesture, a third party acquires such assets. Earlier, even the acquisition of assets by a third party, pursuant to an order of divesture by the CCI, would have required a fresh application for approval to be filed before the CCI. Since this exemption was not available, the third-party buyer, as an abundant caution, used to file a merger notification. Now, the CCI has plugged this loophole and added this exemption.

[12] Sector-Specific Exemptions: Government Notifications

As mentioned earlier, the Central Government can exempt any class of enterprises from application of any provisions of the Competition Act under section 54 under public interest. This power has been exercised to exempt the following enterprises from notification requirements under sections 5 and 6 of the Competition Act:

(i) Banking company in respect of which the Central Government has issued a notification under section 45 of the Banking Regulation Act, 1949.[133]

(ii) Regional rural banks in respect of which the Central Government has issued a notification under section 23A(1) of the Regional Rural Banks Act, 1976.[134]

(iii) All cases of combinations reconstitution, transfer and amalgamation of nationalized banks under the Banking Companies (Acquisition and Transfer of Undertakings) Act, 1970 and the Banking Companies (Acquisition and Transfer of Undertakings) Act, 1980.[135]

(iv) All cases of combinations involving central public sector enterprises operating in the oil and gas sectors under the Petroleum Act, 1934 and the rules made thereunder or under the Oilfields (Regulation and Development) Act, 1948 and the rules made thereunder, along with their wholly or partly owned subsidiaries operating in the oil and gas sectors.[136]

In the context of amalgamation of regional rural banks, it is relevant to note that prior to the exemption granted by the Central Government, such amalgamations triggered the requirement to file a notice to the CCI, even if they were undertaken pursuant to the orders issued by the Central Government and not on regional rural banks' own volition. In fact, in two instances, the CCI has also penalized regional rural banks[137] for consummating the amalgamation without seeking its approval. The CCI reasoned therein that the fact of the decision of amalgamation being taken by the Central Government does not obliterate the Parties from their responsibility to notify the amalgamation to the CCI.

Thus, the granting of exemption by way of the Central Government notification prevents notices for mere technical approval of the CCI, which is unnecessary when such amalgamations have been sanctioned by the Central Government itself.

[C] Open Market Purchases

At present, the Competition Act prohibits parties from acquiring any shares or paying any consideration pending approval of the combination by CCI. We have already discussed how CCI penalizes parties for gun-jumping by part/pre-payment of consideration and placing the consideration in an escrow account. The consequence of this is that any acquisition of shares in the open market, i.e., listed on the stock exchange, including potential hostile takeovers in India, is not allowed. As a result, parties were precluded from capitalizing on open market purchases, which happen nearly instantaneously.

133. Vide Notification S.O. 1034(E) published in Gazette dated 11 Mar. 2022.
134. Vide notification no. S.O. 2561(E) published in Gazette dated 10 Aug. 2017.
135. Vide notification no. S.O. 2828(E) published in Gazette dated 30 Aug. 2017.
136. Vide notification no. S.O. 3714(E) published in Gazette dated 22 Nov. 2017.
137. Section 43A Order against Rajasthan Marudhara Gramin Bank and State Bank of Bikaner and Jaipur, 14 Feb. 2017; Section 43A Order against Sarva Haryana Gramin Bank, 14 Feb. 2017.

The Competition (Amendment) Act, 2023, changes this position by allowing parties to derogate from the standstill obligations for open market purchases so that they can capitalize on open market opportunities. Further, the Draft Regulations require that such transactions have to be notified to the CCI within thirty days from the completion of such on-market transactions. They also specify certain rights that can be exercised before obtaining CCI approval, including: (a) benefiting from economic benefits such as dividends; (b) disposing of shares; or (c) exercising voting rights in matters relating to liquidation or insolvency proceedings. However, the acquirer must not directly or indirectly influence the target enterprise in any way. Upon implementation, it will become easier for parties to initiate and implement open market purchases.

§4.13 TREATMENT OF OFFSHORE COMBINATIONS

There was an erstwhile exemption (which has hitherto been deleted) on offshore combination. Earlier, the un-amended Combinations Regulations envisaged that combinations taking place outside India with *insignificant local nexus and effect on markets in India* would be exempted from the merger control application regime (offshore exemption). However, the 2014 amendment did away with this category of exemption. Hence, offshore combinations are directly amenable to the jurisdiction of the CCI as long as the threshold limit is met.

The CCI has the power to review global transactions by virtue of section 32 of the Competition Act, which states that the CCI '*shall, notwithstanding that a combination has taken place outside India or any party to combination is outside India have power to inquire into such combination if such combination has, or is likely to have, an appreciable adverse effect on competition in the relevant market in India*'.

In its decisional practice, the CCI has noted that once the jurisdictional thresholds are breached, the CCI can enquire into combinations taking place outside India, and the residential status of the parties to the combination is immaterial and, further, an AAEC is not a prerequisite for notification of a proposed transaction to the CCI.[138]

The scope of the Offshore Exemption was first tested in the case of *Tata Chemicals Limited/Wyoming I*,[139] where the CCI was notified of the proposed merger of Wyoming I, which was an offshore wholly owned subsidiary (incorporated in Mauritius) of Tata Chemicals Limited, into its holding company, located in India. The parties claimed, *inter alia*, that the Offshore Exemption was applicable in this instance, given that the transaction was an 'entirely outbound stream of acquisition' by the holding company. However, the CCI did not agree and observed that since the parties exceeded the jurisdictional thresholds in India and one of the parties to the merger was located in India, the Offshore Exemption was unavailable. This interpretation was further

138. Section 43A Order against SABIC International Holdings B.V, 15 Jul. 2022, paras 22-24.
139. Tata Chemicals Ltd. and Wyoming 1 (Mauritius) Pvt. Ltd., Combination Registration No. C-2011/12/12, 28 Nov. 2011.

widened with the CCI holding in *Tetra Laval/Alfa Laval*[140] that if the target enterprise has any *direct or indirect* presence in India through its subsidiaries in excess of the jurisdictional thresholds, there is a *significant local nexus* in India and the transaction is notifiable.

It is by virtue of this expanded interpretation that combinations get captured under the radar of CCI by involving Indian subsidiaries, even if they remain in unrelated businesses, not forming the subject matter of the acquisition.[141] An illustration of the same is the acquisition by Nestle of Pfizer's global nutrition business, which did not have any presence or business operations in India but was notified to the CCI on account of the fact that Pfizer has other subsidiaries in India, which are engaged in completely unrelated business activities, i.e., the pharmaceutical and animal healthcare sector.

For the sake of illustration, let us take an example of a purely overseas transaction:

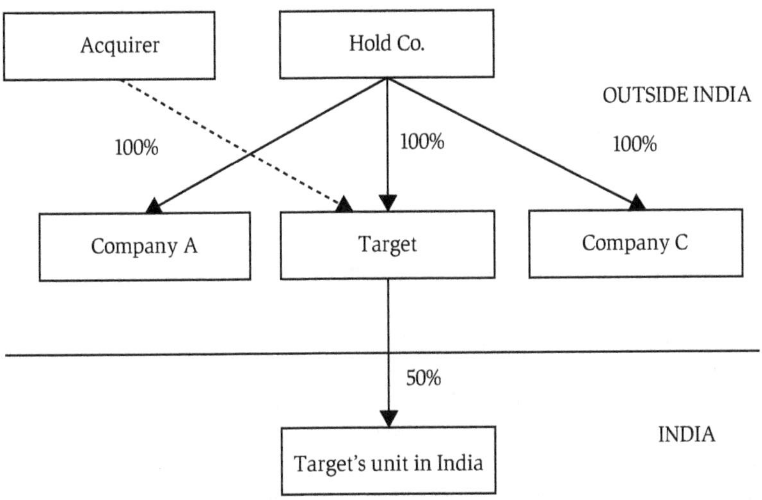

In the structure above, the Acquirer wishes to acquire 25% in Target, which has a subsidiary in India. Further, the subsidiary of Target has different business operations than that of Target, and the Acquirer has no business operations in India. In such a situation, the transaction is purely offshore with no effect on the market in India. Even in such a case, the transaction will be a notifiable transaction if the subsidiary exceeds the jurisdictional thresholds mentioned under the MCA Circular and the transaction crosses the threshold limits mentioned under section 5 of the Competition Act.

140. Tatra Laval B.V. and Alfa Laval AB, Combination Registration No. C-2012/02/40, 12 Apr. 2012.
141. Nestle, Pfizer, Combination Registration No. C-2012/05/57, 1 Aug. 2012; Glory Investments A Limited, Combination Registration No. C-2012/08/76, 11 Oct. 2012; Titan International Inc. and Titan Europe PLC, Combination Registration No. C-2013/02/109, 2 Apr. 2013.

The enforcement regime of CCI with respect to offshore combinations has also strengthened by virtue of imposition of penalties in case of belated filings. For instance, in *Titan International/Titan Europe*,[142] Titan International, Inc., based in the USA, was acquiring the entire share capital of Titan Europe PLC, based in the UK. In its process, Titan International indirectly had to acquire Titan Europe's shareholding of 35.91% equity interest in Wheels India Limited (not a subsidiary of Titan Europe but an associate company of Titan Europe). Though the transaction took place entirely offshore, it only indirectly affected the Indian entity (i.e., on the strength of shares held by the target in an Indian entity), and this shareholding did not even provide the target control over the Indian entity (Wheels India). Yet, CCI considered this shareholding to give the target a local presence in India, and since Wheels India exceeded the prescribed assets and turnover thresholds, the CCI held that a merger notification ought to have been filed to obtain the regulatory clearance from it within the prescribed time-limit under section 6(2) of the Competition Act. Since the application (voluntarily made by parties) was made after the thirty-day time limit, a penalty was imposed by the CCI. Herein, it is relevant to note that as mentioned earlier, the thirty-day time limit to file a notification for CCI's approval after execution of the binding document has been removed.

Now that the Offshore Exemption has been deleted from the Combination Regulations (which in any event was not given accord to by the CCI in its decisional practice), numerous offshore transactions are notified to the CCI which are purely technical filings.

§4.14 PROCEDURE FOR INVESTIGATION OF A COMBINATION

In its decisional practice, to date, the CCI has not refused approval to any combination, even in cases of belated filing or gun-jumping, provided the notice was subsequently filed. When a combination is likely to cause AAEC in India, the CCI undertakes a detailed enquiry into the combination, including inviting opinions from relevant third parties and allows parties to submit voluntary modifications or propose modifications of their own. This procedure has been discussed below.

[A] Phase I

The scheme of the Competition Act and the Combination Regulations provides that the CCI will form a prima facie opinion on whether the proposed combination is likely to cause any AAEC in India.

Regulation 19 of the Combination Regulations provides the prima facie opinion will be formed by the CCI within thirty days of the receipt of the merger notification. In the event that the CCI forms a prima facie view that the combination would not cause AAEC on competition in the relevant market in India, CCI approves the combination,

142. Titan International Inc. and Titan Europe PLC, Combination Registration No. C-2013/02/109, 2 Apr. 2013.

under section 31 of the Competition Act, in Phase I itself. The said period of thirty days of forming a prima facie opinion does not include clock stops. It must be noted that even in Phase 1, Regulation 19 empowers the CCI to call for information from any third party to enquire if the combination has caused or is likely to cause any AAEC in India. As such, the CCI has used Regulation 19(3) of the Combination Regulations to call for information from Air India while approving the *Jet/Etihad* deal.

Regulation 19(2) of the Combination Regulations provides that the CCI may ask the parties to the combination to accept modifications for forming its prima facie order. The CCI has previously sought behavioural commitments in the form of commitments in its combination decisions in Phase I itself, where it asked the parties to review its existing contracts to ensure that they are in compliance with the provisions of the Competition Act and the parties continue to abide by the provisions of the sectoral regulator.

In this regard, it is apposite to note that in July 2015, the CCI amended the filing requirements prescribed under the Combinations Regulations with the aim to make the filing simpler and readily acceptable to various stakeholders, thereby aligning its practice with other matured anti-trust jurisdictions. The key element introduced is the role of third parties in the merger approval process: third parties can give their comments on the likely competition concerns arising in the relevant market as a result of the combination. This has been discussed in more detail subsequently.

A timeline for a Phase I investigation, with the relevant provisions under the Competition Act and the Combination Regulations, is as follows:

<table>
<tr><th>Days</th><th>Procedure</th></tr>
<tr><td>0-30 (thirty days)</td><td>Parties to notify the combination to the CCI within thirty days from the date of trigger of merger/acquisition.</td></tr>
<tr><td>X-30 (thirty working days)</td><td>From the date of receipt of notice, CCI has to form a prima facie opinion on whether the combination causes or is likely to cause AAEC in India.</td></tr>
<tr><td colspan="2">If the combination causes or is likely to cause AAEC in India, then CCI shall issue a show cause notice to the parties directing them to respond within thirty calendar days of the receipt of such notice, furnishing reasons as to why the detailed investigation in respect of such combination should not be conducted under section 29(1) of the Competition Act.</td></tr>
<tr><td>X-30 (thirty days)</td><td>During the continuation of the X-30 days period, the CCI, at any stage, may request the parties to file additional information or accept modification if offered by the parties.

The time taken by parties to furnish information is considered 'the clock stops period' as this period is excluded from the X-30 days (thirty days) period.</td></tr>
</table>

Days	*Procedure*
Fifteen days	In case modification is offered by the parties to the combination, fifteen days are given to the parties to accept them or not. Again, this period is considered 'the clock stops period' as this period is excluded from the X-30 days (thirty days) period.
If the CCI is not satisfied with the response of the parties, it initiates a detailed Phase II investigation.	

[B] Phase 2

In the event that the CCI forms a prima facie opinion that the combination will cause an AAEC in the relevant market in India, it can issue a show cause notice to the parties to the combination to respond, within thirty days, as to why a detailed investigation (Phase II investigation) should not be commenced against them with respect to the combination. On response from the parties to the combination, the CCI may call for a report from the DG to investigate the proposed combination. Thereafter, if the CCI is of the opinion that the proposed combination causes or is likely to cause an AAEC in India, it will direct the parties to the combination to publish details of the proposed combination (Schedule II – Form IV of the Combination Regulations). This aims to bring to the knowledge of or information to the public and persons affected or likely to be affected by such combination and may invite such public or person to file objections, if any. Thereafter, written objection to the combination, if invited by the CCI, will have to be provided within fifteen days from the date of publication of details of the combination by the parties to the combination.

A timeline for a Phase II investigation, with the relevant provisions under the Competition Act and the Combination Regulations, is as follows:

Days	*Procedure*
Y	Issuance of show cause notice
If the combination causes or is likely to cause AAEC in India, then CCI shall issue a show cause notice to the parties directing them to respond within thirty calendar days of the receipt of such notice, furnishing reasons as to why the detailed investigation in respect of such combination should not be conducted under section 29(1) of the Competition Act.	
No timeline specified	From the date of receipt of response from the parties, the CCI may direct the Director General to investigate and formulate a report under section 29(1A) of the Competition Act.
Y + 7 days	From the date of receipt of response from the parties or the report prepared by the Director General, whichever is later, CCI directs parties to publish details of the combination.

<table>
<tr><th>Days</th><th>Procedure</th></tr>
<tr><td>Y + 17</td><td>Parties to furnish such details and the same is brought to public knowledge.</td></tr>
<tr><td colspan="2">Under section 29(2) of the Competition Act, if the CCI is of the prima facie opinion that the combination has or is likely to cause AAEC, it shall direct the parties, within seven working days from the receipt of their response pursuant to section 29(1) or on the receipt of the report of the Director General (whichever is later), to publish the details of the combination within ten working days of such direction to bring it to the knowledge of public and persons likely affected by such combination.</td></tr>
<tr><td>Y + 32</td><td>Under section 29(3) of the Competition Act, the CCI invites third parties to file objections to the combination, if any, within fifteen working days from the date when the details of the combination were published.</td></tr>
<tr><td>Y + 47</td><td>From the expiry of fifteen days from the period in section 29(3), the CCI may ask the parties to furnish additional documents regarding the combination under section 29(4) of the Competition Act.</td></tr>
<tr><td>Y + 62</td><td>Pursuant to section 29(5) of the Competition Act, the parties are to submit the additional documents as required by the CCI within fifteen days from the expiry of the period mentioned under section 29(4).</td></tr>
<tr><td>Y + 107</td><td>Pursuant to section 29(6) of the Competition Act, from the date of receipt of all information by the CCI and within a period of forty-five days from the expiry of the period under section 29(5), CCI will assess all documents on record and proceed to deal with the case in accordance with section 31.</td></tr>
</table>

It is pointed out that under the Competition (Amendment) Act, 2023, the timeline for the CCI to make a prima facie determination on Phase II (or approve the transaction) is thirty calendar days (as opposed to the current thirty-working-day review period under the present law). Further, if the clearance is not issued or an initial order to conduct Phase II is not issued within the thirty-calendar-day period, the transaction would be deemed approved.

[1] Role of Third Parties

As mentioned above, third parties may be involved in both Phase I and Phase II of the combination review process. In Phase I, CCI may reach out to third parties for their comments and observations on the combination. Further, in Phase II, the parties mandatorily have to publish the details of the combination to which any member of the public can file their written objections within fifteen days of such publication.

As stated earlier, a noteworthy aspect of the July 2015 amendment is the insertion of a transparency element in case of merger filing procedure. The amendment provides that the parties to the combination will submit a 500-page summary of the combination (which will contain the details of the combination, parties and the relevant market) to the CCI, and the said summary will be hosted on the website of the CCI. This disclosure would help any stakeholder in the market to provide their comments on the combination to the CCI. The amendment should have been a step forward for the existing regime in third-party to give their comments on the combination. Prior to this amendment, and as discussed above, Regulation 19(3) of the Combination Regulations provided for discretionary powers to the CCI (as it deemed necessary) to call for information from third parties in its inquiry whether the combination has caused or is likely to cause an AAEC in India. Similarly, CCI could seek the opinion of any other agency or statutory authority in relation to combination pursuant to Regulation 34 of the Combination Regulation. Under its own statutory power to regulate its procedure (section 36 of the Competition Act), the CCI holds the power to invite experts or direct persons with respect to the trade in question and gather information. In fact, these provisions have been applied in merger cases such as in the merger between Denki Kagaku Kogyo Kabushiki Kaisha and Mitsui & Co. Ltd. CCI sought the opinion of the Rubber Board, Ministry of Commerce and Industry as well as certain users of chloroprene rubber in India.[143]

This amendment has the following implications. It provides an opportunity for any stakeholder or interested party to provide their comments on a merger application filed with the CCI. However, mere filing of any representation does not give such third party a vested right to participate in the combination proceedings.

Regulation 19(3) of the Combination Regulations empowers the CCI to call for information from any other enterprise while inquiring as to whether a combination has caused or is likely to cause AAEC in India. However, although the CCI is empowered to invite information, the scheme does not entitle any other person other than those who have given notice to participate in the proceedings. This position was clarified by the NCLAT recently *in U.P. Glass Manufacturers Syndicate v. Competition Commission of India & Ors.*[144] The U.P. Glass Manufacturers Syndicate (UPGMS), an industry body of glass manufacturers, sought intervention in CCI's assessment of the proposed acquisition of 100% shares of Hindustan National Glass & Industries Limited by AGI Greenpac Limited, which were two of the biggest market players. The NCLAT held that the right of participation of the general public in the combination assessment process arises when the CCI directs the parties to the combination to publish the details of the combination, for bringing the combination to the knowledge or information of the public and persons affected or likely to be affected. In this case, the stage of direction to publish details of combination had not arisen, since there was no prima facie opinion formed at the second stage review envisaged under section 29(2) of the Competition Act. As a result, UPGMS was rightly not allowed to participate in the combination assessment process by the CCI. Thus, third parties do not have any vested right to participate in a pending combination proceeding until and unless the CCI itself

143. Denki Kagaku Kogyo Kabushiki Kaisha and Mitsui & Co. Ltd, Combination Registration No. C-2015/01/239, 24 Apr. 2015.
144. Competition Appeal (AT) No. 07 of 2023, paras 73, 74.

specifically directs the parties to publish the details of the combination and seeks comments from the public.

Similarly, earlier, the competitors on their own could only make submissions during Phase II of the investigation or when they were asked by the CCI to provide their comments on a combination under Regulation 19(3) of the Combination Regulations. Now, any stakeholder can provide comments in order to assist the CCI in making its determination of merger, and the same can be exercised at any stage, i.e., a prima facie stage or a later stage of merger investigation. As such, as stated above, mere filing of representation does not give such parties a vested right to participate.

In its decisional practice, CCI has frequently sought the comments of third parties in the combination review process.[145] Some of these cases have been discussed below.

The merger between Bayer Aktiengesellschaft (Bayer), Monsanto Company (Monsanto) and KWA Investment Co (Merger Sub), a wholly owned subsidiary of Bayer, raised several competition concerns, *inter alia*, pertaining to the vegetable seeds business due to the presence of several horizontal overlaps in the parties' businesses (Bayer/Monsanto).[146] Further, Bayer's response to the show cause notice did not allay the said concerns. Consequently, CCI asked Bayer to publish the details of the combination, pursuant to which CCI received written objections from several parties, which were considered in the assessment of the merger. Ultimately, the CCI ordered the parties to undertake divestment of certain businesses (as has been discussed under the heading of commitments). Herein, it is relevant to note that after inviting public comments on the combination, CCI generally gives the parties a chance to respond to the comments.

Similarly, in the acquisition of Metso OYJ's mineral business by Outotec OYJ (*Outotec OYJ* decision),[147] the CCI considered the responses of competitors and their submissions regarding Entry Barriers (Technical, Regulatory, etc.), position of parties, countervailing buying power, possession of IPRs & drawing including designs, competitive advantage, etc. This has been discussed in more detail in the next section, under substantive analysis of combinations.

Another example is the merger between PayU and BillDesk, both operating in the market of payment processing (*PayU/BillDesk*).[148] The parties had submitted that payment aggregation services provided by payment aggregators (PAs), such as the parties, were interchangeable with the business model of the merchant integrating itself on a TPAP, wherein the transactions are initiated on the TPAP app. To clarify this, the CCI sought the views of merchant stakeholders who submitted that they do not

145. Schneider Electric India Pvt. Ltd. and MacRitchie Investments Pte. Ltd., Combination Registration No. C-2018/07/586, 18 Apr. 2019, paras 64, 65; Linde Aktiengesellschaft and Praxair, Inc., Combination Registration No. C-2018/01/545, 6 Sep. 2018, para. 14; PVR/DT Cinemas, Combination Registration No. C-2015/07/288, 4 May 2016; Dish TV India Limited & Videocon D2h Limited, Combination Registration No. C-2016/12/463, 4 May 2017, para. 15.
146. Bayer AG and Monsanto Company, Combination Registration No. C-2017/08/523, 14 Jun. 2018, paras 14-18.
147. Outotec OYJ and Metso OYJ, Combination Registration No. C-2020/03/735, 18 Jun. 2020, para. 33.
148. PayU Payments Private Limited, Combination Registration No. C-2022/04/920, 5 Jun. 2022, para. 42.

consider integrating a PA platform on their website/app and services and integrating their store on a TPAP to be interchangeable due to higher cost implications for the merchant, need for high level of monitoring, success rates and transaction management by merchant, concern of discoverability, need for a merchant to integrate with multiple TPAPs in order to provide users with varied options, lack of control over payment logic, lack of data insights, etc. Based on these responses, the CCI of the Online P2M Payment Services is required to be restricted to only PA services, which enable receipt of payments on the merchant website/app.

Hence, it is safe to conclude that the concerns of third parties, which include consumers, competitors and general public, increasingly play an important role in CCI's assessment of combinations.

[C] Voluntary Modifications

In its decisional practice, the CCI has granted approval to combinations which are potentially likely to cause AAEC to be subject to compliance with voluntary modifications offered by the parties at the time of combination assessment if such modifications are sufficient to address the potential competition concerns flagged by the CCI.[149]

Herein, it is relevant to point out that there exists a 'grey zone' between the formation of a prima facie opinion by CCI that a combination will have an AAEC and the decision to launch an investigation. CCI's decisional practice indicates that the parties may submit voluntary modifications during this grey zone.

For instance, in China National Agrochemical Corporation's (acquirer) acquisition of 67% equity shares in and indirect sole control of Syngenta AG, the CCI prima facie found that there were horizontal overlaps between the Parties vis-à-vis crop protection products leading to concerns of AAEC (*China National* decision).[150] Accordingly, the CCI issued a show cause notice to China National as to why an investigation of the proposed combination should not be conducted. The Acquirer filed a response along with a voluntary remedy proposal. The combination was approved subject to compliance with these voluntary modifications, and CCI did not issue commitments of this own.

In the merger between Abbot and St. Jude Medical, Inc. (SJM), the CCI found that the combined market share of the parties in the small-hole vascular closure devices segment was in the range of 90%-100%.[151] As a result, the proposed combination enhanced the combined entity's market power in this segment. The merger was accepted upon the parties submitting a voluntary modification in the form of a plan of

149. Northern TK Venture Pte. Ltd., Combination Registration No. C-2018/09/601, 29 Oct. 2018, para. 18; Tata Sons Private Limited, Singapore Airlines Limited, Air India Limited, Talace Private Limited and Tata SIA Airlines Limited, Combination Registration No. C-2023/04/1022, 1 Sep. 2023, paras 115-133; TRIL Urban Transport Private Limited, Valkyrie Investment Pte Limited and Solis Capital (Singapore) Pte. Limited, Combination Registration No. C-2019/07/676, 1 Oct. 2019, para. 32.
150. China National Agrochemical Corporation, Combination Registration No. C-2016/08/424, 16 May 2017, para. 22.
151. Abbott Laboratories, Combination Registration No. C-2016/08/418, 13 Dec. 2016, paras 9-11.

divesture of all the small-hole vascular closure devices of SJM. The divestiture involved the sale of the entire overlapping business, including products, trademarks, technology, know-how, manufacturing facilities, as well as transitional services for support, to an independent purchaser.

Such voluntary modifications have been accepted by the CCI in the approval of other combinations as well.[152] Subsequently, this option of offering voluntary modifications was formalized by amending the Combination Regulations to allow parties to offer modifications along with their response to the show cause notice during the Phase I review. However, no format was added for the same. CCI's decisional practice indicates a trend that it is keen to approve remedies without progressing to Phase II review provided the voluntary remedies offered by the parties actually allay the AAEC concerns identified by the CCI.[153]

These remedies may not necessarily be in the nature of divestments. For instance, in the proposed acquisition by automobile manufacturers Hyundai and Kia for minority shareholdings in ride-sharing company ANI Technologies (OLA) and its electric vehicles arm, OLA Electric Mobility, the CCI highlighted its concerns that drivers of Hyundai and Kia cars might be favoured in the OLA marketplace. In a first-of-its-kind remedy, the CCI accepted voluntary modifications offered by the parties that the strategic collaboration would be on a non-exclusive basis and that the algorithm/programme of the OLA marketplace would not give preference to the drivers driving Hyundai/Kia cars or discriminate against drivers based solely on the brand of the passenger vehicles manufactured by any other automobile manufacturer. The CCI noted that the above modification would ensure that the radio taxi marketplace would act in an objective manner and that the strategic collaboration would not result in discrimination against any driver who does not drive a vehicle of Hyundai/Kia make.[154]

152. Mumbai International Airport Private Limited, Indian Oil Corporation Limited, Bharat Petroleum Corporation Limited, Hindustan Petroleum Corporation Limited and Mumbai Aviation Fuel Farm Facility Limited, Combination Registration No. C-2014/04/164, 29 Sep. 2014, para. 24; Nippon Yusen Kabushiki Kaisha Ltd., Mitsui O.S.K. Lines Ltd. and Kawasaki Kisen Kaisha, Ltd., Combination Registration No. C-2016/11/459, 29 Jun. 2017, para. 25.

153. ZF Friedrichshafen AG, Combination Registration No. C-2019/11/703, 14 Feb. 2020, paras 75-77; Outotec OYJ and Metso OYJ, Combination Registration No. C-2020/03/735, 18 Jun. 2020 paras 16-20; Canary Investment Limited and Link Investment Trust II, Combination Registration No. C-2020/04/741, 20 Apr. 2019, para. 15; Ipca Laboratories Limited, CCI, Combination Registration No. C-2023/05/1028, 26 Jul. 2023, para. 18; General Atlantic Singapore ACK Pte. Ltd., Combination Registration No. C-2023/04/1017, 6 Jun. 2023, para. 10; Culver Max Entertainment Private Limited, Zee Entertainment Enterprises Limited, Bangla Entertainment Private Limited, and Essel Group Participants, Combination Registration No. C-2022/04/923, 4 Oct. 2022, para. 88; Umang Commercial Company Private Limited and Aditya Marketing and Manufacturing Private Limited, Combination Registration No. C-2022/07/952, 30 Aug. 2022, para. 48; Dish TV India Limited & Videocon D2h Limited, Combination Registration No. C-2016/12/463, 4 May 2017, para. 18; FMC Corporation, Dow Chemical Company, E.I. du Pont de Nemours and Company Combination Registration No. C-2017/06/519, 18 Sep. 2017, paras 24-40.

154. Hyundai Motor Company and Kia Motors Corporation, Combination Registration No. C-2019/09/682, 30 Oct. 2019, paras 23-25.

Similarly, CCI conditionally approved Google International LLC's acquisition of a non-controlling minority stake of 1.28% in Bharti Airtel Limited owing to Google's stake in Jio Platforms Limited (Jio) which is also active in similar businesses to Airtel. The CCI raised concerns of a potential flow of commercial sensitive information between Airtel and Jio which were allayed by certain voluntary behavioural remedies including an information firewall between Airtel and Jio.[155]

Hence, as long as voluntary modifications proposed by the parties are comprehensive to address the anticompetitive concerns emerging from the proposed combinations, the CCI is likely to accept the modification package as it is.

In a build-up of this trend, the Draft Regulations prescribe a format for offering voluntary modifications/remedies to the CCI. The items that must be included are: (a) summary of the modifications offered; (b) details on how the modifications address the identified concerns; (c) various details on the divestment products, if any; and (d) monitoring arrangements. The Draft Regulations also add timelines to the offering of modifications, thereby adding greater certainty to the process.

Therefore, on a comprehensive consideration of the above discussion, it can be said that the CCI has adopted a pro-approval stance subject to compliance in the combination assessment by the parties. If parties themselves propose adequate and sufficient commitments, the CCI is not likely to proceed to a detailed investigation of the combination (Phase II). Thus, it can be said that the cooperation by the parties is central to CCI's approach to approvals.

§4.15 TYPES OF MERGERS

Depending on the nature of the business and at which level of the supply chain the parties are operating, a merger can be categorized into the following three types. The issues arising out of each kind of merger have also been discussed.

[A] Horizontal Mergers

Horizontal mergers occur when companies operating in the same or similar industries and offering similar products or services combine their operations. These mergers typically involve businesses that are direct competitors within the same market segment. It is to be noted that a merger of close competitors can generate horizontal-anticompetitive effects, whether coordinated or non-coordinated if the combined entity significantly constrains the behaviour of other firms active in the market.[156]

155. Google International LLC and Bharti Airtel Limited, Combination Registration No. C-2022/03/91, 30 Jun. 2022, para. 24.
156. Outotec OYJ and Metso OYJ, Combination Registration No. C-2020/03/735, 18 Jun. 2020, para. 35.

[1] Issues with Horizontal Mergers

The following issues need to be considered while assessing the permissibility of horizontal mergers.

First, as in the case of horizontal agreements, it must first be established as to what is the relevant market. This requires a focus on the demand side to establish whether the products are close enough substitutes or not. On the supply side, it is important to identify the market shares of the firms. Clearly, it is not enough to go on current market shares. It is important to assess how the relevant market is likely to evolve in the near future. This would depend on whether entry is easy and whether there are potential entrants that could easily enter, if profitability in the sector increases, how foreign competition is likely to evolve and the growth (or decline) of other incumbent firms.

For instance, in *Bayer/Monsanto*,[157] the CCI observed that the present market shares of Bayer in the market of cotton seeds may undergo change and do not represent near future market dynamics as the other seed companies may be out of the market in the near future. Further, the parties were among very few players with a pan-India distribution network who had across the value chain presence in the cotton seed market, which puts them in an advantageous position as compared to their competitors in the downstream market. Therefore, the CCI concluded that any potential harm to competition in future could not be completely ruled out.

The second important step is to establish whether the higher concentration in the market resulting from the merger will increase the possibility of collusive or unilaterally harmful behaviour. Collusion is more likely in industries producing relatively homogeneous products and characterized by small and frequent transactions, the terms of which cannot be kept secret. The merger is likely to be unilaterally harmful when the two merging firms produce similar products in a concentrated differentiated product market.

The third issue is regarding potential contestability. Even if no potential entrants are immediately visible, a large enough price increase (or high enough profitability) could encourage entry. So, it needs to be established, how high the expected price increase is likely to be. Following this, it is important to consider whether entry is really likely, how quick it will be and whether it will be sufficient to make up for the reduced competition resulting from the merger.

Fourth, the case can be made that even mergers that lead to an uncompetitive outcome could result in certain 'efficiencies' that more than make up for the welfare loss resulting from this.

The fifth concern is the emergence of complementary or portfolio effects as a result of the merger. For instance, in *Bayer/Monsanto*,[158] while Bayer was focused primarily on agrochemicals and vegetable seeds, Monsanto's strengths lied in non-selective herbicides, traits, and agricultural seeds. Generally, portfolio effects included

157. *Bayer/Monsanto*, para. 81.
158. *Bayer/Monsanto*, paras 154, 155.

potential anti-competitive effects that might arise due to a merger uniting complementary products in which one or more parties enjoy significant market power. Thus, CCI concluded that the combined entity would have the ability to bundle their portfolios of crop protection products, seeds and traits which may have a negative impact on competitors and customers. For example, the combined entity may develop new traits for seeds for which only they will be able to develop agrochemical products, and therefore, the rest of the competitors would be excluded from the market.

Similarly, in *PayU/Bill Desk*,[159] an analysis of the complementary relationships between the parties revealed that despite the individual strengths and weaknesses of each party, complementary/portfolio effects of the combined entity were significantly reduced since it did not have a position of strength in any individual market. Upon a holistic consideration of all these factors, CCI concluded that the transaction did not raise competition concerns. Thus, complementary effects cannot be assumed in all situations of horizontal mergers, and a case-by-case analysis has to be done.

[B] Vertical Mergers

Competition Law must not normally have any objections to vertical mergers since they are measures for improving production and distribution efficiencies. The process internalizes the benefits of supply chain management and, as such, cannot be perceived as injuries to competition.

There could, however, be some specific objections to vertical integration, as described below.

[1] Fear of Foreclosure

It is supposed that, through vertical integration, a firm can create captive distribution channels. This will foreclose the rival firms from the market, represented by the captive distribution network. This may be a problem if it threatens competition in general. For instance, in *Bayer/Monsanto*,[160] allegations of anti-competitive practices by imposing unfair and discriminatory conditions in the sub-licence agreements relating to Bt. Technology were made by the downstream competitors of Bayer and Monsanto, who were involved in the market for commercialization of Bt. cotton seed in India. The CCI noted that any foreclosure strategy by the combined entity would have a significant detrimental effect on competition in the downstream market, as it would require potential competitors to enter both the downstream and the upstream level in order to compete effectively in either market. This would raise entry barriers as it would be significantly time- and cost-intensive.

159. PayU Payments Private Limited, Combination Registration No. C-2022/04/920, 5 Sep. 2022.
160. *Bayer/Monsanto*, paras 84, 85.

[2] Entry Blocking

Monopolies can have the ability to prevent the entry of firms into the market. Sometimes, it is claimed that even competitors can come together to prevent a potential entrant. This is sometimes referred to as collective foreclosure. If through integration, firms are able to internalize different levels of production, artificial barriers to entry could be created. This implies that because of the size of the incumbent, a potential entrant's capital requirements will be high.

[3] Price Squeezes

Vertical mergers and integration internalize the process of production and enable a firm to perhaps reduce costs. This will result in a reduction in output prices, which is usually interpreted as a price squeeze. The law should question only those monopolies resulting from vertical mergers (integration) that lead to output restriction rather than preventing vertical integration.

[C] Conglomerate Mergers

A conglomerate merger is a merger that is neither horizontal nor vertical. For example, a merger between a car manufacturer and a textile firm is a conglomerate merger. The theories for 'restraining' vertical and horizontal mergers are well formulated. There, however, is no clear mechanism for similar restraints on conglomerate mergers except those that are based on folklore. There is sufficient evidence to suggest that conglomerate mergers do not pose any threat to competition.

In fact, the green channel route for merger approval, as discussed earlier in the chapter, is an illustration of the fact that CCI ordinarily does not consider conglomerate mergers to be problematic from a competition perspective.

Yet, conglomerate mergers are objected to on several grounds. Some of the objections to conglomerate mergers are:

(a) They create deep pockets which enables that firm to devastate its rivals.
(b) Lower costs below the marginal cost of the industry.
(c) Raise barriers to entry.
(d) Engage in reciprocal dealing to the disadvantage of the rivals.
(e) Eliminate potential competition.

We examine some of these objections below.

[1] The Theory of Deep Pockets

It is believed that firms operating in many markets can devastate their rivals through their potentially infinite capital resources. This suggests that conglomerates can engage in predatory pricing. However, the law cannot presume that possession of capital can lead to harmful pricing practices, even though predatory pricing is a discredited theory. An objection based on the fact of possession of capital cannot be construed as a serious objection.

[2] Raising Barriers to Entry

Conglomerate mergers help in pooling the capital resources. It is believed that conglomerate mergers can lead to the erection of entry barriers. For example, a firm that had a limited promotional budget might now make use of the other firm's promotional expertise. However, if competition is equated with consumer welfare then, one should really ask why is it not a valuable efficiency to bring capital to a firm that can use it? Why is it not good for the consumers if the single-product firm shares the cost savings in advertising and promotion that normally accrue to a multi-product firm?

[3] Loss of Potential Competition

Two arguments are proposed to support this position. First, it is believed that because of the merger, there is less 'space' for new firms. Second, if, instead of the merger, the larger firm had tried to enter a market on its own, the threat of entry would have forced the existing firms to become more competitive and efficient.

§4.16 SUBSTANTIVE ANALYSIS OF COMBINATIONS

Section 6(1) of the Competition Act prevents combinations which cause or are likely to cause AAEC within the relevant market in India. In concluding whether it would cause or is likely to cause AAEC, the CCI takes into account the factors mentioned under section 20(4) of the Competition Act.

The aspect of merger control analysis was done in great detail by the High Level Committee on Competition Law which stated that horizontal mergers would have to be scrutinized more than a vertical or a conglomerate merger. The relevant portions of the High Level Committee Report on the approach to be adopted for merger control analysis and the key issues to be considered are as follows:

> As in the case of agreements, mergers are typically classified into horizontal and vertical mergers. In addition, merger between enterprises operating in different markets are called conglomerate mergers. Mergers are a legitimate means by which firms can grow and are generally as much part of the natural process of industrial evolution and restructuring as new entry, growth and exit. From the point of view of Competition Policy it is horizontal mergers that are generally the focus of attention. As in the case of horizontal agreements, such mergers have a potential for reducing competition. In rare cases, where an enterprise in a dominant position makes a vertical merger with another firm in a (vertically) adjacent market to further entrench its position of dominance, the merger may

> provide cause for concern. Conglomerate mergers should generally be beyond the purview of any law on mergers.
>
> A merger leads to a 'bad' outcome only if it creates a dominant enterprise that subsequently abuses its dominance. To some extent the issue is analogous to that of agreements among enterprises and also overlaps with the issue of dominance and its abuse discussed in the previous sections. Viewed in this way, there is probably no need to have a separate law on mergers. The reason that such a provision exists in most laws is to pre-empt the potential abuse of dominance where it is probable, as subsequent unbundling can be both difficult and socially costly.

Thus, the general principle, in keeping with the overall goal, is that mergers should be challenged only if they reduce or harm competition and adversely affect welfare. Also, the CCI has taken an approach that they will block mergers only if the merger itself causes an AAEC, not issues which are predating the combination. For example, if an enterprise has a 90% market share and it then acquires a company which has a 1% market share, the said merger would not be blocked since the said entity so combined is in a dominant position since even before the merger, the entity was already in a commanding 90% market share position.

Some of the factors routinely analysed in CCI's decisional practice of substantive assessment of combinations have been discussed below.

[A] Combined Market Share

Market share is typically the most important factor in assessing whether the combination will cause or is likely to cause AAEC in the relevant market. Market share can be calculated both in terms of value sales and volume sales. The CCI looks at the combined market share of the parties post the combination, and in the event the market share post the combination is insignificant, the CCI has cleared the transaction in Phase I itself.[161]

Further, the CCI also takes into account whether the market is fragmented and whether there are sufficient competitors in the relevant market which will continue to pose effective competitive constraints on the parties post the combination.[162] It must be noted that the CCI looks at the increment/change in the market share as a result of the combination while analysing a combination. The CCI does not intervene in cases where the increment in market share is negligible/marginal, even if the combined market share of the parties is more than 50%.[163] The rationale for the same is that competition law concerns, if any, was pre-existing the combination, and it is not created as a result of the combination.

161. Indus Ind, Combination Registration No. C-2015/04/268, 15 Jun. 2015; ATC Telecom Tower Corporation Private Limited, Combination Registration No. C-2015/04/269, 26 May 2015.
162. Inox, Fame India, Fame Motion, Big Pictures and Headstrong Films, Combination Registration No. C – 2012/10/84, 23 Oct. 2012, CTLC/TCFSL, Combination Registration No. C-2012/09/78, 4 Oct. 2012.
163. Sutlej Textiles and Industries Limited, Combination Registration No. C-2015/04/266, 15 Jun. 2015; Pfizer Inc, Combination Registration No. C-2015/03/255, 11 Jun. 2015; Johnson Controls Inc., Combination Registration No. C-2015/02/247, 7 May 2015; Torrent Pharmaceuticals

[B] Presence of Overlaps

While analysing a combination, the CCI also looks at pre-existing horizontal and vertical overlaps of the parties to the combination. For analysing overlaps, the CCI assesses whether the parties to the combination operate in different geographic areas in the relevant geographic market.[164]

The CCI has also engaged in price point analysis to see the manner in which the parties to the combination have priced their products in the relevant market to see whether parties operate at different price points to analyse overlaps.[165] It is apposite in this regard to observe the price point analysis of various segments of beverages in the whisky segment, vodka segment, rum, wine and gin segment adopted by the CCI in the merger approval order of acquisition of shares of USL by Relay, a subsidiary of Diageo. The relevant observations of the CCI have been summarized below:

(i) Whisky Segment: Whisky accounted for 60% of the total sales volume, constituting the largest segment. It was further segmented into IMFL Whisky, Scotch Whisky and Imported Whisky:
   - Out of this, IMFL Whisky sales constituted a large chunk of around 98.54% of the total Whisky segment, and all the IMFL Whisky brands were priced below INR 800. None of Diageo's Whisky brands was significantly present below this price point, thereby indicating no significant market concentration in the IMFL Whisky segment post-combination.
   - The Scotch Whisky and the Imported Whisky segments, which together constituted less than 2% of the overall Whisky segment, were characterized by the presence of a large number of brands positioned across various premium and luxury price points starting from INR 800 and going up to INR 10,000 and above. It was observed that the consumers of these segments may have a higher degree of brand affinity, basis the relatively high sales volume of brands like Pernod Ricard's Royal Salute, Chivas Regal 18/12 Year Old, Ballantine's Finest, 100 Pipers, Beam Global's Teacher's 50, Teacher's Original; WM Grant's Glenfiddich, Grant's Family Reserve, Diageo's Johnnie Walker Blue/Red/Black, USL's Black Dog, etc.
   - In the price point segment from INR 800 to INR 1,600 which constituted around 1% of the overall Whisky segment, both USL and Diageo were present with their strong brands like Black Dog 12 Years Old,

---

Limited and Elder Pharmaceuticals Limited, Combination Registration No. C-2014/01/148, 26 Mar. 2014; United Spirits Limited by Relay B.V. (Diageo), Combination Registration No. C-2012/12/97, 26 Feb. 2013.

164. Mahindra and Mahindra Limited, Combination Registration No. C-2013/01/105, 4 Feb. 2013; GSPC Distribution Networks Limited, Gujarat Gas Company Limited, Combination Registration No. C-2012/11/88, 8 Jan. 2013.

165. United Spirits Limited by Relay B.V. (Diageo), Combination Registration No. C-2012/12/97, 26 Feb. 2013.

Black Dog (BII) and Whyte & Mackay in the USL portfolio and brands such as Johnnie Walker Red Label, Black & White and VAT 69 in the Diageo portfolio. As such in this price segment, there was also a significant presence of other brands like Pernod Ricard's 100 Pipers, 100 Pipers (BII), Ballantine's Finest and Passport (BII), Beam Global's Teacher's and its variants, WM Grant's Family Reserve, etc. Further, if USL's Black Dog 12 Years Old had a strong presence at the price point of around INR 1,600, there were equally strong competitive brands of Teacher's 50 and Teacher's Original at around the same price point. Similar was the case with Diageo's Johnnie Walker Red Label and USL's Black Dog (BII) with other competitors like Beam Global with Teacher's and Pernod Ricard with Ballantine's Finest at a price point of INR 1,200. Thus, even if the overall volume in this segment was minuscule, consumers had reasonable choices available at various price points, thereby minimizing any concern about the elimination of competitive constraints. The competitors' brands in the above segment also had high growth rates, and these brands were, therefore, considered to be effective competitors to the brands of the parties to the combination.

- In regard to the narrow price sub-segments in the overall Whisky segment, in which even if the brands of USL and Diageo were considered to be positioned as close competitors, there were multiple other brands effectively competing with USL and Diageo in those segments, and the volume in these price segments was also minuscule in comparison to the overall volume of the Whisky segment.

(ii) Vodka Segment: The Vodka segment constituted around 4% of the overall branded spirits segment in India. In 2011, nearly 88% of the Vodka sold in India was priced at INR 500 or below. Diageo, with its brand Smirnoff and its variants, was present in the INR 500+ price segment, and USL, with its flagship brand Romanov and its variants, was present in the price range below INR 500. However, in both these price segments, other competitors like Radico Khaitan were also present with its brand 'Magic Moments' as well as Pernod Ricard's Absolut and its variants, Brown Forman's Finlandia and its variants, etc., which provided stiff competition to USL and Diageo. Further, the entry of 27 new brands in the market indicated that the vodka segment was rapidly growing and evolving in India.

(iii) Rum, Gin and Wine: The Rum segment constituted around 17% of the overall branded spirits segment in India. Diageo had an insignificant share and marginal presence of less than 1% in all three segments, i.e., rum, gin and wine.

Therefore, despite the existence of overlaps, the market shares of the merging parties were marginal and there was healthy competition in each segment of liquor. On this basis, the merger was approved. Hence, if the presence of overlaps is negligible and the merger is likely to expand consumer choice (like in this case, the proposed combination was likely to bring new products and more variants of the existing brands at different price points), that does not pose a threat to competition in the market.

For global parties to the combination, while there may be global overlaps, the CCI analyses only the horizontal and vertical overlaps in India to analyse the competitive effects to determine whether the combination will cause an AAEC in India.[166] On the aspect of vertical overlap, the CCI will intervene only in situations where there is a likelihood of foreclosure in the upstream or downstream market(s) in which the parties are present in India.[167]

While analysing a combination involving an acquisition by a fund, the CCI looks at the horizontal or vertical overlap between the target and other portfolio companies operating in India, where the acquirer has made an investment.[168] The decisional practice of the CCI suggests that it gives more credence to portfolio companies, over which acquirer has direct control to determine overlaps rather than mere passive investments.[169]

In a first, voluntary modifications in the form of behavioural remedies were accepted by the CCI in relation to potential overlaps.[170] In the acquisition of stake in Ipca Laboratories by Unichem Laboratories Limited, the parties exhibited potential horizontal overlaps in the market for manufacture of formulations and vertical overlaps in the market for the manufacture of APIs (upstream) and manufacture of formulations (downstream). These overlaps were 'potential' in nature because while Ipca sold its formulations in India, Unichem's formulations business was completely export-oriented, with no intention to sell in India. Yet, the CCI undertook a competition assessment of the potential overlaps. Even though the parties had insignificant market share in the concerned markets, they submitted a voluntary behavioural commitment that Unichem would will not re-enter the Indian formulations market for at least thirty-six months from the date of closing of the proposed combination. Although the remedy was voluntary proposed by the parties, this decision has the potential to expose potential overlaps between parties to more detailed scrutiny than was expected earlier.

[C] Barriers to Entry

A combination that materially increases market concentration would not give rise to sustained anti-competitive effects if new firms can enter the market (or existing firms

166. Fujitsu Limited, Panasonic Corporation and Development Bank of Japan Inc. Combination Registration No. C-2014/09/206, 27 Oct. 2014.
167. Hyundai Hysco Co. Ltd. And Hyundai Steel Company, Combination Registration No. C-2015/05/272, 5 Jun. 2015.
168. Sion Investment Holdings Pte. Limited, Combination Registration No. C-2015/03/253, 24 Oct. 2015; TPG Asia VI SF Private Limited and Manipal Health Enterprises Private Limited, Combination Registration No. C-2014/12/234, 15 Jan. 2015; KKR Floorline Investments Pte Ltd and Gland Celsus Bio Chemicals Private Limited, Combination Registration No. C-2013/12/145, 28 Jan. 2014; Vault Bermuda Holding Company Limited, Combination Registration No. C-2014/03/157, 3 Apr. 2014.
169. Caladium Investment Pte. Ltd, Combination Registration No. C-2015/01/243, 5 Mar. 2015.
170. Ipca Laboratories Limited, CCI, Combination Registration No. C-2023/05/1028, 26 Jul. 2023, paras 15-18.

expand) and deter the combining parties (and others) from exploiting their position in the market, post the combination.

Barriers to entry are specific features of the market which give incumbent firms advantages over potential competitors. When entry barriers are low, the combining parties are more likely to be constrained by the entry of new firms, disciplining the existing firms upon entry. Conversely, when entry barriers are high, price increases by the combining firms would not be significantly constrained by entry.

The CCI has, to date, approved most cases of combinations (in Phase I itself) because it has found barriers to entry in the relevant market to be very few and/or negligible.[171] However, in several cases, especially where commitments have been ordered (as discussed in the next section), high barriers to entry have been highlighted by the CCI.[172]

For instance, in *Bayer/Monsanto*,[173] the CCI noted that there were substantial entry barriers in the crop protection segment in the form of upfront R&D costs, regulatory know-how, national distribution network, IPRs, patents, etc. Both parties were integrated R&D players with significant capabilities, and therefore, the entry of a new player so as to be an effective long-term competitor of the parties would be difficult. Further, both Bayer and Monsanto were leading innovators in developing nonselective herbicides as well as corresponding herbicide-tolerant traits and trait stacks. The CCI observed that R&D in traits is characterized by high barriers to entry. Limited number of integrated R&D players have the capability and resources to compete in trait innovation, and the process is also time- and cost-intensive. When coupled with regulatory uncertainty in relation to approvals, it deters other players from entering the market.

[D] Buyer Power

The competitive pressure on a supplier is not only exercised by competitors but can also come from its customers. Even firms with very high market shares may not be in a position, post-combination, to exercise market power if customers possess countervailing buyer power. In this context, countervailing buyer power means the bargaining strength that the buyer has vis-à-vis the seller in commercial negotiations due to its size, the commercial significance of the buyer vis-à-vis the seller and its ability to switch to alternative suppliers.[174]

171. Sg Investors, PDPPL, EPDL, Combination Registration No. C-2012/08/75, 1 Oct. 2012 – CCI observed that there were no significant entry barriers in the relevant market for development and management of commercial and office space in India and therefore approved the combination.
172. Schneider Electric India Pvt. Ltd. and MacRitchie Investments Pte. Ltd., Combination Registration No. C-2018/07/586, 18 Apr. 2019, paras 42-56; *China National decision*, paras 12, 17; Linde Aktiengesellschaft and Praxair, Inc., Combination Registration No. C-2018/01/545, 6 Sep. 2018, paras 68-70; *Outotec OYJ decision*, paras 34-36.
173. *Bayer/Monsanto*, paras 36, 50.
174. Denki Kagaku Kogyo Kabushiki Kaisha and Mitsui & Co. Ltd, Combination Registration No. C-2015/01/239, 24 Apr. 2015.

In *AGI Greenpac Limited/Hindusthan National Glass & Industries Limited*,[175] both parties were the only significant organized players in the market for container class in both the alco-beverage and F&B sub-segments. AGI submitted that since the customers in the glass segment were large conglomerates with deep pockets and the suppliers were dependent on these customers, there was no question of the parties being able to act independently of competitive force post the combination. However, the CCI observed that '*countervailing buyer power is considered more a function of relative differences in concentration on the demand and supply side rather than just the size of customers, unless vertical integration trends are clearly discernible*'. In this case, it was not easy for customers to switch suppliers because of the concentrated nature of the glass market, which would increase post the proposed combination. The CCI held that since the parties were the biggest players in the market, countervailing buyer power was limited, and hence, the proposed combination implied the elimination of the most credible option to switch for customers. Thus, it can be said that even if there is a high degree of buyer power present in the market, the impact of such buyer power on the market from the perspective of the proposed combination has to be seen. If the proposed combination decreases the level of choice and increases the concentration, then even a high degree of buyer power cannot mitigate the likely competition concerns.

In other cases also, the CCI has assessed whether the proposed combination is likely to affect the bargaining power, if any, enjoyed by the buyers and whether it would make them more dependent on the parties post the combination.[176] If the answer is yes, and the proposed combination reduces the competitive alternatives presently available to the buyers, then it means that it is likely to cause AAEC in the relevant market.

[E] Presence of a Sectoral Regulator

The CCI takes into account, while analysing the competitive effects of a combination, whether there is a sectoral regulator which prevents anti-competitive behaviour and promotes competition in a particular sector/industry. The CCI has noted the presence and role of regulators like the TRAI[177] and the Petroleum and Natural Gas Regulatory Board[178] to prevent anti-competitive practices in a sector while approving transactions.

175. AGI Greenpac Limited, Combination Registration No. C-2022/11/983, 15 Mar. 2023, paras 63-68.

176. Culver Max Entertainment Private Limited, Zee Entertainment Enterprises Limited, Bangla Entertainment Private Limited, and Essel Group Participants, Combination Registration No. C-2022/04/923, 4 Oct. 2022, paras 43-48; ZF Friedrichshafen AG, Combination Registration No. C-2019/11/703, 14 Feb. 2020, para. 69; Linde Aktiengesellschaft and Praxair, Inc., Combination Registration No. C-2018/01/545, 6 Sep. 2018, paras 73-76.

177. UTV Global Broadcasting Limited C-2013/01/107; Bharti Airtel Limited and Bharti Hexacom Limited, Combination Registration No. C-2017/05/509, 11 May 2018.

178. GSPC Distribution Networks Limited, Gujarat Gas Company Limited, Combination Registration No. C-2012/11/88, 8 Jan. 2013.

As such, the CCI, in the USL Diageo transaction, looked into the aspects of the manufacturing, distribution and pricing of alcoholic beverages in India which are under the regulatory purview of individual state governments for the production, manufacture, possession, transport, license, bottling, introduction of new brands, pricing, purchase and sale of alcoholic beverages in India. Further, the government's involvement in the market of alcoholic beverages also becomes evident in the distribution channel, wherein the government is involved at both wholesale and retail levels, as well as auctions, lottery systems for distribution to wholesalers, etc. Another aspect is the transportation of alcoholic beverages between the states within India, which is also subject to the imposition of various charges, including export fee taxes, import fees and transportation charges. Thus, the sale or distribution of alcoholic beverages in both the wholesale and retail sectors in India was, in some form or manner, regulated by the State Governments.

[F] Role of Efficiencies as a Defence

The CCI gives a lot of emphasis on efficiencies in the market, which can result from the combination. As such, the CCI has analysed economic efficiencies resulting from a combination which may be consumer and/or administrative efficiencies.[179]

For instance, in the *Jet/Etihad* case, one of the reasons adopted by the CCI while approving the deal was the potential efficiencies that would have resulted from the combination. The CCI undertook a holistic analysis of the sector and identified the cost and administrative efficiencies while approving the combination. The relevant portions of the order of the CCI are summarized as follows:

(i) Airline alliances create substantial opportunities for generating economic benefits, many of which are dependent at least in part on the closer integration achievable. These benefits can be viewed as demand-side -relating to the creation of new or improved services through expanded networks or seamless service, or supply-side – essentially the ability to produce the same services at lower cost, taking advantage of traffic densities, improved utilization of capacity and lower transaction costs.

(ii) In the aviation industry, airlines would benefit by integrating complementary networks, which in turn would result in lower fares for passengers. Further, the possibility of coordinating pricing, fares and inventory/yield management will eliminate inherent inefficiencies in pricing and enable the members to offer more attractive fares to customers.

(iii) One of the most fundamental potential benefits from closer cooperation and integration arises from economies of traffic density. This type of economy of scale is a key feature of airline network models. Airline alliances extend the Hub and Spoke (H&S) network with a large presence at both ends of the market. Feeder routes and services delivering connecting

179. *Jet/Etihad* case.

traffic can increase the traffic density on a city-pair, allowing airlines to operate larger, more efficient aircraft and to spread end-point fixed costs over a larger number of passengers.

(iv) The proposed transaction would generate significant synergies for both airlines in terms of network efficiencies and cost savings. Additionally, the parties to the transaction plan to introduce substantial capacity into the Indian market. Both of these factors could and generally do create downward pressure on fares.

(v) Airline alliance has an increased incentive to harmonize and improve customer service standards and quality experience throughout the processes of ticketing, seat selection, airport lounges, gate location for connecting services, onboard amenities and service quality, baggage policies and problem resolution, frequent flyer plans and refunds and exchanges. As these aspects are integrated and jointly managed, the customer receives a correspondingly simplified and consistent service. This aspect of cooperation is likely to provide consumer benefit without anti-competitive results due to the intense, global competition between alliances for customer loyalty.

(vi) Another potential benefit was the proposed equity infusion and its implication for the Indian aviation sector. Herein, Jet was under a huge financial debt and reported substantial negative equity. Thus, Etihad's equity infusion would be beneficial to Jet as it would strengthen its operational viability and allow it to continue to compete effectively in the relevant markets in India and internationally.

§4.17 COMMITMENTS

Merger analysis is essentially a forward-looking exercise whereby the competition regulators can either unconditionally clear the transaction, prohibit the transaction, or approve the transaction with commitments. It requires considerable analytical skill on the part of the competition authorities to impose commitments. Remedies are employed by competition agencies to resolve and prevent any consequential harm to the competitive process that may result from combinations. As such, the remedies play an essential role in the merger review process, and their careful crafting is of utmost importance to competition agencies conducting the review.

While imposing remedies/commitments, competition regulators must keep in mind the following:

(i) Remedies should only be applied if there is a threat to competition.

(ii) Remedies should be the least restrictive means to effectively eliminate the competition concerns posed by the combination.

Merger remedies are generally classified as either structural, if they require the divestiture of an asset, or behavioural if they impose an obligation on the merged entity to engage in or refrain from a certain conduct. Structural remedies may include both the sale of a physical part of a business or the transfer or licensing of IPRs. They can be imposed either as a condition precedent to a combination, or their completion may be required within a certain period of time after the combination has been approved. Behavioural remedies, however, are always forward-looking in that they consist of limits on future business behaviour or an obligation to perform a specific prescribed conduct for a given, sometimes considerable, period of time following the consummation of the merger.

The CCI has the power under the Competition Act and the Combination Regulations to issue commitments/modifications to the parties to the combination to ensure that combinations, once consummated, will not cause any AAEC in the relevant market in India. As discussed earlier, parties can also voluntarily offer commitments during the combination assessment, and if the competition concerns are not allayed, CCI may propose appropriate modifications to the combination. The parties can accept the modifications proposed by the CCI or respond with amendments, which will again be considered by the CCI. Once the parties to the combination accept the modifications suggested by the CCI, they have to carry out such modifications within the time period specified, failing which such combination will be deemed to have an AAEC in the relevant market in India and hence will be rejected by the CCI.

CCI's decisional practice indicates considerable experience with complex transactions which demonstrate effective engagement with the parties to the combination to address competition concerns. In this light, the structural and behavioural remedies proposed and approved by CCI have been discussed below.

[A] Behavioural Commitments

As mentioned above, the CCI can ask for commitments/modifications even in Phase I review. Regulation 19(2) of the Combination Regulations provides that the CCI may ask the parties to the combination to accept modifications for forming its prima facie order. The decisional practice shows that the CCI has sought behavioural commitments in the form of commitments in its merger approval orders,[180] where it asked the parties to review its existing contracts to ensure that they are in compliance with the provisions of the Competition Act and they will continue to abide by the provisions of the sectoral regulator. Further, the CCI has also sought commitments, during a Phase I review, from the parties to reduce their non-compete period mentioned in the transaction documents.[181]

The behavioural commitments issued by CCI can be broadly clubbed under two heads, i.e., non-compete restrictions and other safeguards. The key trends that have emerged in the adoption of both these categories of behavioural remedies have been discussed below in detail.

180. GSPC Distribution Networks Limited, Gujarat Gas Company Limited, Combination Registration No. C-2012/11/88, 8 Jan. 2013.
181. Orchid Chemicals and Pharmaceuticals Limited, Hospira Healthcare India Private Limited, Combination Registration No. C-2012/09/79, 21 Dec. 2012.

Non-compete restrictions:

(i) As a part of a composite transaction, there may be numerous contractual arrangements (like provisions relating to non-compete, licensing, et al.) which restrict the freedom of the parties to the combination to compete in the relevant market, post the consummation of the combination. Such restrictions are required to ensure that the acquirer receives the full value of the acquired business, and the seller is restricted from entering/venturing into any competing business with the target entity after the consummation of the combination.

(ii) The scope of non-compete clauses must be limited, both in time and geographically, and cannot extend to restrictions which are not *'directly related'* to the implementation of the combination. They must be extremely precise in their product scope and ought to cover only those products in which the target entity and/or its promoters are presently active and not future products. Further, they should be only limited to the geographic operations of the target entity. For example, in the acquisition by PVR Limited of DLF Utilities Limited's film exhibition business, the parties proposed to enter into a non-compete and non-solicitation agreement requiring the target to not engage in the business of operating and managing entertainment theatres/multiplexes for a period of 5 years from the consummation of the proposed combination.[182] It was submitted that the non-compete obligations were necessary to preserve the value of the assets being acquired and to safeguard the target business. However, the CCI found the geographic scope and duration of the non-compete obligations to be unrelated, unnecessary and, therefore, unreasonable to the proposed combination. Consequently, the acquirers committed to reducing the duration from five years to three years and geographic scope from India to Delhi-NCR and Chandigarh.

(iii) The time period of non-compete restrictions cannot be of an indefinite duration. As a general rule, CCI will not allow a non-compete period that extends for a period of three years where goodwill and know-how are transferred and two years when only goodwill is transferred. Such non-compete restrictions can be for a longer duration if the transaction so permits.[183]

(iv) Until 2017, the CCI analysed competition compliance non-compete clauses within its preliminary review and required parties to undertake appropriate modifications. However, the decisional practice of CCI with respect to non-compete clauses has evolved through the removal of the mandatory query in Form I which sought detailed information on any non-compete

182. PVR Limited, Combination Registration No. C-2015/07/288, 4 May 2016, paras 103-105.
183. Orchid Chemicals and Pharmaceuticals Limited, Hospira Healthcare India Private Limited, Combination Registration No. C-2012/09/79, 21 Dec. 2012 – CCI allowed non-compete period up to four years.

obligations. The CCI has reasoned that a one-size-fits-all approach cannot be adopted to non-compete clauses, and now, if the non-compete is not directly related and necessary to the transaction, the CCI will approve the combination without approving the non-compete restriction separately.

(v) However, parties have to remain cautious to ensure that their non-competes are reasonable and competition-compliant. The CCI has emphasized that any competition concerns that may arise from non-compete restrictions can be assessed under section 3 (prohibiting anti-competitive agreements) or section 4 (prohibiting abuses of dominant position) of the Competition Act. This means that while the CCI has reduced the burden on the parties to detail their non-compete restrictions while seeking prior approval of the transaction, the parties are not being exempted from indulging in anti-competitive activities. The amendment simply removes the onus on the parties to provide details of the non-compete in the notification form. All in all, this is a business-friendly step as it will give the parties flexibility in determining non-compete restrictions while also reducing the information burden on them.

Other Safeguards:

(i) CCI's decisional practice indicates other forms of behavioural commitments apart from non-compete clauses. Prominent among these is information control, which is essentially to prevent transmission of sensitive information between the parties, who are usually competitors at some level in the relevant market.

(ii) This can take several forms, such as an information firewall between Airtel and Jio (as discussed earlier)[184] or a 'rule of information control' at the time of completion of combination (basically a prohibition on exchange of sensitive information between the combined entity and the independent businesses of the parties),[185] white labelling, provision of non-exclusive technology licences, price caps[186] and capacity commitments.[187]

(iii) Other variations of information control include prohibition on the directors/officers and the employees of the combined entity from receiving any sensitive information regarding the Non-Integrated Businesses from the directors/officers or employees of the parties, provision of such information to third parties or internally among themselves. A violation of any

184. Google International LLC and Bharti Airtel Limited, Combination Registration No. C-2022/03/91, 30 Jun. 2022, para. 24.
185. Northern TK Venture Pte. Ltd., Combination Registration No. C-2018/09/601, 29 Oct. 2018, para. 18.
186. Schneider Electric India Pvt. Ltd. and MacRitchie Investments Pte. Ltd., Combination Registration No. C-2018/07/586, 18 Apr. 2019.
187. M/s Air India Limited, M/s Tata SIA Airlines Ltd., M/s Tata Sons Private Limited and M/s Singapore Airlines Limited, Combination Registration No. C-2023/04/1022, 1 Sep. 2023, para. 115.

of the above rules will constitute grounds for disciplinary action and punishment. Such disciplinary action could include, for instance, removal from service, denial of promotion, and demotion to a lower rank.[188]

(iv) Other safeguards include the adoption of preventative measures in the commissioning or operation of the combined entity. For instance, the proposed combination for creating a joint venture between Mumbai International Airport Private Limited, IOCL, BPCL, and Hindustan Petroleum Corporation Limited in Mumbai Aviation Fuel Farm Facility Limited (MAFFFL) raised certain concerns about the suppliers of ATF. Consequently, the parties undertook voluntary commitments that MAFFFL shall publish the applicable tariff, maximum storage capacity used by suppliers, change in such capacity, rates approved by the regulatory authority, etc., on its website. Further, the parties also volunteered to, *inter alia*, incorporate a clause in the standard supplier agreement to the effect that each supplier shall comply with competition law principles in relation to the usage of the integrated fuel farm facility.[189]

Interestingly, CCI's decisional practice indicates that it is not averse to the idea of imposing behavioural remedies on a standalone basis, even in cases of combinations involving direct competitors. Cases in point are the merger of Air India Limited with Tata SIA Airlines Limited[190] and the acquisition of the entire electrical and automation business of Larsen & Toubro Limited by Schneider Electric India Private Limited.[191] The intention is to preserve competition by striking a balance between allowing a merger for potential efficiency gains while safeguarding consumers against the adverse effects of reduced competition.

However, behavioural commitments are not always sufficient to assuage the likely AAEC in the market. Often, structural commitments in the form of divestments are the only viable option to prevent anti-competitive effects on the market. Based on the seriousness of the competition concerns, the CCI may also order hybrid remedies incorporating both structural and behavioural commitments.

188. Nippon Yusen Kabushiki Kaisha Ltd., Mitsui O.S.K. Lines Ltd. and Kawasaki Kisen Kaisha, Ltd., Combination Registration No. C-2016/11/459, 29 Jun. 2017, para. 25.
189. Mumbai International Airport Private Limited, Indian Oil Corporation Limited, Bharat Petroleum Corporation Limited, Hindustan Petroleum Corporation Limited, and Mumbai Aviation Fuel Farm Facility Limited, Combination Registration No. C-2014/04/164, 29 Sep. 2014, paras 19-24.
190. M/s Air India Limited, M/s Tata SIA Airlines Ltd., M/s Tata Sons Private Limited and M/s Singapore Airlines Limited, Combination Registration No. C-2023/04/1022, 1 Sep. 2023.
191. Schneider Electric India Pvt. Ltd. and MacRitchie Investments Pte. Ltd., Combination Registration No. C-2018/07/586, 18 Apr. 2019.

[B] Structural Commitments

CCI has amassed a wealth of experience in dealing with cases requiring structural commitments, and in its decisional practice, it has proposed and accepted parties' voluntary proposals for divestments.

In *AGI Greenpac Limited/Hindusthan National Glass & Industries Limited*,[192] both the parties were involved in the manufacture and supply of container glass, and the CCI found that the proposed combination was likely to significantly increase the level of concentration in the relevant market for container glass in India. Consequently, the parties proposed a voluntary modification in the form of divestiture of one of the plants of the target, i.e., the Rishikesh plant. The CCI laid down a two-step test to be followed in examining divestiture as a proposed modification. First, the adequacy of the divestiture to address the adverse impacts of structural changes in the market resulting from the combination has to be seen. Second, the suitability of the specific assets required to be divested has to be considered. In the present case, the Rishikesh plant was involved in all container glass segments that had self-contained assets such as glass melting furnaces, and divestiture appeared to incentivize new entry or augment the capacity of an existing competitor. A new entrant or competitor would gain an overall presence of 5% in the container glass market while gaining a presence in all segments of container glass. Consequently, CCI approved the combination subject to compliance with the modification.

CCI's acceptance indicates the presence of the following trends or key elements in the mode, manner and conditions of implementation of divestitures:

(i) Identifying the divestment business: the necessary components of the business, including, in some cases, key personnel.[193] This involves identifying what shall be divested or not divested and often includes tangible as well as intangible assets such as IPR, necessary licences, permits and authorizations issued by any governmental or statutory authority, contracts, leases, understandings, customer records, credit records and other records related to the business and personnel.[194]

(ii) Transitional Support: Transitional support as may be required by the approved purchaser, which is necessary to enable it to conduct the divestment business in at least the same manner as prior to the purchase,

192. AGI Greenpac Limited, Combination Registration No. C-2022/11/983, 15 Mar. 2023, paras 94-101.

193. *Bayer/Monsanto*, para. 177; Linde Aktiengesellschaft and Praxair, Inc., Combination Registration No. C-2018/01/545, 6 Sep. 2018, paras 147-150, 154-157, 161-164; Sun Pharmaceutical Industries Limited and Ranbaxy Laboratories Limited, Combination Registration No. C-2014/05/170, 17 Mar. 2015; *China National* decision, para. 18.

194. Holcim, Lafarge, Combination Registration No. C-2014/07/190, 30 Mar. 2015; *Bayer/Monsanto*, para. 178; Sun Pharmaceutical Industries Limited and Ranbaxy Laboratories Limited, Combination Registration No. C-2014/05/170, 17 Mar. 2015; *China National* decision, para. 23.

is also offered. This includes training and information delivered by appropriate specialists, supply arrangements, information technology and back end support, etc.[195]

(iii) First Divestiture Period: The divestiture principally takes place in the first divestiture period, which is usually six months from the date of CCI's approval of the combination.[196]

(iv) Preservation of economic viability, marketability and competitiveness: These measures are to be taken to ensure that the business to be divested is run as a viable business, and that the assets are not degraded, and the economic viability, marketability and competitiveness is maintained.[197]

(v) Hold separate obligations: If the business to be divested is part of a broader business, the former is to be kept separate with the appointment of a hold separate manager. In the case of divestment of shares, the divesting shareholders are not to exercise voting rights or be involved in the business from the date of the CCI's decision. Further, the Key Personnel, management and staff of the divestment businesses should have no involvement in any business retained by the Parties and should not report to any individual outside the divestment businesses.[198]

---

195. *Bayer/Monsanto,* paras 180, 187; Sun Pharmaceutical Industries Limited and Ranbaxy Laboratories Limited, Combination Registration No. C-2014/05/170, 17 Mar. 2015, para. 2; ZF Friedrichshafen AG, Combination Registration No. C-2019/11/703, 14 Feb. 2020, Annex A(II) para. 16; Linde Aktiengesellschaft and Praxair, Inc., Combination Registration No. C-2018/01/545, 6 Sep. 2018, paras 151, 154, 158, 165, 166; Dow Chemical Company, E. I. du Pont De Nemours and Company, DowDuPont Inc., Diamond Merger Sub Inc. and Orion Merger Sub Inc., Combination Registration No. C-2016/05/400, 8 Jun. 2017, paras 34.2, 35.2; FMC Corporation, Dow Chemical Company, E.I. du Pont de Nemours and Company Combination Registration No. C-2017/06/519, 18 Sep. 2017, para. 25; *Outotec OYJ,* paras 41-44.
196. *Bayer/Monsanto,* paras 217-222; Dow Chemical Company, E. I. du Pont De Nemours and Company, DowDuPont Inc., Diamond Merger Sub Inc. and Orion Merger Sub Inc., Combination Registration No. C-2016/05/400, 8 Jun. 2017, para. 35.1; FMC Corporation, Dow Chemical Company, E.I. du Pont de Nemours and Company Combination Registration No. C-2017/06/519, 18 Sep. 2017, para. 27; Linde Aktiengesellschaft and Praxair, Inc., Combination Registration No. C-2018/01/545, 6 Sep. 2018, paras 168-172.
197. *Bayer/Monsanto,* paras 223-229; *China National* decision, paras 25-29; Dow Chemical Company, E. I. du Pont De Nemours and Company, DowDuPont Inc., Diamond Merger Sub Inc. and Orion Merger Sub Inc., Combination Registration No. C-2016/05/400, 8 Jun. 2017, para. 35.3; Holcim, Lafarge, Combination Registration No. C-2014/07/190, 30 Mar. 2015; FMC Corporation, Dow Chemical Company, E.I. du Pont de Nemours and Company Combination Registration No. C-2017/06/519, 18 Sep. 2017, para. 28; *Outotec OYJ,* paras 45-47; Linde Aktiengesellschaft and Praxair, Inc., Combination Registration No. C-2018/01/545, 6 Sep. 2018, paras 173-179.
198. Holcim, Lafarge, Combination Registration No. C-2014/07/190, 30 Mar. 2015; *Bayer/Monsanto,* paras 230-233; Dow Chemical Company, E. I. du Pont De Nemours and Company, DowDuPont Inc., Diamond Merger Sub Inc. and Orion Merger Sub Inc., Combination Registration No. C-2016/05/400, 8 Jun. 2017, para. 35.4; FMC Corporation, Dow Chemical Company, E.I. du Pont de Nemours and Company Combination Registration No. C-2017/06/519, 18 Sep. 2017, para. 29; Linde Aktiengesellschaft and Praxair, Inc., Combination Registration No. C-2018/01/545, 6 Sep. 2018, paras 180-184; Agrium Inc. and Potash Corporation of Saskatchewan, Inc., Combination Registration No. C-2016/10/443, 27 Oct. 2017, para. 53; ZF Friedrichshafen AG, Combination Registration No. C-2019/11/703, 14 Feb. 2020, Annex A(II) para. 10.

(vi) Ring-fencing and firewall provisions: The confidential information is not to be shared between the parties and/or their affiliates with respect to the divested business.[199]

(vii) Non-solicitation: The Parties shall not, and procure that their Affiliates do not employ, or make offers of employment to, any member of Key Personnel transferred with the divestment businesses for the period prescribed in CCI's order.[200]

(viii) Due diligence: In order to enable potential purchasers to carry out reasonable due diligence of the divestment businesses, the parties shall, subject to customary confidentiality assurances and dependent on the stage of the divestiture process, provide to potential purchaser(s) sufficient information as regards the divestment businesses; and/or relating to the Key Personnel and Personnel.[201]

(ix) Reporting: The parties must keep the monitoring agency informed of the process and potential purchasers.[202]

(x) No acquisition of influence: the parties are not to acquire direct or indirect influence over the divestment business for a specified period after closing.[203]

---

199. Dow Chemical Company, E. I. du Pont De Nemours and Company, DowDuPont Inc., Diamond Merger Sub Inc. and Orion Merger Sub Inc., Combination Registration No. C-2016/05/400, 8 Jun. 2017, para. 35.5; Agrium Inc. and Potash Corporation of Saskatchewan, Inc., Combination Registration No. C-2016/10/443, 27 Oct. 2017, paras 56, 57; ZF Friedrichshafen AG, Combination Registration No. C-2019/11/703, 14 Feb. 2020, Annex A(II) paras 14, 15; *Bayer/Monsanto*, paras 234, 235; *China National* decision, paras 30-32, 46-49; FMC Corporation, Dow Chemical Company, E.I. du Pont de Nemours and Company Combination Registration No. C-2017/06/519, 18 Sep. 2017, para. 30; Linde Aktiengesellschaft and Praxair, Inc., Combination Registration No. C-2018/01/545, 6 Sep. 2018, paras 185, 186.
200. *Bayer/Monsanto*, para. 236; Dow Chemical Company, E. I. du Pont De Nemours and Company, DowDuPont Inc., Diamond Merger Sub Inc. and Orion Merger Sub Inc., Combination Registration No. C-2016/05/400, 8 Jun. 2017, para. 35.6; FMC Corporation, Dow Chemical Company, E.I. du Pont de Nemours and Company Combination Registration No. C-2017/06/519, 18 Sep. 2017, para. 31.
201. *Bayer/Monsanto*, para. 237; *China National* decision, paras 33, 34; Dow Chemical Company, E. I. du Pont De Nemours and Company, DowDuPont Inc., Diamond Merger Sub Inc. and Orion Merger Sub Inc., Combination Registration No. C-2016/05/400, 8 Jun. 2017, para. 35.7; FMC Corporation, Dow Chemical Company, E.I. du Pont de Nemours and Company Combination Registration No. C-2017/06/519, 18 Sep. 2017, paras 32, 33; Linde Aktiengesellschaft and Praxair, Inc., Combination Registration No. C-2018/01/545, 6 Sep. 2018, para. 188; *Outotec OYJ*, para. 70; ZF Friedrichshafen AG, Combination Registration No. C-2019/11/703, 14 Feb. 2020, Annex A(II) para. 30; Sun Pharmaceutical Industries Limited and Ranbaxy Laboratories Limited, Combination Registration No. C-2014/05/170, 17 Mar. 2015.
202. *Bayer/Monsanto*, paras 238, 239; Dow Chemical Company, E. I. du Pont De Nemours and Company, DowDuPont Inc., Diamond Merger Sub Inc. and Orion Merger Sub Inc., Combination Registration No. C-2016/05/400, 8 Jun. 2017, para. 35.8; Linde Aktiengesellschaft and Praxair, Inc., Combination Registration No. C-2018/01/545, 6 Sep. 2018, paras 189-191; ZF Friedrichshafen AG, Combination Registration No. C-2019/11/703, 14 Feb. 2020, Annex A(II) paras 17-20.
203. Agrium Inc. and Potash Corporation of Saskatchewan, Inc., Combination Registration No. C-2016/10/443, 27 Oct. 2016, para. 58; *China National* decision, para. 35; Sun Pharmaceutical Industries Limited and Ranbaxy Laboratories Limited, Combination Registration No. C-2014/05/170, 17 Mar. 2015; Dow Chemical Company, E. I. du Pont De Nemours and

(xi) Purchaser requirements: Various purchaser requirements are set out to ensure that the purchaser will be an independent and viable player in the market, having no connection with the parties, such as that it should not be their subsidiary, affiliate or associate company, shall have the financial resources, proven expertise and incentive to maintain and develop the divestment business as a viable and active competitive force in competition with the Parties and other competitors.[204]

(xii) Approval of sale and purchase agreement and of the purchaser: The final binding sale and purchase agreement relating to the divestiture shall be conditional on the approval of the CCI.[205] Herein, it is pointed out that in all cases other than Sun Pharmaceutical Industries Limited and Ranbaxy Laboratories Limited, the CCI has permitted the closing of the main transaction pending the closing of the divestment. In the former, the approval of sale and purchase agreement of the purchaser (Emcure) was done during the approval of the transaction itself.

(xiii) Monitoring agency: The CCI generally appoints an independent monitoring agency to supervise the carrying out of the modification.[206]

(xiv) Divestiture Agency: If the Closing of the divestment businesses has not taken place as specified in the modifications to the proposed combination,

---

Company, DowDuPont Inc., Diamond Merger Sub Inc. and Orion Merger Sub Inc., Combination Registration No. C-2016/05/400, 8 Jun. 2017, para. 35.9; FMC Corporation, Dow Chemical Company, E.I. du Pont de Nemours and Company Combination Registration No. C-2017/06/519, 18 Sep. 2017, para. 35; Linde Aktiengesellschaft and Praxair, Inc., Combination Registration No. C-2018/01/545, 6 Sep. 2018, paras 153, 160, 169; ZF Friedrichshafen AG, Combination Registration No. C-2019/11/703, 14 Feb. 2020, Annex A(II) para. 4.

204. Sun Pharmaceutical Industries Limited and Ranbaxy Laboratories Limited, Combination Registration No. C-2014/05/170, 17 Mar. 2015; Holcim, Lafarge, Combination Registration No. C-2014/07/190; *Bayer/Monsanto*, paras 182, 189; *China National* decision, para. 36; Agrium Inc. and Potash Corporation of Saskatchewan, Inc., Combination Registration No. C-2016/10/443, 27 Oct. 207, para. 59; DowDuPont Inc., Diamond Merger Sub Inc. and Orion Merger Sub Inc., Combination Registration No. C-2016/05/400, 8 Jun. 2017, para. 35.10; Linde Aktiengesellschaft and Praxair, Inc., Combination Registration No. C-2018/01/545, 6 Sep. 2018, paras 152, 159; *Outotec OYJ*, para. 67.

205. Sun Pharmaceutical Industries Limited and Ranbaxy Laboratories Limited, Combination Registration No. C-2014/05/170, 17 Mar. 2015, para. 3; Holcim, Lafarge, Combination Registration No. C-2014/07/190; Agrium Inc. and Potash Corporation of Saskatchewan, Inc., Combination Registration No. C-2016/10/443, 27 Oct. 207, para. 62; FMC Corporation, Dow Chemical Company, E.I. du Pont de Nemours and Company Combination Registration No. C-2017/06/519, 18 Sep. 2017, para. 36; Linde Aktiengesellschaft and Praxair, Inc., Combination Registration No. C-2018/01/545, 6 Sep. 2018, paras 192, 193; *Outotec OYJ*, paras 68, 69; ZF Friedrichshafen AG, Combination Registration No. C-2019/11/703, 14 Feb. 2020, Annex A(II) para. 8.

206. Sun Pharmaceutical Industries Limited and Ranbaxy Laboratories Limited, Combination Registration No. C-2014/05/170, 17 Mar. 2015, para. 4; Holcim, Lafarge, Combination Registration No. C-2014/07/190; *Bayer/Monsanto*, paras 242-245; *China National* decision, paras 52-55; Dow Chemical Company, E. I. du Pont De Nemours and Company, DowDuPont Inc., Diamond Merger Sub Inc. and Orion Merger Sub Inc., Combination Registration No. C-2016/05/400, 8 Jun. 2017, para. 35.12; FMC Corporation, Dow Chemical Company, E.I. du Pont de Nemours and Company Combination Registration No. C-2017/06/519, 18 Sep. 2017, para. 37; Linde Aktiengesellschaft and Praxair, Inc., Combination Registration No. C-2018/01/545, 6 Sep. 2018, paras 194-196; *Outotec OYJ*, paras 48-50.

then the CCI shall appoint a Divestiture Agency to divest the divestment businesses.[207]

(xv) Second divestiture period: If the parties fail to divest in the first divestiture period, the CCI may direct the parties to divest alternative divestment products in a second divestiture period.[208]

(xvi) Duties and obligations of parties: The parties are generally required to cooperate with the Monitoring Agency and, if applicable, the Divestment Agency, provide regular reports on the progress of the divestiture, etc. The CCI may also request information from the parties that is reasonably necessary for the effective implementation of the order at any time. The Monitoring Agency and Divestiture Agency shall have full and complete access to any of the Divestment Businesses' books, records, documents, management or other personnel, facilities, sites and technical information necessary for fulfilling its duties under the Order.[209]

Therefore, CCI's remedy packages in divestitures seek to strike a balanced approach between the need to maintain competition in the market and the independence of the parties to the proposed combination.

§4.18 PENALTY FOR MAKING FALSE STATEMENT OR OMISSION TO FURNISH MATERIAL INFORMATION

In its decisional practice, the CCI has penalized parties for not furnishing material information or making false statements at the time of filing the combination notice

207. *Bayer/Monsanto*, paras 246-251; *China National* decision, paras 38-41; FMC Corporation, Dow Chemical Company, E.I. du Pont de Nemours and Company Combination Registration No. C-2017/06/519, 18 Sep. 2017, para. 38; Linde Aktiengesellschaft and Praxair, Inc., Combination Registration No. C-2018/01/545, 6 Sep. 2018, paras 197-202; *Outotec OYJ*, paras 51-59; ZF Friedrichshafen AG, Combination Registration No. C-2019/11/703, 14 Feb. 2020, Annex A(II) paras 21-26.
208. *Bayer/Monsanto*, paras 252-255; *China National* decision, paras 42-44; Dow Chemical Company, E. I. du Pont De Nemours and Company, DowDuPont Inc., Diamond Merger Sub Inc. and Orion Merger Sub Inc., Combination Registration No. C-2016/05/400, 8 Jun. 2017, para. 35.13; FMC Corporation, Dow Chemical Company, E.I. du Pont de Nemours and Company Combination Registration No. C-2017/06/519, 18 Sep. 2017, para. 39; Linde Aktiengesellschaft and Praxair, Inc., Combination Registration No. C-2018/01/545, 6 Sep. 2018, paras 203-206; ZF Friedrichshafen AG, Combination Registration No. C-2019/11/703, 14 Feb. 2020, Annex A(II) para. 6.
209. Agrium Inc. and Potash Corporation of Saskatchewan, Inc., Combination Registration No. C-2016/10/443, 27 Oct. 207, paras 63-68.; *Bayer/Monsanto*, paras 256-261; *China National* decision, paras 53-55; Dow Chemical Company, E. I. du Pont De Nemours and Company, DowDuPont Inc., Diamond Merger Sub Inc. and Orion Merger Sub Inc., Combination Registration No. C-2016/05/400, 8 Jun. 2017, para. 35.15; FMC Corporation, Dow Chemical Company, E.I. du Pont de Nemours and Company Combination Registration No. C-2017/06/519, 18 Sep. 2017, para. 40; Linde Aktiengesellschaft and Praxair, Inc., Combination Registration No. C-2018/01/545, 6 Sep. 2018, paras 207-210; ZF Friedrichshafen AG, Combination Registration No. C-2019/11/703, 14 Feb. 2020, Annex A(II) para. 31; *Outotec OYJ*, paras 60-66.

under sections 44 and 45 of the Competition Act. Although CCI has so far not reversed its approval on this issue, it has penalized the parties for such conduct.

For instance, in the *UltraTech* case,[210] while filing the notice, UltraTech had reported that it is a subsidiary of Grasim Industries Limited which in turn was a flagship company of Aditya Birla Group. However, it did not provide any details in respect of the shareholding/control of the Kumar Mangalam Family Group. The role of the family in determining what constitutes a group for the purpose of competition assessment of combinations has already been discussed in the earlier parts of this chapter. Consequently, UltraTech was penalized under section 44 of the Competition Act.

Noticeably, proceedings were initiated against Amazon for contravening, *inter alia*, section 44 of the Competition Act for misrepresentation, false statement or suppression/concealment of material facts in relation to the scope and purpose of its combination involving FCPL and its failure to identify and notify a relevant commercial agreement, which was an inter-connected part of the combination (as discussed earlier in the section on inter-connected transactions). After granting approval to the transaction, the CCI received intimation that Amazon had suppressed material information about the combination. Upon examination, the CCI found that the purpose of the combination was for investment in FRL and establishing a strategic alignment/partnership between Amazon and Future groups in the Indian retail sector, contrary to what it had submitted in the notice, wherein it had mentioned that the objective of the combination was the gift card business of FCPL and Amazon's interest to expand its portfolio in the payments landscape in India.[211] Further, Amazon had specifically claimed at the time of approval of the combination that it did not have any direct or indirect shareholding in FRL, and certain rights have been granted to it only with respect to FCPL's investment in FRL, which was merely shown as a factor of financial strength.

However, the internal correspondence of Amazon revealed a different picture: that it was all along solely interested in FRL. The CCI held that the object and purpose of strategic rights in a combination is crucial to establishing a proper understanding of the combination and its objective and, accordingly, deciding the appropriate line of inquiry to assess the effects of the combination on competition. In this case, the purpose of securing strategic interest over FRL and commercial partnership with FRL was entirely different from FRL being merely taken as an element of financial strength and protection to the investment in FCPL. Consequently, it was found that Amazon's objective in pursuing the combination was not the potential of the gift and loyalty card business of FCPL, but FCPL was envisaged only as a vehicle to get to FRL. Hence, the present case was held to be a clear, conscious and wilful case of omission to state the actual purpose of the combination in violation of the disclosure requirements mentioned in the Combination Regulations. Therefore, not only did Amazon fail to notify all the inter-connected steps of the transaction (as also discussed earlier), but it also failed to give true and complete disclosure with respect to the substance of its combination in

210. Section 44 Order against UltraTech Cement Limited, 12 Mar. 2018, paras 4-12.1.
211. Sections 43A, 44 and 45 Order against Amazon.com NV Investment Holdings LLC, 14 Dec. 2021, paras 37-44.

violation of sections 44 and 45 of the Competition Act. Subsequently, after a detailed analysis of the factual background and applicable law, the NCLAT stated its 'complete agreement' with the CCI's views that Amazon had intentionally not made known the 'real ambit and purpose' of the combination.[212]

Hence, if a party conceals/suppresses and/or misrepresents the scope and purpose of the combination to obtain CCI's approval, the same would effectively amount to approval/consent having been obtained by way of fraud. Such a breach of trust of the CCI, established under the Competition Act for the benevolent purpose of promoting and sustaining competition in markets in India, manifests a deliberate disregard for the trust-based regulatory mechanism.

The competition assessment undertaken and the consequent decision of the CCI is primarily based on the information provided in the notice. Once the CCI has passed an order, it has no control over the subsequent consummation or non-consummation of a transaction and may only be left with the option of revoking the decision in the event it comes to know that the information was either incomplete or incorrect. Thus, parties to a combination are required to provide complete and correct information on all the aspects asked for in the designated form for filing of notice.

§4.19 MISMATCH OF TIMELINE AND REMEDIES: THE CLASH BETWEEN TWIN REGULATORS

Investments made in a listed company have to adhere to the timelines and procedural compliances mentioned under the Takeover Code and Combination Regulations. For illustration, the merging companies may face a potential mismatch between the timelines for an open offer prescribed under the Takeover Code and the review of a merger notification by the CCI since both regulatory procedures need to be undertaken simultaneously. As discussed in the earlier portions of the chapter, the Competition Act and the Combination Regulations provide for a merger review by the CCI in two phases: (i) CCI to form a prima facie view in thirty days (excluding the clock stops) from the receipt of merger notification & (ii) in case the CCI on a prima facie view is of the opinion that there may be certain anti-competitive effects that can arise because of the combination, it directs an in-depth investigation of the combination, commonly known as Phase II review. Phase II review can be for a time frame of up to 180 days (excluding the clock stops). As mentioned above, the Competition Act and the Combination Regulations provide for a suspensory regime, and the combination cannot be effectuated until the CCI approves the merger notification. However, under the Takeover Code, the acquirer is required to pay the shareholders who have tendered shares within fifteen days from the closure of the open offer process. Post the fifteen days, the acquirer is imposed with the penalty of paying interest until such payment is made. Since the Takeover Code procedure is not suspended while review of the CCI is

212. *Amazon.com NV Investment Holdings LLC v. Competition Commission of India and Others* [2022], (NCLAT) Competition Appeal (AT) No. 01 of 2022.

ongoing, parties cannot claim exemption from paying interest under the Takeover Code on account of a parallel pending regulatory approval.

Similar to the timeline mismatch, the CCI and SEBI may collide on account of a mismatch of remedies. As discussed above, the CCI may impose certain commitments (behavioural or structural) to eliminate the anti-competitive effects of the merger. However, under the Takeover Code (which precedes the scrutiny of the CCI), an acquirer must declare its intention to alienate any material assets of the company in the open offer documents. Therefore, in the event that CCI later imposes structural commitments on the parties which includes divestments, an acquirer may have to obtain a special resolution of its shareholders in order to comply with the requirements imposed by the CCI.

§4.20 CONCLUSION

Since merger assessment is an *ex ante* analysis, it hinges on fair and accurate disclosures pursuant to the trust-based mechanism envisaged in the Competition Act, Combination Regulations and CCI's decisional practice. Thus, adequate and sufficient self-assessment and cooperation by the parties at every step of the process, right from filing of notice to compliance with modifications to the proposed combination, if any, is necessary for CCI to continue with its streak of not refusing approval to any combination. As long as parties comply, CCI is likely to continue with its pro-approval and business-friendly stance.

CHAPTER 5

Intellectual Property and Competition Law

§5.01 FRIENDS IN DISAGREEMENT

The interface between competition law and IPR is an ever- evolving field due to rapid technological advancements in the global economy. While the objective of competition law is to promote fair competition and prevent anti-competitive practices, IPR aims to encourage and safeguard innovation through grant of exclusive rights in the form of patents, copyrights, trademarks, etc.

Although the issue of jurisdiction of CCI in matters concerning IPR has been largely resolved in recent years, with competition concerns having been held to fall squarely within the domain of India's antitrust regulator, new jurisdictional challenges continue to emerge regarding anti-competitive conduct that may arise from the exercise of IPR.

One of the primary concerns in this interface is the potential abuse of IPR by competitors to create or maintain monopolistic positions in the market. There is an apparent antagonism between the IPR law regime and the competition law regime, considering that the essential attribute of IPR is the grant of exclusion, where the state grants a monopoly to the IPR holder, whereas competition law aims at attaining maximum production and allocation of resources, thereby achieving allocative efficiency. However, it has been noticed that IPR and competition law regime work in tandem and perform complementary roles.

Together, they contribute towards spurring innovation. Therefore, the legal regimes of competition law and IPR are often termed as '*friends in disagreement*'. Given that the regime performs a complementary role, the competition authorities must be cautious that the regulatory interventions by them are timely and take place only in cases of abuse of rights guaranteed to the IPR holder, which potentially distorts the competitive structure of the market. Hence, there is a delicate balance to be struck between incentivizing and promoting innovation on the one hand and ensuring that the exclusive rights granted in the form of IPR do not harm competition or restrict consumer choice in any manner on the other hand.

§5.02 JURISDICTION OF THE CCI OVER IPR ISSUES

The issue of jurisdiction of the competition law regulator to hear disputes that sit on the cusp of the interface between competition law and IPR can be traced back to the predecessor regime which existed i.e. Monopolies and Restrictive Trade Practice (MRTP) Commission.

[A] MRTP Commission

In *Dr. Vallal Peruman and Anr. v. Godfrey Phillips (India) Ltd.*,[1] a complaint was filed by a consumer that Godfrey Phillips (India) Ltd. was manufacturing, marketing and selling cigarettes under the brand name Marcovitch Red & White, a reputed foreign company, even though the cigarettes were neither produced in collaboration with or with the knowledge of the foreign company which owned the said mark and brand name. It was alleged that this constituted an unfair trade practice because the complainants were misled by the mark and brand name being used by Godfrey Phillips. At the outset, Godfrey Phillips had argued that the authorities under the Trade and Merchandise Marks Act, 1958 ('*TMM Act*') have exclusive jurisdiction in regard to the complaints pertaining to the use of trademark by the holder of the certificate of registration. Resultantly, the MRTP Commission observed that it is true that there is a potential conflict between IPR and antitrust law because the exercise of the monopoly power conferred upon the holder of IPR may produce anticompetitive effects. However, there are powerful public policy justifications for maintaining these rights as well as a basis to suggest that this potential conflict may not be as severe as it appears at first blush. Reliance was placed on the solution worked out by the ECJ, which has adopted a practical and balanced approach by distinguishing between the mere 'existence' of IPR rights and how they are actually 'exercised'. The same principle was extended to resolve the conflict between the TMM Act and the MRTP Act: a certificate of registration entitles an individual/undertaking to use a trademark so long as such certificate of registration is in operation, and the trade mark is used strictly in conformity with the terms and conditions subject to which it was granted. However, if the holder of the certificate misuses the trademark by engaging in manipulation, distortion, contrivances and embellishments, etc., to mislead or confuse the consumers, then action can be taken against them under section 36A(7) for indulging in unfair trade practices under the MRTP Act. Thus, the provisions of the MRTP Act would be

1. UTP Enquiry No. 180/92; The MRTP Commission in *Manju Bhardwaj v. Zee Telefilms Ltd. and Ors.*; UTPE No. 148/1985, reiterated the findings of *Dr. Vallal Peruman and Anr. v. Godfrey Phillips (India) Ltd.* to hold that if there is misuse of a trademark by manipulation, distortion, contrivances, and embellishments, then the MRTP Commission has jurisdiction to proceed under MRTP Act.

attracted only where there is an abuse in the exercise of the rights protected and granted under the TMM Act.

[B] Challenges to CCI's Jurisdiction

On similar lines, the jurisdiction of the CCI in adjudicating market distortions from abuse of IPRs has been challenged before various High Courts in India. While a majority of the decisions have noted that the CCI has the appropriate jurisdiction to look at the misuse of IPRs under the lens of competition law, a very recent decision of the Delhi High Court has said that the CCI must not exercise jurisdiction due to a similar provision which exists in Patent laws. This has been discussed subsequently in this chapter.

The challenge has been on the grounds that the CCI does not have the requisite jurisdiction to decide on competition issues which have an interface with IPR.

[1] Competition Act Versus Copyright Act

One of the first challenges to the jurisdiction of the CCI was before the Bombay High Court in the case of *Aamir Khan Production Private Limited v. Competition Commission of India.*[2]

The case involved certain film production companies who organized themselves under the umbrella of a trade association and took a collective decision not to release films to multiplexes from 4 April 2009 with the objective of extracting a higher revenue sharing ratio from the multiplex. On receipt of information from the multiplex association, CCI took cognizance of the matter and referred the matter for detailed investigation to the DG.

Post a detailed investigation by the DG, the CCI issued a show cause notice to the film production companies. Thereafter, Aamir Khan Production Private Limited approached the Bombay High Court challenging the jurisdiction of the CCI, raising the following arguments:

(i) The principal point of contention was that the exhibition of a feature film, which is a subject matter of copyright exploitation alone, is specifically excluded under section 3(5) of the Competition Act.

(ii) The Indian copyright law enjoins upon the copyright holder the exclusive right to do or authorize the doing or to authorize to sell or give on hire or offer for sale or hire any copy of the film.

(iii) The producer of the film has the exclusive right to decide as to whom it shall sell or give on hire any copy of the film for communicating the film to the public.

2. *Aamir Khan Production Private Limited v. Competition Commission of India* [2010], (Bombay High Court) 2011 (1) BomCR 802.

(iv) Section 18 of the Copyright Act, 1957 confers upon the owner of the copyright the right to assign to any person a copyright either wholly or partially. Further, section 30 of the Copyright Act recognizes the right of the owner of the copyright to grant any interest in the right by license in writing. Based on the said legal provision, it was argued that when a producer makes a cinematograph film, he has an exclusive right to sell or give on hire any copy of the film, and the show cause notice by the CCI must be quashed on these grounds.

However, based on the reading of the provision of the Competition Act, the Bombay High Court rejected the petition made by Aamir Khan Productions Private Limited. The language of the provisions of the Competition Act clearly indicates that the CCI has the jurisdiction to determine whether the preliminary state of facts (on which the further exercise of its jurisdiction depends) exists.

Further, the question of CCI's jurisdiction is itself a mixed question of law and fact which the CCI is competent to decide. The Bombay High Court held that the CCI has the power to determine whether it has the jurisdiction to entertain a matter and analyse whether the conduct of the parties can avail of the exemption made under section 3(5) of the Competition Act. The contour of the IPR exemption made under section 3(5) of the Competition Act is dealt with in detail later in this chapter.

The issue of the jurisdiction of CCI into IPR-related matters was further discussed before the CCI in the case of *Ms HT Media v. M/s Super Cassettes Industries Limited.*[3] The case concerned Super Cassettes, the largest private publisher of Indian music and allegations that it was abusing its dominant position in contravention of the provisions of section 4 of the Competition Act. The allegations against Super Cassettes involved the following:

(i) charging excessive amounts as licence fees/royalty from the radio operators for grant of rights for the broadcast of its music content; and
(ii) imposing minimum commitment charges to be paid by the radio operators per month irrespective of actual needle hour (each aggregate of sixty minutes of the actual broadcast of sound recordings by FM radio station excluding commercials, advertisements, voice-over, anchor time, etc.) of broadcast of its music content by the radio operators;
(iii) making conclusion of licensing arrangements with radio operators subject to the acceptance of licence fees and minimum commitment charge imposed by Super Cassettes.

It was further alleged that such imposition of exorbitant licence fees and minimum commitment charge by Super Cassettes is an unfair condition imposed by it for granting licence to broadcast its music content on radio under the Competition Act. The licence agreement permitted the licensee to broadcast music subject to acceptance of onerous conditions such as minimum commitment charge obligations, which has the effect of restricting around 30%-40% of the radio stations' broadcast to the music

3. *Ms HT Media v. M/s Super Cassettes Industries Limited*, Case No. 40 of 2011.

content of Super Cassettes. The said action of Super Cassettes limited the choice of music for the end consumers to only the music content of Super Cassettes. Further, such an action of Super Cassettes resulted in denial of market access for other music companies (publishers, copyright societies, etc.) with less market share and bargaining power.

Based on the above facts, the CCI initiated an investigation into the conduct of Super Cassettes. Super Cassettes challenged the jurisdiction of the CCI on the ground that the matter under dispute between Super Cassettes and radio operators vests with the Copyright Board. It was contended by Super Cassettes that the Copyright Board is the only authority to decide whether the terms (not just rates) of a licence between a copyright owner and a radio broadcaster are reasonable and set new terms if existing terms are unreasonable.

Further, it was argued by Super Cassettes that in the event the market is heavily regulated by the Copyright Board, and where the market mechanism is substituted by a regulatory body, the role of competition law is greatly diminished and, in this case, completely ousted.

The CCI did not find merit in the arguments of Super Cassettes and stated that the regulatory domain of the Copyright Board and the CCI are completely different. It was observed by CCI that it is a market regulator which has the mandate of eliminating practices which have an adverse effect on competition in India. The CCI also observed that the ambit of the powers of the Copyright Board and the CCI is different, and they continued with the investigation of the conduct of Super Cassettes under the provisions of the Competition Act. Super Cassettes thereafter preferred to challenge the jurisdiction of the CCI before the Delhi High Court. The Delhi High Court did not grant a stay on the proceedings, and CCI continued the investigation on Super Cassettes and found them guilty of abuse of dominant position. The pricing abuse of Super Cassettes relating to IPRs will be discussed subsequently in this chapter.

On the aspect of jurisdiction, the CCI observed[4] that while the Copyright Board does have the right and obligation to determine licence fee and the reasonableness thereof under the Copyright Act, apart from that, none of the other issues envisaged by section 3 of the Competition Act can be decided by the Copyright Board. Similarly, under section 4 of the Competition Act, the CCI is obligated to adjudicate and give findings on alleged abuse of dominance, *inter alia,* on account of one-sided, discriminatory or unfair terms of the agreement. However, the Copyright Board does not have such jurisdiction.

Further, the rights protected under the Copyright Act are also protected under section 3(5) of the Competition Act. In the present case, the unreasonableness of the licence fee was not the sole reason for referring the matter for investigation. Rather, it was the fact that radio stations had no choice but to accede to the arbitrary and unfair conditions imposed by T-Series by virtue of its dominant position. Since T-Series was the only music company imposing a minimum commitment charge upon the music

4. *Ibid.*, paras 127, 128.

companies, this prima facie amounted to an abuse of dominance, meriting an investigation by the DG. Thus, the CCI exercised its jurisdiction within the four corners of the Competition Act alone and did not encroach upon the areas where the Copyright Board had sole and exclusive jurisdiction, i.e., the determination of the licence fee and reasonableness of the same.

It must be noted that in relation to broadcasting sound recordings, section 31 of the Copyright Act enables a person to seek a compulsory licence. The remedy of compulsory licence applies only when the copyright holder 'refuses' to license that work. As such, entering into a licence agreement subject to acceptance of certain anti-competitive conditions by the licensee may be a subject matter of the Competition Act and, at the same time, could potentially be considered a case of constructive 'refusal' for the purposes of enabling a section 31 proceeding under the Copyright Act. Further, the CCI can also pass any order as it may deem fit, including compulsory licensing if required, to remedy an anti-competitive situation.

This issue will equally spill over even to the patent domain since the Patents Act, 1970, contains provisions relating to compulsory licence. Under the Patents Act, a compulsory licence could be sought by a competitor only after 'refusal' by the patentee to provide a voluntary licence and when other circumstances are established. Current jurisprudence indicates that before seeking a compulsory licence to a patent, the parties must engage in licence negotiations in 'good faith' and therefore, perhaps, refusal to license the patent but for accepting certain anti-competitive conditions may also justify seeking a compulsory licence. It is quite possible that in certain cases, this remedy under the Patents Act and the remedy under the Competition Act may overlap. Most recently, the Division Bench judgment[5] in the *Telefonaktiebolaget LM Ericsson (Publ) v. Competition Commission of India*[6] ('*Ericsson* case') has given primacy to the Patents Act over the Competition Act. This has been discussed in more detail in the next section.

[2] Competition Act Versus Patents Act

The leading case on the overlaps between the Patents Act and the Competition Act is the *Ericsson* case. In this case, Ericsson challenged the section 26(1) orders of the CCI to investigate an abuse of dominance by Ericsson with regards to its SEPs, pursuant to the information filed by Micromax and Intex. The facts of these cases have been discussed in detail in the sub-chapter on SEPs.

However, the *Ericsson* case assumes importance here because the Single Judge of the Delhi High Court made notable observations on the jurisdiction of CCI to hear anti-competitive related matters which had an interface with patent-related matters. Ericsson challenged the maintainability of the orders passed by the CCI before the Delhi High Court, arguing that the CCI lacks the jurisdiction to commence any proceeding in

5. *Telefonaktiebolaget LM Ericsson (Publ) v. Competition Commission of India* [2023], (Delhi High Court) W.P.(C) 8379/2015 & LPA 247/2016, 150/2020, 550/2016 & 246/2016.
6. *Telefonaktiebolaget LM Ericsson (Publ) v. Competition Commission of India* [2016], (Delhi High Court) W.P.(C) 464/2014 & CM Nos 911/2014 & 915/2014.

relation to a claim of royalty by a proprietor of a patent (i.e., a 'patentee') since the same would fall within the scope of the Patents Act.

The CCI in its section 26(1) order expressly held that the pendency of a civil suit in the High Court does not take away the jurisdiction of the CCI to proceed under the Competition Act.[7] However, Ericsson argued before the Delhi High Court that the Patents Act, being a special Act, provided not only the patentee's rights but also a framework for the exercise and remedy for the abuse of such rights. Consequently, a recourse to the Competition Act would be barred.

The Single Judge of the Delhi High Court disagreed and concluded that the same facts may give rise to an action under the Competition Act as well as the Patents Act and that the remedies and legislative intention behind both statutes are distinct and independent of each other. As a result, an agreement which imposes reasonable conditions for protecting patent rights (which concerns specific individual rights) is allowed however, assessing the 'reasonability' of such conditions is the responsibility of the CCI (since it concerns the market at large).

The key observations of the Single Judge of the Delhi High Court have been mentioned below:

(i) Ericsson had argued that it was not an 'enterprise' under section 2(h) of the Competition Act as it was a patentee, and hence, section 4 of the Competition Act would not be applicable to it. In this regard, the CCI observed that the nature of patent rights – the right to exclude without the right to use – does not in any manner exclude patent rights from the scope of 'goods' as defined under the Sale of Goods Act, 1930. All kinds of property (other than actionable claims, money and immovable property) would fall within the definition of 'goods', and this would also include intangible and incorporeal property such as patents. Hence, Ericsson's contention that patents are not 'goods' was dismissed, and it was held to be an 'enterprise' under section 2(h) of the Competition Act.

(ii) Ericsson contended that the CCI would not have the jurisdiction to entertain complaints regarding abuse of dominance in view of the specific provisions under the Patents Act enacted to address the issue of abuse of dominance by a patent holder. The intention of the Parliament in enacting the Competition Act was not to curtail or whittle down the full scope of any other law, and, therefore, it is expressly stated that the Competition Act would be in addition to, and not in derogation of any other Act.

(iii) Section 60 of the Competition Act expressly provides that the provisions of the Competition Act shall have effect notwithstanding anything inconsistent in any other law. However, the said provision must be read in the context of the Competition Act as a whole and the mischief that is sought to be addressed by the Competition Act.

---

7. *Micromax Informatics Limited v. Telefonaktiebolaget LM Ericsson (Publ)*, Case No. 50 of 2013; *Intex Technologies (India) Limited v. Telefonaktiebolaget LM Ericsson (Publ)*, Case No. 76 of 2013.

(iv) The same facts can give rise to an action under both statutes. For instance, in certain cases, threats by a proprietor of a SEP, who is found to be in a dominant position, could be held to be an abuse of dominance. Similarly, certain specific remedies have been provided under the Patents Act in respect of certain practices that may constitute abuse of dominance or may be considered anti-competitive such as grant of compulsory licences under section 84(7) of the Patents Act. Thus, whereas patent laws are concerned with grants of rights enabling the patent holder to exclude others from exploiting the invention, and in that sense promoting rights akin to a monopoly, competition law is essentially aimed to promote competition and, thus, fundamentally opposed to monopolization as well as unfair and anticompetitive practices that are associated with monopolies. The remedies provided under section 27 of the Competition Act for abuse of dominant position are materially different from the remedies available under section 84 of the Patents Act. Hence, the remedies under the two enactments are not mutually exclusive; grant of one is not destructive of the other. Thus, it may be open for a prospective licensee to approach the Controller of Patents for grant of compulsory licence in certain cases. The same is not inconsistent with the CCI passing an appropriate order under section 27 of the Competition Act. It is also necessary to bear in mind that whereas section 84 of the Patents Act provides specific remedy to the person seeking relief, the orders passed by CCI are in rem. Hence, the operative width of the two enactments is different.

(v) The language of the provisions also indicates the legislative intention that the Competition Act and the Patents Act should work harmoniously. The legislature while enacting a law has complete knowledge of the existing laws and, therefore, where an express provision for the repeal of an earlier statute is not provided unless it is concluded that the provisions of the two legislations cannot co-exist, the question of reading the provisions of a statute to have been impliedly repealed does not arise.

(vi) The proviso to section 84(6)(iv) of the Patents Act provides that a prospective licensee who applies for a compulsory licence is expected to have made, prior to his application, efforts to obtain a licence on reasonable terms. However, it further specifies that this consideration would not be relevant where the conduct of a patentee is found to be anti-competitive. This cannot be read to mean that a patentee's anti-competitive conduct would have to be first established in proceedings under the Competition Act before the Controller could take that into account. Rather, it only lists certain factors required to be considered by the Controller. However, if CCI has finally found a patentee's conduct to be anti-competitive and its finding has attained finality, the Controller would also proceed on the said basis and – on the principle akin to issue estoppel – the patentee would be estopped from contending to the contrary.

(vii) Section 3(5) of the Competition Act expressly provides that section 3 would not restrict the right of any person to impose reasonable conditions for protecting its right, *inter alia*, under the Patents Act. Hence, whilst an agreement which imposes reasonable conditions for protecting Patent Rights is permissible, an anti-competitive agreement which imposes unreasonable conditions would not be afforded the safe harbour of section 3(5) of the Competition Act and would fall foul of section 3 of the Competition Act. The question as to whether a condition imposed under the agreement is reasonable or not would be a matter which could only be decided by the CCI under the provisions of the Competition Act. Neither the Controller of Patents discharging his functions in terms of the Patents Act nor a Civil Court would have any jurisdiction to adjudicate whether an agreement falls foul of section 3 of the Competition Act. Thus, there is no irreconcilable repugnancy or conflict between the Competition Act and the Patents Act. And, in the absence of any irreconcilable conflict between the two legislations, the jurisdiction of CCI to entertain complaints for abuse of dominance in respect of Patent rights cannot be ousted.

Hence, the possible overlaps between the competition and patents domain are not contrary to each other and the regulatory authorities for both have separate and distinct mandates to follow. However, in appeal, the Division Bench of the Delhi High Court in the *Ericsson* case[8] has reversed the findings of the Singh Judge Bench. This has been discussed subsequently.

In *Monsanto Holdings Pvt. Ltd. v. Competition Commission of India*[9] ('*Monsanto* case'), Mahyco Monsanto Biotech India Pvt. Ltd. (MMBL) challenged the maintainability of the order passed by CCI to investigate the trait fee charged by MMBL and the other terms and conditions imposed by it through its sub-licence agreement for using the technology for manufacturing Bt. Cotton Seeds.

The facts of the case were as follows: MMBL sub-licensed the technology licensed by Monsanto to various seed manufacturers in India, including the informants (i.e., the sub-licensees) through agreements which were extendable from time to time. The consideration for sub-licensing the said technology was divided into two parts. The first was a non-refundable fee, which was required to be paid upfront (which was as high as INR 50 lakhs), and the second part was a recurring fee, which was referred to as 'trait value' and was determined on the basis of the Maximum Retail Price (MRP) fixed for Bt. Cotton Seeds. The sub-licensees requested MMBL to charge a reasonable trait value considering the increase in the cost of production and fixation of lower MRP of cotton seeds by the State Governments. However, MMBL refused to do so and instead, terminated the licences and also initiated claims for its payments against the sub-licensees.

8. *Telefonaktiebolaget LM Ericsson (Publ) v. Competition Commission of India* [2023], (Delhi High Court) W.P.(C) 8379/2015 & LPA 247/2016, 150/2020, 550/2016 & 246/2016.
9. *Monsanto Holdings Pvt. Ltd. v. Competition Commission of India,* [2020] (Delhi High Court) W.P.(C) 1776/2016 and CM Nos 7606/2016, 12396/2016 & 16685/2016.

Consequently, the informants alleged that:

(i) Monsanto and MMBL abused their dominant position by charging excessive and unfair prices for Bt. Technology. They set prices which are significantly higher than those that would result if there was effective competition in the relevant market. Further, it was alleged that linking the trait value to the MRP of cotton seeds is unreasonable and not reflective of the economic value of the said technology.

(ii) MMBL had imposed unfair conditions in the sub-licence agreements and the same violated section 4(2)(a)(i) of the Competition Act. In terms of Clause 2.05(c) of the sub-licence agreements, the informants were required to notify MMBL in case their affiliates entered into negotiations with any competitor of MMBL/intended to deal with any competitor of MMBL within thirty days of commencement of such negotiations and failure to give such prior notice entitled MMBL to terminate the sub-licence agreement. This clause was alleged to be unfair as commercial negotiations are confidential, and any disclosure of such negotiations would have an adverse effect on the informants. Further, there was a reasonable apprehension that dealing with any competitor of MMBL would invite an adverse action against the informants, such as through selective licensing and refusal to sub-license Bt. Technology.

(iii) Article 9.4 of the sub-licence agreements also imposed an unfair condition as, in terms of the said clause, the informants were required to destroy all parent lines or cotton germplasm, which had been modified to contain Monsanto Technology after the sub-licence was terminated. It was argued that destroying germplasm (parent line) would effectively amount to destroying their intellectual property, which normally takes about five to ten years to develop. It was alleged that through these restrictive and unfair conditions, MMBL had virtually eliminated all potential competition for its technology.

(iv) MMBL and Monsanto Group have violated section 4(2)(a)(i) of the Competition Act as they discriminated against the informants. It was alleged that whereas Bt. Technology was provided to other group companies of Monsanto without entering into any sub-licence agreements containing unfair conditions, MMBL insisted on entering into unfair sub-licence agreements with other seed manufacturers. This had an appreciable adverse effect on the competition (AAEC) in the downstream market of cotton hybrid seeds.

(v) It was also alleged that the sub-licence arrangements contravened section 3(1) and section 3(4) of the Competition Act by causing refusal to deal.

The CCI held that MMBL was dominant in the relevant market of 'provision of Bt. Cotton Technology in India' as well as the downstream market of 'manufacture and sale of Bt. Cotton seeds in India'. It further found the allegations made by the informants to be prima facie merited since the stringent conditions imposed in the sub-licence agreements discouraged the seed companies from dealing with competitors and amounted to restricting the development of alternate technologies. Further, these conditions were harsh and not reasonable for protecting IPR. Accordingly, the CCI passed an order under section 26(1) of the Competition Act directing the DG to investigate the matter.

MMBL sought to oust the jurisdiction of CCI by citing repugnancy between the Competition Act and the Patents Act through a Writ Petition in the Delhi High Court. MMBL argued that:

(i) In order for the CCI to determine whether its conduct is anti-competitive, it would be necessary to have a finding on whether the royalty fee/trait value charged is unreasonable and excessive and the terms of the sub-licence agreement are unreasonable, and these latter issues had to be determined by the Controller of Patents under the Patents Act.
(ii) The Patents Act occupied the entire field in respect of not only the grant of patents but also the exercise of rights granted to a patentee.
(iii) The powers of the Controller of Patents are akin to those of the TRAI in the telecom sector, and in *Competition Commission of India v. Bharti Airtel Ltd.* ('*Bharti Airtel* case'),[10] the Supreme Court held that the regulation of Points of Interconnection (POIs) fell under the jurisdiction of TRAI and not CCI. We have discussed the findings of the *Bharti Airtel* case in the jurisdiction heading in Chapter 1.

However, the Single Judge of the Delhi High Court dismissed these contentions by relying on its observations in the *Ericsson* case. It was held that the CCI is not prevented from exercising its jurisdiction relating to specific rights, such as compulsory licensing under the Patents Act if the same gives rise to anti-competitive conduct or abuse of dominance. While the patentee is free to approach the Controller of Patents for grant of a compulsory licence, the same does not prohibit the CCI from passing an order under section 27 of the Competition Act because the provisions of the two enactments do not intend to substitute one another. Further, although Chapter XVI and section 140 of the Patents Act contain provisions which have a common subject matter with the Competition Act, the remedies provided in the Competition Act are materially different from the Patents Act. Hence, there are dual remedies for the same conduct, but the nature of relief in both enactments is substantially different.

Therefore, there is no irreconcilable conflict between the Patents Act and the Competition Act and the jurisdiction of CCI to entertain complaints regarding abuse of dominance with respect to patent rights cannot be excluded. The key observations of the Single Judge of the Delhi High Court are as follows:

(i) In conformity with the TRIPS Agreement, the Patents Act was amended and now contains provisions for grant of compulsory licences in certain cases. Further, section 140 of the Patents Act also prohibits inclusion of

10. *Competition Commission of India v. Bharti Airtel and Ors.* [2018], (SC) Civil Appeal Nos 11843-11852 of 2018.

certain restrictive conditions in certain contracts – contracts relating to sale or lease of a patented article, licence to manufacture a patented article or to work any patented process. However, the jurisdiction of CCI is not excluded from examining matters relating to certain rights granted under the Patents Act or any alleged anticompetitive conduct of any enterprise, including abuse of its dominant position.

(ii) Although section 60 of the Competition Act expressly provides that it would be given an overriding effect, the same would not whittle down the provisions of the Patents Act. Section 62 of the Competition Act which expressly provides that the Competition Act would be in addition to and not in derogation of the provisions of any other law for the time being in force, clearly expresses the legislative intent that the Competition Act is in addition to other laws and not in substitution thereof.

(iii) Section 84 of the Patents Act provides for grant of compulsory licences in certain cases where reasonable requirement of the public in respect of patented inventions has not been satisfied. Section 85 of the Patents Act provides for revocation of patents if, after the expiry of two years from the date of grant of compulsory licence, the patented invention has not been worked in the territory of India and the reasonable requirements of the public with respect to the patent have not been satisfied. The instances listed in section 84(7) of the Patents Act can in certain circumstances be considered an abuse of dominance if the patentee is dominant in the relevant market. The orders that can be passed by the CCI under section 27 of the Competition Act in respect of abuse of dominant position are materially different from the remedies that are available under section 84 of the Patents Act. In certain cases, it may be open for a prospective licensee to approach the Controller for grant of a compulsory licence. However, the same would not be inconsistent with the CCI passing an appropriate order under section 27 of the Competition Act.

(iv) Under section 21A of the Competition Act, the CCI can make a reference to any regulator where in the course of proceedings, the CCI proposes to take any decision which may be contrary to provisions of any statute, the implementation of which has been entrusted to any statutory authority. Similarly, section 21 of the Competition Act enables any statutory authority, which is charged with administration of any statute, to make a reference to CCI if it proposes to take any decision which may be contrary to the provisions of the Competition Act. These provisions clearly indicate that the intention of the Parliament was to ensure that the provisions of the Competition Act were implemented in addition to the provisions of other statutes. Hence, there was no irreconcilable repugnancy or conflict between the Competition Act and the Patents Act.

(v) A comparison with TRAI in the *Bharti Airtel* case is misplaced since the issue of whether an adequate number of POIs had been provided by service providers for connecting with the service rolled out fell squarely within

TRAI's scope of regulatory powers, which are all pervasive. A 'Controller' does not regulate the exercise of patent rights in such a pervasive manner due to the obvious reason that 'patents' are not an industry. The nature of the role performed by a Controller thus cannot be equated to that of the CCI since the expertise and the nature of inquiry conducted, and the relief that can be granted by both the bodies is materially different. Hence, the Supreme Court's decision in the *Bharti Airtel* case is not an authority for the proposition that wherever there is a statutory regulator, the complaint must be first brought before the Regulator and examination of a complaint by the CCI is contingent on the findings of the Regulator.

On the aforesaid basis, the Delhi High Court upheld CCI's order. However, the position of law has taken a U-turn with the Division Bench judgment in the *Ericsson* case. It held that the CCI cannot exercise jurisdiction over the actions of an enterprise that are in exercise of its rights as a patentee. As a result, it set aside the findings of the Single Judge Bench that there is no overlap between the two enactments and that the CCI has powers that the Controller does not have. It also set aside the finding to the effect that the Patents Act is only defining the contours of patent rights, whereas the Competition Act deals with the abuse of rights, including patent rights, which can also not be sustained. These findings were premised on the following analysis:

(i) The question of whether an agreement under which a patent is licensed will cause an AAEC within India or will amount to an abuse of dominant position is not one that is reserved for the CCI. On the contrary, the factors that the CCI is required to consider under section 19(3) and 19(4) when assessing a potential violation of section 3 or 4 of the Competition Act are not very different from those that the Controller, in exercise of power to grant a compulsory licence, will consider in terms of section 84(6) and 84(7), read with other provisions of the Patents Act. Consequently, the inquiry proposed to be conducted by the CCI in respect of an assertion of patent rights is nearly identical to that which the Controller will conduct under Chapter XVI of the Patents Act.
(ii) The legislative intent of the Patents Act is for the field pertaining to patents, unreasonable conditions in agreements of licensing, abuse of status as a patentee, inquiry in respect thereof, and relief that is to be granted are all to be governed by the Patents Act, and Chapter XVI of the Patents Act is a complete code in itself on all issues in this regard. On the other hand, the Competition Act is a general legislation pertaining to anti-competitive agreements and abuse of dominant position generally. The inclusion of section 84(6)(iv) in the Patents Act by way of an amendment after the Competition Act was passed with section 3(5)(i)(b) is particularly instructive of the above legislative intent as regards anti-competitive agreements.
(iii) For deciding an application for compulsory licensing, the Controller is empowered by the Patents Act to consider the reasonability of conditions

imposed in a licence agreement. The CCI is empowered under the Competition Act to examine anti-competitive agreements and abuse of dominant position. However, under section 3(5)(i)(b) of the Competition Act, reasonable conditions being imposed in an agreement concerning exercise of rights under the Patents Act are exempted from examination. This is indicative of the legislature's intendment as to the exclusive domain of the Patents Act regarding reasonable conditions.

(iv) It also observed that the Patents Act is the special statute and not the Competition Act. Since Chapter XVI of the Patents Act is a subsequent legislation as compared to the Competition Act, an application of the maxims *generalia specialibus non derogant* (i.e., the general does not detract from the specific) or *lex posterior derogat priori* (i.e., the later law prevails over the earlier law), the Patents Act must prevail over the Competition Act on the issue of exercise of rights by a patentee under the Patents Act.

(v) An assessment of even the purpose and policy underlying the two enactments and the clear intendment conveyed by the language of the relevant provisions therein reveals that the Patents Act must necessarily prevail over that of the Competition Act. This is because while the Competition Act deals with the subjects of anti-competitive agreements and abuse of dominant position 'generally', the Patents Act 'deals with these subjects specifically in the context of patents'.

It is pointed out that the Division Bench judgment is likely to be challenged by the CCI. The Supreme Court's finding on this aspect will be critical since the latest decision of the High Court seeks to dislodge the jurisprudence of CCI examining anti-competitive conduct. Further, it may be argued that the Division Bench judgment of the Delhi High Court is contrary to the observations of the Supreme Court in the *Bharti Airtel* case, wherein it has been mentioned that the CCI is the primary regulator which has the mandate to look into anti-competitive practices, even where is an industry regulator.

The Supreme Court in *Competition Commission of India v. Bharti Airtel and Ors.*[11] held that there were no overlaps in the jurisdiction of TRAI (telecom regulator) and CCI (competition regulator) because the function of the CCI is distinct from the function of TRAI under the TRAI Act, and the Competition Act is also a special statute which deals with anti-competition. Moreover, it is within the exclusive domain of the CCI to find out whether a particular agreement will cause AAEC within the relevant market in India. On this basis, the submission that between the two statutes, the TRAI Act would prevail as it is a complete code in itself which regulates the telecom sector in its entirety, including the aspects of competition, was rejected. The said case dealt with a factual matrix wherein the Supreme Court held that the matter under inquiry involved certain aspects which require telecom expertise; hence, the Supreme Court ordered that TRAI must look at such jurisdictional aspects, and thereafter, CCI can look

11. *Ibid.*, paras 86-92.

into the competition law aspect. Hence, the same logic may be argued in the Ericsson matter as well when the CCI decides to appeal the Ericsson order before the Supreme Court.

The issue of jurisdiction of CCI to determine the anti-competitive nature of conduct emanating out of IPRs was also raised in the case of *Biocon Limited v. F. Hoffman-La Roche AG*[12] ('*Roche* case'). Roche had developed a monoclonal antibody called 'Trastuzumab', which targeted a specific form of breast cancer. This was marketed through a drug formulation named 'HERCEPTIN', which was priced at INR 1,20,000 per vial. In 2012, Roche withdrew HERCEPTIN from the market and introduced a low-cost version of Trastuzumab known as 'BICELTIS' which was priced at INR 75,000 per vial, due to the threat of development of a biosimilar version of Trastuzumab by its competitors and to avoid the imposition of a compulsory licence. Subsequently, Biocon and Mylan Pharmaceuticals (informants) collaborated to introduce a biosimilar version of Trastuzumab which was to be priced at INR 57,500 per vial, after receiving a licence from the Drugs Control Department, Karnataka.

In order to prevent the entry of new players into the market of Trastuzumab, Roche filed a suit before the Delhi High Court. The informants filed the information for abuse of dominant position by Roche before the CCI. Roche challenged the maintainability of the information by arguing that the issues raised in the information are squarely covered by the Civil Suit pending before the Delhi High Court. The informants responded by arguing that the reliefs available from both the forums, i.e., the Delhi High Court and the CCI, are distinct. While the issues before the Delhi High Court pertain to the validity of approvals granted by the Drug Controller General of India (DCGI) to Biocon, the primary issue before the CCI was whether the Roche Group's conduct in the market is abusive or not.

The CCI upheld the submissions of the informants by relying on the observations of the Singh Judge Bench Judgment by the Delhi High Court in the *Ericsson* case, as discussed previously. The main issues before the Delhi High Court relate to the propriety of the approvals granted by the DCGI to the informants' products and the alleged passing off by the informants of their products as Roche's products. The CCI in the *Roche* case held that even if various issues have been highlighted by the informants in their defence in the Civil Suit, the Delhi High Court will only adjudicate upon the issues which are pending before it, and it cannot take away their right to approach the CCI for a remedy enshrined under section 27 of the Competition Act. Whether Roche Group is dominant and has abused its dominant position or not is a question that is covered under the provisions of the Act and falls under the exclusive jurisdiction of the CCI under section 61 of the Competition Act. Hence, the pending Civil Suit in the Delhi High Court does not impede the CCI's jurisdiction to look into the present matter.

Once the investigation commenced, the DG sought various information from Roche, including copies of board meetings and marketing arrangements entered into between the petitioner and its parent company, along with pricing structure, etc. Consequently, Roche filed a writ petition before the Delhi High Court seeking a stay

12. *Biocon Limited v. F. Hoffman-La Roche AG*, Case No. 68 of 2016.

against the directions of the DG. Although the Delhi High Court granted the stay, it is important to note that the basis of the same was not an issue of jurisdiction of the CCI but rather the nature of the inquiry being conducted by the DG. The Delhi High Court did not make any adverse observations regarding the power of CCI to cause an investigation into the alleged abusive conduct of Roche.

It is reiterated that this stay on investigation should not be confused as precluding or whittling down the jurisdiction of the CCI in investigating competition issues arising out of patent rights. The stay has been granted owing to the nature of the investigation being conducted and not the right to conduct the investigation in the first place. Thus, the position as it exists today is that the CCI is not excluded from examining the abuse of dominant position emanating out of the conduct of the patent holder as there is no conflict between the Competition Act and the Patents Act.

§5.03 SCOPE OF THE IPR EXEMPTION

As mentioned in the preceding chapter, section 3 of the Competition Act deals with the provision relating to anti-competitive agreements and cartels. There is an exemption provided in section 3(5) which states that the provisions with respect to anti-competitive agreements will not be applicable to agreement entered into by any person for restraining any infringement or imposing reasonable conditions for protecting its rights guaranteed under the IPR statutes in India.

It has been deliberated earlier that section 3(5) of the Competition Act does not simply remove the jurisdiction of the CCI over IPR-related cases. This aspect was highlighted in *Swapan Dey v. Vifor International (AG)* ('*Vifor* case'),[13] wherein it was alleged that Vifor contravened the provisions of section 3(4) and section 4 of the Competition Act by restricting access to its patents of Soluble Ferric Carboxymaltose (FCM) Iron Injectables. FCM is an injectable used for the treatment of iron deficiency/anaemia.

Before making its prima facie opinion, CCI sought the response of Vifor, which challenged the jurisdiction of the CCI and raised several preliminary objections. Instead of filing a response to the CCI, Vifor filed a writ petition before the Delhi High Court, challenging the jurisdiction of the CCI to entertain the present matter. It argued that the CCI neither has the expertise nor competence to decide a matter falling within the domain of Patent Law.

The Delhi High Court, on similar lines mentioned in the *Monsanto* case, as discussed earlier, held that information under the Competition Act would not be sustainable only if the subject matter of such an information relates to the provisions of the Patents Act. Merely because section 3(5) exempts rights under the Patents Act does not mean that the jurisdiction of CCI would be completely ousted from fulfilling its mandate under the Competition Act.

Accordingly, the Delhi High Court directed Vifor to raise its contentions before the CCI. At the outset, the CCI held that the fact that Vifor enjoys patent protection for

13. *Swapan Dey v. Vifor International (AG)*, Case No. 05 of 2022.

its product granted under the patent regime in India and exploitation of this right, albeit in a limited manner, through arrangements with two Indian companies under a licensing arrangement with it, is more relevant to the ascertainment of jurisdiction than the presence of physical office (which is an irrelevant consideration for ascertaining jurisdiction). Section 3(5)(i) of the Competition Act does not absolutely exclude the jurisdiction of the CCI in matters falling under section 3 or merely because the matter is also a subject matter of the Patent Act or any other intellectual property law statute. On the contrary, the very construct of section 3(5)(i) of the Competition Act shows that it is applicable on matters which involve the existence of a right under any of the IPR statutes mentioned therein. It rather allows the CCI to examine whether the alleged anti-competitive agreements have some justifications in relation to protecting any IPR of any person, restraining any infringement of such rights or imposing reasonable conditions, as may be necessary for protecting any of such rights. Such a determination of reasonability can be done only when the CCI examines the condition within the overall contours of the Competition Act. The only limitation is that in appropriate cases, CCI has to determine either the existence or non-existence of a right, flowing through IPR held by the party or derived by it and the reasonability of the exercise of such right when posed as a defence before it, in an allegation of violation of section 3 of the Competition Act. There is nothing that *ex facie* warrants the CCI to circumscribe its powers, in aid of exercise towards sustaining a free and fairer market, when distortions can be induced through an anti-competitive conduct arising out of IPR, the use or non-use of which borders on unreasonableness.

The exemption provided under section 3(5) of the Competition Act provides for two different situations: (i) the right of the party to *restrain* a third party from infringing the relevant IPRs; and (ii) right to impose *reasonable conditions* to protect the rights conferred under the relevant IPR legislation. The ambit of the exemption has been deliberated by the CCI in various cases, as discussed below.

[A] Reasonable Restrictions

The term 'reasonable restriction' mentioned in section 3(5) of the Competition Act was discussed in detail by the CCI in the case of *FICCI – Multiplex Association of India v. United Producers/Distributors Forum.*[14] The facts of the case are similar to the one discussed before the Bombay High Court in the case of Aamir Khan Production Private Limited. It was argued by the United Producers Forum that the copyright owner has the right to exploit the copyright in a manner as it deems fit and that no multiplex owner can demand that the film be released in their theatre and dictate the commercial terms on which such film is to be released.

Furthermore, it was also argued by the distributors forum that based on section 3(5) of the Competition Act, the producers have the right to impose reasonable restrictions for protecting rights conferred upon them under the Copyright Act.

---

14. *FICCI – Multiplex Association of India v. United Producers/Distributors Forum*, Case No. 01 of 2009.

The CCI disregarded the contention of the producers' forum by emphasizing the imposition of 'reasonable' conditions for 'protecting' IPR rights and noted the following:

(i) Intellectual property laws do not have any absolute overriding effect on competition law. The IPR exemption mentioned under section 3(5) only enables the right holder to *impose reasonable conditions as may be necessary for protecting the rights* [emphasis supplied] conferred upon the IPR holders by the IPR statutes mentioned under section 3(5) of the Competition Act.

(ii) The producers/distributors had failed to produce any evidence to show the act of not releasing their movies to the multiplexes is a reasonable condition to protect their rights conferred to them under the Copyright Act. The key word is protection, as opposed to commercial exploitation. The connotation and implication of both the terms are different: while 'exploitation' denotes taking advantage of the copyright and cannot be allowed if it infringes the right to fair access and competition; a 'restriction' can be imposed to protect against the infringement of the rights of the copyright holder, i.e., to prevent commercial exploitation of the copyright by anyone else apart from the copyright owner themselves, so long as it is reasonable. Further, based on the investigation conducted by the DG, it was noted that due to the action of the producers/distributors, the price of tickets of multiplex theatres increased which was borne by the 'common man'. In such a situation, CCI rejected the plea that the collective decision of not releasing the movie to the multiplex was a reasonable condition to protect their rights.

[B] Coverage of IPR Exemption

The CCI had dealt, in great detail, with the coverage of the IPR exemption mentioned under section 3(5) of the Competition Act in the *Shamsher Kataria v. Honda Siel Cars India Limited & Ors.*[15] ('*Automobile Spare Parts* case'). The facts of the case are discussed in detail in the chapter on abuse of dominance. With respect to the exemption under section 3(5) of the Competition Act, the case pertained to an agreement entered into between OEMs (i.e., car manufacturers) and OESs (i.e., suppliers of spare parts) for procurement of spare parts by OEMs for both assembly line and aftermarket requirements. The spare parts to be supplied by the OES were of the following categories:

(i) where the design, drawing, technical specification, technology, know-how, tools (which are large machines to manufacture the parts), quality parameters, etc., are provided by the OEMs. The OES are required to manufacture

15. *Shamsher Kataria v. Honda Siel Cars India Limited & Ors.*, Case No. 03 of 2011.

and supply such spare parts only to the OEMs according to the specified parameters;

(ii) where the patents, know-how, and technology belong to the OES, however, the parts are manufactured based on the specifications, drawings, and designs supplied by the OEM. The tooling/tooling cost may also be borne by the OEM in some of these cases; and

(iii) where the spare parts are developed and sold by the OES and are made to their own specification or designs and commonly used in the automobile industry.

It was observed by the DG that under the agreement entered into between OEM and OES, the OES were prohibited from supplying the spare parts in the aftermarket unless they received the prior consent of the OEM. As such, in practice, it was found that most of the OESs were not selling directly in the aftermarket.

Among other defences raised by the OEMs (which have been discussed in the chapter on abuse of dominance), it was argued by several OEMs that the restrictions of sales on OESs of their proprietary parts to third parties without prior consent would fall within the ambit of reasonable condition to prevent infringements of their IPRs. It was further contended that significant investments are made into research and development facilities based on which these products are manufactured.

The CCI did not agree with the contention of the OEMs and analysed the scope of the exemption and made the following key remarks:[16]

(i) *Scope of the exemption and when can it be availed*: The CCI clarified that section 3(5) of the Competition Act allows an IPR holder to impose 'reasonable' conditions to protect his rights which have been conferred or may be conferred upon him under the relevant IPR statues in India. Therefore, the ambit of the exemption is clear that the IPR must have been conferred prior to availing of the exemption under section 3(5) of the Competition Act. Based on the documents submitted by the OEMs, the CCI concluded that the OEMs have not been able to provide documents to substantiate their claim over a particular type of IPR under the applicable Indian IPR laws. Further, some of the OEMS had contended that the overseas parent corporation of the OEMs had validly held IPRs, which were thereafter transferred to the OEMs by means of a validly executed technology transfer agreement. The CCI, however, noted that the IPR claimed by the parent of the OEMs is territorial in nature and is vested upon the IPR holder only in a particular jurisdiction. Thus, in the event that the parent corporation of the OEMs held such IPR rights in the territories where the IPR rights were originally granted, the said rights cannot be said to be granted to the OEMs operating in India by entering into a technology transfer agreement, unless the rights have been granted upon the OEMs which is recognized under the relevant IPR statutes (mentioned in section

16. *Automobile Spare Parts* case, paras 9.1.10-9.1.15.

3(5) of the Competition Act) in India. Based on the observations of the CCI, for exemption of section 3(5) of the Competition Act to be availed of protection ought to have been granted to the IPR holder, or a process ought to have been initiated for grant of such protection under the relevant IPR statutes in India.

(ii) *Necessary to protect IPRs* – The CCI has adopted an extremely strict *interpretation* and has held that section 3(5) of the Competition Act only allows the IPR holder to impose reasonable conditions necessary for the protection of the IPRs. Although what is necessary and reasonable would necessarily depend on the facts and circumstances of each case, the CCI in this case held that the restriction imposed on the OES by OEMs not to supply the spare parts in the aftermarket is not necessary to protect their rights guaranteed under the IPR statutes since merely selling spare parts which are manufactured end products, does not necessarily compromise the IPR held by car manufacturers in such products. Further, the CCI observed that the car manufacturers could contractually protect their IPR against these dealers and could still permit them to sell their products.

Certain key observations made by the CCI in the *Automobile Spare Parts* case on the IPR exemption under section 3(5) of the Competition Act are as follows:

> In determining whether the agreements entered between the OEMs and the OESs would fall within the ambit of the provisions of section 3(5)(i) of the Competition Act, it is necessary to consider, *inter alia*, the following:
>
> a) whether the right which is put forward is correctly characterized as protecting an intellectual property; and
> b) whether the requirements of the law granting the IPRs are in fact being satisfied.
>
> The DG during the course of the investigation had provided an opportunity to the OEMs to confirm the status of the IPRs held by them in India along with the necessary details justifying the claim of exemption pursuant to section 3(5)(i) of the Competition Act. The CCI noted that none of the OEMs had submitted the relevant documentary evidence to successfully establish the grant of the applicable IPRs in India, with respect to the various spare parts pursuant to which such OEMs have claimed the exemption under section 3(5)(i) of the Competition Act. The important criteria for determining whether the exemption under section 3(5)(i) is available or not is to assess whether the condition imposed by the IPR holder can be termed as 'imposition of a reasonable condition, as may be *necessary* for the protection of any of his rights '*which have been or may be conferred upon him under' the specified IPR statutes* mentioned therein'. The CCI was of the view that the concept of protection of an IPR is qualified by the word 'necessary'. So, the relevant question is whether in the absence of the restrictive condition, would the IPR holder be able to protect his IPR. Further, the statute is clear in its requirement that an IPR must have been conferred (or may be conferred) upon the IPR holder prior to the exception under section 3(5)(i) being available.

Based on the analysis mentioned above and other factors (elaborated in Chapter III on abuse of dominance), the CCI directed (apart from levying hefty fines) that the

OEMs have to put in place an effective system to make the spare parts and diagnostic tools easily available through an efficient network. Further, OEMS must allow the OES to sell the spare parts in the open market without any restrictions.

The matter is currently pending before the Supreme Court; however, it is apposite to mention the relevant observations of the erstwhile COMPAT in this regard. In an appeal before the erstwhile COMPAT,[17] the above findings of the CCI with respect to reasonability and necessity of IPR restrictions were re-affirmed. The erstwhile COMPAT noted that the restrictions imposed on the sale of spare parts were different for different kinds of vendors, and all of them could not be painted with the same brush. Broadly, it identified two such broad categories of vendors based on the OES-OEM relationship and analysed the impact of the restrictions for each of them:

(i) All cases where technology, knowhow, equipment, and tools have been made available to vendors by OEMs themselves, but they are not allowed to sell in the aftermarket. Here, the erstwhile COMPAT observed that if this category of vendors 'are exclusively manufacturing for one OEM and are entirely dependent upon the OEM for knowhow, technology, designs, drawings, specifications, intellectual property even finances in some cases, then they could well be considered as sub-contractors and there is a rationale for them not to sell in the aftermarket'.

(ii) In cases where vendors supply products which are already in their stable but are made to the specifications of the OEMs, they are allowed only with the consent of the OEM. However, no such consent has been ever given. Here, the erstwhile COMPAT observed that those vendors who manufacture their own spare parts but only take the designs and dimensions specific to each model of the vehicle from the OEMs cannot be restricted from selling their products in the aftermarket. This is because, unlike category 1 above, these products are not the exclusive products of the OEMs but the product of the vendor, which has been produced by using its own technology and know-how. Hence, they are dubbed 'matching quality products' because they are specific to the vehicle models (and not generic parts) and can be sold independently in the market. Thus, the erstwhile COMPAT found no reason for such vendors to also seek the permission of the OEMs to sell what is essentially their own products, not exclusive to the OEM. However, the only condition in this case would be that such products cannot be sold under the brand names of the OEMs since they are not produced for/by the OEMs.

An important argument made by the OEMs regarding the necessity and the reasonableness of restrictions was that the Indian aftermarket is full of counterfeit/spurious spare parts, and by imposing these restrictions, they were simply trying to check the potential of mixing the original with the counterfeit. In determining

17. *Toyota Kirloskar Motor Private Limited and Ors. v. Competition Commission of India and Ors.*, Cases 60, 61 and 62 of 2014.

the reasonability of these restrictions, the erstwhile COMPAT found that the appellants were unable to prove that, first, the restrictions were imposed for the protection of their intellectual property and, second, to check the potential mixing of original and counterfeit products in the market. On the first point, it observed that the '*protection of intellectual property*' by itself cannot be considered a reasonable condition, especially in light of the overriding character of the Competition Act. On the second point, it held that making genuine spare parts available at reasonable prices is the solution, as having highly priced spare parts with constrained availability coupled with a lack of regulatory environment was the cause of counterfeiting in the first place. Thus, it became necessary to primarily address the situations that were creating the artificial restraints on the release of genuine spare parts in the aftermarket because the restraint on the supply of genuine spare parts is what caused the counterfeit industry to fill up the deficit in the market. Further, this caused the unavailability of genuine spare parts to independent repairers, and ultimately, the customers did not receive genuine parts, thereby impacting the safety and maintenance of their vehicles. Addressing this situation along with the purpose of protecting IPR could be achieved through contractual means and common law remedies. Therefore, the restrictions imposed by the OEMs were neither reasonable nor necessary.

It is thus important to consider that merely having justifications would not suffice for the purpose of availing the exemption; the Court would only be convinced if such exemption can be given on facts and circumstances of the case, and the ambit of such exemption is very narrow. Hence, the restrictions imposed by OEMs are neither reasonable nor necessary in terms of the IPR exemption. Thus, the restrictions, if any such are imposed, must meet the reasonability and proportionality test.

On this basis, the erstwhile COMPAT generally upheld the directions of the CCI to the OEMs to allow the sale of their respective brands' spare parts in the aftermarket. It also imposed a penalty of 2% on the OEMs' annual average turnover from spare parts for the three financial years preceding the year of inquiry and issued eight specific directions to each of the appellants towards opening the spare parts and repairs and maintenance aftermarkets such as making information regarding their spare parts, warranty, maintenance cost, etc., available in the public domain.

[1] Reasonability Depends on Facts and Circumstances

The scope of section 3(5) of the Competition Act was also clarified in the *Monsanto* case, wherein MMBL relied on section 3(5) to argue that the issue of whether any of the conditions imposed by a patentee is reasonable or not could only be examined in respect of conditions other than those that relate to restraining infringement of any rights granted under the Patents Act. However, the Single Judge of the Delhi High Court dismissed this contention by observing that imposing reasonable conditions to protect IPR is permitted to the extent that such rights fall within the ambit of the specified statutes under section 3(5) of the Competition Act and the conditions are 'reasonable' and 'necessary'. If the conditions are unreasonable or unnecessary, as in the case of MMBL, then the safe harbour of section 3(5) will not be available.

The Delhi High Court observed[18] that the plain language of section 3(5) of the Competition Act makes it apparent that section 3 does not prevent/restrain a person from invoking their right to restrain the infringement of their IPR or to impose reasonable conditions for protecting their IPR. Rather, section 3(5) specifically recognizes these rights of the IPR holder granted under specified statutes such that any agreement entered into with the purpose of infringing a person's IPR falls afoul of section 3 of the Competition Act. However, such rights are not unqualified, and the safe harbour of section 3(5) is only extended to those agreements and only to such extent as is '*necessary for protecting*' IPR. The statutory interpretation of the words '*or to impose reasonable conditions*' placed between two commas must be interpreted as being placed in parenthesis. This means that the safe harbour of section 3(5) allows the IPR holder to impose only reasonable conditions and not unreasonable conditions which are not necessary for the protection of their IPR.

Further, in the case of *K Sera Sera Digital Cinema Ltd. v. Pen India Ltd. and Ors.*,[19] the informant, i.e., K Sera Sera Digital Cinema Ltd., alleged that the producers and presenters of the movie 'Kahaani 2' refused to provide it with the content of the movie but provided the same to other digital cinema service providers alone, in violation of provisions of sections 3 and 4 of the Competition Act. In response, the other digital cinema providers, i.e., UFO Moviez India Ltd. and Real Image Media Technologies Pvt. Ltd., argued that quality and security were the factors for deciding the release of a movie and the informant had caused infringement of copyright in the recent past, by enabling online piracy of another movie called 'Force 2'. Force 2 was screened in the theatres of the informant, but the movie was leaked and pirated from there. In such a situation, it would be counterintuitive for the producers of the movie 'Kahaani – 2' to provide content of the said movie to the informant which was released within two weeks after the incident of piracy.

The CCI held that:[20]

(i) An objective business rationale to protect the commercial interest of the producers and presenters of the movie cannot be overlooked in a proceeding under the Competition Act unless the same is shown to have exclusionary effects or is tainted with an anti-competitive objective. Presently, the movie 'Kahaani – 2' was released on 2 December 2016 which was fourteen days after the release of the movie 'Force 2'. In such a situation, it would be counterintuitive for the producers of the movie 'Kahaani – 2' to provide content of the said movie to the informant which was released within two weeks after the incident of piracy.

(ii) Further, since the producers and presenters of the movie are likely to have spent considerable effort and money to develop their film 'Kahaani – 2', they have every right to decide their business strategy to release the same.

18. *Monsanto Holdings Pvt. Ltd. and Ors. v. Competition Commission of India and Ors.* [2020], (Delhi High Court) W.P.(C) Nos 1776/2016 & 3556/2017, paras 48, 49.
19. *K Sera Sera Digital Cinema Ltd. v. Pen India Ltd.* and Ors., Case No. 34 of 2018.
20. *Ibid.*, paras 10-12.

The producers of the movie 'Kahaani 2' have copyright over the content created by them, and to be protected from any sort of leak/piracy, they must be entitled to take suitable measures to protect their properties from being exploited illegally in the market.

(iii) Section 3(5)(i)(a) of the Competition Act clearly provides that application of section 3 shall not restrict the right of any person to impose reasonable conditions as may be necessary for protecting any of its rights conferred upon under the Copyright Act. The decision of the producers and presenters to refuse to exhibit their movies through the informant's digital service, with whom other producers have had issues of piracy earlier, appears to be taken as a precautionary step to prevent any loss due to piracy.

(iv) In any case, they were availing the services of the informant prior to the incident of the piracy.

Thus, the above decisions of the CCI make it clear that what is reasonable or unreasonable would depend on the facts and circumstances of each case. The CCI must do a balancing analysis to ensure that the exercise of exclusivities guaranteed under the various IPR statutes in India to an IPR holder does not cause a disruptive influence on the market. Also, CCI must be cautious to ensure that the rights guaranteed to the IPR holder under the IPR legislations are not rendered infructuous. In this regard, it must be noted that the balancing test needs to be done wherein equal importance must be given to safeguarding the business interest of the IPR holder as well as the market situation.

Based on the decisional practice of the CCI, it is therefore imperative that the IPR holders are aware that when they enter into any agreement with respect to licensing or otherwise, they cannot enter a practice which may amount to a refusal to deal or other kinds of anti-competitive practices. The IPR exemption is only for the limited purpose of entering into an agreement which may be necessary to protect any of the rights guaranteed under the IPR statutes in India, mentioned therein. As such, the CCI is the body to determine what is necessary and what is reasonable based on the facts and circumstances of each case. It seems like the CCI will allow only those agreements which are least restrictive and totally necessary to protect the rights conferred upon them by the relevant IPR statutes. The key point to be mentioned here is that section 3(5) speaks about the protection of the rights and restrains infringement of the rights under the IPR statutes as opposed to exploitation of the rights guaranteed under the IPR statutes.

Further, as deliberated in the *Automobile Spare Parts* case, unless the IPRs are registered under Indian laws, there is no protection available under section 3(5) of the Competition Act. So, there may be circumstances (like what happened in the *Automobile Spare Parts* case) where a company possesses a valid patent under a foreign jurisdiction, which is licensed to its group company based in India. The group company in India cannot avail of the IPR exemption unless it can be shown by way of clear and unambiguous documentary evidence that the rights of the group company in India are conferred under or will be conferred under the relevant IPR statutes in India.

Further, CCI, as well as the erstwhile COMPAT, have taken a very strict stand on what constitutes 'necessary' to protect IPR rights. Given that the idea of IPR rights is to incentivize innovation, the finding of both bodies that one can allow the licensee to sell spare parts in the open market without affecting the IP rights of the IP holder seems to be an interesting proposition. The CCI opined that merely allowing the open market sale of spare parts, which are manufactured end products, would not necessarily compromise the IPR held by car manufacturers in the spare parts. The CCI was of the view that it was very much possible for the car manufacturers to contractually protect their IPR and permit the OESs to sell their products directly in the open market. In circumstances where the products in question (whether spare parts or otherwise) are being manufactured through sub-contracting arrangements, where the R&D costs and the IP remain with the principal, the sub-contractors as a matter of fact are extensions of the OEM's factory. This is complemented by the opinion of the erstwhile COMPAT that allowing the sale of spare parts in the aftermarket will actually prevent the problem of counterfeiting, which was cited as one of the necessary conditions for imposing the restriction in the first place by the OEMs.[21]

[C] Applicability of Section 3(5) to Trade Secrets

The protection of certain IPRs has long been considered an exception to anti-competitive agreements under the Competition Act. However, only those IPRs specified in the Competition Act for this purpose would be considered an exception to such agreements – i.e., a list of statutes enumerated under section 3(5) of the Competition Act. The report prepared by the DG in the *Automobile Spare Parts* case proceeded on the point that since 'trade secret' is not expressly mentioned in section 3(5), it will be able to avail the exemption mentioned under section 3(5) of the Competition Act. Given the interpretation adopted by the CCI for interpreting section 3(5) of providing protection to the rights which are specifically conferred upon under the specific statues mentioned therein, it was likely that the CCI will not provide a safe harbour to trade secrets.

However, with the introduction of sub-section (g) in section 3(5) of the Competition Act by virtue of the Competition Amendment Act, 2023, in addition to the above-specified legislations, rights under any other law relating to the protection of other IPR would also be considered an exception to anti-competitive agreements. Thus, the scope of this provision has been expanded to all IPRs. Accordingly, protection would now extend to rights accruing under, *inter alia*, the Protection of Plant Varieties and Farmers Rights Act, 2001, Biological Diversity Act, 2002, as well as trade secrets and confidential information (for the protection of which no specific legislation exists), which were previously excluded from the ambit of the provision.

[D] Applicability of IPR Defence to Section 4

The statute provides for IPR exemption only for section 3 and not practices covered under section 4 (provision relating to abuse of dominance) since section 4 does not

21. *Toyota Kirloskar Motor Private Limited and Ors. v. Competition Commission of India and Ors.*, Cases 60, 61 and 62 of 2014.

have a parallel exemption of IPR (on the lines of section 3(5), Competition Act). The Report of the Competition Law Review Committee had recommended the inclusion of IPR as a defence of abuse of dominant position *pari materia* to section 3(5) in the Competition Act. Unlike section 3, which has carved out an exception to anti-competitive agreements if the same is in reasonable exercise of IPR, section 4 of the Competition Act does not provide any such provision. Due to the absence of any such explicit exception under the Competition Act, CCI cannot allow dominant entities to rely on reasonable protection of their IPR in cases of abuse of dominant position.

In light of the above recommendation, section 4A was suggested to be included vide the Competition Amendment Bill, 2020, providing for the protection of IPR holders against section 4 as well, empowering them to impose reasonable conditions in the protection of their IPR. The same was also reiterated in the recommendations of the Parliamentary Standing Committee on Finance for the Draft Competition (Amendment) Bill, 2022. However, this amendment was not accepted by the legislature and has not made its way into the Competition (Amendment) Act, 2023, on the basis that IPR defence need not be explicitly included in section 4 since, in the era of the new age economy, mention of IPR defence explicitly may allow a dominant player to abuse its position of dominance.

Further, the various legal provisions and the decisional practice of CCI with respect to section 4 are covered in the chapter on abuse of dominance. It has also been confirmed by the CCI, in the *Automobile Spare Parts* case, that the safe harbour of IPR exemption is not applicable for abuse of dominance actions mentioned under section 4(2) of the Competition Act. Therefore, if an enterprise is found to be dominant pursuant to Explanation (a) to section 4(2) and is indulging in practices amounting to denial of market access or refusal to deal, it is no defence to suggest that such exclusionary conduct is within the scope of their IPR. In appeal, the erstwhile COMPAT reiterated the observations of the CCI that abusive practices under section 4 of the Competition Act cannot be protected under the defence of section 3(5)(i).

However, the stringent approach to non-applicability of the IPR defence to section 4 has been substantially diluted by the NCLAT to the extent that a dominant enterprise cannot be forced to share its proprietary rights in *Umar Javeed and ors. v. Google LLC and Anr*[22] ('*Google Android* case'), which has been discussed in detail in the chapter on abuse of dominance. In this case, the question arose of access to Google's APIs, i.e., its intellectual property to its rivals, OEMs and app developers. Google owns the IPR to the Android Operating System (OS), and as per its Brand Guidelines, the 'Android' name and the Android logo are property of Google LLC and not part of the assets available through the Android Open-Source Project.

Further, the use of the 'Android' trademark on hardware, packaging or marketing materials of devices is restricted to Android-compatible devices only. Therefore, to use these IPRs, the OEMs must adhere to the obligations imposed by Google. Accordingly, the CCI observed that Google controls the licensing of trademarks related to Android, and OEMs are dependent on Google for using IPR related to Android. Consequently,

22. *Umar Javeed and ors. v. Google LLC and Anr.*, Case No. 39 of 2018.

CCI directed that: '*Google shall not deny access to its Play Services APIs to disadvantage OEMs, app developers and its existing or potential competitors. This would ensure interoperability of apps between Android OS which complies with compatibility requirements of Google and Android Forks...*' In an appeal before the NCLAT, Google argued that it cannot be asked to share APIs as it constitutes the IPR of Google and that the CCI did not demonstrate that Play Services APIs fulfil the criteria of 'essential facility'. Interestingly, the NCLAT affirmed the argument of Google by holding that Google's APIs constitute its proprietary software into which Google has made investments for scientific and technical development. Thus, Google is allowed to enjoy the fruits of its labour. Accordingly, the NCLAT set aside the direction of CCI to allow open access to Google's APIs. This is an important observation as it accounts for one of the rare cases where a dominant firm has been allowed to restrict access to its IPR. The other aspects of this case have been discussed in more detail under the heading of compulsory licensing. It is relevant to mention that the said observations are presently under challenge before the Supreme Court.

§5.04 ANTI-COMPETITIVE PRACTICES EMANATING OUT OF IPRs

With competition law in India having surpassed more than fourteen years of existence, the CCI has discussed the anti-competitive prices emanating out of IPRs on several occasions. Further, the CCI, in its advocacy measures, has highlighted certain practices of abusing IPR rights which may fall afoul of the provisions of the Competition Act. This part of the chapter is divided into two categories based on the decisional practice of the CCI and advocacy initiatives: pricing and non-pricing abuse.

As has been discussed above, the scope of section 3(5) of the Competition Act is very limited, and the decisional practice of the CCI suggests that it will rarely be applicable. Therefore, the licensor must be aware of the nuances of competition law prior to entering into agreements with licensors to monetize their operations by way of earning royalty.

The CCI must consider the fact that the creation of IPRs enhances economic efficiency and that it entails substantial investment. As a result, it is felt that the innovator must not be unduly restricted in the exploitation of valuable IPRs and that licensing as such is pro-competitive. Competition law seeks to strike a balance between rewarding the holder of IPRs by allowing many forms of legitimate exploitation of those rights while at the same time safeguarding competition. Yet, since the licence agreements may contain provisions which may potentially cause market distortions, the same ought to be investigated under section 3 or section 4 of the Competition Act.

[A] Standard Essential Patents

Before explaining pricing and non-pricing abuse, it is important to understand the concept of SEPs.

In *M/s Best IT World (India) Private Limited (iBall) v. M/s Telefonaktiebolaget L M Ericsson (Publ) and Anr*[23] ('*iBall* case'), iBall alleged that the practices adopted by Ericsson with regards to its SEPs in respect of 2G, 3G and 4G patents used in smartphones, tablets, etc., are discriminatory through imposition of unfair terms. The CCI noted that 'standardisation is the process of developing and implementing technical standards. Such technological standards are termed as SEPs. Once a patent is declared as SEP, it faces no competition from other patents until that patent becomes obsolete due to new technology/inventions'. There are three pending investigations (which are presently quashed due to a Division Bench order in the *Ericsson* case) which are being conducted by the DG investigating the conduct of Ericsson on the licensing terms of SEPs, based on information filed by Micromax Informatics Limited,[24] Intex Technologies (India) Limited[25] and M/s Best IT World (India) Private Limited (iBall).[26] The cases deal with the competition law concerns emanating from the licensing of SEPs.

As evident, a patent by nature is a statutory monopoly, but an SEP is above a normal patent (to an extent) because the licensee or implementer has no choice but to take a licence of the SEP. It is in this situation a competition law regulator must be vigilant that the SEP holder is not abusing its power and dictating terms to the licensees. Therefore, SEPs are monitored and ensured that the licences are given by the SEP holders on terms that are really Fair, Reasonable, and Non-Discriminatory (FRAND). As also recorded in the observations of CCI in the *iBall* case, FRAND licences are primarily intended to prevent Patent Hold-up and Royalty Stacking. In the absence of FRAND licences, a licensor can exploit their SEPs for higher royalties because the nature of such patents would make them essential to the business of the licensees, and they would have no other option. It must be noted that licence agreements (especially licence agreements pertaining to SEP) have a lot of benefits and cause efficiencies since the licensee already has access to the necessary production assets, and the licence agreement allows the licensee to gain access to a technology that can be combined with these assets, allows the licensee to exploit new or improved technologies and helps them to launch new products which will, in turn, add consumer benefits. While the investigation against Ericsson has been quashed by virtue of the Division Bench judgment discussed earlier, the same is likely to go up in appeal since, as discussed above, there are some areas of challenge.

Nevertheless, the observations of the CCI assume importance in the context of how misuse of SEPs can distort competition in the market. The CCI observed that[27] since the usefulness of complex products and services depends on their interoperability, competing manufacturers, customers and suppliers engage in standard-setting practices to enhance the value of these complex products by setting technological

23. *M/s Best IT World (India) Private Limited (iBall) v. M/s Telefonaktiebolaget L M Ericsson (Publ) and Anr.*, Case 04 of 2015, para. 8.
24. *Micromax Informatics Limited v. Telefonaktiebolaget LM Ericsson (Publ)*, Case No. 50 of 2013.
25. *Intex Technologies (India) Limited v. Telefonaktiebolaget LM Ericsson (Publ)*, Case No. 76 of 2013.
26. *iBall* case.
27. *Ibid.*, para. 10.

standards for the design and use of such products. Consequently, there is a possibility of a 'hold-up' by the owner of the patent where such standard technologies have patent protection. Hold-up refers to a situation where the patent owner can demand higher royalties or impose more costly or burdensome licensing terms because of the patent having become a market standard, i.e., been declared as an SEP. This can undermine the integrity of standard-setting activities and the competitive process of choosing among technologies because, ultimately, the high costs of such SEPs are transferred to the end consumers. Similarly, a single product may use different patents of the same or different licensors. When this happens, the manufacturer of the product has to add up or 'stack-together' all these different royalties or costs to determine the total royalty burden to be borne by them. This is called 'royalty-stacking.'

In the *Ericsson* case, the Single Judge of Delhi High Court observed that there are grounds to hold that seeking injunctive reliefs by an SEP holder in certain circumstances may amount to abuse of its dominant position. The rationale for this is that the risk of suffering injunctions would, in certain circumstances, clearly exert undue pressure on an implementer and, thus, place him in a disadvantageous bargaining position vis-à-vis an SEP holder. A patent holder has a statutory right to file a suit for infringement, but the Competition Act is not concerned with the rights of a person or an enterprise but the *exercise* of such rights. The position of a proprietor of an SEP cannot be equated with a proprietor of a patent which is not essential to an industry standard. While in the former case, a non-infringing patent is not available to a dealer/manufacturer, in the latter case, the dealer/manufacturer may have other non-infringing options. It is, thus, essential that the bargaining power of a dealer/manufacturer implementing the standard be protected and preserved.

As a result, licence agreements may also foreclose competitors by raising their costs or by denying access to essential inputs (also known as the essential facilities doctrine). While the said decision has been overturned by the Division Bench of the High Court, the matter will most likely be challenged in appeal before the Supreme Court. Notably, the Division Bench of the High Court did not consider some of the aspects which were held by the Single Judge; thus, it would be interesting to see how the Supreme Court addresses such legal issues. In any case, there is an argument to make that the jurisdiction of the CCI cannot be ousted completely due to the express language of section 3(5) of the Act.

Apart from the above, another form of non-pricing abuse emanating out of IPRs is fraudulent litigation, wherein deceptive practices like sham litigation, strategic timing of litigation, enforcement of invalid patents, etc., are employed by an IPR holder to assert their rights and harm their competitors. This has been discussed subsequently under the heading of non-pricing abuse.

[B] Pricing Abuse

There are certain investigation orders passed by the CCI relating to abuse of dominance. The prima facie case was for abuse with respect to imposing excessive and discriminatory pricing, among other non-pricing abuses.

[1] Excessive Pricing

One of the points of investigation in the *Ericsson* case pertains to excessive pricing. Based on the information received, the CCI determined, prima facie, that the relevant product market would be GSM technologies like 3G, EDGE, etc., for 2G, 3G and 4G devices. The CCI observed that Ericsson holds many GSM and CDMA patents. It was observed that Ericsson has 33,000 patents to its credit, with 400 of these patents granted in India. It is the largest holder of SEPs for mobile communications like 2G, 3G and 4G patents used for smartphones, tablets, etc. Further, since Ericsson holds SEPs and there is no other alternate technology in the market, it enjoys *'complete dominance'* over its present and prospective licensees in the relevant product market. On this basis, Ericsson was found prima facie to be a dominant enterprise in the relevant market.

The validity of the terms under a licence agreement on SEPs and the fixing of royalty rates for such SEPs is under investigation. It must be pointed out here that while SEP has immense benefits, it is vulnerable to abuse of market power that it confers upon the SEP holder.

In these two cases, CCI determined that prima facie, the proposed licence terms were both unfair and discriminatory. The information filed by Micromax and Intex stated that Ericsson was demanding unfair, discriminatory and exorbitant royalty for its SEPs. On an examination of the evidence produced by the Informant, the CCI noted that the royalty rates charged by Ericsson had no linkage to the patented product since the technology resided only within the chipset, but Ericsson calculated its royalty on the retail price of the entire phone. Therefore, while the technology remained the same, the royalty may vary for two manufacturers based on the pricing of their phones. Thus, the increase in the royalty for patent holders was without any contribution to the product of the licensee. Charging of two different licence fees per unit phone for use of the same technology prima facie was held to be discriminatory and also reflected excessive pricing vis-à-vis high-cost phones.

Further, the matter pertains to section 4 of the Competition Act, which does not have any IPR exemption. The pricing-related abuse under investigation in this case is excessive pricing and differential pricing. Considering that the CCI has become a very assertive regulator, an IPR holder must be cautious in entering into licence agreements and exercising its statutory right to charge royalty. It will be interesting to gather the regulatory outlook on such an issue once the matter is finally decided.

The CCI has also analysed pricing abuse with respect to excessive pricing relating to the exploitation of rights conferred upon the IPR statutes in the case of *HT Media v. Super Cassettes.*[28] The abuse in question is related to whether the licence fee imposed by Super Cassettes on the radio operator amounts to excessive pricing and whether the minimum commitment charge being imposed by Super Cassettes amounts to abuse of dominant position. On the issue of excessive pricing, the CCI elaborated that the case of excessive pricing can be made out once the cost incurred by the dominant player is obtained and a comparison is made to the economic value of the product vis-à-vis the

28. *HT Media v. Super Cassettes,* Case No. 40 of 2011, paras 193-199.

cost. It was contended by Super Cassettes that cost analysis for setting a licence fee is not possible since the cost of a sound recording is reflected in the acquisition price paid as a royalty to the owners, and in the event the sound recording is developed in-house, the cost is recognized as recording expense. Further, with respect to direct costs, Super Cassettes has various avenues for commercially exploiting the same, and it is very difficult to apportion the cost of acquisition of sound recording to different revenue streams. Based on the same, the CCI noted that in the absence of a cost date, it is not possible to ascertain whether the fee charged at INR 661 per needle hour would amount to an abuse of excessive pricing or not. Further, CCI stated that the price charged by a dominant player cannot be said to be excessive on the sole ground that the price charged is higher than that charged by its competitors.

On the issue of the economic value of the product, the CCI observed that, in this case, the value of a particular sound recording would depend upon its popularity and not its cost. Based on these factors, the CCI held that no case of excessive pricing is being made out.

In the *Roche* case[29] also, the CCI dismissed the challenge of excessive pricing by holding that, being the innovator, Roche might have invested huge sums in the research and development of Trastuzumab. Thus, initial high prices can be attributable to being the reward for innovation.

It must be noted that even internationally, it is challenging for a case of excessive pricing to be made out since it is very difficult for authorities to determine the economic value of the product. The approach of the CCI on excessive pricing also suggests that it is not a straightforward exercise to determine whether a fee so charged is excessive. As also discussed in the chapter on abuse of dominance, the decisional practice of CCI indicates the position that it is not a price regulator and does not intend to be one. Hence, it cannot determine the correct fee to be charged.

While the CCI did not rule out the possibility of reviewing whether licensing fees charged amount to an abuse of dominant position as being unfair and excessive, the finding that one must assess factors beyond just the actual cost in this market segment to analyse the economic value of the product is apt. Such a finding will have very interesting implications when applied in the context of other IP rights, in particular, patents and know-how. Further, in Ericsson's case, the CCI was making a foray into the determination of FRAND royalties to determine whether the practice of Ericsson amounts to excessive pricing.

Further, it is crucial to note that compulsory licence proceedings under the Copyright Act involve the relevant authority in determining the 'reasonable royalties' to be paid to the copyright holder. In the future, an issue that may arise is whether the 'reasonable royalties' determined in a given case under the Copyright Act would become the benchmark to determine unfair pricing issues under the Competition Act to decide the cost of the product. Similar provisions under the other IPR statutes in India, like the Patents Act, 1970, contain provisions relating to compulsory licence, and this proceeding will also involve an assessment of the royalties to a patentee.

29. *Roche* case, para. 80.

Further, another area of overlap may occur in the case of IP infringement proceedings. IP infringement proceedings could result in monetary damages being awarded to the IPR owner, and one of the methods of determining the quantum of damages is 'reasonable royalties' that the IPR owner may have otherwise obtained. In fact, such a dichotomy has already occurred in India, wherein Ericsson was successful in an infringement litigation that entitled Ericsson to receive royalty payments calculated as a percentage of the price of the product. This decision has also recently been affirmed by the Delhi High Court. Whereas, as discussed above, the CCI has ruled that seeking royalties calculated as a percentage of the price of the product as a whole rather than just the chip within that product embodying Ericsson's patent was prima facie an abuse of dominance and ordered an investigation. It will, therefore, be interesting to view the outlook of the CCI in such a case. It is further important to monitor the regulatory outlook because the IPR holders have the right to monetize their rights, enter into a licence agreement and obtain a stream of revenue by way of royalties. However, the IPR holders must be careful that they do not enter into arrangements which seem to be foul of section 4 of the Competition Act.

[2] Differential Pricing

Apart from the issue pertaining to excessive pricing, the CCI is also investigating the issue of differential pricing against Ericsson. Apart from the issue of excessive pricing, it was also alleged that the royalty demanded by Ericsson was excessive when compared to royalties charged by other patentees for patents similar to or comparable to the patents held by Ericsson.

The CCI noted that Ericsson had subjected all its present and prospective licensees to Non-Disclosure Agreements which prohibit the licensees from disclosing commercial terms between similarly placed patent seekers. CCI noted that entering into such a Non-Disclosure Agreement which prohibits such disclosure of commercial terms implies that royalty being charged from a licensee (Micromax, Intex and iBall in this case) may be more than the royalty being charged from similarly placed licensees. The CCI, in its prima facie order, has noted that refusal to share commercial terms with the informant fortifies the accusation of alleged discriminatory commercial terms imposed by Ericsson on the informant vis-à-vis other licensees.

Accordingly, on the issue of differential pricing, the CCI in its prima facie order observed the royalty rates were excessive, unfair, discriminatory and non-transparent because two different licence fees per unit phone were being charged for the use of the same technology.[30] The allegation of discriminatory and excessive pricing was strengthened by the fact that Ericsson forced an Non-Disclosure Agreement (NDA) upon the consumers, after which each user of the SEPs was unable to know the terms of royalty offered to other users. Since transparency is the hallmark of fairness, such

30. *Micromax Informatics Limited v. Telefonaktiebolaget LM Ericsson (Publ)*, Case No. 50 of 2013, para. 17; *Intex Technologies (India) Limited v. Telefonaktiebolaget LM Ericsson (Publ)*, Case No. 76 of 2013, para. 17.

conduct is contrary to the spirit of applying FRAND terms uniformly and fairly to all similarly placed players. Hence, forcing a party to sign such an NDA and imposition of excessive and unfair royalty rates, both prima facie amount to abuse of dominance contrary to section 4 of the Competition Act.

In its prima facie order in the *iBall* case,[31] the CCI opined that the practices adopted by Ericsson appeared to be discriminatory by charging two different licence fees per phone for use of the same technology, as well as contrary to FRAND terms, by imposing royalties linked with the cost of manufacturing product. Further, the royalty rate charged by Ericsson had no linkage to the functionality of the patented product; rather, it had a linkage to the final price of the manufactured product in which the patent is being used. The CCI also held that forcing a party to execute NDA contrary to the spirit of applying FRAND terms fairly and uniformly to similarly placed players and imposing excessive and unfair royalty rates, prima facie, amount to abuse of dominance in violation of section 4 of the Act.

However, mere price discrimination by itself cannot be claimed to be a violation of FRAND terms or abusive in terms of section 4. In the *Vifor* case discussed under the scope of section 3(5) of the Competition Act above, the informant, *inter alia*, claimed that Vifor was engaging in price discrimination between its licensees, i.e., Lupin and Emcure. It was alleged that there was no effective price competition between the brands which were sold by the said licensee companies, which offered a lower price while supplying under the public procurement initiative of the government, as opposed to high-priced retail sale. The differences in prices at which these soluble Iron Injectables were offered in other countries were also highlighted by the Informant. The CCI observed that price differentiation based on reasonable classification can be allowed and did not find the same to be discriminatory in nature:[32]

> *all price differentiations may not be discriminatory, more so when the same is based on reasonable classification of consumers to which they are offered.* Prices offered in government procurement may not be comparable with the products being sold in open market on quantity criteria (bulk vs. individual buying) as well as purpose (public purpose or distribution free of cost vs private consumption).

The approach taken by the CCI gives a very valuable insight for IPR holders to treat their licensees on an equal footing and ensure uniformity in application to similarly placed players. The CCI has noted that FRAND licences are primarily intended to prevent situations of patent hold-up. This means that when standard technologies are protected by patent rights, there is a possibility for 'hold-up' by the patent owner to demand higher royalties or burdensome licensing terms before the standard is chosen. Ultimately, the high costs of such patents get transferred to the final consumers, thus impeding consumer welfare. By standardization, which is a voluntary process, several companies reach a consensus for setting common technology standards under the support of a standard-setting organization, which in the present case is the European Telecommunications Standards Institute. The CCI analysed the policy of the European

31. *iBall* case, para. 14.
32. Case No. 05 of 2022, para. 77.

Telecommunications Standards Institute with respect to licensing of SEPs in the Ericsson matter and noted, based on the IPR policy of the European Telecommunications Standards Institute, that an SEP owner is required to give an irrevocable written undertaking that it is prepared to grant irrevocable licences on FRAND Terms. The same must be applied fairly and uniformly to similarly placed player, i.e., reasonable classification is not precluded.

[3] Minimum Commitment Charge

In the *Super Cassettes* case, CCI also discussed the issue of minimum commitment charge. As discussed above, the radio operators had complained to the CCI that Super Cassettes were imposing a minimum commitment charge to be paid per month by the radio operators to Super Cassettes irrespective of actual needle hour (each aggregate of sixty minutes of the actual broadcast of sound recordings by FM radio station excluding commercials, advertisements, voice-over, anchor time, etc.) of broadcast of the music content of Super Cassettes by the radio operators.

On investigation by the DG, it was noticed that Super Cassettes requires minimum commitment charge to be paid by the radio operators irrespective of the actual number of needle hours of the music of Super Cassettes that is broadcast. It was further noticed by the DG that, except for Super Cassettes, no other music company is imposing minimum commitment charge. Considering the strength of Super Cassettes, the radio operators have no choice but to accept the onerous conditions. On perusal of some of the agreements, the DG found that the minimum committed needle hours for the playoff of the songs of the opposite party imposed by it are as high as 50%.

The CCI agreed with the opinion of the DG that held that imposition of minimum commitment charge is exploitative and exclusionary in nature. The CCI noted that the imposition of a minimum commitment charge by Super Cassettes has an anti-competitive effect on the market as it forecloses other competitors from a substantial share of the market. Since the private radio station is contractually bound to pay Super Cassettes a minimum guaranteed amount, CCI noted that they are likely to broadcast the amount of music that they have already paid for. Therefore, a certain amount of music that plays out on private FM radio stations is already fixed for Super Cassettes. Based on the above, CCI noted that imposition of minimum commitment charge by Super Cassettes is an abuse of dominance.

The ruling of the CCI on the issue of minimum commitment charge in this case is certainly an indication to all IP holders (patentees and copyright holders included) that care must be taken in requiring mandatory minimum royalties. Going by the outlook of the CCI in case of Super Cassettes and prima facie order of Ericsson, it appears that CCI is more in favour of licence fee/royalty that has a nexus to the use or value of the licensed product/work. Once the threshold of dominant position is crossed, minimum commitment charge-type clauses will undergo strict scrutiny.

[4] *The Advocacy Initiatives of the CCI*

Apart from the decisional guidance by the CCI on the issue of interface between IPR and competition law, the CCI has issued an advocacy booklet on the interface between IPR and competition law,[33] highlighting certain enumerative (not exhaustive) pricing practices which may be viewed as anti-competitive and hence void under section 3 and section 4 of the Competition Act:

(i) an agreement which provides that royalty will continue to be paid even after the patent has expired or that royalties shall be payable in respect of unpatented know-how as well as the subject matter of the patent;
(ii) fixing of price by the licensor at which the licensee would sell.

[C] Non-pricing Abuse

From the advocacy initiatives of the CCI, it can be noticed that it gives paramount importance to the rights of the IPR holders while also ensuring that the IPR holders, because of their statutory monopoly do not distort the market in its favour.

In the *Roche case*, as discussed above, the CCI observed that in the pharmaceutical industry, apart from pricing strategies, firms also indulge in non-price strategies to unlawfully raise their rivals' costs or exclude them from the market. Some of these practices which have gained a reasonable degree of acceptance by other competition authorities as being abusive when adopted by dominant entities are as follows:

(i) rendering rivals' products incompatible without adding any technical improvement to the replaced product;
(ii) indulging in vexatious litigation purely aimed at harassing rivals;
(iii) influencing government or regulatory procedures; and
(iv) impeding the entry of generics/biosimilars by denigrating or disparaging rivals' products.

Hence, non-pricing abuse can take many forms, such as discriminatory terms of access to the licence, engaging in vexatious litigation, enforcement of weak or invalid patents, etc. Some of the non-pricing abuses elaborated by the CCI are discussed below:

[1] *Onerous Terms in the Licence Agreement*

Apart from the abuse of excessive and discriminatory pricing, CCI has also shown its inclination to inquire into other terms of the licence agreement, which may be anti-competitive. As deliberated above, the prima facie order of the CCI noted that Ericsson is forcing its licensees to enter into a non-disclosure agreement. The non-disclosure agreement provided jurisdiction of Singapore courts. Based on the same, CCI

33. Advocacy booklet on Competition law, available at https://www.cci.gov.in/advocacy/publications/advocacy-booklets.

has held that apart from imposing excessive and unfair royalties, imposing of jurisdiction clause which debars the licensees from getting disputes adjudicated in the country where both parties were in business and vesting jurisdiction in a foreign land prima facie was also an abuse of dominance. This finding of CCI assumes importance because CCI is looking at the overall conduct of the IPR holder, which can be evidenced in the manner that they are dealing with the licensees and prospective licensees to analyse whether there is a prima facie case of abuse of dominance. It will be interesting to look at the CCI judgment on this issue in the times to come.

In the *Monsanto* case, the Single Judge of the Delhi High Court expressly observed that section 3(5) of the Competition Act does not mean that a patentee would be free to include onerous conditions under the guise of protecting its rights.

In *M/s ATOS Worldline India Private Limited v. M/s Verifone India Sales Private Limited,*[34] ATOS (a provider of Value-Added Services (VAS) as a third-party processor) alleged that Verifone (a manufacturer of point of sale (POS) terminals) abused its dominance while granting licences for its Software Development Kits (SDK) through unfair and discriminatory conditions in the SDK agreement which enabled the operation of POS terminals. *Inter alia,* the SDK agreement had a 'Purpose Clause' which restricted licensees from using any third party to develop or assist in developing any software that it develops or attempts to develop using the licensed software without first obtaining prior permission from Verifone and disclosing certain confidential information, including the names of its customers. Verifone claimed that the restrictive clauses of the SDK agreement are meant for the purpose of protecting its IPRs.

During the investigation, the DG found that this IPR justification was untenable since none of the other POS Terminals vendors have incorporated such restrictive clauses in their SDK agreement. The DG also found that the clauses of the SDK agreement are limiting and restricting the technical or scientific development relating to the prejudice of consumers and the intent of the restrictive clauses in regard to licensing, selling or otherwise transferring any software that the licensee develops was to not allow them its further use.

On this basis, the CCI concluded that the intent of Verifone was to exploit the VAS players by either restricting them or sharing the revenue with them because the VAS market is highly profitable and has recurring benefits.

Being in a dominant position in the relevant market for POS Terminals in India, Verifone was strengthening its position in the downstream market by imposing restrictive clauses in the SDK agreement and by refusing the VAS providers to allow access to development tools like SDK on reasonable terms and conditions. Hence, Verifone's arguments that the restrictions were to ensure the safety of its IPR were rejected, and the terms imposed by Verifone in its licence agreement were found to be unfair and discriminatory.

The decision of the CCI was also subsequently upheld by the NCLAT, which reaffirmed the CCI's observations by holding that the clauses of Verifone's SDK

34. *M/s ATOS Worldline India Private Limited v. M/s Verifone India Sales Private Limited,* Case No. 56 of 2012.

agreement were not as per the prevailing industry practice.[35] Being in a position of strength, the requirement of prior disclosure to Verifone about the VAS developed by ATOS amounted to imposition of unfair condition and also limited the provision of VAS service in the market.

Further, in *M/s. K.C. Marketing v. OPPO Mobiles MU Private Limited,*[36] it was alleged by the informant that certain clauses in the Sub-Super Distributorship Agreement through which it was appointed as the exclusive Sub-Super Mobile Distributor of OPPO mobiles in South and Central Maharashtra were anti-competitive in nature, specifically Clauses 8 and 9 which penalized and restricted online sales and cross-regional sales. It was alleged that such terms amount to using unfair practices. OPPO argued that as far as the restriction on online sales is concerned, the same does not cause AAEC in India and is imposed upon all Sub-Super Distributors pan India without any discrimination because OPPO makes online sales of its products on its own. This OPPO is entitled to do, as being the intellectual property holder of OPPO products, it is free to exploit its intellectual property in any way it pleases.

Even though the CCI observed that OPPO smartphones are freely available in the market at competitive prices and are also easily available for purchase online on all major e-commerce websites at discounted rate and by such restriction, no inter-brand or intra-brand competition has been restricted, it is important to note that the CCI expressly rejected the intellectual property argument put forth by OPPO by stating that the same is not a valid justification for imposition of such restriction.

[2] Denial of Market Access by Fraudulent Litigation

Another manifestation of abuse of dominant position in the context of IPR is through frivolous/fraudulent/vexatious litigation. By misusing the adjudicatory machinery, such as obtaining ex-parte injunctions against smaller players, dominant entities foreclose the market by engaging in sham litigations. This is because such *malafide* proceedings drain the resources of the competitors of the dominant enterprise, prevent them from using their product/service in the market and thereby, lead to the very antithesis of the objective of IPR protection, i.e., to confer an exclusive right to the owner of the IPR to exploit the same for their benefit.

The discussion of denial of market access by fraudulent litigation with regards to IPR emerged in the case of *M/s Bull Machines Pvt. Ltd. v. M/s JCB India Ltd.*[37] Bull Machines (informant) and JCB were engaged in the development and manufacturing of construction and earthmoving equipment. JCB served Bull Machines with an ex parte interim injunction order at the formal launch of the latter's low-cost backhoe loaders called 'Bull Smart'. As a result, Bull Machines was restrained from making, selling, offering for sale, dispatching, advertising, directly or indirectly dealing in/launching backhoe loaders in any manner. Hence, the dealerships of Bull Machines were closed

35. *Verifone India Sales Private Limited v. Competition Commission of India and Anr.* [2020], (NCLAT) TA(AT) (Competition) Nos 1 and 2 of 2017 (Old Appeals Nos 82 and 83 of 2015).
36. *M/s. K.C. Marketing v. OPPO Mobiles MU Private Limited,* Case No. 34 of 2018.
37. *M/s Bull Machines Pvt. Ltd. v. M/s JCB India Ltd,* Case No. 105 of 2013.

even before the formal sale of Bull Smart began; the informant received negative publicity in the market for its new product and its promotional material, documents, components, etc., were seized.

Subsequently, Bull Machines filed a suit for vacation of the ex parte interim stay order before the Delhi High Court and submitted evidence to show that the design registrations of JCB were fraudulently obtained. During the course of the proceedings, the Delhi High Court passed a consent order which, *inter alia*: (i) suspended the interim injunction and (ii) allowed JCB to inspect Bull Smart at a mutually agreed time, date and place within ten days of the passing of the order. However, JCB voluntarily withdrew its application for ex parte interim injunction nearly ten months after filing the original suit without submitting any inspection report or reply. On this basis, Bull Machines sought intervention from CCI.

The entire case of abuse made by Bull Machines was predicated upon the alleged bad faith litigation filed by JCB before the Delhi High Court, alleging that infringement of its design rights was totally false and that the said legal proceedings were only initiated to harass it and prevent the launch of 'Bull Smart', which in effect would have competed with backhoe loaders of JCB in the relevant market. Furthermore, Bull Machines argued that the injunction was obtained on the basis it had allegedly infringed the registered designs and copyrights of JCB while manufacturing 'Bull Smart', which designs/copyrights themselves were obtained fraudulently.

The CCI directed the DG to conduct an investigation into the matter by making the following observations:

(i) On the basis of market share, size and resources, dependence of consumers on it, etc., prima facie, it appears that JCB is a dominant entity in the relevant market for the manufacture and sale of backhoe loaders in India.
(ii) The predation through abuse of judicial processes presents an increasing threat to competition, particularly due to its relatively low anti-trust visibility.
(iii) By abusing their dominant position in the relevant market, JCB sought to stifle competition by denying market access and foreclosing entry of 'Bull Smart' in contravention of the provisions of section 4 of the Competition Act.

In the *Roche* case, which was discussed under the jurisdiction above, with regard to vexatious litigation, the CCI held that unsuccessful litigation is not an indicator that the same was initiated with a mala-fide intention. Even if the litigation initiated by a dominant enterprise fails, it does not change the possible abusive nature of such tactics which drain the resources of smaller competitors.

The CCI also laid down a two-step test to identify if a litigation is vexatious – the legal action (i) must be objectively baseless and (ii) have an anti-competitive intention.[38] If these parameters are satisfied, then there is a prima facie case of vexatious litigation. Under the first limb, it has to be proved that the impugned legal action is

38. *Roche* case, para. 62.

objectively baseless and is being used as a tool to harass the defendant. Under the second limb, it has to be proved that the legal action was conceived with an anti-competitive intent/plan to eliminate the competition. Anticompetitive legislation of this kind by a dominant enterprise as a tactic to exhaust a smaller rival's resources/hinder their entry in the market amounts to abuse of dominance. On application to the facts of the case, CCI did not find the litigations filed by Roche to be baseless or tainted with ulterior motives. Since recourse to legal proceedings is the right of every party, a determination of vexatious litigation should be done in exceptional cases, that too cautiously and sparingly.

It is also apposite to mention that while the allegations of vexation litigation were dismissed by the CCI, the CCI expressed that it was cognizant that the informants' drugs had received approvals from DCGI and had entered the market, despite the attempts made by Roche to discourage and adversely affect the availability of biosimilars in the market. There were a few important observations by the CCI in this regard:

(i) The denial of market access within the meaning of section 4(2)(c) of the Competition Act need not be complete and absolute in nature. Even a partial denial of market access that takes away the freedom of a substitute to compete effectively and on merits in the relevant market may amount to a contravention of section 4(2)(c).

(ii) It is well-acclaimed and acknowledged that the introduction of generics intervenes with the monopoly position of an innovator/originator drug and infuses competition in the market, which not only brings affordability because of reduced prices but also ensures accessibility. However, since competition intervenes with the monopoly position of the innovator drug, such innovators often resort to strategies to delay or oust the entry of generics/biosimilars. While efforts aimed at meeting competition on merits, e.g., reducing prices and improving quality by introducing improved drugs that leave the generic/bio-similar entrants behind, are legitimate under the Competition Act, resorting to anti-competitive strategies to distort genuine competition goes against the very aim that competition law seeks to achieve.

(iii) Competitors, in normal business parlance, indulge in tactics to belittle competitors' products. However, there is a difference between puffery aimed at promoting one's own product and adopting practices which disparage or malign the image of competitors, thereby causing competitive disadvantages. This is even more harmful in the pharmaceutical sector, where such disparagement is made to the doctors who are treating the patients of cancer. The line of difference between these two business strategies is very thin, however, when crossed by a dominant enterprise to its own illegal advantage, it warrants intervention by the competition authority. Such disparagement may also have ripple effects within the medical community. In this scenario, those biosimilar manufacturers who do not have strong marketing channels among doctors may be forced out of the market because of abusive denigration by a dominant player.

(iv) A dominant enterprise is endowed with a special responsibility not to allow its conduct to impair undistorted competition in the relevant market. The Competition Act places a special responsibility on such enterprise not to conduct its business in a manner which is prohibited under section 4(2) of the Competition Act.

Therefore, vexatious or fraudulent litigation under the pretext of IPR protection may not be condoned, and the same can result in a finding of abuse of dominance based on the facts and circumstances of the case. The non-pricing abuse tactics adopted by dominant players are viewed with greater scrutiny owing to the possibility of market distortion and denial of market access to competitors.

[3] Advocacy Initiatives of CCI

As mentioned above, the CCI in their advocacy booklet has highlighted the following practices (which are enumerative and not exhaustive) of practices of IPR holders as anti-competitive:

(i) The practice of patent pooling is where the firms in a manufacturing industry decide to pool their patents and agree not to grant licences to third parties, at the same time fixing quotas and prices. Such a practice will have an anti-competitive effect since the firms will earn supra-normal profits and keep new entrants out of the market. If all the technology is locked in a few hands by a pooling agreement, it will be difficult for outsiders to compete.

(ii) Tie-in arrangement where a licensee may be required to acquire goods (unpatented materials, e.g., raw materials) solely from the patentee, thus foreclosing the opportunities of other producers. There could be an arrangement forbidding a licensee to compete or handle goods which compete with those of the patentee.

(iii) A clause in the licence agreement which restricts competition in R&D or prohibits a licensee from using rival technology.

(iv) Clause in the licence agreement subjecting the licensee to a condition not to challenge the validity of the IPR in question.

(v) The licensee may be restricted territorially or according to categories of customers.

(vi) A licensee may be coerced by the licensor to take several licences in the intellectual property, even though the licensee may not need all of them.

(vii) A condition imposing quality control on the licensed patented product beyond those necessary for guaranteeing the effectiveness of the licensed patent may be an anti-competitive practice.

(viii) Restricting the right of the licensee to sell the product of the licensed know-how to persons other than those designated by the licensor may be in violation of competition.

(ix) Indemnification of the licensor to meet expenses and action in infringement proceedings is likely to be regarded as anti-competitive.

(x) Limiting the maximum amount of use the licensee may make of the patented invention may affect competition.
(xi) A condition imposed on the licensee to employ or use staff designated by the licensor is likely to be regarded as anti-competitive.

From the above-mentioned enumerations provided by the CCI, one may decipher that while the CCI gives due importance to an IPR holder, the CCI would view all practices as anti-competitive, wherein an IPR holder would misuse the rights conferred upon it by the IPR statutes in India. Given the fact that CCI has interpreted section 3(5) to be applicable in limited circumstances and no parallel protection to IPR in an abuse of dominance investigation, it will be interesting to see the jurisprudence in this arena going forward.

§5.05 REFUSAL TO DEAL AND COMPULSORY LICENSING

Section 4 of the Competition Act deals with abuse of dominant position by an enterprise or a group, and one of the abuses of one's dominant position is to indulge in any practice or practices that result in denial of market access in any manner. We have dealt with aspects of abuse of dominance in the previous chapter. A refusal to license IP exclusively held by a dominant enterprise may also be considered a constructive refusal to supply under the provisions of the Competition Act, and such a refusal may be construed to be an abuse under section 4 of the Competition Act.

Section 27(g) of the Competition Act empowers the CCI to pass 'any other order' as it deems fit besides imposing a penalty if it finds that a dominant enterprise has acted in contravention of section 4 of the Competition Act. The term 'any other order' is like an omnibus clause which will include an order by the CCI issuing compulsory licence if the CCI feels that such order will remedy the market situation distorted by the dominant enterprise. Competition authorities in matured antitrust jurisdictions have granted compulsory licences under the competition provisions of their respective statutes, notwithstanding similar provisions in IP laws. One must note that mere refusal to license IPR will not be considered abuse. Internationally also, a mere refusal to license IPRs is not in itself objectionable under competition laws. However, in exceptional circumstances, the refusal by a dominant company to grant a licence under its IPRs can be an abuse under Article 102 of the TFEU. In *Magill*,[39] the ECJ held that the refusal by copyright holders in the United Kingdom and Ireland to grant licences to third parties to provide a new comprehensive television listings magazine was abusive under Article 102 TFEU. In the *Microsoft*[40] decision, Microsoft abused its dominant position by refusing to license the specifications required to ensure interoperability between its operating system and work group server operating systems of competitors.

39. Joined Cases C-241/91 P and C-242/91, *Commission of the European Communities v. Magill TV Guide Ltd*, paras 48-58.
40. Case T-201/04, *Microsoft Corp. v. The Computing Technology Industry Association, Inc. and Ors.*, II-3634, paras 36-41, 330-332, 373-400, 688-712.

Further, the ECJ confirmed that a refusal by a dominant company to license its IPR is an abuse under Article 102 TFEU where three conditions are satisfied, namely: (i) that the refusal is preventing the emergence of a new product for which there is a potential consumer demand, (ii) that it is unjustified, and (iii) that it is such as to exclude any competition on a secondary market.

[A] Decisional Practice of CCI

We have dealt with the concepts of refusal to deal, essential facilities and denial of market access in the chapter on abuse of dominance. There have been some discussions on this doctrine in the CCI so far. In a few of its decisions, the CCI appears to have endorsed the applicability of the 'essential facilities doctrine' under section 4 of the Competition Act.

[1] Refusal to Deal

In *Air Works India (Engineering) Private Limited v. GMR Hyderabad International Airport Limited and Anr.*,[41] the informant entered into a licence agreement with GMR (the operator and manager of Rajiv Gandhi International Airport Hyderabad) to provide Line Maintenance Services to various airlines. As per the facts, there was an understanding among all licensees operating at the airport for the technical support services that as long as they are carrying on their operations, the licence would continue to be granted. It was alleged by the informant that GMR, owing to its sole control over the airport premises, denied access to the informant for providing the Line Maintenance Services, with an intent to give advantage to its group company, i.e., GAT, which competes directly with the informant at the airport in the downstream market for providing Line Maintenance Services. It was also alleged that the termination of the licence was motivated by the fact that GAT was under tremendous financial difficulty and required support from its parent company, GMR.

While assessing the alleged abuse of dominance by GMR in the upstream relevant market for provision of access to airport facilities/premises, the CCI observed that as a general principle, every entity, dominant or otherwise, has the freedom to choose its trading partners. It is a basic and fundamental right to decide with whom an enterprise wishes to deal, and as such refusal to deal is not per se sufficient to conclude contravention of the provisions of the Competition Act. However, there are three guiding conditions, as per the existing literature, where refusal to deal amounts to abuse:[42]

- (i) the refused input is indispensable for an entity in order to compete in the downstream market;
- (ii) refusal shall most likely eliminate competition on the downstream market;

---

41. *Air Works India (Engineering) Private Limited v. GMR Hyderabad International Airport Limited and Anr.*, Case No. 30 of 2019.
42. *Ibid.*, paras 48-59.

(iii) refusal shall most likely damage consumers.

In the context of IPR, the first criterion, i.e., indispensability of the input, becomes important. Substitutability or indispensability is established only when the input refused cannot be obtained through an alternative source.

The doctrine of essential facility originated in the US antitrust law, though it soon gained recognition with various antitrust authorities. As per the existing jurisprudence, an asset is essential facility if it fulfils the following main economic conditions:

(i) the dominant entity controls access to an essential facility;
(ii) the facility cannot reasonably be duplicated by the competitor;
(iii) the dominant entity denies access to the competitor;
(iv) there should be no alternative means of entering the relevant market at a reasonable cost without having access to the essential facility;
(v) there must be spare capacity on the facility in question.

In the case of GMR, all the aforesaid conditions have been met with respect to access to the facilities/premises at the airport for providing Line Maintenance Services. GMR, vide the Concession/Licence Agreement, had the exclusive right and privilege to carry out the development, design, financing, construction, commissioning, maintenance, operation and management of the airport for a period of thirty years, which was further extendable for another thirty years at the option of GMR. Hence, GMR was a government-conferred monopoly which controlled access to the airport premises, i.e., the 'essential facility' here. Further, the Line Maintenance Services pertain to such requirements and procedures which can be undertaken only at the airport itself. An entity providing such services, therefore, cannot do so without being present in the premises as the service is required between the landing and take-off of the aircraft.

Accordingly, the CCI in its prima facie opinion held that given that physical presence at the airport premises is indispensable to provide Line Maintenance Services, non-renewal of the licence arrangement amounts to the informant's exclusion from the downstream market, which may skew the market in favour of GMR's group entity, i.e., GAT. Further, in prima facie contravention of section 4(2)(b), the lack of competitive constraints on GMR in such a case where the very entity which is dominant in the upstream market is providing Line Maintenance Services in the downstream market can potentially lead to over-charging from the airlines and also cause adverse impact on the consumers in the long run.

In the *Vifor* case[43] also, as discussed earlier in this chapter, a contention was raised regarding Vifor's freedom to choose its trading partners. In this regard, the CCI held that this legal position is not absolute: not every company has a right to seek access to the patent of Vifor unless it demonstrates that there is indeed a need for such access based on the existing supply conditions of an essential product/facility as against its demand by the consumers, so as to affect the market adversely by non-dealing on the part of the entity with significant market power. Further, any

43. *Vifor* case, para. 78.

company requesting a grant of access should also demonstrate its ability to the patent holder, to satisfy the requirements specified for receipt of the grant of licence.

However, one cannot state with legal certainty that the 'essential facilities' doctrine is the only basis on which an entity's refusal to license its intellectual property would amount to an abuse of dominance, and a comprehensive analysis must be undertaken. The words used in the Competition Act are denial of market access, which may not be as high a threshold as required for essential facilities.

CCI has also seen issues where market players refuse to license their technology, thereby causing appreciable adverse impact on competition in India. The appropriate relief under the relevant IPR statutes in India in this case would be to force the holder of the technology to license the same, which would be something akin to a compulsory licence. Such refusals under the Competition Act, when limited to decisions of a single entity, will be examined under section 4, though where the refusals involve multiple entities, i.e., 'group boycott', the examination may proceed under section 3 of the Competition Act.

[2] Compulsory Licensing

The leading decision in this regard is the *Google Android case*, wherein the NCLAT decided in favour of Google on the issue of access to Google's APIs, i.e., its proprietary IPR, as discussed in the earlier parts of this chapter. The CCI directed Google not to deny access to its APIs so as to disadvantage OEMs, app developers and its existing or potential competitors. However, the NCLAT set aside CCI's direction and upheld Google's argument that as the owner of proprietary APIs, it is entitled to reap the benefits of the investment made by it into the scientific and technical development of the APIs. The relevant observations of the NCLAT are mentioned below:[44]

> 'The various core device features that Google Play Services provide services relating to security and reliability (through installation of Google Play Protect which provides protection from malware), facility to developers through thousands of continually updated APIs such as "Google Cast" for streaming, Google Maps, provision of accurate location information and sending notifications through a messaging transport layer and enabling core services, such as making emergency call, autofill services, sending and receiving files etc. Thus, it is clear that the APIs which include Google Play Services are APIs that provide essential services to the Apps which are part of Google Play Store. These are privately developed and maintained by Google and are provided by Google to App developers and OEMs.'
>
> 'It is abundantly clear ... that APIs as developed by Google and of which Google Play Services are an integral and important part, are developed and maintained by Google and continually updated through scientific and technical development by the teams of Google and these APIs are necessary for functionality of the Apps in Google Play Store. We are therefore, clear that the APIs and Google Play Services, which are proprietary items of Google cannot be given in through

44. *Google LLC and Anr. v. Competition Commission of India* [2023], (NCLAT) Competition Appeal (AT) No. 01 of 2023, paras 185-188.

> unhindered access to App developers, OEMs and Google's existing and potential competitors. ... proprietary software such as APIs, which are developed through scientific and technical innovation should fetch value to Google and, therefore, remain an incentive for a technological company/Google to further carry out such development and monetize it through its commercial use.'

As a result, the NCLAT set aside the decision issued by CCI on the basis that access to such APIs cannot be provided to Google's competitors without going through necessary technical and commercial engagements with Google. As mentioned earlier, the said observations are presently under challenge before the Supreme Court. In essence, the NCLAT has ruled against allowing compulsory licensing, and in this sense, it has laid down the proposition that there cannot be an absolute rule of licensing under the framework of the Indian competition regime. By recognizing that the IPR holder has a right to innovate and compulsory licensing may affect the enjoyment of this right, the NCLAT has strayed from the earlier jurisprudence of the COMPAT, which in some cases upheld the CCI orders providing for licensing like in the *Automobile Spare parts* case.

[B] Practical Guidance

As mentioned above, some of the IPR statutes in India provide for provisions relating to compulsory licensing. For instance, under section 84 of the Patents Act, 1970, the Controller of Patents has the power to grant a compulsory licence after the expiry of three years from grant of patent in case the patented invention does not meet the 'reasonable requirements of the public', or is 'not available to the public at a reasonably affordable price' or 'is not worked in the territory of India'. In 2012, in an order that was upheld on appeal, the Controller of Patents granted a compulsory licence to Bayer's patent covering a cancer drug to a generic Indian drug manufacturer on all three grounds.[45]

With the ratio of the Division Bench Judgment in the *Ericsson* case, it appears to have become the domain of the Controller of Patents in exercise of its power to grant a compulsory licence under sections 83, 84 and 89 of the Patents Act to look into questions of unreasonable conditions in agreements of licensing of patents, abuse of status as a patentee, inquiry in respect thereof and relief that is to be granted therefor.

There can be similar situations under the Competition Act because the CCI has the power to pass 'any other order' under section 27 of the Competition Act which may include provisions for compulsory licensing. However, there is no guidance presently as to under what conditions will CCI pass an order for a compulsory licence.

The Copyright Act, 1957, contains similar provisions, though of a narrower scope. Compulsory licence may be issued pursuant to section 31(1)(b) of the Copyrights Act, 1957. It may be issued when the Copyright Board is satisfied that the copyright owners have refused to allow communication to the public, and such refusal

45. *Natco Pharma v. Bayer Corporation, Controller of Patents Mumbai*, March 2012; *Bayer Corporation v. Union of India & Ors.* [2013] (IPAB, Chennai).

is not reasonable. This provision extends only to certain types of copyrighted works and not all. In *Music Broadcast Pvt Ltd v. Phonographic Performance Limited*,[46] the Copyright Board issued a compulsory licence to musical works in favour of the FM radio industry on a revenue-sharing model; i.e., 2% of the net advertisement earnings of each FM radio station would be set aside to pay the music providers.

It will be interesting to see whether the CCI would attempt to adopt the factors considered by the relevant IP authorities and fit them within the scope of the Competition Act or whether the CCI would distance itself from such factors and instead assess the issue under other factors and pass appropriate orders if required.

The CCI, therefore, attempts to maintain a critical balance between the rights of the IPR holders and imposing a relief such as compulsory licensing in an abuse of dominance investigation. This appears synonymous with the decisional practice under the EU law where the IP holders do not have a general obligation to license their IPR to competitors, and the ECJ in such context has opined that in 'exceptional circumstances', such refusal could result in an abuse of dominance.

§5.06 IP REMEDIES IN MERGERS

The CCI has grappled with the issue of IP remedies in a merger situation. As mentioned in detail in the chapter on merger control, merger analysis is a forward-looking exercise, and the CCI has the powers under the Competition Act to issue commitments/remedies to the parties of combination to ensure that the behavioural conduct of the parties to the combination, post the consummation of the combination, does not create any competition law concerns. Commitments in a merger situation may be structural or behavioural in nature.

The issue of whether the licensing of IPR constitutes the 'acquisition' or 'transfer' of assets and consequently requires notification has been a topic of debate. IPR can be transferred through many methods, such as assignment, exclusive licensing, non-exclusive licensing. Hence, there is a need to identify situations where such licensing might trigger merger notification. The CCI, in the merger control order of AT&T and Time Warner Inc.,[47] clarified that the licensing of an IP will not in itself constitute a transfer or acquisition if the licence is demonstrably non-exclusive. For this, *inter alia*, the licensor must establish that it itself continues to use the IPR, or indeed licenses out the IPR to others for wider use, and that the licence is not exclusive, irrespective of terminology used in the licence agreements.

Thus, IPR licences that do not meet this requirement will be treated as asset acquisitions that require merger notification to the CCI if no statutory exemption is available.

46. *Music Choice India Pvt Ltd v. Phonographic Performance Limited*, (Copyright Board) (Second Order), 2010.
47. AT&T and Time Warner Inc., Combination Registration No. C-2016/11/456, 13 Feb. 2017.

The CCI has dealt with the issuance of structural commitments which involved IP remedies. Structural commitments consist of a divestment package, and the competition regulator must ensure that the divestment so designed consists of a viable business, which, in the hands of the purchaser, is capable of competing with the merged entity. In order to determine the scope of the business to be divested, all tangible and intangible elements - including IPR, know-how and goodwill - must be specified. Also, the manner in which intellectual property will be transferred must also form part of the divestment package. Generally, the intellectual property is transferred by way of licences, and such licences should generally be exclusive licences, free from field or geographical restrictions, and grant the licensee the ability to compete effectively with the parties to the merger.

[A] Remedies Issued by CCI

In the merger control order of Sun Pharmaceuticals Industries Limited and Ranbaxy Laboratories Limited,[48] CCI discussed the issue of IP remedies/commitments to alleviate the competition law concerns emanating from the merger of Sun and Ranbaxy. Apart from the brands and assets which formed a part of the divestment package, the CCI noted that for intangible assets (including IPR) which contribute to the current operation or are necessary to ensure the economic viability, marketability and competitiveness of products in the divestment package (retained by the Sun/Ranbaxy for use in their other business), the parties will grant a non-exclusive, irrevocable, royalty-free and perpetual licence to the purchaser. Further, CCI also noted that customer and credit records with respect to divestment products must also be given to the purchaser. These IP remedies were designed with the aim of maintaining the existing level of competition in the market by creating a viable, independent and long-term competitor and ensuring that the approved purchaser had the necessary components to compete with the merged entity.

In approving the merger, the CCI directed structural, *inter alia*, ordering the parties to divest seven products under various brand names and assign all trade mark rights related to these Divestment Brands. The parties in return proposed an amendment that in respect of three trademarks, they be allowed to license them exclusively, perpetually, irrevocably and on a royalty-free basis with the right to sub-license to the purchaser of the trademarks instead of assignment. This was allowed by the CCI on the purchaser's commitment that it does not require assignment of the said trademarks as the licence, as above, would suffice to enable it to independently sell and market the said three Divestment Products. Hence, the CCI's order reflected a balanced approach to the transfer of IPR from the IPR holders while ensuring that competitors in the market are able to compete effectively.

48. Sun Pharmaceuticals Industries Limited and Ranbaxy Laboratories Limited, Combination Registration No: C-2014/05/170, 5 Dec. 2014.

Further, in the merger of *Sony/Zee*,[49] the amalgamation of Culver Max Entertainment Private Limited, Zee Entertainment Enterprises Limited, Bangla Entertainment Private Limited, and Essel Group Participants presented several competition concerns, *inter alia*, due to existing licence agreements pertaining to content rights, music rights, broadcasting rights, etc. To allay the concerns of the combination, the parties offered the following voluntary structural modifications:

(i) Divestment of three TV channels engaged in the Hindi GEC and Hindi Films channels market, i.e., Big Magic, Zee Action and Zee Classic. This would include licensing trademarks, channel names, logos, etc., and transfer of applicable licences, permits, authorizations, and applicable agreements on content licensing and employees.
(ii) The purchaser of the divested channels shall, *inter alia*, be independent/unconnected with the combined entity and have the resources and incentive to sustain the same as a viable and active competitor. Accordingly, SIPL and Viacom18 Media Private Limited were disqualified from bidding for the divested channels.
(iii) The parties shall not acquire direct or indirect stake/influence in the divested channels for a period of five years from such sale.

Therefore, it can be seen that in a merger situation, CCI places a lot of emphasis on IPR remedies. It will be interesting to note the stand of the CCI in future where they grant remedies in nature of access remedies, rebranding, etc.

§5.07 CONCLUSION

The totality of the discussion above reveals that the CCI has adopted a nuanced approach in its decisional practice by considering the competitive implications of the exercise of IPR so as to maintain the balance between promoting competition and protecting IPR. While new issues on the interface of competition and IPR may continue to crop up in the future, an attempt has to be made to preserve this delicate balance. Innovation must not be curbed and hence remedies, if any, must spur and not stifle dynamic innovation.

49. Culver Max Entertainment Private Limited, Bangla Entertainment Private Limited, Zee Entertainment Enterprises Limited, Combination Registration No. C-2022/04/923, 4 Oct. 2022.

CHAPTER 6
Digital Markets and Competition Law

§6.01 INTRODUCTION

With digitization, markets have moved beyond the traditional physical realm to the world of the internet. Dubbed 'digital markets', this contemporary shift has given rise to an efficient system which reduces costs for businesses. Correspondingly, it reduces a consumer's search costs, i.e., the cost the consumer would bear to look for the good or service that would best satisfy their want (for, e.g., consider the fuel spent on reaching the markets and the time spent on looking for the desired product). The 'savings' in digital markets go beyond price parameters and include time and convenience, which are essential costs in a fast-paced world. Thus, it is clear that the digital wave presents an opportunity for the country to leverage its potential and increase efficiencies, promote consumer welfare and create a favourable ecosystem for businesses.[1]

However, the specific characteristics of digital markets, such as economies of scale, network effects and the multi-sided nature of the markets, make them more susceptible to anti-competitive conduct as there is an increased likelihood of entrenched market power for the entities operating in the market as compared to traditional industries.[2] Consequently, a winner-takes-all scenario emerges and the concentration of market power is amplified quickly. Given the rapid growth and evolution of digital markets, timely and swift interventions by competition authorities become all the more necessary because the pace at which these markets evolve necessitates proactive regulatory measures to mitigate potential harm to competition and consumers, i.e., an *ex ante* regulatory approach. As digital markets move much beyond nascency and have now become a regular, vital and quintessential feature of the economy, the decisional practice of the CCI and regulatory changes therein merit a

1. Report of the Competition Law Review Committee, 2019, para. 1.1.
2. Case COMP/C-3/37.792 Microsoft, decided on 24 Mar. 2004, at para. 470.

discourse. Accordingly, this chapter shall provide an overview of the features, challenges and developments in the interface between digital markets and competition law.

§6.02 MARKET DEFINITION

The tools and techniques of market definition remain unchanged whether the market is traditional or digital, being born out of the statutory provisions as discussed earlier in this book. However, an analysis of CCI's approach reveals that market definition in digital markets may be slightly nuanced. For instance, new trends have emerged in how the CCI deals with the substitutability of different channels of distribution, the peculiar characteristics as well as the wider scope of the relevant geographic market in the context of platform markets. This has been elaborated below.

[A] Substitutability of Online and Offline Markets

Relevant market determination is based on market realities and an assessment of the factual matrix of each case. An analysis of CCI's decisional practice reveals a shift in determining the substitutability of different channels/modes of distribution.

When CCI received its first case against an online platform in the year 2014,[3] i.e., against 'Snapdeal', an e-commerce platform, it observed that buyers are shifting from offline to online retail market because of heavy discounts, better choices and convenience. However, if the prices in the online market increase significantly, then the consumer is likely to shift towards the offline market and vice versa. On this basis, the CCI opined that online and offline markets were only two different channels of distribution and not two different relevant markets. This view was subsequently followed in other cases also.[4]

In the same year, in *Mohit Manglani v. Flipkart and Ors.*,[5] the CCI considered another piece of information alleging anti-competitive effects arising out of the exclusive agreements between e-commerce websites and sellers for the sale of selected products. Therein, while finding that online platforms and brick-and-mortar companies are distinct channels in the same relevant market, the CCI also observed that '[i]rrespective of whether we consider e-portal market as a separate relevant product market or as a sub-segment of the market for distribution, none of the entities seemed to be individually dominant'. Thus, this marked the initiation of the idea that online channels may be a different relevant market in themselves.

The departure in CCI's stand became more nuanced in 2018 in *All India Online Vendors Association v. Flipkart India Private Ltd. and Anr.*[6] ('*AIOVA v. Flipkart* case').

---

3. *Mr. Ashish Ahuja v. Snapdeal.com and Anr.*, Case No. 17 of 2014, para. 16.
4. *Mr. Deepak Verma v. Clues Network Pvt. Ltd. and Ors.*, Case No. 34 of 2016, paras 10, 11; Bharti Retail Limited and Future Retail Limited, Combination Registration No. C-2015/05/281, 19 Aug. 2015.
5. *Mr. Mohit Manglani v. M/s Flipkart India Private Limited and Ors.*, Case No. 80 of 2014, para. 18.
6. *All India Online Vendors Association v. Flipkart India Private Ltd. and Anr.*, Case No. 20 of 2018, para. 22.

In this case, the CCI discussed the increasing interdependence and integration of online e-commerce platforms and offline business retailers. In order to assess the alleged anti-competitive practices of Flipkart, the CCI defined the relevant market as 'Services provided by online marketplace platforms in India'. This was based on the following reasoning:

> 23. No doubt, *to the end consumers, the distinction line between online and offline sellers is sometimes blurry, yet it cannot be denied that online marketplaces offer convenience for sellers as well as the buyers. For the sellers, they save costs in terms of setting up of a store, sales staff, electricity and other maintenance charges. The benefits afforded to buyers includes comfort of shopping from their homes thus saving time, commuting charges and at the same time they can compare multiple goods* ... .

Hence, the relevant market was defined narrowly for the first time by drawing a distinction between online and offline channels of distribution owing to their distinct and different features. This in itself shows that market definition, particularly in digital markets, is not a static concept but a dynamic concept which changes with time, and the relevant market assessment must be done at each point in time.

The transition from CCI's earlier position becomes clearer when we analyse the travel services market. In 2017, CCI approved the merger of MakeMyTrip and Ibibo, where both parties offered travel-related services through the internet.[7] Therein, CCI observed that online and offline channels of providing travel services were substitutable with each other. As a result, the relevant market was defined as the market of '*sale of travel and travel related services*', based on a substitutability assessment between online travel agents with other distribution channels from the consumers' point of view. However, in just a couple of years and by 2019, while examining the allegations of anti-competitive conduct and abuse of dominance by the same entities, the CCI noted that market realities had changed which necessitated a different market definition. In *Federation of Hotel & Restaurant Associations of India and Anr. v. MakeMyTrip India Pvt. Ltd.*[8] ('*MMT-Go* case'), the relevant market was delineated as the '*market for online intermediation services for booking of hotels in India*' on the basis of the unique features of online platforms such as network effects in terms of customer reach and pricing strategies (discussed later in the chapter). Not only was the substitutability analysis carried out from the hotels' point of view in this case but also the CCI noted that timing is a crucial factor and the assessment in rapidly changing digital markets (such as online travel services) cannot have a static approach. Hence, online and offline channels of distribution were considered to be separate and distinct.[9] Online and offline modes, being characteristically different from each other, do not cater to the same set of consumers and, thus, are not interchangeable from the perspective

7. MIH Internet SEA Pte Limited, Singapore, Combination Registration No. C-2016/10/451, 18 Jan. 2017, paras 8-10.
8. *Federation of Hotel & Restaurant Associations of India and Anr. v. MakeMyTrip India Pvt. Ltd.*, Case No. 14 of 2019, paras 181-191.
9. *Ibid.*, paras 190-216.

of not only hotels but also end consumers. This has been discussed in more detail under the multi-homing and online travel aggregation.

What is important to note is that the legal principles of relevant market delineation remain the same irrespective of whether the firm is digital or traditional; the approach to defining the relevant market will change depending on the market concerned. The approach is: first, the starting point would be the service offered by the enterprise under scrutiny (i.e., MMT-Go, offers to hotels); second, the next step would be to identify such alternate services that are substitutable in terms of price, characteristics and intended use from the perspective of the affected user group (i.e., the hotels' perspective).

The trend that emerges is that in digital markets, there does not exist any one-size-fits-all approach in delineating the relevant market. The peculiar characteristics of the platform, the users served by that platform along with the timing and prevailing market circumstances together necessitate a dynamic approach in conducting the substitutability analysis. Yet, it can be said that the clear takeaway, as upheld in several other cases,[10] is that online and offline channels are not substitutable or even comparable while determining the relevant market because the services offered by online (marketplace) platforms are not substitutable/interchangeable from the consumer's perspective. The focal point of difference is that the services offered by online marketplace platforms are marked differently from offline mode. These services are discussed in more detail in the subsequent sections.

[B] Platform Markets

In the Market Study on E-Commerce in India[11] published by the CCI, it was observed that '*online marketplaces are multi-sided platforms that connect sellers, buyers and advertisers to facilitate transactions between them. A platform offers a multisided environment that internalizes transaction costs and takes advantage of the network effects across the different user groups*'. Intermediation by online platforms allows businesses to have an online presence to access consumers without the need to operate their own websites. The degree of dependence of sellers on online platforms is rising since consumers increasingly rely on these platforms to search for and purchase products on the internet. This tends to create a scenario of a 'winner-takes-all' market.

This was further clarified by the CCI in *AIOVA v. Flipkart* case,[12] wherein the CCI differentiated between online retail stores and online marketplace platforms on the basis that in online retail stores, the seller (who may or may not own a brick-and-mortar store) owns their portal to sell products thorough an online website. However, in online marketplace platforms, the owner of the online portal offers a platform for buyers and sellers to transact. Hence, the sellers would be interested in selling on the

10. *Shri Vishal Gupta v. Google LLC and Ors.*, Case Nos 06 & 46 of 2014, para. 64; *Vijay Gopal v. Big Tree Entertainment Pvt. Ltd. and Ors.*, Case No. 46 of 2021, paras 24-26.
11. Market Study on E-Commerce in India, 2020, para. 34.
12. *AIOVA v. Flipkart case*, para. 24.

online platforms which are able to attract an increasing number of buyers, thus characterizing the online platforms with network effects.

The functioning of platforms was also analysed in the *MMT-Go* case. Therein, the CCI drew a distinction between transaction and non-transaction platforms,[13] as highlighted in the following flowchart:

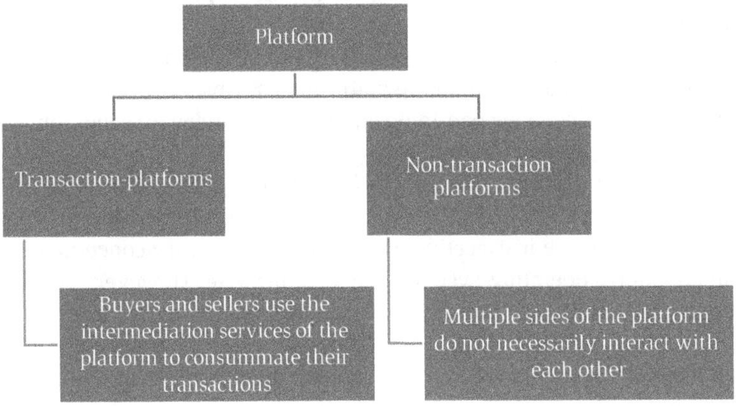

The CCI further went on to observe that:

> *Even within these sub-segments, the platforms may have different features, e.g., the transaction platforms can be purely 'matching-making platforms' where users on different sides of the platform are brought together to effectuate one to one transaction, e.g., cab aggregators like Uber/Ola, or they can be like OTAs where multiple users can see the various options available and decide whether to effectuate a transaction or not.* Given the diversity of platform markets, and their different network effects and pricing strategies, it is imperative that the *specificities of each platform are appropriately factored in while weighing different approaches and alternatives to market definition. One size fit all approach may lead to absurd outcomes in such markets.* Further, the timing is also a crucial factor. *The assessment in rapidly changing digital markets cannot have a static approach.*

Further, platform markets have several unique characteristic features such as network effects, economies of scale, etc., as have been discussed in the subsequent sections of this chapter. The operation of these characteristics makes platform markets distinct and non-substitutable with traditional physical markets. Hence, it emerges that platform markets (which may be further categorized based on the nature of the platform) have distinct characteristics from traditional markets. As a result, assessing the competition concerns and regulating such platforms requires a nuanced and flexible approach so as to adapt to the needs of rapidly evolving digital markets.

13. *MMT-Go* case, para. 191.

[C] Wider Scope of Relevant Geographic Market

The CCI has traditionally taken an approach in *GHCL Limited v. Coal India Limited and Anr.* ('*Coal India* case')[14] that only India can be the relevant geographic market under the Competition Act, and the same cannot be global. The CCI has taken this interpretation based on the technical reading of the provisions of the Competition Act. However, transactions in the digital economy are a global phenomenon. Unlike traditional markets which are confined to physical boundaries, digital markets are borderless and may even span across international jurisdictions. The CCI in its decisional practice pertaining to online platforms has observed that the conditions of competition are homogeneous pan-India and hence, the relevant geographic market in such cases is taken as the entirety of India.[15]

For instance, in *Harshita Chawla v. WhatsApp Inc. and Facebook Inc.* ('*WhatsApp* case'),[16] the CCI observed that the functionality of OTT messaging apps through smartphones is the same irrespective of the region or country concerned in terms of price, functionality, operating system (OS) or otherwise. However, the competitive conditions, regulatory architecture and players may vary in different countries/regions. Since conditions for competition are homogenous in India, the geographic area of India was taken as the relevant geographic market for the purposes of assessment.

Thus, there is already a recognition that the characteristics, features and services offered by the platform under consideration may be consistent across borders. Therefore, there is perhaps a need for relooking at widening the scope of relevant geographic market in appropriate cases when considering digital markets, which tend to be borderless. Therefore, there may be a need to relook at the CCI interpretation in the *Coal India* case and hold that in appropriate cases, the relevant market may be global.

§6.03 CHARACTERISTIC FEATURES OF DIGITAL MARKETS

All digital markets have certain characteristic features on the basis of which they are not substitutable with traditional markets. The collective operation of these characteristics often tends to make online platforms gain and accumulate market power in a short span of time.

[A] Multi-sided Markets

The 'multi-sided' nature of platforms means that they serve multiple distinct groups of users, with users in at least one of those groups valuing the platform more highly as the number or activity of users in the other group increases. For example, an app store

14. *GHCL Limited v. Coal India Limited and Anr.*, Case No. 08 of 2014, paras 28-30.
15. *All India Online Vendors Association v. Flipkart India Private Limited and Anr.*, Case No. 20 of 2018, para. 24; *Baglekar Akash Kumar v. Google LLC and Anr.*, Case No. 39 of 2020, para. 16.
16. *Harshita Chawla v. WhatsApp Inc. and Facebook Inc.*, Case No. 15 of 2020, para. 76.

serves both consumers and app developers, with each group valuing increased participation by members of the other. When a business is multi-sided, the profit-maximizing levels of price and output on one side of the platform may depend, in part, on competitive conditions on the other side. For example, some platform businesses may charge a zero or negative price to users on one side of the platform (e.g., consumers), relying on revenue from users on another side (e.g., advertisers) in order to maximize overall profitability. This has been discussed in more detail subsequently.

In case of two-sided or multi-sided markets, a platform caters to different user groups which may be interlinked and interdependent. In this context, in the *MMT-Go* case,[17] the CCI noted that the intermediation service provided by MMT-Go is provided through a two-sided platform which connects two distinct user groups, i.e., consumers and hotels/hoteliers. Both these user groups positively value the presence of more users on the other side of the platform, as it creates higher visibility and potential sales (for hotels) and a wider variety of options (for consumers). Consequently, any effect analysis needs to take into account both these sets of users to gauge the net effects and to ascertain whether, on a rule of reason analysis, such effects are adverse and appreciable. Similarly, in the *Play Store* case,[18] the CCI observed that app stores can be characterized as multi-sided platforms as they serve different interdependent groups, i.e., OEMs, smartphone users and app developers.

It is plausible that in trying to gain favour with one side of the market, the platform may tend to cause or threaten harm to competition on the other side of the market. Hence, an analysis of CCI's approach reveals that the multi-sided nature of platforms requires an assessment of the interdependence of the different sides on each other, as well as whether the appreciable adverse effects of competition (AAEC) are being felt by both sides of the market.

The interdependence of the different sides of the market and the importance of the platform to the different user groups is assessed on the basis of network effects which enable the platform to create an ecosystem and then 'tip' the market in its favour. These factors are discussed below.

[1] Network Effects

Network effects are characterized as the increased usefulness of a service to the users as the number of users using the service increases. This creates a positive feedback loop for services that are offered, wherein an increase in the number of users/input to a service improves the value of the service to other users and, therefore, further attracts new users. This can be understood from the following flowchart which indicates that if we start from any of the points in the cycle, a positive feedback loop comes into operation:

17. *MMT-Go* case, paras 190, 295.
18. *Play Store* case, para. 116.

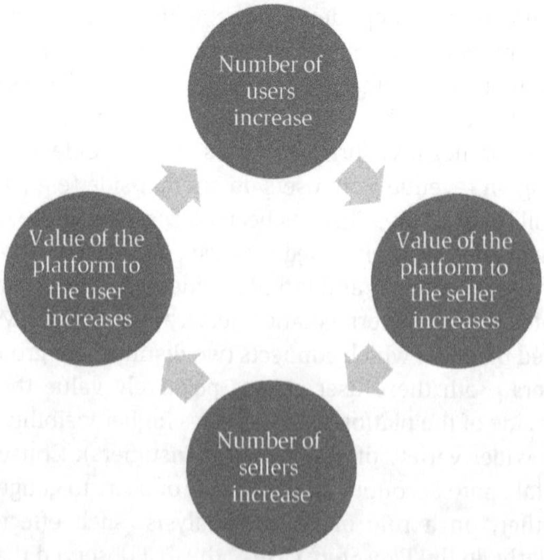

As the value derived by each producer increases, the number of producers finding the economic activity profitable also increases. Consequently, as more producers join the economic activity, the value to the consumer increases (for instance, in the form of increasing choice in the market). This then further attracts more consumers, completing the loop. This is a self-reinforcing loop that can be seen in operation in case of platforms such as e-commerce platforms, wherein the number of consumers increases as the number of sellers providing different and more variety of goods increase, which consequently choose the platform to sell products because of access to more consumers. Similarly, operation of network effects in cases of platforms are observed in case of platform service providers for social networking services, wherein a person joins the network only if a sufficient number of people are already part of the user base. This quality of the platform, as discussed in the next section, has the quality of creating barriers to entry for new entrants.

The operation of network effects has been discussed by the CCI in several cases in the digital market. For instance, in *Umar Javeed v. Google LLC and Ors.* ('*Google Android* case'),[19] it was observed that the Google Play Store, i.e., an app store is a two-sided market which has been able to attract a large number of Android users on one side (due to the presence of a large number of apps) and a large number of app developers on the other side (due to potential to reach a large audience). On one hand, the OS which can run maximum number of apps would be most popular among the users and thus would attract the greatest number of users. On the other hand, app developers would prefer to develop apps for the OS which has the maximum number of users because access to the large user base would result in substantial economies of scale, given the high fixed costs and very low marginal costs associated with the development of such apps. Thus, on this basis, Google was found to enjoy a strong

19. *Umar Javeed v. Google LLC and Ors.*, Case No. 39 of 2018, para. 189.

'network effect' of a large user base and app developers in the market for app stores for Android OS. Similar to the *Google Android* case, cross-side network effects were also found to exist in the prima facie case in *Together We Fight Society v. Apple Inc. and Anr.*[20] ('*Apple* case'), between app developers and app users on Apple's App Store.

In the *Google Android* case, cross-platform network effects were also found to emanate from the linkages between the general web search market and the adjacent web browser market, such that Google's dominance in the general web search market had a significant impact on the web browser market due to close links between the web browser market and general web search market.[21]

Similarly, in *XYZ v. Alphabet Inc. and Ors.*[22] ('*Play Store* case'), the CCI found that OSs exhibit indirect network effects, i.e., the benefit to users of an OS increases with the volume and quality of native apps they can access on that OS, and similarly, the benefit to app developers increases with the number of users they can access on an OS. It further observed that this is 'likely to act as a barrier to new entry and expansion as it creates a 'chicken and egg' problem i.e., an operating system needs a critical mass of users to attract app developers, but also need a critical mass of app developers to attract users.' Thus, network effects result in entry barriers because most consumers prefer an OS for which a large number of apps have already been written, and most developers prefer to create apps for an OS that already has a substantial user base. This 'chicken-and-egg' situation arising out of the barriers to entry means that apps will continue to be written for existing OS, which in turn ensures that consumers will continue to prefer it over new entrant OSs.[23] Hence, it can be said that the positive feedback loop continues and makes it much more difficult for new entrants to achieve a commercially viable scale.

The positive feedback loop is a consequence of the interlinkage and interdependence of the different sides of the market on each other in a multi-sided market. As highlighted in the *MMT-Go* case,[24] through its intermediation service, the platform connects two distinct user groups, i.e., consumers and hotels, both of which positively value the increasing presence of each other on the platform. For the assessment of dominance, what was important was the role of the network effects in understanding the degree of dependence of the aggrieved hotels on MMT-Go's platform.[25]

This was also illustrated in the cases against WhatsApp,[26] which is the most widely used app for instant messaging in India. A communication network/platform gets more valuable as more users join it, thereby benefiting from network effects. This, in turn, causes a strong lock-in effect for users, as switching to another platform gets difficult and meaningless until all or most of their social contacts also switch to the

20. *Together We Fight Society v. Apple Inc. and Anr.*, Case No. 24 of 2021, para. 17.
21. *Google Android* case, para. 290.
22. *XYZ and Ors. v. Alphabet Inc. and Ors.*, Case Nos 07 of 2020, 14 of 2021 and 35 of 2021, paras 82, 102.
23. *Ibid.*, para. 86.
24. *MMT-Go* case, para. 190.
25. *Ibid.*, para. 226.
26. *WhatsApp* case, paras 86, 87; *In Re: Updated Terms of Service and Privacy Policy for WhatsApp Users v. WhatsApp LLC and Facebook, Inc*, Suo Moto Case No. 01 of 2021, para. 26.

same other platform. Consequently, consumers were found to be dependent on WhatsApp, and network effects ensured that customers did not switch to other platforms easily. Barriers to entry may arise indirectly as a result of network effects since they lead to increased switching costs. As a result, new players may be disincentivized from entering the market.

In this context, in the *AIOVA v. Flipkart* case,[27] it was recognized that while it may be possible for new entrants to create online marketplace platforms, it is difficult for them to breach the advantage gained by incumbent players due to network effects.

However, the operation of network effects is not *ipso facto* a factor which contributes to dominance. This means that that there can be certain countervailing market forces that reduce the ability of even a very large platform to insulate itself from competition. This was seen in the case of *Fast Track Call Cab Pvt. Ltd. and Anr. v. ANI Technologies Pvt. Ltd.* ('*Ola* case'),[28] where the CCI was examining the alleged abusive conduct of Ola in the market of radio taxi services. Basis the facts of the case, CCI was of the opinion that despite Ola having the largest network, the network effects were not strong enough to deter entry and rapid expansion of another big and fierce competitor 'Uber' in the relevant market of 'radio taxi services in Bengaluru'. Further, since radio taxi apps could be easily downloaded on smartphones for free and could co-exist on the same handset, multi-homing was found to be possible for both drivers and riders. A successful network/platform requires that both sides of the market be thick, i.e., there are a large number of participants on both sides of the network/platform so that each participant has a substantial number of potential matches on the other side of the market. More riders means more demand scattered across a geographic region owing to a higher density of riders, leading to more ride requests on a particular platform as compared to its competitor, which in turn fuels the demand for more drivers to serve such riders. In this case, both Uber and Ola were found to be aggressively competing with each other to attract participants, i.e., drivers and riders, and hence, the network effects of one platform were not strong enough to deter the expansion of the other platform.

Thus, CCI's decisional practice[29] indicates that network effects play a pivotal role in dominance assessment, and the important aspect is the strength of the network, as that is what enables a large platform/network to stay dominant and insulate itself from potential competition by making it difficult for new entrants to challenge the established network. A comparison of the *Google Android* case and the *Play Store case* with the *Ola* case, for instance, reveals that network effects by themselves are not a factor for dominance because in all cases it cannot be said that they create insurmountable entry barriers. The takeaway is that what has to be seen is not only the size of the network but also its strength, such that it should have an actual effect on the state of competition in the market. At the same time, the role of interdependencies and interlinkages arising

27. *AIOVA v. Flipkart* case, para. 28.
28. *Fast Track Call Cab Pvt. Ltd. and Anr. v. ANI Technologies Pvt. Ltd.*, Case Nos 6 & 74 of 2015, paras 122-132.
29. *MMT-Go* case, para. 232; *Meru Travel Solutions Pvt. Ltd. v. Uber India Systems Pvt. Ltd and Ors.*, Case No. 96 of 2015.

out of the network effects should not be overestimated but should be limited to understanding the impact of such interactions on the substitutability from primarily the aggrieved user side. This has to be assessed based on the facts and circumstances of the case. In the *Ola* case, the effect of Ola's network on riders and drivers was mitigated due to corresponding network effects by Uber. However, in the cases pertaining to Google, the CCI noted that there were no effective alternatives to Google for the OEMs and app developers which could overcome the strength of Google's network and consequently, Google has held to be in a super dominant position.

[2] Tipping Effect

The operation of economies of scale and network externalities not only favour a concentrated market but also erect entry barriers and present the distinct possibility of all consumers in the market deciding to opt for the product of a particular firm or for a particular technology, therefore leading to a 'tipping' of the market in favour of that firm and conferring it with a monopolist position in the market. This results in winner-take-all market outcomes. Thus, digital markets often 'tip' quickly and one or two winners or leading players emerge in a short span of time. Attaining a critical mass of users can lead to firms assuming position of entrenched market power. In such markets, it becomes extremely difficult for new entrants (even if such firms do not face any dearth of capital) to dislodge the incumbent from its position and for new players to enter the market.

This can be illustrated from the findings of the CCI in the *Play Store* case. Once there was a critical mass of app developers and users on the Google Play Store, other app stores found it difficult to dislodge Google from its position because the market had tipped in favour of Google. This could be why Google's Play Store became a 'must have' for OEMs, app developers and app users.

In the *MMT-Go* case,[30] the CCI granted interim relief to the delisted hotels (informants) by ordering MMT-Go to relist them on its platform. These hotels were delisted pursuant to MMT-Go's exclusive arrangement with OYO, which was a competitor of the informants. An analysis of CCI's order reveals that winner-takes-all markets require immediate remedy (here, relisting of the hotels) because otherwise, the market would tip in favour of the incumbent player (MMT-Go and OYO). The following observations of CCI assume importance:

> Thus, as the facts appear before the Commission, *the impugned exclusion under the Agreement has the dangerous probability to irreversibly alter the competitive landscape, especially in the franchisee budget hotel downstream market and may tip the market in favour of OYO causing irreparable harm to competition.* A continued operationalisation of this exclusive agreement will therefore, compel all independent hotels seeking franchise services, for improving their brand recognition and for the purpose of signalling to the consumer the unobservable feature of quality to forcibly tie up with OYO. Any other franchisee arrangement with competitors like FabHotels and Treebo would delist them from the dominant

30. *MMT-Go* case, section 33 Order, para. 114.

> intermediary i.e. MMT-Go reducing their visibility and footfalls. *It becomes a Hobson's choice in as much as the 'market for franchising services for budget hotels in India' is concerned. Such a likely outcome cannot be ignored and hence requires an immediate redressal.* ***In winner takes all platform markets, if the impugned conduct is not based on the merits, eliminating such anti-competitive behaviour at the earliest assumes utmost importance. Network effects coupled with even small actions by the platforms may exclude and marginalize rivals, and further strengthen these effects that may be difficult to dilute at a later stage. Any remedy at that stage will be too little and too late as the suppliers' side of the market, i.e. the franchisee service providers, can be potentially eliminated due to the alleged anticompetitive conduct.***

This case was very interesting since as a matter of practice, the CCI rarely grants interim relief. Therefore, what emerges from this discussion is the tendency of digital markets to tip in favour of a particular player, and thus, there is a discussion on whether India should adopt *ex ante* regulation. It is because multi-sided markets tend to create winner-takes-all outcome that the tipping effect is not only a factor in the assessment of dominance or anti-competitive effects of an agreement but also a factor in determining how abusive that dominance can be or how such an agreement can cause AAEC. This is why anticompetitive actions need to be nipped in the bud. At the same time, it is to be seen in actuality whether the market actually has a tendency to tip in favour of a particular player, viz. Google's lack of competition tipped the market in its favour, and Ola and Uber's competition prevented the tipping from taking place.

[3] Creation of an Ecosystem

The consequence of network effects and market tipping in favour of the incumbent platform is the creation of an ecosystem. Thus, in order to build up their network effects, platforms aim to create an ecosystem which the users find difficult to leave or attractive to stay within.

For instance, in the *Google Android* case, through a combination of its commercial arrangements, such as anti-fragmentation obligations, lack of access to Google's proprietary APIs due to which fork developers could not attract app developers, non-availability of 'must-have' apps like Play Store, Google Search, etc.[31] Google created an ecosystem consisting of the following markets: market for licensable OS for smart mobile devices in India, market for app stores for android smart mobile OS, market for general web search in India, market for non-OS specific web browsers in India and market for online video hosting platforms in India. These ecosystems do not operate in silos but are highly interdependent on each other, where a particular conduct of the platform operator influences various other segments of the ecosystem. It has been the continuous defence of Google that their services are offered for 'free' which is to the benefit of consumers. However, the said defence has not been appreciated by CCI and NCLAT when it notes that Google is building an ecosystem to

31. *Google Android* case, para. 566.

derive advertisement revenue. In appeal, the NCLAT[32] observed that the *substratum of Android OS on which the mobile ecosystem is based is, therefore, the foundation of the Google ecosystem, comprising of Google search-driven apps and other apps that derive data from users and funnel the traffic and data from them into Google Search results which becomes one of the important bases of its advertisement revenue.*

To illustrate in the context of one market, once the OEM has installed a particular app store on its devices, the same becomes a gateway between app developers and the users. An app developer to reach the user base on a particular OS/ecosystem (i.e., Android or iOS), must rely on the app store on that particular OS only. Thus, an app developer cannot reach an iOS user through Google's Play Store and an Android user through Apple's App Store, so they cannot confine their offerings exclusively to one of the ecosystems in order to expand their reach to the maximum set of consumers.[33]

The CCI has also discussed the concept of an ecosystem in the *Apple* case,[34] wherein it noted that the smart device ecosystem of Apple (based on iOS) and Google (based on Android OS) have emerged as the two major mobile ecosystems, former being non-licensable and closed source whereas latter being licensable and open source. Being closed source means that Apple's ecosystem is tightly knit and vertically and exclusively integrated throughout the value chain, wherein it offers apps, an app store as well as smart devices.

This unique strategy of platforms to lock in consumers within the ecosystem of their service offerings by leveraging network effects has to be analysed in the context of securing market control. Therefore, the peculiar tendency of platforms to create an ecosystem to further entrench their position in the market also becomes a crucial factor in determining the anti-competitiveness and abusiveness of their conduct, if any.

[B] Economies of Scale

In the words of the Competition Law Review Committee, 'Economies of Scale' or 'returns to scale' means that 'the cost of production is lesser in proportion to the number of customers served. As the customer base of a digital platform increases, the average cost incurred by such companies in providing services will reduce significantly.'[35] While this characteristic may also be present in traditional markets, the tendency of digital markets is such that the returns are maximized (due to network effects, as discussed earlier), thereby creating competitive advantages for incumbent players. This is attributable to the fact that in digital markets, the cost of producing the information/service/value is much less than what is proportional to the number of customers served.

32. *Google LLC and Anr. v. Competition Commission of India* [2023], (NCLAT) Competition Appeal (AT) No. 01 of 2023, para. 211.
33. *Google Android* case, para. 199.3.
34. *Apple* case, para. 14.
35. Report of the Competition Law Review Committee, para. 1.3.

The Parliamentary Standing Committee on Finance in its Report on Anti-Competitive Practices by Big Tech Companies ('*Big Tech Report*')[36] has also observed that digital markets are essentially different from traditional physical markets because while the former experiences increasing returns to scale (as the size of the firm increases, so do the returns, with rapidly decreasing marginal costs), the latter experiences diminishing returns to scale (as the size of a business entity increases, its returns increase only up to the maximum efficiency point, or the equilibrium point, and then continue to decrease). This means that growing bigger is a competitive disadvantage in physical markets, but in digital markets, it is a significant advantage.

To illustrate, in the *Play Store* case,[37] the CCI observed that the different products and services offered by Google to multiple sides of the market are not only 'intricately intertwined and interwoven with each other, but the products/services offered by the platform operator (Google in this case) derive strength from each other due to economies of scope and scale.' As a result, it becomes extremely difficult for new entrants to replicate such an ecosystem because 'Competition in such a scenario is among ecosystems and not just the verticals or independent services. In such a case, the entire platform has to be taken as one unit to account for the cross-market externalities between platform sides, and revenue generated therefrom has to be seen as a whole.'

An analysis of CCI's approach reveals that economies of scale are interpreted as barriers to entry in the market because the bigger the platform, the more difficult it is for a new or existing player to compete with the strength of that platform. In fact, economies of scale are a rather difficult barrier to overcome because even where entry is not completely deterred, entrants may take time to achieve efficient levels of production, raise capital and build the necessary framework but even despite this entry and sinking of capital, the incumbent could nevertheless retain market power for a substantial period of time. Hence, the existence of such expansion barriers is a key factor in competition assessment and CCI has taken it into account in assessment of large platforms in determining entry and expansion barriers.

[C] Switching Costs

As the name suggests, switching costs refer to the 'costs' incurred by users when they 'switch' from one product/service provider to another. These can be of various types, such as financial, psychological (time, efforts) and technological (learning new technologies, etc.).

In the *Play Store* case,[38] the CCI identified in detail the switching costs of shifting from one OS to another for app developers as well as app users:

36. Standing Committee on Finance, Anti-Competitive Practices by Big Tech Companies (53rd Report, 2022).
37. *Play Store* case, para. 407.
38. *Ibid.*, para. 91.

(i) App developers – Apps developed for one OS cannot be run on another OS due to various platform-differentiating factors, such as programming languages and APIs which are designed and developed specifically for each OS. Porting applications across OS is a tiresome task and requires significant time, resources and effort.[39]

(ii) App users – Since apps and in-app content are OS-specific, switching may result in denial of access to these apps. Further, factors such as consumer inertia, satisfaction with the characteristics of Android devices and brand loyalty also act as switching costs. Switching costs can be tangible, for instance, the cost of switching from low-priced Android OS devices to high-priced Apple devices, as well as intangible, such as learning new interfaces to navigate a different mobile OS, transferring existing data, downloading and purchasing existing apps on the new device, etc.[40]

In contrast, in the *Ola* case, riders could easily switch between Ola and Uber through the touch of a button on their smartphones. This means that there were nil switching costs.

In *Matrimony.com Limited v. Google LLC and Ors.* ('*Google Search Bias*'),[41] while examining Google's dominance in the online general web search and search advertising markets, the CCI observed that '*considering the while high technology services demand continuous innovation, given barriers to entry and Google's scale advantage, it is unlikely that a large number of users would switch to a competing search engine in the short or medium term.*' Network effects can raise switching costs for users and barriers to entry for potential competitors, and hence, users switch less frequently to other suppliers, which has a market power-enhancing effect. However, in this case, the CCI ultimately found that users are free to switch search engines in their browsers and there is no restriction to this effect.

Thus, it can perhaps be said that where there are costs to be incurred, whether financial (e.g., purchasing a new app) or intangible (e.g., loss of data), switching becomes difficult, and we can see 'platform stickiness,' i.e., the tendency of users to stick to a platform. The insistence on default settings is also a key point in analysing stickiness. The trend that emerges from CCI's decisional practice is that switching costs have been assessed in every case pertaining to platform markets, and the substitutability analysis effectively hinges on the same: where switching costs exist, substitutability is low, and where they are absent, substitutability is high. As a result, the presence or absence of switching costs becomes a relevant tool to prove the level of competition and presence of effective alternatives in the market. For example, in the *Ola* case, the CCI found that there is no switching cost for riders and drivers to switch between Ola and Uber; hence, there was no platform stickiness; conversely, in the *Google Android* case, due to the default setting, it was found that there is stickiness due

39. *Ibid.*, paras 124, 126.
40. *Ibid.*, paras 69, 108.
41. *Matrimony.com Limited v. Google LLC and Ors.*, Case Nos 07 and 30 of 2012, paras 118, 199, 367.

to both pre-installation and premium placement requirements imposed by Google on OEMs.

[D] Multi-homing

Multi-homing refers to the ability of users to simultaneously use and interact with multiple competing platforms or service providers. Rather than 'single-homing', i.e., being locked into one platform/service provider, users are free to utilize and choose from multiple competitors.

It is important to note that even the prevalence of multi-homing in a digital market is not a necessary indication of competition in the market. This is because digital platforms often operate in niche markets and target distinct user groups or serve separate purposes which may not be substitutable for other platforms that appear to offer similar services. For instance, in the *Play Store* case,[42] the CCI observed that multi-homing by app developers across Apple's iOS and the App Store on the one hand and Google's Android OS and the Play Store on the other hand, does not tantamount to substitutability as the two OSs serve a different and distinct set of customers. App developers need to maximize their reach and, thus, *would not like to confine their offerings exclusively to one of the ecosystems as it would imply losing a sizable portion of the potential consumers' revenue who are available on the other platform.*

Further, the ability to switch between platforms or substitute one platform with another is not the same as multi-homing. This was clarified by the CCI in the *Google Android* case,[43] wherein it was observed that *(m)ulti-homing by app developers should not be confused with demand-side substitution.*

The app developers have their apps on both licensable and non-licensable mobile OS, but the fact that app developers have apps both on Play Store and Apple app store does not tantamount to substitutability since the app developers need to have their app on both app stores to reach the maximum consumer base. Thus, these are complementary markets – this does not tantamount to substitutability.

This is because they cannot substitute one OS for the other since Android and iOS users are two different and distinct sets of customers. App developers offer their apps in both ecosystems so as to not lose out on a sizable portion of the potential consumers' revenue who are available on the other platform.

In the *MMT-Go* case[44] also, it was argued that consumers multi-home on different channels of hotel booking. On this point, the CCI observed that even if there are consumers who use both these modes (online as well as offline), they did not appear to be using these channels of booking interchangeably for the same booking, given the characteristically different offering that online and offline modes offer. Hence, 'multi-homing even by the same class of customers may not necessarily imply substitution in the sense used for the purpose of defining markets. Even if, most customers use

42. *Play Store* case, para. 110.
43. *Google Android* case, para. 133.
44. *MMT-Go* case, para. 198.

multiple methods to book hotels his in itself implies that these methods/channels are complementary and not substitutable even from a customer's perspective.'

Therefore, the position is that evidence of multi-homing by itself does not mean that CCI will exonerate a firm from dominance. Digital markets and the functioning of platforms in these markets are very complex, such that what may seem to be a perceived alternative may not necessarily amount to demand-side substitution. Further, the key part to analyse here is that the relevant market is defined not from the product perspective (i.e., hotel rooms) but from the service perspective (online versus offline booking service). From the cases discussed above, it can be concluded that even though consumers were multi-homing between online and offline channels of hotel booking in the *MMT-Go* case and app developers had made their apps available across licensable and non-licensable OS in the Google cases, it was not held to be in the same relevant market. Hence, what has to be seen is whether functional substitutes are available and if they are actually substitutable from the perspective of the consumers (both end consumers and B2B).

[E] Prevalence of Zero-Price Strategy

In digital markets, the producer only has to bear the cost of offering and developing an initial service. Once the initial service is produced, the cost of offering an additional consumer the option of using that service is very small or zero. For instance, a software developer needs to first expend capital in creating a new software. However, once the software has been developed, the marginal cost incurred by the developer in serving that software to an additional consumer would be very low in relation to the cost incurred while creating the first copy of the software. This feature of digital markets coupled with the propensity for strong network externalities has led to the emergence of a marketing strategy of providing products for free, or the 'zero-price' strategy.

It is sustainable for firms to adopt this strategy because the digital economy presents many services that may be offered free of charge. Hence, market demand tends to rise which in turn increases the perceived value of the product. Thus, digital firms are able to adopt unique strategies which would not have been viable in a traditional market, such as: introducing free products to leverage network externalities of a market (for instance, as a new entrant in the telecommunications industry); taking advantage of cross-network effects and by pricing services at a zero-price and choosing to earn from other side of the market like advertising revenues instead (e.g., newspapers, free social media, etc.); 'Freemium' models, where firms may offer a basic version of the product for free, and charge for premium versions/added features (e.g., music subscriptions).

In the *Google Android* case,[45] Google had argued that it provided search services to users for free. In this regard, the DG in its investigation report noted that offering a service free of charge is an advantageous commercial strategy for two-sided platforms that connect distinct but interdependent demands: the two sides being general search services and online search advertising. Therefore, advertisers indirectly fund the general search services offered to users. The CCI concluded that the collection and

45. *Google Android* case, paras 208-210.

monetization of user data for funding business operations (as discussed in detail subsequently in this chapter) implies that the provision of general search services is an economic activity, even if it is offered for free. Keeping Android OS open and 'free' of monetary consideration is thus in as much Google's interest as it claims it to be for the OEMs and users.[46]

In appeal, the NCLAT[47] observed that the multi-sided digital platforms, such as the one operated by Google, consist of software that are interconnected and interact at the machine level and the user level through flow of traffic and data, and therefore, the business model, incentives and the revenue streams are a net result of such interplay of software and programs. Thus, while Google purports to offer its mobile OS 'free', there are a number of apps and services on the same device which give rise to huge traffic and data which are effectively monetized through advertisements which bring revenue to Google. The multi-sided nature of these digital platforms is clear from the fact that on one side, there are the OEMs and app developers, while on the second side are the users that generate data and traffic, and on the third side are the advertisers who use these digital platforms for advertising their goods and services. Thus, the substratum of Android OS on which the mobile ecosystem is based, is the foundation of the Google ecosystem, comprising of Google search-driven apps and other apps that derive data from users and funnel the traffic and data from them into Google Search results which becomes one of the important bases of its advertisement revenue. The payment received from advertisers is, therefore, dependent on the data and traffic coming from the various apps, including the search apps feeding primarily in and also other strengthening and refining Google search service.

Therefore, an analysis of the decisions of the CCI and the NCLAT reveals that in competition assessment in digital markets, strictly looking at price from the perspective of one side of the market is insufficient because it is possible that one side does not pay in revenue terms at all (e.g., users pay through their data, but search services are effectively zero priced). Rather, a holistic analysis has to be undertaken to assess how the pricing strategy of the firm is functioning across multiple sides of the same market and even in interdependent markets.

[F] Access to Data

One of the preliminary legal points which may be discussed is whether having access to a large amount of data can be a determining factor in analysing whether an enterprise enjoys a dominant position or not.

The Competition Law Review Committee also noted in its Report that section 19(4)(b) of the Competition Act expressly refers to 'resources of the enterprise' as a factor for determining dominant position.[48] Hence, it is broad enough to include control over data as a factor for determining the dominant position of an enterprise.

46. *Ibid.*, para. 470.
47. *Google LLC and Anr. v. Competition Commission of India* [2023], (NCLAT) Competition Appeal (AT) No. 01 of 2023, para. 210.
48. Report of the Competition Law Review Committee, para. 2.15.

Big tech companies, such as social networking, e-commerce, online search platforms, etc., do not follow the conventional model of charging their customers to make a profit, and most of their services are free. One of the ways by which consumers pay for the services is through their data. Data is what these companies require to provide better services or more personalized services, which ultimately hooks the user to such services. This is why it is often said that 'data is the new oil' because access to data in large volumes in digital markets is crucial to obtaining and sustaining market power. Once an enterprise has enough number of users and their data, as well as the capacity to convert such data into useful information, it is very difficult for a new enterprise to enter the market. The data advantage of market leaders over a period of time overshadows the offerings of newer platforms in terms of quality and data-fed personalization, while a small entrant struggles to attain a critical mass of users and user data. The more users or businesses get onboarded to a tech giant's business, the more data the platform is likely to accumulate. With their data pool constantly increasing, the tech giants continue to entrench their position in the digital market. Hence, access to data also acts as an entry barrier.

In *Vijay Gopal v. Big Tree Entertainment Pvt. Ltd. and Ors.*,[49] while examining the data collection capacity of BookMyShow, an online ticket booking platform, the CCI opined that exclusivity relating to data ownership can increase the bargaining power of the platform over time. This is because access to data strengthens network effects, thereby limiting inter-platform competition. Consequently, the aspect of exclusive ownership of and access to data by the intermediary was directed to be investigated.

[1] Using Data as a Competitive Advantage

In several recent cases, the CCI has discussed the competitive advantage gained by a platform which has access to user data. For instance, in the *Google Android* case,[50] the CCI observed that vertically integrated business operations of Google allowed it to pool the data gathered from each service, and process the same to refine the service offered. This resulted in a superior monetization ability through online ads, thereby conferring a significant and overwhelming competitive edge to Google over its competitors. In its appeal,[51] the NCLAT noted that the business model, incentives and revenue streams of digital platforms such as Google in the present case are interconnected through data. Even services which are seemingly offered for free are essentially aimed at giving rise to huge traffic and data which is subsequently monetized through advertisement revenue. In fact, the different services offered by Google are a channel to derive user data and funnel the same into Google Search to refine its services and improve its monetization. On this basis, that the revenue of Google is fuelled by its data advantage and its bundled and interwoven services, the NCLAT refused to reduce the penalty imposed by the CCI upon Google.

49. *Vijay Gopal v. Big Tree Entertainment Pvt. Ltd. and Ors.*, Case No. 46 of 2021, para. 34.
50. *Google Android* case, para. 263.
51. *Google LLC and Anr. v. Competition Commission of India* [2023], (NCLAT) Competition Appeal (AT) No. 01 of 2023, paras 210-216.

Similarly, in the *Play Store* case,[52] the CCI found on the basis of the DG investigation that Google had access to a significant volume and category of granular data of the app users including complete personal as well as financial transaction information. However, this data was not shared with the app developers, thereby impacting their ability to improve their services and compete effectively in their respective domains. This confiscation resulted in Google having the ability to exploit a vast amount of extremely valuable user data, such as by offering targeted offers and promotions. By having control on the data, Google was also in a position to put its competitors in a disadvantageous position in the downstream markets. What was noteworthy was that CCI took into account that Google's proprietary apps were competing with the other apps in the ecosystem, and such use of data worked to Google's advantage.

The same situation was discussed in the *Apple* case,[53] wherein CCI in its prima facie opinion observed that Apple had access to data collected from the users of its downstream competitors, i.e., app developers which would enable it to improve its own services. However, such competitors may not have access to this data for improvisation/innovation of their own app. This would result in a competitive advantage for Apple over its competitors.

In Re: Updated Terms of Service and Privacy Policy for WhatsApp Users v. WhatsApp LLC and Facebook, Inc.,[54] another aspect of competition vis-à-vis data was considered. WhatsApp was alleged to be sharing the personal data of users with its group companies, i.e., other Facebook companies. The CCI observed that one of the stated purposes of data sharing was to target ad offerings on other Facebook products by building user profiles through cross-linking of data collected across services. Such data sharing by WhatsApp with Facebook amounted to degradation of non-price parameters of competition, such as quality, which resulted in objective detriment to consumers without any acceptable justification. This was found to prima facie amount to imposition of unfair terms and conditions upon the users.

Therefore, the CCI has considered data to be a tool to boost innovation of the controller of the data to the detriment of other players in the market (who may not have access to such data). As more data accumulates, the competitiveness of the firm also increases, and rivals start to get foreclosed on the market. Further, the above cases also highlight that data not only confers a competitive advantage in the existing business but also often grants a competitive advantage to the firm in related markets as well.

[2] Data as a Tool to Create Revenue and New Business Verticals

The primary source of revenue for digital platforms collecting data is through monetization of this data in the form of advertisements. Further, with large data to process, an enterprise has the opportunity to anticipate consumer needs and demand in more than

52. *Play Store* case, paras 278-283, 307, 308.
53. *Apple* case, para. 29.
54. *In Re: Updated Terms of Service and Privacy Policy for WhatsApp Users v. WhatsApp LLC and Facebook, Inc.*, Suo Moto Case No. 01 of 2021, para. 30.

one sector. Armed with this data, the enterprise can create its own products/services which the data shows consumers may prefer. This can be seen in emerging digital markets, as discussed in the later parts of this chapter.

The Big Tech Report also analysed how access to data gives an advantage to digital platforms by enabling them to 'collect and store large amounts of data for comprehensively tracking and profiling end customers and business users. Privileged data from one market may be, thus, used by a leading platform in another market to gain competitive advantage. This further leads to the position of the leading platform getting entrenched.'[55]

In the *Google Android* case,[56] it was found that mandatory pre-installation of Google search (widget on the default home screen) on all Android devices under MADA ensures user traffic and valuable user data for Google that it can collect, combine and leverage for its search advertising business. Hence, through MADA requirements, Google was in a position to leverage its dominant position in the Android ecosystem to maintain and strengthen its dominance in the search advertising sector. The data generated from each app of Google, such as Google Search, Maps, YouTube, etc., can complement the other and, thus, gives '*Google a big data advantage over its rivals*. Importantly, it also *raises the willingness to pay by advertisers. Thus, in presence of cross market data advantage, pushing Android with other apps is a business strategy for Google.*'

In the *Play Store* case[57] also, it was found that Google uses the data of the app developers to support its vast advertisement business by, among other things, selling access to the data back to the developers. This observation was strengthened by virtue of the advertising revenue earned by Google through advertisements in the Google Play Store.

Therefore, an analysis of the CCI and NCLAT's findings on data reveals that data is a factor of market control, and access to large troves of data allows a firm to further entrench its market power. Access to data has wide-ranging implications on competition right from securing a competitive advantage, using it to create entry barriers and foreclosing competition by improving one's own innovation to the exclusion of others and also expanding into new markets. Since firms cannot be stopped altogether from exploiting the data that they have gathered, at best, they need to be cautious about not abusing such access as a tool to prevent their rivals from competing on merits.

[G] Across Platform Parity Agreements

Across Platform Parity Agreements (APPAs), also called Retail Most Favoured Nation (MFN) clauses, are stipulations where the sellers guarantee an online platform, terms (whether price and/or non-price) that are at least as favourable as those granted to any other platform, thus ensuring the former an advantage over its competitors. By

55. Big Tech Report, para. 1.18.
56. *Google Android* case, paras 472, 473.
57. *Play Store* case, para. 282.

securing such favourable terms, the platforms attempt to guarantee the best available price and/or terms for a given product to its final consumers.

The Competition Law Review Committee also noted in its Report that:[58]

> MFN clauses can potentially give rise to both pro-competitive benefits and anti-competitive effects on the market. The extent of the effect depends on various factors such as the market structure, the form of the MFN clause used, and the characteristics of the sellers and buyers in the market. In light of this Committee agreed that such agreements should be analysed under the 'rule of reason' or 'effects' test under Section 3(4) of the Competition Act. Having said that, the Committee noted that in cases where such clauses seek to facilitate a cartel, fix price or supply terms, it will be hit by the provisions of Section 3(3) of the Competition Act.

In the *MMT-Go* case,[59] the CCI discussed the two categories of APPAs, i.e., wide and narrow parity clauses, as described in the following flowchart:

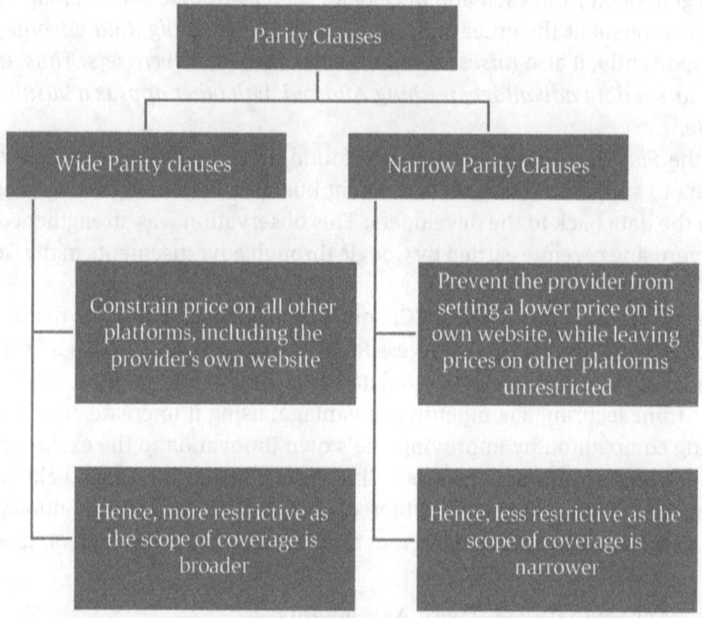

Thus, to illustrate, on the one hand, a wide parity clause prevents a hotel from offering better prices and terms on all other sales/distribution channels (including the hotel's own website and other OTAs). On the other hand, a narrow parity clause prevents a hotel from offering better prices and terms only on its own website, but it can offer better prices on other channels.

58. Report of the Competition Law Review Committee, para. 2.9.
59. *MMT-Go* case, para. 247.

In this case, on the basis of the investigation conducted by the DG, the CCI found that MMT-Go imposed two kinds of wide parity clauses on the hotel partners:[60]

(i) Price/Rate parity obligations – whereby the hotel partners were restrained from offering better prices to other OTAs or on their own websites.
(ii) Room parity – whereby hotels could not refuse to provide rooms on MMT-Go's platform at any given point of time if the rooms were being provided on any other OTA.

MMT-Go's wide price parity obligations were held anti-competitive because of their ability to restrict price competition and, thus, making it difficult for an entrant or an existing player to establish a market presence, thereby creating entry/expansion barriers for new/other platforms due to the hotels' price parity clause with MMT-Go. Parallelly, the room parity condition restricted the hotels from providing differential availability of rooms to other OTAs/alternate portals, including such OTAs that charge lower commission rates or have unmet demand at a given point in time. Resultantly, the hotels were made to relinquish their price-setting freedom on the MMT-Go platform, which decided the final price payable by consumers after a discount on its platform, and also on all other platforms/channels through the price parity condition.

The impact of these parity obligations was that they reduced the incentives for other OTAs to compete with MMT-Go. For instance, even if they offered lower commission than what was charged by MMT-Go, the parity obligations imposed by MMT-Go prevented the hotels from offering better rates to the other OTAs. As a result, the price competition softened and there could be no competition on the prices offered to the end consumer. Given the lack of incentive to compete on commission, the only way to compete would be on the basis of discounts, and consequently, the OTA which would have the maximum capacity to fund discounts would end up intermediating the maximum bookings. Further, the dominant OTA, i.e., MMT-Go, would end up intermediating the maximum number of bookings, and consequently, the hotels would have to pay the maximum commission to MMT-Go. Per the CCI, this had a cascading effect and created an ecosystem which reinforced the strength of MMT-Go and foreclosed competition for other OTAs.

In the *MMT-Go* case,[61] the CCI also observed that parity terms imposed by MMT-Go cannot be justified on the grounds that they are purportedly an 'industry practice'. Rather, 'the effect and implications of a conduct indulged in by a dominant platform on its users and competition in the relevant market is fundamentally different from when a smaller insignificant player does it.' On this basis, the CCI observed that since presence on MMT-Go was indispensable for hotels to access online customers on account of its dominance, hotels, especially budget hotels with no brand recognition had two choices: either accept the terms that MMT-Go offers or forego significant online opportunity of sale and discoverability. Thus, a comparison of the combined effect of deep discounting and parity obligations imposed by a dominant platform (that

60. *Ibid.*, paras 246-260.
61. *Ibid.*, para. 264.

has already reaped the benefits of network effects in its favour) with the parity conditions of other platforms was not held to be a like-to-like comparison. Hence, this is an extension of the principle of special responsibility of dominant players.

In *National Restaurant Association of India v. Zomato Limited and Bundl Technologies Private Limited* ('*Zomato Swiggy* case')[62] also, allegations were raised regarding price parity terms in the agreements/contracts between Zomato/Swiggy and restaurant partners, which prevented the latter from developing their own direct ordering channels or listing on a competing platform by offering more competitive rates. In its prima facie opinion, the CCI observed that such 'widely defined price parity arrangements/restrictions may result in removal of the incentive for platforms to compete on the commission they charge to restaurants, may inflate the commissions and final prices paid by consumers and may also prevent entry of new low-cost platforms'. Thus, agreements were likely to cause AAEC in the market and were directed to be investigated.

[1] Free Riding

CCI's Market Study on E-Commerce[63] noted that price parity clauses can give rise to the following competition concerns:

(i) Existing platforms, in the presence of parity clauses, may not have sufficient incentive to compete on commission rates.
(ii) A new platform could charge lower commissions to service providers that offered a discounted rate in order to gain a toehold in the market. However, parity clauses imposed by incumbent platforms may serve as entry barriers for such low-cost platforms.
(iii) Parity clauses can also help cement coordination or tacit understanding that may exist between platforms by disincentivizing deviation from a consensus rate of commission. Thus, they can potentially lead to higher commission rates and discourage entry.

However, parity clauses can be justified on the grounds that they protect investment incentives by preventing free riding. Platforms make considerable investments to improve and better their functionalities. Free riding means that a service provider may take advantage of these features of a superior quality platform to draw customer attention to its product and then sell the product through its website or another platform at a lower price. As a result, competition would be reduced to price alone, and quality would no longer be a consideration since service providers would want to offer their services where they are charged the lowest price. Thus, without price parity restrictions, competition on non-price parameters may be harmed. However, it is a fact-specific question whether a price parity clause may be justified as

62. *National Restaurant Association of India v. Zomato Limited and Bundl Technologies Private Limited*, Case No. 16 of 2021, paras 77, 85, 86.
63. Market Study on E-Commerce in India, 2020, paras 93-95.

procompetitive in any market and under what circumstances. The analysis of price parity clauses will, *inter alia*, consider how plausible the free-riding concern is and to what extent it would affect the investment incentive for platforms versus the direct loss to price competition caused by a price parity restriction. Hence, mere assertion would not suffice, and it is for the incumbent platform to demonstrate how price parity solves the free-riding problem.

For instance, in the *MMT-Go* case,[64] MMT-Go had argued that parity conditions are necessary to prevent free riding. However, the CCI held that the free-riding concerns were mitigated due to the discounts offered by MMT-Go to build its network as well as the increased competition between OTAs, as these factors together meant that users do not have any incentive to free ride. Further, any investments made by MMT-Go on its platform were not hotel-specific, so even if hotels did engage in free riding, that did not take away MMT-Go's incentives to invest in its platform. Yet, narrow parity clauses were found to be justifiable. The relevant extracts are as follows:

> MMT-Go claims the parity condition to be driven by the need to address free riding concerns. *The Commission is of the view that the potential free riding problem does not have any perceptible relevance in the presence of the discounts that MMT-Go offers over and above the rate at which a hotel lists its rooms. When looked at in light of the deep discounts that MMT-Go has been offering over the years (as the data on record bring out clearly), it does not appear to be a realistic possibility that a user would discover a hotel on MMT-Go and then book it through another channel/OTA at a higher price point.* It is MMT-Go's own submission that discounts were provided to build network. Thus, through its discounting strategy MMT-Go ensured both user footfalls and conversions on its platform. Further, when hotels have more OTA choices, the increased competition between the OTAs may lower fees/commission paid to hotels, so consumers may not have as much incentive to free ride. *Moreover, what emerged from the cases dealt by other authorities, it has been observed that there may not be any concern about the effect of free riding on incentives to invest (in case of OTAs) because the investments of the platform are not "specific" to a particular hotel – thus, if there is free riding on the part of a particular hotel, this does not undermine the incentive of the platform to invest overall.* Be that as it may, the Commission finds some merit in the finding of the DG that the narrow price parity clauses may be justifiable on the grounds of free riding problem. Hotels and OTA are in a contractual relationship and therefore, free riding of hotels on the investment made by OTAs in advertisement and promotion can be detrimental to the business of OTAs. However, wide price parity obligation is not justifiable as it reduces the competition between the OTAs and may have an adverse impact on prices charged to end-consumers.

Therefore, the discussion on parity clauses can be concluded by stating that the free-riding concerns of a platform in terms of its incentives to invest have to be balanced with the freedom of business users to list on multiple distribution channels without being restricted in terms of price since ultimately competition largely boils down to competing on price. It is exactly this balance (which narrow parity clauses seem to meet) that CCI analyses in checking whether parity obligations are anticompetitive or not.

64. *MMT-Go case*, para. 265.

§6.04 EMERGING DIGITAL MARKETS

[A] Technology

Technology is crucial to the development of any digital platform. In this section, platforms whose business revolves around leveraging technology and its derivatives, such as OS, software, etc., have been described.

In the *Play Store* case and *Google Android* case, the CCI on the basis of the investigation of the DG identified several factors which contributed to the dominance of Google. These factors, as outlined below, can be considered common features of technology companies:

(i) Barriers to entry in the form of significant capital and investment for research and development of the platform. These investments are required not only at the stage of initial development, launch and marketing but also subsequently in maintenance, updating, and development of new versions and new features/releases.[65]

(ii) APIs and limited or restricted access to licences and other IPRs of the dominant platform also hinder the entry of new players in the market.[66] Without access to the same, bug fixes, automatic updates, new releases, enhancements included in the new versions of Android, etc., will not be possible. While it is technically feasible to ship a phone without Google Play Services, OEMs who do so will be at a significant disadvantage to OEMs that ship with Google Play Services.[67]

(iii) These restrictions are facilitated through Google's commercial arrangements with OEMs, i.e., MADA/RSA/AFA, etc., through which OEMs were/are restrained from manufacturing and selling devices incorporating the forked version of Android OS (as discussed in detail in Chapter 3).

(iv) Status quo bias in favour of Google because access to the Google Play Store was important for both smart mobile device users as well as app developers. Since Google's Play Store offers the highest number of apps, users seem to have a preference for it and consider it as a 'must have' app.[68]

A combined operation of the above factors makes Google indispensable. As network effects increase, the strength of Google's network increases further. These factors are likely to be present in any dominant technology platform.

[1] Concept of Gatekeepers

The term 'gatekeeper' is used to describe the role and function of dominant platforms in digital markets. In a literal sense, a gatekeeper is a person or entity that controls

65. *Play Store* case, paras 92-95; *Google Android* case, paras 115-116.6.
66. *Play Store* case, paras 98-100.
67. *Ibid.*, para. 184; *Google Android* case, para. 171.
68. *Play Store* case, paras 186, 193.

access to a particular place or service, determining the rules of the ecosystem, i.e., who can enter and under what conditions. In the digital context, the term is applied because these dominant platforms act as intermediaries that control access to specific markets, services, or opportunities.

In the *Google Android* case,[69] the CCI observed that Google governs the running of Android as it determines the roadmap and decides on features and new releases. It also controls the compatibility of derivatives of the Android OS by placing various restrictions on the OEMs. For instance, since Google owns the IPR to the Android, the use of the 'Android' trademark on hardware, packaging or marketing materials of devices is restricted to Android-compatible devices only. Therefore, in order to use these IPRs, the OEMs must adhere to the obligations imposed by Google. Thus, even though the Android mobile OS is released by Google for free under an open-source licence, OEMs are highly dependent on Google as they have to ensure that all the hardware and software features of their devices are compatible with the latest versions of Android released by Google from time to time; otherwise, such devices will become incompatible, and all apps on the same will be dysfunctional. This is one instance of gatekeeping as Google seeks to control access to Android.

Similarly, in the context of online searches, the CCI found that Google has used Android as a vehicle, especially to cement the dominance of its search engine. 'Google's strategy rests on the reach, scale and market power of Android, which allows Google to have control over a vast majority of smart mobile devices that serve as key gateways to the internet. Keeping Android OS open and 'free' of monetary consideration is thus in as much Google's interest as it claims it to be for the OEMs and users.'

For app developers, gatekeepers have also been found to restrict installation of TPAP. A leading example of this is through anti-steering provisions. Primarily linked with app stores, 'anti-steering' provisions refer to prohibitions laid down by app stores which prevent app developers and app users from moving out of the platform of the app store and using alternatives. This issue came to the fore in the *Play Store* case,[70] where the CCI held that Google's gatekeeper position in the Android mobile ecosystem makes it 'well placed to leverage its power to protect and further enhance its dominance in online search by making it difficult for rival search service providers to enter and compete effectively in the mobile search space. The well-regarded benefits of the open-source system of Android cannot legitimize an exclusionary conduct that causes harm to competition in any specific area/markets.'

Accordingly, in the *Play Store* case,[71] the CCI observed that 'gatekeepers like Google should not use their unassailable position to require the app developers, which are dependent on them, to use any of their additional or other service together with its core services viz. app store services'. This is because such conduct by the gatekeeper can be detrimental to app developers '*by reducing their ability to choose their business partners in respect of these additional or other services and also affects their ability to offer innovative solutions*' as they have to accept the gatekeeper's services.

69. *Google Android* case, paras 89-94.
70. *Play Store* case, para. 255.
71. *Ibid.*, para. 268.

In the context of the service fee charged by Google to paid apps and apps offering paid in-app content, the CCI laid down the following proposition:[72]

> in general any conditions (including price related conditions) imposed on business users, by the gatekeepers or platform operators, should be fair, reasonable and non-discriminatory. The pricing and other general conditions should not grant any benefit on the gatekeeper which is disproportionate to the service provided by the gatekeeper to business users.

The NCLAT, in appeal[73] to the *Google Android* case, also observed that Google Search increasingly gains value through network effects as greater traffic on its search engine means a greater volume of data is being generated. This data is then sold to advertisers, thereby helping Google Search gather increased advertising revenue and cement Google's position in the mobile search market. The NCLAT categorically observed that Google's business model makes it clear that:

> there is no single app or service that can be singled out to say that the revenue of Google is derived only out of its user functionality because the user traffic and data comes from not only Google Search and You Tube but also other apps like Google Maps, Google Cloud, Play Store and Gmail etc. In fact, the entire Android System in the mobile device, through tracking device usage, becomes an important source of data for the generic search result. Thus, the data and traffic from multiple apps and service and the entire Android eco-system is funneled into Google Search which is monetized through advertisements.

This illustrates how once gatekeepers have created an ecosystem, they can continue to feed and sustain the ecosystem through a complex interdependence between their various service offerings. An analysis of the above cases reveals that CCI has taken a hard stance on technology platforms owing to their gatekeeper position because the abusive and anticompetitive implications of their conduct have worsened since they control all the key access points to the market for the users. Armed with the powerful tools of digital markets, i.e., network effects, data, etc., they are able to chokehold competition. This is why a need is being felt to perhaps introduce sweeping changes in the statutory and regulatory scheme, as has been discussed in the last part of this chapter.

[B] Social Media and Communication

The leading cases pertaining to social media and communication platforms are the prima facie cases against WhatsApp. In the *WhatsApp* case,[74] the CCI observed that WhatsApp Messenger was the most widely used app for social messaging, followed by Facebook Messenger in the relevant market for OTT messaging apps through smartphones in India. Since WhatsApp Messenger and Facebook Messenger were owned by

72. *Ibid.*, para. 326.
73. *Google LLC and Anr. v. Competition Commission of India* [2023], (NCLAT) Competition Appeal (AT) No. 01 of 2023, para. 211.
74. *WhatsApp* case, para. 84.

the same group, they were not constrained by each other, rather, they possessed combined strength as a group. The key factor was the presence of direct network effects whereby if more people started using WhatsApp, then it would become more valuable to the existing users since they would have more contacts to communicate with. This leads to a win-win situation for both the users as well as the platform.

However, competition concerns arise out of the flip side of the same situation: a stronger network of WhatsApp will deter new and existing messaging apps since no users will be willing to switch to a different messaging app unless all of their contacts also switch platforms.

This allows the incumbent platform to exploit its dominance, as was seen in *In Re: Updated Terms of Service and Privacy Policy for WhatsApp Users v. WhatsApp LLC and Facebook, Inc.*[75] In this case, WhatsApp was found to be prima facie abusing its dominance by sharing data with its group companies, i.e., other companies of Facebook without obtaining user consent. Such data-sharing was allegedly for marketing and advertising and was made a mandatory precondition for availing WhatsApp's services. In a previous instance, similar allegations were raised against WhatsApp, but the differentiating factor was that users had the option to opt out' of sharing user account information with 'Facebook' within thirty days of agreeing to the updated terms of service and privacy policy.[76] However, no such option was granted under the present policy update. In the present case, WhatsApp attempted to abuse its dominant position to exploit user data and compel users to share such data once it had built a strong network by not giving a similar opt-out/carve-out to the policy update. Reduction in consumer data protection and loss of control over their personalized data by the users can also be taken as reduction in quality under antitrust law since it is a non-price parameter of competition. Access to such data can also lead to exclusionary effects since WhatsApp/Facebook would be able to further entrench/reinforce their position and leverage themselves in neighbouring or even in unrelated markets such as the display advertising market.

Thus, these circumstances are an example of how dominant platforms can abuse their dominant position and reduce competition in the market after building a strong network on which users are locked in. CCI's inquiries into WhatsApp also mark a first-of-its-kind investigation into a non-price factor for abuse (i.e., user privacy and data) by an allegedly dominant platform. Therefore, it can also be deduced that CCI's approach is pragmatic and takes into account the immediate (such as unfair imposition in the nature of a take-it-or-leave-it option to users) as well as long term likely effects (such as foreclosure of competition and creation of new business verticals by exploiting user data) of policy decisions.

75. *In Re: Updated Terms of Service and Privacy Policy for WhatsApp Users v. WhatsApp LLC and Facebook, Inc.*, Suo Moto Case No. 01 of 2021, paras 22-32.
76. *Vinod Kumar Gupta v. WhatsApp Inc*, Case No. 99 of 2016.

[C] Online Search

The CCI has examined competition issues in the online search market in two decided cases – *Google Search Bias* and *Google Android* case. Presently, the search market is also being examined in the context of an investigation ordered into the digital advertising market, as described in the next section.

In *Google Search Bias*, the CCI found Google to be dominant in the relevant markets of 'Online General Web Search Services in India' and 'Online Search Advertising Services in India'. On the basis of an investigation by the DG, Google was held to be fixing search results on certain general online searches which meant that users were not seeing organic results but rather the results that were already 'fixed' by Google. Another important finding was that Google collected data from the search side of the platform through its search engines and then monetized it on the search advertising side of the market. This again highlights how platforms use data as a means to leverage and boost their competitiveness on multiple sides of the market. It is made possible by virtue of the critical mass of users that are locked into the platform.

In the *Google Android* case,[77] the CCI noted several characteristics of search platforms, which were also discussed earlier in this chapter, namely:

(i) Presence of status quo bias, i.e., users generally do not download competing search apps where they are presented with an existing pre-installed search app on their mobile devices. This is enhanced by the importance of pre-installation as a distribution channel (enforced through Google's commercial arrangements), wherein a majority of the users tend to stick to the usage of the pre-loaded apps and do not download other apps which may be perceived to provide the same kind of services.

(ii) Presence of barriers to entry and expansion in the form of significant investment required in terms of time and resources, such as acquiring and maintaining sufficient hardware to process the data required, hiring skilled developers to build the necessary algorithms and the software services, building a comprehensive search index, and most importantly, attracting and processing user queries.

A key feature that is relevant for assessment in online search is the volume of search queries since the greater the number of search queries, the faster the ability of the platform to observe user behaviour and refine and update search results. Therefore, any competing search service needs to attract and process user queries to refine its algorithm for populating the most relevant search results. Further, there exists a positive feedback loop between the two sides of the search platform, i.e., general search services and online search advertising also operate as entry barriers. When a search engine does not have a sufficient scale on the search user side, the advertisers would not be willing to use the search advertising services of such a search engine.

77. *Google Android* case, paras 235-237.

Therefore, the key factor that is the focal point of analysis in the online search market is access to user search queries or traffic, i.e., data. The analysis of CCI takes into account the fact that data, which is essentially a non-price parameter of competition, transcends into a crucial price factor because of its capacity to be monetized through valuable targeting and profiling services. This is primarily done through advertisements, as has been discussed in the next section.

[D] Digital Advertising

Platforms which attract consumers for free or negligible fee, target consumers by capitalizing on their data. This business model is called 'digital advertising' wherein, unlike traditional advertising, the firms are able to target consumers with personalized advertisements based on their data. Such targeted advertising is made possible because of profiling of consumers based on search habits and insights gained from their data, such as their browsing behaviour and interests, geographical location, and social, demographic and economic characteristics such as age, gender, income, etc. This data is available because consumers increasingly rely on 'free' services, such as location tracking, general search services, etc., in their daily lives which are offered by digital platforms, thereby generating vast swathes of data which can be used for creating user profiles.

In *Digital News Publishers Association v. Alphabet Inc. and Ors.*,[78] Google was found to be prima facie abusing its dominance in the market for online general web search services in India and market for online search advertising services in India by, *inter alia*, causing denial of fair advertising revenues to news publishers and non-sharing of data pertaining to the amount of revenue earned by Google by placing advertisements on the publisher's websites and fairness thereof. In this context, the following observations of the CCI assume importance:

(i) In consonance with its findings in the *Google Search Bias* case,[79] the CCI observed that the market for online general web search services and the market for online search advertising services are distinct markets. This is because, first, online general web search services cannot be substituted with direct search options by typing the URL of websites in internet browsers, and accordingly, search engines become the first port of call for a user looking for information online. Second, online and offline advertising services are not comparable, and the characteristics, intended use and price of search and non-search advertising are different from one another.[80]

(ii) The relevant market appeared to be characterized by entry barriers resulting from the significant investment required to develop sophisticated algorithms as well as to reach a sufficient scale of search queries. In addition, these markets also exhibited network effects wherein the online

78. *Digital News Publishers Association v. Alphabet Inc. and Ors.*, Case No. 41 of 2021.
79. *Google Search Bias* case.
80. *Digital News Publishers Association v. Alphabet Inc. and Ors.*, para. 16.

general web search and online search advertising are interdependent, and the increase in the number of users on the search engine increases the value of search advertising offered by Google for the advertisers.[81]

(iii) Discoverability of publishers is dependent on search results from Google. This dependence also implies that they primarily rely on the traffic generated by Google to sell advertising space on their respective websites.[82]

On this basis, the CCI observed that the alleged power imbalance between Google and digital news publishers flowed from the alleged position enjoyed by Google as a necessary trading partner for the latter. Google also offered its services as a vertically integrated entity which is present at each level of the digital advertising value chain, i.e., from the demand side to the supply side. Thus, it operated as a gateway for publishers and advertisers to interact with each other. As a result, on the face of it, publishers had no choice but to accept the terms and conditions imposed by Google. Consequently, the CCI directed the DG to investigate the lack of transparency, information asymmetry and other unfair impositions in the ad tech services provided by Google.[83]

The outcome of the investigation is likely to be an important factor in assessing competition issues in digital advertising. At the same time, it is relevant to mention that in *Google LLC v. DRS Logistics P. Ltd. and Ors.*,[84] the Delhi High Court noted the key role played by Google in the digital advertising value chain and held that Google is not a mere passive 'intermediary' in the advertising process but is an active participant at each step of the process.[85] On this basis, it denied the safe harbour exemption which is a protection made available to intermediaries to prevent them from being held liable for third-party information on their platform. The principle may extend to competition law to conclude that platforms cannot shirk their liability by virtue of being mere intermediaries in any process. Therefore, together with the aspect of data discussed earlier, the takeaway is that the ability to monetize and generate revenue through advertisements (which is made possible by having access to large volumes of data) has become a focal point of analysis in almost all investigations pertaining to platform markets. Inevitably, each policy decision is related to some facet of data or advertising.

[E] E-Commerce

In its Market Study on E-Commerce in India,[86] the CCI explained that in the goods category of e-commerce platforms, there exist two types of business models:

81. *Ibid.*, paras 17-19.
82. *Ibid.*, para. 20.
83. *Ibid.*, paras 22, 23, 32-41.
84. *Google LLC v. DRS Logistics P. Ltd. and Ors.* [2023], (Delhi High Court) FAO (OS) (COMM) 2/2022.
85. *Ibid.*, paras 182-186.
86. Market Study on E-Commerce in India, 2020, paras 30, 31.

(i) Marketplace Model – platform operators facilitate transactions between buyers and sellers and can fulfil the orders by handling logistics, deliveries and returns.
(ii) Inventory-based Model – allows online retailers to own inventory and directly sell to consumers through their own platform.

Further, some e-commerce platforms, besides providing marketplace/ intermediation services to connect sellers and consumers, also provide related services such as warehousing facilities, transactional support services, promotion and advertising, centralized payment processing, shipment and delivery of goods, refund and replacement, etc. The nature of the fee charged varies across platforms and can be a fixed upfront fee or a commission per transaction. The other sources of revenue for such platforms are advertisements and customer subscription programs.

The CCI discussed the role and emerging characteristics of e-commerce marketplaces in the market in the *AIOVA v. Flipkart*[87] by observing that e-commerce marketplaces function as a connecting link between buyers and sellers by providing them with a platform to interact and transact their business. Further, it noted that e-commerce companies now offer an integrated shopping experience: while such companies have started opening physical offline stores to offer online buyers the touch-and-feel experience, simultaneously, various offline retailers have started their online ventures or partnered with leading e-commerce companies to attract customers on the electronic marketplace. Thus, it can be said that online and offline businesses are increasingly becoming interdependent.

Further, in *Delhi Vyapar Mahasangh v. Flipkart Internet Private Limited and Amazon Seller Services Private Limited,*[88] the CCI held that Flipkart and Amazon are e-commerce entities, following a marketplace-based model of e-commerce as they provide online intermediation services to sellers on one side and consumers on the other. On the one hand, online intermediation services are key enablers of entrepreneurship by offering sellers access to new markets and increasing consumers' choice of goods; on the other hand, they also result in growing dependence of businesses on these platforms. These platforms/marketplaces and the sellers selling on these platforms also operate at different stages of the vertical/supply chain. Consequently, the CCI found these platforms to be prima facie engaging in four types of anti-competitive agreements:

(i) Preferred sellers on the marketplaces – Amazon and Flipkart have their own set of preferred sellers, and these preferred sellers have nexus with the e-commerce platforms either by way of direct or indirect ownership (through common investors, directors, shareholders, etc.) or some understanding. Hence, it was alleged that these preferred sellers are extension of the marketplaces, operating through different 'proxy' entities blessed with the support of these marketplaces.

87. *AIOVA v. Flipkart,* para. 22.
88. *Delhi Vyapar Mahasangh v. Flipkart Internet Private Limited and Amazon Seller Services Private Limited,* Case No. 40 of 2019, paras 16-26.

(ii) Exclusive launch of mobile phones – Only a few online sellers were observed to be selling exclusively launched smartphones either through Amazon or Flipkart. Thus, prima facie, an exclusive partnership was found between smartphone manufacturers and e-commerce platforms for exclusive launch of smartphone brands.

(iii) Deep discounting – The CCI perused the prices for different smartphone brands sold through Flipkart and Amazon, i.e., original price and discounted price and observed that certain smartphone brands/models were available at significantly discounted price and were largely sold by the preferred sellers identified above.

(iv) Preferential listing/promotion of private labels – The product listings of the preferred sellers dominate the first few pages of search results on the platforms, whereas the products with the same ratings sold by non-preferred sellers are listed on later pages. Hence, competition in the e-commerce marketplace may be influenced in favour of exclusive brands and sellers through higher discounts and preferential listing.

Thus, exclusive launch coupled with preferential treatment to a few sellers and the discounting practices create an ecosystem that may lead to AAEC. Accordingly, the CCI directed the DG to investigate under section 3(1), read with section 3(4) of the Competition Act, whether the alleged exclusive arrangements with preferred sellers, deep-discounting and preferential listing were being used as an exclusionary tactic to foreclose competition and are resulting in AAEC. The order for investigation has also been upheld by the Supreme Court.[89]

In order to understand why this order has far-reaching implications on e-commerce, it is relevant to highlight the key takeaways of the Market Study on E-Commerce in India in terms of the conduct of the e-commerce marketplace. Therein, the CCI found that the issues of lack of platform neutrality, unfair platform-to-business contract terms, exclusive contracts between online marketplace platforms and sellers/service providers, platform price parity restrictions and deep discounts may hinder the realization of the full pro-competitive potential of e-commerce. As a result, the following key takeaways were identified to mitigate any issues in e-commerce:

(i) Increasing transparency to create incentives for competition and to reduce information asymmetry. This includes clearly setting out the platforms' terms and conditions (including discount policy) without disclosure of any information that can enable or facilitate manipulation/exploitation of search results on the platform. Further, the basis of funding the discounts and the implications of participation/non-participation in the discount schemes must also be disclosed.

89. *Flipkart Internet Pvt. Ltd. v. Competition Commission of India and Ors.* [2021], (SC) SLP No. 11558/2021.

(ii) Setting out a clear and transparent policy on data that is collected on the platform, the use of such data by the platform and also the potential and actual sharing of such data with third parties or related entities.

[F] Aggregation

[1] Online Cab Aggregation

In *Meru Travel Solutions Pvt. Ltd. (Meru) v. Uber India Systems Pvt. Ltd. Ors.*,[90] the CCI explained the model of cab aggregation as being digital platforms that connect riders to independent drivers through an app which takes a request for a ride from the prospective rider, searches for available (nearby) taxis on its platform, makes a match and puts the driver and the rider in contact with each other. An algorithm then sets the price, and the revenue is shared between the driver and cab aggregator. Leveraging the technology, the cab-aggregator model reduces transaction costs associated with matching dispersed drivers and riders which also means lower search cost for these two sides of participants. Unlike the traditional asset-owned model, where cabs are owned by radio taxi operators, cab aggregators like Uber and Ola rely on their network of driver partners with their own cars to provide ride services. In order to build a large network size (since a large network implies more riders and thereby more drivers), the platforms design the pricing structure so as to make 'joining' the network and 'staying committed' to it attractive to both sides. This was done through discounts and incentives offered to riders and drivers, respectively. However, as the network grows and reaches a critical mass, the need to offer discounts/incentives gets obviated. The CCI held that in a competitive market where Uber and Ola place competitive constraints on each other, such penetrative pricing strategies (where they price below cost) for the creation of a network seem to be a compelling business strategy to induce loyalty by offering incentives to driver in the early stages of network creation to attract cab-owning drivers. Thus, no reason was found for antitrust intervention.

Further, unlike an e-marketplace platform or an online delivery app, in the cab-aggregator model, there is no opportunity for the rider or driver to choose each other, as may be possible in other digital platform transaction because once a rider books his/her ride at any given time, the same is accepted by an anonymous driver available in the area to whom Uber/Ola allocates such ride. Hence, the drivers do not have any individual identities or brand value vis-à-vis the consumers, e.g., a consumer buying through Zomato App, an online delivery app, may have a preference for a particular restaurant, or a consumer booking a hotel through MakeMyTrip may wish to know the options available in terms of their offerings and characteristics, etc. In the case of a cab aggregator, the consumers have no material information about the drivers available in their area of demand. As such, the rides offered by individual drivers through Uber or Ola App constitute a homogenous composite product where riders are

90. *Meru Travel Solutions Pvt. Ltd. (Meru) v. Uber India Systems Pvt. Ltd. Ors.*, Case No. 96 of 2015, paras 141-151.

indifferent between different drivers registered with a particular cab aggregator. Consequently, despite actually being digital platforms, the cab aggregators are perceived to be the service providers of the 'ride' as a product. On this basis, the CCI held that cab aggregators fall in the same market as the radio taxi service providers operating under the asset-owned model.

In *Meru Travels Solutions Pvt. Ltd. and Anr. v. CCI and Anr.*,[91] an appeal was filed against the CCI's order in the *Ola* case which dismissed the claim of Ola's abuse of dominance on account of its below-cost pricing strategies. The NCLAT held that Ola is a technology company in that it leverages smartphone/internet-based technology to provide the riders not just ease of booking and payment for the ride but also facilitates booking a taxi at a very short notice and almost anywhere in its area of operation. This 'end to end' provision of service from booking to alighting from the taxi with a GPS-based tracking system of the taxi – all provided a high degree of reliability and assurance of availability of taxis anywhere, including security to riders and enough demand to drivers. *This is a new way of doing business, and Ola could translate this concept into reality.* Hence, along with this technology, Ola provided ease of taxi bookings, rider security, payments and drivers' welfare which made many riders comfortable with the network of Ola. Consequently, the customer incentives worked in conjunction with these facilities and conveniences to attract riders to Ola and a certain brand image was created and reinforced over a period of time. In order to compete with Uber which was present in the market at the same time, Ola had to calibrate and change its market strategy, including pricing, to respond to competition of Uber. On this basis, the CCI held that the pricing strategies of Ola were part of a broader strategy to open up a latent market and establish itself firmly in the market. Hence, it did not constitute abuse of dominance or predatory pricing.

The cab-aggregator market is an example of non-intervention by the CCI because there was effective competition in the market between Uber and Ola. This goes on to show that CCI only intervenes when there is harm or likelihood of harm by virtue of the policies adopted by the incumbent platforms. As long as competition exists and is on merits, platform markets do not warrant an intervention merely because factors like network effects may be in existence.

[2] Online Food Services Aggregation

In the *Zomato Swiggy* case, Zomato and Swiggy were observed to be online food delivery platforms operating as online intermediaries for food ordering and delivery. The CCI directed an investigation under section 3(4) of the Competition Act into the following conduct:

(i) A conflict of interest arose because of the presence of commercial interest in the downstream market. These platforms operated cloud kitchens and listed their own private brand which were competing with the downstream

91. *Meru Travels Solutions Pvt. Ltd. and Anr. v. CCI and Anr.* [2022], (NCLAT) Competition Appeal (AT) No. 19 of 2017.

restaurant partners on the same platform. The platforms accorded them with preferential treatment in search ranking. Hence, this violated the principle of platform neutrality as the intermediaries themselves had a vested interest in the competition taking place on their platforms.[92]

(ii) The price parity clauses (as discussed under APPAs) discourage the entry of other platforms because there can be no competition on price if prices are the same across all platforms.

Similar to the discussions on e-commerce above, the outcome of this investigation will have a bearing on how CCI looks at platform neutrality, ranking and exploitation of data. If the trend of the *MMT-Go* case is followed, then the parity clauses imposed by Zomato and Swiggy may warrant intervention only if they are wide, but narrow parity clauses may be allowed to deal with the free-riding concerns of the platform. Having said that, the ambit of such clauses will be seen considering the industry and that there cannot be a one-size-fits-all approach.

[3] Online Travel Services Aggregation

The leading case discussing competition issues in the context of OTAs is the *MMT-Go* case. This case has already been discussed in Chapter 3 on Dominance. However, to recapitulate, the CCI relied on the following factors to conclude that MMT is dominant in the market for online intermediation services for booking hotels in India:

(i) Barriers to entry and expansion inform the state of competitiveness in a market. In this case, the last entry in the market was several years ago, and thereafter, despite the market size growing manifold, there has not been a new entry.[93]

(ii) Due to the wide choice available on MMT-Go's portal, consumers also prefer MMT-Go to other portals, which in turn incentivizes hotels/franchisee service providers to list on it. Further, MMT-Go offers several benefits and features which coupled with its market position have resulted in network effects. In turn, such network effects also create insurmountable entry barriers for existing as well as potential market participants.[94]

(iii) Commercial arrangements in the nature of APPAs, i.e., price and room parity obligations (discussed above under APPAs) further fortified the position of MMT-Go in the market as it caused a *large number of consumers to also book hotels on the said website which then leads to a great influx of hotel owners who are willing to list their hotels on MMT-Go.*[95] Presence on MMT-Go was essential as it was a dominant platform and an important

92. *MMT-Go* case, paras 72-74.
93. *Ibid.*, para. 231.
94. *Ibid.*, para. 232.
95. *Ibid.*, para. 233.

gateway for hotels to reach end consumers. Consequently, hotels did not have any real choice to leave the platform.[96]

(iv) Deep discounting practices, as discussed earlier, meant that competition between OTAs was reduced to their capacity to fund discounts. Since most of the bookings were made through the dominant platform, which was also the one charging the highest commission, the dominant platform was also the one which would end up being most capable of funding those discounts through the commissions earned. The CCI held that this will further make MMT-Go more attractive to end-consumers as compared to its rival OTAs, leading to more bookings through it and more commissions to fund more discount, in a vicious loop, thereby causing foreclosure of competition for other OTAs.[97] While it may be argued that discounts are beneficial for the end-consumers, the net impact may be adverse when seen in light of higher commissions funding the higher discounts, leading to overall higher prices on which the discounts are applied.[98]

Based on the foregoing, the CCI held that the deep discounts, exclusivity condition and parity conditions, in conjunction, create an ecosystem that reinforces MMT-Go's dominant position in the relevant market. This was a seminal decision as it set out the contours for dealing with parity clauses. Further, it also highlights how CCI collectively analyses the entire ecosystem when assessing the conduct of multi-sided intermediation platforms; the CCI does not look at conduct in a silo manner but looks at the collective impact on the market. Most importantly, this decision marks that merely because a certain policy is an industry practice (for instance, the parity and discounting obligations), it does not exonerate the platform yielding market power from the illegality of such a practice. Market assessment is dynamic, and firms need to be mindful of their market power and special responsibility by virtue of that market power, as that has a bearing on all the players at different stages in the market.

§6.05 TRENDS FROM DECISIONAL PRACTICE

In this section, the key trends that have emerged from CCI's decisional practice with regard to big tech and digital markets, as also discussed in the relevant previous chapters of this book, have been briefly summarized.

[A] Exploitative and Exclusionary Abuse

In the *Google Android* case,[99] the exclusionary and exploitative consequences of Google's conduct on the market were explained in detail, as discussed in Chapter 3. As an example, it is helpful to recapitulate one of the practices, i.e., the harm caused by

96. *Ibid.*, para. 249.
97. *Ibid.*, para. 255.
98. *Ibid.*, para. 263.
99. *Google Android* case, paras 373-415.

Google's commercial arrangements with OEMs, i.e., MADA, RSA, AFA/ACC. The CCI on the basis of the DG investigation concluded that these covenants are in the nature of imposition of unfair conditions on OEMs who have no choice but to accept the same. They resulted in anticompetitive harm, viz. pre-installation of the entire suit of GMS as well as prominent placement thereof as:

(i) Due to these arrangements, competitors can only secure a relatively inferior positioning on the second or third screen of the device. Thus, they cannot achieve a more prominent display on the devices and remain inferior to Google's placement, and Google has retained its competitive edge.
(ii) The preinstallation of GMS suite as the default app on any device created a status quo bias in the mind of the users and helped Google attain a 'must have status'. Consequently, rivals lose significant traffic and have no incentive to enter into contractual arrangements with OEMs as they would only have a secondary treatment on the devices.
(iii) By foreclosing the market for rivals, these covenants also reduced the potential choice for users.
(iv) The preinstallation requirement also constituted the imposition of a supplementary obligation on the OEMs.

Hence, the cumulative impact of the restrictions posed by these covenants prohibited alternative vendors from outcompeting Google's apps on merit. They also allowed Google to protect and strengthen its market position in the relevant markets, keeping in mind that its strategy rests on the reach, scale and market power of Android, which allows Google to have control over a vast majority of smart mobile devices that serve as key gateways to the internet. Recognizing Google's gatekeeper position, the CCI held that the *well-regarded benefits of the open-source system of Android cannot legitimize an exclusionary conduct that causes harm to competition in any specific area/market.*[100]

In the *Play Store* case,[101] Google was found to have engaged in exploitative and exclusionary conduct. A clear example of one such conduct was the impact of the mandatory commission charged by Google to app developers by making it necessary for them to use Google's billing system for offering paid apps and paid in-app content, as illustrated in the following flowchart:

100. *Ibid.*, para. 470.
101. *Play Store* case, para. 273.

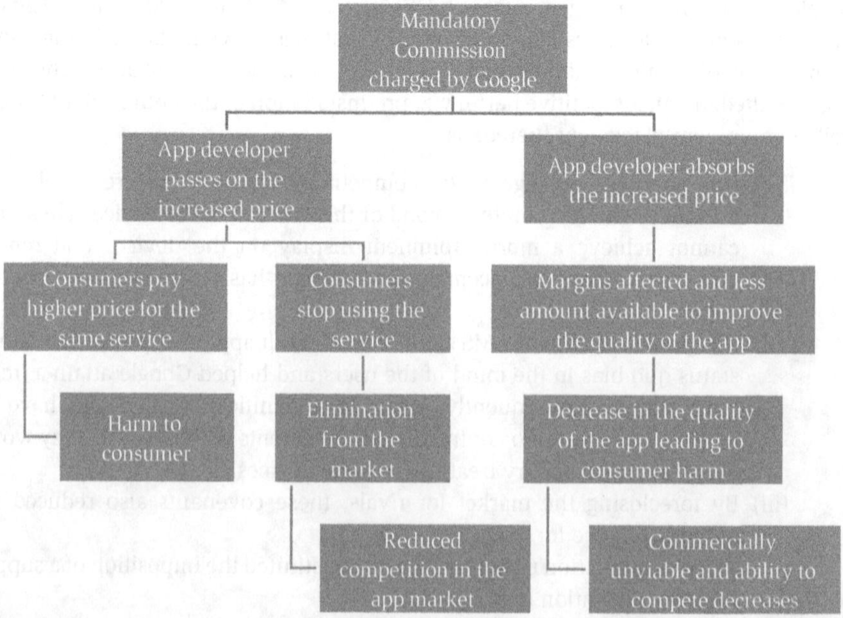

It was found that Google's own apps, such as YouTube, did not have to pay such a commission, and, in any case, if the commission was paid, it would be internalized. Hence, this illustrates how the platform can exploit users on one end of the market, i.e., app developers and also cause their exclusion in order to access the other side of the market, i.e., app users.

Similar conduct has also been found in the prima facie *Apple* case,[102] wherein the CCI noted that Apple's proprietary apps are competing with TPAP on the iOS platform. Resultantly, any commission or fee charged by Apple from these apps (for having access to the platform) would increase the cost of Apple's competitors and thus might affect their competitiveness vis-à-vis Apple's own apps (the fee in respect of which, in any case, would be internalized). This will lead to a competitive disadvantage in the downstream markets and limit the ability of the app developers to offer payment processing solutions of their choice to the users.

Therefore, it is clear that CCI assesses the implications of the platform's conduct in the upstream as well as downstream markets and does not look at it in isolation. The abusive conduct of platforms can turn exploitative and exclusionary when seen in light of the cumulative practices propagated by the platform in its ecosystem.

102. *Apple* case, para. 28.

[B] Special Responsibility

In the context of digital platforms, especially those which act as gatekeepers and host other businesses on their platforms (e.g., online marketplaces), the special responsibility to prevent their conduct from impairing genuine undistorted competition becomes even more important. CCI has reiterated this principle in the context of the various decided cases against Google.[103] Particularly, in the *Google Android* case,[104] the CCI observed that 'Google being a dominant entity has the special responsibility not to impinge the process of competition and ensure fairness and reasonableness in its conduct...Dominant enterprises must not take unfair advantage of their position as such abusive conduct not only impacts the market as a whole but also may affect the entry and sustenance of other market participants into complementary markets associated with the platform.' Hence, Google ought to be mindful of the exclusionary implications of the restrictions imposed on OEMs and should have used more competition-friendly alternatives.

Hence, platforms, being gatekeepers of their respective markets, have a special responsibility to maintain a level playing field and ensure that their conduct does not have adverse consequences for other players in the market.

[C] Efficiency Gains and Competition Harms in Mergers

On the one hand, the characteristic features of digital markets have the potential to increase competition relative to traditional markets by allowing consumers to use multiple services in a single platform simultaneously, the ability to use digital tools to compare prices and features, etc. On the other hand, they also create risks of undesirable concentration by leveraging the advantages of economies of scale and scope, data advantages for incumbents, network effects, etc. These advantages and disadvantages get heightened in case of mergers since the strength of already powerful entities in markets with little competition virtually doubles, thereby making the merged entity into a behemoth with incomparable strength that cannot be challenged by existing smaller players.

In the case of the *Google/Jio* combination,[105] there was an overlap between the activities of the parties in the spheres of mobile app distribution, supply of apps & mobile/web services, supply of advertisement services, and supply of mobile OS. Further, the OTT applications and content of Google and the telecommunication services offered by a subsidiary of Jio were found to be complementary/vertical to each other. Consequently, the CCI assessed the ability and incentive of both platforms to discriminate between competitors in their respective businesses and whether their access to each other's resources created any undue advantages.[106] In particular, Reliance (the parent company of Jio) was found to deploy KaiOS on its mobile devices,

103. *Google Search Bias* case; *Play Store* case.
104. *Google Android* case, paras 557-561.
105. Google International LLC, Combination Registration No. C-2020/09/775, 11 Nov. 2020.
106. *Ibid.*, para. 10.

offering competition to Google's Android OS, and the proposed business collaboration was likely to reduce the incentive for Reliance to continue with KaiOS-based devices. However, since Reliance confirmed that it would continue to sell KaiOS phones and shall not degrade the quality of these phones to favour the new smartphone to be made in collaboration with Google, the CCI concluded that the proposed combination did not raise any competition concerns in relation to supply of Android or customized OS.[107]

Another concern was data-backed market power, arising from possible data sharing between Google and Jio.[108] The CCI observed that the assessment in such instances needs to focus on the incentives of parties to pool or share their databank and monetize such data in the best possible means. In this case, since the proposed combination was an acquisition of 7.73 % stake in Jio by Google, it was observed that it may not result in unrestricted access to each other's resources, including user data. Nevertheless, the parties may have incentives to engage in mutually beneficial data sharing. The CCI consequently allowed the combination by observing that any anticompetitive conduct resulting from any data sharing or otherwise, in the future could be taken up under sections 3 and/or 4 of the Competition Act.

Similarly, in the *Facebook/Reliance*[109] combination, CCI approved the acquisition of 9.99 % stake by a wholly owned subsidiary of Facebook in Reliance Jio Infocomm Limited, which is the largest telecommunications company in India. The investment was aimed at collaborations between the two undertakings in the online advertising and e-commerce sectors: for instance, it envisaged a commercial arrangement to connect the users of WhatsApp with Reliance's e-commerce marketplace, JioMart. Despite a recognition of how data-backed market power can allow firms to pool their data, leading to anti-competitive outcomes and have bearings on platform neutrality, CCI approved the combination while recognizing its pro-competitive effects and the growing synergies between the telecommunication industry and the digital technology sectors. While the parties submitted that they did not intend to share data, this did not have a bearing on CCI's decision, even though there may have been certain complementary overlaps in the data possessed by Facebook and Reliance. In line with its decisional practice in combinations, CCI left the scope open for *ex post* review in the future in case of any anticompetitive effects.

Therefore, the above cases highlight how CCI takes a pro-market balanced approach to regulation so as to focus on market synergies and pro-competitive efficiencies instead of distant possible anticompetitive harm. To date, CCI has not withdrawn any approval but has only subjected combinations that have anticompetitive potential alone to detailed review and subsequent modifications, as required in the factual circumstances.

107. *Ibid.*, para. 14.
108. *Ibid.*, paras 30, 31.
109. Jaadhu Holdings, LLC, Combination Registration No. C-2020/06/747.

[D] Protection of Incentives to Innovate

While it is important to keep a check on the anti-competitive and abusive potential of digital platforms, at the same time, excessive antitrust intervention can reduce the incentives of such platforms to innovate and compete in the market. This can be illustrated qua the *Google Android* case,[110] wherein the CCI directed that Google shall not deny access to its Play Services APIs to disadvantage OEMs, app developers and its existing or potential competitors. This would ensure the interoperability of apps between Android OS which complies with compatibility requirements of Google and Android Forks. This was done in light of the finding that Google used its control and proprietary rights over APIs to obstruct the development of alternative and competing Android fork versions, thereby hindering technical or scientific development, innovation, research and development. Further, by excluding these APIs from the Android OS and not making Google Play services available on forked versions of Android, Google prevented apps developed for Android from being ported onto the forked versions of Android without additional cost and investments.

In appeal, the NCLAT[111] overturned CCI's direction on the ground that the APIs which provide essential services to the apps which are part of the Play Store, are privately developed, maintained and continually updated by Google and are provided by Google to app developers and OEMs. Consequently, unhindered access to such proprietary items of Google cannot be given to app developers, OEMs and Google's existing and potential competitors. Further, such proprietary software which is 'developed through scientific and technical innovation should fetch value to Google and, therefore, remain an incentive for a technological company/Google to further carry out such development and monetize it through its commercial use'. Thus, unhindered access to the same cannot be allowed without going through necessary technical and commercial engagement with Google. The matter is pending appeal before the Supreme Court.

This was also recognized by the CCI in the *AIOVA v. Flipkart*,[112] wherein it observed that since the technology-driven and marketplace-based e-commerce model is still evolving and relatively nascent, regard must be had to the growth potential as well as the efficiencies and consumer benefits that such markets can provide. Hence, *any intervention in such markets needs to be carefully crafted lest it stifles innovation.*

CCI has refrained from acting as a price regulator. In the *Play Store* case,[113] CCI did not hold that the 15%-30% commission charged by Google through imposition of a mandatory GPBS on each transaction pertaining to a paid app/digital in-app purchase was excessive. Similarly, in the *MMT-Go* case, CCI did not give a finding on deep discounting by MMT-Go.[114] Thus, it is clear that CCI has refrained itself from acting as

110. *Google Android* case, paras 530-557, 617.3.
111. *Google LLC and Anr. v. Competition Commission of India* [2023], (NCLAT) Competition Appeal (AT) No. 01 of 2023, paras 183-186.
112. *AIOVA v. Flipkart*, para. 34.
113. *Play Store* case, para. 325.
114. *MMT-Go* case, para. 274.

a price regulator or regulating the commercial wisdom of enterprises. Rather, the CCI has focused on freeing the market at every level of the value chain by removing bottlenecks and promoting dynamic efficiency and innovation in the market (such as by issuing remedial directions). Therefore, the stand taken by the CCI is pro-competition without interfering with the business decisions of the platforms.

§6.06 REGULATORY INTERVENTION

There has been a significant growth of Indian markets and a paradigm shift in the way businesses operate. There have been multiple reasons which have been advanced which bring to the fore the different regulatory challenges facing the digital economy, which perhaps necessitate a new regulatory approach. Some of those factors have been discussed hereinabove.

The rise of the digital economy has accelerated manifold due to the pandemic-induced lockdown in several countries. The regulators need to make sure that the steps towards recovery do not irreversibly alter markets and that competition principles can be respected along the way, especially by '*gatekeeper*' firms that provide online intermediation services. An increasing part of economic activity is going to be facilitated by digital players and channelled through the internet, and a small number of firms have occupied key intermediation positions. This tectonic shift in markets is thus posing challenges for lawmakers and enforcers on how to address the consequent bargaining power imbalance and information asymmetry between platforms and their business users. This imbalance and the resulting concerns were elaborately discussed in the e-commerce market study of the CCI (discussed *supra*). Following the study, multiple issues have been raised before the CCI, showing that these digital platforms have, perhaps, in effect, become private regulators dictating terms and conditions to participants in their ecosystems. Even if the business users are uncomfortable with those terms, there are often few viable alternatives to some of the services offered. Strong network effects increase the value of a digital service for consumers and business users, and switching to newcomers is unattractive. Thus, it becomes very important that the rules of engagement between business users and platforms are such that this unequal power relative to other businesses in a vertical relationship is not exploited by platforms, and competition on merits is preserved. Increasingly, competition regulatory architecture must be mindful of the dynamics of these relationships rather than narrowly focusing on static price competition.

The explosion of online commerce has changed the dynamics of consumer preferences and transactions. As a market regulator, it is thus imperative that the competition regulator ensures that all stakeholders get an opportunity to compete on merits and get a fair chance to be part of digital commerce. The search and comparison functionalities of the intermediary platforms, their reach and scale, and the network effects that work in their favour lead to huge consumer footfalls on these platforms, thereby making presence on these platforms critical for the visibility and competitive ability of sellers/service providers. These trends must not be ignored by lawmakers because the counterfactual – allowing privately owned, democratic legitimacy lacking digital platforms to set the rules of Indian e-commerce without identifying and mitigating the long-term risks and the economic harm they can cause- is a scenario which we cannot afford.

Keeping the above in mind, the government of India constituted the Competition Law Review Committee in 2018, to examine and suggest the modifications in the Competition Act, which submitted its report to the government in 2019. After a review of these recommendations by the Parliamentary Standing Committee, several amendments were mooted, *inter alia*, relating to digital platforms. These have been discussed below.

[A] Competition Law (Amendment) Act, 2022

So far, the following provisions have not yet been notified by the government. Only those amendments which are relevant to digital markets and platforms have been discussed below. The remaining amendments have been highlighted in the relevant chapters.

[1] Deal Value Threshold

The existing merger control framework in India is based on an asset and turnover threshold. As a result, a lot of combinations pertaining to digital markets were escaping antitrust scrutiny. This is because the business model in digital markets is such that they may fail to generate significant revenue in the initial years since the focus is typically on user growth in order to exploit the network effects of such markets. Further, such industries are asset light. Consequently, high-value transactions which did not meet the thresholds specified under section 5 of the Competition Act, were escaping CCI's scrutiny. The most notable example is that of a slew of 'killer acquisitions,' i.e., acquisitions by dominant enterprises of nascent competitors, particularly in digital markets, such as the WhatsApp/Facebook merger, Zomato's acquisition of Uber Eats, Flipkart's acquisition of Jabong.com through its subsidiary Myntra, and Ola Cab's acquisition of TaxiForSure. These deals were significant because the entities involved were tech aggregators with significant market power, but they escaped the scrutiny of the CCI despite likely competition concerns since they did not meet the existing asset/turnover threshold.

In this background, a new deal value threshold has been introduced under section 5 of the Competition Act. This requires that in addition to the criteria of assets and turnover to determine the notifiability of a transaction, if the value of any transaction, in connection with the acquisition of any control, shares, voting rights, or assets of an enterprise, merger or amalgamation exceeds INR 2,000 crore, then it has to be notified to the CCI. The Proviso states that the which is being acquired or taken control of or merged or amalgamated must have substantial business operations in India. Through the CCI Draft (Combination) Regulations, 2023, CCI has defined 'value of transaction' in an expansive manner to include 'every valuable consideration, whether direct or indirect, immediate or deferred, cash or otherwise'. Further, the target will be deemed to have 'substantial business operations in India' if at any point in time in the preceding twelve months of the transaction date, its: (i) users, subscribers, customers, or visitors were from India or; (ii) gross merchandise value was from India or turnover for the preceding financial year derived from all products or services was from India.

Therefore, the swift framing of Draft Regulations immediately after introducing the amendments demonstrates India's resolve and commitment to bring the merger regime at par with international best practices as well as more suited to the needs of India's rapidly growing digital economy.

§6.07 DIGITAL COMPETITION ACT

Anti-competitive behaviour in digital markets has been dealt with through ex-post provisions in competition law around the world, as it has been in India. However, the rise of digital markets has led to new challenges and complexities in the field of competition law. Traditional competition laws were primarily designed for physical markets, and they may not be fully equipped to address the unique features of digital markets. As a result, there is an emerging global consensus to identify and regulate what the Big Tech Report has termed as Systematically Important Digital Intermediaries (SIDIs), which refer to a small number of leading players in digital markets to ensure free and fair markets.

[A] Digital Markets Act: The European Approach

The EU's Digital Markets Act (DMA) is a legislation from the European Commission intended to ensure a higher level of competition in European digital markets by defining gatekeeper platforms and laying down clearly their rights and obligations. It will become fully applicable by 2024. Under DMA, a platform can be designated as a gatekeeper if it:[115]

(i) Provides a core platform service that serves as an important gateway for business users to reach end users. 'Core platform service' includes any of the following: online intermediation services, online search engines, online social networking services, video-sharing platform services, number-independent interpersonal communications services, operating systems, web browsers, virtual assistants, cloud computing services and online advertising services (including any advertising networks, advertising exchanges and any other advertising intermediation services).

(ii) Has a significant impact on the internal EU market, i.e., has an annual turnover of at least EUR 7.5 billion within the EU in each of the past three financial years or an average market valuation of at least EUR 75 billion in

115. Digital Markets Act 2022, Article 2 read with Article 3.

the past financial year, and it provides the same core platform service in at least three Member States.

(iii) Enjoys an (established or expected) entrenched and durable position, i.e., the platform has on average a minimum of 45 million monthly end users established or located in the EU and at least 10,000 yearly business users established in the EU in each of the previous three financial years.

Important prohibitions placed by the DMA on gatekeepers include restrictions on processing personal data of users for online advertising services without taking prior consent,[116] preventing wide and narrow parity clauses,[117] preventing gatekeepers from bundling one core platform service with another core service,[118] restricting end users from switching between different apps and services,[119] etc.

Some key obligations imposed by DMA on gatekeepers include allowing communication and access to content between platform users,[120] ensuring price transparency in advertising in advertising intermediation services,[121] allowing end users to change default settings on their devices and uninstall any apps on an OS besides essential apps,[122] etc.

[B] Does India Need a Digital Competition Act?

The Big Tech Report proposed a set of *ex ante* obligations against SIDIs to regulate the digital market in India. It has been argued that India's digital ecosystem is likely to become the world's largest, and to this end, it must also be open and innovative, as in a globalized world, interconnected digital markets will rapidly demonstrate monopolistic outcomes that prevent fair competition. This will restrict consumer choice, inhibit business users, and prevent the rise of dynamic new companies. Hence, a need was felt to introduce a new regulatory framework for SIDIs.

This ignited a debate on whether India truly needs such *ex ante* regulation through separate guidelines or whether it is an attempt at mirroring the standards adopted by Europe. Long story short, the national and international developing jurisprudence on competition law in digital markets deals with the same gatekeepers and has the same objectives, i.e., to make the digital markets more competitive, protect consumer choice and innovation as well as limit the harm caused by the self-reinforcing position of the incumbent platforms. Although the effects-based approach, as reaffirmed by the NCLAT in the *Google Android* case and discussed in earlier parts of this book, allows sufficient scope for adjudicating the issues arising out of anti-competitive practices adopted by digital platforms, the traditional tools of assessment may not be able to analyse the peculiar characteristics of digital markets. This is

116. DMA, Article 5(2)(a).
117. DMA, Article 5(3).
118. DMA, Article 5(8).
119. DMA, Article 6(6).
120. DMA, Article 5(4)(5).
121. DMA, Article 5(9), 5(10).
122. DMA, Article 6(3).

because while the Competition Act was drafted in a comprehensive, inclusive and forward-thinking manner, it does change the fact that digital markets and platforms were simply not on the horizon at the time it was framed.

This is why *ex ante* approach may be required instead of *ex post* analysis: since traditional investigations take time and digital platforms evolve rapidly, decisions may often lose their relevance since it fails to properly curb the anti-competitive effects in time. This, coupled with the fact that there are delays in market corrections due to the appeal process, paves the way for the entire discussion of having an *ex ante* approach to market corrections by digital gatekeepers. Thus, time is of the essence. At the same time, cautiousness is warranted in adopting an *ex ante* approach so as not to inadvertently stifle innovation in the market.

Some of the key recommendations of the Big Tech Report for ex-ante regulation of SIDIs and digital gatekeepers are as follows:

(i) SIDIs should not condition access to the platform or preferred status or placement on the platform on the purchase or use of other products or services offered by the platform that are not part of or intrinsic to the platform.

(ii) SIDIs must not favour its own offers over the offers of its competitors when mediating access to supply and sales markets, in particular, when presenting its own offers in a more favourable manner; and when exclusively pre-installing its own offers on devices or integrating them in any other way in offers provided by the platform.

(iii) SIDIs should not force business users or end users to subscribe to or register with any further services as a condition for being able to use, access, sign up for or register with any of that platform's core platform service.

(iv) SIDIs should not process personal data of users for providing online advertising services using services of third parties that make use of core services of the platform; combine personal data from the relevant core service of the platform with personal data from any further core services or from any other services provided by the platform or with personal data from third-party services; cross-use personal data from the relevant core service in other services provided separately by the platform, including other core services of the platform, and vice-versa; and sign in end users to other services of the platform in order to combine personal data, unless the end-user has been presented with the specific choice and has given consent.

(v) SIDIs should pre-inform the CCI of any intended concentration, where the merging entities or the target of concentration provide services in the digital sector or enable the collection of data, irrespective of whether it is notifiable to the CCI or not.

(vi) SIDIs should not prevent business users from offering the same products or services to end users through third-party online intermediation services or through their own direct online sales channel at prices or conditions that are different from those offered through the online intermediation services of the platform.

(vii) SIDIs must provide any third-party undertaking providing online search engines, at their request, with access to fair, reasonable and non-discriminatory terms to rank, query, click and view data in relation to free and paid search generated by end users on its online search engines.

§6.08 CONCLUSION

It is clear that the CCI has been quick to adapt to the emerging issues of the digital markets by undertaking timely investigations, approving combinations and swiftly bringing in regulatory changes. It is imperative for competition regulation to keep pace with the digital economy which brings both opportunities for growth and challenges to tackle. As platforms tend to become the necessary gateways of distribution due to a combination of the features outlined above, a question arises regarding what extent such a platform can be allowed to protect its ecosystem and, if so, whether there can be any limits to the same. In the end, it is fair to conclude by saying that in any market, genuine and undistorted market forces should ultimately inform the functioning of the state of competition.

Index

A

Abuse, 5–7, 10, 19, 22, 24, 35, 38, 41, 47–52, 54, 65, 66, 71, 75, 77, 124, 163, 165, 168, 177, 187–284, 369, 370, 379, 389, 391, 393–404, 406–408, 413–415, 417–430, 432–434, 439, 465, 472, 474–476
Abuse of judicial process, 272, 426
Active Risk Management (ARM), 32, 33
Adani Gas case, 220, 221, 227, 242
Added value, 152–154
Adjudicatory, 4, 11, 12, 37–43, 425
Administrative efficiency, 375
Adversarial proceeding, 9
Adverse effect, 1–4, 30, 45, 63, 65, 66, 83, 89, 124, 130, 140, 142, 163, 178, 179, 182, 225, 244, 280, 332, 354, 380, 393, 398, 443
Adverse effect on competition in India, 4, 65, 79–81, 85, 125, 139–144, 164, 172, 175, 179–184, 225, 280, 292, 311, 354, 356–358, 360, 372, 393, 425
Advocacy, 4, 27, 32, 33, 38, 138, 202, 415, 423, 428–429
Affect its competitors or consumers, 187, 192–196, 224, 248
Aftermarket, 73–75, 168, 215, 217, 247–250, 269–271, 278, 406–410, 413
Aggregation, 48, 140, 278, 294, 295, 361, 440, 471–474
Agreement, 5, 79, 189, 287, 392, 438
Airline surcharge cartel, 89, 101, 105, 109
Allocating costs, 247
Allocative efficiency, 3, 389
Appeal, 7, 9, 18, 20, 28, 33–37, 43, 47, 54, 88, 173, 205, 206, 209, 213, 218, 219, 222, 230, 231, 242, 250, 255, 277, 289, 290, 292, 334, 397, 403, 409, 414–417, 433, 449, 454, 455, 464, 472, 479, 484
Apple case, 164, 165, 176, 178, 445, 449, 456, 476
Appreciable adverse effect on competition, 45, 65, 66, 79–81, 83, 85, 89, 124–128, 130, 139–144, 162–165, 168, 170–175, 178–184, 225, 280, 281, 285, 288, 291–292, 311, 313, 325, 326, 328, 334, 350, 354, 356–360, 362, 363, 368, 369, 372, 374, 377, 380, 398, 401, 402, 425, 443, 448, 460, 470
ARM. See Active Risk Management (ARM)
Assets, 28, 211, 265, 285–291, 293–296, 298, 300, 304, 307–311, 313–316, 327, 333, 335, 342, 343, 346–350, 352, 356, 376,

378, 381, 382, 388, 414, 416, 431, 434, 435, 471, 472, 481
Associational link, 275, 276
Audi alteram partem, 12, 41, 42
Automobile Spare Parts case, 21, 71, 73, 74, 166, 168, 179, 181, 195, 203, 204, 215, 217, 246–248, 261, 269, 275, 278, 406, 408, 412–414, 433
Autonomously, 122
Average avoidable cost, 253
Average variable cost, 252, 253, 259

B

Balance of probability, 90
Balancing test, 139, 412
Bargaining power, 60, 130, 223, 227, 239, 244, 292, 374, 393, 417, 455, 480
Barriers, 1, 3, 58, 68, 108, 140–141, 164, 168, 170, 171, 173, 175, 178–182, 192, 202, 209–217, 219, 223, 228, 249, 265, 268, 277, 361, 366–368, 372–373, 444–447, 450–451, 455, 457, 459, 460, 462, 466, 467, 473
Barriers to entry, 141, 168, 180, 182, 202, 213–216, 268, 367–368, 372, 373, 444–446, 450, 451, 462, 466, 473
Behaioural commitments, 357, 372, 377–380
Behavioral remedies, 5, 21–23, 54, 364, 372, 377, 380
Bid price, 104, 113–114
Bid rigging, 11, 15, 47,81, 87, 88, 90, 91, 102–106, 111, 113–123, 125, 128–134, 136, 137, 139
Binding document, 314–317, 319, 328, 356
Bundling, 164, 165, 273, 483
Business justifications, 183, 226, 231, 232, 240, 242, 246, 257
'But for', 90, 100, 343, 394
Buyer power, 202, 216–219, 230, 373–374

C

Cab aggregators, 9, 59, 134, 441, 471–472
Capacity addition, 126
Capacity utilization, 101, 108, 109, 111–112, 126, 129
Capacity utilization index, 112
Cartels, 14, 15, 17, 19, 20, 37, 45, 46, 53, 65, 80–83, 85–128, 130–144, 148–162, 184, 185, 404, 458
CCI. *See* Competition Commission of India (CCI)
Cement cartel, 83, 101, 103, 104, 108–111, 113, 124, 126, 137, 140, 141, 143, 144
Circumstantial evidence, 17, 82–84, 86, 87, 90, 91, 100–122
Civil Court, 13, 49–51, 82, 90, 397
Coal India case, 6, 219, 220, 223, 227, 238, 242, 245, 442
Collective dominant position, 197, 198
Collusion, 86, 88, 105, 111, 130, 133–136, 142, 144, 331–333, 365
Combination Regulations, 285, 294–297, 299, 300, 305, 308, 310–320, 322–326, 334, 336, 337, 339, 341, 347, 349, 350, 352, 356–358, 360, 361, 363, 377, 386–388
Commercial activities, 6, 62, 64, 65, 222–223
Commitments, 5, 23, 53–57, 206, 212, 217, 218, 227, 240, 241, 243, 285, 352, 357, 361, 362, 364, 372, 373, 376–385, 388, 392, 393, 418, 422, 434, 435, 482
Common agents, 90, 105, 106, 134
Common directors, 33, 105, 303

Communication evidence, 82, 85, 86, 88, 101–109, 115
Comparative advantages, 190
Compensation, 37, 55, 162, 236, 237, 239–242
Competition, 1, 79, 187, 285, 389, 437
Competition Act, 1, 79, 187, 285, 391, 442
Competition Appellate Tribunal, 6, 24–26, 36, 37, 41–43, 66, 74, 79, 84, 87–90, 100, 104, 122, 130, 132, 133, 143, 166, 176, 187, 190, 192, 195, 196, 199–202, 206, 209, 218–220, 222, 224, 226, 231, 232, 234–237, 241, 246, 250, 253–255, 257, 258, 267, 277, 279, 281, 320–322, 334, 409, 410, 412–414, 433
Competition Commission of India (CCI), 3, 79, 187, 285, 389, 437
Competition compliance programs, 25, 27, 138
Competition law, 1–77, 79–185, 187–284, 285–388, 389–436, 437–485
Competitive constraints, 65, 66, 69, 70, 75, 173, 177, 178, 194, 195, 208, 213–215, 224, 250, 255, 256, 265, 283, 369, 371, 431, 471
Competitive forces, 2, 4, 58, 66, 182, 187, 190, 192–195, 202, 205, 224, 374, 384
Competitive neutrality, 6, 62
Compulsory licensing, 394, 399, 401, 415, 429–434
Concentration, 1, 59, 65, 69, 108, 136, 175, 177, 205, 228, 323, 365, 370, 372, 374, 381, 437, 477, 484
Concerted action, 82, 91, 110, 136, 141
Conscious parallelism, 83, 85, 87, 100, 135, 136
Consensus ad idem, 82, 227
Constitution of India, 6, 7, 37, 48, 50–51, 137
Consumer benefit, 142, 181, 183, 250, 376, 416, 479
Consumer dependence, 211–213
Consumer efficiencies, 182
Consumer harm, 174, 292
Consumers, 1, 84, 187, 292, 390, 437
Consumer welfare, 1, 2, 60, 139, 182, 236, 368, 421, 437
Control, 1, 79, 190, 285, 396, 449
Convertible instruments, 296
Copyright Act, 184, 391–394, 405, 406, 412, 419, 433
Copyright Board, 393, 394, 433, 434
Corporate veil, 26
Cost benchmarks, 247, 252–254
Cost regulations, 252, 253, 257
Cost structure, 113, 129
Countervailing buying power, 217, 218, 361
Cover bids, 106, 114, 128, 129
Creeping acquisition, 344
Customer allocation, 128, 129

D

Deal value thresholds, 286–288, 481–482
Demand analysis, 126
Demand conditions, 136–137
Demand side substitutability, 67, 68
De minimis, 65, 179, 287
De minimis exemption, 288–295, 310, 327
Depreciation, 308, 309
Differential pricing, 259–261, 418, 420–422
Digital markets, 70, 71, 73, 76, 77, 202, 209, 211, 212, 224, 233, 287, 288, 437–485
Direct evidence, 17, 82, 83, 86, 89–122, 125, 155
Direction simpliciter, 11, 29

Directorate General for Competition of the European Commission, 4
Director General, 4, 82, 203, 357, 391, 453
Directors, 4, 15, 24–27, 32, 33, 38, 105, 106, 123, 253, 287, 297, 300–303, 305, 307, 314, 315, 338–342, 346, 379, 469
Discount, 58, 71, 75, 91, 111, 125, 126, 129, 145, 171–174, 207, 231, 232, 244, 245, 256, 259, 260, 278, 310, 438, 459, 461, 470, 471, 474
Discovery and production of documents, 82
Discriminatory condition, 23, 187, 190, 226, 231–234, 237, 242, 260, 261, 366, 424
Discriminatory pricing, 231, 232, 240, 245–261, 417, 423
Distribution network, 170, 215, 365, 366, 373
DLF Case, 189, 191, 192, 194, 196, 202, 204–206, 208, 217, 227, 234, 236, 237, 279
Dominant position, 5, 16, 19, 22, 38, 41, 47, 48, 52, 54, 70, 72, 149, 166, 179, 187–191, 195–198, 200, 202, 203, 206, 209, 219–223, 225–231, 234–236, 241–245, 248–250, 256, 257, 261, 267, 269, 270, 273–278, 280, 368, 369, 379, 392, 393, 396, 398, 400–404, 414, 417–419, 422, 424–426, 429, 447, 454, 457, 465, 474
Downstream markets, 170, 175, 181, 218, 221, 231, 234, 245, 246, 263–267, 269, 277, 281, 365, 366, 372, 398, 424, 430, 431, 447, 456, 472, 476
Draft Competition, 199, 414
Due diligence, 24, 25, 313, 383
Due process, 12, 20, 37–44, 52, 222
Dynamic efficiency, 3, 480

E

ECJ. *See* European Court of Justice (ECJ)
E-commerce, 14, 58, 71, 72, 167, 168, 171, 209, 425, 438–440, 444, 455, 460, 468–471, 473, 478–481
Economic, 2–7, 19–21, 33, 48, 59, 60, 62–64, 73, 81, 82, 85, 86, 88, 91, 101, 102, 104, 105, 108–123, 126, 129, 135, 136, 142–143, 163, 166, 170, 180, 183, 195, 198, 202, 208–211, 222–224, 236, 246, 248, 249, 255, 257, 261, 265, 269, 273, 284, 289, 302, 309, 311, 319, 328, 329, 346, 354, 375, 382, 398, 415, 418, 419, 431, 435, 444, 454, 467, 480, 481
Economic evidence, 73, 82, 85, 86, 88, 101, 102, 105, 107–122
Economic power, 198, 208–211
Economic value, 246, 248, 289, 329, 398, 418, 419
Effect, 1, 80, 188, 285, 390, 437
Effective competition, 1–3, 27, 138, 193, 201, 202, 249, 250, 279, 398, 472
Efficiency, 1–3, 60, 86, 138–140, 148, 149, 163, 179, 180, 182, 183, 207, 208, 238, 245, 256, 263, 279, 368, 380, 389, 415, 450, 477–478, 480
Efficient competitor test, 190, 246, 254
Eliminate competitors, 169, 201, 257, 264, 265, 272, 430
Enterprise, 1, 79, 187, 285, 395, 440
Entry barriers, 3, 58, 108, 140, 141, 164, 170, 171, 173, 175, 178–182, 192, 209, 213–217, 223, 249, 265, 277, 361, 366, 368, 373, 445–447, 455, 457, 460, 466, 467, 473

Escrow arrangements, 333–334
Essential facilities doctrine, 264–266, 417, 430, 432
European Commission, 4, 21, 143, 281, 323, 482
European Court of Justice (ECJ), 179, 246, 247, 249, 390, 429, 430, 434
Excessive licence fees, 206, 392
Excessive pricing, 246–252, 259, 418–420
Exclusionary, 188–190, 195, 197, 200, 228, 229, 243, 246, 254, 258, 264, 266, 271, 281–283, 411, 414, 422, 463, 465, 470, 474–477
Exclusive distribution agreement, 167–168, 178, 183
Exclusive supply agreement, 166
Exempt transaction, 336–353
Export cartels, 184
Export exemption, 184
Export revenue, 310
Extraterritorial, 5
Extraterritorial jurisdiction, 5

F

Fair, Reasonable, and Non-Discriminatory (FRAND), 416, 419, 421, 422
Film distribution chain, 59–60
Final cost, 129
Fines, 27–28, 32, 89, 90, 92, 408
Foreclosure, 141, 168–170, 175, 176, 178, 179, 181, 200, 263, 264, 273, 274, 277, 281, 283, 366, 367, 372, 465, 474
Frame guidelines, 44
FRAND. See Fair, Reasonable, and Non-Discriminatory (FRAND)

G

General regulations, 12, 13, 19, 28, 29
Geographical allocation, 128
Government procurement, 81, 130, 131, 137, 219, 421
Green channel, 325–326, 367
Group, 19–24, 61, 62, 69, 70, 122, 166, 167, 171, 187, 194, 195, 198, 202, 206, 221, 225, 226, 245–247, 263, 265, 273, 275, 281, 286–287, 291, 293, 294, 296–302, 309, 310, 313, 314, 318, 323, 325, 326, 329, 344, 345, 349–352, 386, 398, 403, 412, 429–432, 436, 440, 442, 443, 445, 452, 456, 465
Gun jumping, 327–335, 353, 356

H

High Level Committee on Competition Policy and Law, 3, 4, 163
Hiranandani case, 176, 226
Homogenous product, 108, 111, 137
Hub-and-spoke cartel, 134, 185

I

Impose, 5, 19–24, 26, 28, 32, 35, 36, 38, 77, 90, 125, 127, 139, 143, 144, 151, 153, 164, 166–170, 173, 175, 179, 184, 193, 194, 196, 197, 217, 218, 220, 226, 227, 230, 231, 233–237, 240, 242–247, 250, 257, 262, 263, 269, 274, 278, 280, 285, 289, 318, 321, 326–331, 335, 352, 356, 376, 377, 387, 388, 392, 393, 395–398, 402, 405–412, 414, 417, 418, 420, 422, 424, 425, 429, 452, 455, 459, 460, 463, 464, 468, 473, 477, 483
Independently, 5, 21, 22, 43, 66, 71, 75, 82, 83, 88, 91, 109, 111, 113, 122, 123, 135, 167, 168, 171, 176, 181, 187, 192–195, 198, 199, 202, 205, 206, 215, 217,

224, 226, 240, 241, 249, 261, 269, 270, 274, 278, 296, 317, 322, 328, 332, 363, 374, 379, 384, 395, 409, 410, 435, 436, 447, 450, 471, 482
Inelastic, 108, 127, 137, 249
Inelastic demand, 127
Information, 4, 9–16, 22, 23, 27–29, 32, 34, 36, 37, 41, 45, 50, 52, 53, 59, 61, 71, 72, 74, 76, 87, 90, 92, 102–105, 109, 112, 125, 130, 132, 134, 135, 144, 147, 149–151, 153–155, 162, 167, 171–173, 176, 191, 192, 200, 206, 213, 219, 220, 224, 234, 244, 251, 255, 271, 292, 303, 310, 312, 316, 321, 323, 325, 328–330, 332, 341, 344, 346, 357, 358, 360, 364, 378, 379, 382, 383, 385–387, 391, 394, 403, 404, 410, 413, 416, 418, 424, 432, 438, 449, 455, 456, 465, 467, 468, 470, 471, 480
Input cost, 110, 113, 129
Input price, 109–110, 113–114
Inquiry, 7–19, 25, 26, 28, 29, 34, 35, 38, 43, 45–47, 49, 52, 53, 55, 57–60, 131, 133, 150, 152, 154, 162, 163, 173, 176, 187–189, 292, 313, 360, 386, 401, 402, 404, 410, 433
Inquisitorial, 4, 12
Intellectual property exemption, 184
Intellectual property rights (IPR), 47, 184, 211, 214, 224, 250, 274, 283, 287, 289, 338, 361, 373, 377, 381, 389–436, 462, 463
Interconnected transaction, 287, 317–324
Interim conditions, 335
Interim relief, 28–31, 35, 41, 447, 448
Investigation, 7, 81, 187, 292, 391, 453
IP remedies, 434–436
IPR. See Intellectual property rights (IPR)
IPR exemption, 392, 404–415, 418
IPR statutes, 404–408, 412, 418, 419, 429, 432, 433

J

Joint control, 302–304, 306, 307, 314, 344–346, 351
Joint liability, 24
Joint venture, 86, 148–149, 218, 294, 295, 299, 315, 329, 380
Joint venture defense, 148–149
Jurisdiction, 5, 19, 34, 44–52, 61, 63, 64, 68, 76, 90, 172, 188, 195, 211, 220, 223, 228, 270, 276, 283, 289, 292, 310, 311, 317, 323, 354, 355, 357, 389–405, 407, 412, 417, 423, 424, 426, 429, 442
Jurisdictional boundary, 44–51
Jute mill case, 84

L

Legal barriers, 213, 214
Lengthy form, 325
Leniency, 36, 37, 53, 112, 149–162, 185
Lesser penalty regulations, 150–155, 162
Leveraging, 165, 187, 274–278, 449, 462, 471, 477
Liaison of intention, 90
Liberalize, 4, 58
License fee, 206, 392–394, 418–422
Licensing arrangement, 206, 392, 405
Limiting production, 109, 126–127, 139
Locus standi, 9, 10
Long run average incremental cost, 253
LPG-I case, 3, 85, 88, 89, 91, 102, 131, 133, 135, 139, 140

M

Marginal cost, 3, 252, 253, 367, 444,

450, 453
Margin squeeze, 245, 246, 282
Market access, 31, 71, 147, 181, 187, 260, 262–273, 282, 393, 414, 425–430, 432
Market distortion, 54, 189, 391, 415, 428
Market power, 60, 66, 69, 76, 163–165, 168, 170, 171, 175, 177–180, 195, 199, 205, 207, 213, 214, 216, 217, 224, 242, 243, 248, 251, 264, 275, 282, 292, 362, 366, 373, 418, 431, 437, 442, 447, 450, 451, 455, 457, 463, 474, 475, 478, 481
Market sharing, 65, 66, 108, 127–129, 137, 140, 164, 177–179, 191, 192, 203–205, 211, 216, 217, 220, 243, 256, 257, 267, 274, 279, 282, 292, 325, 362, 365, 369, 371–373, 393, 426
MCA circular, 288, 293–295, 312, 321, 336, 355
Meeting competition defense, 260–261
Meetings, 14, 38, 55, 81, 83, 84, 89–92, 101–104, 125, 138, 144, 145, 174, 260–261, 302, 303, 317, 321, 403, 427
Memorandum of Understanding, 4, 145
Minimum commitment charge, 206, 217, 218, 243, 392, 393, 418, 422
Mitigating factors, 27, 335
Monopolies and Restrictive Trade Practice commission, 390–391
Monopolies and Restrictive Trade Practice Act, 5, 15, 20, 80, 86, 188, 390
Monopolistic trade practice, 5, 15, 20, 80, 86, 188, 390
Monopolization, 1, 5, 7, 15, 20, 80, 81, 86, 188, 219, 221, 222, 284, 367, 389, 390, 396, 447, 483
Monopoly, 5, 6, 62, 80, 81, 87, 173, 214, 219–222, 241, 242, 250, 389, 390, 396, 416, 423, 427, 431
MRTP. See Monopolies and Restrictive Trade Practice (MRTP)
Multi-homing, 440, 446, 452–453
Multi-product companies, 20, 275
Multi-product firm, 247, 368
Multi-sided markets, 69–70, 442–449

N

National Stock Exchange (NSE) case, 25, 190, 194, 195, 200–202, 204, 213, 245, 253, 254, 258, 270, 275, 276
Necessary to protect IPRs, 408
Negative factors, 139, 180–182
Network effect, 209–211, 213, 219, 234, 259, 280, 437, 439–441, 443–449, 451, 453, 455, 460, 462, 464, 465, 467, 472, 473, 477, 480, 481
Non-compete, 287, 376–379
Non-cooperation, 27–28
Non-filing, 326–335
Non-pricing abuse, 415, 417, 423–429
Notice, 11, 12, 16, 28, 29, 38, 87, 91, 144–146, 188, 199, 242, 248, 250, 258, 269, 270, 287, 289, 290, 293, 296, 298, 299, 308, 310, 312–329, 333–336, 348, 351, 353, 356, 358, 360–363, 385–389, 391, 392, 398, 422, 423, 472

O

Oath, 27, 82
Objective justification, 170, 261, 278–283
Officers-in-charge, 24–27, 32
Offshore combination, 311, 354–356
Oligopolistic market, 88, 100, 109, 135–136, 199
Online distribution, 172, 173, 182
Ordinary course of business, 332, 337–339, 342–344, 346–348
Output control, 126–127

Overlaps, 44, 47, 50, 69, 70, 222, 300, 325, 326, 361–363, 369–371, 394, 397, 401, 402, 420, 477, 478

P

Parallel behavior, 83, 87, 88, 100, 108, 109, 136
Parties to combination, 5, 286, 299, 307, 312, 313, 317–319, 325, 326, 332, 352, 354, 357, 358, 360, 370–372, 377, 378, 434
Patent pool, 428
Patents Act, 47, 184, 394–404, 410, 419, 433
Penalty amount, 36, 154, 174
Perfect competition, 1–3
Per se, 5, 86, 124, 137, 163, 172, 188, 263, 280, 281, 292, 430
Personal liability, 26
Pharmaceutical sector, 58–59, 214, 310, 427
Phase I, 356–359, 363, 369, 373, 377
Phase II, 358–364, 387
Plus factors, 86–89, 101–106, 111, 115, 138
Policy function, 64
Policy guidelines, 65
Position of strength, 65, 66, 70, 175, 187, 189–202, 204, 206, 208, 209, 211, 217, 225, 226, 246, 248, 254, 255, 276, 366, 425
Positive factors, 139, 180, 182–183
Predatory intent test, 252
Predatory pricing, 72, 187, 200, 207, 244–246, 252–257, 259, 368, 472
Pre-deposit, 36
Preponderance of probabilities, 17, 83, 86
Presumptive rule approach, 80
Price bulletin, 104–105
Price correlation, 110–111
Price fixing, 125–126, 134, 139
Price increase, 69, 101, 110, 112, 143, 365, 373
Price index, 112, 287
Price point analysis, 370
Price takers, 3, 217
Prices, 1, 80, 187, 287, 398, 437
Pricing abuse, 245, 246, 254, 259, 393, 415, 417–423
Prima facie case, 11–12, 29, 30, 34, 38, 42, 52, 188, 257, 266, 271, 272, 417, 424, 426, 445, 464
Priority status, 150–153
Procedural gun-jumping, 328
Producer's surplus, 217
Production capacity, 108, 109, 111–112, 126, 129
Production cost, 140, 247
Productive efficiency, 3
Profit margin, 108, 113, 129, 137, 247, 248

Q

Quorum, 39–41, 299, 304

R

Reasonable restrictions, 405–406
Recall, 13, 52–53
Reduce competition, 163, 257, 465
Reference, 9, 10, 13, 17, 34, 61, 165, 199, 211, 292, 316, 340, 400
Refusal to deal, 46, 168–171, 263–266, 398, 412, 414, 429–434
Regulator, 19, 37–39, 45–47, 196, 200, 222, 230, 251, 252, 254, 259, 300, 327, 338, 357, 374–377, 387–390, 393, 400–402, 416, 418, 419, 435, 479, 480
Regulatory, 4, 12, 25, 32, 33, 37, 38, 44–47, 50, 51, 68, 77, 169, 192, 194, 200, 202, 214, 219, 220, 222–223, 241, 260–264, 272, 300, 334, 340, 356, 361, 373, 374–375, 380, 387–389, 393,

397, 401, 410, 418, 420, 423, 437, 442, 464, 480-483, 485
Relevant geographic market, 66, 68–71, 370, 438, 442
Relevant market, 19, 41, 43, 65–76, 124, 134, 163, 171, 173, 175–180, 184, 187, 189, 192–206, 208, 209, 214–216, 223, 224, 231, 240, 242–244, 248, 250, 252, 255–258, 266, 268, 269, 271–273, 275–278, 280, 282, 292, 325, 354, 356–358, 360, 365, 368–370, 373, 374, 376–379, 381, 398, 400, 402, 418, 424, 426–428, 430, 431, 438–440, 442, 446, 453, 459, 464, 466, 467, 474, 475
Relevant product market, 61, 65–69, 72, 73, 176, 211, 418, 438
Relevant turnover, 20, 21, 290
Remedies, 3, 5, 21–23, 49–52, 54, 60, 61, 230, 285, 303, 363, 364, 372, 376, 377, 380, 387–388, 395, 396, 399, 400, 410, 434–436
Report of the High Level Committee on Competition Law, 205, 282
Resale price maintenance, 75, 172–175, 177, 181
Restrictive trade practice, 5, 15, 20, 80, 86, 188, 390
Revolving door, 44
Royalty, 206, 240, 392, 395, 399, 415–424, 435
Rule of reason, 139, 162, 163, 172, 443, 458

S

SAIL case, 1, 11, 12, 16, 29, 33, 42, 49
Sectoral inquiry, 357
Securities and Exchange Board of India (Substantial Acquisition of Shares and Takeovers) Regulations, 46, 84, 300
SEPs. See Standard essential patents (SEPs)
Settlement, 37, 46, 53–57, 233, 234
Several liability, 24
Shares, 4, 81, 191, 285, 393, 465
Short form, 325
Significant market power, 76, 163–165, 171, 177–180, 366, 431, 481
Single economic entity, 122–123, 166
Single notice, 317, 319–324
Sole control, 122, 221, 303–308, 345, 346, 351, 352, 362, 430
Sovereign, 6, 7, 62–64, 219
SSNIP, 75
Stable demand, 137
Standard essential patents (SEPs), 47, 394, 396, 415–418, 420, 422
Standard of proof, 17, 86–91
Statutory monopoly, 62, 214, 219–222, 241, 416, 423
Statutory scheme, 11, 62, 65, 81, 85, 90, 124, 139, 143, 148, 162, 225–226, 260
Strategic barriers, 214–216
Strategic investment, 299, 338, 340, 346
Structural remedies, 5, 23, 54, 377
Sub-contracting, 114
Substance, 101, 102, 215, 295, 308, 322–325, 340–342, 386
Substantive gun-jumping, 328, 329
Summon, 13, 82, 89, 133
Sunk costs, 214, 215
Suo moto, 15
Super Cassettes case, 206, 215, 217, 243, 246, 250, 422
Supplementary obligations, 273–275, 475
Supply conditions, 136–137, 431
Supra normal profits, 110, 194, 196, 201, 249, 254, 428
Supreme Court of India, 11, 85, 133
Suspensory regime, 311, 317, 326, 387
Switching costs, 67, 75, 217, 446, 450–452
Systems market, 73–75

T

Target exemption, 287–295, 323
Telecom sector, 45, 58, 399, 402
Terms of trade, 125
Threshold limits, 285–288, 293, 294, 296, 310, 311, 354, 355
Tipping effect, 447–448
Total avoidable cost, 253
Total cost, 74, 253
Total variable cost, 253
Trade association, 25, 27, 59, 64, 81, 84, 85, 91, 92, 101–105, 127, 137–138, 143–148, 391
Trade secret, 413
Trigger date, 325
Turnover, 19–21, 24, 28, 286–296, 308, 310–311, 327, 335, 355, 410, 481, 482
Tyre case, 88, 103, 109, 110, 135

U

Unilateral conduct, 81, 187, 198, 279
Unilateral novation, 57
Unfair condition, 45, 72, 193, 194, 218, 227, 230–232, 234, 236, 237, 242, 243, 392, 393, 398, 425, 475
Unfair pricing, 23, 245, 246, 248–250, 253–255, 257–261, 276, 277, 398, 419
Unfair trade practice, 2, 61, 80, 390
Upstream markets, 76, 177, 179, 217, 218, 269, 431

V

Vertical agreements, 72, 162–175, 177–182, 184
Vertical integration, 108, 214, 366, 367, 374
Vital disclosure, 150–154

W

With a view, 35, 169, 257, 264, 307
Withdraw, 10, 114, 129, 132, 150, 154, 162, 478

Z

Zero-price strategy, 453–454

www.ingramcontent.com/pod-product-compliance
Lightning Source LLC
LaVergne TN
LVHW020647300926
849161LV00004B/847
* 9 7 8 9 4 0 3 5 3 1 3 7 3 *